Crisis and Critique: Philosophical Analysis and Current Events

# Publications of the Austrian Ludwig Wittgenstein Society
– New Series

---

Volume 28

# Crisis and Critique: Philosophical Analysis and Current Events

Proceedings of the 42nd International Wittgenstein Symposium

Edited by
Anne Siegetsleitner, Andreas Oberprantacher,
Marie-Luisa Frick, and Ulrich Metschl

DE GRUYTER

ISBN 978-3-11-110463-8
e-ISBN (PDF) 978-3-11-070225-5
e-ISBN (EPUB) 978-3-11-070239-2
ISSN 2191-8449

**Library of Congress Control Number: 2021932593**

**Bibliographic information published by the Deutsche Nationalbibliothek**
The Deutsche Nationalbibliothek lists this publication in the Deutsche Nationalbibliografie; detailed bibliographic data are available on the Internet at http://dnb.dnb.de.

© 2022 Walter de Gruyter GmbH, Berlin/Boston
This volume is text- and page-identical with the hardback published in 2021.
Printing and binding: CPI books GmbH, Leck

www.degruyter.com

# Preface

The 42$^{nd}$ International Ludwig Wittgenstein Symposium in Kirchberg am Wechsel (Austria) from 4th to 10th August 2019 was dedicated to the topic "Crisis and Critique: Philosophical Analysis and Current Events." The general premise was that far-reaching changes – whether in the financial or real economy, in Europe's political conditions, in the context of scientific theories, in the field of global (environmental) security, or in gender relations – are also a challenge to philosophical thinking. Precisely at times when fundamental matters seem to transform and are called into question, philosophy can help clarify the bigger picture and sharpen its critique and guidance with perspectives and thorough analyses beyond day-to-day considerations.

Consequently, the symposium was devoted to a philosophical critique of contemporary perplexities. We invited the philosophical community to discuss a wide range of questions such as the following: How can and should philosophy engage with or initiate such transformations? Which current forms of social and cultural criticism are indispensable? How can philosophical critique address current transformations in the fields of politics, economy, and law? What consequences will result from changes in social identities? In consideration of its critical potential, science is especially called upon to accompany societal transformations, not least those brought about by scientific advances themselves. However, how can it succeed in doing so when, at the same time, science is under pressure to justify itself? In these explorations, it seemed of foremost importance to deliberate on diverse conceptions of 'critique' that philosophical thinking has developed and to ask which of these conceptions are applicable to specific societal domains.

In addition to the conference sections devoted to the general topic for 2019, a workshop, organised by Lukas H. Meyer, dealt with "Ethics of Ecology," and a special section was dedicated to all aspects of Wittgenstein's thought as is typical for Kirchberg Wittgenstein symposia. Most of the invited lectures delivered in Kirchberg are contained in this volume. Its divisions follow the sections of the symposium: (1) Philosophical Concepts of Critique; (2) Challenges to Philosophical Critique in Politics, Economy, and Law; (3) Challenges to Philosophical Critique in Culture and Society; (4) Philosophical Critique and Questions of Social Identity; (5) Science and Critique; (6) A Workshop on Ethics of Ecology; and (7) Wittgenstein.

Having organised the "Crisis and Critique" conference just half a year before COVID-19 became a pandemic, we are somewhat awestruck by the recent developments across the globe that amount to a crisis beyond our previous imagination. Neither the pandemic nor the measures taken to contain it defined our daily lives in 2019. It is not without melancholy that we recall our relaxed social intercourse while preparing and delivering the conference. We would also be concerned about the potential losses for academia if we were to be trapped in this state of emergency for too long. The change from pre-pandemic times to our 'new normal' was profound and raised the question of whether we should include contributions on this recent experience of crisis. After an extensive debate, we decided against this option. The reasons are twofold. First, the publication is part of a series of the proceedings of the Kirchberg Wittgenstein symposia, and we did not wish to exceed this scope. Second, the contributions in this volume may inform philosophical analysis and critique of the coronavirus crisis without being explicitly concerned with it or consciously attempting to reflect the *zeitgeist* of 2020. They still illuminate the multifaceted crisis we are facing today in a fresh manner and point to issues that will certainly be of great social relevance in the years to come.

Neither our conference nor this publication would have been possible without the manifold support of various institutions as well as individuals with whom we are grateful to have shared our venture over the last two years. We would like to thank the government of Lower Austria and the board of the Austrian Ludwig Wittgenstein Society for giving us the opportunity to organise this exceptional conference, and the staff of the Wittgenstein Society in Kirchberg, directed by Margret Kronaus, for their valuable practical support. We also thank all the speakers, the authors of the conference pre-proceedings, and the authors of these proceedings. We are particularly grateful to Josef Mitterer for his assistance during the conception and organisation of the conference. Joseph Wang-Kathrein played an invaluable role in processing the conference registrations. Furthermore, we express our sincere thanks to Christoph Schirmer and De Gruyter for the agreeable and professional cooperation. Finally, our greatest gratitude must go to Aaron Tratter for handling the editorial work. Without his diligence and untiring dedication, this book would not be in your hands.

Innsbruck, September 2020
Anne Siegetsleitner, Andreas Oberprantacher, Marie-Luisa Frick,
and Ulrich Metschl

# Table of Contents

**Preface** —— V

**List of Abbreviations** —— XI

## Part 1: Philosophical Concepts of Critique

María Pía Lara
**The Conceptual Semantic Field of "Crisis" and "Critique"** —— 3

Thijs Lijster
**Critical Common/Common Critique**
    Or How to Regain Steam —— 25

## Part 2: Challenges to Philosophical Critique in Politics, Economy, and Law

Richard Amesbury
**Unpopular Sovereignties**
    Democracy and the Paradox of "Peoples" —— 41

Ridha Chennoufi
**Politische Krise und Kritik im historischen Kontext** —— 61

Elisabeth Holzleithner
**Shklar versus Schmitt**
    Kontrastierende Perspektiven eines pessimistischen Menschenbildes in der politischen Philosophie —— 79

Eva Maria Maier
**Zur aktuellen Krise von Demokratie und Rechtsstaatlichkeit**
    Ursachen und Symptome —— 101

## Part 3: Challenges to Philosophical Critique in Culture and Society

Ulrich Frank
**Language, Change, and Possible Worlds**
   Philosophical Considerations of the Digital Transformation —— 117

Sally Haslanger
**Methods of Social Critique** —— 139

Anne Reichold
**Varieties of Resentment** —— 157

Karsten Weber
**Civil Society as a Means against Hate Speech**
   A Baseless Hope —— 175

Eva Weber-Guskar
**Criticizing Moral Criticism**
   Moralism on the Internet —— 189

## Part 4: Philosophical Critique and Questions of Social Identity

Christine Bratu
**Idiots and Assholes**
   What We Should Criticize When We Criticize Sexist Action —— 205

Anke Graness
**Between Necropolitics and Cosmopolitanism** —— 221

Marc Rölli
**Kapitalismus und Identität**
   Zur Dekolonisierung demokratischer Popularität —— 233

## Part 5: Science and Critique

Eva-Maria Engelen
**Testimony and the First-, Second-, and Third-Person Perspective —— 251**

Ulrich Metschl
**Epistemic Disagreement, Doubts, and Coherence —— 269**

Thomas Wallgren
**After Sustainability**
    Modernity, Freedom, and Reason in the Age of Climate Alarmism —— 285

## Part 6: Workshop on Ethics of Ecology

Dieter Birnbacher
**What Is Biodiversity and Why Should It Be Protected? —— 317**

Stephen M. Gardiner
**Should We Embrace a "New," Expansionist Agenda for the Virtues?**
    On Planetary Magnificence and Planetary Magnanimity in the (Alleged) Anthropocene —— 331

Lukas H. Meyer
**Klimagerechtigkeit**
    Ererbte Begünstigungen und Status-quo-Erwartungen —— 343

Susana Monsó
**Is Predation Necessarily Amoral? —— 367**

## Part 7: Wittgenstein

Alice Crary
**Wittgenstein Does Critical Theory —— 385**

Mélika Ouelbani
**Der Status der Mathematik in der Philosophie Wittgensteins —— 417**

Georg Siller
**Hase oder Ente?**
  Wittgensteins Aspektwechsel und Identitätspolitik —— 429

Ilse Somavilla
**Der Verlust an Wahrhaftigkeit**
  Wittgensteins Kritik an Kultur und Wissenschaft der modernen Zivilisation —— 447

**Index of Names** —— 465

**List of Contributors** —— 473

# List of Abbreviations

The following abbreviations have been used within the volume. Bibliographical details can be found in the reference sections of the individual contributions.

## Wittgenstein's works in German

| | |
|---|---|
| BBB | Das Blaue Buch |
| BEE | Wittgenstein's Nachlass: The Bergen Electronic Edition |
| BGM | Bemerkungen über die Grundlagen der Mathematik |
| BPP | Bemerkungen über die Philosophie der Psychologie |
| BÜF | Bemerkungen über die Farben |
| CLF | Briefe an Ludwig von Ficker |
| CLH | Ludwig Hänsel – Ludwig Wittgenstein: Eine Freundschaft: Briefe, Aufsätze, Kommentare |
| DB | Denkbewegungen: Tagebücher 1930–1932, 1936–1937 |
| LUS | Licht und Schatten: Ein nächtliches (Traum-)Erlebnis und ein Brief-Fragment |
| PB | Philosophische Bemerkungen |
| PG | Philosophische Grammatik |
| PU | Philosophische Untersuchungen |
| TB | Tagebücher 1914–1916 |
| TLP | Tractatus logico-philosophicus |
| VB | Vermischte Bemerkungen |
| VE | Vortrag über Ethik und andere kleine Schriften |
| WWK | Ludwig Wittgenstein und der Wiener Kreis |

## Wittgenstein's works in Englisch and French

| | |
|---|---|
| CC | Cambridge Letters: Correspondence with Russell, Keynes, Moore, Ramsey and Sraffa |
| LFM | Cours sur les fondements des mathématiques: Cambridge, 1939 |
| LWL | Wittgenstein's Lectures: Cambridge, 1930–1932 |
| OC | On Certainty/Über Gewißheit |
| PI | Philosophical Investigations |

## Works by other authors

| | |
|---|---|
| EN | Aristotle: *Nicomachean Ethics* |
| WWV | Schopenhauer, Arthur: *Die Welt als Wille und Vorstellung I und II* |

## Other abbreviations

| | |
|---|---|
| AfD | Alternative für Deutschland |
| AI | Artificial Intelligence |
| CGTT | Confédération générale des travailleurs tunisiens |
| DM | Doxastic Morality |
| EMRK | Europäische Menschenrechtskonvention |
| GHG | Greenhouse Gas Emissions |
| IPCC | Intergovernmental Panel on Climate Change |
| LGBTQI | Lesbian, Gay, Bisexual, Transgender, Queer, and Intersex |
| NRA | National Rifle Association |
| PETA | People for the Ethical Treatment of Animals |
| RBV | Reciprocity of the Basic Virtues |
| SSI | Stratospheric Sulfate Injection |
| UGTT | Union générale tunisienne du travail |
| URV | Universal Reciprocity of the Virtues |

# Part 1: **Philosophical Concepts of Critique**

María Pía Lara
# The Conceptual Semantic Field of "Crisis" and "Critique"

**Abstract:** The main goal of this essay is to show the dangers and the goals of political wars as they are very much related to how we use concepts. First, I present a brief explanation of terms that relate to Reinhart Koselleck's conceptual history. I will then discuss the analytical elements and key concepts I will be using to develop my own perspective about his contribution to the thematization of the genealogies of the concepts of crisis and critique. My goal is not to defend Koselleck's views but to help us clarify why these concepts can help trigger change for the better or destroy political enterprises.

**Keywords:** Crisis, critique, conceptual history, semantic battles, political struggles, political agency

## 1 Introduction

I would like to begin by presenting a brief explanation of terms that relate to Reinhart Koselleck's conceptual history. I will then discuss the analytical elements and key concepts I will be using to develop my own perspective about his contribution to the thematization of the genealogies of the concepts of crisis and critique. I will also argue that the semantic differences between crisis and critique, which were introduced by both theorists and agents in different historical eras, are the proof of their internal connectedness to action. In the second part of my discussion, I will focus on how, after struggling to gain clarity about the historical and critical connections between these two concepts, Koselleck developed three different genealogical accounts of crisis. Koselleck preferred to save the concept of crisis as the one that became the hallmark of modernity. My claim is that without the concept of critique, there would be no diagnosis and no modernity at all. In the third part of my contribution, I will argue that the concept of crisis is relevant today in our ongoing political struggles. This concept however can be used as a weapon of a political war. I will also make the claim

---

**Note:** I would like to thank Maeve Cooke, Marie-Luisa Frick, Matthias Kettner, and Andreas Oberprantacher for providing me with critical commentaries and revisions for which I am grateful and for their generosity and care.

https://doi.org/10.1515/9783110702255-003

that the concept of critique has played a key role in politics and its history (we owe this insight to the neo-Hegelians who re-established the initial reconnection of the concept of critique to crisis). These three parts will help us focus on the conceptual frames of concepts, their semantic fields, and their internal co-relation between time and space. It is my hope that they will also enlighten us about the relationship of politics to history. The main goal of this essay is to show the dangers and the goals of political wars as they are very much related to how we use concepts. As I understand the lesson by Koselleck's attempt, my goal is not to defend his views, but to help us clarify why these two concepts can help trigger change for the better or destroy political enterprises.

## 2 The conceptual frame, or the semantic field of concepts

Reinhart Koselleck created an alternative way of thinking about concepts and their history because he understood their effects on social and political history.[1] The importance of his theory has some advantages over other formulations, for example, hermeneutics or the history of ideas, and I will discuss my reasons for this later on. But first let us consider some of Koselleck's key ideas.[2]

First, concepts, especially political concepts, are central for political agency and for thinking about action.

Second, without concepts there are no organizational unities in societies. This does not mean that everything can be reduced to concepts. Rather, concepts provide more than just a linguistic frame. They also help us explore the semantic spaces that are not captured by language alone, such as the nonlinguistic aspects of meaning-making. Just think how Wittgenstein himself was aware of these limitations. Indeed, the most interesting dimensions of his philosophy have to do with the domains of the ineffable.

Third, Koselleck believed that societies are constituted as the result of semantic battles or political struggles between agents and theorists – specifically, about the definition, defense, and occupation of conceptually composed positions.

Fourth, concepts are related to time because, although they are formulated at a particular historical point and define a certain state of affairs, they can also reach the spaces of the future as hopes or expectations, as they are related

---

[1] For the best introduction to Reinhart Koselleck's work, see Olsen (2012).
[2] For an analytical understanding of Koselleck's work, see Andersen (2003).

to the way agents interiorize experiences, which are then sedimented through the history and transformation of their semantics. Because these positions can be seen as disclosing possible changes, they have to be won linguistically. Why? Because concepts are vehicles of action – an issue that I will return to.

Fifth, semantics change at slower pace than factual events. They are articulated through experience, but they can also anticipate possible events, constitute the basis of histories in the plural. New experiences can become part and parcel of language inventories precisely because concepts possess a different timespan from their semantics.

Sixth, concepts possess an inner structure that is different from actual events, and yet they can function as vehicles of action in conceiving or in inciting action. This is the main reason Koselleck was so interested in the semantics of concepts.

Seventh, concepts always relate to their "counter-concepts," that is, their opposite. The interrelation between the concept and the counter-concept helps shape the definition of both. An example is how the concept of democracy was considered the counter-concept of tyranny. The positions of the concept and the counter-concept change, as concepts can be related to the agents' experiences, which allow us to see new relationships with other concepts and to social conflicts as well (cf. Junge/Postoutenko 2011).

## 3 Thematizing the subject of conceptual history

In developing his idea of conceptual history, Koselleck focused on how the shaping of concepts and the transformation of the semantic fields move throughout history and end up designing a future or possible futures. He saw the narrative contents of historical events as structures of repetition or innovation. Actual events are not the same as a concept's narrative contents. In his work, Koselleck also distinguished between diachronic and synchronous analysis.

The diachronic is developed through genealogical traces of the origins of a concept and its transformation throughout history.[3] The synchronous is the field that allows one concept to be connected to another, providing precision for spe-

---

[3] Koselleck (1985: 80) describes this kind of analysis as: "Each history of word or concept leads from a determination of past meanings to a specification of these meanings for us. [...] Precisely because attention is directed in a rigorously diachronic manner to the persistent or change of a concept does the sociohistorical relevance of the results increase." "Persistence, change, and novelty are thus conceived diachronically along the dimension of meanings and through the spoken form of one and the same word." (Koselleck 1985: 83)

cific meanings and their frames. These frames are called "semantic fields." Conceptual history moves back and forth from the diachronic to the synchronous and vice-versa.[4]

So let me now consider the question: what is a concept? A concept relates to the way agents situate themselves within their efforts to provide the spaces of signification where both experiences and expectations are their mediations. Agents situate themselves contextually in relation to the past, the present, and the future. Concepts are not words, and words are not necessarily concepts. A concept unfolds into a process, whereas a word relates to a designation, then acquires meaning and simultaneously refers to an object that is also related to the facts. A similar idea of what a concept is can be considered when we think of Wittgenstein's language games and how his notion of family resemblance grasps similar features that can be ascribed to an umbrella of different meanings attached to a concept.

In order to be a concept, it must have the possibility of becoming generalizable, that is, expandable. Words have specific meanings, found in any dictionary; but concepts cannot be defined once and for all. Their meanings are acquired as they evolve, and they can only be interpreted according to the way they are used over time. Thus, concepts possess what Koselleck called their ambiguity.[5] Concepts must remain ambiguous so their semantics can be developed – though, in spite of their historical changes, they must retain some of their original concentration or condensation of meaning. This is the reason we can go back to a concept's genealogies through its specific uses and transformational semantics.

Koselleck thought that words could become concepts if agents or theorists attached a range of social and political meanings to them in their struggles over definitions. Due to this specific capacity of ambiguity, concepts can move to or occupy a semantic territory and create a new relation between time and space. They can also position themselves against another concept so they become opposites and they gain precision when the comparison between them allows us to see that they are placed as concepts and counter-concepts. Also because of this condition of ambiguity, we struggle over the meaning of certain concepts we would like to place in the battlefield of influencing politics so

---

[4] Koselleck (1985: 89) argues that *Begriffsgeschichte* is therefore capable of clarifying the multiple stratification of meaning descending from chronologically separate periods. This means that it goes beyond a strict alternation of diachrony and synchrony and relates more to the contemporaneity of the non-contemporaneous (*Gleichzeitigkeit des Ungleichzeitigen*) that can be contained in a concept.

[5] To illustrate this condition of ambiguity please read the chapter "The Limits of Emancipation" in *The Practice of Conceptual History* (Koselleck 2002: 248–264).

that actions could take place and transformations would be possible. Without the disagreements about meanings, there would be no battles over concepts.

Finally, concepts in conceptual history are seen as analytical strategies about the semantic or linguistic struggles that take place as agents move forward in occupying territories where actions disclose their possibilities of change.

We can define "semantics," another word that occurs frequently in Koselleck's texts, as repositories of articulated experience and, therefore, the conditions of possibility for historical and political events. If semantics can anticipate what might occur, they cannot be regarded as if they are necessary. Much of it depends on how the battle over concepts unfolds and how they can be successful due to specific features that resonate among agents over the uses and the meaning of certain concepts in relation to the past and future of actions.

# 4 The first attempt to define the semantic field of the concepts of "crisis" and "critique"

As we have seen, for Koselleck, concepts reveal their original meaning only if we focus on when they were initially formulated and by whom. But he erased this genealogical perspective, which I have first to clarify in order to make comprehensible the whole of my journey in reviewing his three attempts at conceptualizing crisis. To understand how the two concepts of crisis and critique configured the same semantic field, it is necessary to realize that both words derive from the Greek verb "κρίνω," which means 'to decide' and 'to judge.' "Crisis" came from "κρίνειν" ('to decide') and turned into "κρίσις" ('decision').[6] "Critique" was synonymous with "judgment," or "κριτική." Thus both "crisis" and "critique" were connected to judgment and decision. Koselleck did not focus on this origin on his first attempt to define the co-relation between these two concepts and we will see why.[7]

The relationship between the concept of crisis and that of critique was the subject of Koselleck's first book (as an earlier draft this was the subject of his habilitation), *Critique and Crisis: Enlightenment and the Pathogenesis of Modern Society* (1988). Since both "crisis" and "critique" belong to the same semantic

---

6 Bizas (2016: 5) noticed that the earlier uses of "κρίνω," namely the Greek verb corresponding to "crisis," used in Homer's sagas deal with notions of "separating," "putting asunder," and "picking out."
7 To learn more about how Koselleck omitted the origins of the Greek conceptions of crisis and critique in his essay, see Bizas (2016).

field, it was possible to trace their diachronic perspective, that is, their genealogy, but Koselleck only focused on the Enlightenment. By focusing on their synchronous field – in how they relate to each other as well as to various concepts – Koselleck was able to develop a topography of the non-sedimented meanings in relation to the historical experiences of enlightened agents, in other words, a semantic field relating critique to crisis.

In tracing this late genealogy, Koselleck discovered that the differentiating meaning of the two words, crisis and critique, took place in the eighteenth century, when "critique" and its semantics were applied to literary works as well as to works of art. As Konstantinos Bizas (2016: 6–7) reminds us, Koselleck already knew that critique had the subjective meaning taken from the earlier uses by the Greeks and from how the Latin literature used the term "*grammaticus*" as relating it to the term "*criticus*" which possessed the meaning of the 'art criticism.' In fact, Koselleck (1988: 104) erased this footnote from his dissertation because he wanted to argue that critique came from the Enlightenment (Bizas 2016: 7). In his narrative, Koselleck argued that as a result of this "professionalization," the judgments became either negative or positive in relation to art. But when this transformation of the meaning of "critique" came to be applied to the current political situation, it had an exclusively negative effect, as all the French Enlightenment theorists used critique as a vehicle to question the absolutist state and all the agents who wanted to incite political change used it to bring it down. According to Koselleck's narrative, the agents in this dramatic event, both civilians and theorists, wanted to hide their political goal – the dissolution of the absolutist state – behind their moral critique. So, they organized themselves in secret. For Koselleck, this was the beginning of the understanding of crisis as a processual concept that eventually acquired the meaning of "endless struggles" – because the role of critique had been to destroy the political authority of the state.

Koselleck was not very clear about why it was not only the absolutist state that he had on his mind, but why he thought that when modern agents wanted to emancipate themselves from sovereign power, they not only separated themselves from previous experiences, but they directed their hopes to envision a new conception of society, of history, and of time. He understood that the semantic field of "critique" in relation to "crisis" was related to the emergence of concepts, such as the "new public sphere" (Kant), the debilitating figure of absolutist sovereignty vis-à-vis popular sovereignty (Rousseau), and the development of a different sense of time. Hegel's notion of modernity as the New Time (*Neuzeit*) or the New Era (*Sattelzeit*) would be the illustrative tropes describing how time was defined by movement – specifically, an acceleration of temporality that would bring about the new perspective of the futures-to-come. The idea of the future was conceptualized in many of the philosophies of history as an emerging space of "salvation" or "redemption." This move relocated the ancient Greek meaning of "crisis" to the Latin term "*judicium*" ('judgment') where the religious semantics referred to the final day of God's reckoning with humankind (Koselleck 2006: 359). Revolutionary theorists "secularized" the Latin semantics. The sense of time as the acceleration of the future was also related to a new meaning attached to the old concept of "revolution," which was no longer seen as a circular process (as in ancient Greece), but as a linear one, marking the beginning of the new time (Svampa 2016: 131–151; Richter/Richter 2006).

It is only after Koselleck had come to a more complete mastery of the role of concepts that we can understand this early negative account of the rise of the enlightened public sphere and the politicization of citizens. We know even more about this negative interpretation because Habermas was able to write a completely different narrative in his *Structural Transformation of the Public Sphere: An Inquiry into a Category of the Bourgeois Society*. For example, Habermas (1995) used the term "structural transformations," which is obviously related to Koselleck's idea about the diachronic and synchronous dimensions. Habermas also took up Koselleck's concept of "critique," but imbued it with a positive meaning. While Habermas had a negative view of absolutist power, he thought that the exercise of critique was a positive enlightened practice that Kant (1991: 116–130) had defined in his *Perpetual Peace* as the right of publicity. Thus, Habermas linked his concept of critique associated with the emergence of the new bourgeois public to the habits and practices that made up the positive semantics of concepts such as modern subjectivity, self-education, emancipation, and, yes, society's normative demand about the checks and balances of state power. Habermas wanted to connect the accountability of the new agents with Kant's idea about the need for checks and balances to ensure a state's legitimacy. State power and its legitimacy were no longer unlimited, and the goal was to provide for a new concept: namely, popular sovereignty.

Habermas saw concepts such as equality and political deliberation, as well as the conceptualization of new public spaces like coffee houses and the encouragement of the impulse to bring about political transformations, as positive steps toward the democratization of a government. He opened up the semantic field of the concept of critique with the new activities of those political agents who engaged in performing their duties of citizenship with well-thought-out critiques. Their interventions in the public sphere marked the future of the new battles to come. He also recovered the Kantian notion of the "public use of reason," an element that I will consider later when we focus specifically on the modern notion of critique.

We can say that, as theorists, both Koselleck and Habermas provided us with different views about what had happened in the past and how that past had modified the future as well as different predictions about the same historical stage of modernity. Each theorist wanted his interpretation to win the battle over the concepts of crisis and critique. Why was Habermas' narrative the one that prevailed? There are many reasons, but probably the most important is related to the conceptual semantic field that I have just explained: Habermas connected the concept of critique to political participation and to the Kantian notion of "publicity" as the space of political contestation against state power. He identified activities such as freedom of expression, freedom of association, and political deliberation as related to the semantic field of this new meaning of critique vis-à-vis political agency.

The concept of critique then came to be seen as the new articulation of democratic habits that were structurally linked to the modern public sphere (the spaces of experiences and horizons of expectations; Koselleck 1985: 267–288). The new ways that agents could participate politically were disclosive of the new hopes to come: with the new sense of political participation and the capacities enabled by the new uses of the concept of critique. The absolutist state had too much unlimited power, and the only way to limit it was by questioning its legitimacy with specific demands about transparency and visibility. A second reason Habermas' narrative won the conceptual battle over the emergence of the modern concept of critique was because he propelled the sense of political agency and endorsed the role of critique with positive political goals about political transformation for the better. In the words of Cooke (2006), he offered a particular representation of "the good society" based on the French, German, and English Enlightened societies that motivated and engaged agents of the twentieth century in an ethically oriented political action. Moreover, he did not locate political agency in relation to crisis, but in connection with the efforts of "limiting state power" and enhancing the spaces of accountability while creating a new conception of power.

Habermas'success was due to his engaged projection of his claim of verisimilitude, that is, the ability of his reconstruction or his genealogy to persuade us with the future project of a participatory deliberative democracy. Koselleck, by contrast, had a very negative opinion of the concept of critique. For him, critique was a hypocritical device that placed the authority of the state in permanent danger. He thought that critique showed its worse side during the Enlightenment, when it was falsely seen as a moral exercise, hiding the truth that it was actually a conceptual political weapon. It opened up the problematic field of allowing non-agents to become political, while they could raise permanent doubts about state authority (Rabotnikof 2005). The problem of anti-statism would become the modern problem of democracies, according to Koselleck.

Koselleck went along with his ex-tutor and friend Carl Schmitt in his condemnation of Hobbes, as each of them charged Hobbes with being the first political philosopher to open the door to the enhancement of critique because of the role played by reason when relating it to state power. According to both theorists, Hobbes thought of politics as related to rationality and to the right uses of reason embodied in the state (cf. Schmitt 2004). In my view, Hobbes saw the state as embodying reason just as Hegel would later do. So, the underlying problematic of the concept of crisis that Koselleck had tried to capture seemed historically limited to absolutist power alone. Indeed as an historian, he did not fully explain why critique was such a dangerous weapon for future generations. He linked its dangers to the acceleration of the political goals that would bring about the new hopes of "revolutions" to come.

A philosopher like Habermas, who had a clear understanding of what Koselleck wanted to explain with his historical narrative, knew that Koselleck could not consider the explicit transition of the conceptual separation between "crisis" and "critique" because his desire to link them had the effect of condemning the critical Enlightenment process whereby the nonpolitical agents could turn into political agents. For Habermas, politics is all about action and participation. The conceptual door opened by this new idea of futures-to-come would allow the new hopes to become disentangled from the old experiences. Koselleck could not see why his interpreters viewed his negative perspective as too conservative, even in our times. Yet some of Koselleck's fears about how to reconnect the concept of critique to the actual crisis of state authority seem prescient. The problem was not only how revolutions of the twentieth century would open the door for experiences that had no previous sediments in the past, but how these events would be the new semantic frame of the battles between communism and fascism. The so-called "crisis" (*pathogenesis*) was a critical interpretation of how non-statists theorists would be permanently questioning the statist views, eroding the role of the state authority on an a priori basis.

Habermas, on the other hand, took up the concept of the public sphere and developed his historical reconstruction by adding two structural dimensions – one normative and one empirical. He connected the semantic field of publicity to public opinion and to deliberation, fulfilling the role of citizens as different agents of a political kind and demonstrating how progressive ideals would benefit his own project of deliberative democracy. *Critique and Crisis* was interpreted as defending Schmitt's thesis and his decisionistic interpretation of Hobbesian sovereignty. But for Habermas as well as for other theorists, Schmitt was also the thinker who claimed that the authority of a dictator was justified with the argument that the failure of the Weimar Republic was the result of the crisis of modern democracy. Thus, the connection between Schmitt's perspective and Koselleck's narrative about the chaos that followed the collapse of the monarchy in eighteenth-century France was so strong that his critics concluded that Koselleck's book was an antidemocratic narrative about the concept of critique and a condemnation of modernity as a whole.

So here we have two examples of how theorists struggled to make their differing conceptual narratives prevail, and how the positive/progressive one was more powerful because it envisioned a transformation – a pictorial view of the good society, in Cooke's words (2006: 124) – which opened up the future expectations that allowed agents' new views about the possibilities of democracy. This perspective helps us understand how Habermas captured the imagination of agents through the uses of concepts that became vehicles of action. The point I want to make here is that Koselleck's narrative failed because of the way he used the concepts to construct a diagnosis that envisioned the futures-to-come as moribund, as suffering from a grave illness. Yet if we look deeper into his critique, we find ideas that deserve to be rescued, ideas that encourage us to reconsider the generally negative judgment about his work. So, we must go back to Koselleck's original concern about how the repeated contestation of state authority can bring understanding to the sedimented meanings of our previous experiences of the twenty-first century (Koselleck 2018: 207–224). It appears that today's expectations about the concept of popular sovereignty are very much on the battles among agents and theorists again even though they are trying to describe the questioning of the state authority on the grounds of another concept: populism. We see that the present political crisis has demonstrated that agents (civilians and theorists) are still questioning the authority, only this time it is the neo-liberal state not the absolute monarchy. Contrary to what many believe, in many countries the crisis of the state is due to the abandonment of social projects and protections that once were provided by the welfare states. But there is a second point I want to make: the current crisis regarding neo-liberal governments has revived the notion of critique as a useful exercise that is supported by the new social movements on both the Right and the Left. As a result of policies dictated by the authority of global financial institutions and as the lives of citizens are becoming increasingly impoverished, activists are questioning how and why state policies have ceased to exist and whether their neo-liberal governments still represent them. The European concept of "governance" is supplanting the idea of state sovereignty, and the goal of some of the contemporary battles is to imbue the concept of "popular sovereignty" with new meanings. All the new social movements that are working to redefine such a concept are all described by the same pejorative term of "populists." Yet we need to distinguish whose critiques possess moral content and can be seen as exclusionary or authoritarian. These activists are linking the "death of democracy" to the social policies of the neo-liberal states and the political policies wrought by globalization. Koselleck's narrative – with its dark diagnosis of this crisis and the prognosis about the futures-to-come – seems more valid than ever, and something with which most of us can find "resonance." Populism is the concept everyone thinks they should struggle against, but the truth of the matter is that neo-liberalism has created the battlefield for conceptual and political struggles of today. We will return to this later on.

## 5 A second attempt to trace the links between "crisis" and "critique"

It must have become obvious to Koselleck that he had to go back and construct a broader account of the concept of crisis than his first one, which was focused only on the Enlightenment. An additional problem was that the concept of crisis had become overgeneralized, almost a catch-all – having so many meanings and being applied to so many nonpolitical situations – as in: emotional crisis, intellectual crisis, psychological crisis, political crisis, and economic crisis. The concept itself had undergone a process of "semantic bleaching," as a result of which it had been stripped of its initial precise meaning (Richter/Richter 2006: 353). Koselleck then, with full confidence about how his method could thematize this problematic, decided to go back to the beginning. He needed to capture the historical transformation of the concept of crisis through its original uses in antiquity and then explore the changes of its semantics in terms of how, where, and by whom these alterations had been made and to what extent some important element had been either preserved or lost.

Koselleck revisited the Greek word "κρίνω" ('to decide' or 'to judge'), which, as we have seen, was the etymological ancestor of "κρίσις" ('crisis') as well as "κριτική" ('critique'), both of which were related to activities of the πόλις. This step enabled him to envision the concept of crisis as a processual concept with a dynamic trajectory over political experiences. Thucydides (1942) first used it when he urged the Greek citizens to decide, correctly as it turns out, to fight the "decisive battle" against the Persian enemy. Both crisis and critique were connected to the need to make choices that were good for the community. They were used in precise ways and were political through and through. Aristotle (1989: 1289b) used the two concepts in the context of writing laws and rendering decisions in tribunals. Interestingly, both concepts could be related to making judgments for or against something (here we can find its original link to the current meanings of critique). No decision could be taken without a previous, careful deliberation. κρίσις was meant to organize society. With the creation of institutional law, crisis became even more strongly associated to the political dimension, as it was related to the process of justice. All government resolutions and policies, including decisions about war and peace, deaths and punishments, information and strategies were included in the meaning of "κρίσις."

Koselleck (1982: 617–650) then proceeded to consider the early Christian era and the medieval period when the translation of the New Testament introduced a new semantic regarding the meaning of "salvation." "κρίσις," or crisis, was then associated with the Latin word "*judicium*," meaning 'judgment.' Religious semantics made the Last Judgment part of the ritual occurring at the end of the world, where the expectations were cosmic and God was the ultimate judge. Thus, judgment was connected to salvation and to apocalyptic expectations, as everyone wanted to be saved when the world came to an end, though this event had no clear date (ideas about the future would return in the eighteenth century, when theories of philosophies constructed prognoses with redemptive powers). The third change in the semantics of crisis comes from the medical profession, where "crisis" refers to a sickness and, to a diagnosis (*judicium*). The expectation was that if the right diagnosis were made, the sick person would be cured and survival would be assured. This semantic was taken from the ancient Greek tome *Corpus Hippocraticum*, a collection of writings by the ancient Greek physician Hippocrates, which was systematized in the second century AD by the physician/philosopher Galen. The concept of sickness-as-crisis lasted for more than fifteen hundred years, all the way into the socio-political domain of eighteenth-century France. Once the semantics of crisis was Latinized as *judicium*, it gradually gained traction in the socio-political domain.

Because, following its juridical semantics, crisis implies a process that must end up in a decision. The decision has not yet been made, but it is imminent. Insofar as crisis is a socio-political concept, Koselleck imbues it with a double semantic content. On the one hand, it is an objective situation where the causes of the sickness can be discussed in scientific terms. But it is also subjective, as the outcome depends on the judgment of individuals who use various criteria to make the diagnosis. Moreover, because the crisis is an illness, a transition from the sickness into health is presumed, thus it is framed by a specific period of time.

All these three semantics – the political, the theological, the medical – are linked by the same concept of crisis. A paradoxical feature is that crisis can be used also as inducing actions and policies when someone like Donald Trump has recently called the "immigrant crisis" as his main political project concerned with "protecting" the USA from aliens.[8] Historians and theorists must move inside the situations that have not been articulated linguistically as they try to reconstruct the circumstances that have not yet been expressed linguistically or put into words so they can influence the outcomes of how the new situations are described. There are times when a concept operates as initiating or inciting change and not simply as indicating that a change has already taken place. This is exactly where the concept of crisis shows its internal tensions and the correlation with the concept of critique. Koselleck argued that modernity – that is, the era from the Enlightenment on – should be thought of as a moment of crisis. This claim connects Koselleck's first book, *Critique and Crisis*, to his later work, his *Lexikon*, with its broader critical perspective. Yet there is no possibility of deciding between two options if there is no judgment attached to a deliberation. So, the point now would be to have a possibility of learning to discriminate between progressive ways of criticism against nonprogressive ones.

It was in the eighteenth century that the secular stage reframed its theological roots with the appearance of the philosophies of history and their constructed redemptive narratives. This new semantics of crisis revealed that the concept offered again two different alternatives about possible futures (the medical and the theological semantics searched for an analogy with the Last Judgment as a final decision). Thus, crisis became a stable concept for modernity. Its determination was based on the historical process of history as unique, but it is at this stage where the transition, or *Sattelzeit*, will begin to deal with new problems associated to the ambiguity of the concept of crisis. The process of modernity chained the historical events under the promise of a salvation and as such, it became the signature of modern times (Koselleck 2002: 236–247).

While Rousseau (1969: 468) used crisis as a diagnostic or indicator of a future, he also followed the new philosophical-historical meaning of making a prognosis. For example, he claimed: "Nous approchons de l'etat de crise et du siècle des revolutions." ("We are approaching a state of crisis and a century of revolutions.") He was right, there were many revolutions to come, and the next century would make up the goals of the future of all revolutions to come. By taking the meaning of salvation from the eschatological origin, he built his diagnosis of new revolutions to come. In his letter to the Princess Dashkova from April 3, 1771, Diderot (1877: 28) claimed that "[n]ous touchons à une crise qui aboutira à l'esclavage ou à la liberté" ("we are touching a crisis that will

---

**8** To envision other ways in which the concept of "crisis" is a constructed weapon, see the special issue "Intersectional Feminist Interventions in the 'Refugee Crisis'," in the journal *Refuge: Canada's Journal on Refugees* 34(1), 2018.

end in slavery or freedom"). Diderot was working also with the conceptual device of a prognosis of a future-to-come that also had a dualistic perspective: He championed the historical outcome of the American Revolution and valorized its social content with his new hopes of freedom. When he referred to the Paris of 1778, he then pointed out the uses of the medical metaphor and used the term to describe an apocalyptic situation similar to the one lived under Nero in Rome. According to Koselleck, both Rousseau and Diderot used the term "crisis" as signaling the need for making the right decision while offering as well a critique implicit in the alternatives. So, critique was smuggled into crisis. They both connected to ancient origins of the meaning of crisis but now the purposes were to liberate new expectations.

The American Revolution helped theorists transform the concept of crisis by imbuing it with the meaning of a last decision to make based on a successful historical event that to them possessed a universal meaning. Thomas Paine named his newspaper *The Crisis*. With the greatest revolution in the world – the American – the concept of crisis would play a leading role linked to this successful uprising. Paine (1984: 370) claimed: "That crisis was then arrived, and there remained no choice but to act with determined vigor, or not to act at all." For Burke (1982), on the other hand, these revolutionary times were more like religious wars, and the concept of crisis would be used with a medical claim that was contrary to Paine's positive semantics. These struggles among theorists were the best examples of how crisis was used to describe opposite political positions just like the ones that I described earlier, involving Koselleck and Habermas about modernity and the uses of critique. Paine and Burke used crisis to propose dualistic alternatives and both claimed that the decision "to act or not to act at all" would have the effect of bringing about a universal kind of transformation.

Such a statement raised Koselleck's doubts about the ways in which the concept of crisis had outlived its usefulness, as it had been "semantically bleached." And rather than only applying to political situations, the term could be used now to describe almost everything. Koselleck was able to demonstrate how concepts carried overlapping old meanings along with new ones and how some of the more recent additions had acquired an entirely different definition. As we have seen with its eighteenth-century uses, concepts also served as weapons in political conflicts, among individual antagonists and, later on, among classes, social strata, and even movements. The changes in the history of concepts also reveal the features that ideologies would play in these battles. Recall what I have said of Donald Trump using the term crisis to refer to the immigration from Latin-American countries to the USA.

## 6 A third and last attempt to thematize crisis

Even though his second attempt to thematize crisis led him to another pessimistic conclusion, namely that the concept of crisis had lost its meaning, Koselleck envisioned one particular case where the concept was used with precision and showed its Greek classical political origin. Marx used the concept of crisis to describe the iterative crisis of capitalism, which was central to his construction of the science he called "political economy."[9] Here we see how the semantics of illness had invested the concept of diagnosis with curative powers, accepting the claim that it was a new science. Marx highly valued his concept of crisis and insisted that "change" (in the form of recovery and renewed health) could only come from an accurate diagnosis of the illness called capitalism. In the end, however, he too succumbed to the use of semantics related to the Last Judgment.[10]

In the same entry from his *Lexikon*, Koselleck reviewed three disparate ways in which theorists had used his semantics of crisis. First, they often described a chain of events culminating in the need to demand decisive action. Second, they focused on how the theological had become secularized in the time period under discussion, as it became the point after which history would be changed forever. Third, they discussed how crisis could refer to any given situation – singular or recurring – that endangered the continuing existence of humanity. This is how Koselleck concluded that crisis had become the signature concept of modernity.

In 1985, Koselleck returned to his concept of crisis, now using Schiller's phrase: "World history is the judgment of the world." We can see how the most definitive feature of the concept of crisis was that it had become a processual concept, one depicting a permanent crisis for humanity who is continually on trial. He observed that crisis was meant to be a "threshold," a passage from one epoch to another. It can be a repetition or not. It can both be an iterative and a periodizing concept. And, last, crisis can point out the end of history, as we have known it. Metaphorically speaking, crisis resembles the Last Judgment. But now, it is exclusively future-oriented, anticipating an outcome and a final decision that cannot be changed or appealed. This is how the apocalyptic meaning of the actual concept of crisis has regained strength. There is no escape from the

---

[9] For an excellent account of how Marx developed a critique of political economy, see Stedman Jones (2016: 172–180).
[10] Koselleck (2002: 244) argues: "The supposedly final struggle between the proletariat and the bourgeoisie is, without doubt, consummated for Marx in the dimension of the Last Judgment, which he did not succeed in defining on purely economic grounds."

ecological destruction, as the world is disappearing, and expectations about the future are being foreclosed. We can think of other examples that would suit this apocalyptic use.

## 7 So, what happened to the concept of critique?

As we have seen, Koselleck observed that when the concept of critique was professionalized in the eighteenth century, its role was appropriated by the citizens as well as by the new theorists of the Enlightenment. But the enlightened thinkers employed the term "critique" with the semantics from the past. For example, Kant (1998) used "κριτική" as a verb meaning 'to organize,' 'to separate.' Its purpose was to establish the foundations of his architectonic of theoretical, practical, and aesthetic rationality. For Kant, *Selbstdenken* was meant to impede reason to be led by either tradition or religious authority. The task was to build up the path to the faculty of reason. Thus, Kant believed that his uses of "critique" were the means to postulate the limits and sources of reason. He used "critique" as opposed to "doctrine." This is the reason why he laid down a complete architectonic plan, and with it, he meant to leave behind dogmatic metaphysics (Wolff and Leibniz) and skepticism (Hume).[11]

Hegel, by contrast, never used the concept of critique. Although many of his interpreters believe that he created the concept of "immanent critique," he, in fact, pursued a different path. Finlayson (2014), for example, claims that although Hegel's notion of critique pertained to how the new sciences of the Enlightenment could delineate the object of knowledge, he reserved the term "critique" to describe the work of other philosophers, like Kant, Fichte, and Jacobi, rather than his own. Hegel (2017) clearly assumed that his method of determinate negation did not concern the object of knowledge but of history. And in so doing, he produced something new – specifically, the idea of a concept moving away from error and gaining determinacy. If Hegel was correct, the meaning of the scientific understanding of historical reality consists in the claim that conceptual thinking moves away from distortion in the direction of truth.

For Hegel, the examination of reality as an immanent object of reflexivity traces the various sources of deception, illusion, and distortion that undermine the journey to absolute knowledge. Hegel was also replacing the previous notion

---

[11] Kant's whole enterprise was connected to the eighteenth century's enormous interest on art criticism where the goals were to lay down rules for taste and establish the standards in the arts. For more on this, see Arendt (1982: 27–33).

of "critique" and its conflicted assumption about the separability of the form of knowledge from its material form. Phenomenology was an historicized integrative perspective (Hegel 2017: 51). Hegel presupposed a conception of liberation from earlier stages of falsehood to new ones of truth. And this was precisely the road taken by the neo-Hegelians, especially by Marx. He made the concept of "ideology" his main weapon, but he ended up conceiving of "ideology critique" as false consciousness. As a result, he granted a privileged role to his own theory, which presupposed true consciousness, that is, a vantage point outside of the closed ideological view, only accessible to theorists like him. Moreover, for Marx, the socioeconomic system assumed the attributes of a collective agent that possessed moral powers (Cooke 2006: 110). Today, this view is largely contested. Maeve Cooke, for example, prefers to focus on the specific ways or forms of ideological distortions that avoid any claim to an epistemically privileged vantage point (Cooke 2006: 13).

Thus, the concept of "critique," recovered at the beginning of the eighteenth century initially had a similar meaning to the one the ancient Greeks had given it: "the one who passes judgment" on an object. But as time passed it was expanded into a much more ambitious concept concerning the new political scenarios of modernity. In its English, Spanish, French, and German uses "critique" – "*crítica,*" "*critique,*" "*Kritik*" – assumed the meaning 'to separate,' 'to distinguish,' which is the way Kant regularly used it. With other enlightened thinkers the concept again pertained to the judgments that originally belonged to the political community as the Greeks had originally conceived of it. Yet a third definition of "criticism," formulated by the neo-Hegelians, was ambiguous. It contained a negative connotation suggesting fault-finding, which is why, with the birth of the concept of "ideology," critique was seen as a weapon. And at the same time, critique also came to possess a positive, normative dimension – that is, a change for the better (connected to the Greek concept of praxis).[12] It acquired an authoritative meaning when it was connected to judgments about social pathologies (Fassin 2017).

As Ricœur (2006) observes, Marx, in his neo-Hegelian phase, initially elucidated the concept of "ideology" with a metaphor taken from physics: False consciousness was like an image inverted on the retina. Thus, the task of ideology-critique was to correct the inversion. In this early theorizing Marx depended on Feuerbach's critique of religion as an inverted image of reality, involving a confusion between subject and object. In a later formulation, Marx refocused his cri-

---

[12] The best work on critical theory and its relation to praxis, in my opinion, is Cooke (2006); see also Celikates (2018).

tique of the concept of alienated labor (Marx 1964; Marx 1970; Marx/Engels 1970). Like Hegel, he presupposed that the concept of alienation pointed to its opposite, in other words, that it was a counter-concept of emancipation. But, as I have said, a privileged vantage point where the theorist stands above alienated reality has proven itself too limited, too simplistic. The critique of "false consciousness" must have a different aim. It must not only accept our pluralist modalities of using critique, but it must also attempt to stimulate the imagination of political agents so that they are motivated to become agents and engage in a praxis of social change for the better. Thus, to reassume Marx's legacy involves two tasks: negatively, to deploy critique to diagnose social pathologies and, positively, to envision more just and fulfilling forms of collective life.

Critical theorists, including Habermas, have moved away from a totalizing perspective because they understand how our finite consciousness can only focus on particular distortions (Gadamer 2010), and also how we are immersed in our own horizons and historical contexts of interpretation. The French critical theorists have attempted to solve the problem of the role of distortions and of constitutive agency as a performative process of political identity by linking the ideology to the positive side of imagination (similar to the role of "the empty signifiers" in Ernesto Laclau's (2005: 91–162) theory). Here again, it has been Cooke who has critically engaged with Laclau's latest conception of ideology. It is well known that Laclau, like Althusser, accepted the possibility of distortions (Laclau 2005: 49–54). But, unlike the French structuralists, he was against imposing a privileged totalizing perspective on social reality. To counter Laclau's negativity to closure, Cooke developed a nonauthoritarian approach that does not abandon the "fictive character of completeness" in relation to validity:

> Becoming aware that the illusion of completeness is necessary to protect against an originary trauma may lead not to ideological closure (and the enjoyment of it) but to the attempt to come to grips with the originary trauma by way of therapeutic process of (collective or individual) self-investigation. (Cooke 2007: 57)

In general, the point is that today many forms of critique are available to us that do not rely on a privileged, which is to say, elitist standpoint. Writers such as Latour (2004), for example, have been making new attacks regarding the modes of critique that presuppose the "reality/appearance" perspective. But that is not my concern here. Rather, my main focus is the original political project of "unveiling" domination, oppression, or distortion and differentiating between the kinds of critiques that have arisen from social movements as well as from theorists, which can help us discriminate among projects leading to positive cognitive transformations. My second concern is therapeutic, that is, to provide an exercise for the imagination that enables agents to invest in political projects aiming at ethical and nonauthoritarian goals. Koselleck was right in his claim that individual agents are not the only ones moved by political interests and goals. Critique is also a political activity that presupposes a moral theoretical standpoint. The crucial point here is that critique can be a weapon of war that helps to destroy a society's ethical projects without transforming them for the better. Lately, we have seen many examples of such happenings thanks to Donald Trump, Viktor Orbán, Matteo Salvini, and the Brexiteers, who want closed frontiers to impede (irregular) immigration and bring back the fiction of past greatness.

My concerns with critique would be to remind us that we must be connected to an antiauthoritarian force – the critical imagination –, which enables us to demonstrate why certain societies, institutions, or political projects are unacceptable. Their distorted views cannot provide us with either an emancipatory potential indicating why action is needed or a proper perspective regarding the positive transformation of reality. As theorists, we must help ourselves by getting the necessary feedback from the claims of social movements and have the capacity to discriminate between them. Critique needs judgment, critical judgments. And, if justice is to be attained, then we must also attempt to formulate a full pictorial vision – "the fictive character" – of positive alternatives.

In all societies, political concepts are used to capture the nature of political conflicts (cf. De Boer/Sonderegger 2012). It is easy to reduce critique either to its fault-finding, "authoritarian" dimensions, or its tendency to be taken as neutral or too general. But critique should be a process of an open dialogue, involving the agents and theorists alike. Critique must be ethically consistent, providing the best possible justifications of why certain states of affairs or institutions exert oppression or domination. Schematically, we can divide critique into two major groups. The first group, whom Ricœur (2006) referred to as "the hermeneutics of suspicion," concentrates on unmasking distorted images of social and political reality. Following Marx and Freud, the members of the first generation of the Frankfurt School were representatives of this approach. Because it presupposes a privileged standpoint from which this unmasking can take place, this group tends toward fault-finding and offers alternatives against the dangers of authoritarianism. Rather than attempting to unmask distorted images, the second group, which contains thinkers like Koselleck and Foucault, employs a genealogical approach. It not only shows how these pictures of the world came into existence, but they suggest how we might move away from them as a change of perspectives allows one to see other angles of the same picture. Both need careful examination, contrasting it with each other, using discrimination as well as judgments.

If critique allows societies to strive to better configure public opinion, or to win battles over different perspectives, or to make people see what they could not see before, then critique, which has played a key role in the history of modernity, reveals itself as the most important concept of political theories (Walzer 2002). Yet it is only by recovering both crisis and critique, as they are intrinsically related to each other, that we can demonstrate how the strategies of both are linked to the conceptual battles of societies and to action. If this fact can be acknowledged, then the enlightened meaning emerging from the different paths that critique has taken gives us multiple ways of envisioning judgments about societies' conflicts or distortions and also the right kind of justifications (Owen 1995). We have learned to use critique as a φάρμακον, just as Nietzsche, Wittgenstein, and Foucault did:

> However distant their theories are from each other, Nietzsche's and Wittgenstein's endeavor to apprehend the way people see the world and make sense of it – from particular perspectives for the former, or via common pictures, for the latter –and their approaches, which imply that these perspectives are historically determined and that these pictures or frames are culturally inherited, which means they can be designated as "genealogies." (Fassin 2017: 17)

Despite his own prejudices, Koselleck could not have developed his own method without making some judgments and strong critiques. Politics without history is not possible. Yet, a historical account that does not focus on allowing us to see how critical ethical constructions have offered not only hope but triggered actual changes for the better is what is needed most. Crisis and critique are complementary concepts, not opposites.

# References

Andersen, Niels Åkerstrøm (2003): *Discursive Analytical Strategies: Understanding Foucault, Koselleck, Laclau, Luhmann*. Bristol: Policy Press.

Arendt, Hannah (1982): *Lectures on Kant's Political Philosophy*. Edited and with an interpretative essay by Ronald Beiner. Chicago, IL: University of Chicago Press.

Aristotle (1989): *Politics*. Trans. into Spanish by Julian Marías and M. Araujo. Bilingual ed. Madrid: CEC.

Bizas, Konstantinos (2016): "Reinhart Koselleck's Work on Crisis." In: *French Journal for Media Research* 5, pp. 2–12.

Burke, Edmund (1982): *Reflections on the Revolution in France*. [1790]. Edited and with an introduction by Conor Cruise O'Brien. London: Penguin.

Celikates, Robin (2018): "Critical Theory and the Unfinished Project of Mediating Theory and Practice." In: Gordon, Peter/Hammer, Espen/Honneth, Axel (Eds.): *The Routledge Companion to the Frankfurt School*. London: Routledge, pp. 206–220.

Cooke, Maeve (2006): *Re-Presenting the Good Society*. Cambridge, MA: MIT Press.

De Boer, Karin/Sonderegger, Ruth (2012): *Conceptions of Critique in Modern Contemporary Philosophy*. London: Palgrave Macmillan.

Diderot, Denis (1877): *Œuvres complètes*. Edited by J. Assézat and M. Tourneux. Paris: Éditions Garnier Frères.

Fassin, Didier (2017): "The Endurance of Critique." In: *Anthropological Theory* 17(1), pp. 4–29.

Finlayson, James Gordon (2014): "Hegel, Adorno and the Origins of Immanent Criticism." In: *British Journal for the History of Philosophy* 22(6), pp. 1142–1166.

Gadamer, Hans-Georg (2010): *Verdad y método*. Vol. II. Trans. from German by Manuel Olasagasti. Salamanca: Sígueme.

Habermas, Jürgen (1995): *The Structural Transformation of the Public Sphere: An Inquiry into a Category of Bourgeois Society*. Trans. into English by Thomas Burger with the assistance of Frederick Lawrence. Cambridge, MA: MIT Press.

Hegel, Georg Wilhelm Friedrich (2017): *Fenomenología del espíritu*. [1807]. Edited and trans. from the German by Gustavo Leyva. México: Fondo de Cultura Económica.

Junge, Kay/Postoutenko, Kirill (Eds.) (2011): *Asymmetrical Concepts after Reinhart Koselleck: Historical Semantics and Beyond*. Bielefeld: Transcript.

Kant, Immanuel (1991): *Political Writings*. Edited and with an introduction by Hans Reiss. New York, NY: Cambridge University Press.

Kant, Immanuel (1998): *Critique of Pure Reason*. [1787]. Trans. by Paul Guyer and Allen Wood. New York, NY: Cambridge University Press.

Koselleck, Reinhart (1982): "Krise." In: Brunner, Otto/Conze, Werner/Koselleck, Reinhart (Eds.): *Geschichtliche Grundbegriffe: Historisches Lexikon zur politisch-sozialen Sprache in Deutschland*. Vol. 3. Stuttgart: Klett-Cotta, pp. 617–650.

Koselleck, Reinhart (1985): *Futures Past: On the Semantics of Historical Time*. Trans. into English by Keith Tribe. Cambridge, MA: MIT Press.

Koselleck, Reinhart (1988): *Critique and Crisis: Enlightenment and the Pathogenesis of Modern Society*. Cambridge, MA: MIT Press.

Koselleck, Reinhart (2002): *The Practice of Conceptual History: Timing History, Spacing Concepts*. Trans. into English by Todd Samuel Presner and others. Stanford, CA: Stanford University Press.

Koselleck, Reinhart (2006): "Crisis." In: *Journal of the History of Ideas* 67(2), pp. 357–400.

Koselleck, Reinhart (2018): *Sediments of Time: On Possible Histories*. Trans. and edited by Sean Franzel and Stefan-Ludwig Hoffman. Stanford, CA: Stanford University Press.

Laclau, Ernesto (2005): *La razón populista*. México: Fondo de Cultura Económica.

Latour, Bruno (2004): "Why Has Critique Run out of Steam? From Matters of Fact to Matters of Concern." In: *Critical Inquiry* 30(2), pp. 225–248.

Marx, Karl (1964): *The Economic and Philosophic Manuscripts of 1844*. [1844]. Edited by Dirk J. Struik. New York, NY: International Publishers.

Marx, Karl (1970): *Critique of Hegel's Philosophy of Right*. [1844]. Trans. into English by Joseph O'Malley. New York, NY: Cambridge University Press.

Marx, Karl/Engels, Friedrich (1970): *The German Ideology*. [1846]. Trans. by C. J. Arthur. New York, NY: International Publishers.

Olsen, Niklas (2012): *History in the Plural: An Introduction to the Work of Reinhart Koselleck.* New York, NY/Oxford: Berghahn.
Owen, David (1995): *Nietzsche, Politics and Modernity.* London: Sage.
Paine, Thomas (1984): *The Rights of Man.* [1791]. New York, NY: Penguin.
Rabotnikof, Nora (2005): *En busca de un lugar común: El espacio público en la teoría política contemporánea.* México: IIF-UNAM.
Richter, Melvin/Richter, Michaela W. (2006): "Introduction: Translation of Reinhart Koselleck's 'Krise,' in *Geschichtliche Grundbegriffe.*" In: *Journal of the History of Ideas* 67(2), pp. 343–356.
Ricœur, Paul (2006): *Ideología y utopía.* Edited by George H. Taylor. Trans. from the French into Spanish by Alcira Bixio. Barcelona: Gedisa.
Rousseau, Jean-Jacques (1969): *Œuvres complètes.* Vol. 4. Paris: Gallimard.
Schmitt, Carl (2004): *El Leviatán en la teoría del Estado de Thomas Hobbes.* Trans. into Spanish by Francisco Javier Conde. Edited by José Luis Monedero Pérez. Granada: Editorial Comares.
Stedman Jones, Gareth (2016): *Karl Marx: Greatness and Illusion.* Cambridge, MA: Belknap Press of Harvard University Press.
Svampa, Lucila (2016): "El concepto de crisis en Reinhart Koselleck: Polisemias de una categoría histórica." In: *Anacronismo e Irrupción: Revista de Teoría Política Clásica y Moderna* 6(11), pp. 131–151.
Thucydides (1942): *Historiae.* Vol. 1. Edited by H. Stuart Jones and J. E. Powell. Oxford: Oxford University Press.
Walzer, Michael (2002): *The Company of Critics.* New York, NY: Basic Books.

Thijs Lijster
# Critical Common/Common Critique

## Or How to Regain Steam

**Abstract:** In the past decade, there have been several philosophical, societal, and artistic critiques of critique. Alain Badiou, for instance, rejects the critical Kantian tradition in favor of being 'true to the Event,' while Bruno Latour concluded in a seminal article that critique had ran 'out of steam.' In certain artistic practices, finally, participation and proximity is preferred over the traditional critical and contemplative attitude of the observer. Although such attacks have their reason, I will argue that we should not give up on critique too hastily, even though that might mean that we have to search for alternative concepts of critique. In order to contribute to that search, I will consider the concept of critique in relation to the concept of the 'common,' that has been widely debated in recent political philosophy and art theory. To do that I will first discuss the tensions between these two concepts, and next try to go beyond this tension by bringing them into a dialectical relationship, by investigating the implications of a 'critical common' and a 'common critique.' I will argue that these categories can strengthen one another: While commons provide fertile soil ('common ground') for critical theory, critique can prevent the romanticization and appropriation of the commons into traditional notions of 'community' or 'common sense.'

**Keywords:** Critique, commons, common sense, community, dialectic

In his 1928 book *One Way Street*, the German philosopher and critic Walter Benjamin bluntly states that only *Narren*, clowns or fools, lament the decay of critique:

> For its day is long past. [Critique] is a matter of correct distancing. It was at home in a world where perspectives and prospects counted and where it was still possible to adopt a standpoint. Now things press too urgently on human society. The "unclouded," "innocent" eye has become a lie, perhaps the whole naive mode of expression sheer incompetence. (Benjamin 1996: 476)

Where does this leave us, worrying about the crisis of critique some ninety years later, when again things seem to be pressing too urgently on human society? Are we indeed *Narren*, clowns or fools, for lamenting its decay? One is indeed tempted to believe so if one considers the recent surge of postcritical or even anticritical discourse. In the past decade, there have been several philosophical, societal, and artistic critiques of critique. Critique is accused of many different things, from many different directions. We can summarize these accusations as follows. First, critique is considered as negative or even nihilistic. This is a point made most famously by Bruno Latour, who in his essay "Why Has Critique Run out of Steam?" (2004) scorns the gratuitous demystifying gesture of the modern critic, who concerns himself only with the shattering of the fetishes of others, thereby neglecting the great fetish of critique itself. We also encounter it, in a different way, in Alain Badiou, who rejects the critical Kantian tradition in favor of being "true to the Event" (Badiou 1999), and even already in Peter Sloterdijk's rejection of the pure negativity of "cynical reason." As diverse as these thinkers may be, all agree that critique is somehow self-defeating, a dead-end-street, that does not and cannot lead to action.

Second, critique is said to be detached and isolated. We recognize this already in Benjamin's abovementioned disavowal of the "unclouded" (*Unbefangenheit*) and "innocent eye" (*freier Blick*). Today this form of anticritique perhaps most prominently features in participation and community art, and the discourse surrounding it. As Claire Bishop has shown, these artistic practices favor the perspective of the participant over the contemplative and detached view of the observer or critic (Bishop 2012). From this point of view, to be critical equals to remain an outsider, to remain uninvolved and unengaged.

Thirdly, critique is said to be conformist. Fredric Jameson addresses capitalism's interest in "'Enlightenment'-type critiques and 'demystification' of belief and committed ideology, in order to clear the ground for unobstructed planning and 'development'" (Jameson 2007: 43). Following Jameson, Stefano Harney and Fred Moten question the status of the academic critic: "He claims to be critical of the negligence of the university. But is he not the most accomplished professional in his studied negligence? [...] Does the questioning of the critical academic not become a pacification?" (Harney/Moten 2013: 39) This disavowal of critique is expressed even more forcefully by the Dutch sociologists Willem Schinkel and Rogier van Reekum:

> Critique has become order, and complains that it is not order enough, that it does not order the order. But critique has been elevated to an ordering principle everywhere. [...] So we are not writing critique, at least we try not to, since critique is a reflex, a privileged second nature built on the order of the first nature of orders [...]. Critique is academic necrophilia. (Schinkel/Van Reekum 2019: 45, 49)

So now we went from clowns, via nihilists, outsiders, and conformists, to necrophiles. What a journey! But what to do with these clownesque necrophiles or necrophile clowns? Should we just give up on the critic and on critique? But then the next question would be: Can we do without it?

In this chapter I will argue, without disregarding the abovementioned shortcomings of critique, that we cannot do without it, that in fact we are in dire need of it, even though that might mean that we have to search for alternative concepts of critique. I want to give a hint of such an alternative concept by relating the concept of critique to the 'common,' a concept that has been widely debated in recent political and social philosophy, as well as in economic and legal theory. To do that I will first discuss the tensions between these two concepts, and next try to go beyond this tension by bringing them into a dialectic relationship with each other, and by investigating the possibilities and implications of a 'critical common' and a 'common critique.' In my conclusion, I will return once more to Benjamin's reflections on the decay of critique.

# 1 Common vs. critique

The 'common,' as a phenomenon, practice, and concept, has been widely discussed in different fields of research, for instance, and most notably by Elinor Ostrom in economic theory (Ostrom 2015), by Michael Hardt and Antonio Negri in political philosophy (Hardt/Negri 2009), by Lawrence Lessig in legal theory (Lessig 2001), by David Harvey and Stavros Stavrides in critical urban studies (Harvey 2012; Stavrides 2016), and Nico Dockx and Pascal Gielen in art theory (Dockx/Gielen 2018). Due to the variety of these discussions and discourses, it is not an easy concept to delineate, alternately referring to certain resources (such as lands, woods, water, or information shared in common) to social relationships, and to organizational forms. Some scholars prefer to speak of "commoning" as an activity rather than "commons" as entities (cf. Harvey 2012). Leaving aside these debates for the moment, I will follow Dardot and Laval, who in their exhaustive study *Common* write:

> [I]f the "commune" is used to name a specific, local, self-governing polity, and the "commons" is the name given to a diverse array of objects or resources managed by the activities of individuals and collectives, "common" is more properly the name of the principle that both animates and guides this activity. (Dardot/Laval 2019: 7)

So, like critique, I will here treat 'the common' first as a concept or principle, rather than as a practice or phenomenon (although, as noted in the quote, practices can be based on this principle). At first sight, the concept or principle of the common might be an unlikely candidate to salvage the concept of critique. If we look at the respective etymologies of these concepts, they almost seem to be mutually exclusive. "Common," from the Latin "*commun*" and the Greek "*koinón*," refers to 'sharing,' 'living,' and 'being together,' a "shared mode of existence" (Dardot/Laval 2019: 11). The concept critique comes from the Greek "*krino*" (κρίνω), 'to separate,' 'divide,' and 'distinguish,' or 'to judge' and 'decide.' Indeed, while "commoning" means 'bringing things together,' "to criticize" is 'to put things apart' (which still resounds in the German "*ur-teilen*").

Furthermore, if we again consider the critique of critique coming from postcritical or anticritical discourse, one can see how the common would 'score' better on all points. The common is neither negative nor nihilistic but designates actually existing and positively formulated alternatives. Although these alternatives often present themselves as emphatically anticapitalist, the common does not emerge as a reaction against capitalism, but rather, as Massimo De Angelis noted, as an alternative and autonomous system that has its own origin and exists next to (and in some cases even within) capitalism (De Angelis 2017: 103–105). If anything, modern capitalism emerged out of an enclosure and appropriation of the commons. The common, finally, refers not to a detached, unengaged, or solitary attitude, but to sharing, collective action, and reciprocal relations.

Before giving the impression that the common is able to right all the wrongs of critique, let us remind ourselves that there is, conversely, also a critical discourse on the common. From the perspective of critique, the common, as expressed in 'common sense' or the power of the 'community' can be and in fact has been considered as a gray, anonymous, and dangerous entity, threatening the critical capacities or even the very existence of the autonomous individual. As Theodor W. Adorno writes in his essay "Critique": "[W]hoever criticizes violates the taboo of unity" (Adorno 2005: 283), and this violation was sometimes punished severely. Or consider Jean-Luc Nancy's words in his essay "The Confronted Community" (2009):

> I could see from all sides the dangers aroused by the use of the word community: its resonance fully invincible and even bloated with substance and interiority; its reference inevitably Christian [...] or more broadly religious as it is used to support an array of so-called ethnicities. All this could only be a warning. It was clear that the emphasis placed on this necessary but still insufficiently clarified concept was at least, at this time, on par with the revival of communitarian trends that could be fascistic. (Nancy 2009: 24–25)

Are critique and the common mere opposites then, or can they be brought into a potentially fruitful interplay with each other, perhaps as a mutual corrective to right each other's wrongs? I would like to emphasize that this is not a mere academic or scholarly issue, as we seem to be living in an era of mass movements and mass protests. In previous years, we have witnessed numerous climate marches, women's marches, and worker's protests. At the same time we sometimes hear critique on such protests: that they are disorganized, uninformed, misdirected, hysterical, or irrational. And this is not only critique coming from right-wing or conservative commentators but also from progressive commentators, such as Nick Srnicek and Alex Williams who criticized the "folk politics" of such movements, their term for the bad and unproductive romanticization of immediate and direct action at the expense of long-term strategy, the critical study of new ideas, and "the long march through the institutions" (Srnicek/Williams 2015). Indeed, we should not step into the pitfall of romanticizing the collective or community per se. Next to all the protests just mentioned, and next to Occupy, Extinction Rebellion, and the Arab Springs we have in recent years also witnessed white supremacists marching Charlottesville, and Polish far-right nationalists, or collectives more difficult to position on either side of the political spectrum such as the yellow vests. Finally, the way the concept of the commons has in recent times been embraced by neoliberal policy makers should also raise some suspicion. One can see how a certain understanding of the common – for instance, David Cameron's "Big Society" – perfectly fits the neoliberal agenda of austerity and further cutting basic social services.

This raises the question of the possibility of a critical common, and/or a common critique. Addressing this question entails a double movement, wherein our understanding of both the common (or community) and our understanding of critique are expanded and adjusted.

## 2 Critical common

Let us start with the possibility of a critical common. In his book *Common Ground* (2014) Jeremy Gilbert discusses the "Leviathan Logic" that has been dominant in the understanding of collectives and communities, which runs from Hobbes onward, and later can be found in writings of several conservative thinkers, such as Gustave Le Bon and Ortega y Gasset. According to Gilbert, this Leviathan Logic is characterized by the following three assumptions: 1) an ontological individualism, i.e., the "implicit belief that social relations are not constitutive of the person and their most fundamental forms of experience" (Gilbert 2014: 31–32); 2) a vertical understanding of the group, namely as constituted by singular relationships of each individual member with the (real or metaphorical) leader; 3) a meta-individualist conception of collectives, which has the properties of and acts like an individual (as illustrated by the famous frontispiece of Hobbes' *Leviathan*). Taken together, these assumptions lead to a conception of the collective as a mere aggregation of individuals, while at the same time considering it as essentially hostile to the individual's autonomy. For Gilbert, this logic prevails in contemporary neoliberalism, which takes the individual as "the basic unit of human experience" (Gilbert 2014: 38). It is strategically deployed when neoliberal politics considers the individual's creativity as the main source of production, and individual responsibility as the legitimization for cutbacks and austerity. Interestingly, however, Gilbert argues that the same Leviathan Logic is present in antiliberal political movements from left to right, although it is of course valued in an entirely different way, such that the power of the group over the singular individual is indeed legitimized for the higher good. Soviet Communism too, considered the crowd as homogenous and with one will, represented by the party, and this logic still pervades in contemporary left-wing notions of populism of Laclau and Mouffe, where individuals gather under the "empty signifier," that is, "the people."

According to Gilbert, the main contemporary political challenge is to conceive of a different understanding of the collective or the community, neither as disorganized rabble nor as totalitarian meta-individual but rather "as a condition of dynamic multiplicity and complex creativity" (Gilbert 2014: x). He makes the useful distinction between "community" and "common." While the first is "dependent upon a shared, but static and homogeneous identity, [that] is often evoked in order to neutralise any possible criticism of the power relations obtaining within 'communities'," the latter "can be understood as that domain of creative potential which is constituted by, and constitutive of, sociality as such" (Gilbert 2014: 164, 167).

The subject of the common (if we can name it such) is indeed not 'the people' nor the traditional community, understood as an identitarian unity, but rather the Spinozean "multitude," which of course has been elaborately discussed by Paolo Virno, Michael Hardt and Antonio Negri. The multitude, in Hardt and Negri's understanding, "is a form of political organization that, on the one hand, emphasizes the multiplicity of the social singularities in struggle and, on the other, seeks to coordinate their common actions and maintain their equality in horizontal organizational structures" (Hardt/Negri 2009: 110). In contrast to the people or the community, the multitude is in a constant process of becoming and cannot be fixed into a unity or identity.

The multitude does not have the clear delineation of Marx's proletariat. Though, like Marx, Hardt and Negri emphasize the link of their political subject to capitalist forms of production, at the same time they note that once capitalist production has become "biopolitical," almost all forms of life can considered to be forms of production. As I see it, the concept of the multitude first and foremost poses the challenge to think of the collective and the individual not as opposing and mutually excluding forces, but to rather think in terms of a productive and fruitful interrelationship between the two. Or more radical, since 'interrelationship' still presumes the ontological distinction and separation between the two, multitude rather implies that the in-dividual is always already part of, and originates in, a common. As Paolo Virno formulates it:

> Precisely because they are the complex result of a progressive differentiation, the "many" do not postulate an ulterior synthesis. The individual of the multitude is the final stage of a process beyond which there is nothing else, because everything else (the passage from the One to the Many) has already taken place. (Virno 2004: 76)

Most importantly for my purposes in this contribution, it puts critique in the heart of the common, since it is only through critique, both directed outward and directed inward, that the multitude remains the dynamic multiplicity that these theorists envision. The self-identification of the collective should never be total if it is still to remain critical. Otherwise, we risk relapsing in traditional notions of 'the people' or 'the community,' governed by the Leviathan Logic that Gilbert was talking about. In contrast, what I call a 'critical common' is precisely characterized by the possibility of self-criticism, dissent, and the potential of transformation.

## 3 Common critique

For the reverse question of how to think of a common (or communal) critique, the notion of critique discussed in the first part – as negative, detached, and distanced – needs to be rethought and contextualized, namely as 1) situated, 2) institutionalized, and 3) politicized. To elaborate on these three features, I will subsequently draw from Donna Haraway, Michel Foucault, Luc Boltanski, and Antonio Gramsci.

Following Donna Haraway and other feminist scholars, we should think of critique as emerging from "situated knowledge" (Haraway 1988: 583). During the 1970s and 1980s decolonial anthropology and feminist theory have revealed the extent to which critics, theorists, and scholars of culture produce their knowledge from a situated perspective. While critical and rational consciousness has long pretended to be a kind of view from nowhere and disqualified any form of knowing that was situated (in a body, a tradition, a particular point of view), Haraway by contrast argues that "knowledge from the point of view of the unmarked is truly fantastic, distorted, and irrational" (Haraway 1988: 587). In recent years, this insight has come more to the foreground in public debates. Critics are increasingly required to account for their own social position and the aesthetic, cultural, and political biases that this position may entail. Critique, then, is always situated, but this obviously does not mean that it accepts its situation, quite the contrary. Michel Foucault famously defined critique as "the art of not being governed like that" that is not "in the name of those principles, with such and such an objective in mind and by means of such procedures, not like that, not for that, not by them" (Foucault 2007: 44). The "like that" in this phrase is crucial, for it excludes from the outset the very possibility of not being governed at all, and therefore indeed principally situates and contextualizes critique. For Foucault, critique is not something that was invented by philosophers in the eighteenth century, and does not come out of nowhere, but is an attitude that exists and has existed everywhere and every time that people revolted against certain (historical and situated) modes of governmentality. In this understanding, then, critique is not some kind of characteristic or skill of the individual, but something thoroughly collective and relational.

This brings us to Luc Boltanski. In his 2011 book *On Critique*, Boltanski distinguishes between a critical sociology and a pragmatic sociology of critique. Critical sociology, which he associates with the work of his former mentor Bourdieu, faces several theoretical and methodological problems. First, the dominated as described by critical sociology are themselves utterly oblivious to the forms of domination exposed by the sociologist. To account for this ignorance, the critical social theorist assumes that these actors suffer from "false consciousness" or a distorted understanding of their own situation. This means, however, that the sociologist or social critic necessarily underestimates, or even ignores, the critical capacities of the actors he or she is analyzing, and at the same time overestimates the explanatory power of his or her own sociological approach. There is, in other words, an "asymmetry between the sociologist enlightened by the light of his science and ordinary people sunk in illusion" (Boltanski 2011: 23). In this way, critical sociology not only overestimates its own range of vision, pretending to know people better than they know themselves, but it eventually also undermines its own emancipatory potential: the contempt for people's critical capabilities and practices ultimately robs critical sociology of an addressee. In *On Justification* (2006) Boltanski and his coauthor Laurent Thévenot responded to these problems with what they call a "pragmatic sociology of critique." This pragmatic sociology of critique is not primarily interested in its own critical perspective but rather in "observing, describing, and interpreting situations where people engage in critique" (Boltanski 2011: 24). This means observing situations in which actors find themselves confronted with indignation and suffering, and the ways in which they deal with these, especially in how they criticize each other and justify their own actions.

This 'pragmatist turn,' however, has several drawbacks of its own. Placing the actors' own critique at the center, the pragmatic sociology of critique made itself dependent on what Boltanski calls the actors' "sense of reality." Actors have a sense of what they consider "normal" – one might also say a "common sense" – and this sense shapes the extent to which they experience feelings of indignation and anxiety, and hence the extent to which they are willing to criticize what they consider as the sources of these feelings. Critique might be happening all the time, the scope of it is often quite local and limited. According to Boltanski, with the exception of revolutionary situations, "ordinary people rarely call into question [...] the general framework in which the situations that provoke their indignation and protests are inscribed" (Boltanski 2011: 32). This also means that the sociologist might miss out on societal developments that occur over longer ranges of time, and that alter the very background against which people justify their actions. This is why in *On Critique* (2011), Boltanski argues that sociology should also develop a "sense of totality," that is a perspective from which the background, within which acts of critique are situated, can be questioned and criticized:

> From the overarching programme [of critical sociology] this framework would take the possibility, obtained by the stance of *exteriority*, of challenging reality, of providing the dominated with tools for resisting fragmentation [...]. But from the pragmatic programme such a framework should pay attention to the activities and critical competences of actors and acknowledgement of the pluralistic expectations which, in contemporary democratic-capitalist societies, seem to occupy a central position in the critical sense of actors, including the most dominated among them. (Boltanski 2011: 48)

According to Boltanski, this combination of critical sociology and the sociology of critique draws special attention to the role of institutions. Social life is characterized by a constant uncertainty about what 'really' is the case. Or in Boltanski's terms: There is a constant gap between reality as "the whatness of what is" and the world as "everything that happens." Critique and institutions can be considered as two distinct ways of responding to this gap: While critique is pointing to it and takes it as a source for indignation, institutions seek to repair the gap, or in some cases obscure it. Hence, institutions and critique are inextricably bound together: While institutions are meant to eliminate the object of critique, critique can take institutions as its addressee. While there is a contradictory logic at work in critique and institutions, in that institutions (sometimes violently) have to circumvent the unmasking work of critique, and in that critique questions the confirmation of reality that is the work of institutions, one can also imagine situations in which the goals of institutions and critique are aligned. These are predominantly situations of crisis, in which the status of 'reality' becomes radically uncertain, and new forms of collective life emerge. As Boltanski writes:

> By recognizing that their fate is bound up with that of critique, institutions would even be consolidated in a sense. It is in fact only through the intermediary of (reformist) critique [...] that institutions can hope to engage with something real, and through that of (radical) forms of existential critique that they can hope to retain contact with the world. (Boltanski 2011: 157)

This brings us, finally, to the question of how the relation between critique and the common might be politicized. Although the politicization of critique has been on the agenda at least since Marx, a good point of departure would be Antonio Gramsci, and his notion of 'common sense,' which he defines as "the diffuse, uncoordinated features of a generic form of thought common to a particular period and a particular popular environment" (Gramsci 1971: 330). While Marx argued that the ideological "superstructure" emerges naturally from the class that ruled over the means of production, for Gramsci it was less one-dimensional than that. Common sense, for Gramsci, is rather an arena of continuously contested and contesting ideas about what the world is like, and what is considered possible, necessary, realistic, etc. Ideological rule does not follow automatically from economic rule but is rather the outcome of a struggle in which the ruling classes eventually gain hegemony over the definition of reality. Thus, for Gramsci it will not suffice for the suppressed classes to cease the economic means of production; the struggle to create a different hegemonic order, that is, to define what is 'common sense,' is also fought through cultural, educational, and media institutions. Each political struggle, then, has to start with challenging and altering common sense. The way to do this, Gramsci argues, is not to start from scratch, but rather exists in "making 'critical' an already existing activity" (Gramsci 1971: 331). This implies that one starts from values and beliefs already acknowledged by a collective (such as 'freedom,' 'equality,' or even 'the common' itself), only to slightly shift them into a different direction. Following Gramsci, Christian Höller thus talked about "un-common sense," and considered the task of critique twofold: "to acknowledge the un-common element in the common, and to start building a new common on the basis of such un-common elements" (Höller 2015: 107).

Following Haraway, Foucault, Boltanski, and Gramsci, one might say that critique both originates and results in a "common" – "origin is the goal," to quote Karl Kraus. A common critique, then, acknowledges that it has no 'God eye's view' but is principally situated, while at the same time sticking to the promise of critique to de-naturalize what 'is the case,' thus laying the groundwork for a critical common.

## 4 Conclusion

An image has emerged of a dialectics of the common and of critique. To summarize, the first part of this dialectic is the idea that the common is dependent on critique to prevent it from relapsing in identitarian and potentially oppressive forms of community. As, among others, Nancy and Adorno have shown, the 'common' is not necessarily progressive – taken as a homogeneous or homogenizing entity, it will pose a threat to both outsiders, and according to a self-defeating logic, eventually also to those inside. In other words: The common depends on open-endedness, porosity, multiplicity, and dissent, and thus on critique.

The flip side of the dialectic, so to say, implies that critique should be situated, institutionalized, and politicized, that is, infused, informed, and operationalized by the common. Critique does not and cannot exist on its own but emerges from the common, not only in form of learning and education, but also as the expression of actually existing forms of indignation and suffering. However, as both Boltanski and Gramsci show us, this cannot mean that critique depends solely on the community's self-understanding ('common sense'), neither should critique put itself entirely in the service of it. After all, that would be precisely the unjustified romanticizing of the 'wisdom of crowds,' while the very purpose of critique is to acknowledge the un-common in 'common sense,' and to build further on it. Furthermore, critical theory can contribute to the self-understanding of mass movements, and I would say that the conceptualization of the commons is itself a perfect example of that, as it allows us to see all kinds of contemporary struggles (e. g., against gentrification, copyrights laws, the influence of big tech, and the climate catastrophe) as inherently connected, namely as struggles for, and in name of, the common.

To conclude, let us once more return to Benjamin's quote on critique. After determining that the time of critique has long past, he goes on like this:

> Today the most real, mercantile gaze into the heart of things is the advertisement. It tears down the stage upon which contemplation moved, and all but hits us between the eyes with things as a car, growing to gigantic proportions, careens at us out of a film screen. […] What, in the end, makes advertisements so superior to [critique]? Not what the moving red neon sign says-but the fiery pool reflecting it in the asphalt. (Benjamin 1996: 476)

An enigmatic statement, to say the least, especially coming from an author who once voiced the ambition to become the foremost critic of German letters, and by many is indeed considered as such. What I think Benjamin is hinting at, most notably with the "reflection in the asphalt," is that critique is only worthwhile if it somehow resonates with 'the street.' In other words: if critique as a theoretical and academic enterprise is connected to critique as part of a collective movement.

This should be our concern today. But for that, it will not help to throw out the baby with the bathwater as the anticritical or postcritical discourse seems to do. In all the accusations on the address of critique (i.e., that it is merely negative, detached, or a mere passive bystander) it is easily forgotten that the one who criticizes often does not have the immediate power to alter the status quo. Thus, such accusations threaten to relapse in what Adorno called "an unctuous sermon admonishing the underlying to keep still" (Adorno 2005: 283). Even in Kant, as Hannah Arendt shows, the *raison d'être* of critique was to think publicly, to connect theory and practice, but also to judge to what extent social movements had genuine emancipatory force. This has been the purpose of critical theory ever since, from Marx via the Frankfurt School to Nancy Fraser. So rather than shooting messengers, or choosing action over words, we should reconnect the two, by finding ways for critique to be common or communal, and the common to be critical. In Karl Marx's words: "The weapon of criticism cannot, of course, replace criticism of the weapon, material force must be overthrown by material force; but theory also becomes a material force as soon as it has gripped the masses." (Marx 1843)

# References

Adorno, Theodor W. (2005): *Critical Models: Interventions and Catchwords*. Trans. by Henry W. Pickford. New York, NY: Columbia University Press.
Badiou, Alain (1999): *Deleuze: The Clamor of Being*. Trans. by Louise Burchill. Minneapolis, MN/London: University of Minnesota Press.
Benjamin, Walter (1996): *Selected Writings*. Vol. 1: *1913–1926*. Edited by Marcus Bullock and Michael W. Jennings. Cambridge, MA/London: Belknap Press of Harvard University Press.
Bishop, Claire (2012): *Artificial Hells: Participatory Art and the Politics of Spectatorship*. London: Verso.
Boltanski, Luc (2011): *On Critique: A Sociology of Emancipation*. Trans. by Gregory Elliott. London: Polity Press.
Boltanski, Luc/Thévenot, Laurent (2006): *On Justification: Economies of Worth*. Trans. by Catherine Porter. Princeton, NJ/Oxford: Princeton University Press.
Dardot, Pierre/Laval, Christian (2019): *Common: On Revolution in the 21st Century*. Trans. by Matthew MacLellan. London: Bloomsbury.
De Angelis, Massimo (2017): *Omnia Sunt Communia: Principles for the Transition to Postcapitalism*. London: Zed Books.
Dockx, Nico/Gielen, Pascal (Eds.) (2018): *Commonism: A New Aesthetics of the Real*. Amsterdam: Valiz.

Foucault, Michel (2007): *The Politics of Truth*. Trans. by Lysa Hockroth and Catherine Porter. Los Angeles, CA: Semiotext(e).

Gilbert, Jeremy (2014): *Common Ground: Democracy and Collectivity in an Age of Individualism*. London: Pluto.

Gramsci, Antonio (1971): *Selections from the Prison Notebooks*. Edited and trans. by Quintin Hoare and Geoffrey Nowell Smith. New York, NY: International Publishers.

Haraway, Donna (1988): "Situated Knowledges: The Science Question in Feminism and the Privilege of Partial Perspective." In: *Feminist Studies* 14(3), pp. 575–599.

Hardt, Michael/Negri, Antonio (2009): *Commonwealth*. Cambridge, MA: Belknap Press of Harvard University Press.

Harney, Stefano/Moten, Fred (2013): *The Undercommons: Fugitive Planning & Black Study*. Wivenhoe/New York, NY/Port Watson: Minor Compositions.

Harvey, David (2012): *Rebel Cities: From the Right to the City to the Urban Revolution*. London/New York, NY: Verso.

Höller, Christian (2015): "'Un-Common Sense': Social Critique and the Struggle over Commonality." In: Lijster, Thijs/Milevska, Suzana/Gielen, Pascal/Sonderegger, Ruth (Eds.): *Spaces for Criticism: Shifts in Contemporary Art Discourses*. Amsterdam: Valiz, pp. 93–108.

Jameson, Fredric (2007): *Late Marxism: Adorno or the Persistence of the Dialectic*. New York, NY: Verso.

Latour, Bruno (2004): "Why Has Critique Run out of Steam? From Matters of Fact to Matters of Concern." In: *Critical Inquiry* 30(2), pp. 225–248.

Lessig, Lawrence (2001): *The Future of Ideas: The Fate of the Commons in a Connected World*. London: Random House.

Marx, Karl (1843): *A Contribution to the Critique of Hegel's Philosophy of Right. Introduction*. https://www.marxists.org/archive/marx/works/1843/critique-hpr/intro.htm, accessed 20 July 2020.

Nancy, Jean-Luc (2009): "The Confronted Community." In: Mitchell, Andrew J./Winfree, Jason Kemp (Eds.): *The Obsession of Georges Bataille*. New York, NY: SUNY, pp. 19–30.

Ostrom, Elinor (2015): *Governing the Commons: The Evolution of Institutions for Collective Action*. Cambridge: Cambridge University Press.

Schinkel, Willem/Van Reekum, Rogier (2019): *Theorie van de kraal: Kapitaal, ras, fascisme*. Amsterdam: Boom.

Srnicek, Nick/Williams, Alex (2015): *Inventing the Future: Postcapitalism and a World without Work*. London/New York, NY: Verso.

Stavrides, Stavros (2016): *Common Space: The City as Commons*. London: Zed Books.

Virno, Paolo (2004): *A Grammar of the Multitude: For an Analysis of Contemporary Forms of Life*. Trans. by Isabella Bertoletti, James Cascaito, and Andrea Casson. Los Angeles, CA: Semiotext(e).

Part 2: **Challenges to Philosophical Critique in Politics, Economy, and Law**

Richard Amesbury
# Unpopular Sovereignties

## Democracy and the Paradox of "Peoples"

**Abstract:** So-called democratic states rest upon acts of violence and exclusion which cannot themselves be justified democratically. Yet, much contemporary political theory takes these configurations for granted as the context for philosophical reflection. This paper explores some of the spatio-temporal paradoxes of popular sovereignty as conventionally understood – i.e., as the authorization of government through the consent of "the people." I argue that, instead of treating the borders of popular sovereignty as given, political philosophy would benefit from greater attention to their continual contestation and critique.

**Keywords:** Popular sovereignty, gerrymandering, American Declaration of Independence, Dred Scott, "We the People"

> *A multitude of men, are made one person, when they are by one man, or one person, represented; so that it be done with the consent of every one of that multitude in particular.*
> – Thomas Hobbes: *Leviathan*

The most significant political question in a democratic nation-state is the question of who "the people" are, and this is not a question that can be answered – on pain of circularity or regress – through conventional democratic procedures, by appealing to the will of the people. For who gets to decide who gets to decide? Another way of thinking about this problem is as a question of borders – of how (and by whom) the line is to be drawn between insiders and outsiders, citizens and foreigners, friends and enemies, us and them. This is a question with profound implications for justice, but it is not straightforwardly a moral question so much as a political one, a question not of *humanity*, to be answered from the standpoint of universality – far from it – but of *sovereignty*, of the will to power.

It is, nevertheless, a striking, if typically unremarked, feature of much contemporary political philosophy and ethics – including accounts of the ethics of citizenship – that the boundaries of civic personhood are treated as given, rather than as inherently contestable and, indeed, vigorously contested. The result of this framing is that insufficient attention has been given to the relation between the political equality sought – if never realized – among citizens and the inequality between citizens and those outside the body politic on which the promise of citizenship is premised.

In what follows I begin by examining the claim – made by Franklin Gamwell, among others – that a liberal state ought to be "self-democratizing," and that this can be achieved on the basis of unrestricted public discourse (Gamwell 2005: 39). There is a tension, I will argue, inherent in such projects between the universalistic dimensions of rational discourse and the assumption that this discourse should or can be limited to citizens, and this tension points to underlying anxieties having to do with what I shall call the *paradox of popular sovereignty* – that the foundation of a democratic state seems to require the very thing it aims to establish, thus embodying a kind of circularity. Turning from ideal theory to the social structures that theory is meant to inform, I argue that the figure of the popular sovereign can be encountered in moments of historical crisis, and that this figure – its bodily morphology – necessarily constitutes a site of ongoing contest. The paper concludes with some reflections on the relation between popular sovereignty and political theology – on how the performative regress involved in constituting the *demos* generates a demand for constatives, for gods, including secular ones.

# 1 Three contemporary controversies

I would like to begin by briefly taking note of three contemporary controversies in the United States.

Donald Trump came to power in 2016 on the dual promises of a ban on Muslims and a wall along the United States' southern border with Mexico, and his term in office was marked by pronounced hostility to immigration and immigrants (with the notable exception of immigrants from Norway). Migration – driven in part by U.S. policies in Latin America which have led to political and economic instability and personal insecurity, and exacerbated by climate change – has been portrayed as an existential crisis – an "invasion" – justifying a series of increasingly cruel and draconian deterrents, including the separation of more than 5,500 children from their parents, the caging of asylum seekers, and mass arrests and deportations.

In addition to hardening external borders, the Trump administration sought to distinguish *among* citizens. The President spent the month of July 2019 waging a *Twitter* campaign against four first-year Congresswomen of color, whom he told to go back to where they came from, and the senior African-American Congressman Elijah Cummings (now deceased), whose predominately African-American district he described as a "dangerous and filthy place" in which "no human being would want to live." What these attacks seem to suggest is a view of America according to which neither legal citizenship nor birth is a sufficient condition of political belonging (all five of Trump's targets were U.S. citizens, and all but one had been born in the United States): that the American body politic is not merely the aggregate of its members, but a body of a particular kind, possessing a determinate color, gender, sexual orientation, etc.

My third contemporary example might seem more obscure, so a bit of background is warranted. The practice of redrawing voting districts to influence electoral results has a long history in the United States, where it has been known, since the beginning of the nineteenth century, as *gerrymandering*. A portmanteau, the term was coined by a Boston newspaper, which noticed that under a redistricting bill signed by Governor Elbridge Gerry, a contorted Senate election district in Essex County, Massachusetts resembled a salamander. Gerrymandering works by effectively diluting votes – devaluing the power of some votes relative to that of others – through "cracking" or "packing" districts – i.e., by dividing a party's voters among multiple districts, so as to ensure that they remain in the minority, or by concentrating them into a single district, so that votes that might have mattered elsewhere are "wasted." In a combined case, *Rucho v. Common Cause*, the U.S. Supreme Court was asked to rule on the constitutionality of the practice. Democratic plaintiffs in North Carolina had argued that partisan gerrymandering by Republicans there "usurped the right of 'the People' to elect their preferred candidates for Congress, in violation of the requirement in Article I, § 2, of the Constitution that Members of the House of Representatives be chosen 'by the People of the several States'" (Supreme Court 2019, § I, A) and Republicans in Maryland had levied a similar complaint against Democrats in that state.

Implicit in such complaints is the intuition that the composition of state legislatures should reflect the partisan affiliation of voters. Yet, Chief Justice John Roberts argued, the Constitution does not guarantee proportional representation, and indeed, winner-take-all electoral schemes have historically not been uncommon.

> Unable to claim that the Constitution requires proportional representation outright, plaintiffs inevitably ask the courts to make their own political judgment about how much representation particular political parties *deserve* – based on the votes of their supporters – and to rearrange the challenged districts to achieve that end (Supreme Court 2019, § III, B)

"But," Roberts claimed, "federal courts are not equipped to apportion political power as a matter of fairness, nor is there any basis for concluding that they were authorized to do so" (Supreme Court 2019, § III, B). The majority concluded that partisan gerrymandering – unlike overtly racial gerrymandering – is "nonjusticiable" – a political, rather than a legal, matter, falling outside the Court's jurisdiction and competence. The Court acknowledged that the results of partisan gerrymandering "reasonably seem unjust." "But," Roberts wrote, "the fact that such gerrymandering is 'incompatible with democratic principles' does not mean that the solution lies with the federal judiciary" (Supreme Court 2019, § III, B).

But if it does not lie with the judiciary, where *does* the solution lie? The Court's view was that this is a *political* question, to be decided by the legislative branch of government. But since the problem is precisely the willingness of legislatures to redraw districts to benefit the ruling party, it seems unlikely that a legislative majority would undertake reform, undermining the mechanism on which it might otherwise hope to be returned to power. There is, moreover, something perverse in the advice to vote the gerrymanderers out, since the effect of gerrymandering is to disenfranchise the voters most likely to object. In a scathing rebuke to the majority, the Court's dissenters – Justices Kagan, Ginsburg, Breyer, and Sotomayor – wrote that "the partisan gerrymanders here debased and dishonored our democracy, turning upside-down the core American idea that all governmental power derives from the people. These gerrymanders enabled politicians to entrench themselves in office as against voters' preferences" (Supreme Court 2019, Intro).

The dissenting justices argued that, by effectively allowing politicians to choose their voters, gerrymandering inverts the core doctrine of American democracy, popular sovereignty:

> "Governments," the Declaration of Independence states, "deriv[e] their just Powers from the Consent of the Governed." The Constitution begins: "We the People of the United States." The Gettysburg Address (almost) ends: "[G]overnment of the people, by the people, for the people." If there is a single idea that made our Nation (and that our Nation commended to the world), it is this one: The people are sovereign. The "power," James Madison wrote, "is in the people over the Government, and not in the Government over the people" (Supreme Court 2019, § I, B).

Partisan gerrymandering "turns it the other way around," they wrote. "By that mechanism, politicians can cherry-pick voters to ensure their reelection. And the power becomes, as Madison put it, 'in the Government over the people'" (Supreme Court 2019, § I, B).

The relation between government and the people is a familiar, if puzzling, conundrum. In an essay comparing Hobbes and Rousseau, Peter Winch wrote:

> The central question of political philosophy concerns the nature of the authority of the state. The concept of such authority generates characteristically philosophical puzzlement because it seems to involve a paradox: on the one hand it seems to involve a power to over-

ride the will of the individual citizen, while on the other hand its existence seems in a certain sense to depend on the wills of the individuals who are subject to it, in that they can decide whether or not to acknowledge it as *legitimate*. (Winch 1972: 100)

One classic answer to this dilemma is the claim – central to social contract theory – that authority ultimately *derives from* the individual wills of those subject to it. As the term implies, social contract theory conceives of political authority as arising out of the will of the people understood individually – "people" in the plural – and this tradition has been central to the idea of democracy as self-rule. But the real-life examples just described suggest that this ideal of rule by the people conceived of individually articulates uneasily with the perceived need to enforce borders and boundaries, to distinguish *among* people, so as to separate those capable of ruling from those outside the body politic. It might be thought that the latter is simply an unfortunate deviation from the norm of popular sovereignty – the inevitable friction the phenomenal world exerts on ideal theory – but I hope in what follows to show that this tension is of political philosophical importance.

## 2 The sovereignty of the people

What is popular sovereignty? On Franklin Gamwell's reconstruction of the basic intuitions implicit in the notion of popular sovereignty, "'the sovereignty of the people' means at least this: First, every member of the political community is sovereign over her or his assessment of actual and proposed governmental activities and thus of any political claim, in the sense that the state may not legitimately stipulate or dictate that assessment." And second, "the final political authority consists in the equal importance of every such person's sovereign assessment" (Gamwell 2005: 35). These, on Gamwell's interpretation, constitute the core of what "religious freedom" is intended to safeguard. If, in other words, we understand "religion" to include "some or other explicit conviction about the ultimate ground of worth for human life as such" (Gamwell 2005: 36), then protecting religious freedom can be viewed as essential for ensuring that individual citizens retain sovereignty over the terms of political assessment, which can be expected to vary among citizens (Gamwell 2005: 36).[1]

---

[1] "Hence, the meaning of 'religion' should be so understood that the principle of religious freedom legitimates all such beliefs about the ultimate terms of political assessment and, thereby, protects the sovereignty of each citizen over her or his assessment of every political claim." (Gamwell 2005: 36)

A liberal philosophical theologian, Gamwell is interested in, among other things, the relation between religion and the state. For as he points out, the diversity of ultimate perspectives authorized by religious freedom poses a significant challenge to the possibility of democratic politics. He writes, "Whatever changes in politics or political thought Western history may include, the abiding purpose of political rule is to create order by which the community as a whole is unified, and there cannot be many unifications of the whole" (Gamwell 2005: 35). Religious freedom seems to be required in order to preserve the sovereignty of each individual citizen over her or his assessment of political claims, but the diversity of ultimate perspectives that is thereby legitimated in turn presents a challenge to the possibility of unifying the political community as a collective "we the people."

To raise the question of how citizens are to act collectively when making political decisions is, Gamwell argues, to inquire into the "proper character of a democratic constitution" (Gamwell 2005: 35). For the function of a constitution, whether written or unwritten, is to specify those principles that comprise the ethics of democratic citizenship and "define how the people act-as-one" (Gamwell 2005: 35).[2] But because the constitution must itself be subject to the sovereignty of the people, who constitute the final political authority, any account of the principles properly belonging to it must be "self-democratizing": "It should so define the political community that this very definition is subject to contestation by the citizens who are thereby defined." (Gamwell 2005: 39)

What sort of constitutional principles would satisfy this requirement? It is not enough, Gamwell argues, for a constitution to provide for its own emendation; if it includes *substantive* principles of justice that specify the ultimate terms of political assessment, it is not self-democratizing, even if it provides formally for its own change, because appeal to any alternative set of substantive principles would violate the stipulated ethics of citizenship. In order legitimately to contest the reigning principles, one would be required paradoxically to endorse them. Nor will a purely "procedural" account of justice suffice, since it would rule out as illegitimate any substantive grounds for political assessment to which citizens might be committed, thereby violating their sovereignty over the ultimate terms of assessment (Gamwell 2005: 41–43). Gamwell argues that an alternative conception of political unity may be discerned as implicit in the idea that every citizen is free to make and contest any political claim. When

---

[2] "Because these principles define how the people act-as-one, explicit adherence to them also defines all members of the community in their status as participants in political rule." (Gamwell 2005: 35)

the political community is conceived as a community of *discourse*, in which all citizens may participate as equals, the unity of the community can be reconciled with the sovereignty of each of its members over the ultimate terms of political assessment.

Drawing on an understanding of political discourse developed by Jürgen Habermas and Karl-Otto Apel, Gamwell posits the following: "Making a political claim, including one that contests another claim, is a communicative act in which one pledges to any recipient that one's claim can be validated and redeemed by argument and, therefore, also concedes that one's claim may be invalidated in the same way." (Gamwell 2005: 44) Constitutional principles are self-democratizing, Gamwell argues, only "if they define the political association as a full and free political discussion and debate or a full and free political discourse" (Gamwell 2005: 45). For "participation in the practice of political argumentation is the one activity that is explicitly neutral to or does not explicitly takes [sic] sides in any possible disagreement" (Gamwell 2005: 45). Democracy, Gamwell argues, "can only be politics through full and free political discussion and debate or politics by the way of reason; only those political claims that can be validated in reasoned discourse should direct the decisions or activities of the state" (Gamwell 2005: 4). On this account, democracy is properly "conceived as rule by way of unrestricted argument" (Gamwell 2005: 48).

Gamwell's account of democracy is presented as an ideal theory, not an empirical description of the discursive structures of historical democratic nation-states. Yet insofar as it is an ideal theory *about* democratic nation-states, it takes for granted the idea of citizenship: Its basic question concerns the relationship between citizens and the state – i.e., of citizens to one another – not the relation between citizens and noncitizens. The idea of citizenship in a state, however, presupposes boundaries and thus articulates uneasily with Gamwell's emphasis on unbounded argument.

## 3 The "way of reason"?

Let us recall Gamwell's contention that the constitution of a state ought to be *self-democratizing* – i.e., that it "should so define the political community that this very definition is subject to contestation by the citizens who are thereby defined" (Gamwell 2005: 39). This is crucial, on Gamwell's account, because it is *the people*, not the constitution, who exercise ultimate authority. He writes, "The constitution is itself authorized by the people, as the opening words to the United States Constitution make clear: 'We the people of the United States, […] do ordain and establish this Constitution'" (Gamwell 2005: 34–35). Notice, however, that his formula that a constitution "should so define the political community that this very definition is subject to contestation by the citizens who are thereby defined" implies that the definition is *not* contestable by those defined as *outside* its borders. Yet why this should be so is unclear on Gamwell's own account of the discursive character of popular sovereignty.

Consider that the philosophical account of discourse on which Gamwell relies, and which he refers to as "the way of reason," makes no reference to the distinction between citizens and noncitizens. Discourse is here conceived as open to everyone precisely because restrictions on participation hinder the search for validity. Reason, one might say, is no respecter of persons. Yet the concept of citizenship is introduced, without comment, in Gamwell's application of the philosophical thesis to democratic politics. Here we are told that "all members of the political community are equal participants" (Gamwell 2005: 45). Notice the slide from "participants in discourse" to "members of the political community," and from "the people" to "citizens." To be sure, Gamwell argues that "[c]ommitment to the way of reason, as we may call it, entails the denial of any principled grounds for political inequality" (Gamwell 2005: 50), but he seems to be thinking of political inequality *among citizens*, rather than of the inequality between citizens and noncitizens.[3] This latter distinction is not itself authorized by, and seems indeed to be in tension with, Gamwell's philosophical account of discourse, which – as he himself points out – is corrosive of all such attempts to arrest the exchange of reasons.

To be clear, my purpose here is not to endorse Gamwell's account of discourse, but to call attention to the way its universalism is constrained by contingent, preexisting boundaries of belonging, which seem to have become sufficiently naturalized to escape philosophical attention. In this respect, I want to suggest, Gamwell's work is not unique. Submerged within liberal theory and under-analyzed, the idea of "peoples," conceived as naturally occurring sover-

---

**3** The purpose of the state, Gamwell argues, "is to unify the community as a whole by governing the associations among individuals" (Gamwell 2005: 90). Although he notes that it is not the state's job to regulate all associations, he attempts to resolve the question of the limits of the state's control by invoking a distinction between the *general* and the *particular*: "Directing it to the general order implies that other norms of human interaction may be properly determined by individuals in or through their diverse other associations, even while leaving underdetermined what general norms should be enforced throughout associational life." (Gamwell 2005: 90) Here the "general order" – which he also identifies as the subject matter of justice (Gamwell 2005: 82) – is understood to be that over which the state exercises control, but no account is offered of how to distinguish it from what lies under the control of *other states*, which presumably operate at this same level. The state thus appears to function not simply as a vertical, but also a horizontal, limit to Gamwell's imaginary.

eign units, continues to exert a powerful influence over contemporary debates about multiculturalism, migration, and the limits of tolerance.

## 4 Dred Scott and the sovereign people

Who are "the People"? The American Declaration of Independence famously begins with an affirmation of popular sovereignty:

> We hold these truths to be self-evident, that all men are created equal, that they are endowed by their Creator with certain unalienable Rights, that among these are Life, Liberty and the pursuit of Happiness. – That to secure these rights, Governments are instituted among Men, deriving their just powers from the consent of the governed [...].

This appeal to the authority of the governed is echoed in the preamble to the Constitution, which speaks of the popular sovereign in the first person: "We the people [...]." Notice that "people" is here being used as a collective noun: Although the pronoun "we" is plural, the noun "people" is singular: "We" as individuals are subsumed within the unique entity of the nation. In this opening line – so frequently cited as a hallmark of democracy – the relation between singular individuals and a collective community is made to seem more straightforward than it would historically prove to be. It is perhaps not surprising that in a republic that claims to derive its just powers from the consent of the governed, the biggest political disagreements and struggles have concerned precisely the question of who belongs to the popular sovereign.

The year 2019 marked, among other things, the 400th anniversary of enslaved persons being brought from West Africa to the British colonies that would eventually become the United States. Thomas Jefferson, who penned the words "all men are created equal," enslaved more than 600 people over the course of his life, and at the time of independence, twenty percent of the population of the new country lived in bondage. How ought we to understand the relation between these facts and the ideal of popular sovereignty espoused by the founders? According to the U.S. Supreme Court's infamous 1857 decision in *Dred Scott v. Sandford*, there is no contradiction, because persons of African descent were never part of "the people":

> The words "people of the United States" and "citizens" are synonymous terms [...]. They both describe the political body who, according to our republican institutions, form the sovereignty, and who hold the power and conduct the government through their representatives. They are what we familiarly call the "sovereign people," and every citizen is one of this people, and a constituent member of this sovereignty. The question before us is, whether the class of persons described in the plea in abatement compose a portion of this people,

and are constituent members of this sovereignty? We think they are not, and that they are not included, and were not intended to be included, under the word "citizens" in the constitution, and can therefore claim none of the rights and privileges which that instrument provides for and secures to citizens of the United States. On the contrary, they were at that time considered as a subordinate and inferior class of beings, who had been subjugated by the dominant race, and, whether emancipated or not, yet remained subject to their authority, and had no rights or privileges but such as those who held the power and the government might choose to grant them. (Supreme Court 1857, § V).

The "class of persons" in question – individuals of African descent – were not, according to the Court, a portion of "the people."

The case involved Dred Scott, an enslaved man who had been brought from Missouri – a state where slavery was legal – to a free territory and back again. Scott argued that, by residing in a free territory – a territory in which slavery was illegal – he had effectively been freed and could not legally be re-enslaved on return to Missouri. However, the Court held, in the passage just quoted, that, being of African descent, Scott was not a citizen and so ineligible to sue in federal court for his freedom. Notice the peculiarly Kafkaesque structure of the Court's argument: As a noncitizen, Scott was said to lack the legal standing necessary to challenge his effective statelessness and the enslavement it made possible. "The people" constitute a kind of closed loop from which Scott is excluded. In the eyes of the law, Scott is rendered voiceless, unable even to lodge an audible complaint. He did not sue for his freedom and lose; rather, he was not permitted to sue. To borrow a phrase from Hannah Arendt, what Scott lacked, in the opinion of the high court, was "the right to have rights" (Arendt 1966: 296). In addition to its manifest racism, the argument is strikingly elliptical: The Court is interpreting the Constitution in light of a particular understanding of "peoplehood," which, while itself maintained by state power – in this instance, by the Court – is said to underwrite the Constitutional powers exercised by government. Who, it might be asked, authorizes the Court to decide who is included in "the people"? The answer: the people. In effect, the Court's decision is self-authorizing.

To be sure, the Court imagined itself to be offering a noncircular argument in support of its refusal to hear Scott's complaint. Its appeal was to the "true intent and meaning" of the founders. "The language of the Declaration of Independence is [...] conclusive," Chief Justice Roger Taney wrote (Supreme Court 1857, § V). It says, he acknowledged that "all men are created equal," and that governments derive "their just powers from the consent of the governed." Nevertheless, he opined, the founders did not intend to include the "African race": "The general words above quoted would seem to embrace the whole human family, and if they were used in a similar instrument at this day would be so understood. But it is too clear for dispute, that the enslaved African race were not intended to be included, and formed no part of the people who framed and adopted this declaration" (Supreme Court 1857, § V). To construe the words of the Declaration so as to include persons of African descent would be to imply a mismatch between the founders' words and their actions, which included enslaving human persons. Since, according to the Court, "the men who framed this declaration were great men – high in literary acquirements – high in their sense of honor, and *incapable of asserting principles inconsistent with those on which they were acting*," they cannot have had in mind "the negro race, which, by common consent, had been excluded from civilized Governments and the family of nations, and doomed to slavery" (Supreme Court 1857, § V; emphasis added).

The Court's claim was that its hands were tied by the meaning of the founding documents, and that any concession to later usage "would abrogate the judicial character of this court, and make it the mere reflex of the popular opinion or passion of the day" (Supreme Court 1857, § V). In other words, in interpreting what the law means when it makes government answerable to the consent of the governed, the Court's responsibility is not to presently existing people – to "the popular opinion of the day" – but to "the people" as conceived according to the Court's reconstruction of the founders' intent. The problem is not simply that the Court is forced to rely upon its own reading of what the law meant to people seventy years earlier, although that is itself a thorny matter. It is possible – if highly controversial – to suppose, as proponents of the doctrine of Constitutional interpretation known as Originalism do, that courts ought to interpret laws according to the meanings that prevailed at the time of legislation. But the work of courts and legislatures – indeed, the Constitution itself, as Gamwell observes – is taken to be authorized by something more basic, namely *the consent of the governed* (Gamwell 2005: 34–35). Beyond the light it casts on the white supremacy at the heart of the republic, what the Dred Scott case reveals is that ostensibly democratic government constructs *the people* from which it purports to draw its authority. In its insistence that "the people" belongs *to* the law and does not name an antecedent, given reality, *Dred Scott v. Sandford* exposes the fiction of auto-authorization on which the law itself depends. The state is materially prior, if conceptually subsequent, to the ostensible source of its legitimation. In effect, the *Dred Scott* decision *gerrymanders* the boundaries of "the people" by constructing a nation that confers legitimacy on the state's exclusions and silences its victims. To put it another way, it is the consent not of the governed as such that seems to matter here, but of those comprised by the *popular sovereign*, where the latter cannot itself on pain of regress or circularity be constituted democratically, by allowing the people to decide who are the people.

# 5 The sacral body politic

The legal theorist Paul W. Kahn has pointed to "a paradox in the constitutional jurisprudence of democratic self-governance: the more the nation believes itself to be a product of the will of the popular sovereign the less democratic it becomes – if we mean by democratic, subject to control through broadly participatory electoral mechanisms" (Kahn 2006: 270). Why, it might be wondered, should the U.S. Constitution – a document drafted and signed by a cadre of eighteenth-century white men – serve as a constraint on United States democratic decision-making in the first place? On what basis can courts declare the will of the majority invalid? And why, when it comes to interpreting the Constitution, should Originalists accord so much weight to the "intent of the founders"? Sometimes called the "counter-majoritarian difficulty," this dimension of American jurisprudence and political life has long puzzled liberal theorists, and some commentators have detected in American Constitutionalism the presence of the sacred. The anthropologist Vincent Crapanzano has noted that Originalists share with American evangelicals an emphasis on *the literal*, and indeed the Constitution functions much like Scripture (Crapanzano 2000).

The counter-majoritarian difficulty is puzzling if viewed from the perspective of democracy considered simply as a process for aggregating and balancing the interests of individual citizens, and difficult to reconcile with popular sovereignty where the latter is conceived – as Gamwell has it – as the equal sovereignty of each party to a political conversation. But if, as I am suggesting, the "people" at issue are understood not distributively – as individuals – but as collectively constituting a *popular sovereign*, a body distinguished by what it is not, then we can begin to make sense of some otherwise puzzling features of American public life, including its sacral dimensions and its anti-Blackness. Kahn writes:

> On this view, the origins of the political community represent a perfect state of grace, in which there is a complete transparency of the individual will to the sovereign will. This revolutionary community has a kind of transtemporal existence: all individuals – present and future – participate as members of the popular sovereign. For this reason, the actions of the Founders can continue to bind future generations: all are part of a single We. The atemporality of Christ has moved from church, to sovereign monarch, to the popular sovereign. (Kahn 2006: 271)

Because it is "the people" considered as a single, enduring locus of sovereignty which gives itself the law, authoring its own founding, its will must prevail in the present as it did in the past. This sacral body is *the people* to which courts appeal for the authority to block the will of mere majorities. The people are dead; long live the People.

## 6 "One actually would need gods"

We come up here against a limit to democratic rationality that has received comparatively little attention in modern liberal political theory. One thinker who grasped its significance, albeit in a slightly different form, was Jean-Jacques Rousseau, who compared the founding of a republic to the problem of "squaring the circle in geometry" (Rousseau 1985: 3). In Rousseau's version of the paradox, the problem is not about constituting the *demos* per se, but about what it is by virtue of which the *constitution* of a new state – in the sense of its *founding*, but by extension its founding *document* – can be invested with *authority*. Commenting on Rousseau, Hannah Arendt writes:

> Theoretically, Rousseau's problem closely resembles Sieyès's vicious circle: those who get together to constitute a new government are themselves unconstitutional, that is, they have no authority to do what they have set out to achieve. The vicious circle in legislating is present not in ordinary lawmaking, but in laying down the fundamental law, the law of the land or the constitution which, from then on, is supposed to incarnate the "higher law" from which all laws ultimately derive their authority. And with this problem, which appeared as the urgent need for some absolute, the men of the American Revolution found themselves no less confronted than their colleagues in France. The trouble was – to quote Rousseau [...] – that to put the law above man and thus to establish the validity of man-made laws, [...] "one actually would need gods." (Arendt 1963: 175–176)

Rousseau's solution to the problem was, famously, the idea of civil religion, which found its realization in Robespierre's 1794 Festival of the Supreme Being. From the vantage point of the twenty-first century, Robespierre's cult might well seem absurd. Indeed, Arendt suggests that it must have seemed that way at the time: "even then it must have looked as though 'the god of the philosophers' upon whom Luther and Pascal had vented their contempt had finally decided to disclose himself in the guise of a circus clown" (Arendt 1963: 176). Yet, she notes,

> we may lose all desire to laugh at the circus clown when we find the same notions, stripped of all ridicule, in John Adams, who also demanded worship of a Supreme Being which he, too, called "the great Legislator of the Universe," or when we recall the solemnity with

which Jefferson, in the Declaration of Independence, appealed to "the laws of nature and nature's God." (Arendt 1963: 177)[4]

To better understand the role these theological invocations play, it will be helpful to consider the paradox of popular sovereignty from a different angle. Earlier I noted that Dred Scott found himself denied the freedom to protest the denial of his freedom. The very exclusion to which he objected was invoked to disqualify the objection. In this sense, the circular logic of popular sovereignty presents itself as something sheer and impenetrable, hermetically closed against the outside world. But the same circularity that allows "the people" to authorize themselves presents itself, from another point of view, as a standing question: Who *are* "we, the people"?

This ambivalence can be detected in the founding documents of the American republic. As Jacques Derrida has noted in connection with the Declaration of Independence,

> this people does not exist. They do not exist as an entity, it does not exist, before this declaration, not as such. If it gives birth to itself, as free and independent subject, as possible signer, this can hold only in the act of the signature. The signature invents the signer. The signer can only authorize him- or herself to sign once he or she has come to the end, if one can say this, of his or her own signature, in a sort of fabulous retroactivity. (Derrida 2003: 27)

By speaking in the name of a community yet to be imagined as such, the Declaration *convenes* the "people" its signatories purport to represent, and from whom they claim to draw their political authority: The American people is imagined to have inscribed itself into existence. In this way, the Founders' "we" can be read as performative, rather than constative: Its referent is not an already existing sovereign unit, but an imagined community in the act of constructing and legitimating itself, a not-yet-fully present referent called into being through the performance of language itself (Derrida 2003: 25).

As Arendt notes, however, the Declaration contains a number of theological gestures beyond itself, to what Derrida calls "another 'subjectivity'." By "appealing to the Supreme Judge of the world for the rectitude of our intentions" – as the Declaration's final paragraph has it – the signers present themselves as co-sign-

---

[4] "Hence, in theory as in practice, we can hardly avoid the paradoxical fact that it was precisely the revolutions, their crisis and their emergency, which drove the very 'enlightened' men of the eighteenth century to plead for some religious sanction at the very moment when they were about to emancipate the secular realm fully from the influences of the churches and to separate politics and religion once and for all." (Arendt 1963: 177)

ers. The performance of language is here imagined to be guaranteed – its "felicity" (to borrow a term from Austin; see, e.g., Austin 1962: 16) ensured – by something beyond itself. Derrida writes:

> It is still "in the name of" that the "good people" of America call themselves and declare themselves independent, at the instant in which they invent (for) themselves a signing identity. They sign in the name of the laws of nature and in the name of God. They pose or posit their institutional laws on the foundation of natural laws and by the same coup (the interpretive coup of force) in the name of God, creator of nature. He comes, in effect, to guarantee the rectitude of popular intentions, the unity and goodness of the people. (Derrida 2003: 28)

On Derrida's reading, these invocations of extra-popular authority represent the Founders' attempts, however oblique, to escape the otherwise vicious circle of self-authorization by anchoring the legitimacy of their new polity in something constative rather than performative, something sovereign outside the circle itself. As Derrida puts it, "for this Declaration to have a meaning and an effect, there must be a last instance. God is the name, the best one, for this last instance and this ultimate signature" (Derrida 2003: 28–29). *God* is here Derrida's shorthand for whatever is imagined to arrest the performative regress inherent in convening a singular "people." Gods – whether religious or secular – are invoked to confer sovereignty from somewhere outside a system that otherwise depends on bootstrapping.

Gamwell's account of popular sovereignty is framed in terms of religious freedom. But "religious freedom" – the ostensible neutrality of the state vis-à-vis religion – is itself predicated on something sacred, namely, the gods said to confer sovereignty on the people. Of course, invoking the gods is itself *part of* the performance, not something that can underwrite it from outside, as it were *metaphysically*. Such invocations belong to politics, not to political theory, which tends accordingly to misunderstand and underestimate their importance. Sylvia Wynter captures this loop when she writes:

> [A]s humans, *we cannot/do not preexist our cosmogonies*, our representations of our origins – even though it is we ourselves who invent those cosmogonies and then retroactively project them onto a past. We invent them in formulaic storytelling terms, as "donor figures" or "entities," who have *extrahumanly* (supernaturally, but now also *naturally* and/or bioevolutionarily, therefore secularly) *mandated* what the structuring societal order of our genre-specific, eusocial or cultural *present* would have to be. (Wynter/McKittrick 2015: 36)

The gods created us, but we created the gods. This is the central paradox of popular sovereignty. As Wendy Brown puts it: "Man generates political sovereignty through the conferral of his own power, but since sovereignty is the divine element within the commonwealth, this process of generation or fabrication is disavowed and covered over." (Brown 2010: 60) Sovereignty is paradoxically generated by the subjects it generates, and the gods do not finally escape the circularity of the logic they are invoked to guarantee.

Arendt notes the irony of America's ostensibly secular founders appealing to God in moments of exception, but it is significant that such appeals have never disappeared from the national conversation. What Robert Bellah famously called "American civil religion" is an archive of repeated efforts aimed at settling the question of popular sovereignty, but the very ubiquity of these expressions – indeed, their ritualized, liturgical structure – suggests that the question has never finally been lain to rest and in fact constitutes a kind of ever-receding horizon of American political life (Bellah 1967).

Bonnie Honig has argued that Arendt failed to take seriously enough the problem which the gods are invoked to solve, insofar as she seems to imagine that such appeals are ultimately unnecessary. "[W]hat saved the American Revolution," Arendt writes, "was neither 'nature's God' nor self-evident truth, but the act of foundation itself" (Arendt 1963: 188). After all, if the truths were truly self-evident, Jefferson would simply have written, "These truths are self-evident." Or rather, he would not have needed to. The fact that he began the sentence with "We hold [...]" not only implies that the claims to be enumerated are contestable, but also – Arendt argues – that it is the "We hold [...]" that is doing the real work – i.e., that the authority of the founding rests not on the constative being invoked but on the performance to which such invocations belongs. On Honig's reading, Arendt would prefer to see the founders' appeals to God as inessential, because she "seeks in the American declaration and founding a moment of perfect legitimacy" (Honig 1991: 106).

> What Arendt does not see is that the American declaration and founding are paradigmatic instances of politics (however impure) *because* of this undecidability, not in spite of it. [...] [I]n every system (every practice), whether linguistic, cultural, or political, there is a moment or place that the system cannot account for. Every system is secured by placeholders that are irrevocably, structurally arbitrary and prelegitimate. They enable the system but are illegitimate from its vantage point (Honig 1991: 106).

It is, however, also possible to read Arendt slightly differently, as recognizing, however inchoately, both the *demand* that motivates the appeal to constatives – the lack or place that the system cannot account for – and the inability of these constatives to satisfy it. Whatever one's view of that interpretive question, the lesson to be drawn from Arendt's discussion, I would argue, is that the self-authorship inherent in moments of revolutionary founding is exposed to the charge of circularity, and that consequently the popular sovereign is always in search of its own legitimacy.

# 7 Conclusion

The underlying problematic that generates the demand met by the gods of American civil religion and their counterparts in a henotheistic international pantheon is inscribed within the aporetic structure of the democratic state itself. It consists in the inability to justify, from within idealized democracy, the founding violence and exclusions on which so-called democratic states depend. The political function of civil religion is precisely to provide the hermeneutical framework needed to rationalize these extra-democratic limits on democracy. As Derrida writes elsewhere,

> the "successful foundation of a state" (in somewhat the same sense that one speaks of a "felicitous performative speech act") will produce *après coup* what it was destined in advance to produce, namely, proper interpretative models to read in return, to give sense, necessity and above all legitimacy to the violence that has produced, among others, the interpretative model in question, that is, the discourse of its self-legitimation (Derrida 1992: 36).

In this sense, to deny the need for gods is, paradoxically, to be already in the interpretive grip of an ideology of legitimation, oblivious to the very problem the gods are invoked to solve.[5] Liberal political theory functions as such an ideology when it accepts "peoples" as given, rather than as sites of ongoing crisis and critique. Because this justificatory circle can never be closed – because legitimation can never quite catch up with itself – the violence required to found a republic coils through its history. On this interpretation, Donald Trump, while not inevitable, is less the exception to the rule than just another extension of it. Derrida writes:

> It belongs to the structure of fundamental violence that it calls for the repetition of itself and founds what ought to be conserved, conservable, promised to heritage and tradition, to be shared. A foundation is a promise. [...] And even if a promise is not kept in fact, iter-

---

5 Arendt suggests that "perhaps the political genius of the American people, or the great good fortune that smiled upon the American republic, consisted precisely in this blindness, or, to put it another way, consisted in the extraordinary capacity to look upon yesterday with the eyes of centuries to come" (Arendt 1963: 198).

ability inscribes the promise as guard in the most irruptive instant of foundation. Thus it inscribes the possibility of repetition at the heart of the originary. (Derrida 1992: 38)

Yet, the very "iterability" of all "foundations" – their historical repetition in novel contexts – is also what makes possible change, i.e., "repetition with a difference."[6] Derrida's analysis emphasizes the need continually to contest and rethink, but also the impossibility of simply doing without, extra-democratic sources of political legitimacy.[7] The construction of a people is always a work in progress, a failure, an aspiration yet to be achieved. God help us all.

# References

Arendt, Hannah (1963): *On Revolution*. New York, NY: Penguin.
Arendt, Hannah (1966): *The Origins of Totalitarianism*. New York, NY: Harcourt.
Austin, J. L. (1962): *How to Do Things with Words*. Oxford: Oxford University Press.
Bellah, Robert N. (1967): "Civil Religion in America." In: *Daedalus* 96(1), pp. 1–21.
Brown, Wendy (2010): *Walled States, Waning Sovereignty*. Brooklyn, NY: Zone Books.
Crapanzano, Vincent (2000): *Serving the Word: Literalism in America from the Pulpit to the Bench*. New York, NY: The New Press.
Derrida, Jacques (1988): *Limited Inc*. Evanston, IL: Northwestern University Press.
Derrida, Jacques (1992): "Force of Law: The 'Mystical Foundation of Authority'." In: Cornell, Drucilla/Rosenfeld, Michel/Carlson, David Gray (Eds.): *Deconstruction and the Possibility of Justice*. New York, NY: Routledge, pp. 3–67.
Derrida, Jacques (1997): *Politics of Friendship*. Trans. by George Collins. New York, NY: Verso.
Derrida, Jacques (2003): "Declarations of Independence." In: Culler, Jonathan (Ed.): *Deconstruction: Critical Concepts in Literary and Cultural Studies*. Vol. 4. New York, NY: Routledge, pp. 24–31.
Gamwell, Franklin (2005): *Politics as a Christian Vocation: Faith and Democracy Today*. New York, NY: Cambridge University Press.
Hobbes, Thomas (1985): *Leviathan*. [1651]. London: Penguin.
Honig, Bonnie (1991): "Declarations of Independence: Arendt and Derrida on the Problem of Founding a Republic." In: *American Political Science Review* 85(1), pp. 97–113.
Kahn, Paul W. (2006): "Political Time: Sovereignty and the Transtemporal Community." In: *Cardozo Law Review* 28(1), pp. 259–276.

---

[6] On Derrida's account, "the structure of iteration […] implies both identity and difference" (Derrida 1988: 53).

[7] Is this democracy? Derrida writes, "Saying that to keep this Greek name, democracy, is an affair of context, of rhetoric or of strategy, even of polemics […] is not necessarily giving in to the opportunism or cynicism of the antidemocrat who is not showing his cards. Completely to the contrary: one keeps this indefinite right to the question, to criticism, to deconstruction […]." (Derrida 1997: 105)

Rousseau, Jean-Jacques (1985): *The Government of Poland*. [1782]. Trans. by Willmoore Kendall. Indianapolis, IN: Hackett.
Supreme Court of the United States (1857): *Dred Scott v. Sandford*, 60 U.S. 393.
Supreme Court of the United States (2019): *Rucho v. Common Cause*, 588 U.S. ___.
Winch, Peter (1972): *Ethics and Action*. London: Routledge and Kegan Paul.
Wynter, Sylvia/McKittrick, Katherine (2015): "Unparalleled Catastrophe for Our Species? Or, to Give Humanness a Different Future: Conversations." In: McKittrick, Katherine (Ed.): *Sylvia Wynter: On Being Human as Praxis*. Durham, NC: Duke University Press, pp. 9–89.

Ridha Chennoufi
# Politische Krise und Kritik im historischen Kontext

**Abstract:** [Political Crisis and Critique in the Historical Context] The aim of this paper is to think about the fall of the former Tunisian political regime (January 2011) by considering it as an event. The latter is not interpreted in the light of the former revolutions but rather in the light of the various political crises that have shaped the history of this country and which have always led to the seizure of power by a new hegemonic alliance. Since 2011, overcoming the crisis seems profound, complex, and uncertain. Therefore, the emphasis is placed on the 'secret forms' of power that the new political actors use, particularly on the functions of ideological discourse and on social norms and practices like that of prestige.

**Keywords:** Political crisis, Tunisia, event, political power, prestige

Um aufzuzeigen, was in Krisenzeiten eine Krise sein kann, haben wir uns entschlossen, den Sturz des tunesischen Regimes (14. Januar 2011) zu analysieren. Es ist offensichtlich, dass diese Reflexion nicht verallgemeinert und auf andere arabische Länder übertragen werden kann, deren autoritäre Regime das gleiche Schicksal erlitten haben. Gewiss teilt Tunesien mit letzteren einige Merkmale wie Sprache, Kultur und Religion. Wie die anderen arabischen Länder hat es auch unter den Krisen des Finanzkapitalismus gelitten, die es Wohlfahrtsstaaten unmöglich machten, minimale Lebensbedingungen zu garantieren, angesichts der Unterwerfung der Bürger und der Plünderung ihres Eigentums.

Aber Tunesien scheint trotz allem das einzige Land zu sein, das von Gewalt relativ verschont geblieben war, sowohl seitens der nationalen Armee als auch von rivalisierenden Milizen. Müssen wir daraus schließen, dass es nicht mehr in Gefahr ist, andere Formen von Herrschaft zu erleben, wie den islamistischen[1] Faschismus, den Erdoğan-Autoritarismus oder den ehemaligen säkularen Autoritarismus „heimtückischer Süßigkeiten" (Hibou 2006: 327–328)? Wir werden keine Antwort geben, die die Form einer Prophezeiung annehmen könnte. Fest

---

[1] Mit „Islamist" meine ich jeden Muslim, der den Koran auf ein von Gott verordnetes und daher durch den legitimen Einsatz von Gewalt erzwungenes rechtliches und politisches System reduziert.

steht jedoch, dass das Land seit fast einem Jahrzehnt nicht aus der Krise, die es erschüttert hat, herausgekommen ist.

Linke Parteien, die in Tunesien weitestgehend in der Minderheit sind, werfen den „postrevolutionären" Regierungen vor, die wirtschaftlichen und sozialen Probleme des Landes nicht gelöst zu haben, weil sie sich vollständig dem Internationalen Währungsfonds und der Weltbank unterworfen hätten. Die islamistische Partei *Ennahda*[2] (*Wiedererwachen*), die als einzige an allen diesen Regierungen teilgenommen hat, führt dieses Versagen auf die Opposition und die staatliche und politische Instabilität zurück, die durch die Implosion jener Partei verursacht wurde, die die Parlamentswahlen von 2014 gewonnen hatte (*Nidaa Tounes*; *Ruf Tunesiens*[3]).

Letztere zieht es vor, demgegenüber den Erfolg des politischen Übergangs hervorzuheben, der gemäß dem Kanon der Transformationstheorie erzielt wurde, und gleichzeitig zu bekräftigen, dass das von der islamistischen Partei gewählte parlamentarische System der Ursprung aller gegenwärtigen Übel Tunesiens sei. Es versteht sich also, dass sich die Diagnose der Krise je nach den Überzeugungen der einen oder der anderen Seite ändert.

Der Ansatz, dem wir folgen, wird viel bescheidener sein. Wir wollen eine Krisensituation verstehen, indem wir die wichtigsten Fakten und Ereignisse des Übergangsprozesses beschreiben, weit entfernt vom Klischee, dass die Krise auf einen Kampf zwischen undemokratischen Islamisten und säkularen Demokraten zurückzuführen ist. Unsere Arbeitshypothese wird darin bestehen, zu überprüfen, ob dieser Übergang tatsächlich in mehrfacher Hinsicht nicht mit denjenigen vergleichbar war, die Tunesien jedes Mal bereits gekannt hat, wenn es notwendig war, ein neues hegemoniales Bündnis zur Überwindung einer politischen Krise zu schließen.

Wir werden erstens unsere Arbeitshypothese testen, indem wir versuchen, die Bedeutung des Abgangs des ehemaligen Präsidenten als Ereignis zu verstehen. Das Verdienst dieses derridaschen Konzepts besteht darin zu erfassen, wie es zu einem Konflikt ideologischer Interpretationen zwischen den politischen Kräften kommt, bei dem es darum geht, sich die Vaterschaft dieses Ereignisses anzueignen. Zweitens werden wir zeigen, wie die Ansammlung dieser Kräfte in hegemonialen Allianzen von ihrer Legitimität und ihrer oft identitätsbasierten Solidarität abhängt. Der dritte Teil befasst sich mit der Funktionsweise von Macht in

---

[2] Mit diesem Namen bezieht sich die islamistische Partei auf eine kulturelle arabische Bewegung des 19. Jahrhunderts, die den Islam mit der Weltanschauung der westlichen Aufklärung zu versöhnen versuchte.

[3] Der *Ruf Tunesiens* ist eine säkulare Catch-all-Partei, die 2012 von dem verstorbenen Präsidenten Béji Caïd Essebsi gegründet wurde.

sozialen Bereichen, das heißt mit dem Zustandekommen von Beziehungen zwischen Individuen auf der Grundlage des Einflusses, den eine Kategorie von ihnen auf die anderen ausübt. Diese Macht des Einflusses wird von 'Abd ar-Rahmān Ibn Khaldūn[4] „das Prestige" (الجاه)[5] genannt, dessen Besonderheit es ist, demjenigen, dem es gehört, mehrere Privilegien zu verschaffen, darunter das Recht, seine Schützlinge zu beherrschen, auf ihre Loyalität zu zählen sowie das Recht, von ihren Diensten zu profitieren. Wir werden sehen, dass Prestige als Vektor der Machtübertragung fungiert und die Bildung von politischen Parteien und sogar der höchsten politischen Autorität bestimmt, die oft von den Eliten verkörpert wird.

## 1 Der Sturz eines Autokraten als ein „Ereignis, das dieses Namens würdig ist"

Von den ersten Tagen nach dem überraschenden Abgang von Präsident Ben Ali (14. Januar 2011) an waren alle Tunesier überzeugt, dass dies tatsächlich „ein historisches Ereignis" war. Aber was ist „ein historisches Ereignis"? In einer ersten grundsätzlichen Bedeutung bezeichnen wir mit (einem) historischen Ereignis(sen) eine reale Tatsache oder reale Tatsachen, die in einer bestimmten Reihe aufeinander folgen, also Tatsachen, die sich in ähnlichen Zusammenhängen wiederholen: erst am 14. Januar in Tunesien, dann am 25. Januar 2011 in Ägypten, dann am 17. Februar in Libyen, am 20. Februar 2011 in Marokko usw.

Hier stellt sich die Frage, ob durch die Reduzierung mehrerer Ereignisse auf eine Reproduktion nicht mehr das wahre Ereignis von dem falschen, das authentische von der Kopie unterschieden werden kann. Um dieses Risiko zu vermeiden, spricht Derrida lieber von einem „Ereignis, das dieses Namens würdig ist" (Derrida 2003: 57) und gibt an,

> dass das Ereignis als solches, als absolute Überraschung, über mich hereinbrechen muss. […] [D]as Ereignis aber ist das, was niemals vorausgesagt werden kann. Ein vorausgesagtes Ereignis ist kein Ereignis. Es bricht über mich herein, weil ich es nicht kommen sehe. […] Bevor es sich ereignet, kann das Ereignis mir nur als unmögliches erscheinen. (Derrida 2003: 35)

---

4 'Abd ar-Rahmān Ibn Khaldūn (geboren am 27. Mai 1332 in Tunis und gestorben am 17. März 1406 in Kairo) war ein Historiker und ein Vorläufer der Soziologie, aber auch ein Politiker. Er ist vor allem als Autor von *Die Einführung (Al-Muqaddima)* bekannt.
5 *Al-Dschah.*

Wenn wir diese derridasche Definition des Ereignisses aufgreifen, können wir sagen, dass Ben Alis überraschender Abgang „durch Gedanken schwer fassbar, einzig und unvorhersehbar" war. Es war besonders überraschend, schnell, folgenreich, voller Emotionen, voller Freude, aber auch und vor allem voller Zorn, vermischt mit einer tiefen Empörung, die eine immer größere Anzahl von Bürgern erreichte, als die Nachricht sich wie ein Lauffeuer im ganzen Land verbreitete. Das Ereignis ist es, was uns dazu bringt, von „es wird sich sowieso nichts ändern" zu „von jetzt an wird nichts mehr so sein wie vorher" zu kommen.

Seltsamerweise hat dieses Ereignis nichts mit dem Tod derjenigen zu tun, die erschossen wurden, vielleicht weil andere Bürger während der Unruhen von 2008, 1984, 1978 usw. das gleiche Schicksal erlitten. In jedem Fall wird es eher durch das Gefühl hervorgerufen, sicher zu sein – ohne zu wissen aus welchem Grund –, dass dieser Aufstand nicht denjenigen gleicht, die ihm vorausgegangen sind.

Wir hätten vielleicht nicht von einem Ereignis gesprochen, wenn der geflohene Präsident durch seinen früheren Premierminister ersetzt worden wäre, wie dies 1987 der Fall war, als Präsident Bourguiba von seinem Premierminister, der kein anderer als Ben Ali war, aus dem Amt entfernt wurde. Wenn dieses Manöver erfolgreich gewesen wäre, wären wir mit einem „Déjà-vu" konfrontiert worden, einer Wiederholung. In der Tat, wie auch Derrida betont, ist nur ein „einzigartiges" Ereignis des Namens würdig. Aus dieser Sicht nehmen wir uns das Recht zu behaupten, dass nur der Sturz des tunesischen Regimes ein historisches Ereignis war. Diejenigen, die folgten, wurden sehr schnell durch die Geschichte überholt.

So sehr die gelebte Erfahrung dieses Ereignisses integrativ war, so kontrovers und sogar widersprüchlich war seine Interpretation. Einerseits wurde es von tunesischen und westlichen Menschenrechtsverteidigern sowie von linken Parteien als Beginn einer neuen Ära der Bürgeremanzipation angesehen. Um darüber zu berichten, zogen sie nach Belieben das revolutionäre Lexikon heran und stritten über die Angemessenheit der Bezeichnungen: Prager Frühling von 1968 oder Frühling der Völker von 1848, Samtene Revolution von 1989, Oktoberrevolution von 1917 oder einfach nur ein Aufstand? Das Problem ist, dass sie, wenn sie hartnäckig Ausdrücke aus dem westlich-revolutionären Lexikon verwenden, das Risiko eingehen, nur den Aspekt zu sehen, der sie beruhigt und ihren Erwartungen entspricht. Der Erkenntnisakt wird also durch Mechanismen und auf die Basis primitiver Gewissheiten eingeschränkt.

Zum Beispiel wurde der Sturz einer Autokratie nur als Entstehung einer Demokratie begriffen. Dann fegte eine Horde von Experten der „Transformationstheorie" mit erstaunlicher Geschwindigkeit über das Land und legte einen fertigen Fahrplan vor: Übergangsphase, Konsolidierung, Verfassungsprozess, Wahl, Verhandlung und Machtteilung, Übergangsjustiz usw.

Von Anfang an schien diese Herangehensweise nicht mit den wahren Ursachen des Aufstandes übereinzustimmen, da die ersten Forderungen junger Menschen bereits 2008 im Bergbaugebiet aufgestellt worden waren und diese vor allem forderten, einen Arbeitsplatz zu erhalten, nachdem Schul- und Universitätsabschlüsse aufgehört hatten, als Zugang zum Arbeitsleben zu dienen.

Um zu überleben, waren sie zu allem bereit: Schwarzarbeit, Schmuggel, Kleinkriminalität, Korruption. Werte wie Freiheit, Gleichheit und Demokratie gehörten also nicht zu ihren primären Anliegen. Wenn wir diese Realität zur Kenntnis nehmen, ist es schwer zu glauben, dass der demokratische Übergang für diesen Teil der Bevölkerung von großer Bedeutung ist. Diese Verzerrung der Realität ist eine der Grundfunktionen der Ideologie, die von Paul Ricœur (1984) bewundernswert beschrieben wurden.

Eine andere Interpretation wurde von jenen präsentiert, die den politischen Islam beanspruchen. Nehmen wir zum Beispiel die Äußerungen eines islamistischen Führers, der von 2012 bis 2013 das Amt des Regierungschefs innehatte, als er nach der Wahl der Verfassunggebenden Nationalversammlung im Oktober 2011 bei einer Kundgebung den Sieg seiner Partei feierte:

> Meine Brüder, ihr seid jetzt in der Gegenwart eines historischen Moments, eines göttlichen Moments, das einen neuen Zyklus[6] der Zivilisation ankündigt, wenn Gott es will, den des sechsten Kalifats[7], wenn Gott es will.[8] (Übersetzung des Autors)

Hier haben wir die beispielhafte Beschreibung eines sehr gewöhnlichen Ereignisses (Versammlung von Wählern, um ihren Sieg zu feiern), das durch die Rede eines der Teilnehmer in eine göttliche Zeitlichkeit gesetzt wird. Und plötzlich wird der Sieg zum Werk Gottes und das „Jetzt-sein-in-Gegenwart-von" wird nicht mehr als interne Zeitlichkeit verstanden, sondern in die ewige Dauer eingeschrieben, in der Vergangenheit, Gegenwart und Zukunft vereint sind. Die Abstimmung bezieht sich nicht mehr auf die Wahl der Verfassunggebenden Nationalversammlung vom 23. Oktober 2011, sondern kündigt die Einführung eines neuen Zyklus an (dieses Wort bezeichnet nach Ibn Khaldūn und zuerst im Koran die Staatsdynastie), und diese Staatsdynastie ist das sechste Staatskalifat.

---

6 Mit dem Wort „Zyklus" bezeichnet Ibn Khaldūn die durch Gewalt unaufhörliche Aufeinanderfolge von dynastischen Staaten.
7 Nach der islamischen Tradition der Sunniten hatten nur die ersten fünf Kalifen nach dem göttlichen Willen geherrscht.
8 Siehe die Rede vom 13. November 2011 in Sousse: „Tunisie – Ennahdha a annoncé le 6ème Califat, avant celui établi par Daech".

Der Schwerpunkt dieser Interpretation liegt darin, dass die Abfolge der Ereignisse (Volksaufstand, Flucht des Staatsoberhauptes, Wahlsieg ...) nicht von sozioökonomischen oder politischen Gründen bestimmt wird, sondern all diese Ereignisse werden vom Willen Gottes diktiert, dessen Pläne unergründlich sind. Darüber hinaus offenbart diese Interpretation die theologisch-politische Bedeutung des Wahlsieges für Islamisten, nämlich die Verpflichtung der Auserwählten gegenüber Gott, den sechsten Kalifenstaat zu errichten. Nach muslimischer Tradition wäre die Pastoralmacht der ersten fünf Kalifen völlig gerecht gewesen, weil sie im Einklang mit Gottes Willen gehandelt hätten. Dagegen wären alle ihre Nachfolger nur Monarchen gewesen, die die Macht für persönliche Zwecke nutzten.

Diesmal ist die Kluft zwischen der politischen Realität und der Rede einiger islamistischer Dschihadistenführer tief. Die Strategen unter ihnen bevorzugten es, sich die Sprache der Menschenrechte anzueignen, und zeigten ihre Bereitschaft, das Programm der „Transformationstheorie" anzuwenden, um die gleichen Ziele der islamistischen Brüderlichkeit zu erreichen.

Es gibt mindestens drei Gründe für das quasi verallgemeinerte Schweigen über die soziale und wirtschaftliche Dimension des Ereignisses vom 14. Januar 2011. Der erste Grund ist, dass eine unorganisierte soziale Kategorie, die der arbeitslosen Jugendlichen, nicht in der Lage ist, ein politisches Regime zu stürzen. Trotz der Stärke, der Macht und der politischen Führung war zum Beispiel die russische Arbeiterklasse gezwungen, das zu bilden, was Lenin „eine ehrliche Koalition" nannte. In seinem Brief „Die erste Etappe der ersten Revolution" (Prawda, 21./22. März 1917) schreibt Lenin:

> Wenn die Revolution so rasch und – dem Anschein nach, bei erster, oberflächlicher Betrachtung – so radikal gesiegt hat, dann nur deshalb, weil sich dank einer außerordentlich originellen historischen Situation *völlig verschiedene Ströme, völlig ungleichartige* Klasseninteressen, *völlig entgegengesetzte* politische und soziale Bestrebungen *vereinigten*, und zwar bemerkenswert „einmütig" vereinigten [...]. (Lenin 1917)

Trotz der unterschiedlichen Kontexte ist dieser Satz ein gutes Beispiel für diese „überraschende Kreuzung", die das Ereignis schafft: ein Bündnis zwischen der Bauernschaft, dem Proletariat und den Beamten in Russland, das Bündnis zwischen arbeitslosen Jugendlichen, Gewerkschaftern, Beamten und Unternehmern in Tunesien.

Der zweite Grund ist, dass die wichtigsten politischen Akteure, die sich dem Volksaufstand angeschlossen haben, die liberale Wirtschaftspolitik des alten Regimes teilen, was für sie bedeutet, dass die wirtschaftliche Komponente nicht antagonistisch gesehen wurde und daher im Hinblick auf den Kampf um die Macht nicht sehr nützlich war. Hier muss klargestellt werden, dass die oben erwähnte „einmütige Vereinigung" eher problematisch ist, da sie in Wahrheit widersprüchliche Interpretationen verbirgt, die in späteren Stadien auftreten werden. Außerdem stimmen Klassenzugehörigkeit und ideologische Klassenposition nicht unbedingt überein. Wie Stuart Hall behauptet,

> gibt es keine Garantie, dass Ideologie und Klasse unter allen Umständen in irgendeiner Weise zusammen artikuliert werden können oder im Klassenkampf eine fähige soziale Kraft für eine Zeit der ihrer selbst bewussten „Einheit in Aktion" hervorbringen.[9] (Übersetzung des Autors)

Der dritte Grund ist, dass in dieser Phase des Machtvakuums die Eroberung des Staatsapparats und der Institutionen im Vordergrund steht, damit der Gewinner die Regeln der neuen Gesellschaftsordnung zu seinem Vorteil gestalten kann. Um diesen letzten Punkt zu verdeutlichen, ist es nützlich, auf die Analyse der drei Funktionen des ricœurschen Ideologiebegriffs und genauer auf die Funktion der Legitimation der Herrschaft und der integrativen Funktion zurückzukommen.

## 2 Der Aufbau hegemonialer Allianzen: Legitimität und kollektive Identität

Ideologie ist für Ricœur nicht nur eine Verschleierung der Realität, sondern auch eine Rechtfertigung, das heißt ein Anbieter von Legitimität. Sie ist, schreibt er, „eine Art Mehrwert des Glaubens, den jede Autorität von ihren Untergebenen erpressen muss"[10] (Übersetzung des Autors).

Die Ideologie hat auch eine integrative Funktion, die in gewisser Weise mit der vorherigen Funktion verknüpft ist, indem sie sich mit der Herstellung der politischen Kohäsion befasst, die stark und intensiv genug für die „Einheit des Handelns" sein muss. Wir werden jedoch feststellen, dass es eine strukturelle Spannung zwischen der Logik der Konstitution eines hegemonialen Bündnisses, das die verschiedenen Kräfte zusammenbringt, und der Konstitution einer politischen Einheit gibt, die darauf beruht. Veranschaulichen wir uns zu diesem Zweck einige Beispiele.

---

9 Original des Zitats: „[...] there is no guarantee that, under all circumstances, ideology and class can never be articulated together in any way or produce a social force capable for a time of self-conscious ‚unity in action', in a class struggle." (Hall 1985: 94–95)
10 Original des Zitats: „une sorte de plus-value de croyance que toute autorité a besoin d'extorquer de ses subordonnés" (Ricœur 1984: 57).

Die Regierung, die nach der Wahl der Verfassunggebenden Nationalversammlung (Oktober 2011 bis Januar 2014) gebildet wurde, stützte sich in Wahrheit auf zwei Bündnisse: zum einen auf ein Bündnis zwischen verschiedenen islamistischen Bewegungen und zum anderen auf ein Bündnis zwischen letzteren und zwei Parteien, die sich als laizistisch präsentierten. Dieses Doppelbündnis war in seinen Anfängen erfolgreich darin, sehr unterschiedliche politische Kräfte zusammenzubringen, wodurch es eine große Legitimität erlangte. Aber es scheiterte später in allen Kämpfen gegen die parlamentarische und außerparlamentarische Opposition und musste die Macht aus einem fundamentalen Grund aufgeben: nämlich seiner Unfähigkeit wegen, ein Kollektiv, ein „Wir", zu formen, das sich selbst in einer politischen Identität erkennt.

Auf der anderen Seite haben diese Kämpfe alle gegnerischen Kräfte dazu gedrängt, eine Catch-all-Partei (*Ruf Tunesiens*) mit agonistischem Charakter zu bilden, um die Umsetzung des islamistischen Projekts zu verhindern. Daher hängt der politische Erfolg eines hegemonialen Bündnisses von seiner Legitimität und insbesondere von seiner Fähigkeit ab, seine politische Vormachtstellung durchzusetzen. Wie wird diese Vormachtstellung erreicht? Wie konnte dieses Bündnis um den *Ruf Tunesiens*, angeführt von einem Achtzigjährigen, einem Vertreter des alten Regimes und daher mit geringer „revolutionärer" oder sogar „religiöser" Legitimation, die Herausforderung der politischen Vorherrschaft erfolgreich bewältigen? Es gelang, weil dieses Bündnis fest in der sozialen und politischen Geschichte des Volkes verwurzelt ist und es diese Geschichte ideologisch nutzen konnte, indem es dafür sorgte, dass bestimmte entscheidende Ereignisse der Übergangsphase als eine Neuverwirklichung der Gründung Tunesiens als Nationalstaat erlebt wurden. In diesem Zusammenhang sind zwei Ereignisse hervorzuheben.

1) Am 7. März 2012, dem Vorabend des Internationalen Frauentags, hinderte eine Studentin mutig einen Salafisten daran, die tunesische Flagge durch das schwarze Banner der Dschihadisten zu ersetzen. Zeugen zufolge rief die Studentin: „Die Flagge ist heilig." Dieses Ereignis geschah zu einer Zeit, als islamistische Führer gegen die 1957 beschlossenen progressiven Gesetze zur Gleichstellung der Geschlechter kämpften. Ohne es zu wissen, beteiligten sich die beiden Studenten an der Neuauflage des Gründungskonflikts des tunesischen Staates, indem sich die Studentin denjenigen widersetzte, die sich aus religiösen Gründen gegen diese Gesetze aussprachen. Der Konflikt zwischen den Studenten betraf eher zufällig zwei Grundlagen der politischen Identität des Staates: die Verteidigung der Gleichstellung der Geschlechter und die Verteidigung der Flagge, dem Symbol der nationalen Souveränität.
2) Am 4. Dezember 2012 wurde eine Demonstration der Allgemeinen Gewerkschaft Tunesiens (UGTT) zum 60. Jahrestag der Ermordung ihres Gründers

durch den französischen Geheimdienst von hunderten islamistischen Milizionären gewaltsam angegriffen. Wie wir sehen können, hat dieses Ereignis die gleiche Struktur wie das vorherige, mit der Ausnahme, dass es zusätzlich durch seine Größe und seine Gewalt einen politischen Konflikt zwischen den ersten beiden Kräften des Landes hervorruft: der islamistischen Partei und der zentralen Gewerkschaft. Hier ist es wichtig zu erwähnen, dass die tunesische Gewerkschaftsbewegung zu Beginn der Zwanzigerjahre des letzten Jahrhunderts gegründet wurde und dass die Geschichte ihrer Kämpfe zur Verteidigung der Arbeitswelt und der Arbeiterklasse im kollektiven sozialen Gedächtnis verankert blieb. Infolgedessen konnte die Aggression, die gegen die Allgemeine Gewerkschaft gerichtet war, nur als Angriff auf die soziale Identität Tunesiens empfunden werden.

Diese beiden Ereignisse zeigen uns also, wie die Ideologie „ein politisches Wir" schafft, indem sie die politische Geschichte verwendet, die in das kollektive Gedächtnis eingraviert ist. Durch verschiedene Mechanismen sind Kämpfe in der Gegenwart (2011–2019) mit früheren Kämpfen (1950–1956) verbunden. Konkret wird der große politische Konflikt zwischen der um die islamistische Partei gebildeten Koalition und der von der Partei des am 25. Juli 2019 verstorbenen Präsidenten Béji Caïd Essebsi geführten Koalition als Reproduktion in Form einer Wiederholung des alten Konflikts zwischen der arabisch-islamistischen sowie der laizistischen und pro-westlichen Elite zu Beginn der Unabhängigkeit dargestellt.

Es ist erwähnenswert, dass die konservative Elite damals aus einem großen Teil der alten Landbesitzer und des Handelsbürgertums bestand, aber auch die Bevölkerung der benachteiligten Gebiete einschloss sowie einen großen Teil derjenigen, die den bewaffneten Kampf gegen die französische Kolonisation führten. Die andere Elite hingegen wurde vom städtischen Kleinbürgertum und insbesondere von der sehr mächtigen Gewerkschaft UGTT unterstützt, die eine entscheidende Rolle für den Sieg des modernistischen Lagers spielte. Aber dieser Sieg war letztendlich gewaltsam, denn das konservative Lager wurde durch Gewalt neutralisiert und sein Anführer ins Exil gedrängt, bevor er 1961 in Frankfurt ermordet wurde.

Dieser Rückblick auf die politische Geschichte des heutigen Tunesiens mit der Parallele zwischen dem Gründungskonflikt des Staates und dem gegenwärtigen Konflikt erlaubt es uns, zwei Thesen vorzubringen. Die erste These ist, dass der 14. Januar 2011 ein Ereignis im Sinne Derridas war, nicht weil es eine Revolution gab, die zum Sturz eines Regimes führte, sondern weil es ein Machtvakuum im Kontext einer Krise des etablierten Machtsystems gab. In der Tat beruhte das autoritäre politische System, wie wir gerade gezeigt haben, auf zwei Hauptkräften, der verfassungsliberalen Partei *Destour* (gegründet 1920) und der Organisation der Gewerkschaftsbewegung (der 1925 gegründeten CGTT, später der 1946 gegründeten UGTT). Die Trennung zwischen Partei und Gewerkschaftszentrale war rein formal, da die Gewerkschaftsführer Parteimitglieder waren und oft mehrere Ministerien leiteten. Mit anderen Worten hat der Abgang von Ben Ali mit Sicherheit zum Sturz der einen politischen Säule des alten politischen Machtsystems geführt; aber die zweite Säule blieb intakt und wurde später sogar zum schärfsten Gegner des arabisch-islamistischen Bündnisses.

Die zweite These lautet, dass dieses System den sozialen und politischen Kräften freien Lauf lassen musste, um die Krise zu überwinden, die das System vollständig destabilisiert hatte, und damit diese Kräfte durch Verhandlungen und/oder Gewalt ein neues hegemoniales Bündnis aufbauen konnten, das es erlaubte, die Hegemonie zu restrukturieren und wieder zu stabilisieren. Es ist anzumerken, dass dies nicht das erste Mal war, dass das Machtsystem eine interne Krise durch Anpassung oder eine hegemoniale Neuzusammensetzung überwindet.

Wir sollten also unter diesem Gesichtspunkt die Kämpfe zwischen den verschiedenen politischen Kräften seit Januar 2011 analysieren. Wir müssen aufpassen, dass wir diese Kämpfe nicht so betrachten, als ob diejenigen, die für den Islam sind, jenen, die für Demokratie eintreten, entgegengesetzt wären. In einem ideologischen Kampf ist religiöser Glaube ein Mobilisierungswerkzeug wie jedes andere oder eher eine Waffe wie jede andere. Um die Einheit einer islamistischen Partei zu formen, benutzt die Ideologie Religion, wie die Laizität benutzt wird, wenn es um eine Partei mit einer modern-laizistischen Ausrichtung geht. Diese theologische oder nationalistische Wut zur Vereinheitlichung (*Tauhīd*) ist von Natur aus blind und kastrierend, da sie darin besteht, die Köpfe zu manipulieren und die Gefühle zu zähmen. Ricœur schildert diesen regressiven Ideologieprozess wie folgt:

> Die Ideologie degeneriert weiter, wenn man bedenkt, durch welche oft grobe Vereinfachung und welche oft arrogante Schematisierung der Integrationsprozess im Legitimationsprozess verlängert wird. Nach und nach wird die Ideologie zu einem künstlichen und autoritären Gitter des Lesens [...] der Lebensweise der Gruppe [...].[11] (Übersetzung des Autors)

---

[11] Original des Zitats: „L'idéologie continue de dégénérer si on considère par quelle simplification souvent grossière er par quelle schématisation souvent arrogante le processus d'intégration se prolonge dans celui de légitimation. Peu à peu, l'idéologie devient une grille de lecture artificielle et autoritaire non seulement de la façon de vivre du groupe [...]." (Ricœur 1984: 59)

Was überrascht, aber gleichzeitig die Analyse von Ricœur stärkt, ist, dass das modernistische Lager, dem berüchtigte Gegner des ehemaligen Regimes angehören (z. B. alte Kommunisten), heute im Kampf gegen die islamistische Front seine Anhänger in Kontinuität mit dem Projekt des Vaters der Nation, Präsident Bourguiba, mobilisiert. Es ist daher an der Zeit, sich auf das Wesentliche zu konzentrieren: den Machtkampf, der mit der Errichtung der Hegemonie einhergeht.

## 3 Hegemoniale Allianz, geheime Machtformen als Prestigeerscheinungen

In „Subjekt und Macht" (Foucault 2005) macht Michel Foucault darauf aufmerksam, dass Macht nicht in Form des Singulars gedacht werden darf und dass vor allem darauf geachtet werden muss, sie nicht, wie dies nur allzu oft geschieht, auf ihre Rechtsform zu reduzieren. Aus dieser Sicht kann die Allgegenwart von Juristen im politischen öffentlichen Raum Tunesiens als ein schönes Beispiel für eine solche Reduktion angesehen werden, die darüber hinaus nicht so unschuldig ist, wie man uns glauben machen will. In der Tat bedeutet Leben in der Gesellschaft, den eigenen Status und die eigene Rolle laufend zu ändern und sich in Institutionen oder in Kreisläufe einzubringen, die für die Legalität unerlässlich sind. Dies bedeutet daher, sich an die Funktionsweise von Herrschaft, Abhängigkeit und Unterwerfung anzupassen, die für jede Institution oder jeden Bereich des sozialen Lebens spezifisch ist.

Um „die Macht in ihrer am wenigsten geheimen Form zu verfolgen", wie wir mit Foucault sagen, verweisen wir auf Ibn Khaldūn, der eine Form von Macht definiert, die nicht aus der unmittelbaren Beziehung zwischen Souverän und Subjekt besteht, sondern unter Bezugnahme auf einen Übertragungsvektor, *das Prestige*, verstanden werden muss, das in allen Erscheinungsformen der Macht zu finden ist. Prestige – genauer gesagt das mit dem Rang verbundene Prestige – ist ein Vektor der Machtübertragung.

Im Arabischen bezeichnet das Wort „*Dschah*" ‚Status', ‚Rang', ‚Respekt', ‚Rücksichtnahme', ‚Einfluss', ‚Gunst', ‚Ehre'. Ibn Khaldūn gibt jedoch an, dass der soziale Rang nicht ausreicht, weil man auch einer niedrigeren Klasse angehören und mehr Prestige haben oder genießen kann. Daher ist Prestige nach seiner Auffassung

> die Fähigkeit [...], die den Menschen dazu antreibt, über die unter ihm Stehenden seiner Gattung frei zu verfügen, indem er erlaubt und verweigert und sie beherrschen kann mit

Zwang und Überlegenheit, um sie dazu zu bringen, die für sie schädlichen Dinge abzuwehren und die nützlichen herbeizuziehen [...]. (Ibn Khaldūn 2011: 350)

Diese Macht wird von oben nach unten ausgeübt, von der Spitze der Hierarchie (dem Potentaten und seinen engsten Beratern) bis zu den untergeordneten, differenzierten und hierarchisch abhängigen sozialen Schichten (religiösen Gelehrten, Rechtsberatern, Magistraten, Beamten, Gelehrten, Bauern, Händlern, bewaffneten Männern und/oder Banditen). Nur die Ärmsten und die Schwächsten haben kein Prestige. Laut Ibn Khaldūn wird Prestige zwischen freien Menschen in dem Sinne weitergegeben, dass jeder sowohl Empfänger als auch Spender ist. Es wird auch betont, dass Macht als Prestige es dem, der sie genießt, ermöglicht, Sachgüter anzusammeln, die von seinen Schützlingen in Form von Geschenken ausgegeben werden.

Dieser Anreicherungsmechanismus resultiert nicht aus der Herrschaft, sondern aus der Beobachtung einer „Tatsachenregel", die stillschweigend von allen akzeptiert wird, weil sie letztendlich für sie rentabel ist. Ibn Khaldūns vorsichtige Darstellung des rangbezogenen Prestiges als Teil einer Reflexion über die Schaffung von Wohlstand zeigt, wie sehr die politische Macht von der Fähigkeit abhängt, Wohlstand anzusammeln.

Diese Analyse eignet sich besonders im vorliegenden Zusammenhang, da sie perfekt zur Strategie aller Akteure passt, die die Macht des Staates erobern wollten. Ihr Erfolg oder Misserfolg wird von ihrer Fähigkeit abhängen, die „angesehensten" Persönlichkeiten anzuziehen. Am beliebtesten waren anfangs militante religiöse Milizen, denn dank ihrer Unterstützung konnten die politischen Parteien die Straße besetzen, möglichst viele Demonstranten mobilisieren, Zusammenkünfte mit ihren Anhängern und Sympathisanten organisieren und sogar die Aktivitäten anderer Parteien verhindern.

Dann, als sich die politische Landschaft weiterentwickelte, war es die Jagd nach Kapitalgebern, Richtern und hohen Beamten, Unternehmern aus Industrie, Handel und Landwirtschaft, Mafiosi, Inhabern von Medien sowie Präsidenten und Spieler von Fußballvereinen usw.

Wenn wir dem Prestigebegriff einen wichtigen Platz einräumen, dann deshalb, weil er in fast allen Gesellschaften, insbesondere aber in hierarchischen Gesellschaften, der Hauptvektor der Machtübertragung ist und weil er, aufgrund seines elitären Charakters, ein strukturelles Hindernis für ein demokratisches Machtverständnis darstellt. Aber Prestige findet sich, wo soziale Beziehungen entstehen. Es bestimmt die Art der Beziehungen in der Familie, der Fabrik, der Schule, den politischen Parteien und der herrschenden Elite. Betrachten wir die letzten zwei Beispiele nun genauer.

## 3.1 Ist politischer Pluralismus ein Bekenntnis zur Demokratie?

Auf den ersten Blick ist der Wechsel von einem Einparteiensystem zu einem Mehrparteiensystem eine gute Nachricht. Aber das Problem ist, dass Parteien, die auf der Grundlage von Rang-Prestige gegründet wurden, in Wirklichkeit nichts mit Demokratie zu tun haben. Und dies aus mehreren Gründen: Der erste ist, dass diese Parteien sehr heterogene Gruppen zusammenbrachten, und zwar unter dem Gesichtspunkt der Werte und Interessen ihrer jeweiligen Mitglieder sowie ihrer unterschiedlichen Loyalität gegenüber der Person des Führers. Der zweite Grund ist, dass die interne Organisation dieser Parteien nicht auf den Normen und Verfahren für die Auswahl einer demokratisch gewählten Führung beruhte. Der dritte Grund ist, dass keine Partei alle diejenigen belohnen konnte, die ihr geholfen hatten, an die Macht zu gelangen, indem sie ihnen Schlüsselpositionen in ihrer politischen Führung, an der Spitze der Ministerien, im Parlament und in der nationalen und regionalen Verwaltung anbot. Der vierte Grund ist, dass das Charisma des Führers heutzutage viel von seiner Ausstrahlung verloren hat: Führung wird immer mehr an den tatsächlichen Gewinnen gemessen, die sie bringt.

Diese lukrative Auffassung von „Loyalität" gegenüber dem Oberhaupt der Familie oder dem Führer der Partei ist nicht ganz neu, da die Autorität des Stammeshäuptlings immer an der Bedeutung der Beute gemessen wurde, die er vom höchsten Oberhaupt (vom Sultan, Kalifen oder vom König) erhalten hatte. Neu ist hingegen die Weigerung der neuen Generationen, so wie ihre Eltern weiter zu leben, indem sie mit der vorgegebenen Arbeit auf den Feldern, in den Fabriken der Zulieferer oder im Tourismus zufrieden wären. Zudem beraubt die fortschreitende Verarmung die Eltern aller Formen der Autorität, weil sie ihre Kinder nicht mehr vor den Folgen der Arbeitslosigkeit schützen können. All dies zeigt, dass die Mehrparteienpolitik noch einen weiten Weg vor sich hat, um mit demokratischen und liberalen Werten in Verbindung gebracht werden zu können.

## 3.2 Die Eliten und die Entstehung eines neuen Machtsystems

Macht als Prestige hat sich bisher viel mehr an der moralischen Dimension des Prestiges als an der Macht im Sinne von Zwang orientiert. Der Begriff des hegemonialen Bündnisses bezieht sich in erster Linie auf die ideologische Überlegenheit. Aber wenn es um die Entstehung eines neuen Machtsystems geht, wie im Falle Tunesiens, müssen wir doch anerkennen, dass das Letztere durch ein für es günstiges Kräfteverhältnis ermöglicht wird.

Unter Bezugnahme auf diesen Punkt erinnert Ricœur daran, dass soziale Vertragstheorien mit Hilfe eines Gedankenexperiments den Moment des Übergangs von einem Kriegszustand in einen Zivilstaat als „eine Art Sprung [...] eine Art der Entsagung"[12] (Übersetzung des Autors) darstellen. Aber dieser Sprung, der eine neue Gesellschaftsordnung hervorbringt, bleibt unklar, ist nicht thematisiert, wird nicht beschrieben oder durchdacht (vgl. Ricœur 1984: 57–58). In der Tat, wenn dem so ist, dann, weil die Sozialvertragstheoretiker nur die Frage der Legitimation der Macht stellen und sich nicht für die Frage interessieren, wie die Macht funktioniert.

Der Unterschied zwischen dem vertragsgebundenen Ansatz und dem foucaultschen Ansatz besteht darin, dass der erste mit Hilfe eines Gedankenexperiments beginnt, indem die Bedingungen festgelegt werden, die die Vision ermöglichen, die er von der legitimen Macht schon hat. Andererseits beschreibt der zweite Ansatz das Phänomen der Macht in seiner Komplexität unter Berücksichtigung aller Elemente, die es ausmachen, wobei die Anwendung von Gewalt unter anderem nur eine Form der Macht ist. Entscheidend ist dabei immer das geografische, kulturelle und historische Umfeld, in dem sich diese Modi entfalten. Nehmen wir zum Beispiel die Elite, die in der arabischen und muslimischen Welt als erste und oberste Quelle des Prestiges gilt.

## 3.3 Das Quartett des nationalen Dialogs oder wie eine Eliten-Allianz die souveräne Entscheidung erwirbt

Das Quartett des nationalen Dialogs setzte sich aus Vertretern von vier angesehenen nationalen Organisationen zusammen: dem Generalsekretär der Allgemeinen Gewerkschaft Tunesiens, der Präsidentin des Arbeitgeberverbandes, dem Präsidenten der tunesischen Anwaltskammer und dem Präsidenten der Tunesischen Liga für Menschenrechte. Es erklärte sich zur Schlichtungsstelle für den Konflikt zwischen den Parteien der Nationalversammlung und der Regierung sowie den politischen Kräften der parlamentarischen und außerparlamentarischen Opposition.

Diese nationalen Organisationen verdanken ihr Ansehen dem Rang, den sie im Kampf für die Unabhängigkeit und für die Verteidigung der Rechte und Freiheiten innehatten. Ihr Rang hängt nicht von der Natur oder der hierarchischen Struktur der Gesellschaft ab, sondern besteht aus einem Kapital moralischer Legitimität. Aber, und das ist das Entscheidende, das Quartett umfasste die beiden

---

[12] Original des Zitats: „une sorte de saut [...] une sorte de renonciation" (Ricœur 1984: 58).

Motoren der Wirtschaft. Infolgedessen wird es zum wahren Machthaber des Landes und es ist die einzige Kraft, die in der Lage ist, wirtschaftliche und soziale Aktivitäten zu dominieren. In einer binären Konfliktkonfiguration (Regierungsmehrheit gegenüber Oppositionskräfte) spielt das Quartett die Rolle eines neutralen Dritten.

Diese Rolle wird auch durch die Einmischung ausländischer Mächte, insbesondere europäischer und amerikanischer, verstärkt. Seit Beginn des politischen Übergangs agierten sie als neutrale Dritte. Laura Baeza, ehemalige Leiterin der EU-Delegation in Tunis, erörtert im Vorwort zum Kooperationsbericht EU-Tunesien 2013 ein entscheidendes Treffen am 27. November 2013 zwischen den europäischen Botschaftern und dem Quartett im Hauptquartier der UGTT mit den Worten: „Das gemeinsame Treffen aller EU-Botschafter mit den Mitgliedern des Quartetts im November während der Krise wird für mich ein Höhepunkt bleiben. An diesem Tag demonstrierte Tunesien der Welt seine Fähigkeit zum Dialog und zur Erfindung seiner eigenen Demokratie."[13] (Übersetzung des Autors; siehe auch Chennoufi 2017) Ziel des Treffens war es zu zeigen, dass die internationale Gemeinschaft das Quartett als die Autorität anerkannte, die befugt ist, den Fahrplan für einen Ausweg aus der Krise aufzustellen. Infolgedessen galt das Quartett nicht mehr als Instanz, um eine Lösung für die politische Krise vorzuschlagen, sondern als Instanz, die befugt war, eine Lösung aufzuzwingen.

Mit anderen Worten: „Der Sprung", von dem Ricœur spricht, ist derjenige, mit dem sich in einem Konflikt oder „einem Kriegszustand" zwischen mehreren Parteien eine von ihnen in eine Instanz der Entscheidungsfindung und vor allem der Anwendung von Entscheidungen verwandelt. Diese Verlagerung von der Schiedsgerichtsbarkeit zur souveränen Entscheidung ist eine konkrete Tatsache. Wenn sie nicht auf ernsthaften Widerstand stößt, markiert sie die Entstehung eines neuen Machtsystems, dessen legale Legitimität rückwirkend ist. Dies ist der Prozess, dem das Quartett folgte. Alle seine Entscheidungen wurden rückwirkend von der Verfassunggebenden Nationalversammlung bestätigt, die daraufhin ihre für lange Wochen ausgesetzte Arbeit wiederaufnahm.

Es ist unnötig darauf hinzuweisen, dass dieses friedliche Ergebnis nicht auf den „außergewöhnlichen Charakter" der Tunesier zurückzuführen ist, die nicht mehr und nicht weniger gewalttätig als andere sind. Dies ist sicherlich auf eine zufällige Verbindung mehrerer exogener und endogener Faktoren zurückzuführen. Dennoch scheint es uns, dass Tunesien das Glück hat, sich seit seiner Un-

---

13 Original des Zitats: „La réunion conjointe de tous les Ambassadeurs de l'UE avec les membres du Quartet en novembre dernier, au cœur de la crise, restera à mes yeux un moment fort. Ce jour-là, la Tunisie a démontré au monde sa capacité à dialoguer et à inventer sa propre démocratie." (Baeza 2013: 5)

abhängigkeit für eine schwache Armee, eine starke Gewerkschaftsorganisation und ein einheitliches laizistisches Bildungssystem entschieden zu haben. Diese drei Optionen haben zu einer sozialen Ordnung geführt, in der Gewalt sowie soziale und politische Solidarität auf eine für die Befriedung von Konflikten recht günstige Weise angeordnet sind.

Es bleibt jedoch zu erklären, warum diese Ordnung die dschihadistischen Milizen nicht davon abgehalten hat, zwei große marxistisch und arabisch-islamisch orientierte linke Führer sowie Soldaten und Zivilisten zu ermorden. Der erste Grund ist die Logik der Eroberung der Macht, die laut den Dschihadisten jeden Muslim dazu zwingt, den Islam zu unterstützen, indem er die Ungläubigen in der „Domäne des Krieges" bekämpft, zu denen Tunesien gehört. Der zweite Grund ist Teil der von Foucault vorgestellten totalitären Logik des modernen Staates. In „Subjekt und Macht" (Foucault 2005) warnt er vor der Versuchung, die Vorherrschaft auf die Mechanismen der wirtschaftlichen Ausbeutung einer Klasse oder auf die Souveränität des Volkes zu beschränken und dabei zu vergessen, dass der moderne Staat eine totalitäre Tendenz hat, Individuen zu unterwerfen. Bezogen auf das 16. Jahrhundert schreibt Foucault,

> dass der moderne westliche Staat in neuer politischer Form eine alte Machttechnik aufgriff, die in den christlichen Institutionen entstanden war. Diese Machttechnik wollen wir als Pastoralmacht bezeichnen. (Foucault 2005: 277)

Diese These ist in mehrfacher Hinsicht interessant. Erstens lenkt sie unsere Aufmerksamkeit auf die Ähnlichkeit zwischen Christentum und Islam in Bezug auf den Machtbegriff und zweitens lässt sie uns verstehen, dass islamistische und nicht islamistische Parteien trotz ihrer Unterschiede ähnlich sind. Sie sind dies sogar bis zu dem Punkt, dass man aus Sicht des klassischen Islam diese Definition der Pastoralmacht fast wörtlich annehmen kann:

> Diese Form von Macht ist auf das Seelenheil ausgerichtet (im Unterschied zur politischen Macht). Sie ist opferbereit (im Unterschied zum Herrschaftsprinzip), und sie individualisiert (im Unterschied zur richterlichen Macht). (Foucault 2005: 277–278)

Wie die christliche ist auch die muslimische Religion auf die Errettung der Seelen im Jenseits ausgerichtet. Sie fordert das Opfer, die Gabe von sich selbst an Gott, den Märtyrer und nicht den Gehorsam gegenüber einem souveränen Willen, sei es der eines Monarchen oder der eines Volkes. Sie kümmert sich um Handlungen, zu denen der Gläubige, als Individuum konzipiert, in allen Bereichen des Lebens berufen ist. Foucault schließt seine Analyse mit der Behauptung, dass die Moderne nicht nur die Pastoralmacht übernommen, sondern sie mit Hilfe des Staates auf das irdische Leben erstreckt hat. Dies ist, was die Islamisten mit der Formel

„Islam ist Religion und Staat" meinen. Es sei aber betont, dass Foucault den modernen Staat nicht auf diese Technik reduziert.

Was die Nichtislamisten angeht, so behaupten sie immer noch, dass der moderne Staat mit dem Islam vereinbar ist, obwohl sie sich zum laizistischen Staat bekennen. Zum Beispiel sagt Präsident Béji Caïd Essebsi immer wieder: „Wir wollen einen Zivilstaat für ein muslimisches Volk!" Was aber genau heißt Islam, Zivilstaat, moderner Staat, muslimisches Volk? Alle diese mehrdeutigen Begriffe und Formeln zeigen die schwierige freiwillige Aneignung der Säkularisation.

## Literatur

Baeza, Laura (2013): *Rapport de coopération Union européenne-Tunisie 2013*. http://www.aleca.tn/wp-content/uploads/2016/04/rapport-cooperation-2013-fr.pdf, Zugriff 6. April 2020.

Chennoufi, Ridha (2017): *Tunisie post-révolutionnaire: Conflits politiques et démocratie*. Tunis: Nirvana.

Derrida, Jacques (2003): *Eine gewisse unmögliche Möglichkeit, vom Ereignis zu sprechen*. Aus dem Französischen von Susanne Lüdemann. Berlin: Merve.

Foucault, Michel (2005): „Subjekt und Macht". In: *Schriften in vier Bänden: Dits et Ecrits*. Band IV: *1980–1988*. Hg. von Daniel Defert und François Ewald unter Mitarbeit von Jacques Lagrange. Aus dem Französischen von Michael Bischoff. Frankfurt a. M.: Suhrkamp, S. 269–294.

Hall, Stuart (1985): „Signification, Representation, Ideology: Althusser and the Post-Structuralist Debates". In: *Critical Studies in Mass Communication* 2(2), S. 91–114.

Hibou, Béatrice (2006): *La force de l'obéissance: Économie politique de la répression en Tunisie*. Paris: La Découverte.

Ibn Khaldūn (2011): *Die Muqaddima: Betrachtungen zur Weltgeschichte*. Aus dem Arabischen übertragen und mit einer Einführung von Alma Giese. Unter Mitwirkung von Wolfhart Heinrichs. München: Beck.

Lenin (1917): „Die erste Etappe der ersten Revolution". In: *Briefe aus der Ferne*. https://www.marxists.org/deutsch/archiv/lenin/1917/bri-fern/brief1.htm, Zugriff 6. April 2020.

Ricœur, Paul (1984): „L'idéologie et l'utopie: Deux expressions de l'imaginaire social". In: *Autres Temps: Les cahiers du christianisme social* 2, S. 53–64.

## Weitere Quellen

„Tunisie – Ennahdha a annoncé le 6ème Califat, avant celui établi par Daech". In: *YouTube*. Hochgeladen von Salah Horchani am 11. Juni 2017. https://www.youtube.com/watch?v=MnM6BJdcSzc, Zugriff 6. April 2020.

Elisabeth Holzleithner
# Shklar versus Schmitt

Kontrastierende Perspektiven eines pessimistischen Menschenbildes in der politischen Philosophie

**Abstract:** [Shklar versus Schmitt: Contrasting Perspectives of a Pessimistic Image of Humanity in Political Philosophy] In her oeuvre, Judith N. Shklar vehemently deals with the abysses of the human character. What people can do to one another, particularly by exercising state power, is terrifying, and this is exactly the foundation of her model of a liberal state. Carl Schmitt's image of humanity is at least as sinister, but he draws completely different conclusions. The paper at hand looks into the premises and political anthropologies of the two authors. It tries to elicit at which junctions they take different paths and prompts the question how plausible these conflicting paths of thought are. The frame for these deliberations is formed by challenges of existing liberal democracies by current developments towards a new authoritarianism in Europe and the United States.

**Keywords:** Philosophical anthropology, liberalism, fear

## 1 Grausamkeit, Furcht und der Mangel an Tugend

Judith N. Shklar hat versucht, aus der Not der Furcht vor staatlich institutionalisierter Grausamkeit eine Tugend zu machen. Ihr Liberalismus ist auf deren Abwehr gebaut. Wir mögen nicht wissen, wer wir sind, oder auch, was gut ist für uns – aber wir haben eine Ahnung davon, was es bedeutet, in Furcht zu leben, und wir wissen, dass wir das nicht wollen. Daraus erwächst eine Art „dissonante Energie" (Robin 2004: 10), aus der die liberale Demokratie zu schöpfen vermag. Weil wir aus historischer Erfahrung damit rechnen – uns davor fürchten – müssen, Opfer staatlicher Macht zu werden, in deren Namen und Schatten staatliche AkteurInnen Grausamkeiten verüben, haben wir daher gute Gründe, den Staat nach liberalen Prinzipien einzurichten: Menschenrechte, Rechtsstaat, Gewaltenteilung. Derart wird auch eine Art Gleichgewicht des Schreckens etabliert, indem Machtkonzentration im Staat möglichst hintangehalten wird. Und Menschen

---

**Anmerkung:** Für kritische Lektüre und hilfreiche Anmerkungen danke ich Hannes Bajohr und Rieke Trimçev; Kati Danielczyk, Isabell Doll, Ralph Janik, Maria Lee, Emanuel Lerch, Ines Rössl und Maria Sagmeister; Marie-Luisa Frick, Andreas Oberprantacher und Aaron Tratter.

https://doi.org/10.1515/9783110702255-007

werden mit Rechten gegen den Staat ausgestattet, dessen Macht sich auch dadurch dezentrieren lässt. Eine der praktischen Folgen dieses Arrangements sieht Shklar darin, dass politische Tugenden nicht erforderlich sind, um ein liberaldemokratisches Gefüge zu realisieren; pointiert übertitelt sie ein Kapitel in *Ganz normale Laster* mit „Schlechte Charaktere für gute Liberale" (Shklar 2014: 249). Shklar will, wie schon Kant, auf den sie sich diesbezüglich gern bezieht, von den Menschen ausgehen, wie sie sind, und das heißt, in all ihrer „Krummheit" (Kant 1977a: 41), in all ihrer Unvollkommenheit und auch Abgründigkeit. Man erinnere sich nur an Kants drastische These, es müsse möglich sein, einen Staat zu konzipieren, der selbst für ein „Volk von Teufeln" funktioniere, wenn sie denn nur Verstand haben (Kant 1977b: 224).

Aus dieser Konstellation heraus ergeben sich einige Fragen: Lehrt uns die Furcht tatsächlich, uns in die Arme eines liberalen Staates zu begeben? Wer ist dieses „Wir", das Shklar hier beschwört; was ist mit den „Tätern", die sich nicht auf der Seite der historischen Opfer und derer sehen, die gute Gründe haben, sich zu fürchten? Und was, wenn die real existierende liberale Demokratie tatsächlich in die Fänge von „schlechten Bürgern" (Shklar 1992: 69) gerät? Diese Fragen sollen vor dem Hintergrund von zwei Herausforderungen exploriert werden: Erstens, der politischen Philosophie von Carl Schmitt, der vor dem Hintergrund einer düsteren Anthropologie die Welt des Politischen in Freund und Feind zerteilt, den Liberalismus verwirft und stattdessen einen totalen Staat favorisiert. Da Shklars Menschenbild zumindest auf den ersten Blick ebenso pessimistisch erscheint wie jenes von Carl Schmitt, stellt sich die Frage nach den Abzweigungen, an denen die beiden je unterschiedliche Wege nehmen, und nach deren jeweiliger Plausibilität.

Die zweite Herausforderung sind aktuelle politische Entwicklungen. Allerorts erstarken populistische, von rassistischen und sexistischen Ressentiments getragene Bewegungen. Sie sind mittlerweile in Parlamenten, teilweise auch in Regierungen repräsentiert. Zwei Beispiele mögen hier genügen: In Ungarn wurde schon vor Jahren die „illiberale Demokratie" ausgerufen; im Zuge der Maßnahmen zur Eindämmung der Verbreitung von COVID-19 hat sich das Parlament dann im März 2020 selbst entmachtet und dem Ministerpräsidenten, Viktor Orbán, eine von existierenden Gesetzen völlig losgelöste Rechtsetzungsmacht zuerkannt (vgl. Scheppele 2020). Und „eine der ältesten und dauerhaftesten Demokratien der Welt" (Bajohr 2017: 8), die Vereinigten Staaten, wurde vier Jahre lang (2017–2021) mit Donald Trump von einem Präsidenten regiert, der jedenfalls in seinen öffentlichen Artikulationen nur wenig Verständnis für die Prinzipien eines liberaldemokratischen Rechtsstaates an den Tag legte. So fehlte etwa jeglicher Sinn für Gewaltenteilung und *checks and balances*, wenn der Präsident Gerichte (wie auch einzelne RichterInnen) für Urteile attackierte, die Maßnahmen seiner Administration für verfassungswidrig erklärten, wie er überhaupt zu meinen schien, dass es im Wesentlichen darum ging, ob man ihn „mochte" oder nicht: „Do you get the impression that the Supreme Court doesn't like me?"[1] Dass die Trump-Administration sich in beiden Fällen gegen den grundrechtlichen Schutz vulnerabler Gruppen gewandt hatte, war bezeichnend; dass der mittlerweile mehrheitlich konservativ besetzte Supreme Court diese Grundrechte hochhielt, kam durchaus überraschend.[2] Trump hielt zwar (gerne in Tweets) „Law & Order" hoch (nicht selten in Großbuchstaben[3]), aber Gesetzesbindung und Rechtsstaatlichkeit schienen ihm bloß als lästige Fesseln seiner imaginierten Allmacht zu gelten. Seine Präsidentschaft ist mit Ende Januar 2021 zu Ende gegangen; die Fragen aber bleiben akut: Hält eine liberale Demokratie solche MachthaberInnen tatsächlich aus, und wie lange? Woran können Versuche möglicher Antworten anknüpfen?

## 2 Ein Liberalismus ohne Illusionen: Judith N. Shklar

Judith N. Shklar hat sich mit Blick auf den menschlichen Charakter im Allgemeinen und jenen von politischen MachthaberInnen im Besonderen keinen Illusionen hingegeben. Davon zeugt ihr gesamtes politisch-philosophisches Werk. Die ganze Pointe von *Der Liberalismus der Furcht* (2013) besteht darin, das verderbliche Wirken von staatlich institutionalisierter Macht im Zaum zu halten und wenigstens die schlimmsten Übergriffe im Namen staatlicher Gewalt als größte Bedrohung[4] menschlicher Freiheit zu verhindern. Derart sollen die „politischen Bedingungen" (Shklar 2013: 26) für menschliche Freiheit geschaffen werden. Darin sieht Shklar die Existenzberechtigung liberaler Ordnungen: Jedem erwachsenen Menschen soll es möglich sein, „ohne Furcht und Vorurteil so viele Entscheidungen über so viele Aspekte seines Lebens zu fällen, wie es mit der

---

[1] Tweet von @realDonaldTrump, 18. Juni 2020, 17:10 Uhr. https://twitter.com/realDonaldTrump/status/1273634152433188865, Zugriff 8. Juli 2020.
[2] Es ging um die Gleichbehandlung von LGBTI am Arbeitsplatz (*Bostock v. Clayton County, Georgia*, 15. Juni 2020. https://www.supremecourt.gov/opinions/19pdf/17-1618_hfci.pdf, Zugriff 8. Juli 2020) sowie um die Aufrechterhaltung der Schutz vor Deportation und Zugang zum Arbeitsplatz verbürgenden Executive Order für „Dreamers"; junge Menschen ohne Staatsbürgerschaft, die als Kinder in die USA gebracht wurden.
[3] Siehe z. B. Tweet von @realDonaldTrump: „LAW & ORDER!", 7. Juni 2020, 00:48 Uhr. https://twitter.com/realdonaldtrump/status/1269400770472001539, Zugriff 8. Juli 2020.
[4] Ob die größte Bedrohung heute von staatlicher Seite ausgeht, wird jedenfalls diskutiert. Zakaria (2007) etwa spricht von einer „Demokratisierung von Gewalt", nicht erst seit 9/11, welche das staatliche Gewaltmonopol in seiner Allmacht durchaus infrage stellt.

gleichen Freiheit eines jeden anderen erwachsenen Menschen vereinbar ist" (Shklar 2013: 26–27). In dieser Formulierung steckt eine wesentliche Grundannahme Shklars: Freiheit wird verunmöglicht durch Furcht, und Furcht wird erzeugt durch jene Grausamkeit, die von staatlicher Seite zu erwarten ist. Diese Furcht ist das „Wogegen" der shklarschen politischen Philosophie.

Der Liberalismus der Furcht ist ebenso deskriptiv wie normativ zu verstehen: Shklar führt seine durchaus stabile, wenn auch mit vielen Mängeln (Stichwort: systemischer Rassismus; Shklar 1991: 1–2) behaftete Etablierung[5] zumal in den Vereinigten Staaten und in diversen europäischen Staaten wie seinen relativen Erfolg auf die Gegenwärtigkeit der Erinnerung an jene Grausamkeiten zurück, die im 20. Jahrhundert von totalitären Regimen verübt wurden, die aber auch, worauf sie vehement besteht, in liberalen Staaten nicht einfach überwunden sind.[6] Das ist der Grund, warum sie ihren „vollkommen nicht-utopisch[en]" Ansatz, unter Verwendung einer Formulierung von Emerson, einer „Partei der Erinnerung" zuschreibt – und nicht einer „Partei der Hoffnung" (Shklar 2013: 37). Letztere würde von liberalen Ordnungen weit mehr erwarten als bloß das von Shklar so genannte *„summum malum"* (Shklar 2013: 43) zu verhindern, nämlich Grausamkeit und die Furcht davor.[7] Darüber hinaus macht sie es, dies ist die normative Komponente, einer wachsamen Zivilgesellschaft im Sinne einer „Vielfalt politisch bevollmächtigter Gruppen" (Shklar 2013: 43) zur Aufgabe, das Wirken politischer Machthaber genau zu beobachten. Weiters sollen auch die Teilung der Gewalten, die *checks and balances* und die rechtsstaatliche Bindung von Exekutive und Judikative an die Gesetze Macht streuen und staatliche Gewalt bändigen. Dazu gehört als Herzstück des Liberalismus, dass die BürgerInnen ihre Rechte gegenüber der Staatsmacht selbst durchsetzen können.

---

5 Ob und inwieweit dieser Liberalismus tatsächlich auf Furcht gründet, so Hess (2016), oder eher ein Liberalismus der Rechte ist, mag an dieser Stelle dahingestellt bleiben, ist doch die Unterscheidung zwischen diesen beiden Liberalismen in der dafür erforderlichen Eindeutigkeit so gar nicht möglich. Ich danke Hannes Bajohr für den Hinweis auf diesen Punkt. Nicht zuletzt bedarf ja auch ein Liberalismus der Furcht einer Verbürgung von Rechten, auch wenn diese ihren Grund nicht in einer vorpolitischen Berechtigung haben, wie dies gemäß der Analyse von Shklar (2017) ein Liberalismus der Rechte vorsieht.
6 Shklar warnt, man dürfe den Blick nicht bloß auf jene „zwanghaften Ideologien" richten, „die sich allein auf den Begriff des Totalitarismus kaprizieren; er ist eine Abkürzung für lediglich die extremste Form institutionalisierter Gewalt und scheint fast nahezulegen, dass alles, dessen Zerstörungskraft weniger radikal ist, uns gar nicht zu beschäftigen braucht" (Shklar 2013: 41).
7 Allerdings kann auch Shklar eine Neigung zur Hoffnung nicht gänzlich abgesprochen werden (vgl. Forrester 2011).

## 3 Gefährliche Menschen und die Verführung der Macht

Dieses Modell ist in vielen Schriften der politischen Philosophie entwickelt worden, ausgehend von der Überwindung des hobbesschen Leviathans, der immerhin das Grauen der religiösen Bürgerkriege beenden sollte, und dessen Staat zwar bereits rechtsstaatliche Züge trägt (Campagna 1998), der Menschen aber doch primär als Objekte staatlicher Gewalt zum Ziel ihrer wechselseitigen Befriedung konzipiert. Die Ratio: Menschen müssen im Zaum gehalten werden, denn Menschen sind gefährlich. Autoren wie Locke, Montesquieu oder Kant sind hinsichtlich der menschlichen Natur kaum weniger pessimistisch. Allerdings meinen sie, dass ein starker Staat hobbesschen Gepräges jene Gefahren, die Menschen füreinander darstellen, noch potenziert. Die Furcht voreinander wird flankiert von der Furcht vor dem übermächtigen Staat und seinen Machthabern, die aufgrund ihrer Machtfülle noch gefährlicher sind als die gewöhnlichen Rechtsunterworfenen.

Locke etwa meinte sarkastisch, einen Herrscher mit absoluter Macht auszustatten hieße, dass die Menschen zwar versuchten, sich vor den Untaten von Iltissen und Füchsen zu schützen, „but are content, nay think it Safety, to be devoured by *Lions*" (Locke 1988: § 93, 328). Genau an diese Formulierung knüpft Shklar an, wenn sie festhält, „dass den Regierungen dieser Welt, mit ihrer überwältigenden Macht zu töten, zu verstümmeln, zu indoktrinieren und Krieg zu führen, nicht bedingungslos zu trauen ist (‚Löwen') und dass jedes Vertrauen in ihre Agenten tiefes Misstrauen voraussetzt" (Shklar 2013: 46–47). Mit dieser paradoxen Formulierung bringt Shklar zum Ausdruck, dass die staatliche Regierung, der an sich nicht getraut werden kann, durch das Machtmissbrauch in Grenzen haltende System der Gewaltenteilung und der *checks and balances* dann doch vertrauenswürdig zu werden vermag.

All das klingt vertraut, und während durchaus Debatten über Feinheiten der Institutionalisierung solcher Ordnungen geführt werden, konvergieren die meisten liberalen, aber auch republikanischen Theorien in wesentlichen Grundzügen, nicht zuletzt in den grundlegenden Prinzipien. Daneben gab und gibt es seit jeher kritische Interventionen, die den real existierenden Liberalismus ebenso wie die ihn begleitenden Theorien von Grund auf infrage stellen. Einer der Paten einer solch fundamentalen Kritik ist Carl Schmitt, bekannt als herausragender Verfassungsjurist, als scharfer Kritiker der Weimarer Republik und ab Mitte der 1930er

Jahre als „Kronjurist"[8] des Nationalsozialismus. Schmitts polemisch zugespitzte Zeitdiagnosen und Analysen politischer Konstellationen werden vielfach als geradezu notwendiges Korrektiv für einen Liberalismus gesehen, der sich typischerweise den Abgründen des sozialen Lebens und den tiefgreifenden Konflikten unter den Menschen nicht angemessen zu widmen vermöge (vgl. Mouffe 1999: 2). Dieser Vorwurf scheint Shklar gerade nicht zu treffen. Aber auch ein so bescheidener, selbstkritischer Liberalismus wie der ihre muss der Kritik von Schmitt standhalten, ihr etwas entgegenhalten können.

In der Folge sollen nun der Reihe nach einige Motive des schmittschen Denkens von einer, wie Bajohr dies formuliert, „negativen Anthropologie" (Bajohr 2013: 138) her mit den Positionen von Shklar verglichen werden. Im Zentrum steht die Frage, welche Schlüsse mehr Sinn ergeben – ob also aus einer negativen Anthropologie im Sinne einer „argumentativen Pfadabhängigkeit"[9] eher eine liberale Staatskonzeption folgt oder eine reaktionär-totalitäre. Gewählt wird der unmittelbare Vergleich an verschiedenen Punkten, um so die Abzweigungen, welche Shklar und Schmitt nehmen, jeweils miteinander zu kontrastieren.

## 4 Grundeinheiten des politischen Lebens

An einer zentralen Stelle ihres Liberalismus der Furcht nimmt Shklar eine ganz elementare Setzung vor: Dessen Grundeinheiten sind „die Schwachen und die Mächtigen" (Shklar 2013: 41). Dabei grenzt sie sich, ohne ihn zu nennen, genau hier von Carl Schmitt ab, wenn sie unter anderem die Unterscheidung von „Freund und Feind" dezidiert verwirft. Auch die Unterscheidung zwischen Schwachen und Mächtigen hat, wie der Liberalismus der Furcht selbst, eine deskriptive und eine normative Dimension: Deskriptiv stellt Shklar – aufgrund reichhaltiger Erfahrung – fest, dass staatliche Macht dazu verführt, ausgenützt zu werden: in Form von „Machtmissbrauch und der Einschüchterung Wehrloser" (Shklar 2013: 41). Und normativ lädt schon die Begriffswahl dazu ein, hier eine Wertung zu treffen, indem wir mit den Schwachen sympathisieren und es uns zur politischen Aufgabe machen, die Verhältnisse so einzurichten, dass die Wahrscheinlichkeit, zum Opfer staatlicher Gewalt zu werden, geringer wird.

Dabei geht es Shklar nicht nur um die selbstbezogene Furcht davor, selbst zum Opfer zu werden, sondern wir fürchten, wie sie meint, auch die Furcht der anderen: „Wir fürchten eine Gesellschaft furchtsamer Menschen." (Shklar 2013: 45) Damit

---

[8] Siehe die zahlreichen Nachweise für diese Titulierung bei Van Laak (1993: 29).
[9] Ich danke Rieke Trimçev für diese Formulierung.

kann zweierlei gemeint sein: Ganz allgemein fürchten wir einerseits eine Gesellschaft, in der Menschen einen Grund haben, sich zu fürchten, weil sie vom Staat institutionalisierte Grausamkeit zu erwarten haben. Und andererseits hat Shklar mit dieser Beobachtung auch die TäterInnen im Visier, wenn sie unter Bezugnahme auf Ausführungen von Montaigne meint, die Furcht würde die TäterInnen grausam machen und das Leiden der Opfer dadurch vergrößern (Shklar 2014: 33).

Schmitt ist bei seiner Unterscheidung zwischen Freund und Feind rein von der Qualität der Kriterien her agnostisch. Wenn er das Politische als jenes Feld fasst, in dem sich alle Handlungen und Motive auf die Unterscheidung zwischen Freund und Feind zurückführen lassen (Schmitt 1963: 26), dann geht es ihm schlicht darum, „den äußersten Intensitätsgrad einer Verbindung oder Trennung, einer Assoziation oder Dissoziation zu bezeichnen" (Schmitt 1963: 27). Politische Feindschaft hat nichts mit Moral zu tun. Vielmehr geht es Schmitt um ein existenzielles Anderssein, eine Art von Fremdheit, die im Extremfall zu Konflikten führt, „die weder durch eine im voraus getroffene generelle Normierung, noch durch den Spruch eines ‚unbeteiligten' und daher ‚unparteiischen' Dritten entschieden werden können" (Schmitt 1963: 27). Die Bestimmung als „Feind" stellt also eine Setzung jener dar, die als Freunde zusammenstehen respektive jener, die innerhalb des Freundeskreises zu solchen Entscheidungen berufen sind, und sie entzieht sich jeglichem Urteil von außen.

Und während Shklars Begriffswahl bereits die Empathie der Autorin mit den Leiden der Schwachen andeutet, werden die Feinde von Schmitt schlicht zu einem Problem erklärt, das aus der Welt zu schaffen ist: Wenn „das Anderssein des Fremden im konkret vorliegenden Konfliktsfalle die Negation der eigenen Art Existenz bedeutet", dann ergibt sich daraus als logische Konsequenz, dass es „abgewehrt oder bekämpft wird, um die eigene seinsmäßige Art von Leben zu bewahren" (Schmitt 1963: 27). Der Fremde, der Feind, ist kein „Mitmensch", den es zu achten gilt, sondern eine Störung, die aus dem Weg zu räumen ist. Voraussetzung dafür, dass dies reibungslos abläuft, ist jedenfalls, dass die Wahrnehmung der anderen Person als Mensch durch die Qualifikation als Feind überspielt wird. Wer vernichten will, muss unempfindlich sein für den Schmerz und das Leiden der anderen Person und darf, wie Meister hinzufügt, auch selbst im Kampf gegen den Feind nicht empfindlich sein (Meister 2002: 121). Schmitt stellt seine Theorie des Weiteren so auf, dass diejenigen, die als Freunde gegen den Feind stehen, auch die entsprechende Macht haben, um als Aggressoren erfolgreich zu sein. Wer sich nicht entsprechend durchsetzen kann, verdient keinen Respekt. Wer die Macht hat, sich des Feindes zu entledigen, hat nachgerade die Verpflichtung, das zu tun. Damit ist freilich auch Schmitts Feindbegriff normativ aufgeladen, denn er fordert – unabhängig von den Gründen, die für die Feindschaft existieren –, den Feind unschädlich zu machen, sei es durch Vertreibung oder durch Vernichtung.

## 5 Grausamkeit, Furcht und die Abkehr von der Religion

Die Grundunterscheidung zwischen Schwachen und Mächtigen findet Eingang in Shklars Definitionen der Grausamkeit. In *Ganz normale Laster* fasst sie Grausamkeit als Verhalten, durch das „einem schwächeren Wesen willentlich körperliche[r] Schmerz" zugefügt wird, „um Furcht und Leid zu erzeugen" (Shklar 2014: 15). Bemerkenswert an dieser Definition ist der Fokus auf den körperlichen Schmerz, und darauf will sie an dieser Stelle auch tatsächlich ausschließlich abstellen.[10] Als eindrucksvolle Illustration dient Shklar Giottos Darstellung des Jüngsten Gerichts, in der „jedes nur vorstellbare Folterinstrument an den Verdammten zum Einsatz kommt" (Shklar 2014: 15). Ausführlicher und umfassender ist die Definition, die sie in *Der Liberalismus der Furcht* formuliert: „Grausamkeit bedeutet, dass einer schwächeren Person oder Gruppe durch eine stärkere absichtlich physischer und, in zweiter Linie, emotionaler Schmerz zugefügt wird, um ein materielles oder immaterielles Ziel zu erreichen." (Shklar 2013: 44) Shklar ergänzt diese Definition dann noch mit Ausführungen zur „öffentliche[n] Grausamkeit", die vom staatlichen Zwangsapparat ausgeht und „durch willkürliche, unerwartete, unnötige und unerlaubte Zwangsanwendung […], durch regelmäßige und weitverbreitete Grausamkeit und Folter" (Shklar 2013: 44) von Seiten des Militärs, paramilitärischer Einheiten und auch der Polizei ausgeübt wird und dadurch illegitime Furcht hervorruft.

Die Feinheiten dieser Definitionen – und die daran gegebenenfalls zu übende Kritik[11] – sind an dieser Stelle nicht der Punkt. Als zentral ist vielmehr herauszustreichen, dass Grausamkeit in ganz grundlegender Weise „ein Vergehen gegen ein anderes Wesen" darstellt (Shklar 2014: 17). Das hat für Shklar eine eigene Pointe, bedeutet es doch, dass es sich um eine ganz und gar innerweltliche Ver-

---

10 Erst spät im einschlägigen Kapitel thematisiert Shklar auch „moralische Grausamkeit", „eine willentliche und anhaltende Demütigung, an deren Ende die Unfähigkeit des Opfers steht, weder sich noch anderen zu vertrauen" (Shklar 2014: 48). Im weiteren Verlauf der Argumentation entkoppelt sie körperliche und moralische Grausamkeit, subsumiert unter letzterer „Ungerechtigkeit" respektive „Selbstzerfleischung und Heuchelei" und gelangt nach einigen argumentativen Volten sogar zur Behauptung, moralische Grausamkeit an erste Stelle zu setzen, wäre mit der Übernahme von „Machiavellis grausamste[n] Maximen" problemlos vereinbar (Shklar 2014: 53).
11 Siehe dazu im Detail und in etwas ungehaltenem Ton Kekes (1996: 836–838).

werflichkeit handelt, eine, die keinen Bezug zum Transzendenten, insbesondere zum Religiösen braucht. Ja, wer wie sie in Anlehnung an Montaigne und Montesquieu vorschlägt, „Grausamkeit an erste Stelle" (Shklar 2013: 45; Shklar 2014: 261) der zu verhindernden Laster zu setzen, würde sich in fundamentaler Weise von der (christlichen) Religion abwenden, indem die „Idee der Sünde" (Shklar 2014: 44) verworfen wird. Denn die Verwerflichkeit der Grausamkeit stehe „an und für sich" und dieses Urteil, diese grundlegende „moralische Intuition" (Shklar 2013: 45), auf welche Shklar den Liberalismus baut, könne nicht „mit Verweis auf etwas Höheres" (Shklar 2014: 17) überspielt werden. In Anspielung auf Franklin D. Roosevelts berühmte Formulierung[12] sieht Shklar im Priorisieren der Grausamkeit als übelstem aller Laster „das Eingeständnis, sich vor nichts mehr zu fürchten als vor der Furcht selbst. Die Furcht vor der Furcht verlangt keine weitere Rechtfertigung, weil sie sich auf nichts Weiteres zurückführen lässt"[13] (Shklar 2014: 261).

Genau diese Verankerung des zentralen Bezugspunkts von Recht und Staat im Irdischen ist einer der wesentlichen Kritikpunkte von Carl Schmitt gegen die politische Philosophie der Moderne. Er formuliert sie gegen Thomas Hobbes: „Friede und Sicherheit" seien die *raison d'être* von dessen Leviathan. Für Schmitt ist es ein Skandalon, dass der Souverän nicht als *defensor pacis* eines auf Gott zurückgehenden Friedens angesehen werden soll, dass er vielmehr allein als Schöpfer „eines nichts als irdischen Friedens, Creator Pacis" (Schmitt 2003: 51) gilt, der durch den Gesellschaftsvertrag begründet wird. Dazu verwirft Schmitt auch noch jene, bei Hobbes ohnehin nur im Kern vorhandene zentrale liberale Errungenschaft, die ein Zusammenleben in einem Europa der Konfessionen überhaupt erst möglich gemacht hat: die Gewissensfreiheit. Hobbes, so Schmitt, habe mit Blick auf den Glauben an Wunder und Mysterien einen „unausrottbaren individualistischen Vorbehalt" (Schmitt 2003: 84) postuliert. Im Einziehen einer Differenzierung zwischen öffentlichem Bekenntnis und privatem Glauben sieht Schmitt die zentrale „Bruchstelle in der sonst so geschlossenen, unwiderstehlichen Einheit" (Schmitt 2003: 84) des Leviathans. Hier öffnet sich die Eintrittspforte für jene Freiheitsrechte, die den liberalen Staat kennzeichnen (Schmitt 2003: 86–87).

Selbstverständlich trifft Schmitt mit dieser Kritik auch Shklar, die durchgängig auf der Zentralität der Differenzierung zwischen Öffentlichkeit und Privatheit und dem dadurch ermöglichten Pluralismus „philosophischer und religiöser Überzeugungen" (Shklar 2013: 34) besteht. Anders wäre ein Liberalismus

---

12 In seiner Rede zur ersten Inauguration betonte Roosevelt: „[...] the only thing we have to fear is fear itself – nameless, unreasoning, unjustified terror which paralyzes needed efforts to convert retreat into advance." https://avalon.law.yale.edu/20th_century/froos1.asp, Zugriff 7. Juli 2020.
13 Bajohr (2019: 91) versteht dies als „formales Argument".

auch gar nicht möglich. Im Kampf dagegen ist für Schmitt selbst jener schmale Raum, den er bei Hobbes durch die Freiheit des Denkens eröffnet sieht, schon zu viel des Zugeständnisses. Schmitt will noch diesen mageren „Gewissensvorbehalt des Einzelnen" durch Techniken der Indoktrinierung „ideologisch überspielt" (Mehring 2001: 79) wissen – oder die Homogenität dadurch herstellen, dass unpassende Elemente „beseitig[t]" werden (Schmitt 1926: 14). Das ist, um es im Geiste von Shklar zu sagen, eine Einladung zur Grausamkeit.

## 6 Das Skandalon der Grausamkeit

Aber was genau ist das Skandalon der Grausamkeit und damit des Schmerzes, der einer schwächeren, einer wehrlosen Person zugefügt wird, in einem staatlichen System, welches dies nachgerade institutionalisiert oder in seinem Schatten in Kauf nimmt? Und was macht die Furcht davor so zentral? Zunächst lässt Shklar mit ihrer Position den empfindungsfähigen Körper zu ihrem Recht kommen: Der Leib und sein Leid zählen ebenso wie die Furcht, welche die Erfahrung von Leid infolge staatlich institutionalisierter oder gedeckter Grausamkeit auslöst. Das ist die ganz grundlegende normative Intuition, und doch reicht diese Shklar zufolge nicht als Begründung aus, droht doch das Verdikt eines „naturalistischen Fehlschluss[es]" (Shklar 2013: 45). Das Grausamkeitsverbot müsse daher „universalisiert und zur notwendigen Bedingung für die Würde von Personen" gemacht werden, um es als „Prinzip politischer Moral" auszeichnen zu können (Shklar 2013: 45–46). Shklar erörtert an dieser Stelle nicht weiter, wie das zu bewerkstelligen ist, sondern referiert in der Folge eine utilitaristische Begründung des Grausamkeitsverbots, um dann anzumerken, sowohl Kantianer als auch Utilitaristen könnten damit zufrieden sein. Bajohr spricht in diesem Zusammenhang treffend von einer „Rechtfertigungslücke, die zu überbrücken sie einer Vielzahl von Erklärungen zugesteht" (Bajohr 2019: 90) und meint in der Folge, sie vertrete eben „keinen Universalismus der Gründe, sondern einen *Universalismus der Zwecke*" (Bajohr 2019: 90).

Allerdings meine ich doch, dass dahinter ein Fundament sichtbar wird. Denn das Skandalon liegt ja in der durch „die Erwartung institutionalisierter Grausamkeit" ausgelösten „systematische[n] Furcht" und der Erkenntnis, dass dadurch „Freiheit unmöglich" gemacht wird (Shklar 2013: 45). An einer Stelle stellt sie sogar die (zu) weit gehende Behauptung auf, dass „Furcht uns auf den Stand lediglich reaktiver Empfindungswesen zurückwirft" (Shklar 2014: 11). Diese extreme Konsequenz hat wohl nur Folter und der dadurch ausgelöste körperliche und seelische Schmerz (Scarry 1985; Sussman 2005). Aber der Punkt, den Shklar hier macht, ist doch ganz deutlich: Am Grund der normativen Intuition liegt das

Prinzip der Freiheit, das Shklar ja auch ganz zu Beginn ins Zentrum von *Der Liberalismus der Furcht* stellt.

Es erübrigt sich fast darauf hinzuweisen, dass Carl Schmitt auch hier eine diametral entgegengesetzte Position vertritt, die aus den vorangegangenen Ausführungen bereits klar hervorgegangen ist. Er will die Freiheit der einzelnen Person im Keim erstickt sehen: Die Menschen sollen sich als Glieder in den Staatskörper einfügen, werden ausgerichtet auf die Ziele jenes Staates, dem sie eingegliedert werden – aber nur dann, wenn ihre Existenz dem entspricht, was staatlicherseits festgelegt ist. Und das bedeutet: Wenn der Staat es so verfügt, dann ist nicht einmal eine freiwillige oder unfreiwillige Unterwerfung unter seine Ziele hinreichend; wenn die Person existenziell nicht „passt", dann liegt es am Staatswesen, sie „zu beseitigen oder fernzuhalten", weil ihm „die Ausscheidung oder Vernichtung des Heterogenen" obliegt (Schmitt 1926: 14). Dass es dabei auch grausam zugehen kann und darf, liegt auf der Hand.

# 7 Grausamkeit und Empathie: Elemente von Shklars Menschenbild

Was kann Shklars Ausführungen über Grausamkeit und Furcht über ihre Vorstellung vom „Wesen" von Menschen entnommen werden? Zunächst ein Caveat: Shklar hat gerade keine Anthropologie im engeren Sinn elaboriert. Ihr Liberalismus beruht auf keinem „umfassenderen Verständnis menschlicher Natur, Geschichte und Gesellschaft" (Benhabib 2013: 69). Und statt einem geschlossenen System aufeinander aufbauender Prämissen und Schlussfolgerungen findet sich in ihren vielfältigen, bisweilen etwas assoziativen Wahrnehmungen historischer und zeitgenössischer politischer Verwerfungen ein prononciert pessimistisches Weltbild, gleichsam als Leitmotiv ihrer politisch-philosophischen Überlegungen. Dieses Denken des Politischen von den Abgründen, von den „dunklen und oft unzugänglichen Seiten" (Hirsch 2014: 671) her ist ganz zentral Shklars Fokus auf die Perspektive der Opfer zu verdanken. Aber worauf gründet die ganz emphatische Parteinahme für die Schwachen? Und wie will sie davon überzeugen?

An manchen Stellen scheint es so, als würde Shklar erwarten, dass ihre LeserInnen ihr bei dieser Positionierung einfach folgen. In dem häufig gebrauchten „wir" steckt die Annahme, dass es eine sie inkludierende, idealerweise universelle Gemeinschaft von Menschen gibt, die sich in Opfer einzufühlen vermögen. Shklar identifiziert als einen der Impulse, die uns dazu treiben, das Mitleid; es umfasst alle, die leiden. Dazu kommt ein „Sinn für Ungerechtigkeit", von dem Shklar annimmt oder zumindest hofft, dass er unter Voraussetzung von

„einigermaßen günstigen demokratischen politischen Bedingungen" zusammen mit dem „Sinn für persönliche Würde gedeihen" (Shklar 1992: 149) wird. Ist er vorhanden, dann wird er offenbar gleichsam automatisch zum Schwingen gebracht, wenn Menschen der „Grausamkeit gegen einen Hilflosen" gewahr werden (Shklar 2014: 34). Wir kämen dann, in den Worten von Liebsch und Bajohr, „nicht umhin, als uns nicht indifferent zu diesen Phänomenen zu verhalten und sogar zu versprechen, ihnen Rechnung zu tragen" (Liebsch/Bajohr 2014: 656).

Freilich ist die Eingemeindung aller über das „wir" in diesem Satz „kaum mehr als ein Problemtitel" (Liebsch/Bajohr 2014: 656–657), angesichts all der historischen und zeitgenössischen Erfahrungen, die das Gegenteil bezeugen. Man denke nur an die nicht selten menschenverachtenden Reaktionen auf das Massensterben von Menschen, die über das Mittelmeer nach Europa flüchten. Wenn etwa, wie im September 2018 geschehen, ein Boot voller geflüchteter Menschen von der Marine eines nordafrikanischen Staates angeschossen und dabei eine Frau getötet wird, dann führt das vielfach zu nicht mehr als einem bestenfalls verquälten Achselzucken – mit Shklar könnte man dies als „habituelle Gleichgültigkeit" bezeichnen (Shklar 1992: 15) –, wenn es nicht gar zynische Zustimmung hervorruft.[14] Damit soll nicht gesagt sein, dass Menschen, die derartige Haltungen aufweisen und kommunizieren, komplett die Empathie oder der Sinn für Ungerechtigkeit abgehen würde – allerdings sind beide Kapazitäten in ganz spezifischer Weise verengt. Denn sie erstrecken sich nicht, wie Shklar sich dies wünschen würde, auf „alle" leidenden Wesen, sondern beziehen sich – schmittianisch zugespitzt – ausschließlich auf diejenigen, die etwa einem ethno-nationalistisch definierten „Wir" als zugehörig erachtet werden. Deutlicher als bei Shklar wird dies bei Richard Rorty. Er sieht in der Unterscheidung zwischen „Menschen wie wir" und den „Anderen" das größte Hindernis für Empathie (Rorty 1993: 113). Christine Unrau spricht in diesem Zusammenhang von „Empathieblockaden" (Unrau 2018: 250).

## 8 Auf der Jagd nach dem Einzelglück: Elemente von Schmitts politischer Anthropologie

Damit wären wir wieder bei Carl Schmitt und seiner Dichotomie von Freund und Feind als Grundunterscheidung des Politischen. Dahinter steht ein zutiefst von

---

[14] Für Beispiele siehe die Kommentarsektion unter https://www.derstandard.at/story/2000088087610/marokkanische-marine-schiesst-auf-auf-boot-mir-migranten-eine-tote, Zugriff 12. April 2021.

Misanthropie durchtränktes Bild vom Menschen. Das beginnt bereits in seiner Habilitationsschrift aus dem Jahr 1914, *Der Wert des Staates und die Bedeutung des Einzelnen*. Menschen sind für Schmitt hier „ein Meer zügellosen und bornierten Egoismus und rohester Instinkte"; „einzeln oder in ihrer Masse" würden sie bloß „trachten, ‚voll Hast ihr Einzelglück zu retten'" (Schmitt 1914: 84). Das Zitat ist aus Theodor Däublers expressionistischem Versepos *Das Nordlicht*. In *Der Begriff des Politischen* vertraut sich Schmitt der philosophischen Anthropologie von Helmuth Plessner (2003) an. Dabei ist Schmitts Anknüpfung eher punktuell, und er gebraucht Plessners Überlegungen im Wesentlichen dafür, um zu etablieren, dass Menschen von Grund auf „problematisch" sind. Denn der Mensch sei „ein primär Abstand nehmendes Wesen" und damit „offene Frage" (Schmitt 1963: 60). Sein „dynamisches ‚Offenbleiben' mit seiner wagnisbereiten Wirklichkeits- und Sachnähe" stehe in einer „positiven Beziehung zur Gefahr und zum Gefährlichen" und sei von daher, wenn man diese Begriffe überhaupt verwenden wolle, „dem ‚Bösen' näher [...] als dem Guten" (Schmitt 1963: 60). In einem nächsten Schritt verschiebt Schmitt die Frage, welches Menschenbild einer Theorie zugrunde liegt, aber ohnehin in den Bereich eines „anthropologischen Glaubensbekenntnisses" (Schmitt 1963: 58). Und gänzlich irrelevant scheint dieses dann zu werden, wenn Schmitt sein pessimistisches Menschenbild schlicht aus der Definition seines Zentralbegriffs des Politischen generiert, indem er apodiktisch formuliert:

> Weil die Sphäre des Politischen letzten Endes von der realen Möglichkeit eines Feindes bestimmt wird, können politische Vorstellungen und Gedankengänge nicht gut einen anthropologischen „Optimismus" zum Ausgangspunkt nehmen. (Schmitt 1963: 63–64)

Man könnte hier entgegnen, dass dem so ist, *wenn* die Sphäre des Politischen über die Dichotomie von Freund und Feind konstituiert wird, nicht weil das der Fall ist. Hier handelt es sich um eine definitorische Prämisse, die man für richtig halten kann – oder auch nicht. Gleiches gilt für eine weitere Grundlage von Schmitts Menschenbild, das sich in seine Verteidigung der religiösen Fundamente des Staates einfügt: nämlich das „theologische Grunddogma von der Sündhaftigkeit der Welt und des Menschen" (Schmitt 1963: 64).[15] Auch daran mag man glauben oder nicht. Schmitt glaubt daran, insistiert aber auf die den Glauben transzen-

---

15 An dieser Stelle konstatiert Schmitt jenen charakteristischen „methodische[n] Zusammenhang theologischer und politischer Denkvoraussetzungen" (er sei „klar"; Schmitt 1963: 64), der sein Werk auszeichnet, das so elusiv zwischen Jurisprudenz, politischer Philosophie und Theologie oszilliert.

dierende Bedeutung[16] des Dogmas: Dieses führe „zu einer ‚Abstandnahme'" und mache „den unterschiedslosen Optimismus eines durchgängigen Menschenbegriffes unmöglich" (Schmitt 1963: 64). Die Formulierung ist etwas eigentümlich, aber die Botschaft scheint klar zu sein: Die säkulare Idee menschlicher Freiheit gilt bloß als menschliche Vermessenheit, die den von Gott und Staat geforderten Gehorsam aufgibt und dadurch das soziale Gefüge radikal infrage stellt.

Die Sündhaftigkeit des Menschen ist für Schmitt auch kein Anlass, Liebe oder Barmherzigkeit ins Spiel zu bringen. Ebenso erlaubt er nicht, das Freund-Feind-Schema auf politischer Ebene mit Hinweis auf die Feindesliebe zu immunisieren – er verfrachtet deren Stellenwert vielmehr in den Bereich des Privaten und spricht ihr die öffentliche, die „politische" Relevanz ab (Schmitt 1963: 29–30). Barbara Nichtweiß formuliert hintersinnig, dass Schmitt das Gebot der Feindesliebe „damit als möglichen Störfaktor für seine Politik-Definition ausschaltete" (Nichtweiß 1994: 48). Wenn er das Private ohnehin als dem Politischen in totaler Weise verfügbar konzipiert und so die Trennung zwischen Öffentlichkeit und Privatheit zur Gänze ausschaltet, ist sein System geschlossen und der Weg für den totalen Staat geebnet; der Ordnung des Staates ist der Stachel der Freiheit gezogen.

## 9 Zur Plausibilität der vertretenen Denkwege

Die vorangegangenen Ausführungen zeigen, dass Schmitt und Shklar, ausgehend von der Diagnose der Gefährlichkeit von Menschen, praktisch an jedem Punkt Abzweigungen in diametral verschiedene Richtungen nehmen. Damit erweist sich ganz plastisch die „normative Kontingenz" (Bajohr 2013: 146) jeglicher politischen Anthropologie. Sie gibt keine eindeutigen Richtungen vor; sie liefert nicht einfach unproblematische, universelle Normen und Prinzipien auf einem, wie Müller dies mit Blick auf Shklar etwas spitz ausdrückt, „sentimentalen Silbertablett" (Müller 2015: 41). Die so unterschiedlichen Denkwege von Shklar und Schmitt könnten damit zusammenhängen, dass Schmitt mehr auf die Schlechtigkeit der Menschen ganz generell fokussiert, während Shklar deren Problematik primär als Ergebnis der Verführung durch die Innehabung von Macht ansieht. Die Anforderungen von Schmitt und Shklar an die Legitimität staatlicher Macht und ihre Überlegungen zu deren Grenzen – bei Schmitt: Grenzenlosigkeit – könnten dann jeweils unterschiedlicher nicht sein.

---

[16] Mit Ironie formuliert Meier (2004: 29): „Wie immer es mit der Ordnung stehen mag, für die der Glaube an die Erbsünde unabdingbar sein soll, sicher ist er es für Schmitts Politische Theologie."

Jedenfalls vertritt Shklar im Einklang mit der liberalen Tradition mitnichten einen „unterschiedslosen Optimismus" mit Blick auf die Menschen, wie Schmitt so despektierlich formuliert. Ganz im Gegenteil ist sie eben zutiefst pessimistisch – man könnte auch sagen: realistisch (vgl. Stullerova 2014: 10) – insbesondere mit Blick auf die korrumpierenden Wirkungen, die von der Innehabung staatlicher Macht ausgehen. Nicht zuletzt war es ja von Anfang an gerade der Witz der Gewaltenteilung, der *checks and balances*, gewesen, menschliches Machtstreben zu bändigen – eine Methode, für die Schmitt im Übrigen nur Spott übrighatte, wenn er sie als „ein System von Hemmungen und Kontrollen des Staates" charakterisierte, „das man nicht als Staatstheorie oder als politisches Konstruktionsprinzip bezeichnen kann" (Schmitt 1963: 61). Die Liberalen aber bestanden und bestehen genau darauf, weil sie aus Erfahrung wissen, dass einsamen Herrschern nicht über den Weg zu trauen ist, und den VolksvertreterInnen wie den Angehörigen der anderen Gewalten in ihrer Vielzahl nur dann, wenn sie einander wachsam im Auge behalten.

Selbstverständlich wird den Menschen im Zuge dessen auch ein gewisses Potenzial zugeschrieben, in liberalen Staaten in ihrem Freiheitshandeln im Rahmen normativer Vorgaben bleiben zu können. Diese Vorstellung verdankt sich aber keinem naiven Bild vom grundguten Menschen, sondern der Idee, dass – legitim ausgeübte – staatliche Macht jenes notwendige „Minimum an Furcht" (Shklar 2013: 44) erzeugt, das Menschen zu legalem Verhalten motiviert. Die darin aufgehobene instrumentelle Vernunft, welche es den „Teufeln" (Kant 1977b: 224) ermöglicht, einen Staat zu bilden, der einen Rahmen für menschliches Freiheitshandeln schafft, muss auch Schmitt voraussetzen, um den „rebellischen Individualismus" (Schmitt 2003: 58) von Menschen im Zaum zu halten. Dazu dient der „Intellekt" (Schmitt 2003: 58). Sobald dieser aber eingeführt ist, muss es Schmitt gehen wie dem Zauberlehrling – der Intellekt ist ein Geist, den er nicht loswird. Hobbes wusste, dass der Staat so total nicht sein kann, dass tatsächlich „keinerlei staatsfeindliche, staatshemmende oder staatszerspaltende Kräfte aufkommen" (Schmitt 1988b: 186) können. Mit dem Verweis auf den Intellekt begibt sich auch Schmitt unausweichlich in die Gasse menschlicher Freiheit, deren Weg er gleichzeitig derart vehement zu verstellen versucht.

Einen muss Schmitt aber ohnehin von der totalen Verfügung durch den Staat ausnehmen, und das ist logischerweise der Führer selbst. Einer muss ja die Richtung vorgeben und entscheiden, was Freund und Feind ausmacht und welche Mittel eingesetzt werden, um des Feindes Herr zu werden. In Hitler glaubt Schmitt, den glanzvollen Führer gefunden zu haben, und er setzt ihm in einer gespenstischen Schrift aus dem Jahr 1934, „Der Führer schützt das Recht", ein Denkmal. Schmitt muss darauf vertrauen, dass jener Führer das Volk stark macht, dass er es nicht in den Abgrund führt. Er hätte besser Anleihen bei Locke genommen. Locke wusste, dass absolute Macht absolut verdirbt, dass absolute Herrscher, umgeben von Günstlingen und SchmeichlerInnen, bald jedes Maß verlieren und ihr Wirken zum Zerstörungswerk wird.

Es sind diese Phasen der Geschichte, auf deren Überwindung der Liberalismus der Furcht ausgerichtet ist. Und so sind angesichts der vielen Hürden, die Liberale für das verderbliche Wirken von Macht aufstellen, nicht sie die Naiven, die Optimistischen, sondern vielmehr Schmitt selbst. Mit Holmes könnte man sagen, dass die Liberalen den Pessimismus geradezu universalisiert haben, während Schmitt mit seinem Führerprinzip einem ganz naiven Optimismus aufgesessen ist (Holmes 1993: 59). Die entsetzlichen Folgen des entfesselten deutschen Führerstaates sind wesentlicher Teil jener (gegenwärtigen) Erinnerung, welche die Grundlage für Shklars Liberalismus der Furcht abgibt. In diesem „Wogegen" eines *„summum malum"* staatlich institutionalisierter Grausamkeit lässt sich in gewissem Sinn der Feind Nummer eins von Shklars Liberalismus erblicken.

Damit erschöpft sich aber auch schon die Parallele in der Denkbewegung zwischen Schmitt und Shklar (Meister 2002: 120). Und wohin im Einzelnen die Wege der Furcht im Bereich des Politischen führen, ist noch einmal eine ganz andere Frage, nicht zuletzt dann, wenn äußere und innere Feinde beschworen werden, um Furcht hervorzurufen: So lautet die Antwort auf Bedrohungen durch Terrorismus kaum „mehr Freiheit", sondern sie wird vielmehr in der sukzessiven Einschränkung von Freiheitsrechten gesucht (vgl. Holzleithner 2017). Fleiner und Schaal fragen daher wohl nicht zu Unrecht, wie „tragfähig" die Furcht als negative Emotion für eine Theorie von Staat und Politik tatsächlich sein kann (Fleiner/Schaal 2012: 189). Dies zumal dann, wenn die Ebene des Legitimatorischen verlassen und die Politik der Furcht im Feld staatlicher Machtausübung und von Seiten rechtspopulistischer Bewegungen in den Fokus genommen wird. Hier werden Ressentiments emotional wirkmächtig gebündelt, und die derart erzeugte Furcht ist mit Lust besetzt, die durch repressive Politik Befriedigung zu erfahren vermag. Shklar spricht hier treffend von „politischen Scharlatane[n], die die Nöte anderer in ihren Vorteil ummünzen" und bezeichnet sie als „gelinde gesagt, schlechte Bürger" (Shklar 1992: 69). Sie wirken mit an der Erzeugung jener „furchtsame[n] Menschen", deren Gesellschaft wir guten Grund haben zu fürchten (Shklar 2013: 45).

## 10 Fazit: Die Politik der „schlechten Charaktere" als Herausforderung für liberale Demokratien

Damit gelangen wir abschließend nochmals zu jenen Herausforderungen, vor denen liberale Demokratien derzeit allen Ortens stehen. Rechtspopulistische Bewegungen und Parteien bekämpfen das Liberale an der Demokratie unter Beschwörung von äußeren und inneren Feinden, die das ethno-nationalistisch konstruierte Volk bedrohen. Es handelt sich hier um eine „Politik der schlechten Charaktere", die antreten, die liberale Demokratie mit ihren eigenen Mitteln zu untergraben. Sie arbeiten mit Lügen und Verschwörungstheorien, bekämpfen die kritische Presse als „Fake News", und wenn sie an der Macht sind, versuchen sie die Institutionen derart in Beschlag zu nehmen, dass ein demokratischer Wechsel schwierig, ja fast unmöglich wird – dafür sorgt dann ein entsprechendes Wahlrecht. So wurde etwa in Ungarn im Jahr 2011 ein neues Wahlgesetz erlassen, das die relativ stärkste Partei massiv begünstigt. Derart konnte die Fidesz-Partei von Ministerpräsident Viktor Orbán mit einer Anzahl von nicht einmal 45 % der Stimmen erneut eine Mehrheit von zwei Dritteln der Parlamentssitze erlangen – und damit auch die Macht zur Verfassungsänderung absichern.[17]

(Wie) Kann die liberale Demokratie dem standhalten? Es kommt darauf an: nicht zuletzt auf die Robustheit jener Institutionen, welche die Liberalität der Demokratie gegen ihre populistischen VerächterInnen aufrechterhalten sollen: Gewaltenteilung, *checks and balances*, Rechtsstaatlichkeit, die Unabhängigkeit der Gerichte, kritische Medien, überhaupt eine vielfältige, wachsame Öffentlichkeit, die, geschützt durch grundrechtliche Verbürgungen, ihr Wächteramt ausüben soll. Ganz zentral ist ein Wahlrecht, das regelmäßigen demokratischen Wechsel ermöglicht. Für diese Mittel der liberalen Demokratie gilt es heute, vielleicht mehr als je zuvor, mit Verve einzutreten.

Es gibt gravierende Anzeichen dafür, dass wir uns an der Schwelle eines neuen autoritären Zeitalters befinden. Jene, die daran mitwirken und die sich für die ProfiteureInnen der herbeigesehnten autoritären Ordnung halten, die TäterInnen, die „schlechten Bürger", auch die „politischen Scharlatane", scheinen blind für die Gefahren, die von solchen Ordnungen ausgehen. Sie sehen sich selbst nicht in der Position der Opfer, dabei lehrt die Geschichte ganz überdeutlich, dass die TäterInnen und passiven BeobachterInnen von heute ganz schnell

---

17 Zur politischen Lage in Ungarn siehe https://www.bpb.de/politik/hintergrund-aktuell/ 308619/demokratie-in-ungarn, Zugriff 9. Juli 2020. Zum Wahlrecht in Ungarn siehe Szigetvári/ Tordai/Vető (2011).

in Ungnade fallen und selbst zum Opfer werden können – und sei es zum Opfer jener Politik von Freund und Feind, die so oft in den Krieg führt. Und so endet der Text, wie er begonnen hat: mit der Beobachtung, dass es die Tugend – ein für das Leid und die Furcht der Opfer waches Mitgefühl und einen universalisierenden Sinn für Ungerechtigkeit – nicht unbedingt braucht. Es würde schon reichen, wenn die „Teufel" ihren Verstand einsetzen, wenn sie Einsicht darin hätten, dass auch sie Grund haben, sich zu fürchten.

In ihrem furchterregenden Werk *How Democracies Die* schreiben Levitsky und Ziblatt, ganz im Geist von Judith N. Shklar: „History doesn't repeat itself. But it rhymes. The promise of history [...] is that we can find the rhymes before it is too late." (Levitsky/Ziblatt 2018: 10) Es gilt, diese „rhymes" auszumachen, die Stimmen der historischen und gegenwärtigen Opfer von Grausamkeit und Gewalt in der politischen Öffentlichkeit deutlich hörbar zu machen und sich energisch für die Aufrechterhaltung jener Institutionen zu engagieren, die eine vitale liberale Demokratie ausmachen. Nur sie ist imstande, die „schlechten Charaktere" zu bändigen – und sei es, indem sie, wie Donald Trump, aus ihren Ämtern gewählt werden. In ihrer Abwehr von Trumps Versuchen, die Wahl für illegitim hinzustellen und seine Abwahl über diverse illegitime Wege zu unterlaufen, erweist sich die Solidität der rechtsstaatlichen Institutionen in den Vereinigten Staaten. Sie mit neuem Leben zu erfüllen, wird Aufgabe der nächsten Administration sein – ebenso wie eine Abkehr von einer Politik der Furcht und des Ressentiments, die in Schmittscher Manier bloß Freund und Feind kennt. Diese Dichotomie ist eine Falle, und liberale Demokratien sind genau darauf ausgerichtet, sie zu überwinden. Letztlich haben alle in Demokratien Lebende Anteil daran, ob dieses Unterfangen scheitert oder gelingt.

## Literatur

Bajohr, Hannes (2013): „‚Am Leben zu sein heißt Furcht zu haben.' Judith Shklars negative Anthropologie des Liberalismus". In: Shklar, Judith N.: *Der Liberalismus der Furcht*. Mit einem Vorwort von Axel Honneth und Essays von Michael Walzer, Seyla Benhabib und Bernard Williams. Hg., aus dem Amerikanischen übers. und mit einem Nachwort versehen von Hannes Bajohr. Berlin: Matthes & Seitz, S. 131–167.

Bajohr, Hannes (2017): „Judith Shklars Liberalismen". In: Shklar, Judith N.: *Der Liberalismus der Rechte*. Hg. und mit einem Vorwort versehen von Hannes Bajohr. Aus dem Amerikanischen und Französischen übers. von Hannes Bajohr und Dirk Höfer. Berlin: Matthes & Seitz, S. 7–19.

Bajohr, Hannes (2019): „Judith N. Shklar über die Quellen liberaler Normativität". In: Fischer, Karsten/Huhnholz, Sebastian (Hg.): *Liberalismus: Traditionsbestände und Gegenwartskontroversen*. Baden-Baden: Nomos, S. 71–97.

Benhabib, Seyla (2013): „Judith Shklars dystopischer Liberalismus". In: Shklar, Judith N.: *Der Liberalismus der Furcht*. Mit einem Vorwort von Axel Honneth und Essays von Michael Walzer, Seyla Benhabib und Bernard Williams. Hg., aus dem Amerikanischen übers. und mit einem Nachwort versehen von Hannes Bajohr. Berlin: Matthes & Seitz, S. 67–86.

Campagna, Norbert (1998): „Leviathan und der Rechtsstaat". In: *Archiv für Rechts- und Sozialphilosophie* 84(3), S. 340–353.

Fleiner, Rebekka/Schaal, Gary S. (2012): „Gegründet auf Furcht und Angst: Demokratietheoretische Überlegungen zur Angstpolitik der Gegenwart". In: Heidenreich, Felix/Schaal, Gary S. (Hg.): *Politische Theorie und Emotionen*. Baden-Baden: Nomos, S. 177–198.

Forrester, Katrina (2011): „Hope and Memory in the Thought of Judith Shklar". In: *Modern Intellectual History* 8(3), S. 591–620.

Hess, Andreas (2016): *The Political Theory of Judith N. Shklar: Exile from Exile*. New York, NY: Palgrave Macmillan.

Hirsch, Alfred (2014): „Furcht vor Verletzungen: Anmerkungen zu Judith Shklars ‚Liberalismus der Furcht'". In: *Deutsche Zeitschrift für Philosophie* 62(4), S. 660–682.

Holmes, Stephen (1993): *The Anatomy of Antiliberalism*. Cambridge, MA: Harvard University Press.

Holzleithner, Elisabeth (2017): „Freiheit und Sicherheit – Konkurrenz oder Synergie?". In: *Zeitschrift für Menschenrechte* 11(2), S. 7–29.

Kant, Immanuel (1977a): „Idee zu einer allgemeinen Geschichte in weltbürgerlicher Absicht". [1784]. In: *Schriften zur Anthropologie, Geschichtsphilosophie, Politik und Pädagogik: Band 1*. Werkausgabe Band 11. Hg. von Wilhelm Weischedel. Frankfurt a. M.: Suhrkamp, S. 31–61.

Kant, Immanuel (1977b): „Zum ewigen Frieden: Ein philosophischer Entwurf". [1795/1796]. In: *Schriften zur Anthropologie, Geschichtsphilosophie, Politik und Pädagogik: Band 1*. Werkausgabe Band 11. Hg. von Wilhelm Weischedel. Frankfurt a. M.: Suhrkamp, S. 193–251.

Kekes, John (1996): „Cruelty and Liberalism". In: *Ethics* 106(4), S. 834–844.

Levitsky, Steven/Ziblatt, Daniel (2018): *How Democracies Die*. New York, NY: Crown.

Liebsch, Burkhard/Bajohr, Hannes (2014): „Geschichte, Negativismus und Skepsis als Herausforderungen politischer Theorie: Judith N. Shklar". In: *Deutsche Zeitschrift für Philosophie* 62(4), S. 633–659.

Locke, John (1988): *Two Treatises of Government*. [1689]. Hg. von Peter Laslett. Cambridge: Cambridge University Press.

Mehring, Reinhard (2001): *Carl Schmitt zur Einführung*. Hamburg: Junius.

Meier, Heinrich (2004): *Die Lehre Carl Schmitts: Vier Kapitel zur Unterscheidung politischer Theologie und Politischer Philosophie*. 2. Auflage. Stuttgart: Metzler.

Meister, Robert (2002): „The Liberalism of Fear and the Counterrevolutionary Project". In: *Ethics and International Affairs* 16(2), S. 118–123.

Mouffe, Chantal (1999): „Introduction: Schmitt's Challenge". In: Mouffe, Chantal (Hg.): *The Challenge of Carl Schmitt*. London/New York, NY: Verso, S. 1–6.

Müller, Jan-Werner (2015): „Fear, Favor, and Freedom: Judith Shklar's Liberalism of Fear Revisited". In: Uitz, Renáta (Hg.): *Freedom and Its Enemies: The Tragedy of Liberty*. Den Haag: Eleven, S. 39–56.

Nichtweiß, Barbara (1994): „Apokalyptische Verfassungslehren: Carl Schmitt im Horizont der Theologie Erik Petersons". In: Wacker, Bernd (Hg.): *Die eigentlich katholische Verschärfung ... Konfession, Theologie und Politik im Werk Carl Schmitts.* München: Fink, S. 37–64.

Plessner, Helmuth (2003): „Macht und menschliche Natur: Ein Versuch zur Anthropologie der geschichtlichen Weltansicht (1931)". In: *Macht und menschliche Natur.* Gesammelte Schriften 5. Frankfurt a. M.: Suhrkamp, S. 135–234.

Robin, Corey (2004): *Fear: The History of a Political Idea.* Oxford: Oxford University Press.

Rorty, Richard (1993): „Human Rights, Rationality, and Sentimentality". In: Shute, Steven/Hurley, Susan (Hg.): *On Human Rights: The Oxford Amnesty Lectures 1993.* New York, NY: Basic Books, S. 111–134.

Scarry, Elaine (1985): *The Body in Pain: The Making and Unmaking of the World.* Oxford: Oxford University Press.

Scheppele, Kim Lane (2020): „Orban's Emergency". In: *Verfassungsblog* 29. März 2020. https://verfassungsblog.de/orbans-emergency/, Zugriff 30. Juni 2020.

Schmitt, Carl (1914): *Der Wert des Staates und die Bedeutung des Einzelnen.* Tübingen: Mohr.

Schmitt, Carl (1926): *Die geistesgeschichtliche Lage des heutigen Parlamentarismus.* 2. Auflage. München: Duncker & Humblot.

Schmitt, Carl (1963): *Der Begriff des Politischen: Text von 1932 mit einem Vorwort und drei Corollarien.* 3. Auflage. Berlin: Duncker & Humblot.

Schmitt, Carl (1988a): „Der Führer schützt das Recht (1934)". In: *Positionen und Begriffe im Kampf mit Weimar – Genf – Versailles 1923–1939.* Unveränderter Nachdruck der ersten Auflage 1940. Berlin: Duncker & Humblot, S. 199–203.

Schmitt, Carl (1988b): „Weiterentwicklung des totalen Staats in Deutschland (1933)". In: *Positionen und Begriffe im Kampf mit Weimar – Genf – Versailles 1923–1939.* Unveränderter Nachdruck der ersten Auflage 1940. Berlin: Duncker & Humblot, S. 185–190.

Schmitt, Carl (2003): *Der Leviathan in der Staatslehre des Thomas Hobbes: Sinn und Fehlschlag eines politischen Symbols.* [Erstausgabe 1938]. 3. Auflage. Mit einem Anhang sowie einem Nachwort des Herausgebers [Günter Maschke]. Stuttgart: Klett-Cotta.

Shklar, Judith N. (1991): *American Citizenship: The Quest for Inclusion.* Cambridge, MA: Harvard University Press.

Shklar, Judith N. (1992): *Über Ungerechtigkeit: Erkundungen zu einem moralischen Gefühl.* Aus dem Amerikanischen von Christiane Goldmann. Berlin: Rotbuch.

Shklar, Judith N. (2013): *Der Liberalismus der Furcht.* Mit einem Vorwort von Axel Honneth und Essays von Michael Walzer, Seyla Benhabib und Bernard Williams. Hg., aus dem Amerikanischen übers. und mit einem Nachwort versehen von Hannes Bajohr. Berlin: Matthes & Seitz.

Shklar, Judith N. (2014): *Ganz normale Laster.* Aus dem Amerikanischen übers. und mit einem Nachwort versehen von Hannes Bajohr. Berlin: Matthes & Seitz.

Shklar, Judith N. (2017): *Der Liberalismus der Rechte.* Hg. und mit einem Vorwort versehen von Hannes Bajohr. Aus dem Amerikanischen und Französischen übers. von Hannes Bajohr und Dirk Höfer. Berlin: Matthes & Seitz.

Stullerova, Kamila (2014): „The Knowledge of Suffering: On Judith Shklar's ‚Putting Cruelty First'". In: *Contemporary Political Theory* 13(1), S. 23–45.

Sussman, David (2005): „What's Wrong with Torture?". In: *Philosophy and Public Affairs* 33(1), S. 1–33.

Szigetvári, Viktor/Tordai, Csaba/Vető, Balázs (2011): „Beyond Democracy – The Model of the New Hungarian Parliamentary Electoral System (Part 2)". In: *Haza és Haladás Közpolitikai Alapítvány* 24. November 2011. https://lapa.princeton.edu/hosteddocs/hungary/Beyond%20democracy%20-%2027%20Nov%202011.pdf, Zugriff 9. Juli 2020.

Unrau, Christine (2018): „Judith Shklars Sinn für Veränderung: Quellen und Voraussetzungen politischen Wandels im Denken Judith Shklars". In: *Zeitschrift für Politische Theorie* 9(2), S. 239–251.

Van Laak, Dirk (1993): *Gespräche in der Sicherheit des Schweigens: Carl Schmitt in der politischen Geistesgeschichte der frühen Bundesrepublik.* Berlin: Akademie Verlag.

Zakaria, Fareed (2007): *The Future of Freedom: Illiberal Democracy at Home and Abroad.* New York, NY: W. W. Norton.

Eva Maria Maier
# Zur aktuellen Krise von Demokratie und Rechtsstaatlichkeit

Ursachen und Symptome

**Abstract:** [On the Current Crisis of Democracy and Rule of Law: Causes and Symptoms] This article deals with the reasons for, and manifestations of, current crisis phenomena of democracy and the rule of law as they are particularly evident in so-called 'defective democracies' but have also reached long-established democratic states. The crisis of democracy is first reflected as a result of the progressive erosion of, and excessive demands on, the traditional concept of sovereignty, driven by globalisation, supranational law, and the multiplication of international legal standards. In this regard, it is also necessary to account for hidden ideological (e.g. anti-republican) roots of the model of the sovereign territorial state. Furthermore, the causes of current crises are located in a trend towards the formalisation and particularisation of the understanding of democracy. This can be observed, for example, in recent suppressions of parliamentary discourse but ultimately also in the decoupling of states from fundamental constitutional requirements, above all from human rights and the principle of human dignity. As symptoms of the crisis of democratic legal culture, two paradigm shifts are described in relation to how the central obligations of the state are perceived. This entails tendencies towards the restructuring of the welfare state, which increase poverty and can therefore also restrict the social framework conditions for democratic self-determination. Yet the dismantling of the welfare state is typically accompanied by the rise of the security state, which is increasingly oriented towards prevention.

**Keywords:** Democracy, majority rule, human dignity, rule of law, sovereignty, welfare state, preventive state, republic

# 1 Einleitung

> Erfährt ein Mensch oder eine Partei [in der Demokratie] eine Ungerechtigkeit, an wen sollen sie sich wenden? An die öffentliche Meinung? Gerade sie bildet die Mehrheit. An die gesetzgebende Gewalt? Sie repräsentiert die Mehrheit und gehorcht ihr blind. An die ausführende Gewalt? Sie wird von der Mehrheit ernannt und ist deren gehorsames Werkzeug. [...] An

> die Geschworenen? Das Geschworenenkollegium ist die Mehrheit mit dem Recht, Urteile zu fällen [...].

So lautet Tocquevilles klassische Kritik an der demokratischen Mehrheitsregel am Beispiel der USA und der darin angelegten Möglichkeit einer – aus aktueller Perspektive „illiberalen" – „Tyrannei der Mehrheit" (Tocqueville 2017: 147–148). Er präzisiert seine partikularismuskritische Sicht der liberalen Demokratie bereits davor: „Was ist denn die Mehrheit im ganzen genommen anders als ein Individuum mit Ansichten und Interessen, die meistens denen eines anderen Individuums, genannt Minderheit, zuwiderlaufen?" (Tocqueville 2017: 145).

Etwa 100 Jahre später, bereits Mitte der 1940er Jahre spitzt der Ökonom Joseph Schumpeter die „Entzauberung" (Offe 2003: 11) der normativen Idee des Volkswillens weiter zu, dies freilich keineswegs nur kritisch, sondern affirmativ hinsichtlich der Ausbildung einer bis heute paradigmatischen elitedemokratischen Theorie:

> Wir sehen uns bei der Analyse politischer Prozesse weithin nicht einem ursprünglichen, sondern einem fabrizierten Volkswillen gegenüber. [...] Die Art und Weise, in der [...] der Volkswillen [...] fabriziert [wird], ist völlig analog zur Art und Weise der kommerziellen Reklametechnik. [...] Wir finden die gleiche Technik der Schaffung günstiger oder ungünstiger Assoziationen, die um so wirksamer sind, je weniger rational sie sind. Wir sehen, dass das gleiche vermieden, das gleiche verschwiegen wird, und wir finden den gleichen Trick, durch wiederholte Behauptung eine Meinung zu schaffen – und dieser Trick ist genau so lange erfolgreich, als er rationale Argumente vermeidet und so auch die Gefahr, die kritischen Fähigkeiten des Volkes zu wecken (Schumpeter 2018: 356–357).

Freilich hat sich der rechtliche und politische Bezugsrahmen, unter anderem im Hinblick auf internationale menschenrechtliche und demokratische Standards einerseits, aber auch durch die Möglichkeiten und Herausforderungen digitalisierter medialer Öffentlichkeit, vor allem durch den Einsatz sogenannter „neuer Medien", dramatisch weiterentwickelt. Dennoch erscheint der Befund beider – im Ansatz höchst unterschiedlichen Vertreter klassischer Demokratietheorie – auch im Hinblick auf neueste Entwicklungen erstaunlich treffsicher.

Die aktuelle Konjunktur populistischer, vor allem rechtspopulistischer Politik in Europa und den USA im Kontext der Krise politischer Ideologien ganz allgemein, die zunehmende Distanz von Bürgerinnen und Bürgern zu Institutionen repräsentativer Demokratie, der Vertrauensverlust in die Parteiendemokratie – und in Politiker und Politikerinnen überhaupt – illustrieren das Selbstgefährdungspotenzial, ja die „Deformationsprozesse" (Offe 2003: 10) des Konzepts liberaler Demokratie in der Gegenwart. Die gezielte parteitaktische Instrumentalisierung von Feindbildern und Angstprojektionen zu Lasten gesellschaftlicher

Randgruppen, die Tendenzen zur weitreichenden Reduktion bzw. Suspendierung des parlamentarischen und außerparlamentarischen, etwa zivilgesellschaftlichen – oder aus spezifisch österreichischer Perspektive „sozialpartnerschaftlichen" – Diskurses lassen in der Tat die ursprüngliche aufklärerische Idee von der Selbstgesetzgebung des Volkes und damit auch das Prinzip der Volkssouveränität nahezu obsolet erscheinen.

Insgesamt zeichnet sich offenbar ein stetiger Trend zur zunehmenden Partikularisierung demokratischer Meinungsbildungsprozesse ab, gleichsam zu einem bloßen „freien Wettbewerb zwischen den Führungsanwärtern um die Stimmen der Wählerschaft" (Schumpeter 2018: 386), ja zu einem ökonomieanalogen „[H]andel" (Schumpeter 2018: 389) mit Stimmen, wie das schon der Ansatz Schumpeters hellsichtig diagnostizierte.

Freilich geht die Krise auch über den – durchaus bedenklichen – skizzierten Verfall demokratischer Kultur und bloße Krisenphänomene der Mehrheitsregel hinaus. Sie reicht selbst in europäischer Perspektive bis zur scheinbar demokratisch legitimierbaren Einschränkung von Grundrechten und anderen rechtsstaatlichen Prinzipien – Phänomene die von Wolfgang Merkel schon in den 1990er Jahren als „defekte Demokratien" (Merkel et al. 2003: 11–37, 65–95) beschrieben wurden. Charakteristisch hierfür sind Grundrechtseinschränkungen, in jüngster Zeit vor allem Eingriffe in die Pressefreiheit, das Asylrecht und kulturelle Rechte von Minderheiten, wie die Religionsfreiheit, einerseits und Eingriffe in die Unabhängigkeit der Gerichtsbarkeit andererseits. Freilich wird moniert, dass der Begriff der „defekten Demokratie" trotz des darin enthaltenen Potenzials kritischer Analyse auch geeignet erscheint, die demokratisch-rechtsstaatlichen Defizite und totalitären Züge von Staaten mit bloß formal-demokratischem Wahlregime zu verschleiern.

Die Anforderungen an demokratische Legitimation erschöpfen sich demnach keineswegs in der Institutionalisierung eines freien und gleichen Wahlrechts. Ja, sie gehen auch noch über die unverzichtbare Wahrung zentraler rechtsstaatlicher Grundsätze und Kerninstitutionen, wie fundamentaler Grundrechte, Gewaltenteilung und gerichtlicher Kontrolle von Exekutive und Legislative, hinaus.

Auch sozialpolitische Maßnahmen – keineswegs nur in sogenannten „defekten Demokratien" – sind als demokratiepolitisch bedenklich zu begreifen, wenn sie etwa die Demontage sozialstaatlicher Institutionen zu Lasten sozial randständiger Gruppen betreiben und armutsfördernd wirken. Denn auch diese schränken in weiterer Folge Freiheit und Selbstbestimmungschancen signifikant ein. Insbesondere aus globaler Sicht ist ferner nicht nur die umwelt-, sondern auch die demokratiepolitische Problematik umwelt- und klimapolitischer Versäumnisse hervorzuheben. Dies gilt nicht nur, weil diese gleichsam die „Naturbedingungen" menschlicher Freiheit in radikaler Weise bedrohen, sondern auch weil deren Folgen weltweit gravierend unterschiedliche regionale (vgl. Jamieson/ Di Paola 2015: 27-28) und generationsüberschreitende Betroffenheiten erzeugen.

Zwar lassen sich die vielfältigen Facetten und Gründe des aktuellen Demokratieschwunds an dieser Stelle nicht abschließend ausloten. Doch möchte ich zwei meines Erachtens zentrale Ursachen dieser Entwicklung hervorheben, nämlich die Krise des modernen neuzeitlichen Souveränitätsbegriffs sowie, in engem Zusammenhang damit, dessen ursprüngliche systematische Implikationen einerseits und den fortschreitenden Trend zur Formalisierung – und damit zur Partikularisierung – des demokratischen Diskurses andererseits.

Diesen beiden Aspekten im Bereich der Ursachenreflexion sollen sodann auf der Ebene der Krisenphänomene von Demokratie im weiteren Sinn zwei exemplarische Paradigmenwechsel gegenübergestellt werden, nämlich hinsichtlich des Begriffs von Sozialstaatlichkeit einerseits – und in direktem Kontext damit – in der Sicherheitspolitik andererseits. Beide Bedeutungswandel in so zentralen Bereichen staatlich-politischer Verantwortlichkeit können dabei zugleich auch als Symptome des Niedergangs des klassischen Souveränitätsbegriffs ebenso wie des Verlusts an demokratischen Partizipationschancen insgesamt verstanden werden.

## 2 Zur Krise des Souveränitätsbegriffs

Die Krise der modernen Demokratie ist wohl nicht zuletzt ein Symptom der Erosion des herkömmlichen nationalstaatlichen Souveränitätsbegriffs. Moderne Demokratien bauen – weitgehend unhinterfragt – auf dem Paradigma des souveränen Territorialstaats auf, ja vom 19. Jahrhundert bis zur Mitte des 20. Jahrhunderts auf jenem des „Nationalstaats" (vgl. Böckenförde 2013: 111–112). Dabei geht es in diesem Zusammenhang nicht vorrangig um die – zurzeit demokratiepolitisch ebenfalls besonders bedeutsame – Frage einer durch Grenzen generierten politischen Identität. Es geht zunächst – noch grundlegender – um das Verständnis von Souveränität als eines „,power-container'" (Giddens 1981: 10), der bereits am Beginn der Neuzeit zum Essential des Staatsbegriffs, ja zum Staatsbegriff schlechthin aufrückte.

Nun signalisiert dieser Begriff eines – ursprünglich vorrangig nach innen gerichteten – Monopols staatlicher Macht nicht nur die Ablöse des konfessionellen und feudalen Staates der Vormoderne, ist daher wesentlich das Produkt eines Säkularisationsprozesses, so die berühmte Böckenförde-These (vgl. Böckenförde 2013: 93–108). Er ist damit in seinem Kern ein Friedensprojekt, das freilich auch die Wende zu einem formellen Friedensbegriff beinhaltet.

Nein, dieses Legitimationsverständnis verdrängt auch ein konkurrierendes Modell politischer Organisation, das am Beginn der Moderne unter veränderten Vorzeichen erneut Aktualität gewann und deutlicher partizipatorisch strukturiert war, nämlich jenes republikanischer Stadtstaaten, konkret historisch greifbar in Oberitalien und im hanseatischen Raum (vgl. Anderson 2004: 20). Dies bedeutet, dass das von seinen Ursprüngen her keineswegs demokratische Modell der souveränen Monarchie mit seinen zentralen Implikationen von Territorialherrschaft und konstitutiver Machtkonzentration – eben jenes des „power-container" – das Konzept der republikanischen Bürgergesellschaft verdrängt (vgl. Giddens 1981: 185), in der die Herrschaft gleichsam vergesellschaftet war (vgl. Riedel 1976: 128– 132). Dies ist eine Weichenstellung, die meines Erachtens von jeher Spannungen zum Verständnis demokratischer Legitimation erzeugt. Der „power-container" des souveränen Staates setzt sich ursprünglich gegenüber dem „politischen Staat" durch. Die freie Bürgerherrschaft muss der konzentrierten Machtfülle territorial definierter Monarchien weichen (vgl. Anderson 2004: 20). In der Folge gilt es, diese abstrakte Machtfülle, die unverkennbar ein monarchisch-absolutistisches Gepräge zum Ausgangspunkt hat, gewissermaßen nachträglich zu limitieren und zu demokratisieren.

Dem „klassischen" Souveränitätsbegriff ist wohl ein Spannungsverhältnis zur Demokratie inhärent – auch wenn das bekanntlich schon Spinoza anders sah als Hobbes. Freilich beruht Spinozas Verständnis staatlicher Einheit nicht auf dem wechselseitigen Machtverzicht aller zugunsten eines Souveräns, wie es zuvor Hobbes einfordert (vgl. Hobbes 2010: 151–156). Vielmehr rekurriert Spinoza auch im Staatszustand in zentraler Weise auf Kooperation (vgl. Spinoza 2010: 27–29), die die „Potenz" der Individuen im Naturzustand verbindet und nicht aufhebt (vgl. Spinoza 2010: 27). Aber auch Locke, der als Vordenker aller liberalen Demokratietheorie gilt, konnte sich bekanntlich nicht dazu durchringen, die Staatsgewalten von der *„political society"* mehr als bloß kommissarisch auf dieser gegenüberstehende staatliche Institutionen zu verlagern (vgl. Locke 1977: 293–294). Dies findet seine Entsprechung wohl auch im englischen Mischverfassungssystem, das nicht auf dem in Kontinentaleuropa entstandenen Konzept der Souveränität gegründet war. Immerhin bezieht freilich gerade die liberale Demokratie in der Folge ihre Legitimation auf eine strikte Unterscheidung zwischen staatlicher Gewalt und Zivilgesellschaft. Damit setzt sie auch die Durchsetzung territorialer Grenzen als eine ihrer zentralen ideologischen Implikationen voraus (vgl. Anderson 2004: 9).

Nunmehr ist eben dieses Konzept von ihren Ursprüngen her territorial konstituierter Souveränität aktuell heftigen Erosionsvorgängen ausgesetzt. Dabei betrifft die fortschreitende Entmachtung nationalstaatlicher Souveränität durch das Diktat von Globalisierung und internationalen Finanzmärkten ebenso wie durch den Ausbau supranationalen Rechts, ja verpflichtender internationaler Rechtsstandards (vgl. Böckenförde 1999: 103–107; Grimm 2012: 78–91) auch das davon bestimmte Modell von Demokratie. Die Krise der Souveränität und des Territorialstaats äußert sich damit auch als Krise des von diesen mitkonstituierten Konzepts demokratischer Legitimation.

Noch bevor diese Krise im vollen Umfang sichtbar wird, ist der Souveränitätsbegriff ab dem 20. Jahrhundert heftiger Ideologiekritik ausgesetzt. In den postmodernen, postsouveränistischen Demokratietheorien Agambens, Derridas und Baumans spitzt sich diese Kritik als Dekonstruktion des politischen Subjekts der Volkssouveränität überhaupt zu (vgl. Derrida 2006: 35–37). Dem Souveränitätsbegriff seien umfassende „Angleichungs- und Homogenisierungstendenz[en]" (Schulz 2012: 105) gleichsam inhärent. Er habe überhaupt seinen Ursprung aus monarchischen Legitimationsstrukturen niemals überwunden (vgl. Derrida 2006: 36). In der Kritik steht etwa der auch im „volkssouveränen" Staat erhaltene „[g]ewaltförmig[e]" (Schulz 2012: 106) Charakter des nur scheinbar demokratisch legitimierten klassischen Gesetzesbegriffs (vgl. Derrida 1991: 15), dem etwa auch ein strikter Territorialbezug von seinem Ursprung her begriffsimmanent sei. Derrida verweist darüber hinaus aber auch auf die „genealogische[n]" Implikationen (Derrida 2018: 155) des herkömmlichen Souveränitätsbegriffs und der darauf bezogenen demokratischen Legitimation. Sie reproduzierten, so die Kritik, in der Konstituierung politischer Identität einen angesichts aktueller Verwischungsprozesse von Grenzen (vgl. Schulz 2012: 115) und Nationalstaatlichkeit anachronistischen „*Schematismus* der Abstammung" (Derrida 2018: 11), ohne das in demokratischen Legitimationsdiskursen ausreichend deutlich zu machen. Ja das Bestreben um Aufrechterhaltung eines längst obsolet gewordenen territorial-zentralistischen Ordnungsmodells frühmoderner Herkunft „in der Definitionsmacht des modernen Staates" (Bauman 2005a: 23) äußere sich nicht zuletzt, so Bauman, in der Produktion des „Ausgeschlossenen", ja „menschliche[n] Abfall[s]" (Bauman 2005b: 48), im „Aussieben, Absondern und Entsorgen des beim Aufbau der Ordnung entstandenen Abfalls" (Bauman 2005b: 50). Dies umfasse „Flüchtlinge, Heimatlose, Asylbewerber, Migranten, alle Menschen ohne Papiere", die eben als „Abfall der Globalisierung" (Bauman 2005b: 85) wie auch jener Ordnungsprozesse begriffen werden, in denen sich die Restsouveränität zu erhalten sucht. Dezidiert knüpft Bauman in seiner Kritik nationalstaatlicher Souveränität auch an Agambens Kategorie des „*homo sacer*" an, dessen „doppelter" Status rechtlicher Ausgrenzung bzw. „Ausnahme" („*una doppia eccezione*") allererst die politische Sphäre der „Souveränität" überhaupt „konstituiere" (Agamben 2005: 92). „Politische Herrschaft" sei, so Bauman, mittlerweile geradezu „teilweise vom abweichenden Anderen und der Mobilisierung von Sicherheitsbedürfnissen abhängig geworden" (Bauman 2005b: 81).

In der Tagespolitik spiegelt sich die Krise der Souveränität dann wohl aktuell auch überdeutlich in der symbolischen Überfrachtung öffentlicher Diskurse und legistischer Vorhaben zu Grenzregimen und innerer Sicherheit, ja insgesamt zu Bedrohungspotenzialen, die Fremden und in der Folge auch anderen sozial randständigen Bevölkerungsgruppen zugeschrieben werden.

## 3 Die Formalisierung des Demokratieverständnisses

Einen weiteren Ausgangspunkt für aktuelle Krisenphänomene bilden die oft dezidierte Abkehr vom „klassischen" – gewissermaßen „republikanischen" (Habermas 2019: 277) – Demokratiebegriff, der Trend zur Entpolitisierung und die weitreichenden Reduktionismen in der Demokratietheorie des 20. Jahrhunderts nach den Krisenerfahrungen von Zwischenkriegszeit und NS-Herrschaft (vgl. Euchner 2005: 18). Dies ist wohl eine Entwicklung, die durch den Bedeutungsverlust spezifisch politischer Ideologie nach dem Ende des Kalten Krieges Ende der 1980er Jahre noch weiter gefördert wurde.

Demokratie ist darin in der Tat zur bloßen politischen „Methode" (Schumpeter 2018: 365) herabgekommen, der der grundsätzliche Anspruch der Universalisierbarkeit demokratisch legitimierter Entscheidungen abhandengekommen zu sein scheint. Insbesondere neuere liberale oder ökonomisch-konkurrenztheoretische Demokratietheorien beschränken sich im Vertrauen auf die regulierende Wirkung von Interessenpluralismus und Konflikt auf eine „minimale Definition von Demokratie" („*la definizione minima di democrazia*") (Bobbio 2014: 4), die sich im Wesentlichen in demokratischem Wahlregime, Parteiendemokratie und Mehrheitsregel erschöpft. Diese formalistische Wettbewerbsdemokratie macht die Grenzen der Mehrheitsregel in ihrer liberalistischen Ausprägung im Allgemeinen allein, aber immerhin, an der Garantie liberaler Grundrechte fest. Konkurrenzdemokratische Theorien der Elitedemokratie, in exemplarischer Weise jene Schumpeters, verschieben den Fokus endgültig zur marktanalogen „Akkumulation von Wählerstimmen" (Saage 2005: 250). Letztendlich ginge es eben, so Schumpeter, um einen „‚Stimmenhandel'" (Schumpeter 2018: 389), der denselben Marktgesetzen gehorche wie der Handel mit Öl (vgl. Schumpeter 2018: 387).

Bereits diese Theorien fördern eine Formalisierung des Demokratieverständnisses, wie es sich wohl kaum an der Aufklärung, gewiss nicht an John Lockes Konzept einer ursprünglichen „*political society*" festmachen lässt. Das gilt aber auch für das von Locke deutlich zu unterscheidende – und etwa aus der Sicht

Ingeborg Maus' – dezidiert *starke* Volkssouveränitätsverständnis Kants (vgl. Maus 2015: 8 – 11, 20 – 42). Dies sei nach Maus zwar strikt prozeduralistisch zu verstehen (vgl. Maus 2015: 10) und trage eben daher nicht in Restbeständen spätfeudal- „[s]ubstantialis[tische]" (Maus 2015: 36) Züge, weil es nicht etwa – wie jenes von Locke – auf die Durchsetzung von vorgängigen materialen Rechtsprinzipien verpflichtet sei. Es sei aber ebenso untrennbar mit der Anforderung eines strikten Universalismus (vgl. Maus 2015: 34) verbunden, durch den sich Gesetze, die einseitig partikulare Standpunkte durchsetzen, selbst delegitimieren. Maus verortet in ihrer Kritik am aktuellen Betrieb von Demokratie gar einen Prozess der „Refeudalisierung" (Maus 2015: 35), in dem Repräsentation zur Vertretung partikularer Interessen und „neokorporatistischen Verhandlungssystemen" (Maus 2015: 34) degeneriert sei, sowie die Volkssouveränität unter anderem durch die Exekutivlastigkeit rechtlicher Steuerungsprozesse stetig weiter ausgehöhlt werde (vgl. Maus 2015: 35). Maus umfasst mit ihrer Kritik freilich auch im engeren Sinn außerkonstitutionelle Phänomene der sogenannten „Verhandlungsdemokratie" (Grimm 2003: 193 – 199), wie sie wohl in der österreichischen politischen Kultur lange insbesondere durch die Praxis der sogenannten „Sozialpartnerschaft", ein teilweise informell institutionalisiertes System der Zusammenarbeit zwischen Arbeitnehmer- und Arbeitgeberinteressenvertretern in Fragen der Sozial- und Wirtschaftspolitik, repräsentiert wurde. Dies entspricht freilich dem Trend, hinsichtlich der komplexen Aufgaben staatlicher Verantwortung „für Bestand und Entwicklung der Gesellschaft in sozialer, ökonomischer und kultureller Hinsicht" (Grimm 1991: 168) auch die – oft informelle – Kooperation von „staatlichen und gesellschaftlichen Entscheidungsträgern" (Grimm 1991: 170) miteinzubeziehen. Jenseits der längst obsoleten liberalen Trennung von Staat und Gesellschaft tritt diese Kooperation vermehrt an die Stelle der klassischen Gesetzesform des punktuellen imperativen Eingriffs. Diese Tendenz zur Entformalisierung mag zwar eine Herausforderung für herkömmliche Rechtsschutzmechanismen darstellen, kann aber auch maßgebliche „deliberative" Aspekte demokratischer Entscheidungskultur beisteuern. Gerade in der jüngeren Vergangenheit wurde etwa in Österreich jedoch der Eindruck vermittelt, selbst hinsichtlich der Wahrnehmung parlamentarischer Verhandlungsspielräume beim Zustand einer exekutivlastigen bloßen Abstimmungsdemokratie angelangt zu sein.

Diese Tendenzen zur „Entzauberung", ja gewissermaßen zur „Entdemokratisierung" der Demokratie, die sich selbst im Rahmen sogenannter *„embedded democrac[ies]"* (Merkel et al. 2003: 14) konstatieren lassen, steigern sich freilich ohne Zweifel signifikant durch die systematische Entflechtung gegenüber Grundrechten und anderen rechtsstaatlichen Garantien. Derartige Entwicklungen werden derzeit in mehreren europäischen Ländern und solchen an den geographischen Rändern Europas mit demokratischem Wahlregime vorangetrieben, die sich dann eben in offen paradoxer Weise als sogenannte „illiberale Demokratien" deklarieren. Ansätze dazu bzw. Sympathien dafür finden sich aber auch in politischen Konzepten, die in jüngster Zeit etwa im deutschsprachigen Raum vertreten wurden.

Freilich manifestieren sich demokratiepolitisch bedenkliche Entwicklungen keineswegs bloß im offenen oder schleichenden Angriff auf zentrale rechtsstaatliche Institutionen. Als charakteristisch für die aktuelle Krise demokratischer Rechtskultur erweisen sich auch Tendenzen zum Umbau des Sozialstaats, die armutsfördernd wirken können und damit ebenfalls geeignet sind, politisch-demokratische Handlungschancen einzuschränken.

Parallel dazu vollzieht sich typischerweise ein Prozess der generellen Überfrachtung – zunehmend präventiv ausgerichteter – staatlicher Schutzaufgaben im Bereich innerer Sicherheit, die bereits einen Paradigmenwechsel von Rechtsstaatlichkeit, zumindest in besonders symbolbefrachteten Kernbereichen, einleiten.

## 4 Vom „aktiven" zum „aktivierenden" Sozialstaat

Längst ist das Modell des unterstützenden Sozialstaats, ja das Bewusstsein von den Realbedingungen selbstverantwortlicher Freiheit und den strukturellen Ursachen menschlicher Armut auf sozialpolitischer Ebene in die Krise geraten. Europaweit – wenngleich mit unterschiedlicher Geschwindigkeit in den Mitgliedsstaaten – zeichnet sich der „Umbau" des „aktiven" zum „aktivierenden" Sozialstaat ab, der einen grundlegenden Bedeutungswandel im Begriff sozialer Gerechtigkeit vollzieht (vgl. Maier 2019: 44–51).

Den Ausgangspunkt bildet die sukzessive Unterordnung der Sozialpolitik unter einseitig ökonomische Modelle der Leistungssteigerung. Das wird bekanntlich in zentraler Weise mit der Optimierung der nationalen „Industriestandortsicherheit" begründet (vgl. Urban 1995: 9–11). Dies führt nicht nur zum pauschalen Trend der „Verschlankung" sozialstaatlicher Garantien. Auch sollen Sozialleistungen selbst nunmehr primär betriebswirtschaftlich reorganisiert werden (vgl. Butterwegge 2017: 161–163). Paradigmatisch ist vor allem die sozialpolitische Wende von der Orientierung am Grundsatz der sozialen Sicherheit zu jenem der sogenannten „Eigenverantwortlichkeit". Das bedeutet, dass Transferleistungen nicht mehr vorrangig nach dem Maßstab der Bedürftigkeit, sondern nach jenem einer quasi-kontraktualistischen „Gegenleistung" zu verteilen sind. Als symptomatisch hierfür kann etwa gelten, dass im „neuen" Sozialstaat wesentliche Fördermaßnahmen nicht durch direkte Transferleistungen, sondern vermehrt auch durch die Einräumung von Steuervorteilen (wie Steuerfreibeträgen) gewährt werden und damit unter einen Leistungsvorbehalt geraten, was gerade die Bedürftigsten von vornherein ausschließt. Komplementär dazu verschiebt sich vor allem im Bereich elementarer Bedarfssicherung der Schwerpunkt von Sozialversicherungsleistungen (etwa Arbeitslosengeld) bzw. sozialstaatlichen Rechtsansprüchen hin zu bloßen Fürsorgemaßnahmen (wie „bedarfsorientierter Mindestsicherung" bzw. „Hartz IV") sowie zu einer Reprivatisierung von Leistungen der existenzsichernden Daseinsvorsorge (vgl. Butterwegge 2017: 125–126).

Darin kommt freilich eine grundlegende Umdeutung des Verhältnisses von freiheitlicher Selbstbestimmung und sozialen Ausgangsbedingungen gegenüber dem Modell des unterstützenden Sozialstaats keynesianischer Prägung zum Ausdruck. Aktive Chancengerechtigkeit soll nahtlos durch die Steigerung – häufig negativ konditionierender – „Leistungsanreize" ersetzt werden (vgl. Butterwegge 2017: 167–172). Im Wandel vom „‚welfare' zum ‚workfare state'" (Butterwegge 2017: 171) vollzieht sich auch ein Prozess der Entpolitisierung in der Bekämpfung struktureller Armutsursachen. Ja mehr noch, dadurch wird gleichsam die vorsozialstaatliche „moralische" Differenzierung zwischen „würdigen" und „unwürdigen" Armen fortgeschrieben. Der Ruf nach mehr „Eigenverantwortung" in Zeiten der Arbeitsplatzknappheit ist häufig von einer Pauschalverdächtigung für soziale Randgruppen, vor allem Langzeitarbeitslose, begleitet. Gleichzeitig werden die – durch individuelle „Tüchtigkeit" und Leistungsbereitschaft eben nicht schlechterdings revidierbaren – sozialen Realbedingungen menschlicher Freiheit systematisch ausgeblendet. Ja, Freiheit und Gleichheit figurieren im „neuen Sozialstaat" in einem prinzipiellen Konkurrenzverhältnis (vgl. Kersting 2000: 202–206).

Dabei kommt es geradewegs zu einer Umkehr des Verhältnisses von freiheitlicher Selbstbestimmung und sozialer Chancengleichheit gegenüber dem Konzept des „aktiven" Sozialstaats. Mit der grundsätzlichen Entrechtlichung von Solidaritätsleistungen und deren intendierter Einschränkung auf die sogenannten „wirklich Armen" (Butterwegge 2017: 177) schreitet der Umbau des „‚Sozialversicherungsstaates für alle' zu einem Fürsorgestaat" (Butterwegge 2017: 180), ja zum „Suppenküchenstaat" (Butterwegge 2017: 178) voran, eine Entwicklung die nicht nur sozial-, sondern auch demokratiepolitisch bedenklich erscheint.

## 5 Auf dem Weg zum Präventionsstaat

Mit der „Verschlankung" des Sozialstaats geht typischerweise auch der Ausbau des Sicherheitsstaats voran – gleichsam als Symptom des Niedergangs des klassischen Souveränitätsbegriffs im postsouveränen Zeitalter mit problematischen rechtsstaatlichen und damit auch demokratiepolitischen Implikationen.

Insgesamt geht es um die Tendenz zur präventiven Vorverlagerung staatlicher Maßnahmen als Gefahrenabwehr, die nicht nur bei konkreten Risiken, sondern auch bei ganz allgemeinen Gefahrenlagen zum Einsatz kommt.

Charakteristisch ist insbesondere der massive Ausbau von sogenannter „Vorfeldkriminalität" im Strafrecht, d. h. der – eben präventiven – selbständigen Inkriminierung grundsätzlich straffreier Vorbereitungshandlungen. Die Konjunktur von Vorbereitungs-, Organisations- und sogenannten „Massendelikten" enthält eine tendenzielle Abkehr vom rechtsstaatlich gebotenen Schuldprinzip und erzeugt Spannungen zum strafrechtlichen Legalitätsprinzip und Bestimmtheitsgebot in Art. 7 EMRK (vgl. Maier 2010: 46–50). Auch die Debatte um die Einführung eines sogenannten „Feindstrafrechts" (Jakobs 2004: 88–95) reflektiert diese Tendenzen einer Abkehr vom Schuldstrafrecht in Richtung auf ein „Gefahrenabwehrstrafrecht" und spitzt sie weiter zu. Die Einführung – und Perpetuierung – des „Ausnahmezustands" in Staaten mit eklatanten Demokratiedefiziten, aber auch in entwickelten Demokratien, wie den USA bzw. Frankreich, als Reaktion auf die Überforderung rechtsstaatlicher und internationaler Institutionen durch das Bedrohungspotenzial des „neuen Terrorismus", aber auch zur Inszenierung von Feindbildern und zur Machtkonsolidierung, rückten scheinbar in das regelmäßige Repertoire staatlicher Sicherheitspolitik auf. Selbst der in Österreich jüngst geäußerte Vorschlag zur präventiven Inhaftierung von als „gefährlich" eingestuften (ausländischen) Personen illustriert diesen Trend eindringlich.

Als besonders exemplarischer Einbruch in demokratisch-rechtsstaatliche Verfassungskultur gelten freilich die Bemühungen zur Legalisierung der Folter in Ausnahmesituationen, die in den USA zur Einführung sogenannter „verschärfter Verhörmethoden" im Rahmen des – als Ausnahmezustand konzipierten – *„war on terrorism"* führten. Aber auch in Deutschland war die Debatte um die sogenannte „Rettungsfolter", nämlich die Frage nach der Zulässigkeit von Folter zur Rettung von Menschenleben, mehr als ein Jahrzehnt Gegenstand von – freilich kategorisch ablehnender – Judikatur und kontroverser wissenschaftlicher Auseinandersetzung (vgl. Maier 2012: 195–202).[1]

Die Palette der rechtsstaatlichen Problematik dieser Maßnahmen reicht somit von Spannungen zum Legalitätsprinzip bis zur offenen Suspendierung von Grundrechten, ja zur Verletzung des Prinzips der Menschenwürde im Namen der

---

[1] Trotz der Verurteilung in der herrschenden Verfassungslehre sowie in der deutschen und europäischen Rechtsprechung als rechtsstaatlicher Tabubruch und Negation des Menschenwürdeprinzips wird der Einsatz von Folter immer noch von einzelnen namhaften Vertretern deutscher Strafrechtswissenschaft im Rahmen des Notwehr(hilfe)rechts als gerechtfertigt angesehen (vgl. dazu Erb 2006: 20–33).

Sicherheit. In jedem Fall scheinen darin Tendenzen eines Paradigmenwechsels weg vom „‚normfolgeorientiert[en]'" Rechtsstaat und hin zum einseitig schutznormlastigen „‚Präventionsstaat'" (Marx 2009: 169) auf. Darin würde die weit vorverlagerte Risikobekämpfung gar zur Normalität der Wahrnehmung staatlicher Schutzpflichten aufrücken. Dies käme letztendlich einer „generelle[n] Umkehr der Beweislast" (Marx 2009: 169) „im Verhältnis Staat-Bürger" (Marx 2009: 169) gleich.

Schließlich kommt wohl in beiden Trends der Wahrnehmung fundamentalster Staatsaufgaben – im „konditionierenden" Sozialstaat wie auch im präventiven Sicherheitsstaat – ein vergleichbares verfehltes Autonomiekonzept zum Ausdruck, das die Anerkennung der Menschenwürde unter einen „Leistungs-" bzw. „Moralvorbehalt" stellt. Dem entspricht eben auch der aktuelle Trend, im sicherheitspolitischen „Präventionsstaat" rechtsstaatliche Garantien zunehmend dem Ziel der sogenannten „Gefahrenabwehr", ja schließlich der strategisch eingesetzten bloßen Befriedigung subjektiver Sicherheitsbedürfnisse, unterzuordnen. Denn in beiden Konzepten kann die allgemeine Vernunftsubjektivität der Bürger und Bürgerinnen nach Maßgabe ihrer „Würdigkeit" (Bielefeldt 2008: 14–15) oder einer sehr abstrakten sogenannten „Gefährlichkeit" relativiert werden. Diese Entwicklungen erweisen sich daher als rechtsstaatlich *und* demokratiepolitisch problematisch.

So soll – abschließend und resümierend – nochmals Tocquevilles kritische Sicht der Rolle der Volkssouveränität zu Wort kommen:

> Das Prinzip der Volkssouveränität, das mehr oder weniger allen menschlichen Institutionen zugrunde liegt, bleibt in der Regel dort begraben. Man gehorcht ihm, ohne es zu erkennen, und wenn es doch einmal ans Tageslicht tritt, so lässt man es eilends wieder in die heilige Finsternis zurücksinken (Tocqueville 2017: 45–46).

## Literatur

Agamben, Giorgio (2005): *Homo sacer: Il potere sovrano e la nuda vita*. Turin: Einaudi.
Anderson, Malcolm (2004): *Frontiers: Territory and State Formation in the Modern World*. Cambridge: Polity Press.
Bauman, Zygmunt (2005a): *Moderne und Ambivalenz: Das Ende der Eindeutigkeit*. Hamburg: Hamburger Edition.
Bauman, Zygmunt (2005b): *Verworfenes Leben: Die Ausgegrenzten der Moderne*. Bonn: Bundeszentrale für politische Bildung.
Bielefeldt, Heiner (2008): *Menschenwürde: Der Grund der Menschenrechte*. Bonn: Deutsches Institut für Menschenrechte.
Bobbio, Norberto (2014): *Il futuro della democrazia*. Turin: Einaudi.

Böckenförde, Ernst-Wolfgang (1999): „Die Zukunft politischer Autonomie: Demokratie und Staatlichkeit im Zeichen von Globalisierung, Europäisierung und Individualisierung". In: *Staat, Nation, Europa: Studien zur Staatslehre, Verfassungstheorie und Rechtsphilosophie*. Frankfurt a. M.: Suhrkamp, S. 103–126.

Böckenförde, Ernst-Wolfgang (2013): „Die Entstehung des Staates als Vorgang der Säkularisation". In: *Recht, Staat, Freiheit: Studien zur Rechtsphilosophie, Staatstheorie und Verfassungsgeschichte*. Frankfurt a. M.: Suhrkamp, S. 92–114.

Butterwegge, Christoph (2017): „Rechtfertigung, Maßnahmen und Folgen einer neoliberalen (Sozial-)Politik". In: Butterwegge, Christoph/Lösch, Bettina/Ptak, Ralf (Hg.): *Kritik des Neoliberalismus*. Wiesbaden: Springer VS, S. 123–200.

Derrida, Jacques (1991): *Gesetzeskraft: Der „mystische Grund der Autorität"*. Frankfurt a. M.: Suhrkamp.

Derrida, Jacques (2006): *Schurken: Zwei Essays über die Vernunft*. Frankfurt a. M.: Suhrkamp.

Derrida, Jacques (2018): *Politik der Freundschaft*. Frankfurt a. M.: Suhrkamp.

Erb, Volker (2006): „Folterverbot und Notwehrrecht". In: Lenzen, Wolfgang (Hg.): *Ist Folter erlaubt? Juristische und philosophische Aspekte*. Paderborn: Mentis, S. 19–38.

Euchner, Walter (2005): „Zur Notwendigkeit einer Ideengeschichte der Demokratie". In: Saage, Richard (Hg.): *Demokratietheorien: Eine Einführung*. Wiesbaden: VS Verlag für Sozialwissenschaften, S. 13–21.

Giddens, Anthony (1981): *A Contemporary Critique of Historical Materialism*. Band 1: *Power, Property and the State*. London: Macmillan.

Grimm, Dieter (1991): *Die Zukunft der Verfassung*. Frankfurt a. M.: Suhrkamp.

Grimm, Dieter (2003): „Lässt sich die Verhandlungsdemokratie konstitutionalisieren?" In: Offe, Claus (Hg.): *Demokratisierung der Demokratie: Diagnosen und Reformvorschläge*. Frankfurt a. M: Campus, S. 193–210.

Grimm, Dieter (2012): *Die Zukunft der Verfassung II: Auswirkungen von Europäisierung und Globalisierung*. Frankfurt a. M.: Suhrkamp.

Habermas, Jürgen (2019): *Die Einbeziehung des Anderen: Studien zur politischen Theorie*. Frankfurt a. M.: Suhrkamp.

Hobbes, Thomas (2010): *Leviathan*. Hg. von Jacob Peter Mayer. Stuttgart: Reclam.

Jakobs, Günther (2004): „Bürgerstrafrecht und Feindstrafrecht". In: *HRRS: Onlinezeitschrift für Höchstrichterliche Rechtsprechung im Strafrecht* 5(3), S. 88–95. https://www.hrr-strafrecht.de/hrr/archiv/04-03/hrrs-3-04.pdf, Zugriff 15. November 2019.

Jamieson, Dale/Di Paola, Marcello (2015): „Klimawandel und globale Gerechtigkeit: Neues Problem, altes Paradigma?" In: Kallhoff, Angela (Hg.): *Klimagerechtigkeit und Klimaethik*. Berlin: De Gruyter, S. 23–37.

Kersting, Wolfgang (2000): „Politische Solidarität statt Verteilungsgerechtigkeit? Eine Kritik egalitaristischer Sozialstaatsbegründung". In: Kersting, Wolfgang (Hg.): *Politische Philosophie des Sozialstaats*. Weilerswist: Velbrück Wissenschaft, S. 202–256.

Locke, John (1977): *Zwei Abhandlungen über die Regierung*. Hg. von Walter Euchner. Frankfurt a. M.: Suhrkamp.

Maier, Eva Maria (2010): „‚Organisierte Kriminalität' oder Ziviler Ungehorsam? Methodische und rechtsphilosophische Anmerkungen zur rechtsstaatlichen Problematik der Strafverfolgung von TierschutzaktivistInnen gemäß § 278a StGB". In: *juridikum: Zeitschrift für Kritik, Recht, Gesellschaft* 21(1), S. 46–57.

Maier, Eva Maria (2012): „Folter und Menschwürde: Zur aktuellen Debatte um die ‚Rettungsfolter'". In: *Journal für Rechtspolitik* 20(3), S. 195–206.

Maier, Eva Maria (2019): „Armut als ‚Dehumanisierung'? Armut und politische Exklusion im rechtsphilosophischen Diskurs". In: Graziani, Enrico/Maier, Eva Maria/Cesolini, Andrea (Hg.): *Forme di deumanizzazione: Umano – non Umano*. Rom: Edizioni Nuova Cultura, S. 27–57.

Marx, Reinhard (2009): „Folter – eine zulässige polizeiliche Präventionsmaßnahme?" In: Furtmayr, Holger/Krása, Kerstin/Frewer, Andreas (Hg.): *Folter und ärztliche Verantwortung: Das Istanbul-Protokoll und Problemfelder in der Praxis*. Göttingen: V&R unipress, S. 143–180.

Maus, Ingeborg (2015): *Zur Aufklärung der Demokratietheorie: Rechts- und demokratietheoretische Überlegungen im Anschluß an Kant*. Frankfurt a. M: Suhrkamp.

Merkel, Wolfgang/Puhle, Hans-Jürgen/Croissant, Aurel/Eicher, Claudia/Thiery, Peter (2003): *Defekte Demokratie. Band 1: Theorie*. Wiesbaden: Springer Fachmedien.

Offe, Claus (2003): „Einleitung: Reformbedarf und Reformoptionen der Demokratie". In: Offe, Claus (Hg.): *Demokratisierung der Demokratie: Diagnosen und Reformvorschläge*. Frankfurt a. M.: Campus, S. 9–23.

Riedel, Manfred (1976): „Herrschaft und Gesellschaft: Zum Legitimationsproblem des Politischen in der Philosophie". In: Batscha, Zwi (Hg.): *Materialien zu Kants Rechtsphilosophie*. Frankfurt a. M.: Suhrkamp, S. 125–148.

Saage, Richard (2005): *Demokratietheorien: Eine Einführung*. Wiesbaden: VS Verlag für Sozialwissenschaften.

Schulz, Daniel (2012): „Kritik der Souveränität und die Grenzen politischer Einheit: Zu postmodernen Demokratietheorien". In: Lembcke, Oliver W./Ritzi, Claudia/Schaal, Gary S. (Hg.): *Zeitgenössische Demokratietheorien. Band 1: Normative Demokratietheorien*. Wiesbaden: Springer VS, S. 97–126.

Schumpeter, Joseph A. (2018): *Kapitalismus, Sozialismus und Demokratie*. Tübingen: Francke.

Spinoza, Baruch de (2010): *Politischer Traktat: Tractatus politicus*. Neu übersetzt, herausgegeben, mit Einleitung und Anmerkungen versehen von Wolfgang Bartuschat. Hamburg: Meiner.

Tocqueville, Alexis de (2017): *Über die Demokratie in Amerika*. Ausgewählt und herausgegeben von Jacob Peter Mayer. Stuttgart: Reclam.

Urban, Hans-Jürgen (1995): „Deregulierter Standort-Kapitalismus". In: Schmitthenner, Horst (Hg.): *Der „schlanke" Staat: Zukunft des Sozialstaats – Sozialstaat der Zukunft*. Hamburg: VSA, S. 9–38.

Part 3: **Challenges to Philosophical Critique in Culture and Society**

Ulrich Frank
# Language, Change, and Possible Worlds
Philosophical Considerations of the Digital Transformation

**Abstract:** This essay aims at the identification and discussion of specific methodological problems related to the study and the support of the digital transformation from the perspective of a discipline that is directly responsible, both as an observer and a driver: Business Informatics. After a short account of the history of information technology and its present constitution, a brief analysis of key aspects of the digital transformation will lead to the pivotal role of language and conceptual models in particular. To prepare systems for change, models need to incorporate abstractions that cover possible future worlds. From an academic perspective, this requirement is fascinating and challenging at the same time. It implies the problem of how to adequately justify the construction of possible worlds. Furthermore, it leads to the question of how we can think possible future worlds that are beyond the limits of the language we speak. Against this background, the paper proposes facets of a methodology of change.

**Keywords:** Artificial intelligence, contingency, induction, justification, language, narrative, research method

> *The transformation we are concerned with is not a technical one, but a continuing evolution of how we understand our surrounding and ourselves – of how we continue becoming the beings that we are.*
> – Terry Winograd and Fernando Flores: *Understanding Computers and Cognition: A New Foundation for Design*

## 1 Introduction

An ever-growing amount of our surroundings is being represented digitally. It does not seem exaggerated to even state: "The world is being rebuilt in code" (Widdicombe 2014: 56). Digitization of this kind does not just mean to create images of a given reality, or to automate tasks previously performed by humans. Instead, it means to open new perspectives on how to conceptualize our surroundings, to reframe familiar patterns of work, of collaboration and of communication. It allows us to overcome traditions and concepts we have been used to for a long time, and to see new options unknown to us in the past. These new options enabled the emergence of new companies that became global giants in less than a decade. At the same time, industries that prospered only a few years ago, lie shattered, swept away by a process of change that is unprecedented in the history of humankind. Therefore, it seems appropriate to think of it as a fundamental transformation or even as a paradigm shift. While it is not clear what the essential characteristics of this change are and what it will bring about, there is a name for it that has been a dominating theme both in academic and public discourses for some time: digital transformation. Even though the omnipresent narrative of the digital transformation suffers from multiple simplifications and dubious contributions, it represents a phenomenon of substantial relevance that will likely change the way we work, live, and think. It is fascinating and ambivalent. It is about opportunities and threats, about creation and decline, about construction and deconstruction, about liberation and domination.

The digital transformation represents a manifold, complex phenomenon that bulks against simple explanations. Nevertheless, it seems not too daring to attribute it to two main driving forces. At first, the Internet provides a common infrastructure that does not only promote the accessibility of digital resources independent from their physical location, but also allows to get access to physical resources, organizations, and people that were beyond our reach in the times before the raise of the Internet. The economic effects of the Internet are tremendous. It enables new services, new business models, promotes bundling of resources, and boosts economies of scale. It is the foundation of new forms of social interaction and promotes the dissemination of knowledge at a previously unknown level. Finally, the Internet paved the way for the second driving force, the growing availability of mass data on almost any aspect of business transactions, of social interaction, and of human life in general. The availability of mass data together with growing computing power enables an extensive use of methods of inductive statistics at relatively low costs. In addition to analyzing data for patterns of correlation which are of use for decision making purposes, approaches to so-called "machine learning" have received particular attention in recent times and contributed to the creation of a remarkable new hype about *artificial intelligence* (AI). Not only has machine learning already produced various impressive software systems, it also holds out the prospect of pushing the limits of automation. Since the functionality of these systems is hard to explain, it is not surprising that they become subject of mystification, which goes along with the emergence of utopian and dystopian scenarios of the future, with promises and warnings.

This is a worrying situation. Decision makers in politics and in organizations are under pressure to invest into research and technology, even though many lack the required appreciation of the subject. This is a clear threat to the idea of rationality and enlightenment. It reaffirms Habermas' critique of technology and science as "ideology" (Habermas 1976) and goes beyond it at the same time: those who (re-)produce this ideology may well become its victims if the assumptions it is based on turn out to be wrong. The remarkable public attention created by the digital transformation and AI does not leave academia unaffected. This is especially the case for disciplines that are directly related to technological and institutional aspects of the digital transformation, like Computer Science and Business Informatics. They benefit from the availability of growing research funds, especially for topics related to AI. At the same time, they also suffer from the growing demand for graduates in the industry because that aggravates filling research positions. In addition, researchers sometimes face a subtle conflict. On the one hand, researchers may benefit from the hype, since research funds are often motivated by daring promises created through the hype. On the other hand, academia should maintain a critical attitude which may lead to unmasking the hype as such.

Apart from that, the digital transformation provides fantastic opportunities, and that also means: formidable challenges, for a wide range of academic studies. This is mainly for two epistemological reasons. First, understanding a system in general is hardly possible without studying how it behaves during change. Often, change will be limited to gradual modifications. The digital transformation, however, goes along with forces that may require radical change in a short period of time. Studying this kind of extensive change provides the opportunity to better understand fundamental system properties such as resilience, adaptability, and consistency. Since the digital transformation concerns interwoven technical, social, and psychological systems, it also allows for studying commonalities, differences, and interdependence of these different kinds of systems, thus contributing to the development of trans-disciplinary knowledge. Second, studying the digital transformation opens a path to an intriguing intellectual adventure. It is like a journey into unknown territory, a territory that is yet to be constructed with measures we do not know of, and that will confront us with questions that were never asked before.

Already today, the digital transformation leads to a plethora of challenging questions. Some of these questions are subject of this essay:
- What are typical drivers of the digital transformation and of automation in particular?
- What are essential differences between traditional programming and machine learning?
- Are traditional research methods still appropriate to study the digital transformation and to develop meaningful and attractive orientations for change?
- What is the role of academia in this process?
- What are convincing options to prepare for future change beyond prediction and prescription?

- In this respect, what is the role of models, theories, and of language?
- Is it possible to develop scientifically grounded orientations for change without transforming academia itself?

To discuss these questions, I will build on my primary academic education in Business Informatics, which mainly relates to the creation and use of information technology in organizations. However, such a specialist perspective is not sufficient to cope with essential facets of the digital transformation. While promoted predominantly by innovations in information technology, the transformation is, at its essence, related to problems that have been the subject of philosophical discourse for a long time. Among others, those problems comprise the ambivalent role of language for recognition as well as for mastering change, the limitations of truth as the pivotal criterion to justify scientific knowledge offerings, or the role of science within processes of social and political change. Therefore, I will, even though not a philosopher by education, dare to enrich the analysis of the digital transformation with a philosophical perspective. I beg the indulgence of those readers who are professional philosophers if my arguments appear too superficial.

## 2 Two principal approaches to automation

The last six decades are characterized by an ever-growing amount of manual work being replaced by software. To better understand this continuing process of automation, it is advisable to analyze general preconditions and objectives of software development. The class of problems to be solved by a software system should be formalized to a certain degree. That involves the data, the software operates on as well as the operations itself. Formalization requires the definition of syntactical and semantic rules that constrain the range of valid representations. General design objectives include integrity, reuse, integration, and adaptability. Integrity means that software should prevent system states that are not consistent with the specification, in other words: states that violate syntactic or semantic constraints. As we shall see, there are remarkable differences between traditional software development and machine learning in that respect. Reuse is, on the one hand, motivated by the demand for integrity. Based on the assumption that professionally developed software artefacts are available, it is valid to conclude that their reuse within the development of a particular software system will contribute to that system's integrity. On the other hand, reuse is the pivotal measure to reduce costs. First, it allows reducing development costs, since developers are not forced to always start from scratch. Second, it enables the reduction of costs per single copy if the software system is being used by many. Integration will often be an important design objective, too. To enable the integration of two systems, they need to have a common semantic reference system (cf. Frank 2011), that is, common data structures or common functions and events. Finally, software is expected to be adaptable since the requirements it is supposed to satisfy will often be subject of change. The more conveniently and safely the relevant modifications on software can be performed, the higher is its adaptability. The following two sections serve the purpose to reconstruct two principle approaches and compare them with respect to the prerequisites of automation and the objectives of software construction.

## 2.1 Reduction of contingency or adaptation to the limitations of machines

Software development requires unambiguous descriptions of problem classes that can be expected to be widely invariant across all present and future use cases. Hence, if propositions characterizing a problem class are true in one context and wrong in another, the automation of reliable problem-solving processes is not feasible. In addition, automation requires representations of data that are readable by machines in an unambiguous and unified way. The history of data processing is essentially characterized by a process of stepwise reduction of contingency. Note that is not relevant here, whether contingency is seen as an ontological property or rather the reflection of an epistemological limitation. The use of punch cards and similar media in the early days of data processing enabled machines to read symbols. In addition, it was required to make sure that the data represented on these media satisfied certain syntactical rules. Furthermore, there was need to reduce ambiguity by defining the (formal) semantics of data. The introduction of data types like String, Integer, etc. addresses this requirement. However, providing for machine readable media was not enough. In addition, the entire task, e.g., payroll accounting, has to be reorganized. Furthermore, the syntactical and semantic diversity of representations and problem-solving approaches needs to be targeted, too. Standardization is a pivotal instrument to reduce this kind of contingency and to promote economies of scale. Standardization also serves the integration of software systems: if they comply with certain standards regarding, e.g., data structures, they are enabled to communicate. Furthermore, standardization fosters economies of scale and protection of investment. In any case, reduction of contingency through the introduction of standards requires adapting problems and problem-solving procedures. In the past, this did not only comprise the reorganization of business processes, but also the reconstruction of entire new business models that are tuned to exploit the potential of software and IT in general.

While automation was possible only because reduction of contingency paved the way, this approach is not without downside. In general, it restricts the freedom of implementing individual solutions. In particular, preparing representations for machine readability may compromise their expressive power and, as a consequence, the quality of communication. A typical example is the use of software to handle customer requests. Standardization may be a threat to differentiation, and, hence, to competitiveness. It may also prevent services that are tailored to specific needs of particular customers. Standardization means to freeze a certain convention. Therefore, it may well be an obstacle to progress because the costs to deviate from a standard will often be prohibitively high.

The Internet is a special case. Its tremendous success seems to be based on both, the reduction of contingency through standardization, and the waiver of rules. On the one hand, the Internet is characterized by an enormous reduction of contingency. Among other things, this reduction is realized through the construction of a unified global address space for resources, organizations, and people that is enabled by a standardized technical infrastructure. As a consequence, the Internet enabled a tremendous wave of automation. On the other hand, the World Wide Web allows for almost total individual freedom regarding the representation of data. Furthermore, the set-up costs for representing data on web pages are relatively low. The lack of constraints promoted the global dissemination of the web. While the web enables the digital representation of the world to an unprecedented extent, it comes with clear downsides as far as automation is concerned. The data represented on web pages will often be of extremely contingent nature. Not only that it lacks semantics, furthermore, it will often be unclear whether it is consistent and up to date. The next approach to promote automation is supposed to deal with contingency, that is to leave contingent representations as they are and let machines cope with them.

## 2.2 "Intelligent" machines that cope with contingency or the pivotal role of data

When the term "artificial intelligence" was coined in the fifties of the last century, it was motivated by the idea of representing the cognitive capabilities of humans on a digital computer. The early enthusiasm created by this prospect was soon replaced by growing frustration and pragmatic adjustments of the original research objectives. No longer was it the claim to develop machines that can think like humans. Instead, the focus was directed toward the formalization of knowledge (cf. Frank 1988). This second wave of AI research was based on three central assumptions. First, qualified knowledge, that is expert knowledge, is pivotal for problem solving. Second, the application of knowledge requires basically logical operations. Third, an expert's knowledge can be formalized. The conception of so-called "knowledge-based" or "expert" systems followed these assumptions. Even though some of these systems achieved remarkable problem-solving capabilities, they did not fulfill the expectations they had created. That was mainly for two reasons. First, it turned out the human problem-solving competence can often not sufficiently be reconstructed with formalized knowledge. Second, these systems did not extend the limits of automation. Like any other software system, they require the specification of solution spaces or, in other words, they allow the automation of tasks only if the problem descriptions they are directed at are free from contingency. However, typically, not necessarily, knowledge-based systems feature a declarative representation of knowledge, which allows for monotonic extensions. Therefore, these systems are in general easier to maintain than procedural program code.

The third wave of AI, even though not well-defined as such, is characterized by a different approach. It does not necessarily require reducing the contingency of a problem representation. Related to that, software that falls into this category, does not have to be specified or programmed manually. Instead, software can be generated through a "learning" process that is based on "training" the structure of a network to gradually produce results from input data that correspond to what is expected from a satisfactory solution. The algorithms that are generated through this kind of "machine learning" (Murphy 2012) are based on induction. Therefore, the availability of mass data is a crucial prerequisite. With a huge number of people leaving their footprints in the net, and a growing armada of sensors, more and more facets of the world are represented by data – which, of course, does not tell much about the quality of this representation. Once a system has been trained sufficiently to produce satisfactory results for a given set of certain input data, it is assumed that it will work for other data of sets of that kind. Apart from the promise that machine learning will reduce software development costs dramatically, it also enables the automation of tasks without a precise specification of the problem or of satisfactory solutions. In other words: it promises to enable software that can cope with contingency, which would substantially extend the limits of automation. Examples of successful and in part very impressive uses of machine learning include natural language translation, face recognition, analysis of medical imaging systems, or so-called autonomous driving.

The success of these systems has fostered remarkable enthusiasm. One of the leading researchers in the field of machine learning claims: "All knowledge – past, present, and future – can be derived from data by a single, universal learning algorithm" (Domingos 2017: 25), "[...] and as a result of all this, our lives will be longer, happier, and more productive" (Domingos 2017: 43). A growing number of startup companies aim at implementing business models based on the promises made by machine learning. Managers regard machine learning as a "game changer" that companies need to take advantage of in order to survive (see, e.g., the survey in Sinclair/Brashear/Shacklady 2018). Politicians are eager to promote research and development of machine learning because it is regarded as a key factor for a national economy's competitiveness (see, e.g., Bundesregierung 2018). Authors of popular literature do not hesitate to make predictions of the economic and ethical impact of machine learning and to propose ideas how to cope with them (e.g., Boddington 2017; Precht 2018). While it is disturbing that many actors, including academics, make affirmative statements about the prospects of a technology most of them do not sufficiently understand, the role of machine learning within the digital transformation must not be underestimated. This is not only because machine learning opens new alleys for automation, but also because it inspires the imagination of millions and their reflection about the future. We will take a closer look at prospects and challenges of machine learning in the next section.

# 3 Methodological challenges

Given the tremendous relevance of the digital transformation, it seems reasonable to ask how science could support it. If we assume that the transformation will leave us with options, predictions that could be developed by studying the past are hardly possible. In other words: focusing on the factual is not sufficient, instead there is need to analyze the possible. Not surprisingly, such an endeavor leads to serious methodological problems. They are also caused by the specific nature of software, since future worlds are more and more penetrated by software, or even (re-)constructed by software. Therefore, I will at first analyze what software essentially is, and how it is developed and used.

## 3.1 The pivotal role of language

Software is an immaterial artefact. From a formal perspective, it can be regarded as an abstract machine that is defined by a set of operations to transform input data into output data. From an engineering perspective, software is realized through the execution of operations of a processor that has read and write access to some kind of data memory. While these views of software are important for formal analysis and the construction of computers, it is not sufficient to adequately describe software as a tool for humans. Software can represent a domain of interest and provide support for users only if it is supplemented with a linguistic representation that is accessible by humans. For that purpose, it is required to map formal structures and operations to concepts that correspond to those known by its prospective users. This kind of mapping is done through designators of software artefacts that refer to concepts known in the targeted domain. In other words, for software to be usable, it is mandatory that is has a conceptual foundation. Otherwise we cannot make sense of it. This is the case for the development of software as well as for its use. Conceptual models are of pivotal relevance when it comes to support the design of a coherent and consistent conceptual foundation. They aim at clear presentation of the concepts that are needed to understand and use the software. To reduce complexity, conceptual models will often focus exclusively on static, functional, or static aspects of software. Conceptual models are created with specific modeling languages the concepts of which should allow a clear mapping to constructs of implementation languages. Figure 1 shows a simple conceptual model and illustrates how it is mapped to code.

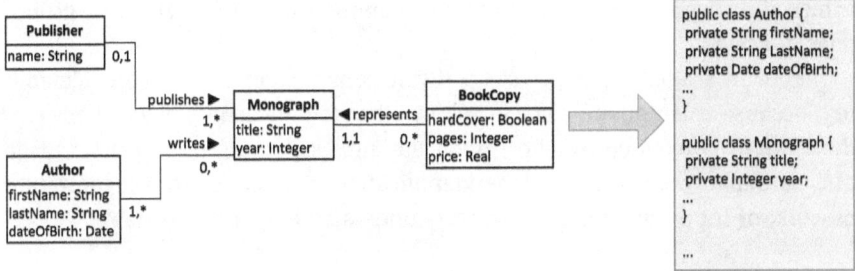

**Fig. 1:** Example of a conceptual model and mapping to code. (Credit: Ulrich Frank)

Note that it is not mandatory to develop an explicit conceptual model as it is shown in Figure 1. It is conceivable that programmers work with implicit conceptual models and represent them rudimentarily in code through designators. It is not only mandatory to conceptualized software when it is developed. If software is not supplemented with a representation that corresponds to concepts known in the relevant domain, it is not possible to use it.

It is not trivial to develop comprehensive and consistent conceptual models. Exceptional requirements may be overlooked. The possible variety of a subject may be inappropriately assessed. For example, in the simple model in Figure 1 a monograph is published by one publisher at the most. However, there are rare cases, where more than one publisher takes care of the publication of a monograph. If a conceptual model does not appropriately represent a domain, it is likely to result in software that does not fulfill the requirements. With respect to the economics of software, its reuse in many particular cases is of pivotal relevance in order to achieve economies of scale. However, that creates the challenge that the variety of requirements across the set of intended use cases needs to be accounted for. To that end, it is required to find, or construct, abstractions, that is, concepts, that are appropriate for the entire range of intended applications, and that allow for convenient and safe adaptation to more specific requirements. Especially in those application areas that are characterized by remarkable variety of requirements the quest for a wide range of reuse is a considerable challenge. A common strategy to cope with contingent requirements is to reduce contingency. This can be done by reducing or reconstructing a problem to fit it to the capabilities of computers: "Many of the problems that are popularly attributed to 'computerization' are the result of forcing our interactions into the narrow mold provided by a limited formalized domain." (Winograd/Flores 1986: 75) Similarly, the variety within a range of intended use cases can be reduced by creating incentives for users to adapt their requirements to a given software. This can be achieved through attractive terms and conditions which are enabled by economies of scale.

From an academic perspective, software construction is even more demanding, because it is not sufficient to ask whether requirements are satisfied. Furthermore, it is required to reflect upon the impact that the technical language of a particular domain has on the identification of problems, the organization of work, or for developing a satisfactory understanding of the domain.

> An awareness of one's own vocabulary is the first step to questioning it with a design attitude and exploring how different vocabularies yield more creative problem representations and enable the development of better designs. (Boland/Collopy 2004: 15)

That leads to the question whether the language we use to conceptualize a domain and to design software systems is adequate. The concepts that are identified during an analysis of a domain might be approved by domain experts. But that does not mean they are an appropriate foundation for structuring the domain, for identifying problems, for organizing work or for developing a satisfactory appreciation of the domain. The example in Figure 1 illustrates these aspects. Without resolving the ambiguity of a term such as "book," by distinguishing between monograph and printed book, it would hardly be possible to develop a consistent information system. At the same time, it is obvious that the concepts presented in the model are not sufficient to cover the variety of publications, since they do not account for edited books, journals, articles, etc.

Therefore, it is not only hard to tell whether requirements are complete, but furthermore whether they are appropriate since they are a reflection of concepts that might have been defined differently. The pivotal and delicate role that language plays for the analysis of requirements, as well as for the construction and use of software, becomes even more apparent in the light of the digital transformation.

## 3.2 In search of new languages

If we assume that the world is more and more constructed through software, it is essential to account for the role of software in times of change. If we further assume that the digital transformation creates new opportunities for the design of products, for the organization of work, or for the arrangement of social interactions, in other words: for new possible worlds, we are confronted with extraordinary methodological challenges. On the one hand, they relate to the evaluation and justification of our constructions. In many disciplines, justification is preferably based on a neo-positivist, "evidence-based" approach that reflects the correspondence theory of truth. However, developing possible future worlds that may serve as an orientation for change can hardly be tested against "reality," because they intentionally deviate from the "factual." In addition, the design of possible future worlds will involve value judgments. On the other hand, the challenges relate to the limits of recognition. Our primary tool to conceive of a possible future is the language we speak. However, at the same time, language limits our imagination, that is, the world we can conceive of (TLP 5.6). This limitation is necessary to cope with complexity and to establish sense. At the same time, we need to be aware of it if we do not want to give up the quest for a critical attitude:

> Our view is limited to what can be expressed in the terms we have adopted. This is not a flaw to be avoided in thinking – on the contrary, it is necessary and inescapable. Reflective thought is impossible without the kind of abstraction that produces blindness. Nevertheless we must be aware of the limitations that are imposed. (Winograd/Flores 1986: 97)

Being aware of this epistemological limitation is a necessary, but not sufficient prerequisite of relaxing it. Against this background, designing a possible future world is confronted with multiple contingencies and overwhelming complexity. Since there are many possible futures, we need to develop a space of possibilities that comprises those options that appear, for convincing reasons (!), to be the most desirable ones. While that requires a new language, it is not sufficient to follow Wittgenstein's advice: "We want to establish an order in our knowledge of the use of language: an order with a particular end in view; one out of many possible orders; not *the* order." (PI § 132) Instead, the choice or construction of a proper language is essential, or, as Rorty put it: "Philosophers have long wanted to understand concepts, but the point is to change them so as to make them serve our purposes better." (Rorty 2000: 25)

But how can we tell how this new, better language should look like, even if we agree with Rorty that it should be suited to foster "democratic politics" (Rorty 2000: 25)? How could we decide for a language that enables us to conceive a possible future world if both the language and the possibilities of the future are beyond our imagination? In any case, this constitutes an epistemologically extremely risky, if not hopeless situation that Derrida characterizes as an "absolute danger":

> The future can only be anticipated in the form of an absolute danger. It is that which breaks absolutely with constituted normality and can only be proclaimed, presented, as a sort of monstrosity. For that future world and for that within it which will have put into question the values of sign, word, and writing, for what which guides our future anterior, there is as yet no exergue. (Derrida 1976: 5)

## 3.3 Prospects and limitations of induction

The enthusiastic promises that accompany the third wave of AI are based on the power of induction and the availability of mass data. The inductive analysis of huge amounts of data may not only reveal patterns shared by many objects, and, thus, increase our knowledge about these objects. In addition, induction may also serve the automated construction of algorithms that enable the transformation of input data toward an intended result. Since induction is also relevant for human learning, especially in early age, it promotes the idea of machines that gradually learn from data to train their "neural" networks to an ever-growing level of "intelligence" that will eventually match or surpass human capabilities. Consequently, AI might be suited to automate scientific research, thus contributing to the growth of human recognition. Pentland, who already predicts the replacement of traditional social sciences by data driven "social physics," outlines an age of groundbreaking scientific achievements:

> For the first time, we will have the data required to really know ourselves and understand how our society evolves. By better understanding ourselves, we can potentially build a world without war or financial crashes, in which infectious disease is quickly detected and stopped [...] and in which governments are part of the solution rather than part of the problem. (Pentland 2014: 18–19)

Based on a similar assessment, Anderson predicts the "end of theory" and of "the scientific method" (Anderson 2008). There is no doubt that induction is suited to uncover facets of the world unknown to us. Induction has been applied to the analysis of, e.g., customer or voter behavior, to the assessment of applicants, or to the translation of natural languages – frequently with impressive results. However, induction as well as its limitations have been known for long. In machine learning, induction is a mechanical process of discovering common patterns. From an epistemological point of view, this is not satisfactory, because induction as pattern detection does not offer a convincing explanation. Rescher who appreciates induction as an instrument of inquiry, therefore proposes to regard induction as an act of "responsible estimation": "it is not just an estimate of the true answer that we want, but an estimate that is sensible and defensible: tenable, in short" (Rescher 1980: 9). Therefore, it does not seem appropriate to speak of inductive inference. Possible conclusions are "not derived from the observed facts, but invented in order to account for them" (Hempel 1966: 13).

Nevertheless, the promises of machine learning may appear intriguing. With large amounts of the world being digitized, and the availability of tremendous computing power, it seems conceivable that all regularities, both static and dynamic, that exist can be discovered by machines. That would leave us with the challenge to somehow justify these estimations. This problem could be addressed in a pragmatic way, that is, by redefining the concept of rational justification. That seems to happen already, when decision makers justify their decisions with patterns produced by inductive analysis of mass data. From an academic perspective, that would hardly be convincing. There is already growing awareness of the problem, which is, among others, expressed in the emergence of a new field of study named "explainable Artificial Intelligence" – a term that reflects a massive criticism of AI research, because it indicates that it lacks an essential part of any scientific knowledge offering, namely justification.

It goes beyond the scope of this essay to investigate the potential of automated induction. In addition to epistemological aspects that would also require accounting for economic and ethical issues. To give one example only: it may seem acceptable that the prediction of consumer behavior fails in some cases, however, this is likely to be different with software to enable "autonomous" driving. Apart from that, the potential of machine learning to replace human inquiry is questionable for two important reasons. First, only those phenomena can be subject of inductive analysis that allow for an appropriate digital representation and are suited for being investigated by machines. That, of course, relates to the old methodological conflict between neo-positivist and hermeneutic approaches. Second, with respect to develop images of possible future worlds in order to provide an orientation for change, induction suffers from a principal restriction. It depends on the analysis of data about the factual world. If we assume that the future is not entirely determined by historical path dependencies, relying on induction would clearly limit our options. Domingos does not deny that, even though he does not regard it as a problem: "We're only interested in knowledge about our world, not about worlds that don't exist" (Domingos 2017: 25).

## 3.4 Recognition and decision making without concepts?

Machine learning is not restricted to the inductive analysis of data that are supplemented with a conceptual definition. There are various approaches to machine learning that lack a conceptual foundation of this kind. Often, these approaches are referred to as "sub-symbolic," (see, e. g., Wichert 2013) which is misleading, because any representation on digital machines has to be symbolic. Solving problems without concepts is in clear contrast not only to the prevalent conception of science, it is furthermore hardly conceivable. Typical examples of this kind of machine learning include image and, in particular, face recognition, but also the detection of tumors. The simplified example in Figure 2 illustrates the principal idea. A traditional approach to software engineering would recommend a conceptualization of the problem, e. g., by introducing concepts like "eye," "nose," etc. Different from that, machine learning is based on digital representations of the images that do not include any conceptual information. After redundant data is removed, the resulting data sets serve as input to a "neural" network, which is trained until its weights are adjusted to produce the same characteristic number for all pictures of that person. If the network is to decide whether a further picture represents the same person, it compares the resulting number to the one that was produced during the training phase. If the number is close enough, it would be concluded that it is the same person. If the result is not satisfactory, the network could be refined through further training data.

The advantage of this approach is obvious. It does not only allow for a substantial reduction of development costs, it may even enable automation in cases where human developers would not be able to cope with the complexity of a

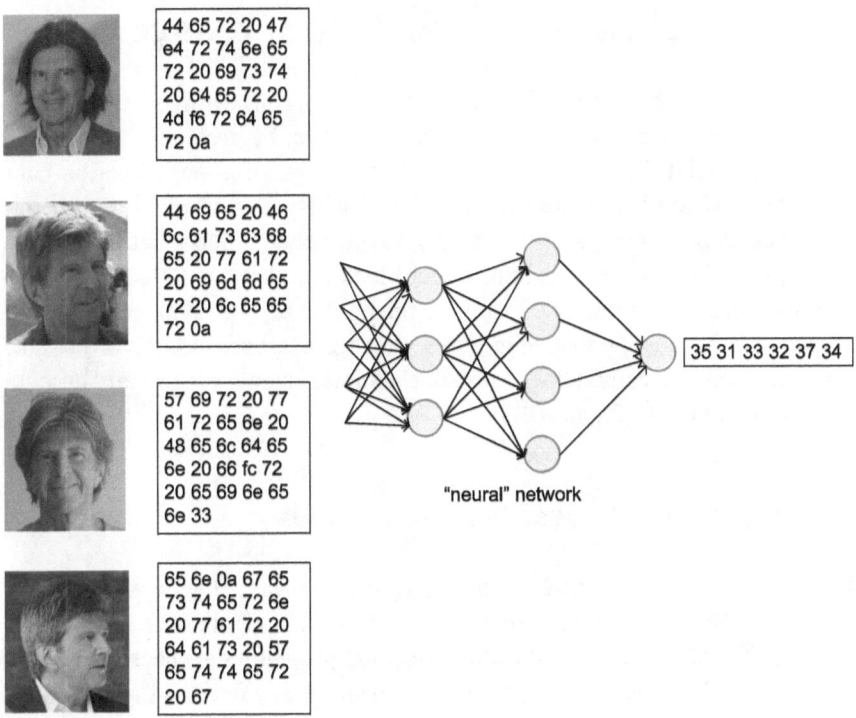

**Fig. 2:** Illustration of face recognition by a neural network, inspired by Murphy (2012). (Credit: Ulrich Frank)

problem. However, this advantage comes at a price. It cannot be guaranteed that the results will always be correct. Depending on the requirements of specific use cases, that may be acceptable or not. It is, in a way, similar to human perception: we can hardly explain it, and it may be deceptive. Nevertheless, it is extremely useful. However, from an academic perspective, it creates a serious problem. Since machine learning is part of university curricula, it should be based on justified recognition. If that is not the case, the approach of choice to evaluate neural networks are benchmarks, that is, testing the performance of a system against given data sets. If these systems perform sufficiently well, it is likely that they are used, and that the decisions they suggest are followed. Such a scenario is critical, because it is suited to shatter the idea of rationality and of enlightenment by giving up the quest for justification.

# 4 In a nutshell: A methodology of change

As we have seen, the methodological challenges that come with the digital transformation are enormous. One could only avoid them by deciding that research is not responsible for designing images of the future. However, taken the huge importance of the digital transformation for society as a whole, and also for the conception of science, that is hardly a convincing option. That leads us to the question how research methods could look like that are suited to develop an orientation for the digital transformation, or, if there is even need for a methodology of change. The following two sections give a brief outlook of possible features of such a methodology (a more elaborate, but still preliminary description can be found in Frank 2017).

## 4.1 Construction of possible future worlds

If the construction of possible future worlds is regarded as a scientifically grounded offering, prevalent research methods are of limited use only. They usually rely on some conception of truth and certain procedures to check the truth of propositions. In its purest form, scientific knowledge is offered as theories. However, as truth is not sufficient to justify possible future worlds, common concepts of theory are not suited to capture our imagination of the future. Giving up on truth or, at least, relaxing its pivotal role in the justification of knowledge, suggests looking for a new kind of methodology. I am reluctant to follow the radical turn that Rorty suggests:

> To say that one should replace knowledge by hope is to say much the same thing: that one should stop worrying about whether what one believes is well grounded and start worrying about whether one has been imaginative enough to think up interesting alternatives to one's present beliefs. (Rorty 1999: 34)

Nevertheless, I feel tempted by the idea to supplement knowledge with hope, which means to supplement the analysis of the factual with the search for the possible. As a consequence, there is need for an extended conception of theory. It should not only reflect descriptions/explanations of the "real," but also emphasize the need for an outlook beyond the factual. In any case, to develop and communicate our imagination of the future, we need models.

> The cognitive artifacts we create are models: representations to ourselves of what we do, of what we want, and of what we hope for. The model is not, therefore, simply a reflection or a

copy of some state of affairs, but beyond this, a putative mode of action, a representation of prospective action, or of acquired modes of action (Wartofsky 1979: xv).

The essential role of models as object and objectivation of our imagination is also emphasized by Wood who uses the term "map" instead. "And this, essentially is what maps give us, *reality*, a reality that exceeds our vision, our reach, the span of our days, a reality we achieve no other way" (Wood 1992: 4–5).

Focusing on models of possible worlds as a subject and outcome of scientific inquiry does not mean to give up on theories as the pivotal representation of scientific knowledge. If we regard theories in the sense of the original meaning as an outlook beyond the ostensible, they would also comprise possible worlds. The concept of "possible worlds" is used in logic to overcome the limitation that a sentence must be either true or false (*tertium non datur*). Modal logic allows for assigning a proposition to many possible worlds. While in each of these worlds the *tertium non datur* postulate is satisfied, the overall picture allows for a contingent truth value. The "many-worlds interpretation" of quantum physics that assumes the co-existence of multiple parallel worlds, has been around for long (cf. Carroll 2019; DeWitt 1970; Everett 1957). An extended concept of theory that would also comprise models of the possible would mean to supplement "committed cognitive claim to truth" (Wartofsky 1979: 2) with the pragmatic claim to usefulness.

With respect to guiding change, models of possible worlds need to satisfy two main postulates. First, a possible future world must be feasible. Second, research should focus on those possible worlds that seem to be particularly attractive, which will usually imply that they are better than the actual world. While both postulates, especially the second, create a substantial challenge with respect to justification, the creation of possible worlds is not supposed to prescribe "scientifically grounded" blueprints of a bright future. Instead, they are intended as knowledge offerings that might serve those who will actually create the future as an inspiration and as a guidance. Regarding the digital transformation, conceptual models are of pivotal relevance, since they form the foundation for software systems, which in turn will chiefly contribute to the construction of the future. But how could a method guide the design of such models if we account for the challenge to somehow overcome the limitations of the language we speak? There is no clear recipe to meet this challenge. There are, however, two approaches that seem useful: stepwise destruction and construction of concepts through abstraction. These approaches are core elements of a new paradigm of conceptual modeling called multilevel modeling (cf. Atkinson/Kühne 2001; Frank 2014). Conventional conceptual modeling is done with a given modeling language that defines the scope of possible models. Multilevel modeling allows to modify the language itself during the act of modeling. Furthermore, an arbitrary number of language levels is possible, where each additional level represents an abstraction of existing terms. The abstraction comprises both, classification and generalization. Adding a further level of abstraction also means to increase the range of possible models, that is, of possible worlds that are covered by that language. In case, multilevel models are executable, one aspect of the feasibility postulate is satisfied. Unfortunately, a more detailed description of multilevel modeling is beyond the scope of this essay. The model in Figure 1 may serve to illustrate the principal idea. The concept "BookCopy" could be abstracted onto a concept like "PaperRepresentation," which could be further abstracted onto "Representation," etc. "Representation" would create the question, what kind of representations are conceivable, which may, among others, lead to the concept of digital representation. From a functional perspective, one could ask for the purpose of a model. At first, it might be "publication," which could then be abstracted to something like "communication" and "documentation." Communication could then be further differentiated to new concepts that enable distinguishing different kinds of communication. This kind of critical deconstruction and reconstruction would not only help to conceive of a future that will be constituted by a language yet not known, it would also broaden our perspective on the current world:

> All formation of new concepts, all change in concepts, involves discovery of the world – that is, the development of a new way of looking at the world [...] which may be more or less borne out as time goes on. Every theory of formation of new concepts is also about discovering the way the world is. (Schön 1963: 34)

However, not every (re-)construction of possible future worlds will be convincing. Therefore, the justification of models of possible future worlds is of crucial importance. Truth in general, and especially the correspondence theory of truth, are of little use in that respect – even though aspects of feasibility will usually include propositions that can be assigned a truth value. The only way to achieve satisfactory justification of what we regard as useful and what we find worth hoping for is through discourse and agreement. But that, of course, comes with the notorious challenge to evaluate whether those who participate in a discourse are sufficiently qualified. With respect to the pivotal role of machine learning, it will be important to emphasize the need for a justification of results achieved through induction, both from an epistemological and an economic point of view.

## 4.2 The role of narratives

The design of conceptual models that describe substantial parts of the organization of future worlds (mainly through software) may provide valuable guidelines for change but is not sufficient. First, conceptual models intentionally fade out all aspects that bulk against formalization and automation. Second, the future is not created through an act of engineering that is guided by models developed by scientists. In the end, it needs to be constructed by those who live in the future. Hence, they have to be involved. That will be possible only if the vision of a possible world makes sense to them. In other words: a possible future world can serve as an orientation for change only if people can imagine how it would be to live in such a world. Only then they can participate in a discourse about its evaluation and contribute to its evolution. But how could sense be mediated? Probably, the most effective approach to mediating sense is story telling. "Narratives are about people acting in a setting, and the happenings that befall them must be relevant to their intentional states [...]" (Bruner 1991: 7). In order to provide for sense-making, a story needs to connect to the practices that form people's lives. However, at the same time, it should support their imagination to overcome the limitations of practices they take for granted. This is a serious challenge. It is needless to say that narratives that serve as a supplement to models and theories must not be confused with science fiction. Instead, narratives of possible worlds should aim at a differentiated picture of possible future worlds that include comprehensible descriptions of prospects, conflicts, and threats. In addition, it should of course be made clear that narratives of this kind address a contingent matter: the future they describe should be possible, but that neither means that it will become reality, nor that there is a deterministic way to achieve it.

Since narratives are not an accepted medium to communicate scientific knowledge, there are no corresponding examples of scientific publications – at least none that I would know of. However, there are a few authors that create images of a possible future who use a narrative like style to reach a broader audience. Lanier, for example, outlines the vision of a future, democratic version of the Internet, not only by describing technical details, but also by using narratives (Lanier 2013). Van Reybrouck performs a reconstruction of the concept of democracy to propose possible future models of democratic politics (cf. Van Reybrouck 2016). In addition to a critical analysis of current implementations of democracy, he also illustrates his ideas with narratives.

## 5 Instead of conclusions

We are living in challenging times, in times of change and contradiction. We cannot predict the future, but we may be able to support a transformation to the better. To that end, it is not advisable to follow the traditional path of scientific inquiry that is restricted to the past and the present. It seems more appropriate to extend the scope of our interest to the investigation of possible future worlds. As I outlined only briefly, such a research program is hardly compatible with established research methods. Furthermore, it is confronted with tremendous methodological problems. The approaches I proposed as elements of a method or even a methodology of change are no solutions but create further challenges. Against this background, one may feel tempted to avoid the risk, that is, to continue focusing on the "factual" and fade out the possible. That, however, would mean to miss a fantastic opportunity. Is it not most inspiring to not only ask why things are, but how they could be? That includes the troubling question, how our cognitive capabilities, how our imagination, how *we* would change if we managed to acquire new languages that include concepts based on abstractions we are not yet aware of. And, of course, we would compromise our credibility if we did not also ask how academia could be changed to serve its purpose better. I agree with Lewis who argues that the idea of possible worlds creates a "philosopher's paradise" (here I would like to add: not only a paradise for philosophers): "We have only to believe in the vast realm of *possibilia*, and there we find what we need to advance our endeavours" (Lewis 1986: 4).

## References

Anderson, Chris (2008): "The End of Theory: The Data Deluge Makes the Scientific Method Obsolete." In: *Wired* 23 June 2008. https://www.wired.com/2008/06/pb-theory/, accessed 21 March 2020.

Atkinson, Colin/Kühne, Thomas (2001): "The Essence of Multilevel Metamodeling." In: Gorgolla, Martin/Kobryn, Cris (Eds.): *"UML 2001" – The Unified Modeling Language: Modeling Languages, Concepts, and Tools*. New York, NY: Springer, pp. 19–23.

Boddington, Paula (2017): *Towards a Code of Ethics for Artificial Intelligence*. New York, NY: Springer.

Boland, Richard/Collopy, Fred (2004): "Design Matters for Management." In: Boland, Richard/Collopy, Fred (Eds.): *Managing as Designing*. Stanford, CA: Stanford Business Books, pp. 3–18.

Bruner, Jerome (1991): "The Narrative Construction of Reality." In: *Critical Inquiry* 18(1), pp. 1–21.

Bundesregierung (2018): *Strategie Künstliche Intelligenz der Bundesregierung.* https://www.bmbf.de/files/Nationale_KI-Strategie.pdf, accessed 21 March 2020.
Carroll, Sean (2019): *Something Deeply Hidden.* Munich: Random House.
Derrida, Jacques (1976): *Of Grammatology.* Baltimore, MD: Johns Hopkins University Press.
DeWitt, Bryce S. (1970): "Quantum Mechanics and Reality: Could the Solution to the Dilemma of Indeterminism Be a Universe in Which All Possible Outcomes of an Experiment Actually Occur?" In: *Physics Today* 23(9), pp. 30–35.
Domingos, Pedro (2017): *The Master Algorithm: How the Quest for the Ultimate Learning Machine Will Remake Our World.* London: Penguin.
Everett, Hugh (1957): "'Relative State' Formulation of Quantum Mechanics." In: *Reviews of Modern Physics* 29(3), pp. 454–462.
Frank, Ulrich (1988): *Expertensysteme: Neue Automatisierungspotentiale im Büro- und Verwaltungsbereich?* Wiesbaden: Gabler.
Frank, Ulrich (2011): *Multi-Perspective Enterprise Modelling: Background and Terminological Foundation.* ICB Research Report No. 46. https://www.icb.wiwi.uni-due.de/fileadmin/fileupload/ICB/research/research_reports/ICB-Report-No46.pdf, accessed 21 March 2020.
Frank, Ulrich (2014): "Multilevel Modeling: Toward a New Paradigm of Conceptual Modeling and Information Systems Design." In: *Business & Information Systems Engineering* 6(6), pp. 319–337.
Frank, Ulrich (2017): "Theories in the Light of Contingency and Change: Possible Future Worlds and Well-Grounded Hope as a Supplement to Truth." In: *Proceedings of the 50th Annual Hawaii International Conference on System Sciences*, pp. 5727–5736.
Habermas, Jürgen (1976): "Technik und Wissenschaft als 'Ideologie'." In: *Technik und Wissenschaft als "Ideologie."* Frankfurt a. M.: Suhrkamp, pp. 48–103.
Hempel, Carl G. (1966): *Philosophy of Natural Science.* Upper Saddle River, NJ: Prentice Hall.
Lanier, Jaron (2013): *Who Owns the Future?* New York, NY: Simon & Schuster.
Lewis, David (1986): *On the Plurality of Worlds.* Oxford: Blackwell.
Murphy, Kevin P. (2012): *Machine Learning: A Probabilistic Perspective.* Cambridge, MA: MIT Press.
Pentland, Alex (2014): *Social Physics: How Good Ideas Spread – The Lessons from a New Science.* Melbourne: Scribe.
Precht, Richard David (2018): *Jäger, Hirten, Kritiker: Eine Utopie für die digitale Gesellschaft.* Munich: Goldmann.
Rescher, Nicholas (1980): *Induction: An Essay on the Justification of Inductive Reasoning.* Pittsburgh, PA: University of Pittsburgh Press.
Rorty, Richard (1999): *Philosophy and Social Hope.* New York, NY: Penguin.
Rorty, Richard (2000): "Universality and Truth." In: Brandom, Robert B. (Ed.): *Rorty and His Critics.* Malden, MA: Blackwell, pp. 1–30.
Schön, Donald A. (1963): *Displacement of Concepts.* London: Tavistock.
Sinclair, Andrew/Brashear, Jeffrey/Shacklady, John (2018): *AI: The Momentum Mindset.* https://www.accenture.com/_acnmedia/pdf-73/accenture-strategy-ai-momentum-mindset-exec-summary-pov.pdf, accessed 21 March 2020.
Van Reybrouck, David (2016): *Against Elections: The Case for Democracy.* London: The Bodley Head.
Wartofsky, Marx W. (1979): *Models: Representation and the Scientific Understanding.* Dordrecht: Reidel.

Wichert, Andreas (2013): "Proto Logic and Neural Subsymbolic Reasoning." In: *Journal of Logic and Computation* 23(3), pp. 627–643.
Widdicombe, Lizzie (2014): "The Programmer's Price." In: *The New Yorker* 24 November 2014, pp. 54–64.
Winograd, Terry/Flores, Fernando (1986): *Understanding Computers and Cognition: A New Foundation for Design*. Norwood, NJ: Ablex.
Wittgenstein, Ludwig (1961) [TLP]: *Tractatus Logico-Philosophicus*. London: Routledge & Kegan Paul.
Wittgenstein, Ludwig (1973) [PI]: *Philosophical Investigations*. Oxford: Prentice Hall.
Wood, Denis (1992): *The Power of Maps*. New York, NY: Guilford Press.

Sally Haslanger
# Methods of Social Critique

**Abstract:** Social critique takes aim at institutions, practices, and structures from a position embedded within those institutions, practices, and structures. It is not a project in ideal theory, but does it depend on ideal theory? This paper considers three methods of nonideal theory: the medical model, the applied ideal theory model, and the critical theory model, with a focus on the latter two. It argues that the method of applied ideal theory, understood as a domain-specific, relatively a priori reflective equilibrium (as Scanlon interprets Rawls), suffers from a version of normative status quo bias. This is inadequate to challenge the effects of ideology. The paper goes on to sketch a version of social critique that draws on oppositional consciousness and suggests that some forms of consciousness raising can provide a better epistemic basis for social critique.

**Keywords:** Social critique, ideal theory, nonideal theory, medical model, critical social theory

## 1 Social critique

The target of social critique is, in the first instance, a practice or set of social practices.[1] For example, social critique might take aim at the consumption of the flesh of dead animals, the hetero-bio-normative construction of families, or the construction of sexual desire through pornography. But because the practices in question are linked to other practices, policies, and laws, social critique quickly widens to target broad social structures and systems. Practices of food consumption occur within and are shaped by the imperatives of capitalist food production and distribution; the practice of traditional marriage, parenting, and gender socialization is an enforcement of compulsory heterosexuality and the sex/gender binary; and the mass consumption of pornography reinforces rape culture. The project of critique is to reveal the systematic and harmful forms of social coordination as they unfold in a particular historical context and to promote change. As a consequence:

---

[1] A further articulation of ideas developed in this paper, with some repetition, will appear in my "Political Epistemology and Social Critique," forthcoming in *Oxford Studies in Political Philosophy*.

- The site of critique is *the social domain*. This includes both individuals and the state. But the primary issues concern what practices we should engage in, what social norms we should embrace, how we should go on, from here, together. Our inquiry is *collective, practice-directed, and embedded*.
- There are many perfectly acceptable ways to organize social life, so the goal is not to ask what the *best* way to do this is; the project is *antiutopian*, but does require imagination and hope (Wright 2010; Solnit 2016). The goal is to identify – from an embedded standpoint – ways in which our practices are inadequate so we can do better. Injustice is rampant. Rectification is a priority.

What methods are apt for social critique? Note that the project of social critique is not the same as the project of political philosophy, narrowly construed, i.e., as concerned with the legitimacy and boundaries of the state. For example, in the context of liberal democracies, there are limitations on what the state can do to interfere in forms of life and cultural expression. These limitations are not, or not obviously, binding on individuals (cf. Murphy 1998). If I am a participant in a community in which the consumption of violent pornography is rampant, or one in which adopted or nonbinary children are ridiculed, it is perfectly reasonable for me to regard these practices as bad for the community and to work to change the social norms and practices that govern us. This is not the same thing as a state passing laws or policies to prohibit such activities. I have argued elsewhere that culture is a proper target of critique, for culture is a crucial component of social structures; state actions alone are not sufficient to bring about social change for the better (Haslanger 2017). Social critique is also not, or not obviously, situated within ethics, narrowly construed. The question is not simply what I should do, as an individual, given my concerns with the actions of others in their personal consumption of pornography, or with actions that marginalize certain children or families. The questions are about what social norms should govern us as a community, what values we uphold, how we should live together.

There are two steps in the project of critique. The first is epistemic: If the community is currently organized to uphold certain values through its social norms, on what basis can an individual or group legitimately challenge these values or norms and make a warranted claim against the community to change the culture, i.e., change the form of life? Even if the state may not intervene, surely there are other measures that might be taken. This happens all the time. Schools and universities articulate mottos, mission statements, and the like, and expect their members to conform their behavior accordingly. Teachers can demand that students in their class interact on terms that cannot and should not be enforced outside the classroom. Parents uphold values in the daily practices of family life. Friends and social groups do the same. In some of these contexts, if one is unhappy with the terms of coordination, one can simply exit; or if a group does not want to hear the complaints of a member, they can be ignored or encouraged to leave the group. But these are not always acceptable or feasible options. More importantly, if there is a warranted critique, then the social practices should be adjusted. This leads us to the second step, which we might consider broadly political: How should warranted critique be taken up? What process should be employed for deciding what changes are apt and how to implement them? Again, this is not a question of state intervention. It is about shaping a community.

My focus in this paper is on the epistemic question. Can social critique rely on the standard methods of political epistemology? What else is available? I will begin by sketching two different models, the "medical model" and the "applied ideal theory model." I will then propose that critical social theory provides a better option. I will not address the political question of what we should do – how we should proceed – in the face of a warranted critique.

## 2 Ideal and nonideal theory

In social/political philosophy, there has been an ongoing debate about the value of ideal theory. Although what counts as "ideal theory" is controversial, one version relies on two related methodological principles. Following Mikkola (2017), they are:
- The (normative) *priority thesis:* We need to know what justice is in order to remedy current injustice.
- The *distancing thesis:* In order to know what justice is, we must abstract away from the messy reality of our lives and understand the nature of justice through reflection on cases that isolate the normative aspects of the phenomenon. This requires consideration of distant and idealized possibilities.

Some theorists endorse only one or the other thesis (or modified versions of each),[2] but Adam Swift embraces the combination quite explicitly:

> [...] only by reference to philosophy – abstract, pure, context-free philosophy – can we have an adequate basis for thinking how to promote justice in our current, radically nonideal, circumstances. (Swift 2008: 382)

---

[2] For example, Shelby (2016: 11, 13) explicitly embraces the priority thesis, but seems to reject the distancing thesis.

The issue of ideal theory has also been raised in other philosophical domains as well: Should we focus first on cooperative (versus uncooperative) communication; on knowledge (versus ignorance)? And the answer has increasingly been no, or not always.

Setting aside the question of how to define ideal or nonideal theory, it is undeniable that in undertaking social critique, we need to understand the complexity of the actual situation to diagnose the problem. We cannot critique the racism in the public-school system, or the sexism in pornography, or the marginalization of the poor, unless we have a theory of where and how the wrong occurs. Empirical research is required. So, insofar as social critique requires application of moral considerations to real world circumstances, it is plausibly a form of nonideal theory. But the question still remains, how should we proceed? How do we undertake nonideal theory in pursuing social critique? What is the relationship between empirical inquiry, moral inquiry, and critique?

## 3 The medical model

In a number of works, Tommie Shelby has described and criticized a "medical model" of social critique. In a critique of Anderson (2010), he says:

> On [the medical] model, the persistent cries of injustice and other grievances of members of society are conceived as symptoms (like headaches, fatigue, and insomnia) to be treated by empirically grounded interventions, which are conceived as potential cures for social ills. The justice doctor, concerned about the health of the polity, attempts to discover the "underlying causes of the complaints" ([Anderson 2010] p. 4), which may differ, perhaps radically, from what those who initially raised the complaints believe is the proper diagnosis. After careful empirical analysis and social experiments, the linchpin of the social problem is identified and actions are taken to remove it, with the hope that the troubling symptoms eventually fade away and the patient is healed. (Shelby 2014: 256)[3]

According to the "social engineering" approach Shelby has in mind, technocrats analyze the problem piecemeal rather than treating it as systematic; they pro-

---

**3** Shelby introduces the medical model in the context of discussing Anderson's (2010) book. He allows that there are different threads in her methodology, and this is only one. I myself interpret Anderson as a more thoroughgoing pragmatist who places great weight on the power of social movements (see Anderson 2014). Moreover, the brief description of the model quoted is a bit misleading, for what is essential is not simply that it provides an empirically informed "diagnosis" of the problem and seeks a "cure." His criticism is aimed at those who offer targeted fixes that make the symptoms go away without addressing the deeper injustice that requires substantive normative theory to identify and address.

pose targeted interventions rather than broad structural changes; they avoid substantive normative inquiry; and they mostly rely on nudging individuals to act in ways that, as judged by experts, further the common good.[4] Examples of such nudges include using "the structure of welfare benefits to deter nonmarital childbearing," and "the promotion of marriage or stable unions and cohabitation between parents who share a child" (Shelby 2016: 121–122).

Shelby (2016: 2) offers several criticisms of the medical model, as it applies to ghetto poverty in particular:

1) *Status quo bias:* "[...] policymakers working within the medical model treat the background structure of society as given and focus only on alleviating the burdens of the disadvantaged." To address the problems systematically, we must make broad structural changes.
2) *Downgraded agency:* "[...] the technocratic reasoning of the medical model marginalizes the political agency of those it aims to help." The oppressed are "passive victims in need of assistance" and resistance is often interpreted as pathology. Instead, we should view the oppressed through a lens that properly recognizes forms of resistance and dissent that affirm self-worth and a commitment to justice (2016: ch. 9).
3) *Unjust-advantage blindspot:* "[...] focusing on the problems of the disadvantaged can divert attention from or obscure the numerous ways in which the advantaged unfairly benefit from an unjust social structure." The advantaged claim credit for agency that is simply enabled by their circumstances. The relationality of oppression is obscured.

Paul Taylor (2017) mentions another concern in the background of Shelby's discussion: On the medical model "the normative and political-theoretic dimensions of the problem too easily drop out, giving way to putatively dispositive appeals to the empirical." This aptly calls attention to Shelby's emphasis on the

---

[4] Titus Stahl has pointed out that these various elements of what Shelby calls the "medical model" might be usefully separated. In particular, setting aside the issues concerning systematic versus targeted approaches and the avoidance of normativity, one might take the essential feature of the medical model to be an epistemic privileging of moral "experts," i.e., the justice doctors. If an adequate approach should not invoke moral expertise, then plausibly all three of the views face this problem in some form. Stahl would suggest that, in contrast, the Frankfurt School Critical Theory tradition avoids this by pointing out the epistemic barriers to coordination on just terms and by empowering communities to rethink their own forms of coordination without such barriers (Stahl 2017; also Celikates 2018). As should become clear in my discussion below, I am skeptical of attempts to draw sharp lines between the epistemic and the moral.

importance of moral theory in the context of policy debates (see 2016: Introduction).

By what method does the medical model promote social justice? According to one interpretation, the project is to employ social choice theory to maximize (informed?) preference satisfaction. We assume that preferences are revealed through behavior (and we adjust for ignorance and irrationality?). We then find ways to incentivize people to form and pursue their preferences in actions that achieve and sustain some state of optimality.

The method just sketched can look very "empirical" and "value neutral": The theorist takes personal preferences at face value without "imposing" their own values; identifies problems that prevent preferences from being satisfied; and proposes empirically tested interventions to produce better solutions, as determined by a more optimal distribution of preference satisfaction.

However, the method has serious drawbacks for social critique. First, the claim that we ought to maximize preference satisfaction is a controversial moral claim that is not "value neutral." The normative assumptions are simply assumed rather than defended. Second, the approach is unable to cope with the problem of ideology or adaptive preferences. Maximizing revealed preference satisfaction is unlikely to achieve justice if individual action is rationally pursued within a choice architecture that unjustly limits one's options. Moreover, choice is constrained by the symbolic resources that are available within a social milieu: What we choose is constrained by what we can conceive or find intelligible. Under conditions of ideology, the cultural frame for agency is distorted. Third, the conception of preference employed by the approach is a poor indicator of what people value and what is valuable. It does not distinguish wants, needs, and commitments; it assumes a monistic conception of value on which all that is valuable is comparable; and it assumes a stability – context independence – of preferences that does not recognize the extent and depth of our sociality. (This third concern is elaborated in, e.g., Anderson (2000); Anderson (2001); Ben-Ner/Putterman (1998); Banerjee/Duflo (2019: ch. 4).) I agree with Shelby's criticisms of the medical model, so I will not offer further critique of it here. Are there other models?

## 4 Applied ideal theory

An alternative to the medical model is the applied ideal theory model. Rather than consider all forms of purportedly ideal theory, I will focus on one, but a familiar one, and argue that it is not well-suited to provide the normative basis for social critique. According to this model, we (philosophers) undertake a form of relatively a priori theory to establish the principles of justice. In spite of controversy over the term 'ideal theory,' a common practice in political theory is to employ a relatively a priori method of *domain-specific reflective equilibrium*. Following Scanlon's interpretation of Rawls, in the domain of normative inquiry, the goal is to provide a consistent theory that does justice to our considered moral judgments and intuitions concerning normative matters, specifically, judgments and intuitions that are empirically and metaphysically uncontroversial. Such a method can be used to generate normative principles about what we owe to each other, how we ought to organize society, and answers to a broad range of other questions; the task is to reflect on the judgments and intuitions from the perspective of a deliberating agent (Scanlon 2003: 148–149). In seeking social justice, an "ideal theory," as I will use the term here, is one that relies on this method to generate the principles governing how we ought to live together in communities.[5]

To apply the resulting "ideal" theory, we consult with social scientists to give us the more controversial facts, and by applying our principles to the facts, we determine where and how our current circumstances fall short of the principles. This presupposes the priority thesis: To make a (warranted) judgment of injustice, one must apply a (warranted) principle of justice. We then rely on policy makers for suggestions about how to bring about change satisfying the principles, making sure that the content and methods for implementation do not violate the normative requirements. Thus, the method distributes labor between (relatively) a priori enquiry, empirical social science, and strategic policy initiatives. On this view, the focus on unjust conditions and *corrective justice* are what make the philosophical project one of nonideal theory.[6] In short, nonideal theory is a form of applied ideal theory.

For our purposes, there are two features to note about this method. First, the reflective equilibrium is domain-specific, i.e., it is concerned only with certain normative judgments and intuitions that "seem to us most clearly to be true about moral matters if anything is" (Scanlon 2003: 145), rather than all of our judgments, intuitions, and other attitudes. The result is not, therefore, what

---

[5] Stemploska (2008) defends ideal theory against those who complain that either it implausibly assumes compliance, that it relies on false premises, that it does not yield "viable recommendations" that can be acted upon, or that it can never be realized. Note that I do not characterize the ideal/nonideal distinction in these terms, nor am I raising these concerns here. Not all mainstream theories of justice employ this method, e.g., the Capability Approach does not, neither is it an ideal theory, on my view.

[6] This is in keeping with the Rawlsian idea that ideal theory assumes full compliance and nonideal theory is theory that does not make this assumption.

would be required of rational agents *per se* (since rational agents should, presumably, take all considerations, all evidence, into account). Second, in order to have wide acceptance, the method must avoid starting with controversial judgments and intuitions; otherwise we could end up with a parochial theory that did not function as a tool for guidance in the face of moral disagreements.

Scanlon considers the criticism that this method of reflective equilibrium can yield only consistency in normative inquiry. Consistency may be necessary for an adequate theory, but it is hardly sufficient, as his example of a consistent but false astrology demonstrates:

> Morality will be in an analogous situation [to astrology] if, but only if, it too has "external commitments" – that is, only if the reasonableness of taking moral judgments seriously depends on claims that go beyond morality itself and lie in, for example, physics, psychology, metaphysics, or the theory of rational choice.
>
> Rawls holds that morality, or at least justice, has no controversial empirical or metaphysical presuppositions. (Scanlon 2003: 146)

In other words, astrology can get things (factually) wrong because it makes controversial empirical claims. Morality cannot get things (factually) wrong because its empirical and metaphysical presuppositions are so obvious and, presumably, hold across all relevant possibilities. This is one place where the distancing thesis plays a role: Because we are seeking principles that capture the nature of justice, we must be prepared to claim that they hold in all possible situations. To achieve this, we must abstract away from actual circumstances to focus on those commonalities that hold between the actual world and others very distant from us. This is why elaborate thought experiments are necessary.

Note that if we do not allow empirical facts specific to our world to impinge upon our moral theorizing, this leaves open the threat of relativism; different individuals (or social groups) will begin with their own judgments, intuitions, and "uncontroversial" assumptions and find their own reflective equilibrium (2003: 152–153). Scanlon suggests that we should accept relativism as a distant possibility, but because "we" are so far from achieving reflective equilibrium, the threat of relativism should not lead us to give up on objective morality (2003: 153). He recommends that those engaged in the different efforts to reach reflective equilibrium – efforts with different starting points – should continue until they get things straight before worrying about whether or not there are fundamental moral disagreements that would lead to relativism.

Moral theory cannot avoid all empirical claims, but on this approach, it cannot get things (factually) wrong because its empirical and metaphysical presuppositions are so obvious and, presumably, hold across all relevant possibilities (see Scanlon 2003: esp. 146). However, if our starting normative judgments and intuitions are misguided, the method is unlikely to reveal it. It would seem, then, that the method builds in a normative status quo bias. If we do not have an uncontroversial description of the phenomenon in question, or do not have an agreed upon normative vocabulary for making judgments about it, then the method treats it as outside the scope of the project and offers no resources for addressing it. Outlier judgments are set aside. However, such redescriptions of the social domain and resulting outlier judgments are typically the source of social critique.

This suggests that applied ideal theory is not the best strategy for social critique. In the next section I will provide reasons for thinking that the priority and distancing theses both limit ideal theory in ways that are problematic. I will then consider whether the limits of ideal theory can be overcome once we draw on empirical methods to provide descriptions of the unjust circumstances we are trying to address. I will argue that, at least in some cases, social critique does not fit the model of applied ideal theory. Rather than relying on theoretically derived moral principles and empirical research, such critique disrupts both our modes of valuing and our understanding of the social world. Because values inform our interpretation of the facts, and the facts, in turn, shape the specification of the relevant values, the distinction between facts and values becomes, at best, blurred.

## 5 Limits of ideal theory for critique

I argued in the previous section that an ideal theory developed through a relatively a priori domain-specific reflective equilibrium is at risk of status quo bias. This is not to claim that it is never useful, or that we should avoid it. My claim is that the social critic needs to draw on other resources and strategies. In particular, the social critic should reject the priority claim. We do not need to *know what justice is* or have a complete moral theory to engage in social critique (thank goodness!) (Wolff 2018; Hampshire 2000: Preface). For example, injustice may not be a proper kind: Iris Young argues plausibly that there are five irreducible faces of oppression (Young 1990). And although we may need something like a moral theory – or modal knowledge of what sorts of things make something an injustice – to solve *all* of our problems, it is surely not the case that such knowledge is required in order to make moral progress or to remedy significant wrongs. After all, even ideal theory *begins with* moral commitments, e. g., that slavery is wrong, that rape is wrong, that we should not cause unnecessary suffering. We do not need *theory* to recognize these wrongs or to make progress in preventing them. We can begin with knowledge of particular forms of injustice.

The distancing thesis is also dubious because some objective values are path-dependent, so reflection on possibilities epistemically accessible from where we are now may not be a good guide to how we should go on from here. Envisioning new ways of life not only needs imagination, but cultural and material change that may not be anticipated or imagined. Jack M. Balkin (1998) makes this point persuasively. What is valuable depends, inter alia, on what is available to value:

> Values are not so much what humans have as what they do and feel. Human beings possess an inexhaustible drive to evaluate, to pronounce what is good and bad, beautiful and ugly, advantageous and disadvantageous. Without culture, human values are inchoate and indeterminate; through culture they become differentiated, articulated, and refined. (Balkin 1998: 27–28)

To develop this idea, Balkin relies on examples of music:

> Before culture there are no electric guitars, violins, or orchestras. There is no art of orchestration, no sonata-allegro form, no idea of jazz or the blues. There is only the human delight in producing and listening to interesting and beautiful sounds. Throughout human history people develop different ways of making and organizing sounds, which they test against their developing sense of beauty and interest. Their sense of the beautiful and the interesting in turn is developed through exposure to and use of the cultural tools available to them within their culture. (Balkin 1998: 28)

More generally, over time, the cultural articulation of value involves both a refinement of old values and a creation of new ones (Balkin 1998: 28). This line of thought also applies to moral value.

> We concretize our indeterminate value of justice by creating human institutions and practices that attempt to enforce it and exemplify it [...]. Hence the institutions that people construct to exemplify justice may be different in different eras and different lands.
>
> It follows [...] that human beings can also generate ever new examples of injustice and oppression through their cultural constructions. In different times and places, human beings find new ways to work evils on their fellow creatures, and to create monuments to brutality and repulsiveness. (Balkin 1998: 30–31)

Balkin here focuses on evolving forms of injustice, but it is easy to think of ways in which our moral landscape changes due to the effects of technology. Consider, e.g., assisted reproductive technology. Normative questions arise about parenthood, surrogacy, parental responsibility, human enhancement, eugenics, all with an overlay of concerns about gender, race, class, sexuality, and disability.

There is no doubt that the biotechnology revolution has disrupted, contested, and changed "family values" as well as what counts as a family and even what counts as human.

If value is path-dependent, a moral theory that makes recommendations based on currently uncontroversial judgments and intuitions misses the evaluative resources provided by the ongoing evolution and creolization of culture. Reflection on and from the values entrenched in the status quo is normatively unreliable. Critique is part of a process of further specifying, elaborating, and creating value and typically relies on resistance and disruption. It is inevitably controversial.

The path-dependency of value does not leave critique without normative resources, however. Social critique can, at the very least, rely on an inchoate and indeterminate sense of justice; and what more is our idea of reciprocity (see Kymlicka 2002: 2–4; Dworkin 1977: 179–183; Wolff 2018)? We rely on such indeterminate ideas about what is valuable when we collect our considered judgments and intuitive principles to begin moral theorizing. But rather than rely on reflection to further specify our intuitions, social critique actively seeks input from experience (especially the conflicting experiences of different participants in the domain in question), from science broadly construed, the arts, the humanities, and the articulation of indeterminate values in other contexts. In short, rather than rely on domain-specific (relatively a priori) reflective equilibrium, social critique begins with concerns about the concrete manifestation of values in our social context to demand better alternatives to the current practices.

Suppose we are considering the division of labor in the family. The question is not how a particular family should divide labor. Rather, it is a question about social norms, the formation of gender identity, and the socialization of individuals through particular practices of intimacy, sexuality, parenting, and economic cooperation. Where do we begin? Do our considered judgments and intuitive principles yield a determinate specification of what form of family we should promote, e.g., that we should form nuclear families? Do they tell us that families should include one man and one woman and their biological offspring? (This is not, after all, a universal family form.) How should we organize intimacy, childcare, the transmission of culture, economic dependence? Should we uphold a gender binary? Historically, philosophers have taken existing gender roles and family structures for granted, and this has been reflected in their considered judgments and intuitions.

Many feminist critics reject the existing gendered division of labor and the processes by which individuals are shaped to fit its requirements. But what are the uncontroversial empirical and metaphysical claims the feminist is entitled to rely on in developing the critique? For example, can we assume that men and women have the same capacities for nurturing young children? This is not only a radical claim in the context of the history of the family, but it remains controversial in many contemporary contexts. Insofar as it is a controversial empirical claim, it cannot play a role in the normative reflective equilibrium that yields our ideal theory. (And neither can its denial, which is also controversial.) So what norms and values does ideal theory offer us for understanding gender relations in the family? Uncontroversial but vague notions such as reciprocity and equal respect do not give the social critic adequate normative resources to challenge the status quo.[7] But such challenges are the task of social critique.

Possibly, ideal theory helps us address some questions about the family, e.g., perhaps it can tell us that individuals rather than families ought to be the unit of political and economic agency. But how culture grows, evolves, and creates new forms of human life is not something that can be decided simply by reflection on our current considered judgments and uncontroversial empirical and metaphysical beliefs. Our embeddedness in culture has deeply shaped us; the necessities of and possibilities for reshaping are conditioned not just by our "bare" humanity but also by who we are as the products of culture. Somehow, we must find a space of critique where we accept our inevitable social embeddedness while also gaining a critical perspective on the particular instance of it at hand. Relatively a priori moral theory tends to either ignore our embeddedness and assume we are just solving a problem for rational agents or embrace our embeddedness uncritically and simply aim to avoid inconsistency in what culture has taught us. Neither of these are adequate.

## 6 Critically applying ideal theory

One might argue, however, that in considering applied ideal theory, I have neglected the role of social science to illuminate the relevant phenomena and the potential for intervention. After all, we are considering *applied* ideal theory, so we must have good grasp of the conditions we are addressing. Current racial injustice in the United States is shaped by the history of slavery, and Jim Crow and the possibilities for moral intervention are constrained by such empirical facts. This can be accommodated within applied ideal theory: We must be informed by social science as we bring the principles of justice to bear on actual

---

[7] This can be seen as a version of Wolff's (2019: 15) point that moral theory under-determines how we should go on.

circumstances. Once we come to know the relevant facts, an application of the principles may yield surprising and controversial conclusions.

For example, much progress toward social justice has been achieved by holding societies accountable for violations of their own explicit principles. It is hard to understand how a government conceived of as "of the people, by the people, for the people" could deny voting rights to so many for so long. It is hard to understand how so many could suffer violations of fundamental human rights seemingly guaranteed by founding documents. Drawing attention to such failures by bringing principles to bear can, of course, be a radical act of critique.

However, there is an important difference between "applying a principle" and, as Balkin puts it, "concretizing our indeterminate sense of justice." (Balkin 1998: 30 – 31) The critic is embedded in a social context that violates her sense of justice, and she challenges the principles – or the interpretation of the principles – that purport to justify it. Iris Young (1990) calls the starting point a "desiring negation":

> Desire […] creates the distance, the negation, that opens the space for criticism of what is. This critical distance does not occur on the basis of some previously discovered rational ideas of the good and the just. On the contrary, the ideas of the good and the just arise from the desiring negation that action brings to what is given.
>
> […] Each social reality presents its own unrealized possibilities, experienced as lacks and desires. Norms and ideals arise from the yearning that is an expression of freedom: it does not have to be this way; it could be otherwise. (Young 1990: 6)

Critique is not (or not always) an exercise applying moral principles. Even if we are able to articulate a principle, it will require interpretation and reinterpretation over time, often prompted by circumstances that were never imagined. We find a principle's unclarity and weakness as we attempt to apply it to controversial, complex, or unforeseen cases. Enduring principles are ones that are suggestive without being precise, for they allow for an evolution of meaning in response to the evolution of our circumstances and our values. So either we establish principles that are precise enough to guide action, and they will be continually overthrown; or we make do with vague articulations of our sense of justice and we reformulate them in response to our confrontation with social reality.

The "desiring negation" of resistance is only a beginning, of course. Emancipatory, or critical, social science may be needed to develop an account of social reality that explains and justifies the resistance. More specifically, a successful critical theory provides the epistemic tools to challenge ideology. One key move is to offer an alternative description or explanation of a phenomenon that reveals morally relevant aspects that ideology masks.[8] The hope is that once these aspects are revealed, or diagnosed, the phenomenon can no longer be viewed as innocent. For example, once one sees industrial agriculture up close, e.g., the animal and human suffering it causes, the wasted natural resources, the damage to public health, one cannot reasonably regard it as a morally innocent or benign economic system (Crary 2016). Social explanation, and with it, social ontology, is central to this effort. Of course, as Erik Olin Wright points out:

> It is not enough to show that people suffer in the world in which we live or that there are enormous inequalities in the extent to which people live flourishing lives. A scientific emancipatory theory must show that the explanation for this suffering and inequality lies in specific properties of institutions and social structures. The first task of emancipatory social science, therefore, is the diagnosis and critique of the causal processes that generate these harms. (Wright 2010: 11)

What counts as morally significant is not given in advance by an ideal theory but emerges through reworking or developing new tools for inquiry; better understanding of our social, material, and cultural milieu; the exercise of our affective and perceptual capacities; and deliberation with others. This is a process of developing an "oppositional consciousness" (Mansbridge/Morris 2001). Rather than rely on theories developed a priori, we aim to "concretize our indeterminate value of justice" in new ways, i.e., not just to "apply" our worked-out principles, but to explore other terms for living together. The work is done by those engaged in a social movement. As mentioned before: it is collective, practice-directed, and embedded. This, more than the applied moral theory model, grants political and moral agency to those directly affected by including them as full participants in normative inquiry.

# 7 Conclusion: Critical social theory

I have argued that the project of social critique is not best undertaken either on the medical model or the applied ideal theory model. I have also suggested that

---

**8** For decades, feminist theorists (and others) have argued that value-laden inquiry is not only inevitable, but more insightful and objective than purportedly value-free inquiry (Anderson 1995). What questions we ask, what methods we choose, and what terms we employ in describing phenomena depend on the goals and purposes of inquiry. Especially in the context of critique, values play a crucial role in the empirical work of identifying, describing, and diagnosing the phenomena that call for intervention (Anderson 1995; 2002; 2004).

critical social theory is a value-laden empirical inquiry that is a crucial part of social critique. How, then, should we proceed in the project of social critique? It is not my aim to provide a *method* of nonmoral moral/political theorizing. My goal, instead, is to highlight the epistemic importance of critical social ontology in undertaking critique.

Very briefly, as social critics, we begin with a "desiring negation" – a phenomenon that we experience or judge to be harmful, unfair, or wrong. This, rather than a theory of justice, is our starting point. The tools that we have to understand the problem are inadequate, so we engage in a process of theorizing to diagnose the problem in ways that reveal its systematic shape, while also preserving the moral and epistemic standing and agency of those affected. The theory should meet a variety of ordinary epistemic norms, e. g., consistency, empirical adequacy, etc. Some experiences of resistance are unwarranted or based on false presuppositions; we can conclude that these do not form a warranted basis for social change.

An adequate theory should also reveal normatively significant facts that give us the resources for critique. As mentioned before: it is collective, practice-directed, and embedded. Rather than rely on theories developed a priori in philosophy seminar rooms, we attend to our current situation and "concretize our indeterminate value of justice" in new ways, responsive to our social and historical circumstances. This, more than applied ideal theory, grants political and moral agency to those directly affected by including them as full participants in normative inquiry.

Note, however, that being able to develop a warranted critique of a practice or a structure does not give one an answer to how we should go on. There will usually be many ways to improve our current practices. We often do not have the information needed to predict outcomes of substantial changes. And rarely can all *pro tanto* political complaints be adequately addressed; solutions to collective action problems distribute, but do not eliminate, benefits and burdens. Danielle Allen reminds us:

> [...] the phrase "the common good" generally ignores the differential distribution of losses and benefits throughout a citizenry that result from collective action, and manages the problem of loss in politics (or, the defeat of a citizen's interests in the public sphere) simply by asking citizens to bear up in moments of disappointment. (Allen 2001: 858)

Trust that the distribution of burdens and benefits will balance over time is essential for democracy. Such trust is eroding, leaving us with critique but little basis for hope. Yet ...

[...] hope is not like a lottery ticket you can sit on the sofa and clutch, feeling lucky. I say it because hope is an ax you break down doors with in an emergency; because hope should shove you out the door, because it will take everything you have to steer the future away from endless war, from the annihilation of the earth's treasures and the grinding down of the poor and marginal. Hope just means another world might be possible, not promised, not guaranteed. Hope calls for action. [...] To hope is to give yourself to the future, and that commitment to the future makes the present inhabitable. (Solnit 2016: 4)

Because critique is not based on an ideal moral theory, but on an awareness of and commitment to the world's unrealized possibilities, we can have hope, and must go on.

# References

Allen, Danielle (2001): "Law's Necessary Forcefulness: Ralph Ellison vs. Hannah Arendt on the Battle of Little Rock." In: *Oklahoma City University Law Review* 26, pp. 857–895.
Anderson, Elizabeth (1995): "Knowledge, Objectivity, and Human Interests in Feminist Epistemology." In: *Philosophical Perspectives* 23(2), pp. 27–58.
Anderson, Elizabeth (2000): "Beyond Homo Economicus: New Developments in the Theory of Social Norms." In: *Philosophy & Public Affairs* 29(2), pp. 170–200.
Anderson, Elizabeth (2001): "Unstrapping the Straitjacket of 'Preference': A Comment on Amartya Sen's Contributions of Philosophy and Economics." In: *Economics and Philosophy* 17, pp. 21–38.
Anderson, Elizabeth (2002): "Situated Knowledge and the Interplay of Value Judgments and Evidence in Scientific Inquiry." In: Gärdenfors, Peter/Woleński, Jan/Kijania-Placek, Katarzyna (Eds.): *In the Scope of Logic, Methodology and Philosophy of Science*. Vol. 2. Dordrecht: Kluwer, pp. 497–517.
Anderson, Elizabeth (2004): "Uses of Value Judgments in Science: A General Argument, with Lessons from a Case Study of Feminist Research on Divorce." In: *Hypatia: A Journal of Feminist Philosophy* 19(1), pp. 1–24.
Anderson, Elizabeth (2010): *The Imperative of Integration*. Princeton, NJ: Princeton University Press.
Anderson, Elizabeth (2014): "Social Movements, Experiments in Living and Moral Progress: Case Studies from Britain's Abolition of Slavery." The Lindley Lecture, University of Kansas. https://kuscholarworks.ku.edu/bitstream/handle/1808/14787/Anderson_Social_Movements.pdf, accessed 26 March 2020.
Balkin, J. M. (1998): *Cultural Software: A Theory of Ideology*. New Haven, CT: Yale University Press.
Banerjee, Abhijit/Duflo, Esther (2019): *Good Economics for Hard Times*. New York, NY: Public Affairs.
Ben-Ner, Avner/Putterman, Louis (Eds.) (1998): *Economics, Values, and Organization*. Cambridge: Cambridge University Press.
Celikates, Robin (2018): *Critique as Social Practice: Critical Theory and Social Self-Understanding*. London: Rowman and Littlefield.

Crary, Alice (2016): *Inside Ethics: On the Demands of Moral Thought.* Cambridge, MA: Harvard University Press.
Dworkin, Ronald (1977): *Taking Rights Seriously.* Cambridge, MA: Harvard University Press.
Hampshire, Stuart (2000): *Justice Is Conflict.* Princeton, NJ: Princeton University Press.
Haslanger, Sally (2017): "Culture and Critique." In: *Proceedings of the Aristotelian Society* Supplementary Vol. 91, pp. 149–173.
Kymlicka, Will (2002): *Contemporary Political Philosophy: An Introduction.* Oxford: Oxford University Press.
Mansbridge, Jane/Morris, Aldon (Eds.) (2001): *Oppositional Consciousness: The Subjective Roots of Social Protest.* Chicago, IL: University of Chicago Press.
Mikkola, Mari (2017): "Dissident Theorising: Tracing, Mapping and Applying a Non-Ideal Philosophical Methodology." Unpublished manuscript.
Murphy, Liam (1998): "Institutions and the Demands of Justice." In: *Philosophy & Public Affairs* 27(4), pp. 251–291.
Scanlon, T. M. (2003): "Rawls on Justification." In: Freeman, Samuel (Ed.): *The Cambridge Companion to Rawls.* Cambridge: Cambridge University Press, pp. 139–167.
Shelby, Tommie (2014): "Integration, Inequality, and Imperatives of Justice: A Review Essay." In: *Philosophy & Public Affairs* 42(3), pp. 253–285.
Shelby, Tommie (2016): *Dark Ghettos.* Cambridge, MA: Harvard University Press.
Solnit, Rebecca (2016): *Hope in the Dark: Untold Histories, Wild Possibilities.* Second ed. Chicago, IL: Haymarket Books.
Stahl, Titus (2017): "Immanent Critique and Particular Moral Experience." In: *Critical Horizons.* https://doi.org/10.1080/14409917.2017.1376939, accessed 26 March 2020
Stemploska, Zofia (2008): "What's Ideal about Ideal Theory?" In: *Social Theory and Practice* 34(3), pp. 319–340.
Swift, Adam (2008): "The Value of Philosophy in Nonideal Circumstances." In: *Social Theory and Practice* 34(3), pp. 363–387.
Taylor, Paul C. (2017): "The Unjustly Disadvantaged: African American Life and Political Philosophy." In: *Black Perspectives* 1 July 2017. https://www.aaihs.org/the-unjustly-disadvantaged-african-american-life-and-political-philosophy, accessed 26 March 2020.
Wolff, Jonathan (2018): "Tommie Shelby, *Dark Ghettos: Injustice, Dissent, and Reform.*" In: *Ethics* 128(2), pp. 510–515.
Wolff, Jonathan (2019): "Method in Philosophy and Public Policy: Applied Philosophy versus Engaged Philosophy." In: Lever, Annabelle/Poama, Andrei (Eds.): *The Routledge Handbook of Ethics and Public Policy.* New York, NY: Routledge, pp. 13–24.
Wright, Erik Olin (2010): *Envisioning Real Utopias.* New York, NY: Verso.
Young, Iris (1990): *Justice and the Politics of Difference.* Princeton, NJ: Princeton University Press.

# Anne Reichold
# Varieties of Resentment

**Abstract:** Expressing resentment is an important way of interpersonal, social, or political critique. In this paper, three types of resentment are distinguished: individual resentment, collective resentment and *ressentiment*. It is argued that individual and collective resentments differ from *ressentiment* not only in their relation to facts and reasons but also in their general aim: collective resentment expresses felt injustices and aims at societal change whereas *ressentiment* is an attitude of carrying a grudge and wanting revenge. Collective resentment and *ressentiment* mark distinct ways of relating to the world and to others and entail different views of society. The conceptual distinctions between varieties of resentment can help to identify and evaluate public expressions of anger.

**Keywords:** Resentment, *ressentiment*, reactive attitudes, revenge, injustice, social critique

## 1 Introduction: Varieties of resentment

Resentment and indignation are important forms of interpersonal, social, and political criticism. They can be expressed in highly informal contexts, on streets, in the kitchen, in classrooms, and via *Twitter*, and they can be expressed in social and political movements. In the history of emancipatory movements like race or gender struggles, resentment plays an important role as a reaction to injustices and as an expression of the demand for acknowledgement of these injustices. Resentment and indignation can serve as a step in raising awareness of existing injustices, and they can contribute to emancipatory social change.

On the other hand, resentment can deepen social and political fission; it can strengthen collective identities and collective distinctions between 'friend' and 'enemy.' Resentment plays an important role in populist movements and identitarian politics that often replace political discourse and foster hatred and exclusion. Justice and equality are not the only standards that resentment applies to and expresses.

Evaluations of resentment differ highly as well: There are forms of resentment that are regarded to be rational, adequate, or well-grounded. Other forms of resentment are criticised due to their emotionality, irrationality, or one-sidedness.

The questions guiding my paper are the following: How can different forms of resentment be distinguished conceptually? And how do these different types of resentment give grounds for normatively evaluating them?

I want to argue that there are structurally and conceptually different forms of resentment that also give rise to different forms of evaluation and criticism. The fact that some forms of resentment express claims in the name of justice should not make us blind to other forms of resentment that call for social hierarchy, exclusion, and social particularity. Also, the fact that some forms of resentment are irrational and closely coupled with violence should not lead to the conclusion that all forms of resentment are irrational and normatively problematic. Not all forms of resentment are structurally similar; rather, there are many types of resentment.

In the following I want to draw a conceptual distinction between three different types of resentment: individual resentment, collective resentment, and *ressentiment*. Apart from clear distinctions between individual and collective subjects and objects of these resentments, each of these types relates differently to reasons and norms. Some forms of resentment are reactive to reasons, information, excuses, or apologies, whereas others seem to resist these changes and seem to be quite stable over time irrespective of facts in the world and the attitudes of others. Some forms of resentment pretend to be rational even though they are not; others seem to be irrational or out of place, though they might turn out to be reasonable and adequate.

In the first part of the paper, I describe forms of individual or intersubjective resentment. The philosophical analysis of intersubjective resentment is strongly influenced by Peter Strawson's concept of reactive attitudes and is developed further in more recent conceptions of blame.

In the second part I broaden these accounts of interpersonal resentment to accounts of collective resentment in social and political contexts. These types of resentment refer to collective terms like nations, gender, race, or religion, and its reasons are more complex than the ones in interpersonal cases.

In a third part I want to distinguish between forms of collective resentment and *ressentiment*. Referring to Max Scheler and Nietzsche's accounts of *ressentiment*, I argue that *ressentiment* is characterised by a different relation between collective emotions and reasons: whereas collective resentment reacts to facts and reasons and aims at changing the resented situation, *ressentiment* is characterised by the inhibition of action and a strong feeling of inability or powerlessness. *Ressentiment* replaces action and tends to decouple from concrete facts and reasons.

It might not always be easy to distinguish between collective resentment and *ressentiment* empirically. Conceptually a clear distinction between these forms can be made, which also has consequences with regards to the normative evaluation of forms of resentment. The conceptual distinction can help to analyse and critically assess and answer instances of resentment and *ressentiment* in social and political contexts.

## 2 Interpersonal resentment

There is a consensus in philosophical literature that interpersonal resentment and indignation are not blind, irrational emotions of anger, but that there is a propositional, inferential structure of reasons backing and leading them. There are reasons for resentment, not only triggers and causes. According to Strawson resentment and indignation are reactive attitudes expressing the felt violation of normative claims by actions of some agent (Strawson 2008). Resentment is one of a number of "non-detached attitudes and reactions of people directly involved in transactions with each other" (Strawson 2008: 5). In contrast to indignation, which can be expressed and felt by an observer or a third party, resentment is an attitude felt and expressed by the offended party herself. Resentment reveals an offence from the viewpoint of the offended party. It is not detached, theoretical or well-balanced. On the contrary, expressions of resentment reveal normative and epistemic views from a subjective, personal perspective. Whereas resentment can be understood or evaluated by third parties, these third persons are not in the right position to themselves resent the injury done to the offended person.

Strawson distinguishes personal resentment from indignation, which he takes to be the "sympathetic or vicarious or impersonal or disinterested or generalized analogue" of non-detached, personal resentment (Strawson 2008: 15). Whereas resentment is expressed from the perspective of the offended party, indignation is expressed from the perspective of a third party observing or witnessing the wrongs or injuries done to others. The impersonal attitudes are taken to be moral attitudes: "Thus one who experiences the vicarious analogue of resentment is said to be indignant or disapproving, or morally indignant or disapproving." (Strawson 2008: 15)

Resentment is not primarily a reaction to pain or the consequences of actions for oneself or others, but it reacts to the violation of an underlying normative interpersonal demand by the offending actor: "The personal reactive attitudes rest on, or reflect, an expectation of, and demand for, the manifestation of a certain degree of goodwill or regard on the part of other human beings towards ourselves." (Strawson 2008: 15) A generalised form of this demand of goodwill towards all human beings underlies the vicarious analogue of indignation. Resentment and indignation express or rest upon a web of normative expectations within interpersonal relationships and social life and an attitudinal and emotional reactivity of human beings with regards to violations of these demands (Reichold 2017). I take Strawson's remarks to point to a normative, inferential structure within reactive attitudes that is broadly recognised within the philosophical discussion: Resentment and indignation occur for reasons; they can and sometimes should be justified, criticised, and modified in the light of reasons. These claims are conceptual claims, not empirical descriptions. Resentment conceptually should be reactive to reasons and modifications; empirically this might not always be the case.

Both types of reactive attitudes, resentment and indignation, serve as forms of normative critique in interpersonal contexts. The resenting criticism is primarily expressed as a resisting or protesting 'no' to an action or attitude of an actor. It focusses on something that should not be the way it is or was from the viewpoint of the resenting person. This 'no' is not just a feeling of unhappiness or resistance, but it expresses a normative claim that is expressed for reasons: Resentment and indignation have an inferential, normative structure and they are responsive to reasons. When asked for reasons for resenting, one might have to think for a while and sometimes one might not immediately know the reasons for resentment, but conceptually it does not make sense to say that one resents without reasons. The reasons consist of normative claims that are regarded as having been violated by a certain action or state of affairs in the world.

The inferential, normative structure of reactive attitudes and their reactiveness to reasons becomes obvious in Strawson's discussion of different kinds of modifications of these attitudes in the light of facts about the world: If I learn that a friend missed our appointment not out of ignorance, but because of a sudden accident in his family, resentment should be transformed into understanding or care. Information about the context, the action, and the actor are important reasons for resentment or the need to transform it. In this sense there is a mind-to-world fit in resentment. New information about the context of action as well as knowledge about the attitude of the actor of the offending action can give reasons to either maintain the resentment or to modify or drop it. The interplay between a normative claim and a description of an action in a certain context forms the basic inferential structure of reasons in any instance of resentment. This inferential structure is open to evaluation and criticism and it calls for specific answers. Resentment is reactive to reasons in the sense that it is defeasible and can or should be modified in the light of further reasons.

Resentment, though, is not only characterised by an (implicit) normative judgement. Being a reactive attitude, there is something distinctive about resenting, something emotional or performative or expressive. Resentment is not the utterance of a judgement, but it is the (temporal and partial) change of attitudes towards the offender. Resentment thus changes the relationship between the resenting person and the offender. The general form of goodwill that should lead our behaviour towards others is in resentment temporally and partially withdrawn. This withdrawal of goodwill takes place for reasons, and thus the resenting person feels justified in withdrawing goodwill and the offender is expected to understand and ultimately to accept this withdrawal. Resentment calls for acknowledgement of the wrong done and it calls for specific answers, e.g. explanations, excuses, apologies. Resentment thus is not primarily judging, but it changes relationships for reasons.

The philosophical discussion on blame analyses specific ways of changing one's attitude in cases of resentment.

Christopher Bennett analyses blame as a type of expressive action (Bennett 2013). Blame is not a means to an end, but it expresses a disapproval by symbolically distancing from the offender. In contrast to punishing or judging or aiming at change, blame operates like a metaphor, "capturing and illuminating some aspect of the situation" (Bennett 2013: 78).

Bennett takes up a Strawsonian term and states:

> Blame is a partial and temporary withdrawal from an offender, (1) carried out because of responsible wrongdoing and (2) carried out in a way that the offender herself can be expected to understand. Because of (1) and (2) blame is a way of treating the offender as a moral agent. It asserts the authority of the violated norms over the offending agent, holds the offender accountable to those norms, and in doing so includes the wrongdoer in the moral community. (Bennett 2012: 76–77)

Blame as an expressive action in Bennett's sense is like a metaphorical 'report' of important features of a situation. There is a clear mind-to-world fit in the reporting aspect and an aesthetic and creative feature in the way of expressing the truth.

Another proposal to analyse the specific nature of blame is Angela Smith's account of moral protest:

> To blame another is to judge that she is blameworthy (i.e. to judge that she has attitudes that impair her relationship with others) and to modify one's own attitudes, intentions, and expectations toward that person as a way of protesting (i.e. registering and challenging) the moral claim implicit in her conduct, where such protest implicitly seeks some kind of moral acknowledgement on the part of the blameworthy agent and/or on the part of those in the moral community. (Smith 2013: 43)

Again the judging is part of blame, but blaming is a way of protesting against the moral claims expressed in the offender's actions. This form of blame is not solely backward-looking, but it aims at acknowledgement of the wrong in the present and for the future.

Smith's account of blame proves to be much broader in the sense that it can be applied also to situations of historical or social blame, where the offender is already dead. It is not primarily the offender as a person that blame is directed at but rather the false normative commitments that are expressed by the wrongs done. The object of blame in this account is a normative structure leading to certain actions, not a person or the offender himself.

This aspect of Smith's account of blame proves to be very fruitful in an account of collective, social, or historical blame that I want to discuss in the next part of my paper.

## 3 Collective resentment

So far the discussed accounts of resentment are accounts of individual, intersubjective resentment reacting to a specific action or situation by an offender. This seems to restrict resentment to interpersonal situations and excludes the analysis of a range of historical, social, or political forms of resentment. Smith explicitly analyses situations of social and political blame with regard to historical wrongs. Her example is a current blaming of slaveholders in the past.

> [...] when I read about the brutal history of slavery in the United States, I am inclined to say not only that I judge southern slaveholders blameworthy; I am inclined to say that I actually blame them [...]. (Smith 2013: 44)

The aim of this protest is not acknowledgement from the offenders, long dead, but acknowledgement from the present community:

> [...] such protest implicitly seeks some kind of moral acknowledgement on the part of the blameworthy agent and/or on the part of those in the moral community. (Smith 2013: 43)

Blame in the protest account has its object in the past but its aims lie in the present and future: normative commitment to non-discrimination in the present community and public expression of protest against the norms of slavery. It is not the resenting person herself who suffered the wrong, and it is not the offender who is the object of blame. Instead, there is a collective perspective introduced, built around national, social, generational, or historical boundaries. The objects of resentment are practices and structural normative commitments: "By continuing to blame, we continue to protest the 'outrageous falsehoods' that the practice of slavery embodied." (Smith 2013: 45)

Resentment regarding historical wrongs expressed in current contexts are not expressed and felt by those who were the primary victims. Referring to examples of resentment by indigenous Canadians, MacLachlan shows that resentment in postcolonial contexts refers to historical contexts that are out of the control of those who live in recent contexts (MacLachlan 2010). The categories of a 'victim' and of an 'offender' do not suffice in an individual form. Instead, collective categories like 'settlers,' 'indigenous people,' 'Germans,' 'women,' or 'people of colour' are used to express the relations between victims and offenders. Katie Stockdale proposes an account of collective resentment in this context:

> Collective resentment is resentment that is felt and expressed by individuals in response to a perceived threat to a collective to which they belong. (Stockdale 2013: 507)

The personal element in individual resentment turns into a belonging to a group in collective resentment. Likewise, the object of resentment is not an individual offender but consists of unjust structures and institutions. Objects of collective resentment can be neoliberal capitalism, structures of cultural supremacy, racism, political liberalism, etc. These collective features of resentment make it a powerful critical attitude in social and political settings.

MacLachlan talks about "complex resentments" in this context, pointing out that "a single resentful reaction may express a multitude of fears, jealousies, and angers, some of which – in isolated form – are more justifiable than others" (MacLachlan 2010: 431). In these cases, resentment can seem unreasonable and more difficult to justify for the resenting people, since a justification might require significant historical and institutional knowledge. The attitude and emotion of resentment can be detached from reasons and thus can seem unreasonable. The politically worrying fact about this is that

> dividing angers as either "reasonable" or "unreasonable" in these complex situations will tend [...] to dismiss the angers of the most vulnerable: those least likely to have their needs and interests represented in a dominant social and moral framework. (MacLachlan 2010: 428)

MacLachlan points to an important political role of resentment: expressing resentment in situations where the injustices and violations of norms or moral standards are not even seen by the resenting person and the social community. Resentment in these cases can be a driver to the articulation and formulation of new norms and values. Resentment might be an alternative form of expression, especially in contexts in which "the source of that is not currently recognizable as injustice" (MacLachlan 2010: 434). MacLachlan points to experiences of lesbian women, of those who live with mental illness, and of illegal immigrants.

> [...] even so-called "unreasonable" resentments may contain morally significant messages of protest, even if those messages cannot yet express moral content. (MacLachlan 2010: 437)

Collective resentment thus not only protests against violations of accepted and known norms, but it is also not always grounded in already known facts. One especially transformative force of resentment lies in the fact that it might lead to a public debate of new norms and more adequate descriptions of complex social and political situations and circumstances. It might give a voice to socially or politically excluded people or groups and thus might lead to societal and moral transformation. The critical potential of resentment goes beyond a rational form of criticism here: It calls for making explicit normative claims that might not be accepted or debated in a society, and it might call for a new or different framing of certain situations or whole practices.

The complexity of collective resentments points to the difficulties and dangers of evaluating collective resentment, anger, or protest. Criticising resentments for being unreasonable or overstretched can be the result of not knowing enough about the circumstances, objects, and contexts of that resentment. Criticising resentment can also be a means of exclusion or discrimination itself. The evaluation and critique of resentment should be aware of their own embeddedness, privileges, and biases.

Myisha Cherry identifies several difficulties in evaluating anger and resentment (Cherry 2018). With reference to Adam Smith's account of resentment, she points to the danger of sympathy-gaps in evaluating anger: We might understand and sympathise with resentment expressed by groups we feel close to and understand better, whereas we might lack sympathy with those we do not feel close to or immediately understand. One might not "be aware of, is not familiar with, or cannot relate to their struggles that brought about the anger. [...] Distance (physical, affective, and cultural) [...] can affect our anger evaluations." (Cherry 2018: 56)

Another failure in anger evaluations is called 'anger-policing': Instead of taking the reasons of anger as a basis for evaluation, being and expressing anger is evaluated with regards to norms of civility or decency.

> It is often people who are most vulnerable to and victimized by unjust and oppressive systems who are punished for speaking their angry truth and recommended to be civil when they express anger. (Cherry 2018: 60)

Evaluations of anger and especially resentment (since this is expressed from the viewpoint and in the name of the offended parties) can be means of "silencing [...] angry agents and their moral concerns" (Cherry 2018: 60). By primarily referring to the emotional qualities of resentment or anger, its rational and normative claims are rejected or pathologised. Evaluations of resentment can be guilty of epistemic or testimonial injustice. Evaluations of resentments might silence and exclude especially the least powerful and privileged people or groups. A philosophical critique of resentment should be aware of these dangers.

Evaluations and critique of resentment might be an expression of power, and they might prolong or contribute to a social or political exclusion of marginalised groups. Reminiscent of a principle of charity in the realm of anger or protest, resentments should be taken seriously, and the reasons for them should be examined even if the resentments initially seem unreasonable. Understanding a resentment before evaluating and criticising – this simple truth is not easy in cases of complex resentments.

Arlie Russell Hochschild in her famous study on anger and mourning on the American Right points to "empathy-walls" between the political camps in the United States (Hochschild 2016). She interviewed many people for several months and reconstructs "deep stories" underlying their resentments. "A deep story is a *feels-as-if* story – it's a story feelings tell, in the language of symbols. It removes judgement. It removes facts. It tells us how things feel." (Hochschild 2016: 135) The stories and reasons for resentment are collective prisms that help to make sense of the world and strengthen collective entities and a sense of belonging. Understanding these deep stories seems crucial to understanding why people protest or resent. Understanding does not mean sympathising or agreeing, though.

These examples show the importance of reconstructing collective narratives behind resentments in order to understand the worldviews of reciprocally resenting groups. The conflicts in these cases go much deeper than a misunderstanding or a partial normative disagreement. These resentments seem to represent collective worldviews and localised positions within it.

Understanding resentment and its reasons, contexts, agents, and norms requires time, communication, knowledge, and empathy. The principle of charity that should guide interpretation and understanding in all contexts is especially required in analysing and understanding resentment. This seems easy in cases of protests that are familiar to us, that we feel close to, and that we know a lot about. It seems to be especially difficult and challenging in cases where we either do not know enough or with which we do not sympathise at all. Evaluating resentment can thus easily become part of resentment's opposition itself: either supporting resentment or opposing it. A philosophical analysis of resentment is in need of a project of understanding resentment as a presupposition of evaluating it.

## 4 *Ressentiment*

MacLachlan points to the danger of excluding legitimate resentments of the weakest parties by ways of calling them "unreasoned." She calls for finding reasons behind collective resentments even in cases where it seems to be unreasoned. In the last part of my paper, I want to raise awareness of a different possibility: Instead of viewing resentment as a reaction to violated norms and potentially being open to public discourse between the resenting subject and the surrounding community, collective protest and anger can be expressions of what I want to call with the French word: *ressentiment*.

There is a tendency of single-sidedness in examples discussing collective resentment, such as resentment expressed by suppressed or marginalised groups fighting against injustice and discrimination. In these cases, MacLachlan's warnings against devaluations of collective resentments are perfectly reasonable. There are different examples of anger and resentment, though, that do not easily fit into this picture: What about Trump resenting migrants and women? What about *Pegida* protesting against migrants? What about anti-Semitic violence and its support in social media? Racist or misogynist norms are explicitly stated, a dehumanising language is used to break social and political taboos, and the will to preserve and strengthen collective identities is expressed. Collective forms of anger are not only expressed by marginalised groups that are partly excluded from political representation and public media; they are also expressed by powerful social or political groups, aiming at social fission and building on long established discriminating narratives of racism, anti-Semitism, or gender discrimination. Besides the above discussed distinctions between individual and collective resentment, be they reasonable or unreasonable, there also exist *ressentiments* sometimes hiding behind a veil of collective resentment.

Max Scheler analyses *ressentiment*, referring to structural elements of Nietzsche's account of *ressentiment*. Like Nietzsche he uses the French word *ressentiment* because there is no adequate translation. Scheler points out that *ressentiment* must be "clearly distinguished from the impulse for [...] self-defense, even when the reaction is accompanied by anger, fury, or indignation" (Scheler 1998: 29).

*Ressentiment* essentially is an attitude of wanting revenge and carrying a grudge that arises in light of impotence or inferiority. Anger and holding a grudge are not transitory feelings leading to action, resolution, or protest; on the contrary, *ressentiment* is characterised by a fundamental suppression or inhibition of actions due to feelings of the inability to act. In *ressentiment* the immediate reaction to a felt deprivation is postponed. In response, the person of *ressentiment* undergoes a process of re-evaluation: that which cannot be achieved due to inferiority or impotence is devalued. Aeschbach, in a broad theoretical approach to *ressentiment*, points to the fable of the fox who cannot reach the sweet grapes and therefore devalues them as being sour (Aeschbach 2017: 9). Whereas resentment in the above sketched sense serves as an engine of change and motivates individuals or groups to act and protest, *ressentiment* develops its attitudinal force by suppressing direct actions and reactions and by revaluating the original scene.

In contrast to resentment directed towards specific objects and events that give rise and reason for resenting, *ressentiment* is largely decoupled from real objects and facts. It is a general attitude that is manifested over a long period of time and whose objects are quite indefinite.

> Impulses of revenge lead to ressentiment [...], the more their direction shifts toward indeterminate groups of objects which need only share one common characteristic, and the less they are satisfied by vengeance taken on a specific object. (Scheler 1998: 32)

*Ressentiment* searches for objects to fuel its structure. Scheler talks about an "indiscriminate criticism without any positive aim" (Scheler 1998: 34). *Ressentiment* is embedded within ideological narratives that are immune to criticism. Whereas resentment protests against that which violates claims of justice, *ressentiment* re-evaluates objects or whole values; due to feelings of impotence, *ressentiment* does not act or protest, but it devalues that which is impossible to gain. Aeschbach distinguishes between weak and strong forms of *ressentiment* (Aeschbach 2017: 95): weak forms of *ressentiment* re-evaluate particular objects (e.g. the grapes are not sweet but sour); strong forms of *ressentiment* re-evaluate the relation between whole values (e.g. cease to place the value of wealth or luxury over that of frugality).

Whereas the sense of injustice in resentment is combined with an element of hope or sense of agency, *ressentiment* develops its distinct form of anger from a feeling of impotence and suppression. The outside is constantly regarded as evil or the enemy. This deeply affective foundation of *ressentiment* is covered or rationalised by moral claims or normative reasons that are the result of re-evaluations. These narrations are not its basis though, but the rationalising veil or surface of a deeply aversive and hateful attitude that is rooted in feelings of powerlessness and a striving for revenge and power.

The general feeling of impotence in *ressentiment* leads to important differences between forms of collective resentment and *ressentiment:* whereas resentment expresses itself in forms of blame and protest, *ressentiment* is characterised by a suppression of action due to feelings of impotence. Instead of publicly expressing protest or speaking out in different ways (as is characteristic for forms of collective resentment), subjects of *ressentiment* are often found among the "sympathizers of violence rather than among the criminals themselves doing violence" (Frings 1998: 7–8). *Ressentiment* is prone to being used as a psychological and political tool for authoritarian political leaders that openly opt for a collective fission between 'us' and 'them.' It is this feature of *ressentiment* that makes it especially interesting in political contexts. Because *ressentiment's* dualist distinction between 'friend' and 'enemy' structures the affective and attitudinal realm and at the same time *ressentiment* is characterised by the inhibition of direct action, authoritarian political leaders can build on these dualist structures and evaluations and motivate action. They combine *ressentiment* with the power and will to act. *Ressentiment* can be used by political leaders as a social and political force that may attract people who feel powerless and unable to act on their own.

Nietzsche uses the analysis of *ressentiment* for a fundamental critique of Christian morality. In his view, moral claims for equality and justice only cover and rationalise an underlying envy and grudge against more powerful social groups. In this view all forms of resentment and indignation, especially those characterised as 'signals of injustice' above, would be instances of *ressentiment:* suppressed social groups envying the privileges of the more powerful and rationalising it by appeals to moral norms.

I do not want to use the critical appeal to *ressentiment* for the purpose of general moral scepticism in the following. Nevertheless, I think a philosophical analysis of varieties of resentment should take into account conceptions of *ressentiment* and distinguish them from interpersonal and collective resentment. The concept of *ressentiment* can not only be used in a general sceptical approach to morality and rationality but also in a more focused way: Not all expressions of resentment are forms of *ressentiment*, but some of them might be and a philosophical analysis of varieties of resentment should have this possibility in mind. Collective forms of resentment-like anger sometimes reveal a structure of *ressentiment:* attitudes that are not reactive to reasons; that do not change in light of explanations, proofs, facts, or apologies and excuses; but that actively search for reasons for anger or even hatred and that consistently react in a resenting way. Some forms of seemingly collective resentment turn out to be forms of *ressentiment*.

Darwall's distinction between second-personal and third-personal attitudes (Darwall 2014) is useful in clarifying the fundamental difference between resentment and *ressentiment*. I claim that collective resentment is a second-person reactive attitude, even in cases of unreasoned resentments, whereas *ressentiment* is fundamentally third-personal. Classifying forms of collective anger as being forms of *ressentiment* implies a fundamental shift of attitudes: Whereas collective resentments protest against felt violations of injustice and call for answers, *ressentiment* expresses an objective attitude towards others, marks a strategy of power, and does not call for mutual acknowledgement by others. Some expressions of *ressentiment* still refer to felt injustices, but the concept of 'injustice' does not seem to be one of free and equal persons. Under the veil of moral concepts, conceptions of power and status are strengthened here.

Emotions and attitudes like envy, status-esteem, jealousy, and a wish for domination, which all characterise *ressentiment*, point to a third-person relationship between the subject of *ressentiment* and its object. Rules, norms, or laws are not referred to as guides for action and evaluation. From the perspective of *ressentiment* the society is hierarchically structured along the lines of status and pride. 'Injustice' from the perspective of *ressentiment* does not relate to fundamentally free and equal persons and a rule of law but to forms of 'honour-respect' and social status for certain groups of people. The distinction between collective resentment on the one hand and *ressentiment* on the other is not just a distinction between different collective attitudes, but it is a fundamental distinction between conceptions of society and respect for human beings. Cherry's and MacLachlan's warnings not to exclude legitimate forms of collective resentment from societal discourse operate on the second-personal level in a double way: (a) they refer to the expressions of resentment in a second-personal way, trying to understand their claims, and (b) they take the subjects of resentment themselves to express second-personal claims for justice and equality.

This is different in cases of *ressentiment*. Calling an attitude one of *ressentiment* entails a whole shift of attitude from a second-personal to a third-personal perspective: (a) the subject of *ressentiment* is regarded to take a third-personal attitude towards other people, treating others as objects of domination or exclusion, and (b) the one calling an attitude *ressentiment* changes her attitude towards the person or group expressing that *ressentiment* from a second-personal to a third-personal attitude. Calling an expression of anger one of *ressentiment* implies the unwillingness or felt senselessness to include the subject of *ressentiment* into a rational discourse in a second-personal way.

Invoking the distinction between second-personal and third-personal attitudes shows that the distinction between collective resentment and *ressentiment* is not just one of different features and characteristics of an attitude. Collective resentment and *ressentiment* mark fundamentally different ways of relating to others and entail different views of society. Calling an attitude one of resentment or of *ressentiment* does not only identify different attitudes, but it also expresses a change of attitudes on the side of the evaluator. Entering the conceptual and attitudinal realm of *ressentiment* involves referring to others much more in a third-personal way.

Conceptually the distinction between collective resentment and *ressentiment* is sharp and fundamental. Empirically, though, expressions of anger might mix elements of both and it is not always easy to distinguish between these forms of attitudes. Furthermore, calling an attitude resentment or *ressentiment* is not just a question of identification according to certain features, but it entails the choice and change of an attitude on the side of those who analyse forms of resentments as well. Identifying an instance of *ressentiment* goes hand in hand with taking an attitude towards this expression: It makes a difference if I try to understand the resentment and anger of a certain group even though I might not share their values and beliefs or if I take an expression of anger to be one of *ressentiment*. In the latter case I come to the conclusion that the attitude is aiming at dominance or social fission and that argumentative dialogue might not make sense. Calling an attitude one of *ressentiment* thus also expresses the willingness to take a third-personal attitude towards the subjects of *ressentiment*. In political contexts this choice is not easy to make, but it seems to be important to have this possibility in mind. Distinguishing between resentment and *ressentiment* is not just a conceptual alternative but also one of attitudes and actions.

Concluding my paper, I want to give an example of the complexities of distinguishing between collective resentment and *ressentiment* by referring to one of the 'deep stories' in Hochschild's study. In her interviews, she identifies the following narrative of unfairness:

> You are patiently standing in a long line leading up a hill, as in a pilgrimage. You are situated in the middle of the line, along with others, who are also white, older, Christian, and predominantly male, some with College degrees, some not. [...] Look! You see people *cutting in line ahead of you!* You're following the rules. They aren't. As they cut in, it feels like you are being moved back. How can they just do that? Who are they? Some are black. Through affirmative action plans, pushed by the federal government, they are given preference for places in colleges and universities, apprenticeships, jobs, welfare payments [...] Women, immigrants, refugees, public sector workers – where will this end? [...] These are opportunities you'd have loved to have had in your day [...] It's not fair. [...] And president Obama: how did *he* rise so high? (Hochschild 2016: 136–137)

This is a good example of a mixture of collective resentment and *ressentiment*. Starting with felt injustices, the deep story continues to blame collectives like women, people of colour, or politicians for causing these felt injustices. Feelings of unfairness, impotence, envy, and fear and a lack of trust in politics are combined with the construction of collective enemies: people of colour, women, refugees. Hochschild presents these deep stories from a second-personal perspective: She calls for understanding, presenting them in the form of collective resentment.

The underlying narratives, though, are clearly misogynist and racist. These collective narratives have been fuelled and used by populist political parties of the American Right. A critical analysis of resentment would have to distinguish between legitimate elements of protest against political and economic deprivation and *ressentiment*-narratives against the collectives of refugees, women, and people of colour blamed in these narratives.

The mixture of ideological *ressentiments* and feelings of unfairness in Hochschild's 'deep story' point to the following complexity: Whereas the concrete facts and the ascriptions of responsibility in the above-mentioned case seem wrong and decoupled from facts, and the collective groups being blamed for the felt injustice reveal racist and misogynist attitudes, there seems to be a link between *ressentiment* and general structures of injustice within society. The feelings of impotence and powerlessness that are constitutive in *ressentiment* reflect, at least potentially and vaguely, structures of power-asymmetry and inequality in societies.

Scheler describes *ressentiment* as a reaction to the simultaneous existence of social structures of inequality and injustice and the normative claims of equality and justice:

> Ressentiment must therefore be strongest in a society like ours, where approximately equal rights (political or otherwise) or formal social equality [...] go hand in hand with wide factual differences in power, property, and education. (Scheler 1998: 33)

At this point a normative ambivalence in the concept of *ressentiment* is visible: On a structural level *ressentiment* seems to arise especially in societies of social and economic injustice. These injustices are not the object of moral indignation though; they fuel *ressentiment* without being hit or addressed by it. A felt powerlessness to answer these injustices leads to a decoupling of criticism where *ressentiment* becomes productive in an ideological way.

The simultaneous existence of claims for justice and equality on the one hand and power asymmetries on the other, which Scheler diagnoses from a philosophical perspective, seems to be covered or hidden by *ressentiment*-ideologies. *Ressentiment*-ideologies do not express or address felt injustices – this is what collective resentment does, as described in the first part of the paper. *Ressentiment*-narratives and re-evaluations are a creative decoupling from social structures and injustices that are not bound to a mind-to-world fit. Their relation to social reality and the facts is not one of representation or description but of overcoming, re-evaluating, and inverting the power-structures in the world, leading to a felt superiority over others. *Ressentiment* thus is an ideological projection that in the thirst for revenge leads to a certain amount of satisfaction and joy and a feeling of power for those who are part of the *ressentiment*-movement. The satisfaction is mostly decoupled from the societal inequalities that remain uncriticised.

A philosophical analysis of varieties of resentment can make explicit the claims in these different forms of protest and especially distinguish between collective resentments and forms of *ressentiment*. Whereas collective resentment can serve as a signal for injustice and thus help to change society normatively towards more inclusion and social justice, *ressentiment* leads to social fission into collective groups of 'us' and 'they,' 'friend' and 'enemy,' that fight one another also on institutional levels.

*Ressentiment* marks a turning-point in the realm of resentments; the second-personal, cooperative, participant attitude of critique and communication is turned into a third-personal power-strategy of social and collective fission. Empirical cases of protest, anger, and resentment very often mix elements of collective resentment and *ressentiment*. The concepts of resentment and *ressentiment* can help to identify and distinguish between levels of social critique that point to existing social injustices and thus should be changed and levels of *ressentiment* that aim at collective fission and the creation of hierarchical power asymmetries. The distinction between resentment and *ressentiment* is especially important, since resentment is a core second-personal attitude that calls for moral acknowledgement and expresses itself in an attitude of legitimacy and moral justification; *ressentiment* invokes a different picture of society and might not be approachable in second-personal ways. A philosophical analysis of resentment should take the possibility of *ressentiment* seriously without forgetting about the dangers of evaluating complex resentments.

# References

Aeschbach, Sébastien (2017): *Ressentiment: An Anatomy*. University of Geneva. Thesis.

Bennett, Christopher (2013): "The Expressive Function of Blame." In: Coates, D. Justin/Tognazzini, Neal A. (Eds.): *Blame: Its Nature and Norms*. Oxford: Oxford University Press, pp. 66–83.

Cherry, Myisha (2018): "The Errors and Limitations of Our 'Anger-Evaluating' Ways." In: Cherry, Myisha/Flanagan, Owen (Eds.): *The Moral Psychology of Anger*. London/New York, NY: Rowman and Littlefield, pp. 49–65.

Darwall, Stephen (2014): "The Social and the Sociable." In: *Philosophical Topics* 42(1), pp. 201–217.

Frings, Manfred S. (1998): "Introduction." In: Scheler, Max: *Ressentiment*. Milwaukee, WI: Marquette University Press, pp. 1–22.

Hochschild, Arlie Russell (2016): *Strangers in Their Own Land: Anger and Mourning on the American Right*. New York, NY: The New Press.

MacLachlan, Alice (2010): "Unreasonable Resentments." In: *Journal of Social Philosophy* 41(4), pp. 422–441.

Reichold, Anne (2017): "Resentment and Societal Transformation: A Rule-Related Argument against Martha Nussbaum's Critique of Anger." In: Brunkhorst, Hauke/Vujadinović, Dragica/Marinković, Tanasije (Eds.): *European Democracy in Crisis: Polities under Challenge and Social Movements*. Utrecht: Eleven, pp. 167–187.

Scheler, Max (1998): *Ressentiment*. Milwaukee, WI: Marquette University Press.

Smith, Angela (2013): "Moral Blame and Moral Protest." In: Coates, D. Justin/Tognazzini, Neal A. (Eds.): *Blame: Its Nature and Norms*. Oxford: Oxford University Press, pp. 27–48.

Stockdale, Katie (2013): "Collective Resentment." In: *Social Theory and Practice* 39(3), pp. 501–521.

Strawson, P. F. (2008): "Freedom and Resentment." In: *Freedom and Resentment and Other Essays*. London/New York, NY: Routledge, pp. 1–28.

Karsten Weber
# Civil Society as a Means against Hate Speech

A Baseless Hope

**Abstract:** On closer examination, the concept of civil society becomes blurred, for instance, on the crucial question of who belongs to civil society. The different answers to this question show how controversial the concept of civil society is, since it cannot be assumed that members of civil society would be morally particularly preferable actors. If, however, the conceptual foundations of and the question of membership in civil society already raise doubts about this concept, the recourse to civil society as a means against fake news and hate speech itself, which is often heard in public debates, becomes doubtful.

**Keywords:** Civil society, political philosophy, social philosophy, religious groups, communication

## 1 Introduction: The good civil society

Whether one looks in mass media, scientific publications, statements of political parties, NGOs, or governments and state authorities: Almost without exception,[1] it seems clear to commentators that a civil society is a good, tolerant, cosmopolitan, plural society. Even if one is skeptical about *Wikipedia*[2] and the information it contains (and in many cases this skepticism would be more than justified) and even if one agrees that the information found there should not be understood as the definitive word on the respective topic, the articles[3] on civil society presented there reflect a widespread sentiment that can be found in rather traditional mass media, in political commentaries as well as on the Internet. The term 'civil society' is generally and explicitly associated with democracy, cooperation, goodwill,

---

[1] One of the few exceptions concerning scholarly papers in a rather extensive research is MacLeod (2019).
[2] Of course, this is not a particularly reliable indicator, but if one looks for the German word '*Zivilgesellschaft*' ('civil society') on *google.de*, the corresponding *Wikipedia* article will be listed first.
[3] Both the English and German *Wikipedia* articles on civil society are very positive and confirm the image that can only be outlined here.

https://doi.org/10.1515/9783110702255-012

and progressiveness – in short: enlightenment in the thoroughly Kantian sense. Even if it is, of course, arbitrary to pick out a single contribution and quote from it, a more extensive research would, in most cases, also provide comments and texts that contain quotations similar to this one:

> There is growing recognition of the role of civil society as both a normative ideal and also a site of democratic and broadly political engagement for social justice. Across the world, civil society organizations play an important role in raising awareness of issues and in campaigning for equity and greater democratic participation. (Kiwan 2009: 83)[4]

The German Federal Agency for Civic Education in turn writes that civil society is seen in a close connection between the ability of a society to organize itself and the resilience of its democratic constitution.[5] The German Federal Ministry for Economic Cooperation and Development states that political scientists describe civil society as a political component necessary alongside the state and market to create an ideal pluralistic society of dedicated citizens.[6] For the *Netzwerk Stiftungen und Bildung*, civil society involvement is associated with the expectation of guaranteeing more democracy and social justice as well as social feedback in political decision-making processes.[7]

The list of similar statements could be expanded almost indefinitely. When people talk about civil society, they most often refer to multicultural district festivals, protest marches against racists, white supremacists, and antifeminists, or to LGBTQI parades such as Christopher Street Day as well as to *Fridays for Future* protests currently (in 2019) taking place in so many countries. In scientific papers, civil society is mentioned, for instance, in relation to the fight against corruption (Kossow/Kukutschka 2017) as well as to good governance or criticism of governments (Grimes 2013). This is civil society as it should be – to paraphrase an advertising slogan of a multinational manufacturer of soft drinks. Almost without exception, civil society is open-minded, diverse, progressive, lively, cool, and environmentally-minded.

However, if one is not willing to allow oneself to be swayed by such images, and if one tries to take a somewhat more distant and perhaps critical look at the concept of civil society, one will hardly be able to avoid realizing that civil society

---

4 See also Williams (2007).
5 https://www.bpb.de/politik/grundfragen/deutsche-verhaeltnisse-eine-sozialkunde/138712/zivilgesellschaft, accessed 16 October 2019.
6 https://www.bmz.de/de/service/glossar/Z/zivilgesellschaft.html, accessed 15 May 2019.
7 https://www.netzwerk-stiftungen-bildung.de/wissenscenter/glossar/zivilgesellschaft, accessed 15 May 2019.

is being idealized. In fact, a critical look would be urgently needed if current developments, for example, in Europe, the United States, and other parts of the world, were taken into account: In many countries, democratic structures are being challenged (to put it mildly), nationalist attitudes are becoming increasingly popular, intolerance, for example, toward ethnic and/or religious groups, is becoming common. These developments are sometimes stimulated by the state, but frequently, if not very often, they find approval in considerable segments of the population in corresponding countries. Societal communication is becoming increasingly extremist, polarized, and irreconcilable; social groups that can certainly be characterized as civil society actors are rather often involved. This raises the question why such a discrepancy exists between a frequently idealized concept of civil society on the one hand and the harsh reality on the other.

## 2 Civil society in theory and reality

If one takes a closer look at the existing scholarly literature and textbooks on theories and concepts of civil society, one does not find a reason to use an idealized concept of civil society:

> Civil society [...] is generally understood to be a social space, namely the pluralistic totality of public associations, unions, and assemblies based on the voluntary interaction of citizens. Associations, federations, and social movements are typical forms of organization. (Adloff 2005: 8; my translation)

This definition says nothing about the social nature of the groups belonging to civil society and it is morally neutral. Civil society might include grassroots initiatives against racism or homophobia, *WikiLeaks* as well as social or environmental movements such as *Fridays for Future*. Empirically, however, it is more than obvious that this range of organizations is only (morally) favorable for a particular portion of society because these groups are actually concerned with the marginalization of people, protest against environmental degradation, or help to reveal the unlawful activities of military and secret services. Perhaps these groups and their activities are in accordance even with the view of the majority of citizens of a given society.

But when one speaks of parts, segments, or portions of society, this already implies that there may be other parts that might express other opinions of such civil society groups. Or to put it another way: It is quite possible that civil society also includes religious fundamentalist, racist, fascist, homophobic, and/or anti-

Semitic groups and all the other marginal and politically extreme groups with (hopefully) comparatively low overall social acceptance. From a historical perspective, Simone Chambers and Jeffrey Kopstein stress that

> [t]he Weimar Republic had a vibrant and well-organized civil society that gave birth to and nurtured the Nazi movement. High levels of associational participation in post-1918 Italy correlate very nicely with support for Mussolini. The new civil societies of Russia and Eastern Europe are home to groups like the Russian National Unity and the Romanian National Union that organize large numbers of citizens around proto-fascist ideologies. (Chambers/Kopstein 2001: 842)

In other words, those groups that are almost never mentioned as members of civil society, at least in *Wikipedia* or on the websites of governmental departments, ministries, or nongovernmental organizations, but are implicitly excluded, also have to be considered as belonging to civil society. Precisely because the concept of civil society, at least in scholarly works, is usually defined in a way that is neutral toward certain groups and also morally indifferent – and thus must be defined because otherwise arbitrary normative stipulations would have to be made, which presumably could not be justified – the identification of civil society with certain social groups, which one might consider morally preferable, is theoretically inappropriate. Such an arbitrary definition of the concept of civil society must inevitably result in rather questionable conclusions such as that civil society is to be regarded as a necessary condition of democracy. In part, this is probably due to the communitarism-liberalism debate of the 1980s and 1990s (e.g., Mulhall/Swift 1992; Sandel 1984). Among others, the writings of Amitai Etzioni as well as Robert Putnam's more sociological works also played a major role in the formation of the (supposed) connection between civil society and democracy. The sociological topic of 'social capital'[8] offers an even broader context.

---

[8] Cf. Gabriel et al. (2002): In many writings of the aforementioned debates it is assumed that there must be a 'core culture' (in German: '*Leitkultur*') in democracies which can give citizens not only moral orientation but whose moral demands must be binding. Such lines of argumentation were (and are) directed in particular against the libertarianism of Robert Nozick and the liberalism of John Rawls; despite all the differences between these two positions and the scholars representing them, they have one thing in common: A democratic society based on the rule of law must do without a moral framework (paradigmatic Rawls 1987; Rawls 1988). If one accepts a communitarian conception of society and/or civil society, then developments such as those observed in Turkey, Poland, Hungary, Italy, or Russia can hardly be legitimately condemned. For it could always be argued that the core cultures of these countries are directed toward a controlled democracy, or that the emphasis on individual rights is not inherent to these cultures. However, this cannot be discussed in depth here.

As indicated above, the popular understanding of civil society is questionable, as it suggests compactness, homogeneity and monolithic identity that is theoretically rather inappropriate. Although Adloff speaks of the "totality of public associations, unions, and assemblies," the reference to this totality should not obscure that civil society itself is constituted of a multitude of very different groups representing both different and conflicting interests. Some civil society groups are committed to saving the environment, others advocate "need for speed"; some want to support migrants, others want to expel them from the country as quickly as possible; some advocate the preservation of lignite mining, others want to save their villages from destruction by mining. Or to put it a little more strikingly: An animal rights protection organization like PETA, the Association for the preservation of kosher (or, for that matter, halal) slaughter and the Association of Bavarian red-game hunters have little in common, with the important exception that they could be counted as part of civil society (assuming that they all really existed) and that they then perhaps actually would see themselves as part of civil society. At least with respect to the first two organizations this is not even fabricated, as in Germany in the past there have always been disputes between animal rights protection organizations and religious associations who want to stick to the tradition of kosher or halal slaughter.

One of the decisive reasons for the usually idealistic popular view on civil society is probably that in democracies certain social groups have often taken on a critical and supervising function vis-à-vis politics and the economy and have pointed to irregularities – in this sense, civil society groups have contributed to constructive communication and thus to the advancement of society. In order to save the concept of civil society, one could therefore be tempted to point out that its formal determinants make it valuable because it speaks – as Adloff and other scholars put it – of "the voluntary interaction of citizens," which makes "public associations, unions, and assemblies" possible in the first place.

If, however, the above-mentioned determining element of voluntariness is understood as a necessary one, religious groups are thus excluded as possible members of civil society. Not only is membership in most religious communities not fundamentally voluntary, since one is born into them and is not asked whether one wants to join. In addition, many religious communities deal very harshly with those willing to quit. Religious groups all too often do not offer the possibility of exit and voice, as Hirschman (1970) called it, as a necessary condition of voluntary membership but demand unrestricted allegiance. The radical Muslim communities which, particularly in Europe or the United States, are frequently mentioned in this context are, however, to be understood only as an example because some Christian religious communities show similar patterns of conduct – think, for instance, of the Jehovah's Witnesses or the Amish. This is probably one of the reasons why, for instance, Jeffrey C. Alexander (1997) argues that religious communities do not belong to civil society (see also Herbert 2002; Kocka 2000).

Although religious groups undoubtedly represent "public associations" (many virtually impose themselves on the public, whether as objects of media coverage or as social actors), they do not necessarily count for being a part of civil society because they (partly) lack the element of voluntary determination – if one understands voluntariness as being a necessary determining element of civil society. But the ambivalence of civil society can also be recognized precisely in the example of the Christian churches: For a long time, Christian churches were regarded as important and morally good (albeit with rough edges) civil society groups, but today deep cracks appear in this portrait. Simultaneously, Christian churches try to control the communication about their internal problems like sexual abuse in order to prevent or weaken public criticism. Since these Christian congregations, being presumed parts of civil society, behave rather dubiously, there exists one more reason to expect that the mostly positive popular view on civil society must become clouded.

## 3 Civil society and particular interests

What has been said so far already calls into question whether civil society groups (can) play an exclusively positive role in shaping public communication and political decision-making processes. However, before going into more detail, the characteristics that civil society groups must have shall be further examined. Adloff names as another determinant of civil society that its actors are characterized both by their distance (or independence) from the state and their being free of commercial interests:

> For example, it is unclear whether the economy or economic organizations should be included in the concept of civil society. Economic liberals and conservatives tend to integrate economic self-reliance into the concept, while left-wing liberals usually draw a clear dividing line between the economy and civil society. (Adloff 2005: 13; my translation)

Of course, one can argue about categories like "economic liberal" or "conservative" used in the quote above. Regardless of this, it remains to be said that it is by no means clear who should or should not belong to civil society with regard to the economic criterion. If one, firstly, accepts distance to the state and, secondly, the absence of economic interests as important determinants, at least for a moment (and thus takes the "left-wing liberal" side), a brief look at reality shows that many supposed civil society groups cannot meet these conditions: The large Christian churches in Germany as well as in many other countries are not characterized by distance and independence from the state since they are closely connected and interlocked with the state both structurally and in terms of personnel at the most diverse levels. Simultaneously, the repeatedly demonstrated claim of religious communities of whatever confession, who undoubtedly see themselves as civil society groups, to participate in state power, is most obvious: With regard to Germany, one only has to consider such conflict-laden debates as those about religious education in state-run schools or about crucifixes in classrooms. In those cases, representatives of particular interests demand a privileged access to state support and power-sharing.

In addition, the claim of the large Christian churches to authority concerning moral questions like abortion, preimplantation genetic diagnosis, or end-of-life-decisions, to name only a few, is without doubt a social and political problem for people belonging to another faith or for nonreligiously bound people because they do not see themselves represented. In Germany, for instance, this claim to authority concerning moral questions results in that probably in any council of some political importance, for example, in councils for public broadcasting companies, ethics committees, and the like, the two large Christian churches are represented, but Muslims, Jews, Hindus, Sikhs, or atheists simply are not. In Germany, this claim can be enforced because the two large Christian churches are organized as public corporations, contrary to many other religious communities which cannot and do not want to organize themselves in this way. Again, this raises doubts about the many above-mentioned determinants of civil society, for it is disturbing that public participation in important decision-making and communication processes should be dependent on the legal constitution of a "public association." The same can be said for secular associations whose political and social impact is created and secured precisely by mutual interlocking of personnel and institutions; with regard (not only) to Germany examples are trade unions as well as business or sports associations.

The determining element of the lack of interest in profit in turn excludes all economically oriented associations; on the one hand, this applies to employers' and professional associations as well as to social associations and trade unions on the other hand. This is because a shortened understanding of profit interest would have to be assumed if business associations were to be excluded from the ranks of civil society groups, while trade unions were to be accepted. Those of us who regularly use public transport have probably already experienced several times by which means interest groups such as trade unions on the one hand and employers on the other try to pursue their particular interests. It is not unusual for them to speak of the common good, but at the same time to accept that immense economic damage is caused and that millions of commuters and rail passengers are degraded to mere means of asserting particular interests. Of course, this is not a plea against the right to strike, but against the idealization of civil society groups – they, too, have (economic) interests and often pursue them with rather harsh means.

Thus, not many candidates for membership in civil society remain. This raises the rather obvious question of why this concept seems so attractive in terms of public communication and political decision-making. One possible answer to this question is that referring to civil society promises a considerable reduction in social complexity, because now one 'only' has to deal with a still large number of civil society actors, but this number is considerably smaller than the number of all actors in a society. Moreover, especially in Germany with its innumerable associations and the tendency to shape their interaction with individuals, other organizations, state authorities, and society as a whole through comprehensive legislation, civil society actors necessarily must have a clearly defined internal constitution – i.e., rules that are intended to shape the "interaction of citizens" within the civil society association. If this inner constitution now includes rules for the appropriate, perhaps even moral, handling of media usage as well as the production and dissemination of media content, one might at least hope that this will quickly constitute a civil society of good actors and thus good communication without hate speech and without fake news.

## 4 Civil society communication = 'good' communication?

But even if something like sincerity, tolerance and solidarity are demanded as moral virtues within a civil society association, such a demand actually always refers only or at least primarily to the members of the civil society association itself, not to the outside world. One only has to keep in mind how political parties, large associations or federations and even Christian congregations react to public criticism: There is a call for unity. This usually means that criticism should remain internal and not become part of a controversial public debate. It is therefore a futile hope that (communicative) conflicts between different civil society groups will be resolved by the mere existence of some kind of an inner constitution or a set of rules that is accepted in those groups. For this constitution or set of rules is usually not even sufficient to pacify internal conflicts – with regard to Germany, this can be seen very well in the example of the right wing or even right extremist political party *Alternative für Deutschland* (AfD).

Chambers and Kopstein (2001) furthermore stress that the structure of collective actors of civil society always requires inclusion and exclusion, because the respective group defines who belongs to it and who does not (see also El-Nawawy/Khamis 2010). As a rule, values such as sincerity, solidarity, or tolerance only apply internally and to the members of a civil society group, but not necessarily externally (Cottle 2005). In addition, by no means all members of a civil society group necessarily enjoy the same opportunities for participation and communication; in many religious and ideologically defined groups women in particular often have only very limited options (cf. Allabadi 2008; King 2009). Chambers and Kopstein therefore draw the conclusion that civil societies are not automatically morally good, fair, or just: There also exists a "bad civil society." It is therefore not surprising that media content, the distribution of which is limited to a certain civil society group, is generally biased, represents particular norms and values and in some cases disseminates anything but contributions to general solidarity or tolerance (e.g., Dallal 2001). Those who expect (communicative) tolerance, for instance, from the National Rifle Association (NRA) with regard to citizen movements that want to restrict the right to bear arms have simply not understood the purpose of the NRA as a "public association" or civil society group, which incidentally fights for the preservation of a constitutional amendment.

Various authors continue to emphasize that the concept of civil society cannot be applied to many actually existing societies at all and that its application nevertheless leads to the mystification of the concept (e.g., Keane 2001). This would be especially true for nondemocratic or authoritarian states where the conditions for the existence of a civil society are lacking.[9] Another concern is that the media tend to secure the status quo rather than support the development of a critical civil society (cf. Klvaňa 2004). With regard to authoritarian or even dictatorial states with strict media control, this indication seems very obvious. Therefore, whether the hopes associated with the Internet as an instrument for promoting (global) civil society are justified (e.g., Castells 2008; Ester/Vinken 2003) remains to be doubted, especially with reference to the events in the Middle East in the context of the so-called 'Arab Spring' and the subsequent developments; the same skepticism applies to the recent developments in Hun-

---

9 Conversely, Tai (2015), for example, argues that in authoritarian states for civil society groups it is necessary to seek state support. It is obvious that in states with tight media control it would be difficult to communicate civil society interests at all without the agreement of the state. This, however, would diametrically oppose the idea that as a defining trait civil society groups must keep distance to the state. Once again it is becoming apparent that the concept of civil society is rather unsuitable for the analysis of communicative processes.

gary, Turkey, Russia, and many other countries in which civil society groups critical of the government can hardly produce any publicity. At the same time, civil society activities in fact are widespread in these countries, but they are not necessarily democratic or critical and therefore cannot meet the criteria of the idealized conception of a good civil society.

When civil society groups use media, they initially do so according to the rules that constitute these groups.[10] From the events surrounding the so-called 'Muhammad cartoons' one can see where this leads: Freedom of expression and tolerance are formulated in a variety of ways. What tolerance is for one civil society group means nothing but (self-)censorship for the other. Olesen (2009) emphasizes that the Muhammad controversy involved civil society groups and that the protests against the publication of the cartoons were a phenomenon of (transnational) civil society activism. Thus, religious groups are seen as part of civil society – which, as indicated above, is controversial. At the same time, Eko and Berkowitz (2009) argue that part of the French press, in particular *Le Monde*, took the position in the Muhammad cartoon controversy that there was an undeniable right to mock religions as part of freedom of expression. The one civil society group thus positioned freedom of expression as an important communicative and ethical norm, the other group demanded religious tolerance and respect. On an abstract level, all participants would probably agree that freedom of expression as well as tolerance and respect are important norms – nevertheless, these norms collide in the concrete conflict. In fact, however, talking about civil society does not help at all at this point, because it neither makes the conflict more understandable nor easier to resolve.

Internally, therefore, media use by civil society groups will often not satisfy ethical requirements that might be considered morally preferable in peaceful democratic societies. Outwardly, there is a great danger that these ethical requirements will even be explicitly contradicted. The sometimes extremely violent events surrounding the aforementioned Muhammad cartoons are an illustrative example (e.g., Powers 2008): When some potential candidates for membership in civil society were publicly demanding the beheading and death of the cartoonist, civil boundaries have long been crossed. But it is also possible to argue that those cartoons and the norms and values associated with them ultimately represent a form of racism as an extreme form of exclusion (cf. Levey/Modood 2009).

---

10 Using the example of the Amish and Mennonites, Kraybill (1998) demonstrates that religious groups, in this case Christian sects, often very restrictively deal with technology in general and with information and communication technology in particular, since from the point of view of these communities the media and their contents represent a grave danger for the very existence of those sects.

This again points out that from a normative point of view a civil society is not necessarily homogeneous and peaceful but may be shaped by clashes of interests and concrete conflicts.

There is another answer to the question why the concept of civil society seems so attractive in terms of public communication as well as from an ethical perspective: There is an unspoken hope that civil society groups are particularly moral. However, as one example among others, the *WikiLeaks* case has shown that the hope for a distinct moral competence on the part of civil society groups is usually unjustified. For such groups also pursue particular interests, which are often represented as a commitment to civil society, but ultimately represent individual interests of exposed persons who try to pursue these interests with the means at their disposal. In such cases the world is divided into good and evil; the self-proclaimed 'good' people demand that different rules apply to them than to the 'bad' people; even serious violations of moral and/or legal norms or the suspicion that such could have taken place are dismissed as irrelevant in view of the self-proclaimed mandate. The Assange case speaks for itself: Only a few newspaper articles pointed out that Assange had fled to the Ecuadorian embassy in London not least because of the rape charges raised against him. A general failure of many civil society groups can and must be attested here, not only with regard to communicative processes, since an alleged crime against two women was simply ignored. Even if one may not share the doubts expressed in this paper about the concept of civil society, it is difficult to deny that membership in a civil society group cannot necessarily be translated into moral integrity.

## 5 Tentative conclusions

In fact, civil society groups are rather inclined to fundamentalism; perhaps they even have to be inclined to it. In this respect they often do not differ in their rigor from those they oppose. This can be seen in many examples in which (communicative) discord was brought into society, sometimes over long decades. The tendency of civil society groups toward fundamentalism cannot, however, come as a surprise, for this promotes cohesion and identification internally, which can only be achieved, however, by demarcation from the outside. There will then be no room for compromise, but it is precisely compromise that is the single reasonable defining element of a civil society – at least if one is willing to translate the term 'civil society' to 'peaceful society.' In short, recourse to civil society does not solve one single communicative problem; on the contrary, the concept of civil society produces new problems far beyond what could be addressed here – for example, the disputed political legitimacy of civil society groups or the problem of group versus individual rights.

# References

Adloff, Frank (2005): *Zivilgesellschaft: Theorie und politische Praxis.* Frankfurt a.M./New York, NY: Campus.
Alexander, Jeffrey C. (1997): "The Paradoxes of Civil Society." In: *International Sociology* 12(2), pp. 115–133.
Allabadi, Fadwa (2008): "Controversy: Secular and Islamist Women in Palestinian Society." In: *European Journal of Women's Studies* 15(3), pp. 181–201.
Castells, Manuel (2008): "The New Public Sphere: Global Civil Society, Communication Networks, and Global Governance." In: *The ANNALS of the American Academy of Political and Social Science* 616(1), pp. 78–93.
Chambers, Simone/Kopstein, Jeffrey (2001): "Bad Civil Society." In: *Political Theory* 29(6), pp. 837–865.
Cottle, Simon (2005): "Mediatized Public Crisis and Civil Society Renewal: The Racist Murder of Stephen Lawrence." In: *Crime, Media, Culture: An International Journal* 1(1), pp. 49–71.
Dallal, Jenine Abboushi (2001): "Hizballah's Virtual Civil Society." In: *Television & New Media* 2(4), pp. 367–372.
Eko, Lyombe/Berkowitz, Dan (2009): "*Le Monde*, French Secular Republicanism and 'The Mohammed Cartoons Affair': Journalistic 'Re-Presentation' of the Sacred Right to Offend." In: *International Communication Gazette* 71(3), pp. 181–202.
El-Nawawy, Mohammed/Khamis, Sahar (2010): "Collective Identity in the Virtual Islamic Public Sphere." In: *International Communication Gazette* 72(3), pp. 229–250.
Ester, Peter/Vinken, Henk (2003): "Debating Civil Society: On the Fear for Civic Decline and Hope for the Internet Alternative." In: *International Sociology* 18(4), pp. 659–680.
Gabriel, Oscar W./Kunz, Volker/Roßteutscher, Sigrid/Van Deth, Jan W. (2002): *Sozialkapital und Demokratie: Zivilgesellschaftliche Ressourcen im Vergleich.* Wien: WUV-Universitätsverlag.
Grimes, Marcia (2013): "The Contingencies of Societal Accountability: Examining the Link between Civil Society and Good Government." In: *Studies in Comparative International Development* 48(4), pp. 380–402.
Herbert, Ulrich (2002): "Liberalisierung als Lernprozeß: Die Bundesrepublik in der deutschen Geschichte – eine Skizze." In: Herbert, Ulrich (Ed.): *Wandlungsprozesse in Westdeutschland: Belastung, Integration, Liberalisierung 1945–1980.* Göttingen: Wallstein, pp. 7–49.
Hirschman, Albert O. (1970): *Exit, Voice, and Loyalty: Responses to Decline in Firms, Organizations, and States.* Cambridge, MA: Harvard University Press.
Keane, Michael (2001): "Broadcasting Policy, Creative Compliance and the Myth of Civil Society in China." In: *Media, Culture & Society* 23(6), pp. 783–798.
King, Anna (2009): "Islam, Women and Violence." In: *Feminist Theology* 17(3), pp. 292–328.
Kiwan, Dina (2009): "Civil Society, Democracy and Education." In: *Education, Citizenship and Social Justice* 4(2), pp. 83–86.

Klvaňa, Tomáš P. (2004): "New Europe's Civil Society, Democracy, and the Media Thirteen Years After." In: *The Harvard International Journal of Press/Politics* 9(3), pp. 40–55.

Kocka, Jürgen (2000): "Zivilgesellschaft als historisches Projekt: Moderne europäische Geschichtsforschung in vergleichender Absicht." In: Dipper, Christof/Klinkhammer, Lutz/Nützenadel, Alexander (Eds.): *Europäische Sozialgeschichte: Festschrift für Wolfgang Schieder.* Berlin: Duncker & Humblot, pp. 475–484.

Kossow, Niklas/Kukutschka, Roberto Martínez Barranco (2017): "Civil Society and Online Connectivity: Controlling Corruption on the Net?" In: *Crime, Law and Social Change* 68(4), pp. 459–476.

Kraybill, Donald (1998): "Plain Reservations: Amish and Mennonite Views of Media and Computers." In: *Journal of Mass Media Ethics* 13(2), pp. 99–110.

Levey, Geoffrey Brahm/Modood, Tariq (2009): "The Muhammad Cartoons and Multicultural Democracies." In: *Ethnicities* 9(3), pp. 427–447.

MacLeod, Alan (2019): "Chavista 'Thugs' vs. Opposition 'Civil Society': Western Media on Venezuela." In: *Race & Class* 60(4), pp. 46–64.

Mulhall, Stephen/Swift, Adam (1992): *Liberals and Communitarians.* Oxford/Cambridge, MA: Blackwell.

Olesen, Thomas (2009): "The Muhammad Cartoons Conflict and Transnational Activism." In: *Ethnicities* 9(3), pp. 409–426.

Powers, Shawn (2008): "Examining the Danish Cartoon Affair: Mediatized Cross-cultural Tensions?" In: *Media, War & Conflict* 1(3), pp. 339–359.

Rawls, John (1987): "The Idea of an Overlapping Consensus." In: *Oxford Journal of Legal Studies* 7(1), pp. 1–25.

Rawls, John (1988): "The Priority of Right and Ideas of the Good." In: *Philosophy and Public Affairs* 17(4), pp. 251–276.

Sandel, Michael J. (Ed.) (1984): *Liberalism and Its Critics.* New York, NY: New York University Press.

Tai, John W. (2015): *Building Civil Society in Authoritarian China: Importance of Leadership Connections for Establishing Effective Nongovernmental Organizations in a Non-Democracy.* Cham: Springer.

Williams, Rhys H. (2007): "The Languages of the Public Sphere: Religious Pluralism, Institutional Logics, and Civil Society." In: *The ANNALS of the American Academy of Political and Social Science* 612(1), pp. 42–61.

Eva Weber-Guskar
# Criticizing Moral Criticism
## Moralism on the Internet

**Abstract:** A moral community depends on its members engaging with each other with appropriate moral praise and blame. Therefore, it is only consistent that such a community should nurture this practice and take note when something goes awry with it, when it is threatened or, conversely, when it is exaggerated. Recently, voices warning of the danger of exaggerating the practice of moral praise and blame in public discourse have become louder. At the same time, a decisive role is attributed to communication via the Internet, or more precisely via digital mass media, in shaping this discourse. This paper makes suggestions concerning what could explain a connection between the two, that is, why digital mass media might promote moralism, and it discusses what is problematic about moralism particularly in digital mass media. First, a working definition of moralism is introduced. Second, a possible connection between digital media use and the rise in moralizing behavior is made plausible by an analysis of the practice of online commenting. This provides the background for the concluding discussion of the normative question of what exactly is deserving criticism in moralism particularly in such digital mass media.

**Keywords:** Moralism, moral criticism, online comments, digital mass media

A moral community depends on its members engaging with each other with appropriate moral praise and blame: The expression of praise and criticism is needed in order to uphold the constitutive norms of society. Therefore, it is only consistent that such a community should nurture this practice and take note when something goes awry with it, when it is threatened or, conversely, when it is exaggerated. In Germany, voices warning of the danger of exaggerating the practice of moral praise and blame have recently become louder. For example, Baden-Württemberg's premier Kretschmann warned in a discussion about the proper way to handle the rise of the political party AfD that people should "stop moralizing" (Kretschmann 2016). In addition to this warning about exaggerated moral

---

**Note:** This article is a shortened and translated version of an article that was first written in German: Weber-Guskar (2020).

criticism in public discourse, a decisive role is attributed to communication via the Internet, or more precisely via digital mass media, in shaping this discourse. Without wanting to make a claim about the extent to which public socio-political discourse takes place on the Internet, it is certainly true that it *also* takes place there. Thus, it makes sense to suspect a connection between the two, namely the current tendency to moralize and the rise of digital mass media.

The empirical question that arises here is whether there is an actual connection between the two: Does digital mass media promote moralism? And in terms of moral philosophy, the question that arises is what is or could be problematic about moralism particularly in digital mass media. My focus in this paper is on the second question. However, to answer it, I will also need to say something about the first. To do that, I am going to introduce a working definition of moralism. I will then emphasize the online commentary feature as a decisive aspect of the transformation in media from the analog to the digital age in order to make plausible a possible connection between digital media use and the rise in moralizing behavior. This provides the background for the concluding discussion of the normative question of what exactly is deserving of criticism in moralism particularly in such digital mass media.

# 1 Moralism

There is an overlap in recent explanations of moralism in the philosophical literature, which can be used here for a broad working definition. According to these explanations, moralizing behavior consists in statements in which critical moral judgements that are distorted in a certain way are made about others. Following this understanding, moralism is a thick concept that has both descriptive and evaluative or normative elements and involves a negative evaluation: Moralistic statements are – prima facie – bad (cf., e.g., Betzler 2020). What exactly is problematic about this will be discussed in more detail later. First, the descriptive part needs to be analyzed.

The characteristic distortion involved in moral judgements can be of various kinds. It can concern the content or the form of the judgement. In other words, something is brought into the moral realm that does not belong there, or something is exaggerated in the moral realm. It is accordingly possible to distinguish more precisely (but still roughly) between three basic types of moralistic statements.

Moralistic statements are statements that either

M1)  make a moral judgement about something that does not concern morality (Driver 2005; Hallich 2020), or
M2)  exaggerate in their moral judgement (Mieth/Rosenthal 2020; Neuhäuser 2020), or
M3)  make a moral reproach without having the necessary standing to do so (Fullinwider 2005; Mayr 2020).

The first type (M1) can be described as moralism in the narrow sense if we understand the word "moralizing" in the sense that someone declares something to be a moral matter which actually is not a moral matter. This means, for example, that someone is morally blamed for a harmless enjoyment, that a purely representative work of art is criticized on moral terms rather than aesthetic terms, or that a bad moral character is attributed to someone because of their (poor) choice of clothing. The mistake made by such a moralist here may simply be epistemic (or even a mistake of moral judgement).

The second type (M2) in the basic characterization of moralism consists in making a moral judgement where a moral judgement is appropriate but exaggerating the judgement. This simply means that something is classified as morally much worse than it actually is. For example, something is considered a great offense, which is actually a pardonable misstep – such as when someone promises to call you in the evening to chat but forgets. A moralist in this sense is someone who holds moral sermons on minor things or threatens draconian punishments in advance. The person does not seem to use the proper yardstick for assessing the degree of moral misconduct. In other words, the mistake here is in the moral judgement: An incorrect moral judgement is made about the severity of the offense.

On the one hand, the exaggeration described here may refer to the assessment of the action (M2a). On the other hand, it may also refer to a judgement about the person as a whole (M2b). An exaggeration relevant to moralism is present in this case if one considers the person only in terms of their moral misconduct and completely leaves out all other aspects of the person (Taylor 2005: 157). In this regard, the moralist does not consider how someone might be painfully aware of their own mistake – and therefore does not need such judgements to be made from the outside, or at least not to that extent. This might be the case, for example, when one friend fails to help another and this is held against them (or is constantly or repeatedly held against them), even though the person in question regrets the failure and has apologized for it. To put this in deontological terms: This testifies to a lack of moral respect for a person capable of change.

The third type of moralism (M3) mentioned here can also be seen in the discussion of "standing to blame," which asks who is in the right position, by virtue of which qualities or circumstances, to morally reproach someone else.[1] There are several reasons why one person might not be allowed to morally reproach another, even if the reproach is correct in substance. One of the reasons is that the person themselves does not live up to the moral standards they use as a measure for the reproach. This is the case, for example, when a regular shoplifter without a guilty conscience accuses another person of the same action. Another reason is that the person is interfering in private matters. That would be the case, for example, if a stranger in public takes sides in a moral way in a disagreement between a couple. And finally, a third reason that speaks against being in the position to make a substantive moral reproach is the fact that this reproach has already been clearly expressed by others such that the accused has already been subject to moral criticism – in that case there is no need to "pile on" the criticism. If this kind of behavior is directed less at the guilty party itself and instead concerns the larger public, it would more accurately be regarded as public denunciation (Mieth/Rosenthal 2020). The relevant mistake here can be formulated in terms of virtue ethics: Moralism in this regard attests to a certain narcissism that leads the person always to present themselves as a particularly committed moral critic and to take pleasure in doing so (Tosi/Warmke 2016: 215).

In what follows, I refer to moralism in this implied sense in order to clarify whether there are good reasons to suppose that the conditions of communication via digital mass media support a tendency toward moralism.

## 2 Moralism in online comments in digital mass media

### 2.1 Online posts and comments

Mass media is a means for the public dissemination of information and public exchange of opinions. Clearly media has changed in the wake of increasing digitization. In addition to classic journalism in print, radio, and television, online journalism has become established, as have online amateur and crowd journalism. There are also new ways of sharing information and opinions, namely in social networks or other platforms, such as *Facebook*, *Instagram*, *Twitter*, etc. But

---

[1] See, e.g., Friedman (2013).

all these variants of digital mass media have one feature that separates them from analog media: comments. Content is not just placed online for others to see; people are able to comment on the content immediately and directly within the same media. Online comments can be used to provide supplemental information or to ask and answer questions. However, for the most part comments are used to make judgements about the people (or events) mentioned in the content. This makes the comments section a forum that allows for extensive criticism – as well as moralism. Because the comments feature represents a major innovation in mass media and because it is widely used, this paper focuses on the question of the extent to which current mass media may promote moralism through this feature.

What conditions characterize communication via online comments in contrast to similar communication options in analog media? Four points stand out here: speed, low effort, reach and, anonymity.

First, the *speed* of the dissemination of information and opinions as well as the reactions to them has increased. You do not have to wait until the next day to read about an incident; reports are produced on an hourly cycle, and you can access them anytime and anywhere with a tablet or smartphone; you do not have to sit in front of the radio waiting for the hourly news for example. Reactions can be written immediately and can immediately be read by others.

Second, you do not have to expend the *effort* to write a letter to the editor, which is only worth doing if it is longer than a sentence, print it out, mail it, and then wait a long time for a response, not knowing whether you will get the privilege of having your editorial printed so that more people than just the editor hear your opinion. Commenting has become extremely easy. The low effort also feeds a culture of commenting without presenting any argumentation. An online comment can consist of a single sentence and this is normally just a comment in the sense of an opinion, given without strong reasoning, or any reasoning at all. The comments feature can actually be used as a kind of chat feature that facilitates the quick and direct exchange of arguments, which may also produce interesting discussions depending on the topic and the kind of platform. But to do this, you have to go a step further, from commentary on the text (which is not an offer to engage in a discussion with the author or commenters) to contributing to the discussion. This tends to happen more with comments on posts among people who are already involved with each other (such as on *Facebook*) rather than with strangers who are commenting on an online newspaper article, even if you do after some time get to know some of the "protagonists" there under their pseudonym.

Third, the *reach* of statements as well as the amount of people who respond quickly to statements has expanded. People do not just read local and national newspapers – some topics go viral throughout the world. In this case it is not just a few selected reader comments that can be seen; there may be thousands.

Finally, fourth, *anonymity* is playing a larger role. Letters to the editor in printed newspapers have not been anonymous since the mid-twentieth century, and if anonymous letters are received, they will not be published. But on the Internet, people can often comment anonymously, or more precisely, under a pseudonym. Depending on the settings, participants are usually known at least to the editorial staff under their real name and address. On the surface, however, at the level of concrete communication, there is anonymity. You can interactively participate in the network without having to reveal your true identity. The lack of a real name or the lack of traceability to a person beyond the specific situation are what makes the communicative situation online special.[2] It is also frequently stressed that the Internet affords a kind of "invisibility" as well: Unlike on the street, where you can also meet people anonymously and not know where they live, online communication takes place without the participants being physically present, that is, without being able to look each other in the eyes, without facial expressions, gestures, tone of voice, or accompanying behavior (see, e. g., Brodnig 2014). Of course, this was always the case with written communication such as letters. However, what is new here is the *combination* of speed and the large reach. In the past, this kind of "invisible" communication was delayed in time. You could not exchange thoughts immediately, and definitely not with as many people simultaneously. It might be objected that telephone calls have for a long time already been conducted in an invisible way without any temporal delay, but at least in this case the person's voice was physically present, and it was also not possible to communicate with so many people simultaneously.[3]

In what follows, I will illustrate the above definition of moralism and the effect of the conditions provided by the online commentary feature with two examples.

## 2.2 Examples of moralism in online comments

The thrust of the scandals in the cases of the former German Bishop Margot Käßmann on the one hand and the former German Federal President Christian Wulff on the other hand can be described as moralizing. Both are also exemplary of cases of public denunciation (M3): The media reported on some moral miscon-

---

[2] On anonymity online see, for example, Thiel (2016: 10–11) and Wallace (1999).
[3] You can of course chat using a webcam, but that is different than using the comment feature.

duct or the suspicion of moral misconduct, and then thousands felt themselves called upon to give their opinion in commentary forums, which primarily meant emphasizing the moral reprehensibility of the action or alleged action – i.e., repeating a reproach that had already been made without being interested in details and distinctions. As mentioned above, people tend to give opinions rather than thoughtful arguments. The rude, spiteful, or malicious tone in which these opinions are given is another problematic aspect of such comments but needs to be distinguished from the actual issue of moralism.[4]

Käßmann was driving with a blood alcohol content of 0.15 percent, disregarded a red light (without anyone being harmed) and was caught by the police. She not only got points on her driving record for violating a traffic regulation, she was also charged for driving under influence. You can of course morally reproach her for her irresponsible behavior which endangered others. But in moral terms, the reproaches in the media went beyond such reproach in at least three of the ways mentioned above: First, there was an exaggeration in the assessment of the gravity of the moral offense with associated sanctions (M2a). It is not clear that the status as a role model associated with being a Bishop would be compromised to such a degree from a single traffic offense that she should lose her position. But the reproaches went in that direction, maintaining that she behaved in an intolerable way and that it was proof that she did not hold herself to the ideal she represented. These demands could be considered exaggerated especially when they are also raised without considering the person as a whole (M2b): You can seriously regret a mistake and refrain from making the same mistake again in the future. This might have been the case with Käßmann, but that was ignored. Third, the kind of moralism associated with "piling on" was also involved, i.e., repeated criticism after many other people had already criticized her (M3).

In the case of Wulff, it also turned out that the allegations of corruption made against him were baseless. But the presumption of innocence in the absence of evidence was suspended. He was accused of not admitting his guilt, which was another moral reproach. He was morally reproached in a case where it was unclear whether a moral offense had actually taken place. In this case, the people reproaching him did not have the proper standing to make such reproaches (M3). It actually turned out later that he had not committed any moral offense. He was also judged very harshly in moral terms where at most something very minor should have been criticized (M2): He had accepted

---

[4] For a discussion about impoliteness or rudeness on the Internet, especially in online comments, see, for example, Santana (2014).

the gift of a buggy from a car dealership, and his wife wore borrowed clothes at a public event. The at most halfway solid reproach was that he had accepted hotel lodging for a night worth 700 euros. The demands that he resign simply seemed exaggerated in view of this. He was ultimately acquitted of the charges, but by that time he was no longer in office.

What speaks for the fact that on the whole there are more such moralistic judgements in the context of online comments than in analog media?

## 2.3 Conditions for moralistic distortion in digital mass media

It might be supposed that it is precisely those characteristics of digital communication in mass media which distinguish it from analog communication as outlined above that provide a breeding ground for moralistic expressions: Speed, low effort, reach, and anonymity or invisibility promote moralizing in the narrow sense, exaggeration in moral judgements, or judgements made without having the necessary standing to do so. This is supported by at least a few existing social-psychological findings, which I will draw upon in what follows.

First, speed, along with reach, seduces us into expressing moral condemnation where others have already done so, without our having the proper standing to do so (M3). This is because reach also means mass participation, and mass participation means the presence of many opinions. Studies in social psychology have shown that people tend toward conformist behavior, and the ease of just clicking to express agreement increases this tendency to conformism, as has been shown in studies of shitstorms and hate commentary.[5] Moralistic "piling on" is thus supported by a psychological mechanism, which is stimulated in the structure of the world of online comments as described here.

The exaggeration in moral judgement (M2) is, so to speak, promoted by all the features of online comments: Given the speed and the large number of participants, in order to be read at all or to attract attention (which is usually at least one motivation among others for even participating), you have to be succinct and pointed – which makes escalation and exaggeration useful. Anonymity is also particularly relevant here. There are scientific studies that confirm the everyday

---

[5] There are studies on conformism in general, outside of the online world, which show that people often agree with the majority opinion, even if they actually hold another opinion – not only with regard to normative issues but with regard to sense perception such as visual impressions. See Pauen/Welzer (2015: 133–147). Regarding online communication, Pauen and Welzer then speak of an "inherent dynamic of social processes that is virtually beyond the reach of individual control" (2015: 251; my translation).

impression that people let loose with all sorts of opinions and are much more uninhibited in anonymous online communication than they would be under their own name and when facing another real person. This is known as the "online disinhibition effect."[6]

The reason online comments also tend toward moralizing behaviors that do not really belong to the realm of morality (M1) can also be explained, at least as a hypothesis, by the continuation of the phenomenon of exaggeration. Moral criticism is usually thought to carry more weight than other forms of criticism. In this sense, the need to make a strong, eye-catching statement online can lead to people making moral judgements where such judgements do not actually belong because it is a way to stand out from the tempest of comments.

All of these aspects mutually reinforce each other, which creates a dynamic that can lead to a negative spiral of morally distorted judgements. Given this background overview of the empirical facts and hypothesis, we can now address the moral-philosophical question of what is *especially* morally problematic about moralism in the context of digital mass media.

# 3 What is problematic about moralism online?

In deontological terms, there is a lack of respect for the criticized person in some cases. And in virtue-ethics terms, some display the vice of narcissism (Suler 2004).[7] The problematic consequences that are central from the point of view of consequentialist ethics, but also play a role in other ethics, can vary depending on the context. In the following, I will look at the problematic consequences for society and the practice of morality.

## 3.1 Social consequences

Apart from concrete consequences for individuals (from damage to reputation to loss of a job without good reason), widespread moralism on the Internet can also have more general morally problematic consequences for society. When moralistic statements get out of hand, they can, first, create a problematic overall social mood. Not only may people feel intimidated about being public about things be-

---

[6] A summary of the study of the disinhibition effect (as well as the "honesty effect") can be found in Thiel (2016: 13–14).
[7] On morality and the virtue of open-mindedness, see Betzler (2020). She makes more precise distinctions and would probably count narcissism as a vice of vanity.

cause they fear harsh criticism; moralism (possibly reinforced by a counteraction) can also lead to a general polarization in the normative debate. This, in turn, can feed populist currents, that is, political debates that are not prudent in differentiating between matters. This may apply to online criticism in general such that online moralism just has the same negative impact here as other forms of harsh criticism.

A second point, however, shows a more specific problem associated with moralism. Moralistic expressions are specifically problematic in political discourse when they are of the variety that something that should not be evaluated morally is criticized on moral terms. The criticism of Angela Merkel's refugee policy in Germany could be seen as an example of such moralism:[8] When people discuss the moral integrity or depravity of the Chancellor that may have led her to take the step of opening the border in 2015, this really goes beyond what actually needs to be discussed. What is at issue is the best political decision in this situation, something which is unlikely to be decided without some moral compromises. Political decisions should, of course, be informed by proper moral judgements, but they do not always coincide with moral judgements and, accordingly, they are not primarily to be evaluated as moral judgements but as political judgements. The relationship between these two kinds of judgement is, however, something that deserves its own discussion. In any case, it sometimes complicates, slows, and poisons the debate when one has to argue why this or that moralistic judgement is inappropriate (i.e., why we should not be talking about the Chancellor's virtues or vices) instead of discussing the matter itself (i.e., what would be the right thing to do in such a complex situation).

## 3.2 Consequences for the practice of morality

Regardless of these consequences, there is another dimension of problematic consequences of widespread moralism that we can discuss. If participants in public discourse tend more toward moralism when being online, and if public discourse becomes more and more moralistic as more and more parts of public discourse take place on the Internet, it could be a danger to the moral community insofar as it would be a danger to the practice of morality itself. Why would this be the case?

One might initially think that even if moralistic statements are problematic, they still take place, as we have seen above, within the realm of morals. Moral-

---

[8] For a more detailed discussion of the subject of refugees and moralism, see Wendt (2020).

istic statements are based on a moral standard and are motivated by the desire to promote morality. A thief in contrast makes a moral misstep, without following the rules of morality at all. Why should the practice of morality be damaged if mistakes are made in its name? Indeed, it might seem as if moralistic statements support existing morality insofar as they insist on the observance of the rules and thereby make them particularly clear, even if they overshoot the goal in doing so.

However, the problem is the kind of mistake involved in moralism. There are mistakes in the moral judgement of actions – either in terms of the seriousness of an offense or regarding whether the action is one that is subject to moral criticism at all. And these mistakes implicate problematic consequences for the existence of the practice of morality in at least three respects.

First, moralizing is accompanied by unnecessary moral outrage. This leaves little room in the rarer cases of truly serious moral offenses for mustering the amount of energy or making the critical distinctions that would be required to do justice to those cases in comparison to the others (Tosi/Warmke 2016: 211). Moralism in this way undermines the power of appropriate moral reproaches.

Second, moralism can lead to a feeling of excessive burden on those who are unsure of their moral judgement or behavior. Morality itself can be placed in a bad light when it is associated with demands that would require a great deal of effort to meet, or that are pedantic, voiced by the wrong people etc. This creates a distorted image of morality that makes some people less motivated to pursue it. Just as too little moral criticism can lead to fewer people acting in moral ways, so too can "too much" moral criticism.

Finally, third, certain forms of moralizing with regard to morality are similar to what Harry Frankfurt calls "bullshitting" with regard to factual arguments (Frankfurt 1988; Tosi/Warmke 2016: 209). Bullshitting involves making statements that appear in the guise of arguments or as contributions to discourse about the truth but are not interested in truth at all. Bullshitting is a threat to the functioning of discourse that is actually interested in the truth. Moralizing can in this regard be seen as a form of expression of moral evaluations that are not actually interested in the practice of morality. This is the case at least when moral statements are ultimately used, whether consciously or not, in an instrumental way to present oneself as better than others, to enforce political ends, or to harm others. When this happens, moralizing threatens to corrode moral discourse from the inside.

As I have shown, there are good reasons to believe that the conditions surrounding online comments encourage moralistic statements, and there are good reasons to think that moralism online is particularly problematic because its negative effects are greater online than offline.

## 4 Outlook

Should we conclude then that something needs to be done, perhaps even in the legal domain, to combat moralism online? That is another question I have not discussed here. In another essay, I discuss and explain why I believe there is no justification for systematically preventing or selectively eliminating it.[9] That is because such an approach would mean a restriction of freedom of expression and moralizing behavior is not as serious in comparison. But that also does not mean that nothing should be done about it. What then can be done?

First, one could try to prevent the damage from moralism by engaging directly with the consequences. For example, one could try to prevent a Federal President from losing public confidence and from being condemned socially in such a way that he had to resign before any judicial conviction – even if this is confusing terrain and the processes in which public opinion is formed are difficult to control. Politicians would have to take it upon themselves here to speak out publicly online as well as in traditional media.

In addition, all those involved in the public moral and socio-political discourse should do everything in their power to work toward reducing such moralism. It would be difficult to directly address the subtle topic of moralism in campaigns and events run by political foundations and similar organizations. It should, however, be part of the effort to set a good public tone for discourse.[10]

Finally, one might consider whether something could be done to change the technological conditions that, as described above, fuel moralism in online comments. There are already some ideas in this direction for reducing hate comments and the like: Some have considered doing away with anonymity by using real names, and some experiments have been done in this direction.[11] There have also been experiments on slowing down the speed by having people who would like to leave comments first answer three simple questions about the text before they can post.[12] Of course such efforts still need to be examined systematically.

---

9 I have set out my answer to this in a longer article. See Weber-Guskar (2020).
10 One organization that is bringing together such initiatives is das-nettz.de.
11 On this discussion, see, for example, Weber-Guskar (2019).
12 Griffin (2017).

# References

Betzler, Monika (2020): "Moralismus und die Tugend der Aufgeschlossenheit." In: Neuhäuser, Christian/Seidel, Christian (Eds.): *Kritik des Moralismus*. Berlin: Suhrkamp, pp. 106–133.
Brodnig, Ingird (2014): *Der unsichtbare Mensch: Wie die Anonymität im Internet unsere Gesellschaft verändert*. Vienna: Czernin.
Driver, Julia (2005): "Moralism." In: *Journal of Applied Philosophy* 22(2), pp. 137–151.
Frankfurt, Harry (1988): "On Bullshit." In: *The Importance of What We Care About: Philosophical Essays*. New York, NY: Cambridge University Press, pp. 117–133.
Friedman, Marilyn (2013): "How to Blame People Responsibly." In: *The Journal of Value Inquiry* 47(3), pp. 271–284.
Fullinwider, Robert K. (2005): "On Moralism." In: *Journal of Applied Philosophy* 22(2), pp. 105–120.
Hallich, Oliver (2020): "Was ist Moralismus? Ein Explikationsvorschlag." In: Neuhäuser, Christian/Seidel, Christian (Eds.): *Kritik des Moralismus*. Berlin: Suhrkamp, pp. 61–82.
Griffin, Andrew (2017): "News Site Makes Readers Answer Questions to Prove They Understand Story Before Posting Comments" In: *Independent* 2 March 2017. https://www.independent.co.uk/life-style/gadgets-and-tech/news/nrk-norwegian-news-site-comments-read-story-understand-post-quiz-questions-a7607246.html, accessed 19 July 2020.
Kretschmann, Winfried (2016): "Schluss mit dem Moralisieren." In: *Die Zeit* 7 October 2016. https://www.zeit.de/2016/42/die-gruenen-kritik-winfried-kretschmann-afd-aufstieg, accessed 19 July 2020.
Mayr, Erasmus (2020): "Moralismus und die Zuständigkeit für moralische Vorwürfe." In: Neuhäuser, Christian/Seidel, Christian (Eds.): *Kritik des Moralismus*. Berlin: Suhrkamp, pp. 83–105.
Mieth, Corinna/Rosenthal, Jacob (2020): "Spielarten des Moralismus." In: Neuhäuser, Christian/Seidel, Christian (Eds.): *Kritik des Moralismus*. Berlin: Suhrkamp, pp. 35–60.
Neuhäuser, Christian (2020): "Moralismuskritik und vernünftige Erwartbarkeit." In: Neuhäuser, Christian/Seidel, Christian (Eds.): *Kritik des Moralismus*. Berlin: Suhrkamp, pp. 383–405.
Pauen, Michael/Welzer, Harald (2015): *Autonomie: Eine Verteidigung*. Frankfurt a. M.: Fischer.
Santana, Arthur D. (2014): "Virtuous or Vitriolic." In: *Journalism Practice* 8(1), pp. 18–33.
Suler, John (2004): "The Online Disinhibition Effect." In: *CyberPsychology & Behavior* 7(3), pp. 321–326.
Taylor, Craig (2005): "Moralism and Morally Accountable Beings." In: *Journal of Applied Philosophy* 22(2), pp. 153–160.
Thiel, Thorsten (2016): "Anonymität und der digitale Strukturwandel der Öffentlichkeit." In: *Zeitschrift für Menschenrechte* 10(1), pp. 7–24.
Tosi, Justin/Warmke, Brandon (2016): "Moral Grandstanding." In: *Philosophy and Public Affairs* 44(3), pp. 197–217.
Wallace, Kathleen A. (1999): "Anonymity." In: *Ethics and Information Technology* 1(1), pp. 21–31.
Weber-Guskar, Eva (2019): "Ambivalente Anonymität: Demokratische Debatten in Online-Kommentaren?" In: Behrendt, Hauke/Loh, Wulf/Matzner, Tobias/Misselhorn,

Catrin (Eds.): *Privatsphäre 4.0: Eine Neuverortung des Privaten im Zeitalter der Digitalisierung*. Stuttgart: Metzler, pp. 199–212.

Weber-Guskar, Eva (2020): "Der Online-Kommentar: Moralismus in digitalen Massenmedien." In: Neuhäuser, Christian/Seidel, Christian (Eds.): *Kritik des Moralismus*. Berlin: Suhrkamp, pp. 422–447.

Wendt, Fabian (2020): "Moralismus in der Migrationsdebatte." In: Neuhäuser, Christian/Seidel, Christian (Eds.): *Kritik des Moralismus*. Berlin: Suhrkamp, pp. 406–421.

# Part 4: Philosophical Critique and Questions of Social Identity

Christine Bratu
# Idiots and Assholes
## What We Should Criticize When We Criticize Sexist Action

**Abstract:** In this paper I argue against a cognitivist understanding of sexist action, according to which an action is sexist insofar as it can be traced back to the agent's belief that some people have a subordinate social position in virtue of their gender. We see this conception at work whenever people defend themselves against the charge of sexism by saying, e.g., that it is impossible for them to act in a sexist way as they do not subscribe to a sexist worldview. I contend that we should reject this conception because it cannot make sense of the intuition that sexist actions wrong their targets. To do so, proponents of the cognitive conception would have to assume that there is doxastic morality in the strict sense, i.e., that we can wrong each other simply in virtue of the beliefs we entertain about each other. But at least against the backdrop of liberal moral philosophy, we cannot make this assumption as it conflicts with our freedom of thought.

**Keywords:** Sexism, doxastic morality, doxastic wronging, freedom of thought

## 1 Introduction

In her influential essay on sexism, Marilyn Frye claims that individual acts are sexist insofar as they reinforce and support structures "which divide the species, along the lines of sex, into dominators and subordinates" (Frye 1983: 38). The understanding of sexist action Frye employs here raises many questions. For instance, do sexist actions result in domination and subordination in a normative or in a descriptive sense? How can an individual action contribute to structural domination and subordination? And should we not rather be talking about gender, as opposed to sex, as the base of sexism? These open questions notwithstanding, I consider Frye's understanding to point us into the right direction, i.e., *toward a consequentialist understanding of sexist action*, as for Frye an action is sexist depending on what it potentially does in the world.

Over the last years I have had quite a few discussions about sexist action and from these I conclude that many people reject such a consequentialist understanding in favor of what I call a cognitivist one. According to *a cognitivist understanding*, an action is sexist insofar as it can be traced back to some sexist belief on the part of the agent performing it. That people subscribe to such an understanding, often becomes apparent when they are accused of having acted in a sexist way. In most cases, such a charge leads to a strong emotional reaction, ranging from indignation to outright outrage, and often the accused try to dismiss it by pointing out that they do not believe that some people are inferior or have a subordinate social position because of their gender, similar to how Donald Trump denied the blatant racism of his hateful tweets about four congresswomen of color by stating "I don't have a Racist bone in my body!" (cf. Fabian 2019). Pointing to the purity of their beliefs only makes sense as a defense strategy if they assume (at least implicitly) that whether their actions are sexist or not depends on what they believe rather than on the consequences of what they did.

In this paper, I argue against a cognitivist understanding of sexist action. My aim thus bears a strong resemblance to what has been called "solving the location problem" in the philosophy of race, where people try to establish what makes an action racist (cf. Glasgow 2009: 65–71). In the philosophy of race, this discussion is mainly driven by counterexamples as those arguing against a cognitivist understanding present cases in which our intuitive assessment clashes with such understanding. Racism cannot be "in the head," or so they claim, given that we also consider some structures and practices to be racist even though neither have any mental life of their own. Socio-psychological research on implicit bias is also often cited as a counterexample since this research strongly suggests that many of us consistently disadvantage people we presume to be of a different race without (at least explicitly) subscribing to any negative beliefs about them.[1] Personally, I find these counterexamples convincing; but I assume that a firm believer in the cognitivist understanding will see them as attempts to beg the question, since such examples presuppose what adherents of a cognitivist understanding deny, i.e., that there can be racist action without racist belief. To avoid a similar impasse in this paper, I pursue a different strategy. My aim is to show that *we should reject a cognitivist understanding of sexist action because it fails to accommodate an intuition even proponents of such an understanding accept, namely that sexist actions (however we conceive of them) wrong their targets.*

I proceed as follows: In section 2, I present the cognitivist understanding in more detail and introduce a condition of adequacy. In section 3, I spell out that

---

[1] The debate about an adequate understanding of racism is very interesting, but too complex for me to provide an extensive overview here. For an emotivist understanding, cf. Garcia 1997 and 2004; for a defense of the cognitive position, cf. Shelby 2002; for a structural position, cf. Haslanger 2004; for a hybrid position, cf. Blum 2002 and Dummett 2004.

in order to satisfy this condition, the cognitivist understanding has to assume that there is doxastic morality in the strong sense, i.e., that we can wrong people in virtue of the beliefs we have about them. In section 4, I show that we have to reject this assumption, at least if we want to hold on to certain liberal tenets about people's comprehensive liberty. Since this implies that the cognitive understanding cannot fulfill the condition of adequacy I introduced, I conclude that we should also reject the cognitive conception. Section 5 sums up my results.

## 2 "Sexism is in the head": The cognitivist conception

In this section I want to set the stage for my argument by elaborating on the cognitivist conception as well as on the condition of adequacy I believe a philosophically useful understanding of sexist action has to live up to. Let us start with the cognitivist conception which we can put like this:

**Cognitive conception$_{short}$:** A's action x is sexist if and only if and because x is traceable to A's sexist belief that p.

Before I go on to explain how we should understand the central notion of *being traceable to*, I first want to address a potential worry. A critic might suspect that I deliberately set up the cognitivist conception in an uncharitable way as its explanans relies in part on the notion it is meant to explain. If the cognitive conception cashes out the notion of *sexist action* by referring back to the notion of *sexist belief*, does that not already presuppose some understanding of what renders something sexist? This worry strikes me as misguided. As I stated in the introduction, the cognitive conception is best understood as an answer to *the location problem*, so its main aim is not to spell out the content of sexism, but rather to pin down where it manifests. And understood as an answer to the location problem, the cognitive conception is illuminating, as it informs us that an action is sexist in virtue of its agent's beliefs rather than, say, in virtue of its consequences or its symbolic meaning. To dispel the critic's (albeit misguided) worry even more, we can also draw on Frye's suggestion and specify the beliefs to which sexist actions can supposedly be traced back to. An elaborate version of the cognitivist conception would amount to the following:

**Cognitive conception**~elaborate~: A's action x is sexist if and only if and because x is traceable to A's belief that some people have a dominant or subordinate social position in virtue of their gender.

Both the short and the elaborate version of the cognitive conception center on the idea that actions are sexist in virtue of standing in a particular relation to the agent's beliefs. But how are we to understand the idea of an action being traceable to a specific belief? Presumably, many of those who accept some version of the cognitive conception in everyday life do not have a worked-out position on the issue of mental causation; to avoid putting words into their mouth, I therefore refrain from spelling out the notion of *being traceable to* in an overly technical way and adopt, instead, the following contrafactual understanding:

**Being traceable to:** A's action x is traceable to A's belief that p if and only if A would not have performed x, had she not believed that p.

On this understanding, A's catcalling after some woman B is sexist if A also believes, say, that women should be available for men at all times and if A had not shouted after B had he not held this belief. Without such belief, A's catcalling might still be considered scary or even humiliating, but not sexist. Similarly, it counts as sexist when an employer pays his female staff less than their male co-workers for comparable work if he does so because he believes women's contributions to be generally less valuable and if he had acted differently had he not subscribed to this belief. In contrast, if the same employer pays his female employees less because he already factors in the additional cost the company will (presumably) have to bear when they drop out due to pregnancy, his behavior might still be seen as exploitative but not as sexist. On the cognitive understanding, to accuse him of sexism in the latter case would amount to misunderstanding his actions.[2]

As I stated in the introduction, many of us take accusations of sexism very seriously. Such accusations often result in feelings of indignation or outrage on the part of the accused. Also, such accusations often carry with them the explicit

---

[2] I believe that sexist actions targeting women (understood as those people perceived to be women because of their gender presentation) are more pervasive than those targeting men (understood as those people perceived to be men because of their gender presentation) and therefore more pressing to address both socially and politically. This is why the examples I present focus exclusively on women as the targets of sexist action. Nevertheless, I do not think that we should adopt an understanding that makes sexist action against men impossible on conceptual grounds.

demand that the perpetrators apologize to their targets. All this indicates that (at least implicitly) *we assume that sexist actions wrong their targets and that people have a moral claim against each other not to be targeted by sexist action* as well to some compensation, for instance in the form of an apology, by the perpetrator if they violated this claim. I contend that this assumption is acceptable to both proponents and critics of the cognitive conception, which is why, in what follows, it will serve as my condition of adequacy for a philosophically useful account of sexist action.

**Criterion of adequacy:** A philosophically useful conception of sexist action accommodates the intuition that sexist actions wrong their targets and, consequently, that the targets of sexist action have a moral claim to not be targeted in such a way.

As I hinted at in the introduction, there are other considerations we might want to introduce as criteria of adequacy. For instance, we could insist that a philosophically useful account of sexist action also has to make sense of the intuition that it is not only people who can act in a sexist way, but that institutions can do so, too. Alternatively, we could demand that a useful account of sexist action makes it fairly easy for us to assess whether an action was sexist or not – a demand which, given the opacity of the human mind, the cognitive conception cannot meet. Personally, I consider these valuable suggestions from which to start an ameliorative analysis of sexist action.[3] Nevertheless I do not incorporate them here, as I suspect that proponents of the cognitive conception (or those who, in general, are not very invested in gender justice) reject both of them and the idea of using ameliorative analysis to increase gender justice. In what follows, I will therefore work with this sole criterion of adequacy.

---

[3] According to Haslanger, the point of an ameliorative analysis is to come up with an understanding of a term that suits our practical purposes (cf. Haslanger 2012: 386). The guiding question of any ameliorative analysis thus is: "Which concept (if any) would do the work best?" (Haslanger 2012: 386) But when it comes to sexism, different people have different purposes; feminists, for instance, want to do away with it, whilst those profiting from patriarchy want to hold on to it. An ameliorative analysis of "sexist action" will therefore be as contested as the different practical purposes are.

## 3 The cognitive conception and doxastic morality

After introducing the cognitive conception of sexist action as well as my criterion of adequacy, I now argue that *to fulfill this criterion the cognitive conception has to rely on the idea of doxastic morality in the narrow sense, i.e., on the idea that we can wrong each other in virtue of the beliefs we have about each other*. My argument runs as follows:
(1) Sexist actions (inter alia) wrong their targets in virtue of being sexist.
(2) A's action x is sexist in virtue of being traceable to A's sexist belief that p.
(3) A's action x (inter alia) wrongs its targets in virtue of being traceable to A's sexist belief that p.
(4) If A's action x (inter alia) wrongs its targets in virtue of being traceable to A's sexist belief that p, it either constitutes a wrong that x is traceable to a sexist belief or holding sexist beliefs constitutes a wrong in itself which spills over to the actions that are traceable to it.
(5) There is nothing morally problematic about the property of being traceable to.
(C) Therefore A's holding the sexist belief that p constitutes a wrong in itself which spills over to the actions that are traceable to it.

Let us take a look at each of the premises in turn. (1) articulates the intuition captured by my criterion of adequacy but adds the complementary aspect that sexist actions are wrongful not only in virtue of some *other* feature they might exhibit as well, but also simply in virtue of being sexist. As I said in section 2, it may well be that in a specific instance of sexist catcalling, A also wrongs his target B by scaring or humiliating her; but in addition, A also wrongs B simply because he acted in a sexist way toward her. Put differently, (1) makes explicit that sexist action constitutes a wrong in its own right which cannot be reduced to other wrongs. The intuition I discussed above bears this out, since the reactions of indignation and outrage that often follow accusations of sexism are usually responses to this particular charge (i.e., the charge of sexism) and not to, say, the charge of having acted in a scary or humiliating way. (2) states the cognitive conception in its short version. (3) follows from (1) and (2); in addition, it sets up the question (4) addresses. For if (3) holds and A's action x (inter alia) wrongs its target in virtue of being traceable to A's sexist belief that p, this raises the question what about this fact – i.e., what about the fact that x is traceable to A's believing that p – is so morally problematic as to constitute a wrong. (4) takes a stance on this, claiming that there are just two possible answers to this question: Either the relation "being traceable to" is in itself morally problematic (as, for instance, the property "being cruel" is), so that an action which displays it is thereby morally wrongful; or this relation is morally neutral, so that x inherits its moral wrongness from its connection to A's sexist belief that p. (5) then states that the first of these two answers is not convincing as there is nothing morally questionable about the relation "being traceable to." Together (4) and (5) bear out the conclusion (C), i.e., that the wrong we detect in A's sexist action x is at least in part a spill-over from A's holding the sexist belief that p. Since they do most of the philosophical work in this argument, (4) and (5) deserve particular scrutiny. But at least to me, both seem plausible. If the wrongness of A's action x is constituted by x's being connected to A's sexist belief that p, where else shall x's wrongness stem from if not either from that to which x is connected or from the mere fact of being connected? But what could possibly be morally dubious about the mere fact of being connected? Therefore, I contend that proponents of the cognitive conception should accept that their understanding of sexist action commits them to the idea that entertaining sexist beliefs constitutes in itself a moral wrong.

At first glance, this might seem like a strange commitment. But recently, a similar idea has enjoyed increasing support in the debate about doxastic morality (DM), whose the central claim is precisely "that beliefs can wrong and that there is *something* we epistemically owe to each other" (Basu 2019a: 915). More specifically, defenders of doxastic morality argue that we can wrong each other simply in virtue of holding certain beliefs about each other, independent of whether we are epistemically warranted in holding the offending beliefs as well as of the consequences that holding these beliefs might have. To bring this idea into focus, consider the following example (which is a version of a case Rima Basu discusses, cf. Basu 2019a: 917):

**(Suspicious)** Mark has an alcohol problem but has been sober for eight months. At a work dinner, he successfully withstands the temptation to have a drink, but a colleague accidentally spills some wine on his sleeve. When Mark comes home late at night and smelling of alcohol, his partner John concludes that he has fallen off the wagon. John is disappointed in Mark, but he keeps his suspicion and reproach to himself, as he is resolved to be unconditionally supportive of Mark.

Note that, even though he is mistaken in believing that Mark has given in to temptation, John is justified in this belief as the available evidence (i.e., the late hour, the smell of wine) suggests that Mark has been drinking. Note also that John does not articulate his belief that Mark has fallen off the wagon, so that his entertaining it does not have any further consequences, for instance to enrage Mark or to hurt his feelings. Basu claims that John, his justification and restraint notwithstanding, wrongs his partner and that Mark has reason to demand an apology from John and should do so if he ever found out about John's suspicion. According to Basu, cases like "Suspicion" show that we have an interest not only in how other people treat us, but also in what they think of us; in fact, we care about this to such degree that we can wrong each other simply by (not) holding certain beliefs about each other.

Before I go on to show how the idea of DM refers back to the cognitive conception, I first want to spell it out in more detail. First, I want to highlight that, given the way Basu argues for it, *DM is best understood in a strict (as opposed to a wide) sense*. Basu does not contend herself with claiming that by (not) having certain beliefs, we contribute to a morally better or worse state of affairs. By claiming this, i.e., by claiming that our mental lives have moral value, she would be arguing for DM in a wide sense. But Basu's insistence that cases like "Suspicious" warrant an apology by the epistemic agent and that they constitute doxastic wrongings (cf. Basu 2019b: sec. 4; as well as Basu/Schroeder 2019: sec. 1.1) shows that she has a stricter conception of DM in mind. For these phenomena presuppose not only that there is value to, but that there are directed moral duties regarding our mental lives. Put differently, Basu assumes a strict version of DM which states that we have morally grounded epistemic duties, i.e., morally grounded duties to (not) believe certain things about each other, and that, in consequence, we can wrong each other simply in virtue of the beliefs we have about each other.

The second aspect I need to clarify is the content of these duties. Which beliefs should we (not) have, lest we fall short of what we epistemically owe to each other? The example I cited above centers on what people epistemically owe to each other in close personal relationships. But for the most part, Basu focuses on racist beliefs, albeit contending that her arguments "can also be easily extended to cover [...] *sexist* beliefs, *homophobic* beliefs, and other morally objectionable beliefs of this kind" (Basu 2019b: 2498) The common thread running through these morally objectionable beliefs is that they violate what Basu calls "the moral standpoint" (Basu 2019a: 928). Drawing on Peter Strawson's work, Basu claims that we have a moral duty to adopt this standpoint vis-a-vis one another and that *this requires seeing each other "as we see ourselves, not as we are expected to be on the basis of our race, gender, sexual orientation, class, etc."* (Basu 2019a: 928; emphasis added).

This is where the debate about DM and the cognitive conception finally converge. At the start of this section I argued that proponents of the cognitive conception find themselves committed to the claim that entertaining sexist beliefs constitutes in itself a moral wrong. Sexist beliefs fit Basu's characterization of beliefs that violate the moral standpoint as they are judgments about people on the basis of their gender. According to Basu, entertaining beliefs that violate the moral standpoint constitutes in itself a moral wrong, regardless of whether these beliefs are epistemically warranted or acted upon in any way – the agent wrongs their target just by having them. So proponents of the cognitive conception can back up the claim their conception commits them to, i.e., that entertaining sexist beliefs constitutes in itself a moral wrong, by pointing to the debate about DM where people defend the exact same claim. Conversely, this implies that the fate of the cognitive conception rises and falls with DM, as the cognitive conception can only fulfill its criterion of adequacy if there is indeed such a thing as DM, i.e., as wronging each other simply by (not) holding certain beliefs about each other.

## 4 Liberal moral philosophy and the impossibility of doxastic morality

In this section, I use the connection between the cognitive conception and DM to argue against a cognitivist understanding of sexist action. More precisely, I argue that given some (as I hope fairly uncontroversial) liberal assumptions we have to reject the possibility of DM. From this it follows that the cognitive conception cannot make sense of the intuition that sexist actions wrong their targets. But a philosophically useful conception of sexist action should be able to accommodate this intuition. That it fails to do so thus speaks against the cognitive conception.

The argument I am going to present against the possibility of DM differs from the ones the literature focuses on. For the most part, these are concerned with issues of control and coordination (cf. Basu/Schroeder 2019: secs. 2.1–3.2): On the one hand, if we assume (as DM does) that there is a morally grounded duty to (not) believe that p, we also have to assume that we can exercise at least some degree of control over our beliefs; otherwise we would posit a duty we are not able to fulfill and thus run afoul of the principle that ought implies can. But, as critics of DM point out, such doxastic voluntarism is implausible, since what we believe is (and should) not be up to us but to the evidence available to us. On the other hand, critics also highlight that positing a morally grounded duty to (not) believe that p might result in problems of coordination in cases where this duty and our epistemic norms (such as "do not hold contradictory beliefs" or "do not believe on insufficient evidence") collide. It is unclear how to even assess which of the conflicting prescriptions would take precedence in such cases. I consider the problems of control and of coordination pressing criticisms which defenders of DM have to address; *my own objection, though, stems from a different concern, namely from the comprehensive liberty right liberal moral philosophy posits*. My reasoning runs as follows:

(1) According to liberal moral philosophy, A has a comprehensive liberty right.
(2) A's comprehensive liberty right consists in a number of concrete liberty rights such as A's concrete liberty right to (not) develop her talents as well as A's concrete liberty right to (not) shape her own body.
(3) A's comprehensive liberty right also includes A's concrete liberty right to (not) believe that p.
(4) According to liberal moral philosophy, A has the concrete liberty right to (not) believe that p.
(5) According to DM, A has a morally grounded duty to (not) believe that p.
(6) A cannot have both the concrete liberty right to (not) believe that p and a morally grounded duty to (not) believe that p.
(C) Therefore, we have to reject either DM or liberal moral philosophy's claim that A has a comprehensive liberty right (or both).

Again, let us take a look at each of these premises. Premise (1) needs much further elaboration since there is *no one such thing* as liberal moral philosophy, as the liberal tradition comprises a number of distinct approaches. To name just a few, John Locke's proto-libertarian liberalism differs from Immanuel Kant's perfectionist liberalism as well as from John Stuart Mill's individuality-based approach and from John Rawls' political liberalism, and depending on which author we draw on, the comprehensive liberty right stipulated in (1) covers different types of action (cf. Gaus 2004). This complexity notwithstanding, I do not commit myself to one particular approach here, as I hope that all of them bear out what follows. Instead, I limit myself to unpacking the understanding of "liberty right" I rely on. In general, "A's liberty right to phi" is best understood as a paired privilege, so that A "has a privilege [no duty not] to phi, and also has a privilege [no duty not] *not* to phi" (Wenar 2005: 226). Put differently, A is normatively free with respect to performing phi, i.e., she is allowed to either perform or not perform phi, just as she pleases. From this it follows not only that other people are not allowed to interfere with A's phi-ing or to force A to phi; it also implies that other people do not have any moral claim on A regarding her phi-ing. This holds true even if it would be morally better for A to (not) phi, for instance, because her (not) phi-ing would lead to a better state of affairs or because it would exemplify some virtue on the part of A. In such cases, others might justifiably wish or hope for A to (not) phi, but they cannot rightfully demand it of A nor can they blame A if she refuses. In sustaining that A has a comprehensive liberty right, moral liberal philosophy claims in effect that there is a large number of action types regarding which A has a paired privilege to (not) perform them.

Most versions of liberalism go on to spell out this comprehensive liberty right into more concrete ones, thereby specifying which types of actions we are normatively free to perform. (2) contends that there will be an overlap between different liberal approaches at least regarding two concrete liberty rights, namely the right to (not) develop one's individual talents and the right to (not) shape one's own body. To see what speaks for this, imagine a moral theory that allowed others to make moral demands on us to make good use of our natural abilities (as some versions of utilitarianism might) and to take good care of our bodies (as could follow from some versions of perfectionism); regardless of whether we would find such a theory plausible, it would certainly be a stretch to consider it liberal. Another way to defend (2) is by highlighting the values at least some versions of liberalism use to justify why they posit a comprehensive liberty right in the first place. Mill, for instance, stresses that such right is necessary for us to develop our individuality (cf. Mill 2008: ch. 3); similarly, Joseph Raz points out the importance of liberty for our autonomy (cf. Raz 1988: ch. 15). But clearly, how we treat our own bodies and whether we cultivate our talents and abilities is central to our individuality and to our autonomy. Versions of liberalism that emphasize the importance of these values will therefore grant us those concrete liberty rights as they help foster these values.

Premise (3) takes us back to the issue of DM because according to (3), another concrete liberty right that follows from liberalism's commitment to comprehensive individual liberty is the liberty right to (not) believe that p. (3) thus foreshadows (6), as A having a paired privilege to believe and not believe that p is incompatible with a morally grounded duty to (not) believe that p. A critic could therefore suspect that by introducing (3), I distort the whole argument to my favor, as (3) straightforwardly states what DM denies. In reply, I want to point out that (3) has additional explanatory value as *it elucidates why* we should have the concrete liberty right which then conflicts with DM. For (3) highlights that the liberty right to (not) believe that p is simply part of the comprehensive liberty right liberalism argues for and thus on a par with concrete liberty rights such as the right to (not) develop our talents or to (not) shape our own bodies. If liberalism allows us to unrestrictedly decide what to make of our natural abilities as well as of our bodies, how could it not also allow us to unrestrictedly make up our own minds? How could liberalism possibly fail to grant us what we might call *freedom of thought*, given how crucial our mental lives are for the values liberalism centers on such as individuality and personal autonomy? Put differently, (3) highlights that it is hard to imagine how the liberty right to (not) believe that p could not be among the concrete liberty rights that follow from liberalism's commitment to comprehensive liberty. This insight is captured in (4).

(5) simply restates DM's core claim. (6) then spells out the tension I already alluded to between DM and liberal moral philosophy's commitment to comprehensive liberty, as A cannot be duty-bound to (not) believe that p on the one hand and have discretion over whether or not to believe that p on the other. So in (C) the argument concludes that, as the core claims of DM and liberal moral philosophy are incompatible, we have to reject one of these positions (or both). Faced with these two options, I propose that we reject DM. Admittedly, I will not offer any additional argument for this, as defending comprehensive individual liberty is well beyond the scope of this paper; but I hope that most readers agree that it is both too plausible and too important to give up. If we reject DM, though, it follows that there is no way for the cognitive conception to fulfill the criterion of adequacy I proposed. As I have shown, on the cognitive conception, the only way to make sense of the idea that sexist actions wrong their targets is by assuming that we can wrong each other in virtue of our beliefs. But once we reject DM, we cannot make this assumption anymore. Thus, if we reject DM, we also have to reject the cognitive conception.

A critic could object to this argument by claiming that I overstate my case. More specifically, they could point out that the tension in (6) only arises if A's freedom of thought is unrestricted and thus does not leave any conceptual room for a morally grounded duty regarding belief. But most concrete liberty rights liberal moral philosophy argues for come with at least some limitations. For instance, our freedom of movement stops short of other people's homes much like our freedom of speech does not cover libel or the public incitement of violence. Put more generally, many concrete liberty rights are somewhat limited so as to prevent harm to other people which their unrestricted exercise would likely cause. The critic could continue by stressing that the point of examples like Basu's is precisely to show that we can indeed harm each other in virtue of the beliefs we have about each other. This speaks in favor of restricting our freedom of thought, which in turn makes room for a morally grounded duty regarding belief and thus for DM. Put differently, a critic could insist that we have to amend premises (4) and (5) in the following way:

(4*) According to liberal moral philosophy, A has the concrete liberty right to (not) believe that p, as long as by (not) believing that p A does not harm some other person B.

(5*) According to DM, A has a morally grounded duty to (not) believe that p, if by believing that p A harms some other person B.

(4\*) and (5\*) are compatible so that there is no tension between the core claims of liberal moral philosophy and DM. But then, so a critic could conclude, there is no need for us to reject either of them (or both) or, in consequence, the cognitive conception.

To this objection, I reply the following. I agree that many of the concrete liberty rights liberal moral philosophy posits come with restrictions. I also agree that the point behind these restrictions is to avoid harm to other people. Finally, I also accept that examples like Basu's show that we can indeed harm each other with our beliefs. We can spell out this last point in more detail than even Basu herself does by drawing on an interest theory of wellbeing (as Simon Keller suggests, cf. Keller 2018: 21–22). According to this theory, wellbeing consists in the fulfillment of our interests, while harm consists in their frustration. Cases like Basu's show that most of us want other people to think well of us. We do not want them to believe, say, that we have relapsed into a disease (as in "Suspicious") or to see us through the lens of some negative stereotype. If they fail to do so (either because they hold unfriendly beliefs about us as particular persons or because they despise a whole social group to which we belong), they frustrate this interest and thus harm us.[4] So if we accept an interest theory of wellbeing and if we also assume that we care about other people's opinion about us, there is a sense in which we can harm each other in virtue of our beliefs, just as the critic posits.

While I am willing to grant the critic all these points, I do not think that they support the conclusion. For even though liberal moral philosophy does restrict concrete liberty rights as to avoid potential harm to others, the rationale behind such restrictions is more complex than the critic's objection suggests. In particular, we cannot assume that if the unrestricted use of some concrete liberty right causes some harm to others, this will automatically warrant its restriction. To assess whether restricting some concrete liberty right is justified, we have to at least also consider the weight of the harm we could avoid through this restriction as well as how central this particular liberty right is to our understanding of comprehensive liberty. For instance, people could hesitate to argue for more comprehensive limitations on freedom of speech because they believe either that the harms caused by unrestricted speech are not damaging enough (thus subscribing to the optimistic idea that sticks and stones might break our bones, but

---

[4] Note that they do so even if we are not aware of their disdainful beliefs, since our interests can be frustrated without us realizing it. Note that they also harm us even if their disdainful beliefs are epistemically justified, since what we desire is often just that other people think well of us and not that their good opinion of us also be justified.

that words will not) or that this particular liberty right is very much at the heart of comprehensive liberty.

Providing a detailed account of how liberal moral philosophy should balance the weight of potential harms against the importance of concrete liberty rights is, again, beyond the scope of this paper; but I am positive that even without a worked-out account it is reasonable to assume that the harm we cause each other by frustrating our interest in being thought of well is not weighty enough to justify limitations on our freedom of thought. To see this, just think of the harms which can result from the exercise of our concrete liberty rights to (not) develop our talents or to (not) shape our bodies. For instance, we grant people the normative freedom to endanger their own bodily integrity by smoking or by engaging in risky sports even though by doing so they frustrate the interests of all the people who care about their health; similarly, we allow people to waste their talents even if they could contribute to an overall better state of affairs by choosing different life plans. Intuitively, these harms can be considerable, but still they are not considerable enough to warrant the restriction of these important concrete liberty rights. To defend their claim that the harm potentially caused by the unrestricted use of our freedom of thought warrants its restriction, the critic would thus have to argue either that these potential harms are weightier than the potential harms entailed by the unrestricted exercise of the two concrete liberty rights just discussed, or that freedom of thought is less central to the idea of comprehensive liberty than the liberty rights to (not) develop our talents or to (not) shape our bodies are. Neither alternative seems promising which is why we should conclude that the critic has failed to provide the conceptual room necessary to make DM and liberal moral philosophy compatible. But then we also have to reject the cognitive conception since without DM it cannot succeed at accommodating the criterion of adequacy.

## 5 Conclusion

My aim in this paper was to argue against a cognitive conception of sexist action according to which an action is sexist only insofar as it goes back to a sexist belief on the part of the agent. I claimed that we should reject such an understanding because it fails to account for an intuition even people who are not particularly invested in gender justice share, namely that sexist actions wrong their targets qua sexist actions.

To show that the cognitive conception cannot accommodate this intuition, I had to take a look at the debate about doxastic morality, because proponents of doxastic morality assert that we can wrong each other in virtue of our beliefs, which is precisely what those who defend the cognitive conception have to sustain to account for said intuition. Engaging with examples like the ones Basu provides showed that there is indeed doxastic morality in a wide sense. People with bigoted beliefs about the members of whole social groups (i.e., people with sexist, racist, abelist, ageist beliefs, etc.) do indeed harm their targets by frustrating their interest in being thought of well and thus contribute to a morally worse state of affairs. We might add that they also contribute to an epistemically worse state of affairs, as across-the-board judgments about all members of a social group are (almost) never epistemically justified. So to put it bluntly, we can say that people with bigoted beliefs are idiots.

But I also showed that, at least if we want to hold on to a liberal commitment to comprehensive liberty, we cannot say that bigots also wrong their targets in virtue of their bigoted beliefs. For a commitment to individual liberty entails freedom of thought, which, in turn, entails that people are neither bound by any morally grounded duty to (not) have certain beliefs nor at risk of wronging others by violating such a duty. To put it bluntly again, as long as their bigotry remains confined "to their heads," bigots do not wrong their targets and thus avoid turning from idiots into full-fledged assholes.[5] So contrary to what its proponents claim, we cannot make sense of the idea that there is doxastic morality in the strict sense, i.e., that we can wrong each other in virtue of our beliefs.

This result brought me full circle as it implies that, at least against the backdrop of liberal moral philosophy, the cognitive conception of sexist action fails to accommodate the crucial intuition that sexist actions wrong their targets. Therefore, I concluded that we should reject this conception. If we want to criticize sexist action in the way I assume that we do, i.e., if we want to criticize those who act in a sexist way for wronging their targets (and not simply for being idi-

---

[5] Obviously, it is hard to imagine that bigots will manage to confine their bigotry "to their heads." People tend to act on their beliefs and so it is reasonable to assume that someone who thinks that, say, women should have a subordinate social position will eventually treat them as if they did. A critic could take the connection between our mental lives and our actions to speak against the liberal argument I presented: If bigoted beliefs often lead to bigoted actions, should we not say that the former wrong their targets just as much as the latter? In response to this I want to stress that once they start acting on their beliefs, bigots step outside the protected sphere established by their comprehensive liberty right, as the harm they cause by acting on their bigoted beliefs exceeds the one they cause by simply entertaining them. Put differently, the argument I presented why *entertaining bigoted beliefs* is protected by liberal moral philosophy's core claim by no means entails that *acting in a bigoted way* is protected, too. Liberal moral philosophy has ample resources to condemn bigoted action (for instance by pointing to the right not to be discriminated against) and does not have to accept the idea of DM to do so.

ots), we are well advised to accept a consequentialist understanding like the one Frye proposes.

# References

Basu, Rima (2019a): "What We Epistemically Owe to Each Other." In: *Philosophical Studies* 176(4), pp. 915–931.
Basu, Rima (2019b): "The Wrongs of Racist Beliefs." In: *Philosophical Studies* 176(9), pp. 2497–2515.
Basu, Rima/Schroeder, Mark (2019): "Doxastic Wronging." In: Kim, Brian/McGrath, Matthew (Eds.): *Pragmatic Encroachment in Epistemology*. London: Routledge, pp. 181–205.
Blum, Lawrence (2002): *"I'm Not a Racist, But...": The Moral Quandary of Race*. Ithaca, NY/London: Cornell University Press.
Dummett, Michael (2004): "The Nature of Racism." In: Levine, Michael/Pataki, Tamas (Eds.): *Racism in Mind*. Ithaca, NY/London: Cornell University Press, pp. 27–34.
Fabian, Jordan (2019): "Trump: I Don't Have a Racist Bone in My Body." In: *The Hill* 16 July 2019. https://thehill.com/homenews/administration/453253-trump-i-dont-have-a-racist-bone-in-my-body, accessed 21 February 2020.
Frye, Marilyn (1983): "Sexism." In: *The Politics of Reality*. New York, NY: Crossing Press, pp. 17–38.
Garcia, J. L. A. (1997): "Current Conceptions of Racism: A Critical Examination of Some Recent Social Philosophy." In: *Journal of Social Philosophy* 28(2), pp. 5–42.
Garcia, J. L. A. (2004): "Three Sites for Racism: Social Structurings, Valuings, and Vice." In: Levine, Michael/Pataki, Tamas (Eds.): *Racism in Mind*. Ithaca, NY/London: Cornell University Press, pp. 35–55.
Gaus, Gerald (2004): "The Diversity of Comprehensive Liberalisms." In: Gaus, Gerald/Kukathas, Chandras (Eds.): *The Handbook of Political Theory*. London: Sage, pp. 100–114.
Glasgow, Joshua (2009): "Racism as Disrespect." In: *Ethics* 120(1), pp. 64–93.
Haslanger, Sally (2004): "Oppressions: Racial and Other." In: Levine, Michael/Pataki, Tamas (Eds.): *Racism in Mind*. Ithaca, NY/London: Cornell University Press, pp. 97–126.
Haslanger, Sally (2012): "What Good Are Our Intuitions? Philosophical Analysis and Social Kinds." In: *Resisting Reality*. Oxford: Oxford University Press, pp. 381–405.
Keller, Simon (2018): "Belief for Someone Else's Sake." In: *Philosophical Topics* 46(1), pp. 19–35.
Mill, John Stuart (2008): *On Liberty and Other Writings*. [1859]. Edited by Stefan Collini. Cambridge: Cambridge University Press.
Raz, Joseph (1988): *The Morality of Freedom*. Oxford: Oxford University Press.
Shelby, Tommie (2002): "Is Racism in the 'Heart'?" In: *Journal of Social Philosophy* 33(3), pp. 411–420.
Wenar, Leif (2005): "The Nature of Rights." In: *Philosophy and Public Affairs* 33(3), pp. 223–252.

Anke Graness
# Between Necropolitics and Cosmopolitanism

**Abstract:** Today the world seems to be torn between two extremely different worldviews: nationalism, on the one hand, which aims to defend the interests of a certain group of people (citizens) only, and cosmopolitanism on the other hand which considers all human beings as members of a single human community. How do philosophers describe, explain, and conceptualize these two contradicting worldviews? In this paper, I will discuss two controversial views on this topic. While the Ghanaian-English philosopher Kwame Anthony Appiah considers separation and enclosure as something alien to humans and pursues the possibility of a cosmopolitan community in which both the individual's local loyalties and friendly relationships with strangers are cultivated, Cameroonian historian Achille Mbembe argues that separation and enclosure lie at the root of modern democracies and continue to shape today's "politics of enmity." For Mbembe, the slave trade is the key phenomenon to understanding today's deadly "necropolitics," which still cause hate and terror around the world. After Mbembe's analysis, the question arises if there is a future for such universal concepts like cosmopolitanism.

**Keywords:** Necropolitics, Achille Mbembe, cosmopolitanism, Kwame Anthony Appiah, slavery, colonialism

## 1 Necropolitics

The historian, political theorist, and public intellectual Achille Mbembe is today considered as one of the most important philosophers from the African continent. His book *De la postcolonie* (2000; English edition: *On the Postcolony* 2001) in particular sparked widespread debates and is considered one of the key twenty-first-century works of postcolonial theory. In this book, Mbembe describes the postcolony as a place of persistent excesses, of violence, terror, and a deep economic crisis manifested in permanent deficiencies and enormous poverty. The postcolony, he concludes, differs little in violence and arbitrariness from the colony, which it replaced.

But his diagnosis of "Western" liberal societies is also not very flattering: Violence, marginalization, and arbitrariness mark the beginning of modern democracy, too, and continue to shape it to this day. In *Politiques de l'inimitié* (2016;

English edition: *Necropolitics* 2019) Mbembe argues that those who want to understand today's "politics of enmity," in which people are marginalized, new walls are built, or people in distress at sea are left to drown, must hark back to the age of the slave trade and colonialism and face what he calls "*the nocturnal body*" (Mbembe 2019: 22) of democracy: the colonial empire, particularly the plantation and the penal colony, and the pro-slavery state, such as the United States of America, which was for a long time a "pro-slavery democracy" (Mbembe 2019: 17). Mbembe argues that from the beginning, modern democracies were shaped by two coexisting orders, namely a *community of fellows* governed by the law of equality, and a *category of nonfellows*, a group of people without participation rights who were governed by the "law of inequality" (Mbembe 2019: 17), that is denied full freedom and protection by the law.[1] Their inequality is based above all on the "prejudice of race" (Mbembe 2019: 17), which is at the heart of Mbembe's analysis.[2]

The colony was impossible without the slave trade and the primacy of race, which made the division of humanity possible. The colony and the plantation system are places of separation in which there are people with rights (the owner/the colonizer/the white) and people without rights (the slave/the Black). Here, human beings are turned into slaves, that is, they become "subject to a deep symbolic and social devaluation through their abasement" (Mbembe 2019: 166) to the status of a commodity: "[...] the slave is not a subject of right but instead a commodity like any other" (Mbembe 2019: 18). The ability to transform human life into an object of economic exchange – slaves – within the plantation system was essential for the progress of capitalist economies. Thus, the primacy of race and the reduction of people to the status of a commodity were prerequisites for global capitalism, i.e., for an accumulation process on a global scale. The industrial revolution is inseparably intertwined with colonial imperialism and its technologies of race and power.

The "camp" as a place of separation was also invented in the colonies. Mbembe states: "From a strict historical viewpoint, the camp-form emerged on the cusp of the twentieth century (between 1896 and 1907) as part of colonial war in Cuba, the Philippines, South Africa, and the then-German-controlled Af-

---

[1] "[...] those without part have no rights to have rights." (Mbembe 2019: 17) Note the reference to Hannah Arendt's famous phrase: "a right to have rights" (Arendt 1968: 177).
[2] In this respect, it is crucial to note that nonparticipation is not only based on racial prejudice but also on gender difference. The latter is touched on by Mbembe only marginally. However, the colonial difference is always linked to a gender difference, as feminist postcolonial scholars underline (cf. Spivak 1988; Lugones 2010; in Lugones see particularly the concept of coloniality of gender) and, thus, should be an integral part of such an analysis.

rican Southwest" (Mbembe 2019: 23). He concludes: "Democracy, the plantation, and the colonial empire are all part of the same historical matrix" and, thus, "at the heart of every historical understanding of the violence of contemporary global order" (Mbembe 2019: 23). It follows that if we want to understand today's necropolitics, we have to go back to its roots, or as Mbembe puts it, "[a]ny historical account of the rise of modern terror needs to address slavery, which could be considered one of the first instances of biopolitical experimentation" (Mbembe 2003: 21).

Mbembe coined the term *Necropolitics* in 2003 in an article under the same title, in order to demonstrate "that the notion of biopower[3] is insufficient to account for contemporary forms of subjugation of life to the power of death" (Mbembe 2019: 92). According to Mbembe, the Foucauldian idea of biopower is not sufficiently able to explain the modern forms of submission; it ignores the continued existence of necropolitical techniques within liberal democracies and underestimates the central importance of colonial slavery as a condition for the development of Western capitalism.

He starts from the hypothesis that

> the ultimate expression of sovereignty resides, to a large degree, in the power and the capacity to dictate who may live and who must die. Hence, to kill or to allow to live constitute the limits of sovereignty, its fundamental attributes. To exercise sovereignty is to exercise control over mortality and to define life as the deployment and manifestation of power. (Mbembe 2003: 11–12)

Mbembe uses the notions of necropolitics and necropower

> to account for the various ways in which, in our contemporary world, weapons are deployed in the interest of maximum destruction of persons and the creation of death-worlds, new and unique forms of social existence in which vast populations are subjected to conditions of life conferring upon them the status of living dead. (Mbembe 2003: 39–40)

Until the nineteenth century, the ensuing violence has been carried mainly abroad, to the colonies, but later the aggression turned increasingly inward,

---

[3] For Foucault, whose thinking was largely focused on the history of Central Europe, modernity is characterized by the replacement of the necropolitical understanding of sovereignty (in which power asserts itself through violence) with the biopolitical administration of the population. See Michel Foucault's notion on "biopower," which describes the practice of modern nation states and their regulation of their subjects through "an explosion of numerous and diverse techniques for achieving the subjugation of bodies and the control of populations" (Foucault 1981: 140) and the division of people into those who must live and those who must die (Foucault 2003: 241, 256).

for example, as hatred against the Jews which ended in extermination. The camp – the concentration camp – was thereby relocated inside and has since become a "structural feature of our globalized condition. It has ceased to scandalize" (Mbembe 2019: 60). The force of separation that caused the Holocaust and Apartheid in the twentieth century continues today in the war on terror "that claims the right to cruelty, torture, and indefinite detention" (Mbembe 2019: 38).[4] It is a form of war beyond all territorial restrictions that constantly produces new enemies, who must be banned from infiltrating and corrupting one's own ethnicity, culture or nation by walls, fences, entry bans, and internment camps. Today, building impermeable borders and other forms of keeping strangers, enemies, and intruders away appears to be a central concern of democracies. And thus, "[b]orders are no longer sites to be crossed but lines that separate" (Mbembe 2019: 3).

And this also has psychological causes. Mbembe argues that the new "State of Insecurity" was born by creating anxiety in entire peoples about being invaded or losing their identity. Such anxieties are based on what Mbembe calls an "imaginary surplus" (Mbembe 2019: 55), fears fostered by a media environment where "[c]ertainties and convictions are held to be the truth. Reason needs not to be employed. Simply believing and surrendering oneself is enough" (Mbembe 2019: 55). Irrational fears that have to be constantly reinvented, such as fear of Muslims or of veiled women, dominate people, especially in the industrialized countries. Because of such irrational fears, "Western" societies are increasingly being pushed to exit democracy to transform into societies of enmity. Inhumane policies, a dulling of empathy for the suffering of the other, who is not "one of us," and even the use of brute force against the unfortunate are hallmarks of today's democracies, where a state of exception provides "the normative basis of the right to kill" (Mbembe 2019: 70). The "war on terror" increasingly leads to the abolition of fundamental democratic principles and the rule of law and is increasingly directed against the citizens themselves of democratic states.

To sum up: Mbembe argues that today's "politics of enmity" or "necropolitics," in which it has become the norm to "live by the sword" (Mbembe 2019: 31), has a genealogy: the tradition of dirty war has its historical roots in the colonial wars, and the force of separation has its origins in the racially based enslavement of people. Neither slavery nor colonialism were incompatible with democracy; on the contrary, the democratic order is notoriously ambivalent and the

---

[4] The phrase "war on terror" was coined in 2001 by the incumbent U.S. presidential administration to justify measures taken after the attack on the World Trade Center, ostensibly to combat 'Muslim' terrorists. Mbembe seems to use the term in a broader sense.

"planetary-scale renewal of the relation of enmity and its multiple reconfigurations" (Mbembe 2019: 1–2) can only be understood in this context.

## 2 Cosmopolitanism

Mbembe's rigorous analysis draws attention to important historical settings frequently neglected in political and public thinking, in particular the roots of the project of European modernism in slavery and colonialism – practices which were not morally questioned by thinkers who framed European modernity, like Locke, Hume, Kant, or Hegel; on the contrary, they often legitimized these practices.[5] Such strategies of legitimization also belong to the "nocturnal body of democracy." However, what can be done to overcome an ideology of exclusion and separation? Mbembe's "Ethics of the Passerby" (Mbembe 2019: 184–189) provides only a vague hint. Is the project of cosmopolitanism the *pharmakon* Mbembe is searching for? (Mbembe 2019: 2)

One of the most important theoretical contributions to the concept of cosmopolitanism during recent years was published by Kwame Anthony Appiah in his *Cosmopolitanism: Ethics in a World of Strangers* (2006). Unlike Mbembe, who argues that a politics of separation is a driving force of the modern state, Appiah considers separation and closure as something alien to people. He is convinced that "the way of segregation and seclusion has always been anomalous in our perpetually voyaging species. Cosmopolitanism isn't hard work; repudiating it is" (Appiah 2006: xx). In view of the Holocaust, Apartheid, racism, and the almost daily media reports about deaths at border rivers, border walls, or in the Mediterranean Sea, this sentence sounds almost anachronistic. After a period of great enthusiasm due to the possibilities of new transport and communication technologies and the European unification processes in the 1990s that began with the fall of the Berlin Wall, cosmopolitanism today seems to be an idea

---

[5] John Locke, for example, authored *The Fundamental Constitutions of Carolina* (1669), which explicitly supported slavery: "Every freeman of Carolina shall have absolute power and authority over his negro slaves [...]." (Locke 1669: § 110) Moreover, Locke owned stock in the Royal African Company, which ran the African slave trade for England. And even though Locke states in his *Two Treatises of Government*: "Slavery is so vile and miserable an Estate of Man [...] that 'tis hardly to be conceived" (Locke 1988: 141) that anyone would support it, he still justifies slavery as punishment for a crime. Or see David Hume who claims the natural inferiority of Black people (see Hume 1964: 252).

that is currently in decline, particularly a concept of cosmopolitanism which goes beyond the idea of being a world traveler who is at home everywhere.[6]

The core idea of a philosophical concept of cosmopolitanism is the idea of a unity of humanity which extends our moral duties to all human beings, not just to our family members, fellow citizens, or other groups we belong to. As Appiah puts it:

> One truth we hold to [...] is that every human being has obligations to every other. Everybody matters: that is our central [cosmopolitan] idea. And it sharply limits the scope of our tolerance. (Appiah 2006: 144)

Contrary to nationalist aspirations, "cosmopolitans share [the idea] that no local loyalty can ever justify forgetting that each human being has responsibilities to every other" (Appiah 2006: xvi). In a similar manner Thomas Pogge, an influential proponent of a cosmopolitan approach to global justice, claims that all cosmopolitan positions are marked by three features: individual human beings are what ultimately matter; they matter equally; and nobody is exempted by distance or lack of a shared community from potential demands arising out of counting of everybody equally (Pogge 1994: 89). This basic idea is fundamentally questioned today in both public opinion and national politics.

In his approach, Appiah tries to find a balance between cosmopolitanism and nationalism by giving more weight to the individual's local relations. His book documents a search for a cosmopolitan ethic that finds a balance between universal, inalienable values, on the one hand, and respect for the different types of world views and experiences (the local) on the other. The starting point of his reflections is the question: "What do we really owe to strangers?" which is a central question in the current debate on global justice. And he argues:

> Whatever my basic obligations are to the poor far away, they cannot be enough, I believe, to trump my concerns for my family, my friends, my country; nor can an argument that every life matters require me to be indifferent to the fact that one of those lives is mine. (Appiah 2006: 165)

In other words, one's own life must still be worth living, and thus, no meaningful representation of our duties toward strangers may ignore the variety of things

---

[6] It should be noted that the idea of a world traveler is still an elitist idea, which can be realized by only a small percentage of the world's population. The majority of humanity is denied such a life due to their economic situation or passport and entry regulations.

that are meaningful in human life. In a critique of Peter Singer, Appiah considers the following principle to be correct: "If you are the person in the best position to prevent something really awful, and it won't cost you much to do so, do it." (Appiah 2006: 161)

Here, Appiah touches on something important about how social ethics seems to operate: Whatever obligation one might have to another human being, especially a stranger, that obligation does not supersede the obligations one has to those people most familiar to one. This idea, as well as his view that the nation state is primarily responsible for the protection of fundamental human rights, points to a rather restricted or conditional concept of cosmopolitanism, and, thus, Appiah calls his approach a "partial cosmopolitanism" (Appiah 2006: xvii), i.e., a cosmopolitanism that gives importance to local identities and loyalties. Appiah has a critical distance from what he calls "immoderate cosmopolitans," that is, scholars who deny the importance of nation states, national boundaries, and borders and who look at friends and fellow citizens with "icy impartiality" (Appiah 2006: xvii). Appiah argues that local loyalties and allegiances are important because they determine who we are. Thus, we must show the most benevolence to those who are closest to us: "A creed that disdains the partialities of kinfolk and community may have a past, but it has no future." (Appiah 2006: xviii) Appiah encourages us to embrace both local and universal loyalties and allegiances and denies that they necessarily come into conflict with each other. He votes for a kind of cosmopolitanism that involves continuous rebalancing of interests and problems, a cosmopolitanism which recognizes the universality of fundamental human rights without neglecting particularist interests and vice versa. He advocates a cosmopolitanism that appreciates the individual's local ties and maintains friendly relationships with strangers. This is not an easy undertaking; it has to be negotiated again and again. Appiah sees a solution in the conversation between people from different societies and with disparate lifestyles, in which national, religious, and cultural differences are explored and made understandable.

Appiah's "partial cosmopolitanism" is not the only part of his text that raises many questions, for instance, concerning power asymmetries in this world. The following passage is also problematic:

> It was terribly wrong that slaves were worked to death building the pyramids – or, for that matter, in building the United States – but it is not therefore terrible that those monuments, or this nation, exist. Not all values have a single measure. If the founders of this nation had dealt only with the most urgent moral problem facing them – and let us suppose that it was, indeed, slavery – they would almost certainly not have set in motion the slow march of political, cultural, and moral progress with its sallies and its retreats, that Americans justly take pride in. (Appiah 2006: 166)

Particularly with regard to Mbembe's historical analysis, which shows that the cultural and material wealth of "Western" societies was barbarically bought through the plantation system, slavery, and every conceivable violence associated with them (Mbembe 2019: 19–20), Appiah's argument seems almost cynical and points to the roots of the problem Mbembe tries to bring to light: the trivialization or even legitimation of the violence and cruelty of slavery and the conception of colonialism as an inevitable phase of the development of capitalism. Slavery and colonialism have made the wealth of colonizing societies and their enormous economic, technical, and scientific progress possible – albeit at the price of exclusion, separation, oppression, and the extreme exploitation of entire groups of people. For Mbembe, the close connection between liberal, democratic societies and colonialism is one of our current system's basic flaws, which has been successfully repressed and neglected. But only the recognition of the scandal of slavery can pave the way for the decolonization of "Western" societies and thus for overcoming racism, violence, and the exclusion of others.

## 3 Emancipatory cosmopolitanism

Mbembe demands a break with a *Zeitgeist* that is concerned with exclusion and segregation of human beings. In this respect, Appiah's "partial cosmopolitanism" must be criticized for drawing a line, i.e., for giving preference to family, friends, and nation. However, Mbembe remains vague on the question of how a global, exclusion-free coexistence can be realized, and he leaves many moral questions unanswered, which, in turn, Appiah tries to address in his detailed normative project.

An alternative approach in this regard is the concept of a "critical" (Mignolo 2002b) or "emancipatory" cosmopolitanism (Nederveen Pieterse 2006). Such an approach tries to overcome the conventional Eurocentrism of dominant forms of cosmopolitanism by including non-European approaches to the concept. Nederveen Pieterse, for example, criticizes "[t]he strange double life of conventional cosmopolitanism [...] that while claiming universality [...] reflects a regional parochial order" (Nederveen Pieterse 2006: 1252). Nederveen Pieterse calls for an act of epistemic justice designed to resuscitate the cultural and human contributions of oppressed or marginalized communities: the development of a new, emancipatory form of cosmopolitanism which engages with "alternative cosmovisions beyond Eurocentrism" (Nederveen Pieterse 2006: 1255).

One of the main proponents of the Latin American concept of *decoloniality* is Walter Mignolo. He underlines even more strongly the need for alternative concepts of cosmopolitanism since the dominant concepts are inextricably linked to a modern/colonial world system. He coined the term "critical cosmopolitanism" (Mignolo 2002b) and introduced it as a concept that has to emerge from the spatial and historical locations of colonial difference (and not from national or cultural differences); a difference which is produced, reproduced, and maintained by the global world order and continues to determine our understanding of modernity, says Mignolo. Racially grounded colonial difference leads to the representation of the "Other" as both inferior and radically different, hence incorrigibly inferior. As Mignolo puts it, colonial difference is first

> a consequence of the coloniality of power (in the making of it) and second [...] an epistemic location beyond right and left as articulated in the second modernity (i.e., liberal, neoliberal; socialism, neosocialism). The world became unthinkable beyond European (and, later, North Atlantic) epistemology. The colonial difference marked the limits of thinking and theorizing, unless modern epistemology (philosophy, social sciences, natural sciences) was exported/imported to those places where thinking was impossible (because it was folklore, magic, wisdom, and the like). (Mignolo 2002a: 90)

But the colonial difference is not only the space where the coloniality of power is enacted. It is also the space where subaltern knowledge and where "border thinking," that is, "the recognition and transformation of the hegemonic imaginary from the perspective of people in subaltern positions" (Mignolo 2002b: 174), takes place, where global designs (globalization) meet local histories and are adapted, adopted, rejected, integrated, or ignored: "Border thinking" can become a "tool" of critical cosmopolitanism. Moreover, critical or emancipatory cosmopolitanism "contributes to *rebalancing corporate, political and social globalization* and enables legitimate political institutions and social forces to act as countervailing power and re-regulate corporate globalization and thus transform overall globalization" (Nederveen Pieterse 2006: 1248; emphasis in original).

Critical cosmopolitanism is defined as a project "located in the exteriority and issuing forth from the colonial difference"[7] (Mignolo 2002b: 160). Today, Mignolo argues, cosmopolitanism can no longer be articulated from one point of view or within a mono-logic[8] discourse, and certainly not from a view which considers cosmopolitanism as a benevolent form of control (Mignolo 2002b: 179). Thus, it is time for the discourse on cosmopolitanism to open up

---

[7] Mignolo defines this exteriority not as something "untouched beyond capitalism and modernity, but the outside that is needed by the inside [...] the borderland seen from the perspective of those 'to be included' as they have no other option" (Mignolo 2002b: 160).
[8] The term refers here not only to "a single speaker," but that the whole discourse is based on one logic or epistemic frame of a certain dominant culture only.

to concepts from different regions of the world – to become a truly cosmopolitan debate.

"Emancipatory" or "critical" cosmopolitanism seems to offer alternatives to reconceptualize cosmopolitanism. First, emancipatory cosmopolitanism underlines the relational character of human beings and conceptualizes the individual human being as transcending cultural traditions, symbolic classifications, and identifications and the structuration of belonging and exclusion particular to the community in which an individual is born. Moreover, it embraces both individuality and universality: While being conscious about one's own contextuality or positionality in the world, a cosmopolitan approach looks beyond superficial differences to the essential sameness of human beings. Such cosmopolitanism identifies culture as a rhetorical practice for the provision of common symbolic forms (Geertz 1973) and not as a thing in itself. Taken in this way, cosmopolitanism is a kind of emancipation that liberates the individual to freely explore the space between what he/she is or could become, on the one hand, and how he/she might wish to join collectivities and lifeworlds on the other. A cosmopolitanism of this kind would not negate differentiation into discrete parts such as nations, ethnicities, religions, castes, or classes, but handle them as secondary, formal, and superficial distinctions. Also, the concept of "border" needs to be reconceptualized in a similar way, namely as a point of connection for complementary relationships. A new conceptualization of a border as a link and not as something divisive can be achieved if boundaries are conceptualized as places of complementation.

Mbembe argues that "a genuine deconstruction of the world of our time begins with the full recognition of the perforce provincial status of our discourses and the necessarily regional character of our concepts – and therefore with a critique of every form of abstract universalism" (Mbembe 2019: 9). Decolonization is not a project for former colonies and colonized people alone but has to be applied to societies of the Global North – and the knowledge (concepts, ideas, terminology) produced here while being intertwined with colonialism and racism. Particularly concepts with a claim to universality such as humanism, human rights, democracy, and cosmopolitanism should be subject to such a critique.

# References

Appiah, Kwame Anthony (2006): *Cosmopolitanism: Ethics in a World of Strangers.* New York, NY: W. W. Norton.
Arendt, Hannah (1968): *The Origins of Totalitarianism.* [1951]. New York, NY: Harcourt Brace Jovanovich.

Foucault, Michel (1981): *The History of Sexuality.* Vol. 1. Trans. by Robert Hurley. London: Penguin.
Foucault, Michel (2003): *"Society Must Be Defended": Lectures at the Collège de France, 1975–76.* Edited by Mauro Bertani and Alessandro Fontana. Trans. by David Macey. New York, NY: Picador.
Geertz, Clifford (1973): *The Interpretation of Cultures.* New York, NY: Basic Books.
Hume, David (1964): "Of National Characters." [1748]. In: *The Philosophical Works.* Vol. 3. Edited by Thomas Hill Green and Thomas Hodge Grose. Reprint of the new ed. London 1882. Aalen: Scientia, pp. 244–258.
Locke, John (1669): "The Fundamental Constitutions of Carolina: March 1, 1669." In: *The Avalon Project.* https://avalon.law.yale.edu/17th_century/nc05.asp, accessed 7 May 2020.
Locke, John (1988): *Two Treatises of Government.* [1689]. Edited with an introduction and notes by Peter Laslett. Cambridge: Cambridge University Press.
Lugones, María (2010): "Toward a Decolonial Feminism." In: *Hypatia* 25(4), pp. 742–759.
Mbembe, Achille (2000): *De la postcolonie: Essai sur l'imagination politique dans l'Afrique contemporaine.* Paris: Karthala.
Mbembe, Achille (2001): *On the Postcolony.* Berkeley, CA: University of California Press.
Mbembe, Achille (2003): "Necropolitics." Trans. by Libby Meintje. In: *Public Culture* 15(1), pp. 11–40.
Mbembe, Achille (2016): *Politiques de l'inimitié.* Paris: La Découverte.
Mbembe, Achille (2019): *Necropolitics.* Durham, NC: Duke University Press.
Mignolo, Walter D. (2002a): "The Geopolitics of Knowledge and the Colonial Difference." In: *The South Atlantic Quarterly* 101(1), pp. 57–96.
Mignolo, Walter D. (2002b): "The Many Faces of Cosmo-polis: Border Thinking and Critical Cosmopolitanism." In: Breckenridge, Carol A./Pollock, Sheldon/Bhabha, Homi K./Chakrabarty, Dipesh (Eds.): *Cosmopolitanism.* Durham, NC: Duke University Press, pp. 157–188.
Nederveen Pieterse, Jan (2006): "Emancipatory Cosmopolitanism: Towards an Agenda." In: *Development and Change* 37(6), pp. 1247–1257.
Ngcoya, Mvuselelo (2015): "*Ubuntu:* Toward an Emancipatory Cosmopolitanism?" In: *International Political Sociology* 9(3), pp. 248–262.
Pogge, Thomas W. (1994): "Cosmopolitanism and Sovereignty." In: Brown, Chris (Ed.): *Political Restructuring in Europe: Ethical Perspectives.* London: Routledge, pp. 89–112.
Spivak, Gayatri Chakravorty (1988): "Can the Subaltern Speak?" In: Nelson, Cary/Grossberg, Lawrence (Eds.): *Marxism and the Interpretation of Culture.* Chicago, IL: University of Illinois Press, pp. 271–313.

Marc Rölli
# Kapitalismus und Identität
Zur Dekolonisierung demokratischer Popularität

**Abstract:** [Capitalism and Identity: On the Decolonisation of Democratic Popularity] The current form of the liberal critique of populism is generally based on a problematic elitist self-image that is incapable of perceiving neoliberal power relations as anti-democratic. The post-democratic conditions of the present are characterised by economic power centres without democratic legitimacy. This diagnosis reveals a discursive power that understands the culture of modernisation as a guiding culture (*Leitkultur*). Theories of the 'mass' are part of its genealogy and clearly demonstrate that the racism identified in postcolonial discourse takes on a new form when applied to an inferior part of the European population as a mass. The concept of the mass exhibits colonising traits in its wild, unbridled, irrational nature and finds its way into political and economic propaganda strategies that reproduce the despotic leadership style assigned to it. The critical models of mass consumption, mass media, and mass society are still uncritically in their traditional line. Their contemporary manifestation is described by so-called populism although its critique only succeeds where social inequalities are taken into account in a radical democratic sense or where the democratic response to the sovereignty of the people is fragmented and multiplied in the response to a crowd (*multitudo*).

**Keywords:** Popularity, populism, mass, propaganda, crowd, bell hooks, Gustave Le Bon, Edward Bernays, Michel Foucault

In den gegenwärtig geführten Diskussionen über neu erstarkte rechtsextreme Strömungen in Europa dominiert eine Populismus-Kritik, die sich Demokratie, Menschenrechte, Pluralismus, Liberalität, Multilateralismus und andere Errungenschaften der modernen westlichen Zivilisation auf die Fahnen geschrieben hat. Rechtspopulisten gelten als antipluralistische Traditionalisten, die sich an kulturellen und nationalen Identitäten festhalten – und damit gleichsam rechtmäßig ein Monopol auf Identitätskonflikte beanspruchen. Dies scheint ganz einfach und nahezu selbstverständlich zu sein. Die Folge dieser Sichtweise ist eine fortschreitende Polarisierung der europäischen Gesellschaften. Unversöhnlich stehen sich die Lager der Modernen, die eine ‚progressive' Globalisierung vertreten, und die Traditionsbewussten eines eher ‚regressiv' beschriebenen Kulturverständnisses gegenüber. Nicht zuletzt dividieren sich die dogmatisch verhärteten Weltanschauungen anhand der Themen Klima und Migration auseinander.

In dieser Situation eines selbstbewussten Kosmopolitismus und seiner Gegner ergibt es schon aus strategischen Gründen Sinn, Voraussetzungen zu berücksichtigen, die von beiden Seiten geteilt werden. Diese sind vielfältig und unterschiedlich gelagert. Besonders auffällig sind bestehende Missverhältnisse zwischen ökonomischen Interessen und politischer Repräsentation. Etwas böse gesagt, zielen die einen rhetorisch darauf ab, den Wohlstand für eine homogene, national und kulturell (oft implizit rassistisch) ausgezeichnete Volksgruppe zu sichern, während die anderen stärker Gesellschaftsgruppen adressieren, die um ihre Einbindung in globale Märkte wissen. In diesem Fall treten traditionelle Strukturen eher in den Hintergrund. In beiden Fällen werden bestehende ökonomische Ungleichheiten und damit auch entsprechende Machtstrukturen reproduziert. Und während die einen vom Volk reden, auch wenn sie nur einen Teil von diesem meinen, sprechen die anderen von demokratischen Verhältnissen, meinen aber faktisch stets eine privilegierte Bevölkerungsschicht.

Die Gemengelage ist insofern neuartig, als Rassismus bekanntlich die längste Zeit aus einem kolonialen Diskurs resultierte, der mit imperialen Machtansprüchen verbunden war. Die globalen Eliten der Gegenwart weisen rassistische Positionen weit von sich, während sie dort wieder hoffähig gemacht und artikulierbar werden, wo wenigstens ‚rhetorisch' die internationalen Wirtschaftsbeziehungen als problematisch gelten. Rassismus bedeutet im Kontext der aktuellen rechtsradikalen bis rechtsextremen Positionen keine offensive Ausbeutungs-, sondern eher eine defensive Abgrenzungsstrategie. Zumindest liegt darauf der Akzent.

Mit Ernesto Laclau kann Populismus als ein Prozess beschrieben werden, der, gegen vorherrschende Machtverhältnisse gerichtet, eine neue Hegemonie performativ konstruiert, indem mittels leerer Signifikanten und Äquivalenzketten ein einigermaßen stabiles Bedeutungssystem kollektiver Identität hergestellt wird (Laclau 2005: 74). Die fungierende Identität ist ein Volk – seine Konstruktion bedient sich in den neuen rechten Parteien (bzw. ‚Bewegungen') Vorstellungen von einer nationalen, kulturellen und ethnischen Homogenität. Zu bemerken ist hier nun allerdings, dass gleichsam übergeordnete Identitäten auch dort eine wichtige Rolle spielen, wo es im Selbstverständnis eines liberalen Pluralismus um die demokratische Teilhabe autonom agierender Individuen geht. Es handelt sich bei ihnen um Identitäten einer Mehrheitskultur, die ebenfalls mit Popularität aufgeladen sind: z. B. um Vorstellungen eines kreativen, offenen, toleranten, aufgeklärten Individuums, das sich im Wettbewerb der Interessen durchzusetzen versteht. Kritisch wird diese Situation oft als eine ‚neoliberaler' oder normalistischer Verhältnisse beschrieben. Damit ist zugleich gesagt, dass vielerorts demokratische Ideale relativ auf den neuen Geist des Kapitalismus limitiert sind. Die Ignoranz gegenüber sozialen Ungleichheiten verhindert ein radikaleres Verständnis von Pluralismus, Öffentlichkeit und Demokratie. Popularität zu dekolonisieren bedeutet daher, Identitäten zu problematisieren, die in den gegenwärtigen Prozessen der Ökonomisierung der Existenzweisen genauso ihr Unwesen treiben wie in den vermeintlich auf stabile nationale Traditionen zurückverweisenden reaktionären Tendenzen.

Im ersten Teil der folgenden Ausführungen werden die impliziten Beziehungen zwischen den gegensätzlich aufgestellten modernistischen und traditionalistischen Sichtweisen quasi ‚intersektional' betrachtet, indem bell hooks Arbeiten zur US-amerikanischen Geschichte des Feminismus thematisiert werden. Für sie ist es entscheidend, diese Geschichte unter Berücksichtigung der einerseits ökonomischen und andererseits rassistischen Kontexte zu schreiben. Die berühmte Frage von Sojourner Truth „Ain't I a woman?", die bell hooks als Titel ihres Buches gewählt hat, macht deutlich, dass eine schwarze Frau um 1850 darum ringen musste, überhaupt als Frau anerkannt zu werden (vgl. hooks 1982). Der weiße Feminismus, der für Frauenrechte im Allgemeinen eintrat, erweist sich dabei als eine Bewegung, die etablierte Privilegien weißer Männer für sich zu erlangen suchte. In ihr begegnen sich rassistische Abgrenzungs- und klassenspezifische Besserstellungsstrategien, die sich den geltenden Regeln des Zusammenlebens in der US-amerikanischen Gesellschaft ziemlich bruchlos fügten.

Im zweiten Teil wird die demokratische Popularität unter dem Gesichtspunkt der Massentheorie genauer betrachtet. Meine These besagt, dass das Konzept der Masse nicht nur mit dem Entstehen einer homogen organisierten Arbeiterschaft – und damit verbunden: mit ihrem neu gewonnenen Selbstbewusstsein, wie Ortega y Gasset sagen würde – gegen Ende des 19. Jahrhunderts auftaucht; vielmehr ist ‚Masse' ein Konzept, das es ermöglicht, den gegen andere gerichteten und kolonial bestimmten Inferioritätsdiskurs (im anthropologischen, psychiatrischen, politisch-ökonomischen Zusammenhang) innerhalb der ‚eigenen Kultur' auf einen bestimmten Teil der Bevölkerung zu beziehen. Die Masse von Eliten zu kontrollieren, so der Tenor der frühen massenpsychologischen Literatur, entspricht wahren demokratischen Forderungen – während ein Verlust dieser Kontrolle zum Chaos einer „Hyperdemokratie" (Ortega y Gasset 1952: 159) oder zum Untergang des Abendlandes (Barbarei) führen müsste.

# 1

Der schwarze Feminismus markiert eine Randzone in der Literatur der *postcolonial studies*. In ihm verbindet sich das feministische Anliegen mit den postkolonialen Ansätzen, politisch-ökonomische und diskursive Machtverhältnisse, Kapitalismus und Rassismus in ihrer Verschränkung zu analysieren. Und zugleich verbirgt sich in ihm eine Praxis der Dekolonisierung, die mit den Bürgerrechtsbewegungen oder einer wiedererlangten nationalen Unabhängigkeit von den Kolonialmächten zu keinem Abschluss gekommen ist. In dieser vermittelnden Position steckt wiederum ein Popularitätspotenzial, das ganz aktuell in der Formulierung „we should all be feminists" zum Ausdruck kommt (vgl. Adichie 2014).[1] Es signalisiert eine radikaldemokratische Handlungsmacht, die in beiden Richtungen der Rassen- und der Klassenzugehörigkeit von ihren Möglichkeiten getrennt gehalten wird. Mit den Worten von bell hooks: „The 19th century women's rights movement could have provided a forum for black women to address their grievances, but white female racism barred them from full participation in the movement." (hooks 1982: 161) Der weiße Feminismus erhielt den Mythos der gleichwertigen sozialen Stellung *aller* Frauen in der US-amerikanischen Gesellschaft am Leben. Und wenn in späteren Jahren, zwischen Mitte der 1920er und Mitte der 1960er Jahre, der Kampf für die Schwarze Befreiung in den Vordergrund rückte, so wurde diese Befreiung synonym „with gaining full participation in the existing patriarchal nation-state and their demands were for the elimination of racism, not capitalism or patriarchy" (hooks 1982: 176). Hier wie dort wird eine produktive Allianz (schwarzer Frauen und Männer bzw. schwarzer und weißer Frauen) unterbunden, aus gleichermaßen strategischen Erwägungen, die sich einmal rassistischer Vorurteile bedienen und die das andere Mal feministische Forderungen nach Gendergleichstellung bzw. Überwindung der Zwänge des Sexismus marginalisieren.

Die Überlegungen von bell hooks machen deutlich, dass sich die kolonialen Machtverhältnisse gerade in ihrer Ausprägung ökonomischer Unterschiede mit Diskursen verbinden, die eine machtlose, mindere Stellung bestimmter Menschengruppen behaupten. Gruppen, die von anderen Gruppen nach Geschlecht, Rasse oder Eigentum und sozialem Status differieren – und die deshalb *anders* sind als die Gruppe, die für sich reklamiert, den Menschen im Allgemeinen (und damit auch die Humanität) zu repräsentieren. Wie insbesondere die historische Erfahrung des schwarzen Feminismus lehrt, kann das Freiheitsbegehren verschiedener unterdrückter Gruppen leicht gegeneinander ausgespielt werden. Wenn Freiheit bedeutet, frei zu sein wie diejenigen ‚Herren', die es zu sein behaupten oder zu sein scheinen, weil sie an der Spitze der gesellschaftlichen Hierarchie stehen, dann kann dies leicht zur Abwehr der nichtprivilegierten anderen (der Schwarzen, der Frauen ...) führen: „Women's liberationists, white and

---

[1] Schon im Titel ist die Referenz auf bell hooks (2000) evident.

black, will always be at odds with one another as long as our idea of liberation is based on having the power white men have." (hooks 1982: 156) bell hooks legt großen Wert darauf, die ideologische Dimension dieser Macht von ihrer historischen Realität zu unterscheiden. Oder anders gesagt: Zwischen der Macht des Diskurses und den politisch und institutionell sedimentierten Machtverhältnissen gilt es zu unterscheiden, weil genau dies den Ort markiert, wo ein Hebel angesetzt werden kann, die im Diskurs angelegte performative Reproduzierbarkeit der Verhältnisse zu unterbrechen:

> To perpetuate the notion that all men are creatures of privilege with access to a personal fulfillment and a personal liberation denied women, as feminists do, is to lend further credibility to the sexist mystique of male power that proclaims all that is male is inherently superior to that which is female. A feminism so rooted in envy, fear, and idealization of male power cannot expose the de-humanizing effect of sexism on men and women in American society. (hooks 1982: 192)

Die mit dem anthropologisch-humanistischen Ideal verknüpfte Superiorität und die aus ihr folgende Dehumanisierung des anderen Geschlechts bzw. anderer Rassen bezeichnet den strukturellen Moment der Herabsetzung, der aus einer gleichzeitig feministischen und postkolonialen Perspektive zum Problem gemacht werden muss. Seine fortdauernde Geltung – und Verquickung mit emanzipatorischen Zielen – ist eine dogmatische Festsetzung, die den feministischen Kampf nach bell hooks zur realhistorischen Wirkungslosigkeit verurteilt. An vielen Stellen ihres Buches wird die konkrete Bedeutung ‚weißer Ideale' erläutert, die ein patriarchales Geschlechterverhältnis fortschreiben, indem sie z. B. das Frausein (im Fernsehen der 1950er Jahre) auf eine ‚passive' Rolle im gesellschaftlichen Leben und damit auf Aufgaben im Haushalt verpflichten, etwa auf Kindererziehung und Pflege der Alten. Der elitäre, liberale Gestus vieler weißer Feministinnen, die nicht in der Lage waren, die besondere Situation schwarzer Frauen zu verstehen oder anzuerkennen, führte zu schwierigen Konflikten.[2] „Rather than black women attacking the white female attempt to present them as an Other, an unknown, unfathomable element, they acted as if they were an Other." (hooks 1982: 151) Damit aber akzeptierten sie die ihnen auferlegten kolonialen Strukturen:

---

2 „White women were assuming that all they had to do was express a desire for sisterhood, or a desire to have black women join their groups [...]. They saw themselves as acting in a generous, open, non-racist manner and were shocked that black women responded to their overtures with anger and outrage. [...] Their unwillingness to distinguish between various degrees of discrimination or oppression caused black women to see them as enemies." (hooks 1982: 144–145)

> Black and white women have for so long allowed their idea of liberation to be formed by the existing status quo that they have not yet devised a strategy by which we can come together. They have had only a slave's idea of freedom. And to the slave, the master's way of life represents the ideal free lifestyle. (hooks 1982: 156)

Paradox formuliert: Das Ideal des freien Menschen ist nicht frei von bestimmten Bedingungen, an die die Freiheit gebunden bleibt. Was theoretisch eine Schwierigkeit bezeichnet, ist praktisch leicht nachvollziehbar. Nach Kant wäre der allgemeine Mensch vom besonderen weiter entfernt als jeder Stern am Himmel. Und doch finden sich in ihm Bestimmungen einer moralischen Natur, die sich im Feld der Empirie wiederfinden lassen.[3] Die Herabsetzung der nichteuropäischen Rassen genauso wie der Frauen ergibt sich daraus. Dies scheint ganz leicht zu sein. Und das ist das Problem. Mit bell hooks könnte ich sagen, dass nicht notwendig jede Idee der Freiheit eine ist, die sich aus dialektischen Beziehungen von Herren und Knechten ergibt.[4] Aber historisch betrachtet ist nicht zu übersehen, dass die Idee sich erst in ihrer Bindung an ein geschichtliches Dasein konkretisiert. Das kann zweierlei heißen: Zum einen werden Idealbilder konstruiert, die den freien Menschen anschaulich machen, indem sie ihn auf welchem Weg auch immer mit bestimmten Vorstellungen von Freiheit ausstatten. Zum anderen werden empirische Voraussetzungen der vorgestellten Freiheit ignoriert oder unsichtbar gemacht. Gesund ist, wer gesund ist – oder es sich leisten kann. Der normative Aspekt des idealisierten Menschen verbindet sich historisch mit einer hierarchischen Position, die bei Abweichungen vom Idealzustand Defizite verzeichnet. Und wiederum ist dies ein Problem, sofern entweder mit festen ‚Charakter'-Identitäten (im Sinne des älteren anthropologischen Diskurses: weiß-schwarz, männlich-weiblich) hantiert wird oder aber die genauen Bedingungen der privilegierten Stellung mit Stillschweigen übergangen werden.

## 2

Eine aussagekräftige Verschränkung kapitalistisch-traditionalistischer Motive findet sich im Diskurs über die Masse – und seine kritische Analyse kann als ein Schritt auf dem Weg zu einer Dekolonisierung des europäischen Denkens verstanden werden. 1895 publiziert Gustave Le Bon seine *Psychologie der Massen* im Anschluss an die früheren kulturanthropologisch-orientalistischen Arbeiten, die

---

[3] Einige Kritikpunkte dieses anthropologietypischen Vorgehens hatte bereits Wittgenstein in seiner Auseinandersetzung mit James G. Frazer erörtert. Vgl. dazu Nordmann (2015).
[4] Vgl. hierzu bereits die Hegelkritik des differenzfeministischen Ansatzes in Lonzi (2013).

bereits mit völker- und rassenpsychologischen Überlegungen durchsetzt waren (vgl. Le Bon 2009; Le Bon 1894). Masse folgt auf Rasse, denn auch sie ist wie diese eine Kollektivseele, in der das individuelle Bewusstsein des Einzelnen „schwindet" (Le Bon 2009: 29).[5] Im Unterschied zur Rasse handelt es sich bei ihr um ein sozialgeschichtliches Phänomen, das mit dem „Eintritt der Volksklassen in das politische Leben", dem „Umsturz" eines „primitiven Kommunismus" zusammenhängt (Le Bon 2009: 23). Das „Zeitalter der Massen", das Le Bon heraufziehen sieht, bedroht die Grundlagen der europäischen Kultur (Le Bon 2009: 22). Von „Mikroben" ist die Rede oder auch von „blinden Massen", die den Zusammenbruch des „Gebäudes" der Kultur herbeiführen (Le Bon 2009: 25).[6]

Wie aus der anthropologischen Literatur des 19. Jahrhunderts bekannt, korrespondiert mit der menschlichen Natur ein ungeformtes, von (sinnlichen) Neigungen und (vererblichen) Dispositionen beherrschtes Seelenleben, das vernünftig entwickelt werden muss (vgl. Rölli 2011). Charakteristisch gilt, dass Frauen oder Wilde nur ein begrenztes Entwicklungspotenzial der menschlichen Anlagen besitzen. Le Bon überträgt genau diesen Aspekt von der Rassen- und Völkerpsychologie auf die Massenpsychologie, indem er das in der Vermassung aufkommende „Machtgefühl", Teil eines Ganzen zu sein, auf eine „Triebhaftigkeit" bezieht, die jeden bewussten Skrupel ausschaltet, jedes Gefühl der Verantwortung eliminiert (Le Bon 2009: 35). Damit stellt er zwischen den unbewussten Trieben, die die Massenseele organisieren, den „vererblichen" Aspekten ihres Charakters und den von ihrer Sinnlichkeit dominierten „Frauen und Kindern" oder „Primitiven" einen direkten Zusammenhang her (Le Bon 2009: 50, 40).[7] Er schreibt:

> Verschiedene besondere Eigenschaften der Massen, wie Triebhaftigkeit, Reizbarkeit, Unfähigkeit zum logischen Denken, Mangel an Urteil und kritischem Geist, Überschwang der Gefühle und noch andere sind bei Wesen einer niedrigeren Entwicklungsstufe, wie beim Wilden und beim Kinde, ebenfalls zu beobachten. (Le Bon 2009: 40)

Die Masse ist aufgrund ihrer psychologischen Struktur leicht zu lenken, zu verführen oder zu manipulieren. Sie denkt lediglich assoziativ oder „in Bildern",

---

5 „Die bewusste Persönlichkeit schwindet, die Gefühle und Gedanken aller einzelnen sind nach derselben Richtung orientiert. Es bildet sich eine Gemeinschaftsseele […], [eine] psychologische Masse." (Le Bon 2009: 29)
6 „Bisher wurden die Kulturen von einer kleinen, intellektuellen Aristokratie geschaffen und geleitet, niemals von den Massen." (Le Bon 2009: 25)
7 „Unsere bewussten Handlungen entspringen einer unbewussten Grundlage, die namentlich durch Vererbungseinflüsse geschaffen wird. Diese Grundlage enthält die zahllosen Ahnenspuren, aus denen sich die Rassenseele aufbaut." (Le Bon 2009: 34)

weshalb sie beliebigen Einflüssen ausgesetzt werden kann, die sich in ihr auf unkontrollierten Übertragungswegen ausbreiten (Le Bon 2009: 45). Auch von Ansteckung (*contagion*) ist die Rede (Le Bon 2009: 36). Neben epidemiologischen (und proto-medialen) Metaphern bedient sich Le Bon des psychiatrischen Begriffs der Hypnose. Der Geist der Masse befindet sich gleichsam in einem hypnotisierten oder verzauberten Zustand.[8] Moralische und kulturelle Regeln, selbst der Wille, sich selbst zu erhalten, sind dabei vorübergehend außer Kraft gesetzt. Massen sind unfähig, „Meinungen zu haben außer jenen, die ihnen eingeflößt wurden" (Le Bon 2009: 27). Genau in ihrer Beeinflussbarkeit oder Verführbarkeit liegt das (scheinbar massenpsychologisch aufgeklärte) Mittel, dessen sich die Politik zu bedienen hat, wenn sie nicht zur Marionette der Macht der Massen verkommen will. „Die Kunst, die Einbildungskraft der Massen zu erregen, ist die Kunst, sie zu regieren." (Le Bon 2009: 72)[9]

Mit diesen Überlegungen zur Psychologie der Massen verbinden sich diagnostische Motive, Erklärungsansätze, kritischer Zynismus und nicht zuletzt Handlungsanweisungen. Auch wenn Gabriel Tarde eine deutlicher ausgefeilte Theorie vorlegte, indem er – bereits vor Le Bon – eine Soziologie der Nachahmung entwickelte und (etwas später) in einem Aufsatz Masse und Publikum unterschied – Le Bon wird dort wegen seines unwissenschaftlichen Vorgehens streng getadelt (vgl. Tarde 2015: 17) – so steht dennoch die breite Rezeption der Massentheorie in der Folgezeit ganz unter dem Eindruck Le Bons. Ob Freud, Lippmann oder Ortega y Gasset: Sie alle orientieren sich an ihm. Eine Konsequenz dieser enormen Wirksamkeit liegt in der Entstehung der Konzepte von Massenkultur und Massengesellschaft, eine andere im Verständnis von öffentlicher Meinung und überhaupt von Öffentlichkeit.

In der *Propaganda*-Schrift (1928) von Edward Bernays werden diese Aspekte zusammengeführt. Bernays begreift die Propaganda als eine Kunst der Public Relations, die auf massenpsychologischen Grundlagen operiert (Bernays 2014: 49). Sie ist eingebunden in eine demokratische Struktur, die nach dem „Modell" des „freien Wettbewerb[s]" organisiert ist (Bernays 2014: 21). Aus seiner Sicht schließen sich Propaganda und Demokratie keineswegs aus; vielmehr stehen sie in reziproken Beziehungen zueinander:

---

**8** „Da das Verstandesleben des Hypnotisierten lahm gelegt ist, wird er der Sklave seiner unbewussten Kräfte, die der Hypnotiseur nach seinem Belieben lenkt. [...] Ungefähr in diesem Zustand befindet sich der einzelne als Glied einer Masse." (Le Bon 2009: 37)
**9** Wie Le Bon meint, zeichnet sich ein „großer Führer" durch die besondere Fähigkeit aus, „Glauben zu erwecken" (Le Bon 2009: 113). In der Gegenwart allerdings, z.B. aufgrund der Bedeutung der Presse, gelingt es den Regierungen immer weniger, „die öffentliche Meinung zu lenken" (Le Bon 2009: 139).

> Die bewusste und zielgerichtete Manipulation der Verhaltensweisen und Einstellungen der Massen ist ein wesentlicher Bestandteil demokratischer Gesellschaften. Organisationen, die im Verborgenen arbeiten, lenken die gesellschaftlichen Abläufe. Sie sind die eigentlichen Regierungen in unserem Land. [...] [D]ieser Zustand ist nur eine logische Folge der Struktur unserer Demokratie. (Bernays 2014: 19)

Es handelt sich um eine „logische Folge", weil die moderne Gesellschaft „Steuerungsprozesse dieser Art unumgänglich" macht (Bernays 2014: 19). Bernays zeigt nicht nur auf, wie Propaganda funktioniert, sondern auch, warum sie (in kapitalistischen Verhältnissen liberaler Demokratien) notwendig ist. Er kritisiert sie nicht grundsätzlich, sondern plädiert für eine ethisch legitimierte und zugleich für eine neue Propaganda. „Dieses Buch erläutert die Strukturen und Mechanismen, mit denen das öffentliche Bewusstsein gesteuert wird." (Bernays 2014: 26) Nicht die ältere Kriegspropaganda und die ihr zugeordnete mechanistische Reaktionspsychologie steht im Vordergrund, sondern eine komplexe, plural ausdifferenzierte Gesellschaft, die durch Massenproduktion und Massenmedien gekennzeichnet ist. In einer solchen Situation liberaler, ökonomischer Konkurrenzverhältnisse muss eine erfolgreiche Unternehmensstrategie der Produktvermarktung daraufsetzen, die Öffentlichkeit für sich zu gewinnen.[10] Die Gegenwart zeichnet sich nicht einfach durch eine Herrschaft der Volksmassen aus:

> Mittlerweile hat [...] eine Gegenreaktion eingesetzt. Die herrschende Minderheit hat ein mächtiges Instrument entdeckt, mit dem sie die Mehrheit beeinflussen kann. Die Meinung der Massen ist offensichtlich formbar, sodass ihre neu gewonnene Kraft in die gewünschte Richtung gelenkt werden kann. (Bernays 2014: 27)

Massen gibt es also nicht ohne Eliten, die sie steuern. Sie tun dies, indem sie „bestimmte Assoziationen und Bilder in den Köpfen der Massen erzeugen" (Bernays 2014: 31). Hier greift Bernays auf massenpsychologische Einsichten zurück: „Anstelle von Gedanken stehen bei der Gruppe Impulse, Gewohnheiten und Gefühle. Um zu einer Entscheidung zu gelangen, neigt sie gewöhnlich als Erstes dazu, dem Vorbild eines Führers zu folgen, dem sie vertraut." (Bernays 2014: 51) Den Thesen Le Bons oder auch Freuds werden die von Lippmann über die Bedeutung von Stereotypen zur Seite gestellt: „Steht kein Vorbild eines Führers zur Verfügung, muss die Herde für sich selbst denken. Dabei greift sie zurück auf

---

10 Bernays gibt folgende Definition: „Moderne Propaganda ist das stetige, konsequente Bemühen, Ereignisse zu formen oder zu schaffen mit dem Zweck, die Haltung der Öffentlichkeit zu einem Unternehmen, einer Idee oder einer Gruppe zu beeinflussen." (Bernays 2014: 31)

Klischees, Schlagworte oder Bilder, die für ein ganzes Bündel von Ideen und Erfahrungen stehen." (Bernays 2014: 51)

Massen sind nicht nur manipulierbar, weil sie seelisch – und d. h. nach Le Bon: assoziativ, emotional, imaginativ – einheitlich organisiert sind. Sie unterliegen unbewussten Kräften, die libidinös bestimmt (vgl. Freud 1974) oder durch Wiederholungsmuster (vgl. Lippmann 1922) geprägt sind. Sie kennen die wahren Beweggründe ihres Handelns (z. B. ihrer Kaufentscheidungen) zumeist nicht, weshalb ein psychologisches Wissen an diesem Punkt, durch die Fachleute der Propaganda oder Öffentlichkeitsarbeit, eine elitäre Funktion besitzt: „Die Maschine Gesellschaft hat als Motor die Wünsche und Sehnsüchte der Menschen. Nur wenn der Propagandist sie kennt und begreift, kann er den riesigen, lose verbundenen Apparat namens moderne Gesellschaft steuern." (Bernays 2014: 53) Die Eliten lenken die Massen, indem sie auf die öffentliche Meinung dauerhaft und systematisch mittels Propaganda einwirken. Sie sind die Aktivitätszentren der amerikanischen Demokratie; sie fördern ihre Entwicklung oder ermöglichen ihren Fortschritt, da ihr „Eigeninteresse mit dem öffentlichen Interesse zusammenfällt" (Bernays 2014: 35). An anderer Stelle unterstreicht Bernays: „Die Lücke zwischen den Intellektuellen und der Masse wird in der komplexen modernen Gesellschaft mithilfe von Propaganda überbrückt." (Bernays 2014: 98)

Wie aber lässt sich die moderne Gesellschaft als ein Massenphänomen beschreiben? Die Gesellschaft zerfällt in eine Vielzahl unterschiedlichster Gruppierungen. Anhand endloser Listen von Vereinen und Verbänden, Zeitschriften oder Tagungen macht Bernays deutlich, wie komplex dies „unsichtbare Geflecht aus Gruppierungen und Verbindungen" eigentlich ist (Bernays 2014: 25). Es wäre daher auch verfehlt, ihm ein kompaktes, homogenes, von kulturellen, nationalen oder ethnischen Identitäten geprägtes Massenverständnis zu unterstellen. Tatsächlich spricht er von einer „gigantische[n], *heterogene[n]* Masse", die erst durch die Bearbeitung der öffentlichen Meinung – im Rahmen ökonomischer, dann aber auch politischer Verhältnisse – homogenisiert wird (Bernays 2014: 99; Hervorhebung hinzugefügt). Ausdrücklich wehrt er den quasi vormodernen Massenbegriff ab, der „körperliche Nähe zur Voraussetzung" hat (Bernays 2014: 22; vgl. Tarde 2015: 10). Mit Tarde könnte hier von einer Masse in „zweiter Potenz" gesprochen werden, sofern sie aus der medial vermittelten „Suggestibilität allein durch Ideen, [...] Ansteckung ohne Berührung" als ebenso abstrakte wie reale Gruppenbildung entsteht (Tarde 2015: 13). Mit der Idee der zweiten Potenz verbindet sich nicht nur eine besondere Akzentuierung der Medialität – und die spezifische Bedeutung des Journalismus und überhaupt der Publizität –, vielmehr unterliegt die Gesellschaft einer „Segmentierung [...] in Publika" (Tarde 2015: 25, 55).

Bernays *Propaganda*-Buch ist aus zweierlei Gründen eine lehrreiche Lektüre. Verdeutlicht wird erstens die gegenseitige Abhängigkeit von Massen und Eliten. Die einen gibt es nicht ohne die anderen. Es sind in erster Linie ökonomische und mediale Bedingungen, die es nicht nur möglich, sondern geradezu notwendig machen, die Massen zu ‚informieren' oder öffentliche Meinung hervorzubringen. Dabei werden nicht nur bestimmte Meinungen generiert, die mit Dynamiken interagieren, die als Moden oder Trends bezeichnet werden können. Zugleich macht Bernays auch Propaganda für Propaganda, indem er ihren generellen ökonomischen und politischen Wert herausarbeitet. Masse wie auch Eliten werden damit immer auch im Diskurs konstruiert. In jedem Fall handelt es sich bei ihnen nicht um reine Positivitäten. Masse wird im Bezugsfeld von Märkten ins Spiel gebracht – und d. h. im Kontext der massenpsychologischen These, dass sie von Eliten geführt wird und werden kann, weil sie so leicht zu beeinflussen ist.

Zweitens reflektiert sich in Bernays' Buch eine moderne Gesellschaft, die den älteren Begriff der Masse – vielleicht mehr implizit – auch problematisiert. Masse ist bei ihm ein heterogenes Phänomen, und sie wird pluralisiert. Zwar unterliegt sie recht fügsam einer klugen Strategie, die sie bei ihren sogenannten unbewussten Begierden packt. Aber dieser Vorgang wird genauer bestimmt als eine identitätsstiftende Maßnahme, die nicht auf die basalen Eigenschaften einer naturalisierten Psyche reduziert werden kann. Moderne Massenphänomene entstehen aus einer Vielfalt neuer Medien und den mit ihnen koexistierenden Publika. Es stellt sich hier die weiterführende Frage, inwiefern populäre Kulturen und Massenkulturen unterschiedlich konzipiert werden können. Stehen diese immer mit ‚antiliberalen' Führungseliten in Kontakt, so liegt in jenen eine Aufwertung des Populären, die nicht länger die Masse als fasziniertes Tier oder getaktete Maschine begreift, die aufgrund ihrer widerstandslosen Beherrschbarkeit, durch Ideologien oder Werbekampagnen, ihr nichtdemokratiefähiges Wesen zum Ausdruck bringt.[11] Es ist bekannt und kaum Zufall, dass die Aufwertung des Populären und die Zurückweisung ihres allzu voraussetzungsvollen Massendaseins in der amerikanischen Soziologie und Literaturwissenschaft in den 1950er Jahren den Begriff des ‚Postmodernen' hervorbrachte.

# 3

In Bernays' Buch mischen sich enthüllende und propagandistische Aspekte. Es macht deutlich, wie die öffentliche Meinung bearbeitet wird und werden soll –

---
11 Vgl. Hall/Whannel (2018: 66–87).

und es reflektiert diesen Vorgang. Es nimmt die komplexe Ausgangssituation der modernen Gesellschaft wahr – und reproduziert zugleich den einfachen Dualismus von Elite und Masse. Es greift zu kurz, die privatwirtschaftlich interessierte Steuerung des Massenkonsums kritisch zu thematisieren, weil die Massenlenkung selbst ein problematisches Konstrukt ist, das mit einer ökonomischen wie auch politischen Funktion ausgestattet ist. Wenn Habermas von einer „Refeudalisierung der Öffentlichkeit" spricht, die sich mit „ihrer Gestaltung durch public relations" ergibt, so bleibt er im Bann der instrumentellen Vernunft der massenmedialen „Meinungspflege" (Habermas 1962: 233). Er zitiert Bernays mit dem Buchtitel *The Engineering of Consent*, das ist ein Konsens, der zwar aus rationalen kommunikativen Prozessen zu resultieren scheint, eigentlich aber nur „privilegierte Privatinteressen" für sich „adoptiert" (Habermas 1962: 231–232).[12] Die entlarvende Kritik bleibt damit zu eng auf ihren Gegenstand (und seine Selbstbeschreibungen) bezogen. Und sie vermeidet es, den Strukturwandel als einen der Rationalität selbst zu begreifen. Wenn Medien, wie McLuhan sagen würde, eine hypnotisierende Wirkung haben, weil sie sich strukturell hinter dem verbergen, was sie inhaltlich mitteilen, dann muss keine Massenseele für diese unter anderem technisch bedingte Suggestibilität herhalten. Und die medientheoretische Reflexion muss mit einem blinden Fleck umgehen – sie kann diesen nicht durch elitäre Einsichten auffüllen.

Foucault hat in seinen Vorlesungen der ersten Monate des Jahres 1979 am Collège de France, die unter dem Titel *Naissance de la biopolitique* (dt.: *Die Geburt der Biopolitik*) veröffentlicht wurden, eine weitreichende Skepsis an der Massentheorie sowohl ihrer Vertreter als auch ihrer Kritiker*innen („von Sombart bis Marcuse") geäußert (Foucault 2006: 169). Mit ihr schließt sich der Kreis. Masse firmiert bei ihm als ein dem Liberalismus entgegengesetztes Konstrukt, das schon gar nicht in die Lage versetzt, die spezifisch neoliberalen Verhältnisse der Gegenwart kritisch aufzuschlüsseln.

> Die Kritiker irren sich einfach, wenn sie eine „Sombartsche" Gesellschaft in Anführungsstrichen anprangern, ich meine, eine vereinheitlichende Massen-, Konsum-, Unterhaltungsgesellschaft usw., sie irren sich, wenn sie glauben, daß sie das kritisieren, was das gegenwärtige Ziel der Regierungspolitik ist. Sie kritisieren etwas anderes [...], etwas, das zweifellos [...] im [...] Horizont der Regierungskunst der Jahre zwischen 1920 und 1960 lag.

---

[12] „Der hergestellte Konsens hat natürlich mit öffentlicher Meinung, mit der endlichen Einstimmigkeit eines langwierigen Prozesses wechselseitiger Aufklärung im Ernst nicht viel gemeinsam [...]. Dem im Zeichen eines fingierten public interest durch raffinierte opinion-molding services erzeugten Konsensus fehlen Kriterien des Räsonablen überhaupt. [...] Publizität hieß einst die Entblößung politischer Herrschaft vor dem öffentlichen Räsonnement; publicity summiert die Reaktionen eines unverbindlichen Wohlwollens." (Habermas 1962: 232–233)

> Über dieses Stadium sind wir jedoch hinaus. Wir befinden uns nicht mehr dort. Die um die 1930er Jahre von den Ordoliberalen programmatisch entworfene Regierungskunst, die jetzt für die meisten Regierungen kapitalistischer Länder zum Programm geworden ist, nun, dieser programmatische Entwurf strebt keineswegs nach der Errichtung jener Art von Gesellschaft. Es geht im Gegenteil darum, zu einer Gesellschaft zu gelangen, die sich nicht an der Ware und an der Gleichförmigkeit der Ware ausrichtet, sondern an der Vielzahl und der Differenzierung der Unternehmen. (Foucault 2006: 211)

Den Ordoliberalen geht es nach Foucault darum, die Informationsgewalt der Marktwirtschaft zur Organisation der Gesellschaft produktiv zu machen – und daher den Wettbewerb als formalen Mechanismus der Regelung des Marktes (als regulatives Prinzip der Gesellschaft) zu analysieren. Nicht die ‚Handels'- oder die Massengesellschaft (und damit die Warenform und der Tauschwert) sind das Ziel ihrer Regierungskunst, sondern eine Gesellschaft, „die der Dynamik des Wettbewerbs untersteht" (Foucault 2006: 208). Mit ihr verbinden sich eine Reihe von Dingen, die den neuen Geist einer nicht länger an der Massengesellschaft ausgerichteten kapitalistischen Wirtschaftsordnung ausmachen: die Vervielfachung der Unternehmensform, die im Gegensatz zur Planwirtschaft entwickelte spieltheoretische Rahmenanalyse (vgl. Foucault 2006: 241–245) und die Konzepte der Vitalpolitik (vgl. Rüstow 1957) oder auch des Humankapitals, indem Arbeit quasi vom Standpunkt des Arbeiters aus als ökonomisches Verhalten bestimmt wird (vgl. Foucault 2006: 311–324). Damit ist er als eine „Kompetenz/Maschine" begriffen, die in sich selbst als eine Art von Unternehmen Kapital investiert (Foucault 2006: 315). Der Arbeiter wird nicht länger in einen inhumanen Apparat eingegliedert und damit der Entfremdung ausgesetzt (als Objekt oder Rädchen im Getriebe), sondern als ein ‚aktives Wirtschaftssubjekt' begriffen. Dass dies so ist, macht es allerdings auch nicht besser, nur deutlich anders. Die aktuellen kapitalistischen Machtverhältnisse beziehen sich mehr auf Strategien, sich selbst als zukunftsträchtiges Wesen effizient zu steuern und zu vermarkten, und weniger darauf, Individuen gleichmäßig zu unterwerfen, zu disziplinieren oder zu vorgegebenen kollektiven Einheiten zusammenzusetzen.

Foucaults machtanalytische Perspektive kann verdeutlichen, inwiefern das Schema einer von Eliten gesteuerten Masse sowohl mit einem geläufigen Begriff der Demokratie als auch mit einer grundsätzlichen Ablehnung des Populären in einen Zusammenhang gestellt werden kann. Masse ist nichts anderes als eine Menschenmenge, die – im Hinblick auf ihren psychologischen Charakter – als minderwertig und riskant (verblendet, fehlgeleitet, triebgesteuert) angesehen wird. Ihre Popularität überträgt sich auf die Unterhaltungs- oder Kulturindustrie, die sie als ihren Begehrenswert produziert. Masse ist damit kein eigentlich demokratisches Konzept, weil es die Menge der Leute nicht nur einheitlich repräsentiert, sondern zur Unmündigkeit verurteilt. Mit einer Aufwertung der populären Kulturen (und womöglich selbst der ‚Volkskulturen') ändert sich das Bild. Es ist nicht länger die aufgeklärte bürgerliche Öffentlichkeit, die der Massengesellschaft ihren Maßstab entgegenhält.[13] Vielmehr sind es umgekehrt häufig populäre Kulturen, die die älteren anthropologischen Idealvorstellungen problematisieren. Wenn die ökonomischen Verhältnisse der Gegenwart nicht in Begriffen der Massenmanipulation wirkungsvoll kritisiert werden können, dann macht die Kritik der veränderten ‚neoliberalen' Verhältnisse einen anderen Anfang notwendig. Machtstrukturen einer durchgreifenden Ökonomisierung der Gesellschaft, wie sie von Foucault anhand der Verallgemeinerung der Unternehmensform herausgearbeitet worden sind, können nur vor dem Hintergrund einer nicht vorschnell als Masse repräsentierten Menge (in ihrer radikal pluralistischen Auflösung) rekonstruiert werden.

Aus ihrer Perspektive der Geschichte des schwarzen Feminismus konnte bell hooks die populären Seiten des Rassismus und des Kapitalismus zeigen, indem sie die Identitätspolitiken von weißen Frauen oder schwarzen Männern mit einer allgemeineren demokratischen Popularität konfrontierte, die exemplarisch von der schwarzen Frau und ihren sozialpolitischen Ansprüchen getragen war. Ihre Potenziale können dabei nur zur Entfaltung kommen, wenn das Ideal der Freiheit von seiner exklusiven (anthropologischen) Anbindung an ein patriarchales *und* koloniales Ideal losgekoppelt und damit dekolonisiert wird. Das Massenthema verschiebt den Fokus von anthropologischen Fragen des Rassismus und Feminismus direkter auf die mit ihnen zusammenhängenden kapitalismustheoretischen. Massetheorie bringt Massen stets gleichzeitig mit einem Selbstverständnis von Eliten hervor, das die demokratische Kultur ruiniert. Mit der Theorie der Masse und ihrem Konzept von Volk oder Popularität gelingt es nicht, die Schwierigkeiten der aktuellen Machtverhältnisse adäquat zu thematisieren, weil es sich beim Begriff der Masse – und dem stets als homogene Einheit präsentierten Kollektiv – selbst um eine revisionsbedürftige Kategorie handelt. Ihre Eliten begreifen sich als politische, ökonomische oder auch intellektuelle Führung – und ihre privilegierte Stellung überfliegt die Niederungen der anderen, die nur als angeführte Masse in den Blick gerät. Ein kritischer Blick auf diese demokratischen Defizite kann daher erst gelingen, wenn hinter dem Phantasma der Masse die Multiplizität der Menge zum Vorschein kommt.[14] Erst mit ihr wird es

---

[13] Es geht nicht länger darum, mit Habermas den Verfall der bürgerlichen Öffentlichkeit in Massenmedien und Kulturindustrie zu beklagen. Vielmehr kann in der bürgerlichen Gesellschaft (und ihrer Beschreibung bei Ferguson) die Vorgeschichte einer neoliberalen „Mechanik der Interessen" herausgelesen werden (vgl. Foucault 2006: 412).

[14] Vgl. zu diesem Konzept die breite Wirksamkeit der Spinoza-Lektüren von Deleuze z. B. in Hardt/Negri (2004).

möglich, die neoliberalen Verhältnisse in ihren konkreten Veranstaltungen nachzuvollziehen – und die mit ihnen produzierten sozialen Ungleichheiten aufzudecken. Deshalb ist das auf die Menge bezogene Minoritärwerden der Bevölkerung stets und in sich selbst immer bereits ein Demokratischwerden, das über die Grenzen der real existierenden liberalen Demokratien hinausweist.

## Literatur

Adichie, Chimamanda Ngozi (2014): *We Should All Be Feminists*. London: Harper Collins.
Bernays, Edward (2014): *Propaganda: Die Kunst der Public Relations*. [1928]. Übers. von Patrick Schnur. Berlin: Orange Press.
Foucault, Michel (2006): *Die Geburt der Biopolitik: Geschichte der Gouvernementalität II*. Vorlesung am Collège de France 1978–1979. Hg. von Michel Sennelart. Aus dem Französischen von Jürgen Schröder. Frankfurt a. M.: Suhrkamp.
Freud, Sigmund (1974): „Massenpsychologie und Ich-Analyse". [1921]. In: *Fragen der Gesellschaft: Ursprünge der Religion*. Studienausgabe. Band 9. Frankfurt a. M.: Fischer, S. 61–134.
Habermas, Jürgen (1962): *Strukturwandel der Öffentlichkeit: Untersuchungen zu einer Kategorie der bürgerlichen Gesellschaft*. Neuwied/Berlin: Luchterhand.
Hall, Stuart/Whannel, Paddy (2018): *The Popular Arts*. [1964]. Durham, NC/London: Duke University Press.
Hardt, Michael/Negri, Antonio (2004): *Multitude: Krieg und Demokratie im Empire*. Frankfurt a. M.: Campus.
hooks, bell (1982): *Ain't I a Woman: Black Women and Feminism*. London: Pluto.
hooks, bell (2000): *Feminism Is for Everybody*. London: Pluto.
Laclau, Ernesto (2005): *On Populist Reason*. London: Verso.
Le Bon, Gustave (1894): *Les lois psychologiques de l'évolution des peuples*. Paris: Félix Alcan.
Le Bon, Gustave (2009): *Psychologie der Massen*. [1895]. Übers. von Rudolf Eisler. Hamburg: Nikol.
Lippmann, Walter (1922): *Public Opinion*. London: Allen & Unwin.
Lonzi, Carla (2013): *Sputiamo su Hegel*. [1970]. Milano: Et Al.
Nordmann, Alfred (2015): „Der Ursachen-Bär: Wittgensteins anthropologische Anthropologiekritik". In: Rölli, Marc (Hg.): *Fines Hominis? Zur Geschichte der philosophischen Anthropologiekritik*. Bielefeld: Transcript, S. 119–136.
Ortega y Gasset, José (1952): „Der Aufstand der Massen". [1930]. In: *Signale unserer Zeit: Essays*. Stuttgart/Salzburg: Europäischer Buchklub, S. 151–304.
Rölli, Marc (2011): *Kritik der anthropologischen Vernunft*. Berlin: Matthes & Seitz.
Rüstow, Alexander (1957): „Vitalpolitik gegen Vermassung". In: Hunold, Albert (Hg.): *Masse und Demokratie*. Erlenbach-Zürich/Stuttgart: Eugen Rentsch, S. 215–238.
Tarde, Gabriel (2015): *Masse und Meinung*. [1901]. Übers. von Horst Brühmann. Konstanz: Konstanz University Press.

Part 5: **Science and Critique**

Eva-Maria Engelen
# Testimony and the First-, Second-, and Third-Person Perspective

**Abstract:** This paper discusses the notion of testimony in the case of transmission of knowledge, both in the case of expert knowledge and in the case of witnessing historical events. These terms are not entirely different concepts of testimony. Nevertheless, in order to do justice to the specific difficulties and questions associated with them, it is necessary to apply the concepts of first-, second-, and third-person perspective from philosophy of mind. This step also permits us to resolve the inherent tension between a social epistemological approach in the transmission of knowledge in which testimony is a key term and an approach focusing on the giving testimony, whose starting point is primarily subjective, irrespective of whether one adheres to a reductive or an anti-reductive theory of testimony. What is revealed thereby as well is the importance of understanding the witness and their body both as having been part of an historical event and as being part of the process of witnessing itself.

**Keywords:** Testimony, social epistemology, evidence, perspective, trust

'Testimony' is a topic frequently discussed in epistemology as well as in the ethics of witnessing. Some philosophers maintain that the notions of 'testimony' used in these different academic contexts should be clearly distinguished. Others, however, demand that they be discussed together in order to prevent the loss of ordinary meaning whenever the terminologies become too specialised. In this paper we will introduce some concepts from philosophy of mind in order to specify the particular characteristics of the term as it is used in different contexts, without having to insist that the notions of testimony used in these discussions are in fact dissimilar. The concepts from philosophy of mind that are relevant here have to do with the notion of perspective: first-person perspective, second-person perspective, and third-person perspective. These concepts occasionally make an appearance within debates on testimony, but quite often they appear not at all. Nevertheless, depending on the context, at least one of the perspectives should be an integral part of any discussion of 'testimony.' This allows us to work with a general concept of testimony and, at the same time, to take into account the necessary distinctions that are specific for the respective usage. Furthermore, as this investigation will reveal, there is an inherent tension between a social epistemological approach and the concept of testimony itself.

# 1 Interest in testimony and an unresolved tension

Recent years have seen an intensifying interest in the topic of testimony. The ethics of witnessing has attracted considerable attention from different viewpoints, most prominently from philosophy, literature, history, as well as from film studies. The reasons for this are quite heterogeneous. One reason is certainly the impressive body of survivor literature that has forced thinkers to consider the significance of testimony and its impact on our understanding of the atrocities of the past.

The increased focus on testimony in epistemology has very different reasons. Among them is the rise of social epistemology, which coincides with a general turning away from the concept of an epistemic subject based on direct experience as the principal source of genuine knowledge.

Moreover, philosophers have begun to understand more clearly that testimony is part of the process of gaining knowledge and therefore of the practice of generating knowledge. Most of what we take to be knowledge has been learned from experts, as it would be impossible to have direct, personal experience of everything we are told and taught. This is not only the case in academic and scientific work but also in early language acquisition and later in everyday life. It remains, in effect, continuous throughout our whole existence. Testifying in court or giving testimony of a spiritual experience are therefore only rare instances of a practice that is quite common; and yet these instances exhibit some features that are significant for the general practice of giving testimony.

In the main, the concept 'testimony' indicates that certain information is offered as evidence (Coady 1992: 42). This includes the intention to convey such information to someone else and to show it as evidence to another person. In specific discourses, as in epistemology or in the ethics of witnessing, different aspects are emphasised or added to this broad term according to the requirements of the context.

Now, one could leave it at this, i.e. by stating that 'testimony' has different meanings according to the philosophical context in which it is used. But this would abet the tendency to lose sight of the broader philosophical standpoint for which 'testimony' is a key term. The most important consideration in this respect is the turn away from self- or subject-oriented philosophy, with its concentration on the first-person perspective, towards one that takes into account social relations as a condition for the possibility of knowledge, language, and ethics.

There is an inherent tension, however, between a social epistemological approach and the concept of testimony, a tension that has scarcely been addressed in the literature. Anti-reductionist theories like the assurance view have an implicit focus on the first-person perspective in so far as the speaker's willingness to "stand by their word," giving their assurance, entitles others to believe them. It is the personal assurance for the truth of one's testimony that provides justification for belief. This renders such testimony inherently subjective as a source for belief.

The situation is a bit different when we look at reductive theories, but it turns out that here too the first-person is indispensable. As the credibility of a testimony depends on empirical sources like perception, memory, and induction, for a reductionist testimony the first person provides the evidential basis in terms of direct experience of the facts or on working out conclusions for oneself.

But giving testimony is per se a social activity, and the acquisition of both language and knowledge depends on it. Nevertheless, its starting point is primarily a subjective one, irrespective of whether one adheres to a reductive or an anti-reductive theory of testimony. In the following we will present a way of resolving this conflict, at least for anti-reductionist approaches. For now, let us merely hint at the multifaceted solution: For one thing the speaker is standing by their word, giving their assurance, and assuming responsibility for what they assert and for the truth of it – this constellation does not render their testimony intersubjectively accessible, but it does imply the speaker's assertion that they were part of the event to which they testify. And in so far as the witness has been part of the event, the testimony is at least in part intersubjectively accessible from a third-person perspective. This will be explained in more detail hereafter.

In the case of knowledge tradition, however, where the witness has not been part of the event they are speaking about, the situation is different. The passing on of testimony is not primarily guaranteed by an assurance but by being involved and engaged in a knowledge system or a life form.

## 2 The evidential status of testimony

When we take it for granted that certain information is being offered as evidence by testimony, we are confronted with certain questions: To what extent are we justified in believing such testimonies? What would be a plausible theory to explain how testimony can convey knowledge and evidence?

Mainly two issues are discussed in the literature in order to give an answer to these questions: (1) Is testimony a source of knowledge? Or, to put it differently: Is the statement of an eyewitness a source of knowledge, or, for that matter, is the report of a colleague? And (2), is testimony an autonomous source of epistemic authority when it comes from an eyewitness or originates from a colleague? The second question is of less interest in our context and will not be given further consideration here. It is presupposed, however, that testimony can be an autonomous source of knowledge.

The question of testimonial evidence is closely related to this topic. As hinted above, when it comes to the subject of testimonial evidence, there are mainly two positions that are taken up in the literature, namely a reductionist and an anti-reductionist one. For a reductionist, testimony is not a fundamental or autonomous source of warrant. Its credibility is seen to depend on empirical sources like perception, memory, and induction. The reliance on these empirical sources already implies a certain tendency towards a self- or subject-oriented philosophy. It is therefore not a very good candidate from the outset, if one is interested in the key role of testimony in turning away from precisely such a philosophy.

For the anti-reductionist, by contrast, testimony is indeed an independent source of warrant, which may, nonetheless, depend on the sources that the reductionists mention[1] (Adler 2017). If we take testimony to be an independent source of knowledge, it can play a role in the transmission of information between people when it comes to learning language, gaining knowledge, or acting in an ethical manner. It is therefore primarily to the anti-reductionist positions that we will turn our attention in what follows.

## 3 The locus of testimonial knowledge

What is the hearer's justification for belief in the testimony of a speaker? Or, to put it differently, what is the locus of testimonial knowledge? Is it the words of the speaker, that is to say, the reliability of the words and of the speaker herself? Is it her knowledge? Her having been part of an historical event?

Someone who offers testimony gives the hearer, according to the assurance view, a non-evidential justification for belief by assuming responsibility for the

---

[1] And then there are positions like that of Paul Faulkner, who endorses a pluralism about testimony when the claim is made that it is possible "to give different and overlapping explanations" of how testimony works (Faulkner 2011: 198).

truth of their testimony (Gelfert 2014: 227). Or, as Jonathan Adler (2017) has put it: "A speaker's assertion is not evidence for what he believes or the truth of what he asserts. The hearer's entitlement to belief resides in the speaker's standing behind his word, giving his assurance." The reason for belief is that the speaker assumes responsibility for what they assert as well as for the truth of it. It is, in short, the speaker who constitutes their utterance as a reason for belief. Nevertheless, when presenting evidence, the epistemic import is independent of the presenter (Adler 2017). According to the assurance view, the reason for belief in testimony is therefore the utterance of the witness, not their knowledge. As we hope to make clear, it is the aforementioned constitution as a reason for belief that opens up the subject of testimony to observations within the philosophy of mind.

When evidence is presented by a photo, for instance it is the photo that induces knowledge, thoughts, etc. about what happened when it was taken. The photo represents a third-person perspective with respect to the photographed event. The epistemic import is independent of the presenter. When evidence is presented by the words of a speaker it is them who induce belief, hence the epistemic import is not independent of the presenter. The act in the latter case is of a first-person perspective, although it must be shareable by the interlocutor (Moran 2018: xii).² The utterance is given from the perspective of the speaker: It is their view on the world, their understanding of the world, as well as their way of experiencing it that is being presented.

An obvious question to be asked here is this: What does this first-person perspective add to the knowledge and understanding of the hearer of a personal testimony compared to an impersonal testimony? Does it add anything when it comes to testimonial knowledge, or is it simply less certain and thus more doubtful?

Take for example the testimony of an eyewitness to a massacre or to the atrocities that took place in Nazi concentration camps.³ What does the witness' testimony add to the historical evidence? Their first-person perspective is related to subjective experience, emotional experience, feelings, etc., which are ex-

---

2 Moran also occasionally uses the notions 'second person perspective' and 'first person perspective' but with another focus. He addresses the different characteristics of intentionality as well as the different evidential statuses that come along with giving testimony and being a witness. He does not, however, deploy these notions in order to characterise the different aspects of the concept of testimony in the various debates nor to offer a conceptual tool for viewing them together from different angles.

3 Later on we will see what role the second-person perspective plays in such cases.

pressed in their utterances.[4] By contrast, the evidence that comes from files, photographs, etc., which we can examine intersubjectively, is linked to a third-person perspective independent of the presenter.

Witness experiences, articulated and presented in utterances that show that the witness is standing by their words and giving their assurance, can be a locus of testimonial knowledge as such. The assured utterances give us information about the historical incidence that is not inherent in the historical facts. How did people experience the situation? What did they feel? We know this from their reports.

But here a question confronts us: Might the eyewitness herself also be called a locus of testimonial knowledge? Or are only her utterances a locus of testimonial knowledge? In other words, since she has been part of the historical event that we are trying to understand and about which we want to know more, is she herself – including her body – therefore not also a locus of testimonial knowledge?

We might hesitate to say so because presenting oneself as such a locus might not be considered part of an assurance for standing by one's words. Nevertheless, this is not what legal psychology teaches us. If we take the findings of this discipline into account, the physical gestures (facial and bodily expressions) are certainly part of standing by one's words. We therefore have to widen our understanding of what it means to constitute an utterance as a reason for belief.

If it is true that facial and other bodily expressions are part of standing by one's words, then both the first- and third-person perspectives are implied. The witness' utterances express a first-person perspective, but their bodily expressions are accessible intersubjectively. Hence the first- and third-person perspectives are both essential in these cases, although with different degrees of importance.

In addition to the fact that bodily expressions are a visual representation of standing by one's words, they are also inscriptions of the historical event. The encounter with a witness who has been part of a situation that we want to understand and comprehend is an encounter with someone whose body is part of the historical evidence because their bodily expressions, including the prosody of their voice, will be different from those of someone who was not part of the event. We might say that the historic event is inscribed in the body. This shows inter alia why utterances of an eyewitness constitute a special reason

---

4 Avishai Margalit distinguishes between the moral witness who testifies from a first-person perspective in this respect and a political witness who does it from a third-person perspective (Margalit 2002: 168).

for belief when it comes to testimony. (It also explains why a witness has to be present in court personally.)

Yet, having been part of an event does not imply infallibility with respect to particular observations. A witness' testimony might therefore not be hard evidence regarding every detail. But it does imply that one cannot err about how one has experienced the situation. Therefore, Descartes' (and Augustine's) observation that we cannot err about our own subjective conscious mental life represents another reason for being warranted in trusting a speaker's assurance, in spite of the general possibility that our sense perceptions might deceive us.[5]

Does the first-person perspective add anything over and above what has already been mentioned? Is there not also a surplus with respect to our understanding of the historical incident when we encounter a first-person perspective? In order to answer this question, we might revert to the question of the locus of testimonial knowledge and ask more generally what the locus of testimonial knowledge is. Usually this points to the following alternative: the speaker's words or the speaker's knowledge. What (or who) might be a source of epistemic authority? The answers usually given do not go far enough. Not only might the speaker's knowledge or their utterances be a source of testimonial knowledge, as is often observed, but they themselves, as an embodiment of the experiences they have had, are a source of testimonial knowledge. They did not merely observe the events they witnessed but were part of them, and they are therefore marked by this participation.

Thus, the data that are intersubjectively accessible from a third-person perspective are not the only evidence. Both the utterances of a person, which represent their first-person experience and their embodied experiences, which are partly accessible from a third-person-experience, are part of the testimonial evidence.

## 4 Testimony, doubt, and truth

To emphasise that personal experience might be part of the evidence base for a long chain of utterances seems to be quite the opposite of the strategy that we also come across in philosophy with respect to testimony. Testimony that accounts for testimonial knowledge, whose evidential status we might never have investigated for ourselves, has also been a subject in other philosophical de-

---

5 The additional problem of lying will not be discussed here.

bates. But the strategy of argumentation is quite different there. One refrains altogether from referring to personal experience.

Take for example Saul Kripke's "causal chain" (Kripke 1980: 91–97). Kripke separates what we know about the historical figure 'Aristotle' from the person who was initially named 'Aristotle' when it comes to passing on the name 'Aristotle.' Kripke does this in order to render the reference necessary and therefore unassailable. And, although she approaches the question from quite a different position, Elizabeth Anscombe (Anscombe 1981: 88) nevertheless does something similar in claiming that there are certain historical truths (such as that Caesar was assassinated) which serve as groundless propositions and which are therefore "exempt from doubt"[6] (OC § 341;[7] cf. Adler 2017). Utterances like "This is Aristotle" or "Caesar was assassinated" are exempted from doubt by different philosophical strategies and are therefore thought to serve as a sound basis in a knowledge tradition.

Kripke and Anscombe show that it is, at least under certain conditions, irrelevant for the knowledge tradition whether a historical event has taken place or not and whether the claims concerning it might have been true or not. The whole discourse is exempted from the question of truth and error. By the way, the assurance view does something similar, when it claims that it is only the utterances of the witness that are a locus of evidence in testimony. It exempts the discourse from the question of truth and error.

Kripke and Anscombe each present a view that separates the truth of a historical assertion from its validity in a discourse, or as the case may be, in a knowledge tradition. What is claimed here is that the personal evidence of an eyewitness has a similar purpose. It separates, to a certain extent, truth and necessary validity.

Now, how are we to classify the testimony of personal experience by comparison to these strategies? As it is not the only decisive factor for counting as testimony whether the knowledge of the witness is infallible or not, nor whether the truth of her assertions is objectively establishable or not, the latter case is comparable to the two strategies just mentioned, but also to the assurance view.

---

[6] "They are to be default-accepted for those who participate in these historical inquiries, serving to confirm a historical chain's accuracy, rather than conversely confirming the historical truth of the event (Coady 1992 [...]). But they need not be taken for granted in other contexts of inquiry." (Adler 2017: sec. 3, par. 15)

[7] Kusch (2019) also refers to Wittgenstein's *On Certainty* with respect to testimony. His concern, however, is "to analyse the 'linguistic despair' expressed by many Holocaust survivors when trying to put their horrendous experiences into words" (Kusch 2019: 979).

Even if the witness errs with respect to some historical details, they are still a locus of testimony with respect to their experiences.[8]

## 5 Testimony that has been handed down

What has been presented so far is the case in which, although the actual information provided by a witness might be wrong in parts, the witness themselves are part of the evidence. Furthermore, as we have seen, there are already positions with respect to the tradition of knowledge that separate evidence and validity. Within these perspectives on the tradition of knowledge, the notion of truth is to some extent eliminated.

But what guarantees the correctness of our statements and judgements? As Wittgenstein (with his position in *On Certainty*), or Kripke (with his causal chain theory), as well as Anscombe (with her groundless propositions, which are exempt from doubt) show, the knowledge tradition itself exempts us to a certain degree from this responsibility. We might also say that these traditions are like certainties of a life world.

This should be kept in mind when we consider the a priori argument in the testimony debate, according to which it is a basic requirement for the practice of testimony and the status of our justifications for beliefs acquired thus, that regular correlations obtain between assertive utterances and the conditions under which they would be true. Otherwise, it would not be possible to assign content to the speaker's utterances. The assertions of a community of speakers have to bear all in all a reliable correlation with the facts: "For assigning *content* to the utterances of the hypothetical speaker requires [...] regular correlation between assertive utterances and the conditions under which they would be true." (Moran 2018: 39; taking up the position of C. A. J. Coady 1992) If this were not the case, the practice of making or accepting assertions would break down in the long run.

This kind of a priori argument is most likely inspired by Wittgenstein's remarks in *On Certainty*. The human practice of passing on information, which only reaches us through a long chain of utterances and whose evidential status we have never investigated for ourselves, appears to function fairly well. If there were no regular correlation between assertive utterances and the conditions under which they would be true, it would not.

---

[8] Cf. Alloa (2019) for a detailed discussion of an exemplary case.

## 6 Special access of the subject to evidence

Richard Moran has noticed an "apparent clash between the kind of epistemic relations involved and the classic empiricist picture of genuine knowledge basing itself either on direct experience of the facts or on working out conclusions for oneself."

> Recent interest in the epistemology of testimony has focused attention on what justification we may commonly have in the vast areas of life where we are dependent on what other people tell us. This dependence is not restricted to what we are told in face-to-face-encounters, for we also take ourselves to know all sorts of things that only reached us through a long chain of utterances [...], whose evidential status we have never investigated for ourselves [...]. In part it is the enormity of this dependence that makes for the interest in the subject of testimony, combined with the apparent clash between the kind of epistemic relations involved here and the classic empiricist picture of genuine knowledge basing itself either on direct experience of the facts or on working out conclusions for oneself. (Moran 2018: 36)

One may also say that the "apparent clash" originates when the relations between the first-, second-, and third-person perspective are widely separated through a long chain of utterances whose evidential status we have never investigated for ourselves.

But is the genuine knowledge that is based on *direct conscious experience* of facts really indispensable when it comes to testimony? All of us know quite well that the utmost care must be taken with testimonies about experiences. Should we therefore not refrain from taking them into account *when* truth and knowledge are in question? Well, the crucial point as to why we do not do this, is that *the subject* has a special access to evidence and that it plays a fundamental role in knowledge theory. Just think of Descartes' *cogito ergo sum*, which could also be rephrased as *sento ergo sum*. The *cogito* argument (as well as the *sento* argument) is inter alia about the question of whether we can trust our sensory perception or not, and to what extent we do *not* have to trust our conscious experience because there is no space for an error. (If there is no possibility for an error there is no need for trust.) This is one of the central motifs of the classic empiricist picture of genuine knowledge, although it originates from the point of view of a rationalist philosophy.

Let us therefore go back to the first-person perspective. Somebody who gives testimony is preassigned to give a statement or a judgement from the first-person perspective. For this judgement she has to take responsibility. Put this way, it is not first and foremost a result of the academic debate on testimony but an essential aspect of the practice of being a witness and of giving testimony. To take responsibility means (in this case) that you make a commitment with respect to your statements, according to which you have perceived things in this way and not in another;[9] and that it has therefore – from your subjective perspective – not been otherwise. To take responsibility does not render this form of testimony intersubjectively accessible in the way, for example, a photo is. But the interlocutor may well question me, watch me, etc. and this is also a form of intersubjective access.

Let us not forget, however, that the special status of an eyewitness in testimony is not only based on the utterances and assurance by the witness but also on the fact that they were part of the situation about which we want to know more. Even as a deaf, they could be a witness in this sense. Their bodily reactions would then give testimony about what they have endured.

# 7 Testimony of experts

The statements of experts have to be analysed differently. An expert is likely to provide documentary evidence like photos, statistics, material samples, etc. Such evidence does not bring with it a first-person perspective but rather a third-person perspective. In relying on documentary evidence, the expert does more than merely objectify their statements. The documents also induce opinions, beliefs, and assumptions. Thus, the expert guarantees for their statements not only on the basis of their personal expertise but also on the basis of documented evidence, which is evidence in its own right. This evidence can induce a certain level of expertise or knowledge within other persons. Therefore, the expert does not have to guarantee for the correctness of their statements and judgements all alone. As an expert, they have merely to guarantee that the evidence is achieved according to scientific criteria and that no deception is involved. Thus, the first-person perspective is not relevant in the same way it is for a non-expert who gives testimony in court, for example.

The knowledge and the perception of the expert are already trained and "objectified" in a certain way, whereas the perception of a personal witness is more or less strictly personal, and there might not be any further evidence with which it could be substantiated. A body of evidence, on the other hand, is accessible from a third-person perspective. Strictly speaking, a body of evidence does not need an oath as guarantee.

---

[9] The situation is more complex with regard to the "moral witness" Avishai Margalit (2002) writes about. The authenticity of the moral witness, which stands for the truth of their statements, cannot be affirmed with an oath, as in the case of a court witness, nor can it be affirmed with an affirmation formula, as in the case of a messenger.

So far, we have explained why the first-person perspective is relevant when it comes to testimony that is not by an expert. And we have explained the degree to which this is different when it comes to an expert's testimony. But to what degree, if at all, is the first-person perspective also relevant when we are dealing with expert testimony? Could we not just leave it out entirely in this case?

As a rule, an expert uses some piece of evidence which allows for a third-person perspective and therefore for a judgement that is intersubjectively transparent. The expert expresses themselves as somebody who relies on scientific methods and results. But unless they are a mathematician or a statistician, there will have been some experiments involved at the outset. When one traces the expert opinion back to the initial scientific findings that entitle the expert to utter their opinion in the first place, one will arrive at the initial experiments set up by a scientist who made certain observations from a first-person perspective.

Therefore, in the end, every empirical approach comes down to a first-person perspective in one way or the other – somebody has to have a direct (or indirect) experience. We have to experience ourselves the empirical object science is talking about, in order to know empirically what we are referring to in the world, and hence what in the world we are talking about in the first place.

## 8 Trustworthiness

Nevertheless, the question remains whether the fact that the witness has been part of the situation about which we want to learn means that their assertions are to be considered evidence?

We do generally assume that the epistemic import of evidence is independent of the presenter. But a personal witness is offering what one might call their subjective "truth," which is per se no evidence. There are, in this case, no objective data that might induce a certain belief. Nevertheless, they are offering their experience of the situation, which has been part of the event itself.

In order to make this clearer, and to say at the same time a little more about the concept of trustworthiness, let us consider three scenarios. This will bring in certain relevant aspects that we have been neglecting so far, and it will help us develop a more nuanced picture of evidence and trustworthiness.

(A) You and your colleague are looking at a photograph of a red parrot. It is supposed to prove that a certain species has been newly discovered in some isolated place in the primeval forest. This photo is the evidence for the scientific claim of your colleague who has been on a research expedition to this far off place.

(B) You and your colleague are looking at a red and yellow spot on a scintigram. You try to interpret it together.
(C) You are a contemporary historian and you interview an old woman who has, as you have been told, survived a massacre.

The evidence of a red parrot in a photograph that anyone can see is independent of the trustworthiness of the speaker who talks about it. This impersonal evidence is lacking in the case of someone who assures us that they have seen a red parrot in the zoo. You have to believe them that this is what they saw. The difference with the evidence of a photo is that you do not relate to an object in this case, but to a narrative, and therefore to the narrator themselves. And here, the trustworthiness of the narrator (in this case, a speaker) becomes relevant. This is obviously the main reason why the trustworthiness of a witness is so important in court and elsewhere.

In one case the photo is "inducing" the knowledge, thought, etc. about the red parrot. It is a third-person perspective. In the other case it is the words of the speaker that are inducing a belief. The act in the latter case is one of a first-person perspective, although it must be shareable by the interlocutor. The piece of evidence to which we can relate intersubjectively from a third-person perspective has a special significance when it comes to trust because we can relate to it again and again together with other people or even with experts. The amount of trust that we have to invest in an expert's opinion when we rely on such a piece of evidence is therefore comparatively low because the risk of error is reduced by control mechanisms. In the case of an expert testimony, both aspects – the third-person perspective as well as the inducing words of the speaker – are relevant: the evidence of the experimental data as well as the trustworthiness of the speaker. The trustworthiness of the speaker inheres in their role as an expert and the trustworthiness of the experimental data depends on the general reliability of control mechanisms in science. In the end there is not much difference here because the role of an expert also depends on the reliability of control mechanisms in science. In the context of academia, we consider somebody to be an expert precisely because they have successfully undergone academic training. As mentioned above, however, "it must be shareable by the interlocutor." This is an important point, and it leads us to a further question: What are the requirements for the "shareability" or rather, communicability, of an experience – not just for words?

Take example (B) above. You and your colleague are looking at a red and yellow spot on a scintigram. It is not obvious which belief the scintigram is inducing, not even for the two of you who are experts. In short, it has to be interpreted.

This is done from a third-person perspective because the scintigram is intersubjectively accessible.

On the other hand, when you are confronted with the trustworthiness of a person, or rather their narrative, you cannot rely on the high degree of academic control that ensures a certain level of correctness. What you trust in (or not) is the personal evidence of the other. We have already seen what role the bodily expressions of the witness play in such situations. Yet another important aspect comes into view when we reflect on the trustworthiness of a person. Personal evidence is testified by a "you," that is, by another person. The implicit second-person perspective involves some proximity to the person with whom you share a perspective. This closeness is one component, among others, when it comes to the trustworthiness of a speaker.

Take example (C) above. You are a contemporary historian and you interview an old woman who has, as you have been told, survived a massacre. There are historical facts you can rely on. When you listen to the narrative of the old woman you can match her report with the relevant facts of the time. If they do not match, you might have difficulty believing her statements from the start. But if they do match, you might be inclined to rank her narrative as oral history. But this is not all that matters here.

Why is somebody who gives their personal evidence trustworthy? While there are no "hard" criteria for it, one might very well speak of a bundle of indicators. For example: One has encountered the reliability of the person, their story is credible. The narrative is plausible (for contextual reasons that cannot be discussed here). One has made similar observations or appraisals oneself, or others with whom one has communicated have done so. In the end, it is personal experience that you are able to share to at least some degree – however small. The trustworthiness depends on an encounter between two persons, and not on the reliability of a system or an institution. The tradition of knowledge-transfer is, as has already been stated, a social process.

The evidence of a red parrot in a photograph is independent of the trustworthiness of the speaker – leaving aside for now the possibility of digital manipulation of images etc. This impersonal evidence is lacking in the case of qualia and in the case of narratives. If somebody assures you that they perceive a red parrot in the zoo, you have to believe that this is what they see, once the possibilities of lying or hallucinating are excluded. (You might check with the help of an apparatus whether a certain region in their brain is activated or not. This would help you to have confidence in the claim that they are at all feeling or perceiving something. But even in this case you do not know exactly what they are feeling and how it is for them to do so.) As already mentioned, the difference with the evidence of a photograph is in this case that, when somebody tells you something, you do not relate to an object but to a narrative and therefore to the narrator themselves.

If you are listening to the narration of somebody else whom you consider to be a human being, you will treat them as an Other and not as a set of scientific data, and therefore also not as an object. The narration is itself a testimony in this case, and the other shares his personal evidence with you.

# 9 The role of the other for giving testimony/Otherness

It has been widely recognised that to give testimony, i.e. to induce a belief by words, is an act of a first-person perspective. But although testimony is per se given from a first-person perspective, the second-person perspective, the "you," also plays a crucial role for the tradition of knowledge. This is already obvious when one realises that one cannot testify to oneself ("self-confession" or reflexive self-assurance are something else): Another person is needed to whom you testify.

A dialogue requires addressing the interlocutor as a second person, and as Moran adds, "the possibility of believing the speaker (and not just the proposition affirmed) requires a mutually acknowledged dependence of the interlocutor on the speaker herself [...]. The nature of this dependence on the person as such [...] is what we need to clarify in order to understand the role of 'otherness' that the idea of a 'social act of mind' requires." (Moran 2018: 195)

In order to understand the statement of another person, however, one has to be able to share their experiences and to understand their meaning at least to some extent. One has to be able to understand the perspective of the other and therefore some kind of perspective-taking and empathy is also required. (Unfortunately, I will not be able to discuss this here.)

In a second-person perspective we regard the other as a person rather than an object. And we therefore perceive them as a subject with whom we can enter into dialogue and as a human being to whom we owe respect. The second-person perspective presupposes a reciprocal relation. I perceive the other as a person with whom I can share an experience. This is always implicit when it comes to testimony, and it involves a certain closeness between the speaker and the hearer. This closeness is one important component, among others, when it comes to the trustworthiness of a speaker. One should share the speaker's life world to a certain extent in order to be able to judge their statements and narratives. It is a certain prerequisite for trust in the statements of others.

Moreover, the cases in which trust is prerequisite and the ones in which, because of intersubjectively shared evidence, it is either less so or not at all, are usually not as clearly separated as philosophers of knowledge make us think. This becomes inter alia clear in the following quotation by Lutz Wingert:

> This other person is an Other which is also an I. [...] For this reason, the second person has certain things in common with the addressor. That is, she has the status of a member. She is not simply one being among many beings. The second person is not an *alius*, but a *secundus*. She lives in an intersubjectively shared world [...]. (Wingert 2009)

In this last remark, the second-person perspective and the third-person perspective are mentioned together. The second-person perspective is named explicitly, the third-person perspective implicitly when the author hints at an intersubjectively shared world. In an intersubjectively shared perspective, we can look at something from the very same perspective. In so far as this is the case, we can call it a third-person perspective.

This intersubjectively shared world does not exist when we listen to the testimony of a survivor who has endured scenarios that we are not even able to imagine ourselves. The witness to such historic monstrosities speaks from their first-person perspective, but there is no third-person perspective because the intersubjectively shared world is missing. Moreover, we cannot regard the survivor as a neutral observer like the *testis*[10] (the witness) in court.

We have seen, however, that there is a third-person perspective involved on a different level even in these cases. The bodily expressions of the witness are intersubjectively accessible.[11] But when we look at such a testimony from this perspective, it is that of the person who is listening to it, not that of the witness. For her, the significance of giving testimony is altogether different. The first-person perspective allows (among other things) for a re-subjectification[12] of the witness through herself by presenting herself in her report as a person who has endured barbaric crimes. Yet the process of re-subjectification is a social one that affects not only the witness but also the person or persons who receive her testimony. In accepting the other to be a witness, the listener enters into a second-person per-

---

**10** Giorgio Agamben was among the first who made this observation in *Remnants of Auschwitz* (2002: 17); cf. also the more detailed analysis on this topic by Aleida Assmann in *Der lange Schatten* (2006: 90). A good overview over the discourse on survivor testimonies is given by Sybille Schmidt in *Ethik und Episteme der Zeugenschaft* (2015).
**11** Cf. also Avishai Margalit's (2002) observations in "The Moral Witness" concerning the relevance of the body of a moral witness for our comprehension of the National Socialists' crimes.
**12** This term is normally not used in this context. However, it illustrates the effect of recognition of "the you" by a counterpart.

spective with the person who is giving testimony;[13] he accepts her as an Other, a person; and this, over and above the communication of testimonial content, aids the survivor in overcoming the very dehumanisation to which she, as victim, had been subjected. Nor is this all: for the moral witness, by being heard, creates a moral community.[14]

# References

Adler, Jonathan (2017): "Epistemological Problems of Testimony." In: *The Stanford Encyclopedia of Philosophy* (Winter 2017 Edition). Edited by Edward N. Zalta. https://plato.stanford.edu/archives/win2017/entries/testimony-episprob, accessed 17 April 2020.

Agamben, Giorgio (2002): *Remnants of Auschwitz: The Witness and the Archive*. Trans. by Daniel Heller-Roazen. New York, NY: Zone Books.

Alloa, Emmanuel (2019): "Der Fall Serena N. im Brennpunkt von Holocaust-Forschung, Psychoanalyse und Philosophie." In: *Deutsche Zeitschrift für Philosophie* 67(6), pp. 1008–1023.

Anscombe, G. E. M. (1981): "Hume and Julius Caesar." In: *From Parmenides to Wittgenstein. The Collected Philosophical Papers of G. E. M. Anscombe*. Vol. 1. Minneapolis, MN: University of Minnesota Press, pp. 86–93.

Assmann, Aleida (2006): *Der lange Schatten: Erinnerungskultur und Geschichtspolitik*. Munich: C. H. Beck.

Assmann, Aleida (2016): *Shadows of Trauma: Memory and the Politics of Postwar Identity*. Trans. by Sarah Clift. New York, NY: Fordham University Press.

Coady, C. A. J. (1992): *Testimony: A Philosophical Study*. Oxford: Oxford University Press.

Darwall, Stephen (2006): *The Second-Person Standpoint: Morality, Respect and Accountability*. Cambridge, MA.: Harvard University Press.

Faulkner, Paul (2011): *Knowledge on Trust*. Oxford: Oxford University Press.

Gelfert, Axel (2014): *A Critical Introduction to Testimony*. London: Bloomsbury.

Kripke, Saul A. (1980): *Naming and Necessity*. Cambridge, MA: Harvard University Press.

Kusch, Martin (2019): "Das Zeugnis der Holocaustüberlebenden: Gewissheit, Skeptizismus, Relativismus." In: *Deutsche Zeitschrift für Philosophie* 67(6), pp. 979–991.

Margalit, Avishai (2002): *The Ethics of Memory*. Cambridge, MA: Harvard University Press.

---

[13] Darwall also discusses testimony as a candidate for second-personal reason for belief (Darwall 2006: 57), but the way he uses the notion 'second-personal' differs somewhat from the notion of a second-person perspective as it is used here. Darwall calls "the second-person standpoint the perspective you and I take up when we make and acknowledge claims on one another's conduct and will" (Darwall 2006: 3). McMyler points out that a second-personal relation always requires recognising the other as a person, to address claims to one another and to reciprocally recognise one as another (McMyler 2011: 161).

[14] Assmann merges the positions of Avishai Margalit and Bernhard Gießen with regard to this aspect; cf. Assmann (2006: 91).

McMyler, Benjamin (2011): *Testimony, Trust and Authority*. Oxford: Oxford University Press.
Moran, Richard (2018): *The Exchange of Words: Speech, Testimony and Intersubjectivity*. Oxford: Oxford University Press.
Schmidt, Sybille (2015): *Ethik und Episteme der Zeugenschaft*. Konstanz: Konstanz University Press.
Wingert, Lutz (2009): "The Authority of the Second Person." Manuscript of a paper presented in a plenary talk at the 32nd International Wittgenstein Symposium *Language and World*. Kirchberg am Wechsel.
Wittgenstein, Ludwig (1969) [OC]: *On Certainty/Über Gewißheit*. Edited by G. E. M. Anscombe and G. H. von Wright. Oxford: Basil Blackwell.

Ulrich Metschl
# Epistemic Disagreement, Doubts, and Coherence

**Abstract:** Epistemic disagreement has not ranked high as an issue in the history of epistemology. In recent decades, however, epistemic disagreement has become more widely appreciated as an opportunity for rational agents to revise and eventually improve their initial credal states. However, a willingness to open one's mind for potential revisions requires that rival views be accepted as possibilities that merit serious consideration. Clearly, not every position with which one disagrees will qualify as a serious possibility. The question to be addressed in what follows is whether coherence provides a suitable criterion to distinguish rival beliefs that are apt to induce reasonable doubts from beliefs that can be dismissed as unsubstantiated (from an agent's point of view). I will try to argue, however, that such an idea can be best defended when coherence is specified as (wide) reflective equilibrium. This, in turn, points rather to a criterion of reciprocity in responding to evidence and argument instead of coherence narrowly conceived.

**Keywords:** Epistemic disagreement, coherence, rival beliefs, reasonable doubts, (wide) reflective equilibrium

## 1 Epistemic disagreement

In human affairs, unanimity is rather the exception than the rule. Of course, differences in matters of taste, preferences, or interests are familiar enough, and they are, in our better moods, even borne with some equanimity. Conflicts in value judgments are presumably of more concern and they may account not only for recalcitrant moral controversies but also for quite a few equally intractable theoretical debates in moral philosophy. Compared to disagreement on norms and values, however, disagreement on matters of fact might at first appear unproblematic. To be sure, agents do disagree about what is or is not the case, or about how likely it is that something is (or will become) true. The available evidence on which judgments must be based is often inconclusive and therefore will not permit an unequivocal resolution for epistemic disagreement in favor of one side.

Nevertheless, it is in the end purely a question of matters of fact who is right and who is wrong (assuming that the rival positions are definite enough), or so one might contend. Although this move seems to reflect a decidedly realistic perspective, putting the blame for epistemic disagreement entirely on the cognitive side, not much is gained if instead an epistemic perspective is taken, where disagreement in factual assessments must also appear as either almost intractable or completely trivial. This is because it seems that beyond an appeal to incomplete evidence or asymmetry in information nothing is left that could account for a genuine divergence in beliefs (discounting psychological factors that always may result in blunders, miscalculations, hasty conclusions, etc.). According to this picture, where rational agents disagree with respect to factual assessments, this is entirely due to circumstantial differences in their information states and not to any leeway that reason would grant for the processing of information.

In this spirit, a widely held assumption in game theory, known as the Harsanyi doctrine, explicitly rules out that rational agents can rationally disagree: On the basis of identical information they must come to identical conclusions, and even their prior probabilities will eventually be the same (Binmore 2009: 73). This assumption is supplemented by Robert Aumann's result that rational 'Bayesian' agents, whose prior probabilities are 'common knowledge,' cannot agree to disagree in their posteriors, even when they update their beliefs on different items of evidence (Aumann 1976). Moreover, under Bayesian requirements updating will automatically lead to a 'merging of opinions' so that priors get 'washed out,' irrespective of the agents' prior probabilities.

Given the settings of Bayesian rationality, epistemic disagreement thus cannot be an issue of much concern, or so it seems. It simply reflects temporary deficiencies in the epistemic situation of rational agents to be overcome with ongoing deliberation, i.e., by updating on new evidence. Whatever was initially controversial will eventually be cancelled out. But then, if we were omniscient, we would all agree on what is and is not the case anyway. For not so ideally rational persons, however, the situation is perhaps less benign and epistemic disagreement may well present itself as a real challenge instead of a negligible cognitive accident.

Epistemic disagreement is a natural consequence of the imperfections of evidential circumstances and the cognitive shortcomings of common reasoners. The available evidence often leaves room for diverging assessments, and what is or is not the case can at best be judged only as more or less likely. Even rocket scientists may sometimes, no matter how seldom, fail in their calculations, given human fallibility. As we all may well err on different sides, epistemic disagreement must seem inevitable unless agents are willing to renounce their individual judgments for the sake of peace and harmony, or out of an unhealthy bias to conformity.

David Christensen, having us reminded that epistemic disagreement is our daily lot for all the reasons just mentioned, argues that instead of simply lamenting this situation we should greet it as an opportunity for improving one's epistemic situation (Christensen 2007). And indeed, to accept that our factual assessments can rarely be expected to be exempt from revision and correction is to acknowledge a kind of skeptical reservation regarding one's own beliefs. Skeptical reservations can be a first step to open one's mind and to give rival views a hearing that closed minds would deny. We may thus agree with Christensen that agents who find themselves in epistemic disagreement should not simply accept their different views as equally and simultaneously maintainable but should rather seek convergence by mutual concessions. Where agents disagree, a fair compromise will often be a recommendable solution, unless one or more of the clashing opinions is flatly wrong or obviously misguided such that outright dismissal is an adequate response.

Christensen's favored approach specifies the details for a compromise solution as a weighted average of the different degrees of confidence of the agents in disagreement so that, when Alice's degree of confidence in proposition $p$ is, say, 0.7 while Bob's is 0.3, their weighted averages are $a \times 0.7 + (1 - a) \times 0.3$ and $b \times 0.3 + (1 - b) \times 0.7$ respectively, where $a$ and $b$ ($0 \leq a, b \leq 1$) reflect Alice's and Bob's degree of trust in their own judgment, respectively. Under ideal circumstances, when Alice and Bob respect each other as 'epistemic peers,' the agents should be willing 'to split the difference' evenly so that, for the given example, they both end with a degree of confidence of 0.5. More generally, however, Christensen's approach will also allow that agents in disagreement can recognize that they both are not exactly competent experts for the issue under dispute, so that they might then not only attach different (but not complementary) weights $a_1$, $a_2$, $b_1$, $b_2$ to their individual judgments (where $a_1 + a_2$ and $b_1 + b_2$ respectively add up to less than 1) but might even opt for a suspense of judgment altogether.[1]

Christensen does not elaborate on the details of these possibilities, and he is reluctant to discuss explicitly the option of suspense of judgment. But then, his main concern is to argue against 'epistemic permissiveness' that would allow epistemic disagreement to persist. Instead, Christensen tries to make a convinc-

---

[1] This may look like a somewhat questionable psychological move, bringing the agents close to cognitive dissonance when they first believe proposition $p$ with degree $r$ and then, realizing their disagreement, believe $p$ with degree $a \times r$ ($0 \leq a \leq 1$), having modified their initial judgment by a concession that as a judgment it may have not been fully reliable. But this is precisely the point of epistemic disagreement: that it invites second thoughts that then belong to a modified and slightly different state of belief.

ing case for compromise solutions as just sketched above. To accept unmitigated epistemic disagreement seems indeed hardly compatible with a commitment to truth, though there is perhaps a certain temptation to advocate it at least as sound political advice for toleration.

Isaac Levi, at any rate, has seen in Isaiah Berlin's reading of John Stuart Mill's essay "On Liberty" a plea for 'skeptical respect' over 'contemptuous toleration' with regard to dissenting views, where both are furthermore to be preferred to oppression or persecution (Levi 1997). The questions Mill was addressing in his essay, or, for that matter, Berlin in his reading of Mill, were arguably different from those that prompted Christensen's discussion of epistemic disagreement. Nevertheless, Levi's warning, targeting Berlin's distinction between skeptical respect and contemptuous toleration, that not any rival view presents a 'serious possibility' from an agent's perspective that would deserve a fair hearing (albeit in skeptical respect), is clearly in order. Even Christensen's proposal to go for an epistemic compromise depends critically on the condition that the agents in disagreement can accept each other (roughly) as epistemic peers.

Clearly, a rival view must qualify as a credible alternative if it is to deserve due consideration, and this will hardly be the case unless the proponent of a rival view is seen as sufficiently dependable (with respect to the issue under dispute). A further requirement is obviously that agents can harbor some skeptical reservations regarding their own beliefs, and a good deal of Christensen's discussion of epistemic disagreement is devoted to the demonstration that opening one's mind to a rival, but epistemically trustworthy position is a demand of reason. But there is yet more to it, as Levi reminds us with his reservations against an unqualified preference for skeptical respect over contemptuous toleration (to say nothing of oppression). While open-mindedness may well count as a cognitive virtue, it should be practiced, as all virtues, with measure. We must not forget the Peircean insight that we need reasons to doubt no less than we need reasons to accept beliefs, or so Levi seems to suggest.

All this would perhaps not deserve much belaboring were it not for its wider political implications. Public decisions are typically made under conditions of conflict and uncertainty. This, as such, is neither surprising nor reason for deep concern. To cope with differences in normative attitudes, stemming from, at times, incompatible value commitments due to diverging "comprehensive views" (John Rawls), is daily business for liberal, pluralistic societies. The social, political, or economic consequences of various policies are rarely foreseeable, but decisions often cannot be postponed until the information is sufficiently complete to turn them into a choice under certainty.

Precisely because public decision-making takes place under less than ideal conditions it should be done with a commitment to diligence and responsibility.

Public decisions should be based on, or at least should be informed by robust assessments of the relevant matters of fact, assessments that in turn are to be undertaken in accordance with sound methodological standards. Science plays a crucial role in this context. In current public debates, be they on issues like energy production, public health, migration policies, or environmental protection, it is not only opinions strictly in line with scientific findings that get voiced. Views that promote fringe theories or otherwise dissenting positions without credible backing must perhaps be tolerated but they rarely mandate skeptical respect. When 'Mad' Mike Hughes took off in his homemade rocket to prove that the Earth is flat, we found this perhaps mildly amusing, but it was no reason to call our belief in a spherical planet into question.[2]

More irritating, however, is the fact that even a scientific verdict can be controversial and sometimes for the wrong reasons. Criticizing the obfuscating strategies of so-called climate skeptics, Dale Jamieson has urged that their attitude of denialism must not be confused with a "healthy skepticism" which is an essential element of the scientific method (Jamieson 2014). Although they advocate their position as skeptical, a climate change denialist "is neither a skeptic nor a contrarian. [...] Denialists, unlike both skeptics and contrarians, are dogmatists" (Jamieson 2014: 86). Of course, resistance or even open contempt regarding scientific consensus is not confined to climate change debates. Support for complementary medicine or a firm vaccination hesitance may likewise result from a distrust of mainstream science or even from a resolute opposition to scientific reasoning tout court. Still worse, however, than discontent with scientific authority, which may strengthen a penchant for pseudoscientific methods in the context of medicine but also in other fields, is the fabrication of spurious doubts against scientific results out of vested interests.

Even more frustrating than the existence of dissenting views, or their resonance in a wider audience, is the fact that these are not necessarily an expression of ignorance or partisan machinations but may also crop up in the scientific community itself, and often for perfectly legitimate reasons.

The possibility of epistemic conflict is, as Christensen has rightly emphasized, a source for reasonable doubts. Accordingly, Jamieson's appeal to a 'healthy skepticism' should be read as an injunction to allow for epistemic dis-

---

**2** While assembling the final version of this paper I learned that daredevil Mike Hughes, having for some time provided a convenient example for not quite so highly respected ideas, has passed away. According to media reports, he died in an accident when the parachute of his rocket malfunctioned. It should be emphasized that Mike Hughes himself probably never seriously believed in a flat Earth, and he associated with the Flat Earth Society presumably only with the aim to crowdfund his rocket project.

agreement as an opportunity to improve one's epistemic situation (or the epistemic situation of the scientific community), just as Christensen advocates. Reasonable doubts serve a zetetic function and bear a commitment to truth-seeking. But one must still bear in mind Isaac Levi's warning that not any view with which one disagrees merits serious consideration. Our predicament is therefore to tell apart cases of epistemic disagreement, where a skeptical attitude toward one's own initial beliefs is a proper response, from those cases where the position with which one finds oneself in disagreement can (or even should) be safely dismissed.

We may be fairly confident that a flat-Earth hypothesis is not a serious option, and we may likewise feel certain that U.S. Senator James Inhofe's claim that anthropogenic global warming is "the greatest hoax ever perpetrated on the American people" is a sign of deplorable ignorance. At the other end of the spectrum, we find those positions that, while in conflict with established beliefs, led to new insights via the revision of erstwhile held doctrines. A case in point is Barbara McClintock's discovery of 'jumping genes,' i.e., genetic transposition. Although a major breakthrough in genetics, it was fully appreciated only with some delay.

Nevertheless, unclear cases unbound. It is in general far from evident which claims are unfounded or are advanced out of ignorance or bad faith. Should publications by Christopher Monckton and Willie Soon prompt reasonable doubts among climate researchers (see, e.g., Monckton et al. 2015)? Is Richard Lindzen's position an expression of a 'healthy skepticism' directed against mainstream consensus in climate research (e.g., Lindzen 2012)? Should their statements rather be dismissed as just another attempt to fabricate doubts where doubts are unfounded? The fact that doubts will sometimes be nurtured for purely strategic reasons, as Naomi Oreskes and Erik Conway have shown, implies that where laypersons are bewildered even experts will have a hard time to distinguish claims that should induce serious doubts from spurious ones (Oreskes/Conway 2010). Still, our efforts to separate views we deem potentially instructive from those we take for bogus are not always in vain, troublesome as the separation must be. Mark Kaplan puts the point succinctly:

> [...] we quite properly distinguish between contentful theories and narratives that [...] are worthy of assertion in the context of inquiry and those that, like mad conspiracy theories, are not. How can we be expected to distinguish between those whose assertion in the context of inquiry is worth the risk of error required and those whose assertion is not? (Kaplan 1998: 122)

The answer suggested by Kaplan points to coherence as a litmus test.

## 2 The price for contrarian positions

It is doubtful that we can reasonably expect a robust and unequivocal criterion that will sift dissenting views reliably into two distinct classes, the reasonable beliefs on the one side and weird, unreasonable beliefs on the other. Presumably, no uniform standard will cover all potential cases. Just as there are different standards for risk assessment, so there will be different standards for evaluating the epistemic merits of competing claims. However, Kaplan's remarks support the intuitively attractive idea that coherence can at least roughly indicate when skeptical respect is due, even if not by way of a necessary and sufficient condition. This idea is motivated by the observation that theories obviously missing the mark, such as, e.g., conspiracy theories, often betray a degree of incoherence that seems unacceptable for serious scientific theories.

An analysis of climate change denialism, as a paradigm case of a scientifically unfounded attitude, undertaken by Stephan Lewandowsky, John Cook, and Elizabeth Lloyd, lends independent support to the idea that coherence is a filter holding back views that are pointless for truth-seeking purposes (Lewandowsky/ Cook/Lloyd 2018). Drawing on various sample cases, Lewandowsky and his colleagues argue that denialism concerning climate change or similar issues is often characterized by a subscription to contradictory statements. Coherence is then restored by an ascent to a higher level where it is claimed, e.g., that climate research is biased anyway. The coherence emerging from this ascent is political in the sense that it proclaims for example a "uniform and unifying opposition to GHG emission cuts" (Lewandowsky/Cook/Lloyd 2018: 190).

Lewandowsky and colleagues emphasize that it is in general not one single person who simultaneously holds contradictory beliefs as expressed by these statements, although instances can be found where even that is the case. Rather, incoherence affects a denialist position as a collective attitude, or so we may understand their claim. Of course, this will not salvage denialism. As Lewandowsky and colleagues rightly note, scientific theories aim at coherence and they try to present themselves as coherent bodies of propositions (or beliefs). Where a scientific theory is exposed as incoherent, its proponents will seek to rectify the situation. In contrast, the complacency regarding incoherence that one finds in denialist positions is a familiar feature of conspiracy theories. Summarizing their argument Lewandowsky and colleagues write:

> The lack of mechanisms to self-correct the scientific incoherencies manifest in denialist discourse further evidences that this is not the level at which rational activity is focused, and we must move to a higher level, looking at the role of conspiracist ideation in the political

> realm. At that political level, climate denial achieves coherence in its uniform and unifying opposition to GHG emission cuts. (Lewandowsky/Cook/Lloyd 2018: 190)

The observations that Lewandowsky, Cook, and Lloyd bring to our attention strongly motivate the idea that reasonable doubts may be a proper response to coherent systems of belief and are less justified, if at all, when one is confronted with incoherent beliefs (where these are accepted with indifference and no efforts are made to restore coherence).

However, coherence, and accordingly incoherence, are notoriously ambiguous concepts. Even proponents of coherence theories (for truth, for knowledge, etc.) frankly admit that a generally accepted definition or explanation of coherence is missing. The exposition given by Lewandowsky and colleagues already operates with at least two distinct concepts of coherence. The inconsistencies they identify among various denialist statements violate a standard of coherence that differs from the one they find in the denialist attitudes concerning climate action. Coherent support for certain policies, for instance, policies that will not impose significant reductions in GHG emissions, can exist in harmony with an inconsistent set of statements about the causes and effects of global climate change.

Desirable as pragmatic coherence may be, one would nevertheless expect that what recommends a position for serious consideration is ultimately found at the theoretical (propositional) level where coherence is a relation between beliefs, or statements expressing beliefs. Support for this expectation originates in assumptions about the epistemological merits of coherence. As John Welch put it succinctly:

> Why should coherence be an epistemic desideratum? A standard answer is that coherence is truth-conducive: mutually coherent propositions are more likely to be true than mutually incoherent ones. (Welch 2014: 2241)

Truth-conduciveness aside, coherence is, in Erik Olsson's words, something like the antiskeptic's last resort (Olsson 2005: vii), and as such the proper means to dispel unfounded skeptical reservations. Of course, all of this immediately calls for qualification. The initial plausibility of the propositions under consideration, due to the reliability of the sources of information, will likewise play a role for the credibility of assertions. Nevertheless, given such an "all things considered" assessment, one might still subscribe to the conclusion that coherence is a benchmark for the confidence in statements or beliefs, simply because missing the mark must raise suspicions. If only we knew what coherence means.

## 3 Probabilistic coherence

A convenient point of departure to survey the candidates that currently dominate the scene is an account of probabilistic coherence as pioneered by Frank P. Ramsey (Ramsey 1990). Interpreting probabilities as degrees of belief, Ramsey suggested that coherence in beliefs can be read off from hedged betting behavior: An agent $A$ holds incoherent beliefs when $A$ is susceptible to a 'Dutch book,' with degrees of beliefs measured as real-valued probabilities. A Dutch book is a system of bets or lotteries, each individually rationally acceptable, that, when jointly accepted by an agent, will induce a sure loss for the agent. Susceptibility to a Dutch book thus means that the beliefs harbored by the agent are incoherent because they violate the laws of probability. To complete Ramsey's suggestion one must add the complementary idea that an agent respecting the laws of probability is not susceptible to Dutch books, as Alan Hájek has pointed out (Hájek 2009: 177).

For a brief illustration of Ramsey's ingenious idea, consider the case of Bob who correctly believes that, for a fair die, the probability for the outcomes $\{1, 2\}$ or $\{5, 6\}$ is ⅓ respectively but that the probability for a throw resulting in 1, 2, 5, or 6 $\{1, 2, 5, 6\}$ is ¾ instead of ⅔. Bob, purely going by expectations, should then find the following bets individually acceptable. (Bet 1): accept 33¢ for the prospect to pay $1 if the result is 1 or 2; (bet 2): accept 33¢ for the prospect to pay $1 if the result is 5 or 6; and (bet 3): pay 75¢ for the prospect to gain $1 if the outcome is one of 1, 2, 5, or 6. The bets should be acceptable because the prices (for buying or selling) match the probabilities. The combination of these bets, however, forms a Dutch book with a sure net loss for Bob. Assume that the die is cast, and the outcome is 5. Then Bob gets 33¢ from (bet 1) (having nothing to pay), pays 67¢ for (bet 2), and wins 25¢ from (bet 3), with a net loss from all three bets of 9¢.

If the outcome were 3 or 4, so that none of the three bets wins, Bob would find that he earned 66¢ from selling (bet 1) and (bet 2), and lost 75¢ from buying (bet 3).

Despite their ingenuity, however, Dutch book arguments do not establish a notion of coherence that allows one to distinguish between reasonable systems of belief and unreasonable ones. Just as it is with related conditions for coherent preferences, the notion of coherence here is deliberately designed to be weak, leaving as much as possible to an agent's discretion. It is weak enough, at any rate, so that even some run-of-the-mill conspiracy theories will pass muster.

Addressing the need to invoke a stronger concept of coherence, Mark Kaplan suggested what he calls structural soundness (Kaplan 1998: 121–132). Intuitively, the idea underlying structural soundness is that a set of propositions can be arranged in a sequential order $s_1, s_2, ...$ so that the initial element $s_1$ is accepted as sufficiently likely and each later element in the sequence is conditionally backed by all the earlier elements, thereby becoming at least as likely as the first element. More precisely (and simplifying just slightly): A set $S$ of propositions is structurally sound, given an agent $A$'s epistemic state, if $S$ is consistent and the elements of $S$ can be ordered as a sequence $s_1, ..., s_i, ..., s_n$ so that for a probability function $P$ (representing $A$'s degrees of belief): $P(s_1) \geq r$, for $1 \geq r > 0.5$, and for all $i$: $P(s_i \mid s_1, ..., s_{i-1}) \geq r$. For a structurally sound set of propositions (representing beliefs) we may say that, given a belief whose credibility passes a certain 'threshold level' $r$, all further beliefs are supported jointly by all the preceding ones so that the threshold level is maintained throughout. The support for any proposition by those preceding it in the order is a quasi-inferential relation, captured by probabilistic conditionalization. But is this sufficient to keep unreasonable beliefs at bay?

Structural soundness is a fine specimen for the concept of coherence because it spells out in some detail how the idea of a supportive structure among coherent beliefs can be conceived. However, structural soundness is not utterly helpful when it comes to defending the idea that coherence is indeed truth-conducive. Given the requirement that all the elements of a structurally sound set $S$ match a certain confidence level, truth-conduciveness is almost a built-in property. Note in this context that degrees of belief or levels of confidence are purely subjective. Accordingly, it is unclear how, in the absence of any external constraint, structural soundness can be sufficiently strong to rule out 'mad conspiracy theories' as intended by Kaplan. All that we can concede is that if it still be madness, there is, thanks to structural soundness, at least method to it.

More general reservations against the idea that coherence is a criterion for reasonable beliefs that deserve serious consideration against unreasonable, spurious ones can be distilled from Erik Olsson's broader argument against coherence (Olsson 2005). Olsson's target is the claim that coherence implies truth, or, with more modest aspirations, that more coherence makes truth more likely. To show instead that coherence per se is not truth-conducive, Olsson starts with a paradigm case of coherence: agreement among testimonies. The idea, prominently elaborated in C. I. Lewis' *An Analysis of Knowledge and Valuation* from 1946, is that when testimonies agree on some proposition then, even when the testimonies individually seem rather unreliable, the proposition's truth becomes highly likely. Granting the assumption "that full agreement among testimonies must be regarded as a case of coherence" (Olsson 2005: 2) one will find that the standard situations in which the addition of an agreeing testimony has a positive effect on the likelihood of truth are such that the reports satisfy the further conditions of being collectively independent and individually to some degree credible (Olsson 2005: 2).

Without the conditions of independence and initial credibility, however, agreement is not much of an asset. To illustrate: The fact that a group of young men all testify that Bob, our suspect, was with them in a near-by bar when the bank was robbed, will not lower our belief that Bob committed the crime when we know that the group is a bunch of mobsters anyway.

It is instructive to compare Olsson's warnings that the truth-conduciveness of coherence (in probabilistic terms) is conditional on favorable circumstances with the requirements for Condorcet's Jury Theorem.[3] This theorem is a result about the majority principle and it states that for a choice between two alternatives $a$, $b$ of which one is objectively correct (e.g., "the plaintiff is guilty" vs. "the plaintiff is not guilty") and a jury of $n$ members, each of them being uncertain and fallible, the majority's verdict will be correct with a higher probability than the minority judgment if the individual judgments of the jury members are independent and for each jury member the probability to be right is higher than 0.5. In addition, the likelihood that the majority judgment is correct is increasing with increasing group size. However, Condorcet's positive result depends on conditions that match the conditions under which probabilistic coherence can be truth-conducive: independence and initial plausibility for the individual judgments. How crucial these conditions are for Condorcet's Jury Theorem can be seen from its flip side when the jury members are supposed to be 'incompetent,' so that their individual probability to come up with a true judgment is lower than 0.5. In that case it is more likely that the majority verdict will be wrong, the likelihood again approaching 1 with increasing group size.[4]

Given these observations, I suggest as a tentative conclusion that coherence is not in itself a sufficiently reliable criterion to separate beliefs worthy of serious consideration from beliefs that can be given short shrift. The fact that examples of fully coherent beliefs can be formulated so that despite their coherence the beliefs lack any credibility suggests that it is not the 'uniformity in direction' alone that turns beliefs into promising candidates for acceptance under epistemic disagreement. It may be unlikely, as Lewandowsky and colleagues have

---

[3] For a presentation of Condorcet's Jury Theorem, see Young (1995).
[4] The negative side of Condorcet's Jury Theorem is captured in Heiner Müller's quip that of course ten Germans are more stupid than five, assuming for the moment that the average German's ability to deliver a correct (political) judgment is sufficiently low.

shown, but sometimes even weird conspiracy theories appear as fully coherent systems of belief.

## 4 Coherence as balanced beliefs

If, then, coherence is not sufficient, is it at least a necessary condition for the reasonableness of (rival) beliefs? This is likewise doubtful. Examples from the history of science provide evidence that even eventually successful theories may, in an initial phase, contain incoherent assumptions. Galileo's achievements in classical mechanics surely should not be dismissed because of his wrong account of the tides, and Newton's formulation of mechanics is not to be deemed nonsense because Newton was unwilling to accept energy conservation, although it is a consequence of his own theory. Even outright inconsistent theories can lead to insights and improved understanding of a subject matter, as Frege's failed attempt to reduce arithmetic to logic illustrates. Similar benefits can hardly be claimed, though, for bogus theories like climate change denial, Holocaust denial, or an alleged moon landing hoax.[5]

However, if coherence is neither necessary nor sufficient for the reasonableness of beliefs that might prompt reasonable doubts for the settlement of epistemic disagreement, do we have to conclude that our initial intuition, backed by the observations of Lewandowsky et al., was misguided?

The argument so far, stripped to its core, was that the conjecture that coherence automatically lends higher credibility to beliefs irrespective of their initial plausibility cannot be fully vindicated because there is a possibility that, under adverse conditions, coherent beliefs collude for a deceptive impression of trustworthiness. And just as their coherence is not a reliable sign that one should open one's mind for (a set of) rival beliefs, their lack of coherence should only with caution be taken as a sign that it is safe to close one's mind.

Note, however, that the operating notion of coherence, couched in terms of probabilities, was highly specific and therefore quite restricted. For a first description one might say that it was a static conception of coherence from which more dynamic versions may be distinguished. A dynamic conception of coherence, in contrast to a static one, is not so much a relation between beliefs or propositions at one instance of time but rather a condition on belief acquisition or updating one's beliefs, given new evidence. Dutch book arguments do

---

[5] Benefits may of course accrue indirectly through efforts to refute conspiracy theories or wild arguments against vaccination, anthropogenic climate change, etc. by diligent fact checking.

also exist for a dynamic, diachronic version of coherence where the aim is to demonstrate that rational systems of belief are subject to a constraint of coherent updating via conditionalization:

$$P_{new}(A) = P_{old}(A \mid E)$$

where the belief state $P_{new}$ results from learning evidence $E$, and $P_{old}(A \mid E)$ is the initial conditional probability for $A$, assuming $E$. Notwithstanding the force one may or may not find in Dutch book arguments as arguments for coherence, it is far from obvious that this is a form of coherence prompting skeptical respect for rival views.

There is, however, a different approach to coherence, one that is arguably better suited to model a dynamic conception and perhaps also closer to the assumptions regarding coherence as we find them in the discussion of Lewandowsky and colleagues, namely coherence as wide reflective equilibrium (Daniels 1979). Reflective equilibrium is a familiar method in ethics. Moral principles are seen as justified when intuitive moral judgments and theoretical moral principles can be brought into balance by a process of mutual adaptation and revision so that considered moral judgments are backed by moral principles, which in turn do not lead to judgments offensive or counter-intuitive to our considered moral persuasions. For a wide reflective equilibrium a balance must hold between judgments, principles, and background theories, where the background theories are to some degree independent from the basic judgments (Daniels 1979: 258–260). How does this relate to our predicament of specifying a notion of coherence that bestows distinctive epistemic qualities to beliefs whereby they qualify at least for skeptical respect?

The essential feature, or so I would like to argue in concluding, is the process of deliberation that is supposed to lead to reflective equilibrium. What Lewandowsky and his colleagues bring to our attention in their exposition of the shortcomings of denialist accounts or conspiracy theories is that these positions, compared to a scientific approach, are based on a skewed weighing of evidence. Such biased reasoning leads to distorted conclusions whose aim is rather to confirm already entrenched, dogmatically held convictions.

From the perspective of wide reflective equilibrium, the failure of conspiracy theories then is a lack of (reference to) an independent, neutral background theory, relative to which an equilibrium is sought by a check on the more basic judgments. The lack of a controlling and supportive background theory results either from willfully ignoring available sources of information or from concocting a home-spun theory that fits one's ideological needs. Sweeping accusations addressed against 'the system,' which Lewandowsky and colleagues rightly see as an attempt to simulate coherence, perhaps exemplify the latter strategy. In any case, the assessment of evidence for or against climate change is an issue that must not be confused with questions about the integrity of science or the trustworthiness of government agencies, even if answers to the latter questions are relevant for what citizens may learn with regard to the former.

If these considerations have some force, then the claim seems justified that rational agents, in a situation of epistemic disagreement, should be wary of positions that betray a nonchalant, noncommittal attitude toward balanced reasoning, as it characterizes the quest for reflective equilibrium. In positive terms, rival systems of belief whose commitment to coherence in this sense is evident are beliefs that rational agents can greet with skeptical respect, if only for the reason that the quest for reflective equilibrium is an expression of epistemic responsibility.

Of course, ambiguities remain. For example, what is the range of the background assumptions over which a reflective equilibrium must be sought? Is a physicist proposing a promising physical hypothesis disqualifying herself if she confesses not to believe in evolution? Does it make a difference when her rejection of Darwin's theory is motivated by religious beliefs? Obviously, it is a matter of degree how far the cast must be thrown in search of a wide reflective equilibrium.

Nonetheless, the notion of a wide reflective equilibrium, in which a balance is reached between considered judgments, justifying principles, and wider background theories, is an appealing candidate to elucidate the concept of coherence for factual beliefs as well. Because of its procedural character, resulting in responsibly weighing the evidence for a judgment against the background of wider assumptions, beliefs that are in reflective equilibrium deserve serious consideration, unless they must be ruled out on a priori grounds. Furthermore, agents who can be trusted in their commitment to bring their beliefs in reflective equilibrium should be seen in debates as opponents whose views, even if we disagree with them, tentatively deserve skeptical respect.

Accepting the argument so far, there is then a further thought that can be added as a concluding remark. In situations of epistemic disagreement, epistemic agents face the challenge to decide when they should give rival views a fair hearing by greeting them with skeptical respect. The opponent who claims that our climate model is based on wrong assumptions about the tropopause may rightly bring us to critically reexamine our theory. A person who claims that climate change will not happen as long as there is a divine being 'up there' should not prompt doubts about our initial scientific views. The point here is that, in making this distinction and trying to identify cases where reasonable doubts are due, agents with that commitment can now themselves be taken as engaging in the quest for reflective equilibrium. Thus, the reflective equilibrium of rival beliefs is of value especially for those who themselves are trying to align their beliefs in the appropriate way. Where truth-seeking is a symmetric commitment, coherence, when all things are considered has its merits for rational agents in epistemic disagreement.

# References

Aumann, Robert J. (1976): "Agreeing to Disagree." In: *The Annals of Statistics* 4(6), pp. 1236–1239.
Binmore, Ken (2007): *Playing for Real: A Text on Game Theory*. Oxford: Oxford University Press.
Binmore, Ken (2009): *Rational Decisions*. Princeton, NJ: Princeton University Press.
Christensen, David (2007): "Epistemology of Disagreement: The Good News." In: *The Philosophical Review* 116(2), pp. 187–217.
Daniels, Norman (1979): "Wide Reflective Equilibrium and Theory Acceptance in Ethics." In: *Journal of Philosophy* 76(5), pp. 256–282.
Hájek, Alan (2009): "Dutch Book Arguments." In: Anand, Paul/Pattanaik, Prasanta K./Puppe, Clemens (Eds.): *The Handbook of Rational and Social Choice: An Overview of New Foundations and Applications*. Oxford: Oxford University Press, pp. 173–195.
Jamieson, Dale (2014): *Reason in a Dark Time: Why the Struggle against Climate Change Failed – and What It Means for Our Future*. Oxford: Oxford University Press.
Kaplan, Mark (1998): *Decision Theory as Philosophy*. Cambridge: Cambridge University Press.
Levi, Isaac (1997): "The Ethics of Controversy." In: *The Covenant of Reason: Rationality and the Commitments of Thought*. Cambridge: Cambridge University Press, pp. 239–254.
Lewandowsky, Stephan/Cook, John/Lloyd, Elizabeth (2018): "The 'Alice in Wonderland' Mechanics of the Rejection of (Climate) Science: Simulating Coherence by Conspiracism." In: *Synthese* 195(1), pp. 175–196.
Lewis, C. I. (1946): *An Analysis of Knowledge and Valuation*. La Salle, IL: Open Court.
Lindzen, Richard S. (2012): "Climate Physics, Feedbacks, and Reductionism (and When Does Reductionism Go Too Far?)." In: *The European Physical Journal Plus* 127(5), https://doi.org/10.1140/epjp/i2012-12052-8.
Monckton, Christopher/Soon, Willie W.-H./Legates, David R./Briggs, William M. (2015): "Why Models Run Hot: Results from an Irreducibly Simple Climate Model." In: *Science Bulletin* 60(1), pp. 122–135.
Olsson, Erik J. (2005): *Against Coherence: Truth, Probability, and Justification*. Oxford: Clarendon Press.
Oreskes, Naomi/Conway, Erik M. (2010): *Merchants of Doubt: How a Handful of Scientists Obscured the Truth on Issues from Tobacco Smoke to Global Warming*. London: Bloomsbury.
Ramsey, Frank P. (1990): "Truth and Probability (1926)." In: *Philosophical Papers*. Edited by D. H. Mellor. Cambridge: Cambridge University Press, pp. 52–109.
Welch, John R. (2014): "Plausibilistic Coherence." In: *Synthese* 191(10), pp. 2239–2253.
Young, Peyton (1995): "Optimal Voting Rules." In: *Journal of Economic Perspectives* 9(1), pp. 51–64.

Thomas Wallgren
# After Sustainability

Modernity, Freedom, and Reason in the Age of Climate Alarmism

**Abstract:** The debate about climate change is best seen as a part of larger debates about the future of the liberal West and the crisis of modernity. A diagnosis of the liberal self-confidence typical in the Western world in the 1990s and of the reasons for its demise in the early 2000s is presented. A comprehensive "polycentric" framework for the analysis of the cultural era of modernity and its current formation, High Modernity, is outlined. A "sceptical" reading of Wittgenstein's later philosophy provides formidable resources for a solution to the impasse in the debates between modernists and postmodernists about the emancipatory power of reason. Because of the ecological crisis, High Modernity nevertheless faces an insoluble cultural contradiction. The contradiction is not, as many have claimed, between the quest for affluence and for global justice but between the quest for affluence and the quest for the quintessential ideal of modernity, self-determination, or, the rational pursuit of freedom.

**Keywords:** Crisis of modernity, sustainable development, climate change, limits to growth, self-determination

## 1 Introduction and overview

This is an exercise in a philosophically informed diagnosis of our times. My framework is the philosophical discourse of modernity. Resources from Wittgenstein's later philosophy are brought to bear on the debate.

The structure of the argument is the following. The notions of climate alarmism, modernity, and High Modernity are introduced and defined (section 2). Next there is a discussion of what is called a certain mood of liberal self-confidence that was widespread in the modern West around thirty years ago. This age of self-confidence can be seen as a culmination point in the history of High Modernity (section 3). I proceed to the unsurprising proposal that among liberals the time of optimism has meanwhile given way to confusion, pessimism, and dispersion. This proposal is given some precise content (section 4). It is suggested that one reason for the erosion of liberal self-confidence is the perception that in the late 1900s high-profile philosophical debates about the normative foundations of

High Modernity resulted in a dead end (section 5). I next explain how ways can be found to bring us out of the philosophical dead end through what is called a "sceptical" reading of the philosophy of the later Wittgenstein (section 6). In the remaining, longest sections the conceptual resources presented so far are put to use in a diagnostic discussion of climate alarmism and, more generally, of the environmental crisis. Since the 1960s it has become common for "ecologists" to claim, that because of the "limits to growth" it is impossible for all to gain entry into "consumer paradise," and that therefore, the modern quest for everlasting economic growth is incompatible with ethical universalism. Now, as long as we understand it as an empirical claim about factual conditions, *this* thesis about limits to growth is false, for the simple reason that we cannot know what new possibilities technological development will bring. I shall argue that the underlying intuition is nevertheless correct and that there is indeed a contradiction between two promises that define High Modernity. The contradiction is, however, not between ethical universalism and the quest for economic growth. The real contradiction is between the quest for economic growth and the quest for freedom with reason. This cultural contradiction is, I shall argue, impossible to resolve and, hence, we are indeed living in the time of the inevitable end of High Modernity as we have known it (sections 7 and 8).

## 2 Conceptual starters: Climate alarmism, modernity, High Modernity

A person is a *climate alarmist* in the sense intended here when she has the following beliefs. One of her beliefs is that unless drastic measures are taken greenhouse gas emissions resulting from human activity are likely to lead to considerable climate change in a relatively near future, say, in less than a hundred years. A climate alarmist also believes that the change is likely to alter the ecological conditions greatly in such ways that a rapid reduction in the number of people and species on the planet may be difficult to avoid. It seems to me that today all people have very good reason to share these beliefs. To the extent that this is true it is today irrational for any well-informed person not to be a climate alarmist in the sense defined here.[1] Climate alarmism gives rise to fear and mo-

---

[1] This fact needs to be acknowledged alongside with acknowledgement of the necessity to avoid any immaturity about what follows. All forms of alarmism (including climate alarmism) run the risk of serving as a licence for giving up on reason, respect for the other, and democracy, etc. Well-founded climate alarmism can only, it seems to me, be, or become, benign if it is taken

bilises people for action. It leads to depression, denial, cynicism, political engagement, and to other reactions at the individual level. The more people there are who are climate alarmists and the more culture and society is shaped by the practices that follow, and by the reactions and counter-reactions to those practices, the more appropriate it is to speak of the age of climate alarmism.

In order to understand the emergence of climate alarmism, we need to conceptualise it as an event within the cultural epoch of modernity, an event upsetting modernity's self-understanding. The conception of our times as modern times takes its cue from the philosophical diagnosis of the times in which Rousseau, Kant, and Hegel are defined as classics (Gumbrecht 1978; Koselleck 1985; Habermas 1985; 1987; Taylor 1975; 1989). It also builds on the enrichment of the concept of modernity achieved in the debates, since the 1970s, over eurocentrism, postcoloniality, transmodernity, ecofeminism, ecological democracy, the pluriverse, and related topics. In the light of these recent debates, I will occasionally prefer to use the term favoured by Mohandas K. Gandhi, *the modern West*, for this same epoch (Gandhi 1986a; 1986b; 1987; 2010).[2] The era of modernity, as I understand it, emerges gradually over time as the result of efforts to realise practices inspired by eleven new imagined possibilities and ideals, or, as we also might say, as the result of the development of eleven new ideal practices.[3] Five of the ideal practices that have shaped the modern West have a history going back to pre-Christian antiquity. They have been formed around the ideals of (i) rationality, (ii) ethical universalism, and (iii) democracy, and around (iv) new conceptions of being and time, and (v) the new moral imagination and social practices allowed by money. Christianity introduced two further creative sources for the development of new ideal practices without which the modern West as we know it is unthinkable: (vi) The linear conception of time and (vii) the call to

---

as a call to ever deepening engagement in reflection and practices in which the intrinsic connections between democracy, non-violence and reason are fully recognised.

2 See also Nandy (1988), Kothari (1988), Escobar (2018), Dussel (1985), De Sousa Santos (2006; 2016). I will assume without argument, that the notion that we live in the era of modernity, whether defined as late modernity, postmodernity, transmodernity, or modernity *sans phrase*, provides richer resources for self-understanding in our times than competing theoretical frameworks, especially as compared with that offered by the increasingly popular notion of our era as the "Anthropocene." It seems to me that the discursive power-effect of the term "the Anthropocene" is de-intellectualising, as it invites discussants to ignore the achievements of most traditions associated with the term "critical theory."

3 I do not claim that any of the ideals and associated practices introduced originate in Europe or "Western" civilisation or that they are exclusive to the West. – The overview I introduce is the conceptual skeleton of a book project with the working title *Polycentric Modernity: A Polyvocal Approach*.

proselytise. From the Renaissance to the nineteenth century new ideal practices which have defined modernity were formed around (viii) individualism, (ix) the political secularisation of linear time, (x) the new valorisation of daily life and the promise of affluence for all, and (xi) "the death of God."

By *High Modernity* I refer to the cultural constellation for which it was typical that many people lived, more or less self-reflectively, in the belief that the eleven new forms of ideal practices, which define and contribute to modernity, were all worthwhile and mutually compatible so that the ever richer pursuit of each one of them would be conducive to the realisation of all others, or at least not detrimental to any one of them. High Modernity in this sense lasted, I suggest, during roughly 150 years, between 1850 and 2000. One culmination point was what we may call the time of the self-confident liberal West.[4]

## 3 The self-confident liberal West

For a brief moment of time, it seemed to some observers in the so-called advanced Western world that after the collapse of the Soviet Empire the Cold War would be over, the Global South would "develop," the countries of the Warsaw Pact would go through an economic and democratic transition, and there would be a happy end of history bringing all nations together in a harmonious global community of modern liberal welfare democracies. This self-congratulatory proposal was of course, already at the time, controversial. Nevertheless, the fact that what we now see as, at best, a naive chimera, was taken seriously three decades ago is one measure of the transformations that have taken place in the dominant mood of the times between then and today. I suggest that we single out four pillars for closer inspection that contributed to and shaped the liberal self-confidence of the late twentieth century.

(i)  One pillar was the hope invested in the formation of regional transnational entities which gained their legitimacy and popular support from a triple promise. The promise was that free trade would bolster economies and enhance welfare for all, that free trade would also promote peace, and, thirdly, that regional governance would serve the historical evolution of democracy as it steadily moves from the small scale of the ancient *polis* over the modern nation state to global democracy. The battle cry of the times, repeated in myriads of academic publications and political debates, was the notion that

---

[4] The "we" assumed here without further ado is the "we" of what is sometimes called "the Global North" or "the consuming classes" (Ulvila/Pasanen 2009).

the so-called globalisation of the economy and the new scale of corporate power has brought challenges to politics which necessitate a shift from national to post- or transnational political governance. The most perfect expression of the post-national ambition of the times was EU integration or what we may also, following Habermas, refer to as the "European project." The high time of this project occurred between 1986 when the Single European Act was signed and 1992 when the Maastricht Treaty was finalised.[5]

(ii) The second pillar was, as already suggested, the enthusiasm that followed the collapse of the Soviet Union. There seemed to be an empirical basis for the enthusiasm. Russia and many other countries that were part of the former Soviet Union and its sphere of influence, together with Vietnam, parts of Latin America and Africa, and even China under the leadership of Deng Xiaoping, seemed to undergo similar political transitions. Were these not signs that the dream of gradual progress towards world peace, prosperity, and liberal democracy for all was becoming real?

(iii) The third pillar was the idea of *sustainable development*. Since the 1980s the notion of sustainable development has been a central ingredient in the discursive regime of global political ecology. The fundamental idea propagated by advocates of sustainable development has been that the environmental problems of our times can be solved by means of improved governance and technology. These advocates have agreed that concerns about distributive justice and environmental responsibility today and over time are justified. But they have added that we should all be optimists and search together for such ways forwards that there will be no need to question High Modernity's commitment to all the splendid ideal practices, which give our epoch its identity.[6]

---

[5] Here is Nancy Fraser's summary of a widely shared view: "So there's a mismatch in scale between Europe as a political unit and Europe as an economic unit and that's already bad enough but then you plug it into this worldwide context where essentially private economic powers have wildly outstripped the public political powers at all levels. We don't have the capacity to develop for example global financial regulation that could prevent the bond markets dictating to states what they can do, how much they can spend on social programmes and so on. This is a deeply undemocratic situation, and I think the only way to resolve it is to scale up political power in a democratic way to cope with this huge runaway of economic and financial power. I think the challenges are really enormous and Europe's situation is part of a much bigger set of problems." (Sadinmaa 2013: 9) For theoretical elaborations see, for instance Habermas (2001; 2006), Habermas/Derrida (2003), Held/Patomäki (2006). For critical discussion, see Sehm-Patomäki/Ulvila (2007) and Wallgren (2014).

[6] The classical statement is the so-called Brundtland Report (World Commission on Environment and Development 1988). See the discussion in section 7 below.

(iv) The fourth pillar of liberal self-confidence was the perception that it was theoretically well-founded. With the publication of John Rawls' *A Theory of Justice* in 1971 and *Political Liberalism* in 1993, Habermas' *The Theory of Communicative Action* (*Theorie des kommunikativen Handelns*) in 1981 and *Between Facts and Norms* (*Faktizität und Geltung*) in 1992, and with the publication of other similar treatises, the modern, liberal, green, and reformist left took pride in understanding its global aspirations and dominance as morally and intellectually well-founded.

# 4 The erosion of liberal self-confidence

In the new millennium the liberal self-confidence of the preceding decades has rapidly eroded. The dream of gradual progress towards post-national democratisation has been weakened, above all, by the frictions in "the European project." The problems first came to a clear view with the rejection of the Treaty establishing a Constitution for Europe in the French and in the Dutch referenda in 2005. Since then, liberal confidence in the future of the EU has been hurt by several problematic developments. One important factor has been the controversies over the handling of the financial crisis since 2008. A key point has been the debate about the social and economic consequences of the Growth and Stability Pact and the so-called austerity regime, especially in South Europe, including Greece, Italy, and Spain. Further trouble has been brought to the liberal mind by the departure of the United Kingdom from the EU and by the electoral successes of xenophobic and illiberal political formations in several member countries. The dream of a smooth transition from the Cold War to global peace has been disturbed, since the late 1990s, by the derailing of the ambition to rebuild the relations of Russia and the NATO countries on the basis of trust and friendly cooperation and later also by 9/11 and the global war on terror proclaimed in its aftermath. Globally, the hope of accomplishing economic stability and prosperity for all has been shaken by the threat of financial meltdown in the autumn of 2008 and the growth of economic disparity and volatility after that. (Presently the COVID-19 pandemic further aggravates the concern.) The dream of ecological sustainability has been upset by increasing concern about climate change leading more and more to climate alarmism and uncertainty about the capacity of democracies to respond with sufficient speed. The dream, finally, of providing a convincing theoretical grounding for the progressive liberal dream, is not doing too well either.

How can we understand the rapid change of mood from the High Modern optimism of 1990 to the lurking pessimism of today? My proposal is that no progress can be expected in debates about this familiar topic unless the cultural ambitions that define High Modernity are clearly identified and subjected to criticism. I will discuss two aspects. I first take stock of the philosophical discourse of modernity. My focus is on the question whether liberals and leftists should still, under the pressure of populism, climate alarmism, "post-truth," and in the light of the many disappointing developments in recent decades remain committed to the idea that reason and freedom (and perhaps also the good) are intrinsically connected. I suggest that the kind of sceptical philosophy whose biggest champions are Wittgenstein and Socrates provides much needed resources for a self-critical appraisal and transformation of some of the ideal practices, which have defined and shaped High Modernity. I then discuss some aspects of the history and current dynamics in the political semantics of sustainable development.

# 5 Crumbling foundations of liberal self-confidence

The Kantian and Left-Hegelian project of providing normative foundations for a critical self-understanding of our times – and hence, also, the intellectual basis for the moral self-confidence of liberal democracy – resurged as a key theme in philosophy on both sides of the North Atlantic Ocean in the 1960s. Let us revisit some aspects of the debates up to the 1990s.

The impetus to the debate came when pressures was felt from many sides: The analytic tradition found trouble in explaining the "scientism" it inherited from Vienna in relation to the question of the autonomy of the humanities and the charge of reductionism in moral philosophy; Nietzscheans equated search for knowledge with search for power; Heideggerians claimed that all moral philosophy is sentimental humanism and that it can have no place in a serious philosophy of Being; Horkheimer and Adorno argued that Auschwitz represented the ultimate realisation of the ideal practices of reason that the modern West committed itself to more than two millennia ago; postcolonial theorists saw modern rationalism as adding "epistemicide" to the oppressive practices of the old colonial masters; and historicists, linguistic idealists, and social constructivists, who claimed that contingent identity formation is basic to morality, cast yet one more shadow over the notion that modern liberals could explain the normative advantage of their social, moral, or political vision as compared with others. In different strands of critical theory these pressures were productive in different ways.

One camp, significantly represented by Karl-Otto Apel and Jürgen Habermas, argued for the unity of the rational and the morally right. Another tendency, articulated in works by Derrida, Lacan, Žižek and others was to proclaim, and sometimes celebrate, the capacity of philosophy to unmask the empty core, the void, at the centre of all foundational aspirations in the philosophy of modernity. A third strand of thinking, eloquently propagated by Foucault and Rorty in their various ways, proposed the rejection of the question of normative foundations as just one form of enlightenment blackmail. The fourth option spearheaded by Axel Honneth and others preferred, after witnessing the stalemate of the debates between these competing positions, to ignore the question of normative foundations altogether in order to address, as they insisted, more directly substantial issues in a critical theory of the times. Rawls combined elements of the first, third, and fourth position in a titanic search, which, as he maintained, remained inconclusive.

My suggestion is that around the shift of the millennium the overall outcome of the said debates was a widely shared sense of fatigue with respect to the classical programme of Kantian or Hegelian enlightenment to create a philosophy that would legitimise reason's commitment to its own realisation. I also suggest that this erosion of philosophical self-confidence is the intellectual corollary of the loss of self-confidence of the liberal modern West as a universal paradigm for social and political progress.

## 6 Wittgenstein and sceptical philosophy

I have elsewhere argued that intellectually, morally, and politically enriching resources for addressing again the question of normative foundations of critical theory are available in Wittgenstein's later philosophy and that his philosophy constitutes (i) a transformational intervention in the debates about foundations such that (ii) it opens new prospects for productive dialogue with the many competing strands in the philosophy of modernity and more generally in diagnostic debate about the times (Wallgren 2006; 2012; 2013a; 2013b; 2017).

In order to bring this abstract notion to bear on the present topic I suggest that we ask: How did Wittgenstein's thinking unfold? Here is one answer, which brings out the intimacy of his intellectual evolution with key elements in the philosophical discourse of modernity: Young Wittgenstein wanted to solve Frege's problem. Frege's problem was the legitimacy of arithmetic, a problem which in the hands of Russell took the form of a search for a general theory of the legitimacy of reason's confidence in itself. Frege's and Russell's logistic programme reached a first pinnacle in the work of the young Wittgenstein.

The history of analytical philosophy after the *Tractatus* has often been written as the history of making good the basic idea inherited from Frege, Russell, and young Wittgenstein that *a theory of meaning* is our best candidate for a first philosophy.[7]

From this perspective, Wittgenstein's later philosophy has then often been incorporated into the narrative as built around a core theory of "meaning as use." Four main lines of interpretation have emerged. According to *the transcendental interpretation* later Wittgenstein proposes a theory of the conditions of possibility of sense. According to *the grammatical interpretation*, his philosophy should be seen as a methodological guide to the establishment of objective criteria of sense and nonsense. According to *therapeutic interpretations* later Wittgenstein offers a method of analysis that, in principle at least, enables each individual to achieve, case by case, understanding of where the realm of meaning ends and the realm of pure nonsense begins. Fourthly, according to *postmodern, historicist, and neo-conservative interpretations* Wittgenstein's theory of meaning as use shows that all claims to meaning gain their significance against the background of the unquestionable authority of tradition or contingent agreement in practice.

Now, we may wonder, which interpretation is correct? Insofar as we use this question as our point of departure, we consider Wittgenstein's later philosophy from the perspective of a certain, conventional understanding of philosophy. According to this understanding, philosophy is as an activity in which (i) the aim is the solution of problems, or perhaps, their dissolution; (ii) the method is argumentative (or descriptive); (iii) arguments (or descriptions) are taken to carry objective or intersubjectively binding authority; and (iv) the arguments (or descriptions) have the effect that they induce convergence of rational participants towards agreement or truth about how things are, about the correctness of theoretical positions or about what makes sense and what does not make sense. When this view is in place, the question "Who is right?", or, the question "Which position is right?" will easily invite themselves. An investigation that is orientated towards answering such questions will make it difficult to gain a correct understanding of some of Wittgenstein's most important achievements. Other options are possible. One is to interpret Wittgenstein's later work as work on the problems he inherited from Frege and Russell and as leading him to a transformation of his views on what kind of problems those problems are, what kind of work on them one (anyone who is as strongly as possible com-

---

7 Von Wright (1957), although only available in Swedish and in Finnish translation, is one of the best presentations of the career of early analytical philosophy.

mitted to reason) may at best do, and what we may expect to learn from such work. The transformation that Wittgenstein achieved and its importance for present purposes can best be seen if we look at Wittgenstein's later philosophy as a revival, or rediscovery, of certain ideas which are central to philosophy as imagined by Sextus Empiricus and, before him, by Socrates.

In the very first paragraphs of his work *Outlines of Pyrrhonism*, Sextus Empiricus identifies his own philosophy as sceptical. The philosophy Sextus wishes to outline is equally different from, or equally distant to, what seems to Sextus to be two other major forms of philosophy. One he calls dogmatic, which he describes as formed by philosophers who claim that they have found truth. The other he calls academic of which he says that it is characteristic to claim that truth cannot be found. Sextus has no quarrel with the dogmatic or academic philosophers. He is not engaged in any movement of thought that seeks competition with other movements of thought. He is also not engaged in doubting the truth or meaning of what dogmatists or academics say or argue. So, if we think that sceptical philosophy is marked by an effort to doubt what can be doubted, or if we think of it as a critique that tries to define or establish limits of thoughts or meaning, then Sextus is not at all a sceptical philosopher. Instead Sextus is, as he quite explicitly states, a sceptical philosopher in the quite different sense of one whose activity consists in searching, or, in investigating (Sextus Empiricus 1933).

Enter Wittgenstein: Anyone who is acquainted with his *Philosophical Investigations* will be familiar with the frustration that comes from efforts to get out of it results in the form of valid arguments or true statements, theses, theories, or doctrines to which Wittgenstein was committed. Countless proposals have been offered, but all remain shrouded in controversy. Nevertheless, it is also difficult to read the work without being excited by the intensity of the search it presents. We should, I propose, take seriously the possibility of reading it as central to what goes on in the *Philosophical Investigations* that Wittgenstein there, in his effort to come to terms with the crisis in the debate about philosophical foundations, brings to new life the notion of philosophy as unending search practised by Socrates and self-reflectively explicated by Sextus. We might call such philosophy true or real sceptical philosophy. At this point, two aspects are crucial for our purposes. The first key aspect of real sceptical philosophy in the sense of Sextus and Wittgenstein is that they have nothing to do with the notion that sceptical philosophy undermines our belief in the power of reason or in our grounds for committing ourselves to reason. The second is that neither Sextus nor Wittgenstein satisfies either of the two characterisations of sceptical philosophy that dominate contemporary discussion. According to one common characterisation, scepticism – especially modern "Cartesian" scepticism – turns around doubt. On this view scepticism challenges us not to accept as true that to which rational or reasonable objections can be made and, on the same view, a person who maintains that no such truths can be found is a sceptic. This characterisation obscures the decisive difference for Sextus between sceptical philosophy and academic philosophy. According to a second characterisation common in contemporary philosophy, the main attraction of scepticism – especially in antiquity – is that it promises peace of mind, or tranquillity, as a consequence of its efforts. That view may be legitimate with respect to Sextus (see however Næss 1968), but it comes too close to an instrumental conception of the relation between reason, freedom, and wisdom to do justice to some features of the sceptical philosophy of Wittgenstein, which are important for present purposes.

Now consider Socrates: In Plato's dialogues we find Socrates searching, but not alone as in the case of Sextus, but in dialogue with several others. We also find him claiming that his inquiries do not lead to the discovery of truth or to knowledge. Thirdly, we find Socrates claiming that the dialogic inquiries he has engaged in have been inquiries of what our words mean and that the engagement has given him advantages in terms of human wisdom (see *Apology* esp. 20 – 21, 38, 43; *Laches* 200e).

My simple suggestion is that Wittgenstein in his later philosophical investigations of language and meaning achieves a liberating transformation of how commitment to reason can at best be realised. He achieves this transformation by, first, laying bare the opacity of the paralysing notion that foundationalism and anti-foundationalism are clear, exclusive, and exhaustive options in the philosophical self-scrutiny of reason. Secondly, he offers a basis for a very different notion of what a truly radical commitment to reason may at best be like, which has profound parallels in the philosophy of Sextus and Socrates. According to this notion radical critical and self-critical philosophical reasoning has, among other things, the following three features:

(i) It is a study of what words mean.
(ii) It takes the form of polyvocal dialogue.
(iii) It is a search with no end in sight.

In order to add some flesh to these bones we may, first, remind ourselves of some characteristics of the Socratic dialogues. In them Socrates discovered, or created, philosophy as an investigation of the sense we give to the words we live by. Such philosophy can find its place only when it is unclear to us what some of our words mean to one of us or to us all. The lack of clarity about the meaning of a word is a lack of clarity about how to live. Philosophy is inquiry propelled by the discovery of such lack of clarity. If that is so, then the occasion for philosophy comes whenever we realise that we do not understand a word in the sense of understanding of how to place it in our lives, or, of "how to go on" (cf. PI § 150, § 151, and passim).

Socrates stressed the intrinsic link between not knowing how to give an account of the meaning of the word and not knowing how to be guided by that word in one's life.[8] Socrates is explicit and emphatic about what follows. The consequence is what Gregory Vlastos called Socrates' *principle of sincerity* (Vlastos 1991: 14, 44, and passim; Wallgren 2006: esp. 47, 70–72). The basic idea is simple: It is analytic that if we do not commit ourselves to our words, we do not say anything, at least not about the matter at hand, namely the question of what we can take the word to mean.[9]

Now, a second feature of the idea of philosophy as a search for what our words mean that Socrates discovers is the need for philosophers to turn to others. When Socrates comes back from, say, a military campaign, he does not seek isolation to reflect on and understand his experience. He goes to the palaestra to speak with his peers (*Charmides* 153a). Words have been shared with others and have the potential of being shared also in the future. Others, too, have experience of lives in which the words I live by have a meaning. Their experience, their sense of that experience, how to understand it and what to do with it – not only my experience and my understanding – is part of what the word means. It does not follow that we should expect agreement about the meaning of words, past or future. But it does follow that when I search for the meaning of words it matters to me what you say. Such mattering is a complex thing. One feature is that when I turn to you, I show my dependence on you for finding and achieving myself as my self: We might speak of the unity or search for self and search for community in philosophy. This is also the key to why Socrates said that his philosophy is *real politics* and why there are reasons to say that conceptual analysis, moral philosophy, and political philosophy all coincide in Socratic philosophy (*Gorgias* 521d; see also *Apology* 36c; *Gorgias* 464a, 513e–514a; *Euthydemus* 292).

A third feature is – as Socrates stresses more perhaps than any other philosopher in our tradition – that the other person can be *anyone* who lives with the words that I depend on for my life.[10] There is no position, no experience, no life,

---

**8** Of all the Socratic dialogues the *Laches* may be the most pedagogical illustration of this aspect of Socratic philosophy.
**9** This feature of the Socratic conception of philosophy undermines the relevance of the distinction between the everyday and the philosophical which has played a rather significant role in the discussion of Wittgenstein's conception of philosophy.
**10** We gather from the opening sections of the Socratic dialogues that Socrates is keen to speak with friends and foes, with people he knows well and with people he does not know, with older

that is in principle excluded as a resource that can provide me with clues that I need for my understanding and formation and that hence become a part of what we need for our understanding and formation. This we might call the principle of polyvocality, or the principle of democracy, in Socratic philosophy. When the task is to decipher the differences between typically modern scientific claims to reason and knowledge on the one hand and philosophical claims to reason and wisdom on the other, there is, I believe, no other point of contact between the Socratic dialogues and Wittgenstein's later philosophy that is as important as their convergence around methodological polyvocality.

A fourth feature of Socratic philosophy is the openness of the search. When we, through polyvocal conversation, investigate how to place a word which we – or at least one of us – have discovered difficulties with, there is no place for any default view of what kind of result will follow. It may follow that we easily arrive at conclusions (about meaning of words) which we find illuminating and helpful and agree on between us. It may follow that we come to see that we depart from each other in various ways. We may, for instance, come to see that what satisfies one of us does not satisfy another, or that we do not meet each other in what we find important or less important. The experience that our ways do not meet, or that they fall apart, can take many forms. They can be conflictual, or leave us with a sense of solidarity, or with a sense of serene solitude or despondent abandonment and so on. Let us note, finally, that the discovery of meanings shared and not shared, of companionship and conflict, of distance and proximity is, I think we can say, a transformational learning process about words, ourselves, and others.

Now, there certainly are interesting differences between the conceptions of philosophy as developed by Socrates and Sextus and between both of these and that of Wittgenstein. But the picture I am driving at is the following: Differences aside, there is overlap and commonality between Sextus, Socrates, and later Wittgenstein about philosophy. Not about what philosophy has to be, but what it might be, or what it might be at best. Here is a summary:

1. Their philosophy is about the meaning of words, typically, about words which seem familiar to us, but which have lost their familiarity, or lose it on closer inspection.
2. Their study of words takes the form of polyvocal dialogue in which a view which the philosopher seeks to defend is nowhere to be found.
3. Their philosophy is a public enterprise open to all.

---

and with younger people and in the *Meno* he even brings in a slave lad into the dialogue. (Women remain absent.) The notion that anyone's opinion counts is basic to Socrates' method.

4. They see philosophy as searching without end: It is typical of all three authors that the question whether the search will arrive at results such that all should agree with them, or even that just one person should find an end to her search, is of no consequence. Hence, they agree that the lack of a promise that philosophy would bring knowledge or truth about what our words mean, or about something else, is in no way disappointing.
5. They all agree that the dialogic democratic search for word meaning that their philosophy amounts to is transformational in a sense which has to do with the quest for wisdom.
6. The potential for transformation of the meanings of words that sceptical philosophy involves, is always constitutive both of subjectivity and of community. Any such philosophy is therefore intrinsically always both a moral and a political engagement.

We may see Wittgenstein's journey from logicism to the *Philosophical Investigations* as a learning process that leads to a rediscovery of real sceptical philosophy as a morally and politically transformative practice driven by a relentless commitment to reason and freedom. This philosophical event enables a fresh look at the fatigue in which twentieth century debates about a philosophical basis for critical standards ended. Philosophers asked: "Can we reach and defend bedrock? Can universal doubt, relativism, historicism, constructivism, deconstruction, and irony explain themselves to themselves? Can we answer the questions if we reframe them? Should we reject them?" Many locked themselves into dogmatic camps and others gave up, satisfying themselves perhaps with an empirical turn, austere formalism, or social relevance. The sceptical philosopher will not expect discussion of these issues to lead her to a "position," on say, the Lacanian void, Apelian universal pragmatics, Derridean *différance*, Rortyan ironism, naturalised transcendentalism, empirically informed philosophy, or descriptive or therapeutic dissolution of the problems of philosophy, and she will not see this as a failure or as a reason for disappointment about reason.

The relation between the notion of the best possible practices of reason suggested here and the future of modernity is of course not straightforward. It is also easy, in times of disappointment with Enlightenment, to underestimate the power of ideas, and of how we understand ideas and ideals. I turn, in the spirit of self-scrutiny and "optimism of the will," to my case study: the discourse of environment and climate change and to what I call the political-conceptual history of sustainable development.

## 7 Past and future of sustainable development

We may identify the following four phases in the history of the discourse of sustainable development: The time of innocence, which lasted from around 1500 to around 1950; the time of civilisational dilemma, from the 1950s to 1987; the time of sustainable development, from 1987 to 2008; and the time of disappointment, confusion, and climate alarmism from 2008 to the present.

(i) In the first phase, "sustainable development" was not a point of discussion in the present sense. Nevertheless, the cultural dynamic that prepared the ground for it was certainly in place: There would be no notion of a global problem of sustainability as we know it without colonisation and globalisation, the ensuing global quest for affluence without limit, and the promise of realising affluence for all with the help of "techno-science" as envisioned by Francis Bacon and others since the early seventeenth century (Bacon 1999; Von Wright 1986; Toivakainen 2018). The idea that science and technology by enabling an industrial growth model of progress pave the way for universal liberation from scarcity to affluence, was for a long time predominantly greeted with enthusiasm. High-profile early criticism and concern was voiced, by Rousseau, the Luddites, Malthus, Dostoyevsky, Tolstoy, Heidegger, Spengler, and, most incisively perhaps, by Gandhi, but optimism remained the modern mainstream attitude. We may call this the time of innocence about growth, sustainability, and ecology.

(ii) In the 1950s and 1960s a new worry about environmental degradation as the downside of modern development gradually emerged. It first took the form of concern about individual issues. Threats to ecosystems through changes in land use, as in the case of the east African savannahs, and to biodiversity due to toxic waste, caught people's attention and inspired new initiatives, such as the World Wildlife Fund which was founded in 1961. Soon, the concerns were generalised and in the 1960s individual issues were ever more often re-framed as reference points in apocalyptic narratives about an impending global ecological crisis. This discourse inspired action and gave birth to the new environmental movement or "green" movement. The specific worry that gave the movement its radical political identity was that the environmental crisis is a cultural crisis. It coalesced around the notion that High Modernity as a cultural epoch, which believes in the compatibility of all its other ideal practices with ideal practices of affluence, is coming to its end. From the point of view of the green movement both the main camps in contemporary politics, the socialist left and the market-friendly right were equally and catastrophically blind to the most fundamental facts about the emerging ecological crisis. The new rallying call from the environmental movement was that modernity must choose between affluence for some and solidarity with all. The best articulation of this message came from Norwegian eco-philosophy, especially from the intellectual-activist Sigmund Kvaløy (Kvaløy 1976). Internationally more well-known was the 1972 report from the Club of Rome called *The Limits to Growth* (Meadows et al. 1972). We may call this the time when the ecological crisis was perceived as a civilisational dilemma.

(iii) The third phase, the phase of sustainable development, began with the publication of the *United Nations Report on Sustainable Development*, submitted in 1987. It is not by chance that this landmark report to the UN Secretary General was produced under the leadership of another Norwegian, the former Norwegian prime minister, Gro Harlem Brundtland, (World Commission on Environment and Development 1988). The innocence of the title notwithstanding the political message of the report was clear and strong. The report wanted to tell the world that the environmentalists are wrong; that the environmental problems do *not* force the modern world to give up the search for ever-increasing affluence for all. According to the report there will be no limits to growth, no need to give up industrial growth society, and no need for a reform of the cultural imagination of High Modernity if only we make science, technology, the market economy, and governance good enough. This *cultural domestication* of the environmental crisis was the essence of the political semantics of sustainable development. In view of the implications for public debate and policy the new catchword "sustainable development" was, then, already from its inception indistinguishable from a call for sustainable growth.[11]

For some years, the discursive battle between environmental radicals calling for civilisational change and domesticating reformists calling for sustainability was an open affair. Our best witness to the openness of the con-

---

11 The report defines sustainable development as "development that meets the needs of the present without compromising the ability of future generations to meet their own needs." The report stresses that, while "overriding priority should be given" to "the world's poor," limitations on the environment's ability to meet present and future needs are only "imposed by the state of technology and social organization" (World Commission on Environment and Development 1988: 8). Hence, the definition and the discussion that follows allowed – and in actual fact it encouraged – the inference that with better technology and better organisation present limits can be stretched without limit. This notion was quickly picked up and it became the mainstream view in public debate that technical fixes and improved governance will be sufficient to solve any environmental problem. Therefore, no cultural reorientation and no critical reconsideration of the ambitions that define the cultural epoch of High Modernity is needed.

troversy is the American president George H. W. Bush. Feeling the pressure from the radical environmentalists, Bush, prior to the United Nations conference on sustainable development held in Rio de Janeiro in 1992, told the world, "The American way of life is not negotiable." (Drexhage/Murphy 2010: 7) The fighting spirit with which Bush addressed the world shows that the debate between Kvaløy and Brundtland was undecided at the time. What Bush did was that he threw the full political weight of his country into the Brundtland camp. Soon he and Brundtland won the day. The most formidable evidence of the success of Brundtland and Bush came in 2004 when the quasi-constitutional treaty of the European Union was agreed. The treaty committed the member states and the EU to the promotion, not only of sustainable development but of "balanced economic growth."[12] My claim, then, is that between 1987 and 2008 the default conviction in liberal-left-green mainstream politics in the Global North was gradually established, that Brundtland and Bush are right and that the most responsible way to address the mounting environmental problems is to promote sustainable development and economic growth. In this spirit the General Assembly of the United Nations passed the United Nations Millennium Declaration on 8 September 2000.[13] During that time other concepts than sustainable development were also launched to produce the said domesticating effect. "Ecological modernisation" or "eco-modernism," "green growth" and "Green New Deal" stand out together with sustainable development and sustainable or balanced growth as flags raised in those years to defend High Modernity's continued commitment to industrial growth society in the time of environmental crisis.

(iv) In recent times, problems for the dream of sustainability have mounted. I suggest that we see the years after 2008 as a new, fourth phase in the history of the political semantics of sustainability. We can call this period the time of disappointment, confusion, and climate alarmism.

---

12 The so called Lisbon Treaty, or The Treaty establishing a Constitution for Europe, was signed by representatives of all EU governments in 2004 but rejected by France and the Netherlands in national referenda in 2005. Article 3 Section 3 in the sequel to the Treaty of Lisbon, the Treaty on European Union, states, "The Union shall establish an internal market. It shall work for the sustainable development of Europe based on balanced economic growth and price stability, a highly competitive social market economy, aiming at full employment and social progress, and a high level of protection and improvement of the quality of the environment. It shall promote scientific and technological advance." (European Union 2012)
13 United Nations General Assembly, 8 September 2000. 55/2. United Nations Millennium Declaration.

I turn first to the disappointment. Consider emission of greenhouse gases: Twenty-five years after the adoption of the United Nations Framework Convention on Climate Change and fifteen years after the Kyoto Protocol, emissions of greenhouse gases continue to grow.[14] Consider also the more general issue of decoupling. The idea of decoupling is the idea of getting more of the same output and welfare that we enjoy now with less impact of energy and other material resources. Without decoupling, there can be no sustainability as promised by Brundtland and intended by the European Union and the United Nations. Here, too, the empirical record is alarming.[15] One reaction to the disappointments comes from intellectuals and activists of the "Degrowth Movement" who rediscover the rallying call from eco-philosophy and the Club of Rome from the 1970s about limits to growth as a comprehensive civilisational issue.[16] Another reaction comes from those who defend the High Modern consensus and claim that the disappointments are only temporary and that technology and global governance are on a path towards solutions. Some will even insist that if we still want to remain true to the project of modernity as progressive self-determination, the only rational policy is to maximise economic growth, because only if we maximise economic growth, will we be able to maximise our capacity for scientific and technological progress and only if we do so, will we be able to fully realise the aspirations which have defined High Modernity.

Where does this line of debate between proponents of growth and proponents of degrowth leave us? As noted earlier the question whether growth and technological progress will inevitably lead to environmental disaster cannot be answered definitely on the basis of empirical findings. Nevertheless, the empirical, historical record is important, morally and politically. A comparison with the post-war history of discourse of so-called real socialism may be instructive: When the Soviet experiment was young, there was a fair deal of youthful optimism. But as time passed and as more and more people felt that the gap between the promises and realities of socialism was widening the dream collapsed (Habermas 1990).

I submit the following suspicion. One reason for the rising support enjoyed by right wing populism today is that more and more people perceive the difference between Donald Trump and Barack Obama, or between Angela Merkel and

---

[14] According to Crippa et al. (2019: 33) the global total $CO_2$ emissions were 22,637.134 Mt in 1990 and 37,887.224 Mt in 2018. See also IPCC (2014).

[15] For an overview of the evidence see, for instance Wiedmann et al. (2015) and Ward et al. (2016).

[16] See the material collected at https://www.degrowth.info/en/library/, accessed 20 August 2020.

Matteo Salvini, or between Narendra Modi and Rahul Gandhi to be one of degrees of honesty, not of policy. Angela Merkel, described in 2019 by the *Financial Times* as the de facto leader of the liberal West, was highly praised by many good socially conscious liberals for her words *"Wir schaffen das"* ("We will manage it"), uttered at the height of the so-called European refugee crisis in 2015–2016. But Merkel was also, as head of government, together with a number of respected liberal, green, left, and social-democratic leaders from other EU countries, responsible for the 2016 deal between Turkey and the European Union on migration from Syria and other countries.[17] After the assassination and dismembering of Jamal Khashoggi at the Saudi Arabian consulate in Istanbul in October 2018, liberal democracies have continued business as usual with Saudi Arabia. And, as we already noted, greenhouse gas emissions have continued to rise throughout the modern West regardless of who has won elections. So why not go for Trump or Salvini who at least are honest about their choice: "America First, damn liberal, left, and green dreams of solidarity and ecological justice." The point is *not* that there are no differences. But it strikes me as terrible, and sad, and strange, that from the perspective of those who live in refugee camps in Turkey or Libya or who walk in the migrant caravans in Guatemala or Mexico it is often not as easy as one might hope to recognise the big differences between the heroes of the liberal and the illiberal West.

The relative lack of attention in North Atlantic public debates to the issues just mentioned is, as I submit, a symptom of a wilful blindness, which is spreading and causing, insofar as the observation is correct, a shift which I suggest we identify conceptually as a shift from the era of High Modernity as defined above to the new cultural era Cynical Modernity. The shift occurs to the extent that a sense prevails that we have to choose, and are, surreptitiously, already choosing, between the desire to remain true to the dream of ethical universalism and the desire to remain true to the affluent dream for the privileged. The empirical measure of the shift from High Modernity to Cynical Modernity is the extent to which the political forces, who promote the optimistic notion that it is the task of the "developed countries" to bring development to all people, have lost support to other forces, who no longer proclaim global welfare as their goal.

This diagnostic suggestion about present moral regress and birth of Cynical Modernity is relevant for present purposes in the following way. The cultural-ecological criticism of past decades brought attention to the difficulty of combining the quest for affluence with the quest for growth. We have learnt that the debate between de-growthists and pro-growthists is undecidable as long as we

---

17 For critical analysis see, e.g. Elitok (2019) and Gkliati (2017), as well as Gogou (2017).

think of it as a debate to be decided empirically or perhaps, scientifically. Hence, as long as we see the affluence-universalism issue in ethics as the only potential cultural contradiction of modernity that follows from the ecological crisis, the rise of Cynical Modernity is difficult to explain. Keys to a clearer understanding of the present predicament must therefore be sought elsewhere. I suggest that we need to see clearly how the ecological crisis implicates tensions between our search for affluence and two ambitions other than ethical universalism, which have defined the project of modernity. The tension is with respect to the quests for reason and freedom. If we pay attention to this we may, as I shall next suggest, gain recourse to intellectual, moral, and political resources for dealing with climate change and other ecological problems, which have so far been grossly underestimated.

## 8 Sustainable development, technology, and freedom

Here are two starting points for the discussion in this section.
(i) One aspect of the High Modern valuation of freedom is that freedom should comprise, as at least one of its aspects, self-determination. The idea of self-determination is, we may say, the idea that human freedom is progressively realised in secular linear time when life conditions are increasingly shaped through choice and action that have been scrutinised by reason, such that reason is constantly also concerned with progress in the conditions for its own realisation.
(ii) In what we may call the standard defence of sustainable development and growth it is assumed that growth is good only if it is compatible with ethical universalism. It follows that for sustainable development to be a good idea, decoupling as defined above is necessary. Decoupling is possible only if progress in technology and governance happens. But this dependence on technology may, for reasons to be explicated next, be incompatible with the High Modern ideas of reason and freedom which I just mentioned. I will present two concerns. The concerns are closely linked. While the dynamic of the linkage is important, I here discuss the issues individually only.[18]

---

[18] For some discussion of how the concerns are linked, see Wallgren/Toivakainen (forthcoming).

## 8.1 Is freedom to throw oneself into the unknown real freedom?

Since Bacon published his landmark essay, power has been a key trope in the modern discourse of technology. According to Bacon's vision technology can give humans power that is transparent to its master in the sense that the development of new technology allows him or her to achieve what s/he wanted in the ways s/he wanted. This is the positive vision of the relation between technological development and freedom. Bacon, and many after him, have failed to take interest in the other side of the coin: in the ways in which we are not masters of the technology we create and in how technological development therefore destroys freedom. Technology can be non-transparent to its master in numerous ways. Here is one conceptual breakdown which alerts us to five different dimensions of the negative relation between technology and the High Modern search for self-determination. First, any new technology can be used successfully by others for purposes other than the ones which those who created the technology had in mind, thus putting the future designs of the original creators at risk. Second, new technology as used by the original creators for their original purpose can have unforeseen effects of known kinds, in the sense that the effects can be described on terms already familiar to us. (One example would be "the silent spring" of the 1960s.) Third, new technology as used by others for other purposes than imagined by the original inventors can have unforeseen effects of known kinds in the sense just defined. Fourth, new technology as used by the original creators with their original purpose in mind can have unforeseen effects of hitherto unimagined kinds, that is, effects such that their appropriate description on terms, or with concepts, familiar to us may seem impossible. Fifth, new technology as used with intentions foreign to those of the original creators can also have unforeseen effects of unimagined kinds in the sense just defined. This is one way of explaining how what we might call the ontology of technological change may change our imagination, our conception of the possible and the realm of meaning. For all these reasons the idea that technology is a source of power and that this power has a positive relation to freedom is obscure. While it is true that technology may allow us to fly to Mars and to clone our loved ones (whatever we could take human cloning to mean), it also brings unforeseeable effects and changes the range of the possible, of what we can do, imagine, and hope for in unexpected and unforeseeable ways.

I therefore suggest the usefulness of the term, *the opacity of technological progress*, and the obscurity of the notion of the neutrality of it. Debates about artificial intelligence (AI), genetic engineering, robotics, cyborgs, and transhumanism may be the most obvious examples today for the moral and political relevance of the opacity of technological progress. Fears have grown that pursuit of economic growth aided by technological progress may spell the end of human civilisation and for most species on the planet and that climate change is only the most visible aspect of the dangers (Barnosky et al. 2011).

We can say that a new tension has emerged in the conceptual landscape that defines the cultural constellation of High Modernity. The tension is between two ideas of how to understand the relation between freedom and technological advances. If every technological novelty carries the unknown in its wake, then what is a responsible attitude to this? Some will say: "We are already moving too fast and danger is growing. The responsibility of freedom involves the responsibility for intended and unintended consequences. Freedom calls upon us not only to reduce maximal risk but also to avoid uncertainty. We must therefore reduce the speed of change." Others will say: "There is no greater moral aspiration than the willingness to affirm the unpredictable. The only responsible freedom is the freedom to throw oneself into the unknown. If humans had not done that, we would all still live in caves."

Can we say which position is better? Which is more rational, more free? The question opens up in many directions. One thing which is quite straightforward is this: It is a mark of confusion if people promise that High Modern culture, including "the American way of life" as one its incarnations, can be preserved if we invest more in sustainable growth and technological development. Because of the rational opacity of technological power such investments are by conceptual logic investments in the advancement of freedom defined as freedom to throw oneself into uncharted territory. It therefore means that we say goodbye to that other dream of freedom that has defined High Modernity: freedom as self-determination, or, as we might also say, as conscious design of future life conditions (Theunissen 1982; Habermas 1985; Tugendhat 1986; Escobar 2018).

When this is clearly seen, we may ask two questions:

Do we want to call such blind rush into the unknown freedom – can we accept *this* as a legitimate use of the word freedom?

If we say: "Yes you can call that freedom if you like. (Who would I be to police how you want to use a word?)", are we then also ready to say that freedom as thus conceived is a good thing?

I think both questions are illuminated better perhaps than in any other philosophical treatise in the Socratic *Apology*. In the *Apology* Socrates asks why the oracle in Delphi claims that no one is wiser than he is. His investigations turn around a search for an answer to the question of what wisdom is. What does it mean to say that someone has wisdom? What do we mean with the word? What meaning can I, or you, or we, freely, wish to give to the word? How can I be guided in my life by wisdom, by the word and the meaning I can give to it? Will the questions we put when we search for wisdom, and the answers we give, tear us apart or bring us together? The questions are open. Nevertheless, it seems to me that, pace the eloquent protests of Nietzsche, Schumpeter, Deleuze and Guattari, and other champions of freedom as creative destruction, important arguments can be given in favour of negative answers to both questions. I will not pursue those arguments here, but I hope that what I have said gives some sense to the following thesis:

For reasons indicated above ecological activists and climate alarmists are wrong when they say that it is an objective fact that technological progress cannot save us from a planetary environmental catastrophe unless we give up the pursuit of economic growth. But their original intuition about the cultural contradictions of our times is nevertheless correct. The reason is that the pursuit of technological progress that is necessary in all efforts to realise sustainable development and affluence for all is incompatible with reasonable allegiance to the High Modern aspiration to realise reason, freedom, and progress.

## 8.2 Functional dependencies, responsibility, and democracy

A popular argument in contemporary pro-growth discourse of sustainability has been that economic growth that is part of a comprehensive, socially and politically balanced development policy will allow people increasing capacity (or "capabilities") to meet their needs and pursue their dreams and that, hence, economic growth goes hand in hand with the growth of human freedom (Sen 1999). However, such arguments, which put the focus on individual freedom are, arguably, incapable of making sense of the social and political dimensions of freedom which must be integral to any adequate theory of how humans can be free *together* (Rousseau 1973; Kant 1996; Rawls 1971; Read 2020).

Here is one way of fleshing out the elementary but crucial point: The kind of affluence and growth that has been achieved in the modern West and that is imitated and pursued by all, or almost all, governments across the planet requires deployment and large-scale use of highly complex technical devices, such as satellite-transmitted communication and robotised trade in derivatives, as well as reliance on complex organisational designs, such as the Energy Charter Treaty or the Brexit deal. It follows that the daily lives of all who have "made it" to the consuming classes are deeply embedded in a web of functional dependencies, which will to a large extent remain opaque to them and which make them involved in relations to unknown others which have enormous consequences socially and materially. These relations can, on the secular terms one may assume in modern times, earn moral legitimacy only through democratic procedures (Habermas 1996). We can ask ourselves: Is this political condition of entanglement in webs of dependence which are difficult to understand something new? Or have the political conditions under which people live been inscrutable long before social media and the World Trade Organization "connected people"? There were caravans on the Silk Road long ago, and long ago large amounts of silver were brought to Europe from the mines of Potosí – so, what is the correct question here?

Clearly the problem of what meaning can be assigned to the idea of freedom in history is not endemic to the questions brought to us by the complexity that is characteristic of High Modernity. But this fact should not blind us to the radical change in scale and the ensuing growing intensity of the tension between complexity and political freedom. It is central to what Marx achieved that he was the first to realise that this tension lies at the heart of capitalism. There are two fundamental insights in his analysis. One is that capitalism is inherently expansive and will, if its "logic" is left untamed, lead to global market integration and to the social and political upheavals required for their functioning, that is, to "globalisation." Marx's second and deeper insight concerns the moral implications of what involvement in the global market implies. The main point is that the expansion of market dependencies is always accompanied by ever greater indifference to the concrete individuality of others.[19]

The challenges to moral responsibility and freedom brought by market expansion, technological development, and functional dependencies have been subject to rich theorising also after Marx. One culmination of this theoretical tradition was the debate between Habermas and Niklas Luhmann in the 1970s. Habermas' solution to the problem of democratic legitimacy in societies marked by growing technological and systemic complexity was, as we know, that in societies where communicative democracy flourishes there is no limit in principle to the capacities of citizens to realise common self-determination (Habermas/Luhmann 1971; Habermas 1981a; 1981b; McCarthy 1985; see also Marglin 1974; 1975 and 2008). The new problem that Habermas' solution faces in the age of climate alarmism is this: What happens if free and equal citizens who exercise their radically reflective self-determination together are divided over the following question: Ought we to continue the quest for affluence, even when it implies that we give up the quest for freedom as freedom to understand consequences of what we do together? Ought we to embrace the quest for freedom as freedom to affirm as radically as possible the unknown?

---

**19** I here follow Georg Lohmann's analysis in his *Indifferenz und Gesellschaft: Eine kritische Auseinandersetzung mit Marx* (1991).

Kant had a perfect answer to this question in his essay on *Perpetual Peace*. He noted that because there will be cases when democratic communities wish to realise mutually incompatible but morally defensible policies, or what Rawls might have called different reasonable comprehensive doctrines, there must in global democracies be a possibility for voluntary migration from one polity to another (Kant 1973; Rawls 1993). But we live today in a world in which a problem that even Kant did not foresee looms large. The problem is that the planetary expansion of capitalism and the rise of the ecological crisis has made Kant's answer obsolete insofar as the planetary expansion of one democratic community, the community of High Modernity, already effectively forecloses emigration from it.[20]

Although I cannot within the limits of the present essay explain this, it seems to me that Habermasian democratic optimism has also become unrealistic: The average citizen is, simply, not in a position to invest the time and effort that would be required for her to achieve the minimum level of insight into the dependencies she is involved in that she would need in order to exercise her citizenship responsibly. Perhaps Trump, Modi, Bolsonaro, and Brexit are empirical proof that the time investment requirement for insightful citizenship has already become unrealistic and that citizens already carry a greater burden than can realistically be expected and morally demanded?

Also for these reasons sceptical citizens may say that sustainable development is more a threat than a solution if we wish to remain true to High Modern ideals of freedom and reason in the time of climate alarmism.

## 9 Concluding remarks

So where have we reached? Consider first this proposition:

If there is, or to the extent that there is, some truth worth preserving and fighting for in the idea of a link between the concepts of freedom, reason, and the good, these links are, one might argue, jeopardised by all claims typically offered under the rubric of sustainable development. More promising avenues for our moral and political imagination and practices can be found under the banners of local self-reliance, eco-feminism, degrowth, commoning, and, perhaps of *ubuntu, buen vivir,* and *swaraj* (Pratap 2004; Solón 2017).

---

**20** See, for instance, https://www.lifegate.com/nahua-tribe-poisoned-by-mercury, accessed 20 August 2020, and https://www.msn.com/en-us/news/world/illegal-mining-threatens-brazils-last-major-isolated-tribe/ar-BB15YeD1, accessed 20 August 2020.

Is the proposition true? Or: What is the place of truth and argument and reason in relation to it? Here is one response:

In such matters everyone must as a citizen speak for herself or himself. The matters involved are complex and while philosophy may provide some conceptual clarification philosophy has little to say about the correct political position.

Here is another response:

In such matters, everyone must as a citizen speak for herself and himself. But to be a citizen is to be a philosopher. This is so to the extent that we understand citizenship as a form of freedom and agree that there is truth in the Socratic idea that we are free only to the extent that we seek to exercise our best judgment in moral life and that best judgment will only be available to us if we are always also open to engagement in sceptical philosophy.

Here is a third and last response:

Enough now of academic philosophising about democracy and freedom and reason and what not: The whole planet is at risk and we have no time to lose on academic matters or unending Socratic deliberation. We must throw ourselves now with all our strength into the battle for (or, perhaps, against) sustainable development.

Commitment to the second ethos may define an emerging community searching, perhaps, for a transformed modernity. Commitment to the ethos of the first and third responses unites, I think, many idealistic corporate bosses with many sincere Weberians in important administrative positions and with many good Marxists and non-Marxist academics and with many liberal and socialist and green active citizens across the planet. Such commitment to High Modernity may, for reasons I have tried to indicate above, lead to ever deepening misery for ever greater numbers of people and to accelerated loss of biodiversity across the planet.[21]

# References

Bacon, Francis (1999): *Selected Philosophical Works*. Edited by Rose-Mary Sargent. Indianapolis, IN: Hackett.
Barnosky, Anthony D./Matzke, Nicholas/Tomiya, Susumu/Wogan, Guinevere O. U./Swartz, Brian/Quental, Tiago B./Marshall, Charles/McGuire, Jenny L./Lindsey, Emily L./Maguire,

---

[21] I dedicate my essay to the memory of Berta Cáceres, who was a leader in a campaign to protect the sacred river of the Lenca people, the Río Gualcarque, against the building of a hydroelectric power plant. Cáceres was assassinated in her home on 2 March 2016.

Kaitlin C./Mersey, Ben/Ferrer, Elizabeth A. (2011): "Has the Earth's Sixth Mass Extinction Already Arrived?" In: *Nature* 471(7336), pp. 51–57.

Crippa, Monica/Oreggioni, Gabriel/Guizzardi, Diedgo/Muntean, Marilena/Schaaf, Edwin/Lo Vullo, Eleonora/Solazzo, Efisio/Monforti-Ferrario, Fabio/Olivier, Jos /Vignati, Elisabetta (2019): *Fossil $CO_2$ and GHG Emissions of All World Countries: 2019 Report*. JRC Science for Policy Report. Luxembourg: Publications Office of the European Union.

De Sousa Santos, Boaventura (2006): *The Rise of the Global Left: The World Social Forum and Beyond*. London/New York, NY: Zed Books.

De Sousa Santos, Boaventura (2016): *Epistemologies of the South: Justice against Epistemicide*. London/New York, NY: Routledge.

Drexhage, John/Murphy, Deborah (2010): *Sustainable Development: From Brundtland to Rio 2012*. Background paper prepared for consideration by the High Level Panel on Global Sustainability at its first meeting, 19 September 2010, United Nations Headquarters, New York.

Dussel, Enrique (1985): *Philosophy of Liberation*. Maryknoll, NY: Orbis.

Elitok, Seçil Paçacı (2019): *Three Years On: An Evaluation of the EU-Turkey Refugee Deal*. MiReKoc Working Papers 04/2019. Istanbul: Migration Research Center at Koç University. https://mirekoc.ku.edu.tr/wp-content/uploads/2019/04/Mirekoc_Elitok_2019_Report_ThreeYearsOn-AnEvaluationOfTheEU-TurkeyRefugeeDeal.pdf, accessed 17 August 2020.

Escobar, Arturo (2018): *Designs for the Pluriverse: Radical Interdependence, Autonomy, and the Making of Worlds*. Durham, NC: Duke University Press.

European Union (2012): "Consolidated Version of the Treaty on European Union." In: *Official Journal of the European Union* 55(C 326), pp. 13–45. https://data.europa.eu/eli/treaty/teu_2012/oj, accessed 16 August 2020.

Gandhi, Mohandas Karamchand (1986a): *The Moral and Political Writings of Mahatma Gandhi*. Vol. 1. Edited by Raghavan Iyer. Oxford: Clarendon Press.

Gandhi, Mohandas Karamchand (1986b): *The Moral and Political Writings of Mahatma Gandhi*. Vol. 2. Edited by Raghavan Iyer. Oxford: Clarendon Press.

Gandhi, Mohandas Karamchand (1987): *The Moral and Political Writings of Mahatma Gandhi*. Vol. 3. Edited by Raghavan Iyer. Oxford: Clarendon Press.

Gandhi, Mohandas Karamchand (2010): *M. K. Gandhi's Hind Swaraj: A Critical Edition*. Annotated and edited by Suresh Sharma and Tridip Suhrud. New Delhi: Orient BlackSwan.

Gkliati, Mariana (2017): "The Application of the EU-Turkey Agreement: A Critical Analysis of the Decisions of the Greek Appeals Committees." In: *European Journal of Legal Studies* 10(1), pp. 81–123.

Gogou, Kondylia (2017): "The EU-Turkey Deal: Europe's Year of Shame." In: *Amnesty International* 20 March 2017. https://www.amnesty.org/en/latest/news/2017/03/the-eu-turkey-deal-europes-year-of-shame/, accessed 29 June 2020.

Gumbrecht, Hans Ulrich (1978): "Modern, Modernität, Moderne." In: Brunner, Otto/Conze, Werner/Koselleck, Reinhart (Eds.): *Geschichtliche Grundbegriffe: Historisches Lexikon zur politisch-sozialen Sprache in Deutschland*. Vol. 4. Stuttgart: Klett-Cotta, pp. 93–131.

Habermas, Jürgen (1981a): *Theorie des kommunikativen Handelns*. Vol. 1: *Handlungsrationalität und gesellschaftliche Rationalisierung*. Frankfurt a. M.: Suhrkamp.

Habermas, Jürgen (1981b): *Theorie des kommunikativen Handelns*. Vol. 2: *Zur Kritik der funktionalistischen Vernunft*. Frankfurt a. M.: Suhrkamp.

Habermas, Jürgen (1985): *Der philosophische Diskurs der Moderne: Zwölf Vorlesungen.* Frankfurt a. M.: Suhrkamp.

Habermas, Jürgen (1987): *The Philosophical Discourse of Modernity: Twelve Lectures.* Cambridge: Polity Press.

Habermas, Jürgen (1990): *Die nachholende Revolution.* Frankfurt a. M.: Suhrkamp.

Habermas, Jürgen (1996): *Between Facts and Norms: Contributions to a Discourse Theory of Law and Democracy.* Cambridge: Polity Press.

Habermas, Jürgen (2001): *The Postnational Constellation: Political Essays.* Trans., edited, and with an introduction by Max Pensky. Cambridge: Polity Press.

Habermas, Jürgen (2006): *The Divided West.* Edited and trans. by Ciaran Cronin. Cambridge: Polity Press.

Habermas, Jürgen/Derrida, Jacques (2003): "February 15, or What Binds Europeans Together: A Plea for a Common Foreign Policy, Beginning in the Core of Europe." In: *Constellations* 10(3), 291–297.

Habermas, Jürgen/Luhmann, Niklas (1971): *Theorie der Gesellschaft oder Sozialtechnologie: Was leistet die Systemforschung.* Frankfurt a. M.: Suhrkamp.

Held, David/Patomäki, Heikki (2006): "Problems of Global Democracy: A Dialogue." In: *Theory, Culture & Society* 23(5), pp. 115–133.

IPCC (2014): *Climate Change 2014: Synthesis Report: Contribution of Working Groups I, II and III to the Fifth Assessment Report of the Intergovernmental Panel on Climate Change.* Edited by The Core Writing Team, Rajendra K. Pachauri, and Leo Meyer. Geneva: IPCC.

Kant, Immanuel (1973): *Zum ewigen Frieden: Ein philosophischer Entwurf.* Stuttgart: Reclam.

Kant, Immanuel (1996): "An Answer to the Question: What Is Enlightenment? (1784)." In: *Practical Philosophy.* Trans. and edited by Mary J. Gregor. General introduction by Allen Wood. New York, NY: Cambridge University Press, pp. 11–22.

Koselleck, Reinhart (1985): *Futures Past: On the Semantics of Historical Time.* Trans. by Keith Tribe. Cambridge, MA: The MIT Press.

Kothari, Rajni (1988): *Rethinking Development: In Search of Humane Alternatives.* Delhi: Ajanta.

Kvaløy, Sigmund (1976): *Ekologisk kris – natur och människa: En inledning i eko-filosofi och eko-politik.* Stockholm: By & Bydg.

Lohmann, Georg (1991): *Indifferenz und Gesellschaft: Eine kritische Auseinandersetzung mit Marx.* Frankfurt a. M.: Suhrkamp.

Marglin, Stephen A. (1974): "What Do Bosses Do? The Origins and Functions of Hierarchy in Capitalist Production, Part I." In: *The Review of Radical Political Economics* 6(2), pp. 60–112.

Marglin, Stephen A. (1975): "What Do Bosses Do? Part II." In: *The Review of Radical Political Economics* 7(1), pp. 20–37.

Marglin, Stephen A. (2008): *The Dismal Science: How Thinking like an Economist Undermines Community.* Cambridge, MA: Harvard University Press.

McCarthy, Thomas (1985): "Complexity and Democracy, or the Seducements of Systems Theory." In: *New German Critique* 35, pp. 27–53.

Meadows, Donella H./Meadows, Dennis L./Randers, Jørgen/Behrens III, William W. (1972): *The Limits to Growth: A Report for the Club of Rome's Project on the Predicament of Mankind.* New York, NY: Universe Books.

Næss, Arne (1968): *Scepticism.* Oslo: Universitetsforlaget.

Nandy, Ashis (1988): *The Intimate Enemy: Loss and Recovery of Self under Colonialism.* New Delhi: Oxford University Press.
Nussbaum, Martha/Sen, Amartya (Eds.) (1993): *The Quality of Life.* Oxford: Clarendon Press.
Pratap, Vijay (2004): *Politics, Morality, Identity: An Intimate Quest.* Delhi: Vasudhaiva Kutumbakam.
Rawls, John (1971): *A Theory of Justice.* Cambridge, MA: Belknap Press of Harvard University Press.
Rawls, John (1993): *Political Liberalism.* New York, NY: Columbia University Press.
Read, Rupert (2020): *Wittgenstein's Liberatory Philosophy: Thinking through His Philosophical Investigations.* London: Routledge.
Rousseau, Jean-Jacques (1973): *The Social Contract and Discourses.* London: J. M. Dent & Sons.
Sadinmaa, Antti (2013): "Crisis, Critical Theory and the Question of Emancipation: An Interview with Nancy Fraser." In: *Helsinki Collegium for Advanced Studies Newsletter* 6(2), pp. 8–10. http://www.helsinki.fi/collegium/english/publications/HCASnewsletter_spring2013/Newsletter_2013spring.pdf, accessed 12 August 2020.
Sehm-Patomäki, Katarina/Ulvila, Marko (Eds.) (2007): *Global Political Parties.* London: Zed Books.
Sen, Amartya (1999): *Development as Freedom.* Oxford: Oxford University Press.
Sextus Empiricus (1933): *Outlines of Pyrrhonism.* With an English trans. by R. G. Bury. Cambridge, MA: Harvard University Press.
Solón, Pablo (Ed.) (2017): *Systemic Alternatives.* La Paz/Paris/Bangkok: Fundación Solón/Attac France/Focus on the Global South.
Taylor, Charles (1975): *Hegel.* Cambridge/New York, NY: Cambridge University Press.
Taylor, Charles (1989): *Sources of the Self: The Making of the Modern Identity.* Cambridge: Cambridge University Press.
Theunissen, Michael (1982): *Selbstverwirklichung und Allgemeinheit: Zur Kritik des gegenwärtigen Bewußtseins.* Berlin/New York, NY: De Gruyter.
Toivakainen, Niklas (2018): "Automation Technology in the Dynamics of Modernity: An Essay on Technology, Social Organization, and Existential Concerns." In: Tzafestas, Spyros G. (Ed.): *Information, Communication, and Automation Ethics in the Knowledge Society Age.* New York, NY: Nova Science, pp. 237–270.
Tugendhat, Ernst (1986): *Self-Consciousness and Self-Determination.* Cambridge, MA: The MIT Press.
Ulvila, Marko/Pasanen, Jarna (2009): *Sustainable Futures: Replacing Growth Imperative and Hierarchies with Sustainable Ways.* Helsinki: Ministry for Foreign Affairs of Finland.
Vlastos, Gregory (1991): *Socrates: Ironist and Moral Philosopher.* Cambridge: Cambridge University Press.
Wallgren, Thomas (1990): "Some Remarks on the 'Brundtland' Report." In: *Lokayan Bulletin* 8(3), pp. 21–33.
Wallgren, Thomas (2006): *Transformative Philosophy: Socrates, Wittgenstein, and the Democratic Spirit of Philosophy.* Lanham, MD: Lexington.
Wallgren, Thomas (2012): "Philosophy without End: Wittgenstein and Pyrrhonian Scepticism." In: Somavilla, Ilse/Thompson, James M. (Eds.): *Wittgenstein und die Antike/Wittgenstein and Ancient Thought.* Berlin: Parerga, pp. 163–213.

Wallgren, Thomas (2013a): "The Genius, the Businessman, the Sceptic: Three Phases in Wittgenstein's Views on Publishing and on Philosophy." In: Rothhaupt, Josef G. F./Vossenkuhl, Wilhelm (Eds.): *Kulturen und Werte: Wittgensteins Kringel-Buch als Initialtext*. Berlin: De Gruyter, pp. 113–139.

Wallgren, Thomas (2013b): "Radical Enlightenment Optimism: Socrates and Wittgenstein." In: Perissinotto, Luigi/Ramón Cámara, Begoña (Eds.): *Wittgenstein and Plato: Connections, Comparisons and Contrasts*. Basingstoke: Palgrave Macmillan, pp. 298–330.

Wallgren, Thomas (2014): "Cosmopolitan Futures for Europe." In: Silva, José Filipe/Lorite Escorihuela, Alejandro (Eds.): *Dictatorship of Failure: The Discourse of Democratic Failure in the Current European Crisis*. Helsinki: University of Helsinki, pp. 244–298. http://www.helsinki.fi/collegium/journal/volumes/14/volume14_full.pdf, accessed 12 August 2020.

Wallgren, Thomas (2017): "Wittgenstein's Modernist Political Philosophy." In: Matar, Anat (Ed.): *Understanding Wittgenstein, Understanding Modernism*. London/New York, NY: Bloomsbury, pp. 75–91.

Wallgren, Thomas/Toivakainen, Niklas (forthcoming): "The Question of Technology: From Noise to Reflection." In: Heikkurinen, Pasi/Ruuska, Toni (Eds.): *Sustainability Beyond Technology: Philosophy, Critique and Implications for Human Organization*. Oxford: Oxford University Press.

Ward, James D./Sutton, Paul C./Werner, Adrian D./Costanza, Robert/Mohr, Steve H./Simmons, Craig T. (2016): "Is Decoupling GDP Growth from Environmental Impact Possible?" In: *PLOS ONE* 11(10).

Wiedmann, Thomas O./Schandl, Heinz/Lenzen, Manfred/Moran, Daniel/Suh, Sangwon/West, James/Kanemoto, Keiichiro (2015): "The Material Footprint of Nations." In: *Proceedings of the National Academy of Sciences of the United States of America* 112(20), pp. 6271–6276.

Wittgenstein, Ludwig (1976) [PI]: *Philosophical Investigations*. Trans. by G. E. M. Anscombe. Oxford: Basil Blackwell.

World Commission on Environment and Development (1988): *Our Common Future*. Oxford: Oxford University Press.

Wright, Georg Henrik von (1957): *Logik, filosofi och språk: Strömningar och gestalter i modern filosofi*. Helsinki: Söderström.

Wright, Georg Henrik von (1986): *Vetenskapen och förnuftet: Ett försök till orientering*. Helsinki: Söderström.

Part 6: **Workshop on Ethics of Ecology**

Dieter Birnbacher
# What Is Biodiversity and Why Should It Be Protected?

**Abstract:** For a philosopher biodiversity is a challenge on at least two counts: 1. How is biodiversity defined? What constitutes biodiversity? 2. Why is the conservation of biodiversity important? Is biodiversity an intrinsic value or dependent of other values? The article makes an attempt to clarify the first issue by isolating a number of component factors that influence the appraisal and measurement of diversity. The second question is answered by a want-regarding and future-oriented ethics: Biodiversity is important because of the diversity of the aspects humans seek in nature and the expectation that with the process of civilisation nature will become more and more of a scarce and correspondingly valuable resource.

**Keywords:** Biodiversity, diversity, intrinsic value, ecological ethics

## 1 Introduction

Biodiversity is what is called in ethics a "hard case," in two respects. First, it is not easy to say what biodiversity is, how biodiversity is defined. Though there have been several attempts to answer the question (cf., for example Oksanen/Pietarinen 2004; Lanzerath/Friele 2014) it still is far from clear what it means to say of a natural system that it is "diverse." What is the thing of which diversity is predicated – biological species, alleles or ecosystems taken as wholes? Are only biological properties relevant, or does diversity include cultural properties such as aesthetic or symbolic ones? Is the number of items relevant, or should biodiversity be defined by a qualitative measure, perhaps one that takes account of the differences between the relevant items?

The main difficulty does not seem to be specific to the concept of *biodiversity* but concerns likewise the more comprehensive concept of *diversity*. Like simplicity – a concept that plays an important role as a methodical ideal in the philosophy of science – the concept of diversity, in spite of its seeming familiarity, has its own complexity. As in the case of simplicity, it is by no means simple to define diversity, or to operationalise it in a way that makes it amenable to measurement.

The second difficulty is to explain why biodiversity, however defined, is a value and should be protected. Is the value of biodiversity *intrinsic* or *extrinsic*?

Is biodiversity valuable in itself, or does its value depend on other values? In this case, as in the first, the difficulty is not specific to biodiversity. The same difficulty applies to diversity as an overarching value. Why should diversity be preferable to homogeneity? In the tradition of philosophy, diversity was often credited with an intrinsic value, especially by philosophers inspired by theology. Augustine was convinced that a world that contains something bad and sinful in addition to the good is preferable to a world that contains only the good. A world with only good things might possibly be better but not more perfect:

> When sinners are unhappy, the whole is perfect in spite of this. Provided that souls themselves are not lacking, whether those which are made unhappy when they sin or those which are made happy when they do right, the whole, having beings of every kind, is always complete and perfect. (Augustine 1955: 167)

Thomas Aquinas thought in a similar way. He wrote that

> a great beauty would be lost to creation in the removal of the order of distinct and dissimilar beings, one better than the other. A dead level of goodness would be a manifest derogation to the perfection of creation. A higher grade of goodness consists in there being something which cannot fall away from goodness; a lower grade, in there being that which can fall away. The perfection of the universe requires both grades of goodness. (Thomas Aquinas 1905: 242)

And Leibniz postulated that a universe that mirrors the perfection of its creator should exhibit an even infinite variety:

> The wonderful thing is that the sovereign wisdom has found the means by the representative substances to give variety to the same world infinitely. Though the world has already an infinite variety in itself so that it is already expressed variously by an infinity of different representations, it receives an infinity of infinities, and could not better correspond to the nature and the intentions of its inexpressible author who surpasses in perfection everything one can think thereof. (Leibniz 1965: 554; my translation)

These authors, however, typically fail to justify why it is that diversity is a more plausible sign of perfection than the maximum quantity of good. One gets the impression that they simply pursue apologetic strategies and want to make the attribution of omnipotence and infinite benevolence to God compatible with reality. In this, secular metaphysical defences of diversity such as those of Nicholas Rescher (1980) or Ulrich Steinvorth (1994: 121) are less exposed to criticism. But even with them, it remains ultimately unclear why variety should be preferable to homogeneity and why we should preserve variety, and especially natural variety, for its own sake, in preference to other goods.

## 2 Kinds and components of diversity

How can we characterise diversity? The first thing to say is that diversity is characterised by two general semantic conditions: Diversity is a *second-order property* which depends on and refers to other properties, and it is not a classificatory but a *gradable* property.

As to the first condition, it is obvious that diversity is a property of wholes composed of many different elements, and that diversity describes a quality of the whole resulting from the differences between the properties of these elements. Diversity is a property of properties. For diversity to be present, the elements have to exhibit a number of differences between their properties, whatever these properties may be. As to the second condition, diversity is a property that admits of a more or less. One whole can exhibit more diversity than another. Usually, this kind of grading is done more or less intuitively and without reflecting on the dimensions or components that go into these intuitions. The grading of diversity and homogeneity is done by an unconscious weighing of various factors. It might be interesting, however, to make these factors explicit by identifying them and, as it were, mentally experimenting with them.

In the following, such an experiment will be carried out. For each putative factor two hypothetical examples will be given, one coming from art and one from zoology.

In order to identify the first factor, imagine a monochrome painting, which, though having only one colour, exhibits a number of distinct shades of this colour. The painting gives a strong impression of homogeneity but is in fact differentiated, though with a very small margin of variation. Would we be justified to talk of a diversity of colours in this case? Certainly not. A painting with more colours – though otherwise with the same properties – would exhibit a higher amount of diversity. One might describe the difference by saying that the monochrome painting shows a certain micro-diversity, but little *macro-diversity*. As far as the painting exhibits diversity, it is a diversity within the bounds of a single property while the painting is otherwise perfectly homogeneous. With each additional diversity the *diversity content* of the painting, as it may be termed, would increase. Something similar could be said of a hypothetical world of animals which consists only of ants. There would certainly some diversity in this world, but – in comparison with alternatives – only to a certain degree. There would be micro-diversity without macro-diversity. On the macro-level there would be homogeneity.

A second factor of the diversity content of a whole is the number of dimensions or categories to which the qualitative differences between the items of the whole belong. For example, a painting can contain a great variety of elements with different shapes, which, however, do not differ in colour. Diversity is completely located in the dimension of shape. Analogously, a painting can contain elements with a great variety of colours, but of only one single shape. Diversity would be completely located in the dimension of colour. A painting would be more diverse if the diversity extended over more than one dimension. A biological analogue would be a hypothetical world of animals with only butterflies. Again, this world would exhibit a great amount of diversity, but this would be limited to relatively few dimensions, among them shape, size, and colouring. A world of only birds would probably be more diverse only because there are more dimensions in which birds can differ among themselves, e.g. by sound. This factor might be called the *breadth* of diversity. Diversity has the more breadth the greater the number of dimensions in which diversity exists. A maximum diversity of the kind Leibniz postulated with his "principle of plenitude" (cf. Lovejoy 1972), would be a diversity with the maximum macro-diversity and the maximum breadth.

A third factor of diversity concerns the distribution of diversity in the relevant whole. There might be a collection of paintings which as such exhibits a great diversity of shapes and colours, but where these shapes and colours are concentrated in only one painting, while all the other paintings are monochrome and otherwise completely homogeneous. Such a collection would be more diverse than a collection of completely homogeneous paintings. But a collection with the same overall diversity, in which, however, diversity extends over a greater number of pictures, would have a larger diversity content. Analogously, a world of animals would be more diverse which exhibited not only a great diversity of forms in only one class of animals but in which diversity extends to more or even to all classes. Thus, a hypothetical world inhabited only by the really existing mammals and beetles would certainly exhibit a considerable diversity. This diversity would, however, be concentrated in the realm of beetles. A hypothetical world in which diversity were shifted to some degree from the class of beetles to the class of mammals would be, on the whole, more diverse. Diversity would be more equally distributed among the classes.

If there is something in these considerations, some important conclusions can be drawn. First, that diversity, including biodiversity, itself exhibits a certain degree of diversity. Diversity is determined by a diversity of factors. Above all, diversity cannot be measured simply by the number of distinct types of elements of a whole. Diversity depends on qualities as well as on quantities, which does not exclude that quantities (such as the quantity of species) might pragmatically function as indicators of diversity in cases in which there is no better way of measuring diversity. However, even the quantity of distinct properties within a given whole is no adequate measure of diversity because diversity essentially depends on the relations between these properties and especially on how different they are. The more similarity there is between these properties, the less diversity can be attributed to the relevant whole.

Another conclusion is that we cannot expect the analysis to replace intuitive judgement. The analysis is unable to yield systematic and operational criteria which make away with intuitive judgements. Without exception, the factors mentioned involve intuitions, especially on the similarities and dissimilarities between elements or properties. Intuitive judgements on diversity and homogeneity are replaced by judgements on similarities and dissimilarities. The level on which intuitions work has changed. They have not become redundant.

# 3 Is biodiversity worthy of protection?

The above reflections correspond, to a large degree, to the provisions made by legal documents concerning preservation. The kind of biodiversity recognised by legislatures is throughout determined by the factors macro-diversity and breadth of diversity. For example, article 2 of the UN Convention on Biological Diversity of 1992 describes biological diversity as "the variability among living organisms from all sources including, inter alia, terrestrial, marine and other aquatic ecosystems and the ecological complexes of which they are part; this includes diversity within species, between species and of ecosystems." (United Nations 1992)

In a similar vein, § 7, 1, of the German *Bundesnaturschutzgesetz* defines biological diversity as "diversity of animal and plant species, included the diversity within species, as well as the diversity of forms of habitats and biotopes" (Germany 1992). According to these documents, protection of biodiversity is more than protection of species. Not only the diversity of existing species should be preserved but also the diversity of ecosystems in which they live and the diversity of alleles within species. Protecting biodiversity means to protect diversity on all levels of the biological hierarchy: on the level of genes, of individuals, of species, of communities, and of ecosystems (cf. Wägele 2014: 24).

It is remarkable that in the standard theories of the ethics of nature this array of different levels is frequently missed by reducing them to only one, preferably to individuals or ecosystems. An example is Paul W. Taylor's ethics of "respect for nature" (Taylor 1986), which is exclusively focused on the protection of animal and plant individuals, ignoring structural properties. Another example is Aldo Leopold's "land ethic" (Leopold 1949), which is focused on the protection of ecosystems, but not on the protection of biological species and genetic diversity. The last example shows that even holistic approaches to nature ethics sometimes are, from the perspective of biodiversity protection, not holistic enough and, for example, make no provisions for protecting species as long as these are irrelevant for the functioning of ecosystems or do not provide significant services (cf. Ehrenfeld 1978: 188).

One of the few contemporary philosophical approaches to the protection of biodiversity as a principle of man's relation to non-human nature is Nicholas Rescher's "evaluative metaphysics" of natural variety (Rescher 1980). Rescher postulates natural variety as a metaphysical value which should be respected in addition to moral values and norms. While moral values, in Rescher's view, are inherently related to human interests, metaphysical values stand apart from the sphere of human interests but are nevertheless binding. Though, for Rescher, there are also genuinely moral grounds for the preservation of biodiversity – in particular, grounds referring to the interests of future generations –, the obligation to preserve natural variety is primarily justified by reasons provided by his "evaluative metaphysics" (which, to distinguish it from moral reasons he calls "ethical reasons"). Differently from Leibniz, to whom Rescher's principles bear an evident affinity, this metaphysics does not include a divine creator or observer who values the variety of his creatures. The value of variety is not based on its origin in a divine will but on the inherent value of natural species.

Rescher's ethics of biodiversity is a courageous step into a normative *terra incognita*. Nevertheless, it may be doubted whether it can do the work it is designed to do, i.e. to give convincing reasons for the preservation of biodiversity. To achieve this, it would have to rely on less controversial premises. Both pillars of Rescher's theory are open to doubt. First, that the mere being of species is held to be a value. How can mere existence be a value, independently of the qualitative nature of what exists? (cf. Meyer 2003: 87) Within a theological conception of creation the assumption that existence implies value might be defensible (compare the formula in Genesis that "God saw that everything was good"). But this cannot hold in the framework of a secular metaphysics. The second problematic premise is that we can assume that biodiversity is an *intrinsic* value independent of all other values. This assumption is hardly plausible. If biodiversity were an intrinsic value independent of its consequences for other values we should have to conclude that the existence of a diversity of ebolaviruses is more valuable, *ceteris paribus*, than the existence of only one unitary type (cf. Marggraf/Streb 1997: 238). But a diversity of evils is not better than one single evil. Diversity seems to be valuable only in conjunction with other kinds of positive value. To what degree biodiversity is valuable seems to depend on how far that to which diversity is ascribed has a positive value of its own. The value of diversity is, as we might say, *complementary*. It makes whatever is valuable become more valuable. But this is only the case if what it makes more valuable is valuable in its own right. In this respect, diversity, taken as a value concept, can be compared to the concept of *rarity*. Like diversity, rarity cannot reasonably be taken to be an intrinsic value. The fact that something is rare does not entail that it deserves to be preserved (cf. Krieger 1973: 449). Nevertheless, rarity increases the urgency of the need, and the importance of the corresponding norm, to preserve whatever has a value of its own. The fact that a natural individual, an ecosystem or a landscape is rare is an additional reason to preserve it.

If biodiversity cannot be seriously taken to be an intrinsic value, the value of biodiversity, and the necessity to preserve it, must be founded on *extrinsic* values. Which values? I think that there is no single answer to this question, but that the answer must be differentiated according to whether the biodiversity in question is primarily of a *global* or primarily of a *local* kind. On the global level, the relevant extrinsic values are mainly *instrumental* values, on the local level, mainly *inherent* ones. "Instrumental" and "inherent" are in this context understood in the sense given to them by C. I. Lewis and made popular in environmental ethics by William Frankena (1979: 13). According to this usage, natural items have an *instrumental* value as far as they are actually or potentially useful for human beings or for sentient animals, for example as conditions of intrinsically valuable states such as health, safety and subjective well-being. Inherent values of natural items, on the other hand, are such that they become, or are able to become objects of intrinsically valuable states, for example as objects of contemplative (aesthetic, religious or metaphysical) attitudes. Biodiversity has instrumental values to the extent that it contributes to the usefulness of nature for men and other sentient animals. It has inherent value to the extent that it has qualities of beauty, sublimity, or holiness.

The instrumental value of biodiversity is of a direct or an indirect kind. Its direct value lies in maintaining and improving human living conditions, its indirect value in securing the functioning of ecosystems and in functioning as potential sources of natural resources, medicines and bionic models. These services are rendered by biodiversity to mankind as a whole, independently of the geographical location at which it can and should be protected. What is important is that a sufficiently diverse stock of species, alleles, and types of ecosystems is preserved. For the ongoing replacement of antibiotics by new medicines for infectious diseases, for example, the only thing that matters is that as many biological species as possible are preserved that might serve as components of the required new substances. It does not matter where exactly these species are preserved.

This is different with the inherent values of biodiversity. These are more frequently bound to certain regions and landscapes and less substitutable. Inherent values of natural diversity cannot, as a rule, be "transplanted" without serious loss. The reason is that they are much more dependent on cultural context. Aesthetic value is highly dependent on culturally framed perceptions, and relative to local traditions and narratives. It is true, biodiversity can hardly be said to be an aesthetic value of its own. But biodiversity completes and enriches the aesthetic value of nature (cf. Pimlott 1974: 41). There may be some aesthetic value even in a uniform hypertrophied meadow without any natural variety. But "how much more powerful," an enthusiastic biologist writes, "is the beauty of a natural meadow in which a myriad of species and colours meet in the smallest spot, against a background of thousand shades of green" (Erhardt 1996: 133). Like the old towns of big cities with their historically grown, irregular and diversified houses in the midst of uniform modern blocks of offices, the oases of natural diversity with their richness of trees, hedges and meadows in the midst of monocultures are an aesthetic attraction. Though the relations between diversity and aesthetic are complex – some people find monotonous landscapes inspiring, others may prefer a less diverse but more familiar kind of nature to a more diverse but less well-known kind of nature –, it can hardly be doubted that aesthetic reasons are among the strongest to maintain a high level of biodiversity.

Cultural context is important also for the preservation of natural diversity for historical reasons. Local biodiversity is a cultural value and should be preserved where it constitutes a tradition. As far as biodiversity has cultural value, its preservation is a matter of preserving the cultural heritage and providing for opportunities of face-to-face encounters with earlier stages of natural history. In this case, the diversity that matters is the diversity of "local" nature, the diversity characteristic of the "traditional" landscape, and the diversity we find represented in cultural products of the past such as art and literature. In this, natural items are paramount that carry symbolic meaning and have become objects of allegory, such as (in Europe) eagle, fox, bear, wolf, and serpent.

## 4 Why preserve biodiversity?

It is widely agreed that preserving biodiversity is an important political objective. But people are deeply divided on the reasons why this should be so. There are, roughly, two fundamentally distinct avenues (which, however, can be combined). The first avenue is what might be called *ontological*. It ascribed to biodiversity, or to the natural items by which it is constituted, an intrinsic value independent of all present and future human valuations and which is not in any way affected by value changes. In respect of the aesthetic value of nature, a value of this kind is defended by the American philosopher and preservationist Holmes

Rolston: "It takes considerable straining even after studying philosophy, to accept the idea that the beauty of the sunset is only in the eye of the beholder." (Rolston 1986: 44) An approach of this kind provides a strong, but possibly too strong, defence of the preservation of biodiversity. It meets, above all, with a metaethical objection. It is far from clear what it means that a value exists independently from all valuation. Values are not simply given, they originate in valuations. It is certainly not accidental that the values for which philosophers like Plato, Scheler, or Jonas claimed an objective status independent of any kind of valuation, were, in each single case, in one-to-one correspondence with the personal values of these philosophers and exhibited obvious traits of temporal and cultural relativity. If there were such values, this correspondence must seem strange.

The alternative is a "want-regarding" approach that bases obligations of preservation on instrumental and contemplative values of which it can be assumed that they persist in future generations of human and other sentient animals and which depend for their satisfaction, wholly or partly, on the preservation of the natural heritage (Birnbacher 2014). This kind of approach starts from much weaker value premises but is otherwise much more robust. That something that satisfies the needs of a human or other animal is something valuable is a nearly universally shared value premise. In comparison to an ontological axiology, a want-regarding axiology is universalisable to a much greater extent. It is definitely better suited to meet the universalisation requirements of a corresponding morality.

However, it might seem that this basis is too weak to do the work it is expected to do and to function as a foundation for obligations of preserving biodiversity. This impression might be corrected by three considerations:

First, the concrete wants and desires of later generation are difficult to predict. We cannot make any safe prognoses about which values later generations will adopt. The only thing we know from history is that there is sometimes rapid, sometimes slow value change which does not leave unaffected cultural ideals and the loyalty to traditions. In view of the uncertainties about the directions in which cultural preferences, including preferences for natural variety, will develop, there is, thus, at least a prima facie obligation to preserve the existing natural capital. This was already recognised by the "want-regarding" moral philosopher John Stuart Mill who replied to the proposal of his correspondence partner Auguste Comte to systematically eradicate all animal and plant species without evident usefulness to man: "As if anyone could presume to assert that the smallest weed may not, as knowledge advances, be found to have some property serviceable to man" (Mill 1969: 357). We should not restrict the options open to future generations by making present needs and values the standard of which natural items deserve to be preserved and which do not, and to irreversibly destroy what seems dispensable from our present perspective. The same holds for inherent natural values. The aesthetic and other uses of nature beyond instrumental value are themselves of a great variety, and this can be expected to remain so in the future. There is, however, no better reason for the preservation of diversity than the diversity of what is loved and valued in nature.

A second consideration in favour of preservation is that many people value the preservation of natural and cultural resources independently of whether they make use of these resources or intend to use them in the future. As the social science method of contingent valuation shows, there are other dimensions of value in these resources than their instrumental value: *option value* – the value of leaving open the option of using it in the future (people want woods to be preserved without making any kind of use of it), *existence value* – the value of knowing that public good exists and will exist in the future, and *legacy value* – the value of knowing that a public good is saved for later generations (cf. Pommerehne 1987: 178). It is true, one has to be cautious against overinterpreting values found by testing willingness to pay. Since these tests require no real but only hypothetical negotiations between values, there can be no guarantee that the people claiming to recognise these values would stick to these values if confronted with the costs and opportunity costs of realising them. Not everyone who has strong opinions on the preservation of natural diversity is prepared to accept higher taxes for financing it. What is brought to light by contingent valuation is rather desire than will. But this method is none the less useful because it shows that individual preferences extend far beyond individual utility. Of course, how far these values make themselves felt in political strategies of resource use will strongly depend on the economic well-being of the respective society.

A third consideration refers to the change of preferences that goes together with continued economic growth and, in consequence, with a decrease in the part of income necessary for subsistence. It is highly probable that there will be further progress in well-being (possibly interrupted by periods of stagnation) in the future, due, amongst others, to the continuing progress of science, technology and medicine. In contrast to popular scepticism, a progressive scenario is clearly suggested by the global trends of the last decades. It is also reflected in the perception of the majority of people. Most people would prefer, if they could choose, to live in the future than in the past or in the present – obviously because they think that they will then be able to make use of even more means that alleviate life. Though extrapolations like Ronald Inglehart's theory of a "postmaterialist" society (Inglehart 1977) have not fully stood the test of reality, it can be expected that, with the increasing saturation of basic needs, "higher" needs will become more and more important, including preferences for natural and aesthetic values. It is probable that the interest in experiencing nature in a state unspoiled by civilisation will increase, if only as a consequence of its increasing rarity. There are only few areas on the planet where civilisation recedes. The general tendency is that more and more areas are permeated by human activities, with the consequence of a simplified and impoverished nature.

If the preservation of biodiversity can be justified with a view to the probability of increased future interest in a differentiated experience of nature, it seems plausible not only to postulate the preservation of biodiversity in a conservative sense, but also – wherever possible without jeopardising other legitimate ecological or non-ecological aims – its deliberate production. Though a principle of actively enriching nature is not part of the predominantly conservative tendency of preservation ethics – an extreme case is David Ehrenfeld's *Noah principle:* "Long-standing existence in nature is deemed to carry with it the unimpeachable right to continued existence" (Ehrenfeld 1978: 208) –, a principle of exclusively conservative protection of biodiversity is unsatisfactory. As an absolute principle it would imply the obligation (indorsed by Ehrenfeld) to protect even Variola, the pathogen producing smallpox. More importantly, it neglects the enrichment brought to nature by human interventions such as by cultivation and breeding. Among the approaches to nature ethics this avenue has been taken, notably, by Nicholas Rescher's theory of biodiversity protection (Rescher 1980: 90–91). Remarkably, this further step was also made by some of the legal codifications of preservation. The German *Bundesnaturschutzgesetz*, for example, goes so far as to proclaim in its first paragraph the aim of *developing* nature and landscapes along with the aims of *preserving* and *protecting* it. "Development" encourages active interventions over and above the restoration of an earlier or "original" state of nature. Biodiversity, it seems, is too important to leave it to nature itself.

# References

Augustine (1955): *The Problem of Free Choice*. Trans. and annotated by Dom Mark Pontifex. Westminster, MD/London: The Newman Press/Longmans, Green and Co.
Birnbacher, Dieter (2014): "Biodiversity and the 'Substitution Problem'." In: Lanzerath, Dirk/Friele, Minou (Eds.): *Concepts and Values in Biodiversity*. London/New York, NY: Routledge, pp. 39–54.
Ehrenfeld, David (1978): *The Arrogance of Humanism*. New York, NY: Oxford University Press.
Erhardt, Andreas (1996): "Die Schönheit der Natur aus der Sicht eines Biologen." In: Lesch, Walter (Ed.): *Naturbilder – Ökologische Kommunikation zwischen Ästhetik und Moral*. Basel: Birkhäuser, pp. 127–145.

Frankena, William K. (1979): "Ethics and the Environment." In: Goodpaster, Kenneth /Sayre, Kenneth M. (Eds.): *Ethics and Problems of the 21st Century*. Notre Dame, IN: University of Notre Dame Press, pp. 3–20.
Germany (2009): *Gesetz über Naturschutz und Landschaftspflege*. https://dejure.org/gesetze/BNatSch
Inglehart, Ronald (1977): *The Silent Revolution: Changing Values and Political Styles among Western Publics*. Princeton, NJ: Princeton University Press.
Krieger, Martin H. (1973): "What's Wrong with Plastic Trees?" In: *Science* 179 (4072), pp. 446–455.
Lanzerath, Dirk/Friele, Minou (Eds.) (2014): *Concepts and Values in Biodiversity*. London/New York, NY: Routledge.
Leibniz, Gottfried Wilhelm (1965): "Eclaircissement des difficultés que Monsieur Bayle a trouvées dans le systeme nouveau de l'union de l'ame et du corps." In: *Die philosophischen Schriften*. Vol. 4. Edited by C. J. Gerhardt. Hildesheim: Olms, pp. 547–571.
Leopold, Aldo (1949): "The Land Ethic." In: *A Sand County Almanac and Sketches Here and There*. New York, NY: Oxford University Press, pp. 201–226.
Lovejoy, Arthur O. (1972): "Plenitude and Sufficient Reason in Leibniz and Spinoza." In: Frankfurt, Harry G. (Ed.): *Leibniz: A Collection of Critical Essays*. Garden City, NY: Anchor Books, pp. 281–334.
Marggraf, Rainer/Streb, Sabine (1997): *Ökonomische Bewertung der natürlichen Umwelt: Theorie, politische Bedeutung, ethische Diskussion*. Heidelberg: Spektrum Akademischer Verlag.
Meyer, Kirsten (2003): *Der Wert der Natur: Begründungsvielfalt im Naturschutz*. Paderborn: Mentis.
Mill, John Stuart (1969): "Auguste Comte and Positivism." In: *The Collected Works of John Stuart Mill*. Vol. 10. Edited by John M. Robson. Toronto: University of Toronto Press/London: Routledge and Kegan Paul, pp. 261–368.
Oksanen, Markku/Pietarien, Juhani (Eds.) (2004): *Philosophy and Biodiversity*. Cambridge: Cambridge University Press.
Pimlott, Douglas H. (1974): "The Value of Diversity." In: Bailey, James A./Elder, William/McKinney, Ted D. (Eds.): *Readings in Wildlife Conservation*. Washington, D.C.: Wildlife Society, pp. 31–43.
Pommerehne, Werner W. (1987): *Präferenzen für öffentliche Güter*. Tübingen: Mohr Siebeck.
Rescher, Nicholas (1980): "Why Save Endangered Species?" In: *Unpopular Essays on Technological Progress*. Pittsburgh, PA: University of Pittsburgh Press, pp. 79–92.
Rolston III, Holmes (1986): "Can and Ought We to Follow Nature?" In: *Philosophy Gone Wild: Essays in Environmental Ethics*. Buffalo, NY: Prometheus Books, pp. 30–52.
Steinvorth, Ulrich (1994): *Warum überhaupt etwas ist: Kleine demiurgische Metaphysik*. Reinbek: Rowohlt.
Taylor, Paul W. (1986): *Respect for Nature: A Theory of Environmental Ethics*. Princeton, NJ: Princeton University Press
Thomas Aquinas (1905): *Of God and His Creatures*. An annotated translation (with some abridgement) of the *Summa contra Gentiles* of Saint Thomas Aquinas by Joseph Rickaby S.J. London: Burns & Oates.

United Nations (1992): *Convention on Biological Diversity.* https://www.cbd.int/convention/articles/?a=cbd-02

Wägele, Johann-Wolfgang (2014): "The Necessity for Biodiversity Research: We Are Responsible for the Quality of Life of Coming Generations." In: Lanzerath, Dirk/Friele, Minou (Eds.): *Concepts and Values in Biodiversity.* London/New York, NY: Routledge, pp. 23–38.

Stephen M. Gardiner
# Should We Embrace a "New," Expansionist Agenda for the Virtues?
On Planetary Magnificence and Planetary Magnanimity in the (Alleged) Anthropocene

**Abstract:** Does the evolving influence of humanity on the Earth's environment call for new virtues? How might such virtues be seen as contributing to human flourishing? In this paper, I develop Aristotle's discussion of magnificence and magnanimity to provide a framework within which to discuss such claims. I also defend the controversial view that even if genuinely new virtues may be involved, these may be virtues to which we should not aspire (now, or perhaps ever).

**Keywords:** Virtue ethics, Aristotle's ethics, unity of the virtues, Anthropocene, planetary virtues

> *Most of all, we must not see the Anthropocene as a crisis, but as the beginning of a new geological epoch ripe with human-directed opportunity.*
> – Erle Ellis: "The Planet of No Return: Human Resilience on an Artificial Earth"

Does the recent, dramatic upsurge in humanity's influence on the Earth imply that we need a new virtue ethics? Does the increase in humanity's reach entail an *expansion* of the field of virtue beyond its traditional limits? In particular, might it unleash new, hitherto inaccessible virtues? And would this open up transformative possibilities for human flourishing? These are live questions in what some term a new geological era on the planet, the Anthropocene or age of humans. Notably, some wish to embrace expansion, calling for new virtues and positive visions of flourishing that embody them (e.g., Jenkins 2016; Thomp-

---

**Note:** This paper is part of a broader project. Earlier versions were presented at the International Wittgenstein Symposium (2019), the University of Bergen (2019), the University of Vienna (2017), the American Philosophical Association (2017), the University of Reading (2019), the Institute for Future Studies in Stockholm (2019), and the Cerisy Conferences (2019). I thank these audiences, and especially Paul Bowman, Matthew Coffay, Jamie Draper, Goran Duss-Otterstrom, Augustin Fragniéré, Espen Gamlund, Sally Haslanger, Clare Heyward, Gérald Hess, Dale Jamieson, Willis Jenkins, Angela Kallhoff, Catriona McKinnon, Alex McLaughlin, Lukas Meyer, Ed Page, Corine Pelluchon, Barbara Reiter, Allen Thompson, Steve Vanderheiden, and Josh Wells. A French-language version will appear in the conference proceedings for the Cerisy Conferences, translated by Gérald Hess.

https://doi.org/10.1515/9783110702255-023

son 2012). Others, by contrast, find the whole idea irresponsible and objectionable (e.g., Hamilton 2013).

My aim in this paper is to provide a framework within which to understand these issues. (It is not to defend a particular view, which I defer for another occasion.) In general, I argue that my earlier, Neo-Aristotelian account of the basic and nonbasic virtues provides a good starting-point for thinking about the place of virtue in the (alleged) Anthropocene, and also about expansions of the domain of virtue in other settings (Gardiner 2001).

More specifically, I suggest (first) that there may well be reasons to identify new virtues of "planetary management" that occupy a similar conceptual space to Aristotle's magnificence and magnanimity, and (second) that these virtues – "planetary magnificence" and "planetary magnanimity" – may well be genuine virtues. Nevertheless, I argue (third) that this alone does not guarantee that we have good reason to pursue them and the associated expansion of the field of virtue. Put crudely, the virtues of the (alleged) new era may (paradoxically) be virtues to which we should not aspire, at least not yet, and perhaps not ever. Consequently, positing new virtues serves only to raise central questions about the ethics of human expansion; it does not resolve them. Instead, a deeper debate is needed. While planetary management is my example in this paper, the overall lesson applies to the ethics of human expansion in general.

## 1 Two puzzles

I begin with two puzzles. The first is theoretical. From the point of view of the classical tradition, the whole idea of expanding the domain of virtue to reveal new virtues looks problematic. Most classical virtue ethicists, including Socrates, Plato, and Aristotle, assert the *universal reciprocity of the virtues* (URV): a person can have one of the virtues if and only if she has all of them. Yet URV creates difficulties for the notion of expanding the field of virtue to include new virtues, since it invites an unhappy dilemma.

The first horn of the dilemma emerges from the most obvious interpretation of expansion, as involving genuinely new virtues, that is virtues that are of the same kind and standing as the traditional virtues, yet which were hitherto inaccessible. In light of URV, this vision of expansion appears to have radical implications. Specifically, if all of the virtues are needed in order to have any virtues, it seems that *no one can have the traditional virtues without having the new virtues as well:* for instance, no one can be genuinely brave, temperate, or generous without also having the virtues of planetary management. Unfortunately, this view is unattractively demanding. One reason is that it implies that at this point in human history no one has ever been virtuous, or even ever *could* have been virtuous. Thus, Socrates, for example, had none of the traditional virtues (e.g., courage, temperance, generosity) and neither has any other human being who has yet existed. Achieving any virtue must await the time when virtuous planetary management becomes possible. Prior to that point, none of the other virtues are accessible.

The other horn of the dilemma emerges from a more conservative reading of "expansion." Suppose we concede that talk of "new" virtues is misleading and say instead that expanding the field of virtue merely involves increasing the domain of the traditional virtues. Thus, the "new" virtues of expansion actually only require something "old" (the traditional virtues), which we effectively already have when we have normal virtue, but which now needs to be opened out into an expanded field. On this view, adjusting to expansions of agency may well be a substantial task, and one that involves reorienting the traditional virtues. Still, since adjustment does not require genuinely new virtues, it need not fall under the universal reciprocity thesis. Thus, it might avoid "disenfranchising" Socrates and other past moral exemplars.

One problem with the conservative approach is that it appears deflationary. "Expansion" merely increases the domain of existing virtues. At a minimum, the rhetoric of "new" virtues looks exaggerated, inappropriate, and misleading. Moreover, in context the proposed transformation of virtue ethics for the (alleged) new age of humans becomes much less dramatic. Since what is needed is still the traditional virtues (albeit in expanded domains), it is unclear why a fundamental reorientation of virtue ethics itself is required.

A second, more important problem is that the conservative account suggests that those with the traditional virtues already have all the virtue they need to deal with a changing world, even one that is changing very radically. This may seem unduly optimistic. For instance, we appear to be left saying that Socrates and his fellow moral exemplars are already more or less equipped to become virtuous planetary managers. Yet this might appear to attribute a kind of omnipotence to the virtuous that seems highly complacent, and perhaps naïve. Again, this is a troublingly bold and unattractive view.

In summary, universal reciprocity presents us with a dilemma. On the one hand, if the virtues of expansion are genuinely new virtues, then URV appears to make virtue troublingly inaccessible for vast periods of human history. On the other hand, if the virtues of expansion are mere aspects of traditional virtues, filling in previously inaccessible domains of those virtues, then we appear to embrace an overly ambitious account of the (ordinarily) virtuous person that fails to take seriously the extent to which expansions of the field of virtue may require new skills and perceptual abilities. The (ordinarily) virtuous appear to be ascribed extreme abilities that, at the extreme, amount to a kind of omnipotence.

In light of this dilemma, virtue ethicists should be open to considering alternative theoretical frameworks. Fortunately, a second puzzle provides independent motivation for rejecting universal reciprocity. URV is already under pressure in Aristotle's ethics. As T. H. Irwin has observed, Aristotle treats two apparent domains of virtue differently, positing two virtues in each rather than the usual one. For wealth, the virtues are generosity and magnificence; for honor, (a nameless virtue that Irwin calls) "proper pride" and magnanimity. Moreover, Aristotle's comments on the relationships between these virtues appear to conflict with URV. Specifically, he says: (1) magnificence requires generosity, but generosity does not require magnificence (EN 1122a28); (2) magnanimity requires proper pride, but proper pride does not require magnanimity (EN 1125b1–8); and (3) temperance does not require magnanimity (EN 1123b5–6) (Irwin 1988; passages in Irwin 1985).

Why does Aristotle posit multiple virtues for wealth and honor? Irwin suggests that the rationale concerns scale: generosity and proper pride are "small-scale" virtues; magnificence and magnanimity are "large-scale" virtues. Irwin is clearly correct that Aristotle's magnificence and magnanimity concern great wealth and great honor. Still, the distinction between large- and small-scale virtues is not really sufficient to explain why two virtues are needed in each domain. Why should scale make a difference, and why only here? Why does the "large-scale" and "small-scale" distinction not arise in other domains, and generate two separate virtues there? For example, why are there not distinct virtues for, say, large-scale temperance (dealing with large pleasures and pains) and small-scale temperance (handling small, or more normal pleasures and pains), or for large-scale courage (confronting large fears) and small-scale courage (addressing small fears)?

## 2 Basic and nonbasic virtues

There are many ways in which a virtue ethicist might approach such questions. My suggestion, based on earlier work, is that Aristotle can be understood (on textual and theoretical grounds) as adopting a more subtle account of the unity of the virtues than URV. Interestingly, this account resonates well with the question of whether there are new virtues of planetary management. The key elements of my account are as follows.

First, Aristotle accepts a distinction between basic and nonbasic virtues. The basic virtues are the familiar core virtues, such as courage, temperance, and generosity. Magnificence and magnanimity are key examples of nonbasic virtues. (For current purposes, I will focus on magnificence, as magnanimity is a more controversial virtue.)

Second, Aristotle endorses the reciprocity of the basic virtues (RBV): a person can have one of the *basic* virtues if and only if she has all of the *basic* virtues. Thus, for example, to have genuine courage, one must also be temperate, generous, and so on; similarly, to have genuine generosity, one must also possess courage, temperance, and the other basic virtues.

Third, the nonbasic virtues stand in a more complex relationship to the basic ones. On the one hand, the nonbasic virtues are dependent on the basic: a person can have a nonbasic virtue if and only if she has the basic virtues. So, for instance, one cannot have magnificence without also having courage, generosity, and the other basic virtues. On the other hand, the reverse is not true. The basic virtues are independent of the nonbasic: a person can have the basic virtues without having any nonbasic virtues. For instance, one can be genuinely brave or temperate or generous (and so on) without having either magnificence or magnanimity, and this is true for the basic virtues as a group.

Fourth, the nonbasic virtues are isolatable from one another: one can have one nonbasic virtue without having any other nonbasic virtues. Hence, for instance, one can be magnanimous without having magnificence, and vice versa.

## 3 Virtues for systematic relative advantage

The complex structure just elaborated calls out for explanation and justification. Here, however, I will argue only that we can make some progress through a more limited account, and that this account is of particular relevance to the issue of planetary management.

My suggestion is that the crucial feature of the large-scale virtues is not their scale as such, but rather that each governs *an essentially relative advantage*: magnificence requires being *relatively* rich; magnanimity requires having *relatively* higher capacities. More explicitly, both virtues concern appropriate conduct when someone is *systematically better placed* than most people, in such a way that this brings on a challenge for ethical action that is *sufficiently different in degree to open up a new difference in kind*.

The idea that new virtues might be needed in such domains has some intuitive appeal. For instance, take magnificence. It seems plausible that being virtuous in handling normal resources (e.g., as governed by generosity) is not the same as being virtuous in handling having dramatically more resources than other people, and that a distinct set of skills is required. Aristotle, for example, sees the virtue of magnificence as associated with the role of being a public benefactor, a person with the resources to make substantial contributions to the public good in ways unavailable to the ordinary citizen.

In our time, we might think of the role of billionaires in public life, including in politics and philanthropy. It is not strange to think that managing this role might require a distinct set of skills, such as abilities to discern the public good, to earn the trust of others in promoting it, to refrain from using the resources to exert inappropriate political power, and so on. Given this, one might say that it is not enough for a billionaire merely to have the regular virtue of generosity. They must also have special abilities for managing the distinctive power that their relative wealth gives them and the corresponding role in the community. Moreover, these skills are distinctive enough to constitute a new virtue, with its own subject-matter, internal logic, and sensitivities. For instance, it seems reasonable to think that acquiring these skills takes an additional period of moral training and habituation beyond those required for the basic virtues. Suppose, for example, that a normally virtuous person suddenly becomes a billionaire. It is not obvious that they are immediately equipped to handle their new wealth well and to take on the role of a public benefactor. The standard (i.e., basic) virtues may not be sufficient to guide them, including the (normal) virtue of generosity in standard settings. Perhaps then their best course of action would be to step back for a while, learn more about their new position of privilege and develop the skills necessary for occupying that role well.

As well as having initial plausibility, the relative advantage account gives a *pro tanto* rationale for why only some people need extra virtues, so that magnificence and magnanimity are not required by everyone in order for them to achieve virtue. Since both nonbasic virtues concern *relative* advantages – advantages that mean that the holder is systematically better placed than other people – these virtues are not of a kind that everyone *could* have *even in principle*. One cannot have a society in which everyone is *relatively* rich compared to others all things considered or has relatively superior capacities; that would be a contradiction in terms. Put another way, the virtues governing systematic relative advantages are inherently what we might call *elite virtues*. They presuppose the existence of various elites (financial and otherwise). Therefore, it makes no sense to say that magnificence and magnanimity are virtues that everyone could have, and perhaps even should have.

Interestingly, the proposal that the elite virtues correspond to essentially relative advantages provides one rationale for the complex structure of basic and nonbasic virtues outlined above. In particular, it is natural to think that while reciprocity applies to the basic virtues, but not the nonbasic, nevertheless the nonbasic virtues remain both dependent on the basic, yet isolatable from one another. The proposal also suggests that special, nonbasic virtues will not be needed in other domains where relative advantage is not an issue or does not give rise to a substantive difference in kind with respect to the ethical challenges to be faced. So, for example, there is no initial reason to propose extra, nonbasic virtues for domains such as fear or temptation. Unless someone can make a convincing case that some people face systematically different relative advantages or disadvantages in these areas (e.g., qualitatively different kinds of fear or temptation), there is no need to posit nonbasic counterparts to the traditional virtues of courage and temperance.

## 4 Planetary virtues

How might the basic-nonbasic virtues framework help us understand the "new" virtues of the (alleged) Anthropocene? In general, those attracted to the idea of an expansion that reveals new virtues appear to be supposing that humanity is attaining a level of power over the rest of nature that opens up the field of special virtues with respect to planetary responsibility that become accessible once humans embrace the task of becoming planetary managers. Given this, I propose that the idea they are reaching for is that the (alleged) new era reveals a need for what we might call distinctive *planetary* virtues of magnanimity and magnificence. In the case of planetary magnanimity, they are enthused about a *new state of superiority* that the advent of the Anthropocene suggests that we now have. In the case of planetary magnificence, they want to embrace the specific role of becoming *potential planetary benefactors*, and the largesse that it enables us to exercise.

Many questions arise about these (alleged) new virtues that cannot be considered here. Still, before moving on, let me highlight one: who are the "we" that are supposed to embody these new positions of systematic relative advantage? The most natural reading of the rhetoric of planetary management is usually that the *"we" are humanity as such*, so that the new virtues are then in some sense for *all of us*, as we (humanity) seek to manage our new superiority over nature as *an elite species*. By contrast, I want to emphasize that a rival, arguably much more realistic, possibility is that the "we" should really be taken to refer to *an elite subsection of humanity*, as determined by social class, nationality, or other relevant factors. In other words, the new virtues of the Anthropocene may turn out to be the virtues needed by those who exercise systematic relative advantages *over the rest of humanity, as well as over the rest of nature*. Like the traditional nonbasic virtues of magnificence and magnanimity, they are virtues for an (allegedly) elite group *of humans*. As we shall now see, in raising this possibility I am not endorsing it, nor am I saying that it is in any way a good thing.

## 5 Resistance to the elite virtues

Resistance to pursuit of the planetary virtues is likely to come from two main sources: from skepticism that they are really realizable, and from opposition based on competing ethical ideals. My focus will be on the second; but let us begin by at least mentioning the first.

Some may worry that the planetary virtues (even if real virtues) are not realizable, and so that it is not virtuous to aspire to them. For instance, they may maintain that planetary magnificence and magnanimity are not appropriate objectives due to technical or political or moral limitations. Consider, for example, radical geoengineering techniques to combat climate change, such as injecting sulfates into the stratosphere to reflect more sunlight and so cool down the surface. It is often observed that such techniques are currently "technological imaginaries," things that are not yet within our capabilities. I have also claimed that they are currently *socio-political imaginaries* – interventions for which we lack the right kinds of institutions, political will, and so on – and *ethical imaginaries* – where we lack the robust ethical frameworks within which such institutions might operate and be conceived.

Notably, some limitations may not be eternal. For instance, perhaps we may yet develop the science and ethics required to make stratospheric sulfate injection (SSI) a reality rather than an imaginary. Still, some constraints may be genuinely permanent. For example, perhaps humanity will never achieve the institutions needed to responsibly govern a genuinely global, multigenerational intervention that lasts hundreds, or perhaps thousands, of years. Another possibility is that some limitations will turn out to be *effectively permanent* given the timescales of our current predicament. For instance, perhaps we are not capable of developing the science necessary for safe SSI quickly enough for it to have any relevance to our current predicament (e.g., if we could manage it by 2300, but not by 2050). In such cases, it may not be consistent with virtue to pursue such expansions.

Let us turn now to resistance based on competing ethical ideals. We can begin with a notable parallel. The classical virtues of magnanimity and magnificence are often regarded negatively from the contemporary point of view, at least among philosophers, as out of keeping with the (alleged) broadly egalitarian ethos of the age. To say that deploying qualitatively superior wealth well or behaving well with respect to one's inherent superiority as a person, seems, to the ear of many in the twenty-first century, to express morally and politically problematic attitudes toward others. Similarly, aspiring to a situation where such virtues become relevant also seems dubious. There are ethical reasons to resist such self-aggrandizement, including that social arrangements that reflect them are toxic in many respects, such as for community, human relationships, and the individual well-being of those of both sides of the (alleged) "superior" and "inferior" divide.

It is not difficult to see parallels between egalitarian resistance to Aristotle's virtues of magnificence and magnanimity, and environmentalist resistance to planetary magnificence and planetary magnanimity. To many, the idea that we should *seek out and then embrace achieving human superiority* over nonhuman nature, and to become *self-styled benefactors of nature* also seems deeply problematic. For one thing, it seems very much in keeping with *past attitudes of domination, arrogance, and hubris* that many believe brought us to the point of environmental crisis in the first place. For another, it seems to display a willingness to take on *burdens of responsibility* for life on the planet to which it is far from clear that it is virtuous to aspire.

Given these parallels, it seems that we can say that even if it may be a genuine human excellence to possess the elite virtues of the (alleged) Anthropocene – e.g., to govern the field of planetary management well – it does not follow from this that these are virtues to which we should aspire. Just as there are egalitarian reasons to resist expanding the field of virtue so that we can pursue the elite virtues of Aristotelian magnificence and magnanimity, so there may be ecological reasons to resist the expansion of virtue into planetary management and its associated virtues. In short, simply noting the possibility of new, previously unattainable virtues becoming accessible is not sufficient to justify pursuit of expansion. That the nonbasic virtues are genuine virtues is not enough; further argument is needed.

## 6 Goodness and flourishing

Aristotle associates the unity of the virtues with those virtues required for being "unconditionally (ἁπλῶς) good." Reading the unity thesis conventionally, as universal reciprocity, he is thereby maintaining that all of the genuine virtues – including magnificence and magnanimity – are required to be genuinely good. If magnificence and magnanimity are understood as elite virtues, virtue would only be within the reach of a few, the elite. If one also accepts my relative good interpretation of the large-scale virtues, this would be necessarily so: since magnificence and magnanimity are by definition only accessible to a limited portion of society, only some can have all the virtues and most will be left out. If goodness requires all of the virtues, then it too will be beyond the grasp of the majority; again, by definition. On this view, goodness is only for the elite.

By contrast, my structural account of the basic and nonbasic virtues suggests an alternative possibility, that only the basic virtues are required for being unconditionally good. Indeed, it is tempting to think that this is what generates and *underwrites* the distinction between basic and nonbasic virtues in the first place: the basic virtues are those required for unconditional goodness, and the nonbasic virtues are those not required for unconditional goodness. This has an important implication. Given that the basic virtues govern nonrelative goods, they are (at least in some sense) accessible to all. Hence, genuine goodness is open to everyone; it is not the province only of an elite.[1]

So, what is meant by "unconditional goodness," and what role does possessing such goodness play? My suggestion is that unconditional goodness is the kind of goodness it is necessary to have in order to count as a virtuous person. Hence, the link with the basic virtues is that the basic virtues are those it is necessary for someone to possess in order to be a genuinely virtuous person. The nonbasic virtues, by contrast, are those not required to be a virtuous person. In light of this, we might say that the basic virtues constitute virtue *proper* (or "simple," "plain," or "basic" virtue), and therefore entail goodness *proper* (or "simple," "plain," or "basic" goodness). Indeed, one might surmise that this is the appropriate sense of "ἁπλῶς" in this context. It signifies the unqualified nature of the assertion of virtue.

Ancient virtue ethicists typically posit tight relationships between virtue, goodness, and human flourishing. Although the exact nature of the connection varies, all agree that virtue is at least necessary for flourishing, while some hold that it is also sufficient. Within my new framework, I propose that we develop this minimal claim by saying that the basic virtues (as a set) are necessary for flourishing, but the nonbasic virtues are not. The importance of virtue proper for flourishing then lies in the basic virtues. Among other things, this delivers the *nonelitist* conclusion that flourishing is accessible to those with only the basic virtues, and so to everyone. The nonbasic virtues are not critical to, or indeed even involved in, that core relationship that stands at the heart of ancient virtue ethics.

The upshot of all this is that the nonbasic virtues stand in a very different relationship to the core concerns of virtue ethics than the basic virtues. In par-

---

[1] On the idea that some kind of universal accessibility is an important requirement for a virtue ethical theory, see Annas (2011).

ticular, whereas the basic virtues are quite central to the project of becoming a virtuous person, and to the pursuit of human flourishing, the nonbasic virtues are not. Critically, we do not have the same, strong reasons to pursue the nonbasic virtues as we do to pursue the basic virtues.

Most notably, the nonbasic virtues do not appear to be necessary for human flourishing. This has important implications. First, it becomes unclear that there are *any* flourishing-based reasons to pursue the nonbasic virtues. Second, even if there are some such reasons (e.g., if the nonbasic virtues add to flourishing in some way), these appear to be of a different order to the reasons to pursue the basic virtues. For acquiring the basic virtues is necessary for goodness and for flourishing; but any contribution to goodness and flourishing that might be made by the nonbasic virtues appears less central.

This framework is useful when we return to understanding our previous discussion. Consider the egalitarian objections to Aristotle's magnificence and magnanimity. Even if these are genuine virtues, since they are nonbasic, there may still not be good reason, all things considered, to pursue them. Since the ordinary virtues (i.e., the basic virtues that constitute virtue proper) are already sufficient for flourishing, there may be no strong grounds based in human flourishing to enter the expanded domain where magnificence and magnanimity are accessible. Moreover, there may be compelling (e.g., egalitarian) reasons to resist expanding the field of virtue.

Turning to the planetary virtues, our framework can also make sense of environmentalist objections to expanding the field of virtue to embrace planetary management. Planetary magnificence and planetary magnanimity may be genuine virtues. Nevertheless, since they are nonbasic virtues, they remain unnecessary for unconditional goodness, virtue proper, and human flourishing. Hence, there may not be good overall reason to expand the domain of virtue in order to pursue them, especially if doing so brings on new risks and there are wider objections.

# 7 Conclusion

I have argued that there may be genuine human excellences to be had relating to human expansion – for example, in governing the field of "planetary management" well in the (alleged) Anthropocene – however, it is not yet clear that these "new" virtues are ones to which we should aspire. This is partly because our limitations imply that opening up the field of virtue in this way may not be something that we should welcome at this point in human history, or perhaps ever. However, it is also because the sense of human excellence involved is nonbasic, and so not necessary for virtue proper or flourishing proper. Both reasons suggest that it may be better to focus more on promoting virtue in existing domains – to achieving a more just, temperate, and generous world, for example – than on pursuing an aggressive expansion of the field of human endeavor into new domains, especially if there are wider objections to expansion. I have not made that argument here. Instead, my claim is the more limited one that my theoretical account provides a valuable framework within which to have the necessary debate. My leading example in this paper concerns planetary management and the possibility of nonbasic virtues of planetary magnificence and planetary magnanimity. However, this is just one, central case. I contend that my framework provides a useful way to think about the ethics of expansion much more generally, whenever agents confront the possibility of opening up new fields of virtuous activity, and especially when thinking about human expansion.

# References

Annas, Julia (2011): *Intelligent Virtue*. Oxford: Oxford University Press.
Ellis, Erle (2011): "The Planet of No Return: Human Resilience on an Artificial Earth." In: *The Breakthrough Journal* 2, pp. 37–46.
Gardiner, Stephen M. (2001): "Aristotle's Basic and Non-basic Virtues." In: *Oxford Studies in Ancient Philosophy* 20, pp. 261–295.
Hamilton, Clive (2013): *Earthmasters: The Dawn of the Age of Climate Engineering*. New Haven, CT: Yale University Press.
Irwin, T. H. (1988): "Disunity in the Aristotelian Virtues." In: *Oxford Studies in Ancient Philosophy* Supplementary Vol. 1988, pp. 61–78.
Irwin, T. H. (1985). *Aristotle: Nicomachean Ethics*. Hackett. 1$^{st}$ edition.
Jenkins, Willis (2016): "The Turn to Virtue in Climate Ethics: Wickedness and Goodness in the Anthropocene." In: *Environmental Ethics* 38(1), pp. 77–96.
Thompson, Allen (2012): "The Virtue of Responsibility for the Global Climate." In: Thompson, Allen/Bendik-Keymer, Jeremy (Eds.): *Ethical Adaptation to Climate Change*. Cambridge, MA: MIT Press, pp. 203–221.

Lukas H. Meyer
# Klimagerechtigkeit

Ererbte Begünstigungen und Status-quo-Erwartungen

**Abstract:** [Climate Justice: Inherited Benefits and Status Quo Expectations] One of the important debates in climate justice is the internationally fair allocation of the remaining intergenerationally just budget of emissions. One important dimension is the historical, namely the contentious issue of the normative significance of past emissions. The paper analyses two arguments in terms of both their shared presuppositions and differing normative implications. The inherited benefits argument is relevant for the international distribution of the remaining permissible emission rights. The argument reflecting special costs of the frustration of legitimate status quo expectations is relevant for an understanding of the just distribution of the costs of the transformation to net-zero emissions within states.

**Keywords:** Climate change, climate justice, inherited benefits, status quo expectations, emission-generating activities, net-zero emissions

**Anmerkung:** Der Beitrag beruht auf früheren Aufsätzen, nämlich insbesondere einerseits auf Meyer/Roser (2010) und Meyer (2013) zur Relevanz historischer Emissionen für die gerechte Allokation des verbleibenden globalen Kohlenstoffbudgets und andererseits auf Meyer/Sanklecha (2011; 2014) zur Relevanz legitimer Erwartungen für die faire Verteilung der Kosten der Transition zu einer so gut wie emissionsfreien Gesellschaft. Die jeweils entwickelten Argumente scheinen in einem Spannungsverhältnis zu stehen. Dieses zu klären war schon der Gegenstand von Vorträgen an der Observer Research Foundation, New Delhi (am 25.09.2018 mit Kommentaren von Shashi Motilal und Sanjay Vashist), an der Universität Marburg, Institut für Philosophie (30.10.2018), an der Princeton University – organisiert von Environmental Institute, Climate Futures Initiative, University Center for Human Values (04.12.2018, zusammen mit Pranay Sanklecha und mit einem Kommentar von Peter Singer) und auf dem Workshop des Internationalen Wittgenstein Symposiums (08.08.2019). Die sehr hilfreiche Kritik und die vielen konstruktiven Hinweise haben zur Entwicklung der neuen These dieses Aufsatzes beigetragen. Für Diskussion danke ich auch insbesondere meinen Grazer Kollegen Gottfried Kirchengast (Klimaphysik) und Karl Steininger (Klimaökonomie). Besonderer Dank auch an Benedikt Namdar (Studentischer Mitarbeiter im Arbeitsbereich Praktische Philosophie der Universität Graz) für die Hilfe bei der redaktionellen Bearbeitung des Beitrags.

https://doi.org/10.1515/9783110702255-024

# 1 Einleitung

Um den globalen Temperaturanstieg auf höchstens 1,5 Grad Celsius zu beschränken, müssen die globalen Emissionen substanziell reduziert werden (siehe United Nations 2015). Unter dieser Vorgabe sind Emissionen (bzw. Emissionsrechte) eine beschränkte Ressource. Das sogenannte verbleibende globale Kohlenstoff- bzw. Emissionsbudget gilt es fair zwischen Staaten aufzuteilen.[1] Angesichts der positiven Korrelation zwischen Wohlergehen- und Emissionsniveaus wird eine solche Verteilung einen erheblichen Einfluss auf die Handlungsmöglichkeiten von Staaten und die innerhalb von Staaten zukünftig realisierbaren Wohlergehenniveaus haben. Die faire Allokation des verbleibenden globalen Kohlenstoffbudgets ist daher von großer Bedeutung.

Schon rein normativ betrachtet sind mehrere Faktoren bei dieser Allokation unter Staaten zu berücksichtigen. Eine der wichtigen und politisch sehr umstrittenen Fragen ist, ob vergangene bzw. historische Emissionen für die Festlegung der Verteilung des verbleibenden globalen Kohlenstoffbudgets zu berücksichtigen sind und, falls ja, wie genau (siehe Meyer/Sanklecha 2017b).

Das nationale Eigeninteresse bestimmt nachweislich die von Staaten in den Verhandlungen vertretenen Positionen auch zu dieser Frage. Zum Beispiel sind die Verpflichtungen, die Staaten unter dem Paris Agreement eingegangen sind, stark abhängig vom historisch erreichten Emissionsniveau (für empirische Evidenz siehe Williges et al. u. B.: Supplementary Information). Offenbar vertreten viele der Akteure mit weit überdurchschnittlichem Emissionsniveau (kurz: hohe Emittenten) die Position, dass sie aufgrund des von ihnen heute erreichten hohen Niveaus Anspruch auf einen höheren Anteil am verbleibenden Emissionsbudget haben, auch wenn sie diese als „*grandfathering*" (Bestandssicherung) bezeichnete Auffassung nicht oder selten öffentlich vertreten. Die gegenteilige zweite Position, dass nämlich der Anteil der hohen Emittent*innen am verbleibenden globalen Budget aufgrund der bereits von ihnen verursachten Emissionen niedriger sein sollte, wurde und wird häufig von Staaten mit historisch und bis heute geringen Emissionsniveaus vertreten, die damit zugleich einen höheren Anteil des verbleibenden Budgets für sich beanspruchen. Gemäß beiden Positionen sind historische Emissionen normativ signifikant. Beide Auffassungen scheinen rechtfertigbar und Begründungen beider Positionen liegen vor (siehe Meyer/Roser 2010; Meyer 2013; Meyer/Sanklecha 2011; 2014).

---

[1] Siehe Williges et al. (u. B.) für eine Diskussion, was als faire Allokation gelten kann und welche Budgets daraus resultieren.

In diesem Beitrag wird gezeigt, inwiefern die beiden Positionen theoretisch miteinander verknüpft sind. Dafür wird zunächst erläutert, welche prinzipiellen Gründe dafürsprechen, ungleiche Begünstigungen aufgrund historischer und vergangener Emissionen zu berücksichtigen, nämlich im Sinne der zweiten oben genannten Position. Dann werden entsprechende Gründe für die erste Position dargelegt. Diese beziehen sich auf die Idee legitimer Erwartungen von hohen Emittenten. Interessanterweise sprechen ähnliche prinzipielle Gründe, vergangene Emissionen für normativ signifikant zu halten, für beide Positionen. Das scheint dafür zu sprechen, dass beide Positionen Gründe ausweisen, die für die Allokation des verbleibenden Emissionsbudgets relevant sind, aber in gegensätzlich gerichteter Weise, nämlich in einer den Anteil der hohen Emittenten entweder herab- oder heraufsetzenden Weise. Das ist aber nicht richtig, weil, wie hier argumentiert, die normativen Implikationen beider Positionen, obgleich sie auf ähnlichen Prämissen beruhen, je andere sind. Das erste Argument spricht, so wird hier argumentiert, für die Herabsetzung des Anteils der (historisch) hohen Emittenten, das zweite nicht für die Heraufsetzung ihres Anteils. Vielmehr sind besonders hohe Kosten der Transformation Einzelner aufgrund der Frustration ihrer legitimen Status-quo-Erwartungen bei der Wahl der staatlichen Strategien der Transformation zu berücksichtigen und gegebenenfalls auszugleichen.[2]

## 2 Die normative Signifikanz von Begünstigungen aus Emissionen generierenden Aktivitäten früher lebender Menschen

Zunächst muss genauer erläutert werden, warum wir über eine faire Verteilung der noch zulässigen Emissionen nachdenken. Es geht um die Verteilung der Begünstigungen, die Personen durch Emissionen generierende Aktivitäten realisieren – durch Handlungen, die Emissionen als unvermeidliche Nebenfolgen haben. Derzeit haben fast alle unserer Aktivitäten, wie etwa die Produktion industrieller Güter, Landwirtschaft oder Flugverkehr, Emissionen als unvermeidliches Ne-

---

[2] Im Weiteren ist davon die Rede, dass Individuen Anspruch auf einen Anteil am verbleibenden globalen Budget haben. Hierbei wird unterstellt, dass alle Menschen einen Anspruch auf gleiche Berücksichtigung haben (für eine Begründung siehe Meyer 2013) und, sofern Unterschiede im Anspruch zwischen Individuen nicht gerechtfertigt werden können, der legitime jeweilige Anteil der Staaten gemäß dem Prinzip der Pro-Kopf-Gleichverteilung von der Zahl der heute und zukünftig lebenden Bewohner*innen der Staaten abhängt. Demnach beruht die faire Allokation des verbleibenden Emissionsbudgets unter Staaten auf der gerechten Verteilung unter Menschen.

benprodukt. Emissionen zu verursachen, ist eine *conditio sine qua non* in Bezug auf die meisten Handlungen, die potenziell zu unserem Wohlergehen beitragen. Während wir keinen unmittelbaren Grund haben, uns für Emissionen als solche zu interessieren, haben wir starke Gründe, an unserem Wohlergehen interessiert zu sein, und daher Interesse an der Erlaubnis, Emissionen zu verursachen, solange sie ein unvermeidliches Nebenprodukt unserer Handlungen sind. Diese Erlaubnisse werden häufig als „Emissionsrechte" bezeichnet. Emissionen zu verteilen ist demnach gleichbedeutend mit der Verteilung von möglichen Begünstigungen, die durch Emissionen generierende Handlungen erzielt werden können.

Die Konsequenzen aus Aktivitäten, die Emissionen als Nebenprodukt haben, unterscheiden sich auf dramatische Weise: Das Wohlfahrtsniveau eines Landes oder einer Region korreliert stark positiv mit den historischen und derzeitigen Emissionsniveaus dieser Länder und Regionen. Hoch industrialisierte Länder sind kausal für über drei Mal so viele Emissionen zwischen 1850 und 2002 verantwortlich wie Entwicklungsländer (vgl. Baumert/Herzog/Pershing 2005). Obwohl die Industrialisierung der heutigen einkommensstarken Länder einen sehr großen Anteil der Treibhausgase in der Atmosphäre verursacht hat, haben Menschen, die in Entwicklungs- oder Schwellenländern leben und leben werden (und das sind weit mehr Menschen als in den einkommensstarken Ländern), durchschnittlich nicht nur weniger Begünstigungen aus Emissionen generierenden Aktivitäten, sondern leiden überproportional stärker unter den Konsequenzen des Klimawandels (vgl. United Nations Population Fund 2014). Hier sehen wir ab von der ebenfalls kontrovers diskutierten Frage, wer für Kompensationsmaßnahmen für nichtvermiedene und als unvermeidlich geltende Klimaschäden aufzukommen hat (siehe aber Meyer 2013: 609–614; Wallimann-Helmer et al. 2019). Es soll nur um die ungleichen Begünstigungen gehen, die heute und zukünftig Lebende aufgrund der Konsequenzen vergangener Emissionen generierender Aktivitäten realisieren.

Sollten die begünstigenden Konsequenzen historischer Emissionen für eine gerechte Verteilung der verbleibenden zulässigen Emissionen unter gegenwärtig Lebenden als relevant erachtet werden? Wenn ja, wie? Wir können mehrere Haupteinwände gegen das Ausgleichen vergangener Emissionen unterscheiden:
1. Die Vereinigten Staaten beispielsweise haben über die Hälfte ihrer Emissionen vor 1975 verursacht. Posner und Weisbach (2007) weisen darauf hin, dass die Hälfte aller heute lebenden amerikanischen Bürger*innen nach 1975 geboren wurden und über 27 Prozent jünger als 20 Jahre sind (Posner/Weisbach 2007: 103). Diese jungen Amerikaner*innen könnten einwenden: „Warum sollten wir für das Fehlverhalten unserer Vorfahr*innen verantwortlich sein?" Dieser Einwand hält fest, dass gegenwärtig lebende Menschen nicht für die

Handlungen ihrer Vorfahr*innen verantwortlich gemacht und nicht allein deshalb benachteiligt werden sollten, weil jene, die zuvor in ihrem Land lebten, zu viel emittiert haben.
2. Anderen Autor*innen folgend schlagen Posner und Weisbach (2007) vor, zwischen jenen Treibhausemissionen, die entstanden sind, bevor das Problem des menschlich verursachten Klimawandels gut bekannt war und weithin als solches anerkannt wurde, und denen danach zu unterscheiden (Posner/Weisbach 2007: 104). Für die Zeit davor könnten viele einwenden: „Wir wussten nichts vom Treibhauseffekt." Dieser Einwand hält fest, dass Personen Handlungen, die andere tatsächlich schädigen, nur vorgeworfen werden können, wenn sie von den schädigenden Konsequenzen ihrer Handlungen wussten oder hätten wissen sollen. Es scheint zweifelhaft, dass die meisten Menschen vor z. B. 1990 über die schädigenden Effekte von Emissionen wissen konnten (vgl. Posner/Weisbach 2007: 104, 110; Posner/Weisbach 2007: 110–116, Diskussion des *„culpability problem"*).
3. Ein dritter genereller Einwand interpretiert das Nicht-Identitätsproblem für die Konsequenzen vergangener Handlungen gegenwärtig und zukünftig lebender Menschen wie folgt: Niemand kann behaupten, dass es ihm oder ihr schlechter oder besser geht, als es ihm*ihr gehen würde, wenn früher Lebende eine andere Umweltpolitik verfolgt hätten. Denn dann hätte es die Personen, die heute leben, als Personen mit genau ihrer personalen Identität mit hoher Wahrscheinlichkeit nicht gegeben.[3]

Die Einwände betreffen unterschiedliche Teilmengen der in der Vergangenheit verursachten Emissionen. Der erste Einwand ist für Emissionen von Menschen relevant, die nicht mehr leben; der zweite Einwand betrifft Emissionen, so soll hier angenommen werden, die vor der Veröffentlichung des ersten Sachstands-

---

[3] Das Nicht-Identitätsproblem beruht auf der Annahme, dass zukünftig Lebende durch Handlungen nicht geschädigt (oder begünstigt) werden können, die zu den notwendigen Bedingungen ihrer Existenz als Individuen zählen. Vgl. hierzu Parfit (1984: 351–379). Hier wird angenommen, dass dies gilt. An anderer Stelle wurde erstens gezeigt, dass diese Annahme unter anderem ein bestimmtes Verständnis von Schädigung bzw. Begünstigung voraussetzt: Menschen werden durch eine Handlung geschädigt bzw. begünstigt, wenn es ihnen aufgrund dieser Handlung schlechter bzw. besser geht, als es ihnen ginge, wäre die Handlung unterblieben. Zweitens kann das alternative Schwellenwertverständnis von Schädigung dem Nicht-Identitätsproblem ausweichen: Menschen sind durch Handlungen geschädigt, wenn sie dadurch unter einen bestimmten Schwellenwert des Wohlergehens fallen. Auf den Vergleich, wie es ihnen ergangen wäre, wäre die Handlung unterblieben, kommt es nicht an. Demnach können solche Handlungen als schädigend für zukünftig Lebende ausgewiesen werden, selbst wenn sie konstitutiv für ihre Existenz sind. Für eine Diskussion dieser Themen siehe allgemein Meyer (2003).

berichts des Intergovernmental Panel on Climate Change (IPCC) aus dem Jahre 1990 verursacht wurden;[4] und der dritte kann in Zusammenhang mit Emissionen (und Regelungen, die Emissionen beeinflussen) aufgebracht werden, die früh genug passierten, um ein einflussreicher Kausalfaktor für die personale Identität heute lebender Menschen zu sein.

Trotz dieser Einwände sind aber, so wird hier argumentiert, historische Emissionen, wenn auch nicht alle, für die gerechte Verteilung des verbleibenden Emissionsbudgets unter heute und zukünftig lebenden Menschen relevant. Die drei Einwände sprechen nicht dagegen, einen gewissen Teil vergangener Emissionen einzubeziehen, nämlich die folgenden zwei Arten von Emissionen: erstens die von heute lebenden Menschen in ihrer Lebenszeit verursachten Emissionen und zweitens die Emissionen generierenden Aktivitäten von früher Lebenden, soweit sie begünstigende Konsequenzen für heute und zukünftig Lebende haben.

Der erste Vorschlag, vergangene Emissionen zu berücksichtigen, beruht darauf, dass Personen bei der Zuteilung der verbleibenden Emissionen in Bezug auf die von ihnen in ihrer Gesamtlebenszeit realisierten Begünstigungen aus Emissionen generierenden Aktivitäten fair berücksichtigt werden. Nehmen wir an, das hier gültige Verteilungsprinzip sei die Pro-Kopf-Gleichverteilung von Emissionsrechten.[5] Nun könnte man meinen, Menschen sollten Tag für Tag über gleich viele Emissionsrechte verfügen. Für Gleichverteilung über die Gesamtlebenszeit von Menschen spricht, dass Menschen Emissionen nicht von Zeit zu Zeit verursachen (siehe Holtung/Lippert-Rasmussen 2007 sowie Hurka 1993: 9–22). Die Notwendigkeit, Emissionen zu verursachen, kommt nicht nur sporadisch auf. Vielmehr gilt, dass Emissionen generierende Tätigkeiten gar nicht vermieden werden

---

[4] Siehe Houghton/Jenkins/Ephraums (1990). Dies ist eine stark vereinfachende Annahme. Zur Diskussion, ab wann Menschen Wissen um die Konsequenzen des Klimawandels zuschreibbar und ihr Nichtwissen vorwerfbar ist, siehe z. B. Gosseries (2004: 36, 40) (Auflistung und Diskussion einiger Daten, die als eine Alternative zu 1990 angesehen werden könnten: 1840 (wie im Brazilian Proposal vorgeschlagen), 1896 (erster wissenschaftlicher Text über den Treibhauseffekt von Svante Arrhenius), 1967 (erste ernsthafte Modellierungsversuche) und 1995 (der zweite IPCC-Bericht)). Der Ansatz, einen Zeitpunkt festlegen zu wollen, ab welchem für alle Akteur*innen gleichermaßen gilt, dass sie über die relevanten Wissensbestände verfügen konnten bzw. ab dem ihnen ihr Nichtwissen vorwerfbar ist, macht bereits stark vereinfachende Annahmen, wie Stephen M. Gardiner in Diskussion hervorgehoben hat. Möglich scheint, diese Frage als eine des Grades von Wissen zu verstehen und zwischen individuellen Personen und Akteur*innen zu unterscheiden. Diese Diskussion wird hier nicht geführt, sondern stark vereinfachend 1990 als Datum gewählt.

[5] Es lässt sich zeigen, dass ohne historische Emissionen zu berücksichtigen, auch nicht strikt egalitäre Prinzipien der Verteilung, insbesondere die sogenannte Vorrangsicht, wenigstens gleiche Verteilung von Emissionsrechten verlangen.

können. Emissionen zu verursachen ist heute für nahezu alle Tätigkeiten und in allen Lebensphasen notwendig. Dies wird in der vorhersehbaren Zukunft auch weiterhin so bleiben. Die Transformation zu einer nahezu emissionsfreien Wirtschaft und Gesellschaft ist, so der weitgehende Konsens unter den Klimawissenschaftler*innen, bis 2050 zu realisieren, sollen die Konsequenzen des sogenannten „gefährlichen Klimawandels" vermieden werden, die ab einer Erhöhung der globalen Durchschnittstemperatur von über 1,5 oder 2 Grad Celsius erwartet werden (siehe United Nations 2015: Artikel 4 in Verbindung mit Artikel 2). Die Transformation setzt voraus, dass Treibhausgase in hohem Ausmaß vermieden werden oder, nachdem sie verursacht wurden, kompensiert oder extrahiert werden. Die Kosten, die diese Transformation für Einzelstaaten, Regionen, aber auch für Individuen mit sich bringt, werden voraussichtlich stark davon abhängen, wie viele Emissionen diese Akteure im Prozess der Transformation noch werden verursachen dürfen. Denn davon (und dem jeweiligen derzeitigen Emissionsniveau) hängt ab, wie hoch die durchschnittliche Reduktionsrate sein muss, um das Ziel einer emissionsneutralen Zukunft in ca. drei Dekaden zu erreichen, also wie einschneidend die Reduktionsmaßnahmen und wie umfänglich die Kompensations- und Extraktionsmaßnahmen dafür sein müssen.

Bezieht sich die Forderung auf einen fairen Anteil des verbleibenden Emissionsbudgets auf die Gesamtlebenszeit von Individuen, sind die Emissionen, die gegenwärtig Lebende bisher in ihrem Leben verursacht haben, einzubeziehen. Dabei handelt es sich offenbar nur um einen kleinen Teil aller bisher von Menschen verursachten Emissionen. Steht ein fairer Anteil von Emissionen für einen fairen Anteil an Begünstigungen aus Emissionen generierenden Aktivitäten, haben Menschen in hoch industrialisierten Ländern bereits jetzt typischerweise in hohem Umfang Begünstigungen aus ihren eigenen Emissionen generierenden Aktivitäten realisiert. Wollen wir eine gleiche Pro-Kopf-Verteilung von Begünstigungen erzielen, dann gilt Folgendes: Ein großer Teil der Erlaubnisse für begünstigende Emissionen generierende Tätigkeiten müsste an jene gehen, die in Entwicklungsländern leben und bisher typischerweise viel weniger solcher Begünstigungen in ihrem Lebensvollzug realisiert haben. So kann für überdurchschnittlich hohe Pro-Kopf-Emissionsrechte für die meisten Menschen in Entwicklungsländern argumentiert werden – auf Basis der Ungleichheit vergangener Emissionen, die gegenwärtig lebende Menschen im Laufe ihres Lebens produziert haben.

Nachdem es sich bei diesen Emissionen um jene handelt, die gegenwärtig lebende Generationen selbst verursacht haben, sprechen sowohl der erste als auch der der dritte Einwand klarerweise nicht dagegen, sie einzubeziehen. Menschen haben aber möglicherweise manche ihrer vergangenen Emissionen in unverschuldeter Unwissenheit der Konsequenzen dieser Handlungen für den

Klimawandel verursacht. Hier wird vereinfachend angenommen, das gilt für Emissionen vor 1990 (siehe Fußnote 4). Man könnte dementsprechend auf den zweiten Einwand Bezug nehmen und dafür argumentieren, einen Teil der vergangenen Emissionen heute Lebender zu entschuldigen: Sofern sie nicht wissen konnten, durch ihre Emissionen generierenden Aktivitäten zum Klimawandel beizutragen, oder ihr Unwissen ihnen nicht vorzuwerfen war, können diese Handlungen ihnen unter dieser Beschreibung nicht vorgeworfen werden. Das dem Argument zugrundeliegende Verteilungsprinzip bezieht sich aber nicht auf vorwerfbare Handlungen, sondern auf ungleiche Verteilungen von Wohlergehen aufgrund der je eigenen Emissionen generierenden Handlungen unter der Annahme, dass Menschen, gleich wo sie leben, einen gleichen Anspruch auf Begünstigungen aus Emissionen generierenden Aktivitäten haben. Das Argument rechtfertigt die Idee, Emissionsbegünstigungen über die Gesamtlebenszeit von Individuen hinweg anzugleichen. Für das Verteilungsprinzip ist es bedeutend, dass ein Individuum bereits Begünstigungen aus Emissionen generierenden Aktivitäten realisiert hat. Es kommt nicht darauf an, ob dies wissend und zu Unrecht passierte. Es geht nicht um Kompensation für Fehlverhalten von Personen aus industrialisierten Ländern.

Da es nicht um Emissionen als solche, sondern um Begünstigungen für Menschen aus Emissionen generierenden Aktivitäten geht, können und sollen auch die sie jeweils begünstigenden Emissionen generierenden Aktivitäten anderer Personen, einschließlich früher lebender Personen, im Sinne einer fairen Verteilung der verbleibenden erlaubten Begünstigungen aus Emissionen generierenden Aktivitäten berücksichtigt werden. Auf diese Weise wird ein weiterer Teil der vergangenen oder historischen Emissionen, nämlich die Emissionen, die mit der Generierung von Begünstigungen heute und zukünftig Lebender durch Aktivitäten vergangener Generationen einhergegangen sind, für die faire Verteilung des verbleibenden Emissionsbudgets berücksichtigt. Die von unseren Vorfahr*innen verfolgte Industrialisierung hat bis zum heutigen Tag begünstigende Auswirkungen – weitaus mehr für Menschen in hoch industrialisierten Ländern als für jene Menschen, die in Entwicklungs- oder Schwellenländern leben. Diese Begünstigungen beinhalten beispielsweise die Bereitstellung von komplexen Infrastrukturen einschließlich Bildungseinrichtungen, Krankenhäusern, Straßen und Zugverbindungen, welche häufig schon eingerichtet und gebaut wurden, als heute Lebende noch nicht geboren waren. Dass die Produkte der Emissionen generierenden Tätigkeiten früherer Generationen eine ungleiche Verteilung von Begünstigungen unter den gegenwärtig Lebenden mitverursacht haben, ist aus der Perspektive der Verteilungsgerechtigkeit zu berücksichtigen, geht es doch um die faire Verteilung von Begünstigungen aus Emissionen generierenden Tätigkeiten unter heute Lebenden.[6]

Die Berücksichtigung dieser gewissermaßen ererbten Begünstigungen geht nicht damit einher, heute Lebenden Verantwortung für die Emissionen generierenden Handlungen früher Lebender zuzuschreiben. Auch die Frage, was früher oder heute Lebende über den Klimawandel und seine Ursachen wissen konnten, ist offensichtlich nicht relevant. Folglich sprechen die ersten zwei der oben genannten Einwände nicht gegen die Berücksichtigung dieses Teils der historischen Emissionen. Der dritte Einwand, der sich auf das Nicht-Identitätsproblem beruft, scheint aber gegen die Berücksichtigung von Begünstigungen aus Handlungen früher lebender Menschen zu sprechen. Bei genauer Betrachtung ist dies aber nicht der Fall. Das Argument verdankt sich einer Perspektive distributiver Gerechtigkeit: Das Argument zugunsten der Berücksichtigung dieser Begünstigungen aus Emissionen generierenden Aktivitäten beruht weder auf der Behauptung, dass es den Personen, die heute als Individuen in Entwicklungsländern leben, schlechter geht, als es der Fall wäre, wenn es die Industrialisierung nicht gegeben hätte, noch auf der Behauptung, dass es den Individuen in den hoch industrialisierten Ländern aufgrund der ererbten Begünstigungen aus der Geschichte der Industrialisierung besser geht, als es ihnen ginge, hätte es diese Industrialisierung nicht gegeben. Darauf weist das Nicht-Identitätsproblem hin: Niemand kann behaupten, es gehe ihm oder ihr besser als es ohne Industrialisierung der Fall wäre, da sie bei einer anderen Geschichte der ökonomischen Entwicklung höchstwahrscheinlich als die Personen, die sie sind, gar nicht zur Existenz gekommen wären. Dies zu behaupten steht jedoch in keinem Widerspruch zu der für das Argument zugunsten der Berücksichtigung ererbter Begünstigungen relevanten Behauptung: Die Umstände, in denen Menschen sich seit ihrer Zeugung befinden, sind mehr oder weniger begünstigend für sie. Menschen erhalten und realisieren Begünstigungen abhängig davon, ob sie in der industrialisierten Welt aufgewachsen sind. Offenbar wäre es einem Individuum anders ergangen, wäre es bald nach seiner Geburt in einem hoch industrialisierten Land in einen Slum in einem der Entwicklungsländer übersiedelt worden. Dieser Person wäre es dort höchstwahrscheinlich schlechter gegangen.

Bestimmte Teile vergangener Emissionen sollten also für die faire Verteilung des verbleibenden Emissionsbudgets berücksichtigt werden, nämlich zumindest jene vergangenen Emissionen, die Nebenprodukt der sie selbst begünstigenden

---

6 Unter der Annahme, dass das Gut „Begünstigungen aus Emissionen generierenden Aktivitäten" als solches Gegenstand einer Untersuchung aus distributiver Sicht sinnvoller Weise sein kann. Zu dieser Debatte siehe Baatz/Ott (2017).

Aktivitäten gegenwärtig Lebender sind, sowie jene vergangenen Emissionen, die Nebenprodukte von Begünstigungen aus Emissionen generierenden Aktivitäten anderer sind, deren Konsequenzen heute und zukünftig Lebende nach wie vor begünstigen.[7] Da durch diese beiden Argumente nur ein Teil der vergangenen Emissionen berücksichtigt wird, bleiben große Ungleichheiten bei der Verursachung von Emissionen unter den früher Lebenden unberücksichtigt: Jene historischen Emissionen, die auf Emissionen generierende Aktivitäten früher Lebender zurückzuführen sind und die häufig die Verursacher selbst begünstigt, aber zu keinen Begünstigungen für gegenwärtig Lebende geführt haben, sind gemäß dieser Sichtweise ohne normative Signifikanz.

Verstehen wir die Verteilung von Emissionsrechten als ein Problem distributiver Gerechtigkeit, beziehen wir uns nicht auf Schaden oder Unrecht. Die Idee ist vielmehr, die Begünstigungen, die mit Emissionen generierenden Aktivitäten einhergehen, unter den gegenwärtig Lebenden für ihre Gesamtlebenszeit gleich zu verteilen. Wie argumentiert, werden wir dieses Ziel nicht erreichen, wenn wir den Menschen aus Entwicklungsländern nicht höhere Anteile an Emissionsrechten zuschreiben. Dies ist der ungleichen Ererbung von Begünstigungen geschuldet sowie den ungleichen Begünstigungen, die Menschen durch ihre eigenen Emissionen generierenden Handlungen erzielen konnten.[8]

Hier geht es nicht darum, die genauen Implikationen dieser Auffassung der Signifikanz historischer Emissionen zu bestimmen (siehe Williges et al. u. B.). Vielmehr soll darauf hingewiesen werden, dass die Überlegungen, die dem Argument zugrunde liegen, das Potenzial haben, auch andere und womöglich anders gerichtete Ansprüche für die zukunftsorientierte Distribution des verbleibenden erlaubten Emissionsbudgets auszuweisen, wenn diese Ansprüche sich auf andere distributiv relevant ungleiche Konsequenzen von vergangenen Emissionen beziehen. Konsistenz scheint dann zu verlangen, dass wir beide Typen von Ansprüchen für die Allokation des Emissionsbudgets berücksichtigen.

---

**7** Für alternative Vorschläge der normativen Signifikanz historischer Emissionen und ihrer Konsequenzen siehe die Beiträge in Meyer/Sanklecha (2017a).

**8** Die drei Einwände sprechen nicht gegen die zwei Vorschläge, vergangene Emissionen zu berücksichtigen, weil gemäß diesen Vorschlägen die Konsequenzen historischer Emissionen distributiv relevant sind und auf keine Art und Weise auf der Idee der Kompensation von vergangenem Unrecht beruhen. Das Argument zugunsten der Berücksichtigung dieser Teilmengen historischer Emissionen ist nicht, dass durch diese Emissionen vorwerfbare Schäden verursacht wurden, so dass der oder die Schädigende (oder jene, die aus den unrechten und schädigenden Handlungen vorwerfbar Begünstigungen beziehen) Kompensationsleistungen an die zu leisten hat, die (mittelbar) geschädigt werden. Die drei Einwände sprechen gegen ein solches, auf der Idee kompensatorischer Gerechtigkeit beruhenden Verständnis der normativen Signifikanz historischer Emissionen und ihrer Konsequenzen. Siehe dazu Meyer (2013).

In den nächsten Abschnitten wird ein solcher vermeintlich anders gerichteter, die Emittenten mit hohem Emissionsniveau unterstützender Anspruch untersucht, nämlich der Anspruch von hohen Emittenten auf einen größeren Anteil an den Emissionsrechten aufgrund ihrer historisch ausgebildeten „legitimen Erwartungen": Denn, so das Argument, die von ihnen ausgebildeten Erwartungen, auf weit überdurchschnittlichem Niveau emittieren zu dürfen, sind nicht ihnen, sondern der von ihnen nicht zu verantwortenden historischen Entwicklung der Emissionsniveaus innerhalb der hoch industrialisierten Länder zuzuschreiben, und aufgrund dieser Erwartungen haben, so die empirische Behauptung, die hohen Emittenten, sollen sie ihre Emissionen in kurzer Frist drastisch, nämlich auf netto Null reduzieren, höhere Kosten als Menschen, die dieses Ziel von einem niedrigeren Emissionsniveau ausgehend anstreben. Diese höheren Kosten der hohen Emittenten sind distributiv relevant, so das Argument, sollen die Begünstigungen aus Emissionen generierenden Aktivitäten insgesamt fair verteilt werden.

## 3 Die normative Signifikanz historisch geformter legitimer Erwartungen

Erwartungen können als eine Art von Vorhersage über die Zukunft verstanden werden.[9] So verstanden sind Erwartungen durch drei Merkmale gekennzeichnet. Erstens spielen Erwartungen in der Lebensplanung von Menschen und bei der Durchführung ihrer Projekte eine große Rolle, und wenn ihre Erwartungen sich nicht erfüllen, schadet ihnen das, indem es unmöglich, schwierig oder kostspielig für sie wird, ihre Pläne weiterhin zu verfolgen. Zweitens ist die Erfüllung oder Nichterfüllung von Erwartungen im Prinzip unter menschlicher Kontrolle; ob Erwartungen sich erfüllen, hängt von den Handlungen und Unterlassungen von Menschen ab. Drittens wird hier unterstellt, dass die hier untersuchten Erwartungen epistemisch gültig sind, in dem minimalen Sinne, dass Menschen, die sie haben, auch gute Gründe dafür haben zu glauben, dass sie sich erfüllen werden. Aufgrund dieser Merkmale können Erwartungen und die Handlungen von Menschen, welche sich auf deren Erfüllung oder Nicht-Erfüllung auswirken, Gegenstand normativer Beurteilung sein: Haben Menschen gültige Ansprüche darauf, dass ihre Erwartungen erfüllt werden? Sollten andere Menschen davon absehen,

---

9 Im dritten und vierten Abschnitt werden einige der Forschungsergebnisse aus Meyer/Sanklecha (2011) und Meyer/Sanklecha (2014) präsentiert. Deren Signifikanz wird in diesem Beitrag neu gedeutet.

die Erfüllung dieser Erwartungen zu untergraben? Welche Ansprüche kommen Menschen zu, wenn ihre legitimen Erwartungen enttäuscht werden?

Um zwei Beispiele zu verwenden, betrachten wir zunächst einen Dieb, der ein Auto stiehlt und nun erwartet, mit dem Diebstahl davonzukommen. Weil er diese Erwartung hat, geht er verschiedene finanzielle Verpflichtungen ein, aus denen herauszukommen ihm Kosten verursachen bzw. ihm Schaden zufügen werden. Nehmen wir an, die Polizei erwischt ihn und seine Erwartung wird frustriert, bevor er vom Diebstahl profitieren kann. Er wurde sicherlich durch die Frustration seiner Erwartung geschädigt, aber intuitiv würden wir nicht glauben, dass er irgendeine Art von Anspruch auf Entschädigung oder allgemein irgendeine Art von gültiger Beschwerde hat. In diesem Fall erzeugt die Tatsache, dass ein Akteur eine bestimmte Erwartung hat und durch seine Frustration geschädigt würde, keinen gültigen normativen Anspruch des Akteurs, nicht so geschädigt zu werden.

Betrachten wir nun den zweiten Fall. Dieser Fall betrifft eine Zusammenarbeit, die auf Vertrauen und Zuverlässigkeit basiert. Seit geraumer Zeit essen die zwei Mitbewohner*innen A und B freitags zusammen zu Abend und bereiten abwechselnd das Abendessen vor. Angenommen, A bereitet diesen Freitag das Abendessen vor, weil sie an der Reihe ist. A verlässt sich auf ihre Erwartung, dass B zum Abendessen zu ihr kommt. Diesmal erscheint B jedoch nicht. A ist frustriert. In der Tat erleidet A einen Schaden aufgrund der Frustration ihrer Erwartung. Obwohl die Frustration von As Erwartung relativ unbedeutend ist, würde man normalerweise annehmen, dass B ihr etwas schuldet. B schuldet A zumindest eine Erklärung, zudem wahrscheinlich auch eine Entschuldigung. So interpretiert ist die Erwartung von A normativ bedeutsam. Wird sie frustriert, erfordert dies eine Reaktion von B und A hat Grund sich darüber zu beschweren, dass ihre Erwartung frustriert wurde.

Vereinfachend wird hier angenommen, dass die beiden Fälle legitime bzw. illegitime Erwartungen veranschaulichen (für die nicht vereinfachte Version siehe Meyer/Sanklecha 2014). Ferner wird angenommen, dass eine der Implikationen einer legitimen Erwartung darin besteht, dass ihr Träger einen gültigen normativen Anspruch hat, dass der Schaden, der ihm aus der Frustration seiner Erwartung erwachsen kann, berücksichtigt wird, wir über Handlungen und Maßnahmen entscheiden, die zur Frustration seiner Erwartungen führen können.

Geht es um die hohen Emittenten, dürfte unumstritten sein, dass Menschen, die in Ländern mit einem durchschnittlich besonders hohen Emissionsniveau leben, typischerweise ein breites Spektrum von Erwartungen haben, deren Frustration wahrscheinlich ist, wird mit dem Klimawandel angemessen umgegangen. Man denke an Erwartungen hinsichtlich der Höhe der in Zukunft zulässigen persönlichen Emissionen bei privaten Aktivitäten (etwa in Bezug auf Emissionen durch die Nutzung ihrer Privatwagen mit Verbrennungsmotoren), Erwartungen hinsichtlich der zukünftigen Nachfrage nach den Fähigkeiten, in denen Menschen ausgebildet wurden (wenn sie z. B. ausgebildete Automechaniker*innen sind und Verbrennungsmotoren warten und reparieren können), Erwartungen an die zukünftige Zulässigkeit und Erschwinglichkeit von Langstreckenflügen (z. B., wenn Menschen auf einem anderen Kontinent ein Studium verfolgen, aus privaten Gründen aber regelmäßig nachhause fliegen möchten), Erwartungen an die Möglichkeit, weiterhin in Gebieten leben zu können, in denen aufgrund des Klimawandels das Risiko extremer Ereignisse besteht (was z. B. auch in österreichischen Alpentälern ein Thema geworden ist) usw. (siehe Ortner et al. 2017). Darüber hinaus und allgemein gesprochen werden diese Personen Erwartungen an die ihnen offenstehenden Lebensweisen haben, nämlich konkret die Erwartung, dass sie diese auch in Zukunft pflegen und verfolgen können. Dies ist Teil des Hintergrunds, vor dem Akteur*innen langfristige Pläne und Projekte auswählen und verfolgen, und die Fähigkeit, dies zu tun, ist ein wesentlicher Bestandteil des guten Lebens (Rawls 1999: 358–360; Williams 1973: 116–117).

Diese Erwartungen, die auf dem Status quo beruhen, sind entweder direkte Erwartungen, weiterhin auf dem derzeit hohen und, global gesehen, weit überdurchschnittlichen Niveau emittieren zu können, oder Erwartungen, aus denen die Erwartung, weit überdurchschnittlich hohe Emissionen verursachen zu können, abgeleitet werden kann. Frühere Untersuchungen hatten zum Gegenstand, ob und unter welchen Bedingungen solche Erwartungen, weiterhin auf so hohem Niveau emittieren zu können, als legitim angesehen werden sollten und was es normativ und praktisch hieße, anzunehmen, dass diese Erwartungen legitim sind (Meyer/Sanklecha 2011; Meyer/Sanklecha 2014).

Die Situation ist komplex. Einerseits ist es notwendig, dass die globalen Emissionen erheblich reduziert werden, wenn der Temperaturanstieg auf unter 2 oder 1,5 Grad Celsius beschränkt werden soll, und es wird für Menschen, die heute auf besonders hohem Niveau emittieren, in der Regel nicht möglich sein, weiterhin auf dem aktuellen Niveau zu emittieren, wenn diese Reduzierungen umgesetzt werden sollen. Darüber hinaus scheinen Fairnessüberlegungen wenigstens zu erfordern, dass Menschen mit derzeit hohen Emissionen zumindest an der Minderungslast beteiligt werden. Zusammenfassend können wir sagen, dass Überlegungen der Generationengerechtigkeit die Forderung stützen, die globalen Emissionen erheblich zu reduzieren, und Überlegungen zur internationalen Verteilungsgerechtigkeit die Forderung stützen, dass die Belastungen dieser Transformation zu möglichst Netto-Null-Emissionen gerecht aufgeteilt werden.

Andererseits sind wir mit den folgenden Überlegungen konfrontiert. Erstens erleiden die Akteur*innen, deren Erwartungen frustriert werden, häufig Schaden. In einigen Fällen kann der Schaden sehr bedeutsam sein, da er dazu führen kann, dass der oder die Akteur*in langfristige Projekte und Pläne aufgeben muss, in die er oder sie bereits (und nicht nur finanziell) stark investiert hat. Die Frustration der Status-quo-Erwartungen hoher Emittenten und die Änderung ihrer Lebensweisen innerhalb kurzer Frist, so dass sie Netto-Null-Emissionen verursachen, geht, so eine Vermutung, weil die durchschnittliche Reduktionsrate über die kurze Zeitspanne besonders steil sein muss, womöglich mit besonders hohen Kosten einher und höheren Kosten als die Reduktion auf Netto-Null-Niveau bei Menschen, die von einem viel niedrigeren Niveau starten.

Zweitens wird es in vielen Fällen schwierig sein, den oder die Akteur*in für die Erwartungen, die er oder sie hat, und für die Pläne und Projekte, die er oder sie auf der Grundlage seiner oder ihrer Erwartungen entwickelt und verfolgt hat, verantwortlich zu machen. Dafür spricht, dass auch in den Ländern mit durchschnittlich sehr hohen Emissionen die Menschen ihre langfristigen Pläne und Projekte aus den Optionen, die in diesen Ländern typischerweise und realistisch verfügbar sind, ausgewählt haben und, da dies eine der Bedingungen für den Erfolg von Projekten ist, auch auf der Grundlage der Erwartung, dass sie diese Pläne und Projekte werden langfristig weiterverfolgen können. Wenn solche Erwartungen bestimmten Bedingungen genügen,[10] können zumindest einige davon als legitim angesehen werden. Denn auch wenn die historischen Prozesse, die für die Ausbildung dieser Erwartungen konstitutiv waren, heute als unzulässig anzusehen wären (z. B. in dem Sinne, dass die Staaten, in denen diese Prozesse stattgefunden haben, für ihre schädlichen (langfristigen) Folgen innerhalb und außerhalb ihrer Staatsgrenzen haften; siehe Thompson (2017) und Butt (2017)), sind die heute lebenden Menschen, deren Erwartungen durch diese Prozesse gebildet werden, für diese Prozesse nicht verantwortlich, da sie Aktivitäten vor ihrer Geburt nicht beeinflussen konnten oder einen vernachlässigbaren Einfluss auf diese Prozesse und deren Entfaltung sowie Institutionalisierung hatten.

Dass eine Erwartung legitim ist, bedeutet allerdings nicht, dass sie unbedingt geschützt werden muss. Im Zusammenhang mit dem Klimawandel gibt es wichtige Gründe, sehr viele der womöglich legitimen Erwartungen der hohen Emittenten zu vereiteln – also deren Erwartungen, Emissionen verursachen zu können, die weit über das hinausgehen, was eine gleiche Pro-Kopf-Zuteilung erlaubte. Wie oben skizziert, wäre der Schutz der Erwartungen der hohen Emittenten mit ganz grundlegenden Überlegungen zur Generationengerechtigkeit und internationalen Gerechtigkeit unvereinbar: Die globalen Emissionen müssen erheblich

---

**10** Die Erwartung, weiterhin hohe Emissionen zu verursachen, ist unzulässig, wenn so viele Emissionen zu verursachen nicht erforderlich ist, um das Projekt zu verfolgen, oder wenn das Projekt durch ein anderes weniger emissionsintensives Projekt ersetzt werden kann, dass es dem Akteur ermöglicht, dieselben oder sehr ähnliche Begünstigungen zu realisieren. Für Einzelheiten des Arguments siehe Meyer/Sanklecha (2011) und Meyer/Sanklecha (2014).

reduziert werden und dieses reduzierte globale Kohlenstoffbudget sollte fair auf die Staaten verteilt werden. Mit anderen Worten, dass solche Erwartungen der hohen Emittenten legitim sind, dürfte in aller Regel keine normativen Ansprüche nach sich ziehen, welche höheres Gewicht haben als die Erfüllung der Pflichten intergenerationeller und internationaler Gerechtigkeit. Dass aber ein Anspruch als weniger gewichtig angesehen wird oder anderen normativen Forderungen unterzuordnen ist, ist nicht dasselbe, wie dass er ignoriert wird (oder dass er zu Recht ignoriert wird). Vielmehr bedeutet, dass bestimmte Emissionserwartungen legitim sind, dass sie nicht ignoriert werden sollten.

Die hier vertretene Auffassung lässt sich also so zusammenfassen: Die Frustration legitimer Erwartungen kann als erlaubt angesehen werden, da der Grund für den Schutz legitimer Erwartungen durch Überlegungen zur internationalen Gerechtigkeit und zur Gerechtigkeit zwischen den Generationen aufgewogen wird. Zugleich zieht die schädigende Frustration einer legitimen Erwartung im Kontext des Klimawandels einen Pro-tanto-Anspruch darauf nach sich, dass diese Kosten berücksichtigt werden, wenn die verbleibenden generationenübergreifend zulässigen Emissionen verteilt werden. Unter dem Gesichtspunkt der Verteilungsgerechtigkeit ist es wahrscheinlich, dass andere Ansprüche (insbesondere die Ansprüche auch zukünftig Lebender auf Schutz ihrer Suffizienzrechte) einen größeren Unterschied machen (Meyer 2009; Meyer/Pölzler i. E.). Damit ist aber der Anspruch, dass die Kosten für die Frustration legitimer Erwartungen zu berücksichtigen sind, nicht ungültig und zu analysieren ist, welchen normativen Unterschied seine Berücksichtigung machen soll.

## 4 Wie die Argumente sich ähneln

Beide Argumente – das Argument zugunsten der Berücksichtigung von Begünstigungen aus früheren und historischen Emissionen generierenden Aktivitäten (kurz: Argument der ererbten Nettobegünstigungen) (Abschnitt 2) und das Argument der Berücksichtigung der besonderen Kosten aufgrund der Frustration von Erwartungen, die sich historischen Entwicklungen verdanken (kurz: Argument der legitimen Erwartung) (Abschnitt 3) – beruhen auf der Idee, dass wir an den (begünstigenden wie schädlichen) Konsequenzen historischer Emissionen generierender Aktivitäten interessiert sind und nicht an den Emissionen selbst. In den folgenden Abschnitten dieses Beitrags wird argumentiert, dass es aus Gründen der Kohärenz erforderlich ist, dass, wer das Argument der ererbten Begünstigungen unterstützt, auch das Argument der legitimen Erwartung unterstützen muss (und umgekehrt). Zugleich, so die hier vertretene Auffassung, haben die beiden Argumente aber unterschiedliche normative Implikationen.

Beide Argumente sind relevant ähnlich. Wie ausgeführt gilt für ererbte Begünstigungen: Zwar gibt es ernsthafte Schwierigkeiten, Fehlverhalten in Bezug auf historische und vergangene Emissionen festzustellen. Es muss jedoch kein unrechtmäßiger Schaden festgestellt werden, um Grund zu haben, auf die höchst ungleichen Folgen historischer und vergangener Emissionen gemäß der Idee der Verteilungsgerechtigkeit reagieren zu sollen. Das Argument zugunsten der Berücksichtigung ererbter Begünstigungen setzt voraus, dass Menschen aufgrund der Emissionen generierenden Aktivitäten früher Lebender als benachteiligt oder begünstigt angesehen werden können, ohne diese Ungleichheit zu verdienen (und ohne für die Aktivitäten verantwortlich zu sein), und mit einer daraus resultierenden Verteilung, die gemäß einem ergebnisorientierten Prinzip der Verteilungsgerechtigkeit als unfair oder ungerecht zu erachten ist. Dann stehen Menschen unter Pflichten der Verteilungsgerechtigkeit, nämlich der Redistribution der relevanten Güter mit dem Ziel einer gerechten Verteilung. Und für legitime Erwartungen wurde festgehalten: Die Frustration legitimer Erwartungen zum Zwecke der Implementierung eines intergenerationell und international gerechten Regimes der Transformation zu Netto-Null-Emissionen ist erlaubt; die Protanto-Gründe für den Schutz legitimer Erwartungen können durch Pflichten intergenerationeller und internationaler Gerechtigkeit aufgewogen werden, denen durch das Transformationsregime entsprochen wird. Die Frustration dieser Erwartungen wird jedoch häufig schädlich sein, da langfristige Pläne und Projekte entgegen legitimer Erwartungen nicht weiter verfolgen zu können, Menschen typischerweise erheblichen Schaden (im Sinne von Kosten der Adaptation, Substitution und des Verlusts wertvoller Güter) zufügt. Das heißt, der Schaden, der durch die Frustration legitimer Erwartungen verursacht wird, sollte als ein Fall nicht vorwerfbarer (erlaubter) Schädigung verstanden werden. Die Schädigung bleibt aber normativ relevant und Schäden aufgrund der Frustration legitimer Status-quo-Erwartungen zählen zu den Nettokosten, die Menschen bei der Transformation zu einer emissionsarmen Gesellschaft entstehen. Diese Schäden sind zu berücksichtigen.

Beide Argumente zeigen, dass die Folgen historischer Emissionen generierender Aktivitäten unter dem Gesichtspunkt der Verteilungsgerechtigkeit behandelt werden können, und beide Argumente stützen sich dabei auf die Idee, dass die derzeit lebenden Menschen für zumindest einige der Folgen historischer Emissionen nicht verantwortlich sind oder sein können: Das Argument der ererbten Begünstigungen besagt, dass derzeit lebende Menschen für die Nettobegünstigungen, die sie aufgrund ungleicher historischer Emissionen genießen, weder verantwortlich sind noch diese verdienen. Das Argument der legitimen Erwartungen besagt, dass derzeit lebende Menschen zumindest für einige der Erwartungen, die sie aufgrund historisch hoher Emissionen gebildet haben, nicht verantwortlich sind und daher auch den Schaden nicht verdienen, den sie aufgrund der Frustration dieser Erwartungen erleiden werden.

Entsprechend sind gemäß dem Argument der ererbten Begünstigungen zu berücksichtigen (und, wie schon oben argumentiert, für die Verteilung der verbleibenden zulässigen Emissionen relevant): erstens, die tatsächlichen und absehbaren ungleichen Begünstigungen, die derzeit lebende Menschen während ihrer Lebenszeit durch ihre eigenen Emissionen generierenden Aktivitäten erzielen; zweitens, die ungleichen Nettobegünstigungen, die derzeit lebende Menschen seit ihrer Konzeption aufgrund der (begünstigenden und schädlichen) langfristigen Folgen der Emissionen generierenden Aktivitäten zuvor lebender Menschen realisieren. Das sind die tatsächlich realisierten und erwarteten Begünstigungen aus historischen Emissionen heute lebender Menschen sowie die tatsächlichen und erwarteten Anpassungskosten derzeit lebender Menschen in ihrer Lebenszeit und die nicht vermiedenen Schäden bzw. Verluste, die sie während ihrer Lebenszeit erlitten haben oder wahrscheinlich erleiden werden. Und gemäß dem Argument der legitimen Erwartungen sind die folgenden Kosten unter Fairnessgesichtspunkten zu berücksichtigen: die aufgrund der Frustration historisch geformter legitimer Erwartungen tatsächlichen und erwarteten Anpassungs- und Substitutionskosten derzeit lebender Menschen und im Falle, dass die Projekte nicht fortgesetzt werden können, die Verluste daraus.

Zusammengefasst stimmen die Argumente der ererbten Begünstigungen und der besonderen Schäden aufgrund der Frustration legitimer Erwartungen darin überein, dass ungleiche begünstigende und schädliche Folgen früherer Emissionen generierender Aktivitäten aus Gründen der Verteilungsgerechtigkeit relevant sind, wenn derzeit lebende Menschen nicht für diese Folgen verantwortlich gemacht werden können. Aber jedes der Argumente konzentriert sich auf etwas Anderes. Während es dem Argument der ererbten Begünstigungen um die ungleichen positiven Konsequenzen vergangener Emissionen für das Wohlergehen heute Lebender geht, konzentriert sich das Argument der legitimen Erwartungen ganz auf die ungleichen schädlichen Folgen, die bei der Transformation von einem emissionsreichen zu einem emissionsarmen Regime durch Frustration legitimer Status-quo-Erwartungen entstehen. Weil die Argumente auf derselben Grundüberlegung beruhen – der Gerechtigkeitsforderung des Ausgleichs ungleicher unverdienter Begünstigungen und Belastungen – erfordert Kohärenz, die Gültigkeit beider Argumente anzuerkennen, wenn man der Gültigkeit eines der Argumente beipflichtet.

## 5 Warum die Argumente unterschiedliche normative Implikationen haben

Man könnte meinen, die legitimen Emissionserwartungen hoher Emittenten könnten eine Erhöhung ihres Anteils am globalen Emissionsbudget begründen. Zum Beispiel könnten die behaupteten besonderen Kosten für hohe Emittenten bei der radikalen Reduktion auf netto Null durch ein vorübergehendes *„grandfathering"* (eine vorübergehende Bestandssicherung) berücksichtigt werden. Die eventuelle Zuteilung von Emissionsrechten würde dem Ziel einer Transformation zu Netto-Null-Emissionen bis 2050 entsprechen und in einem, wenn auch neu gedeuteten und verdrehten Sinne der Idee gleicher Emissionen pro Kopf: Anstatt diese Zuteilung sofort hinsichtlich der Anteile am verbleibenden globalen Emissionsbudget umzusetzen, könnten die legitimen Erwartungen der Individuen in Ländern mit besonders hohen Emissionen als Grund gesehen werden, die Allokation des verbleibenden globalen Emissionsbudgets gemäß dem Ansatz *„contraction and convergence"* (Verringerung und Konvergenz) vorzunehmen, nämlich Verringerung der Emissionsniveaus ausgehend von je unterschiedlichen tatsächlichen Ausgangsniveaus mit schrittweisem Übergang zur gleichen Netto-Null-pro-Kopf-Verteilung der Emissionen und der Realisierung des Ziels einer kohlenstoffarmen Wirtschaft und Gesellschaft im Jahr 2050 (Implikationen werden diskutiert in Williges et al. u. B.).

Dieses Argument ist allerdings fragwürdig.[11] Das betrifft einerseits die empirische Seite des Arguments und insbesondere die behauptete normative Implikation. Es scheint zumindest fragwürdig, dass es kostspieliger ist, Emissionen von einem hohen zu einem sehr niedrigen Level in kurzer Zeit zu reduzieren. Staaten mit weit überdurchschnittlichem Emissionsniveau auf dasselbe niedrige Level in einer kurzen Zeit zu reduzieren, könnte sich als weniger kostspielig im Vergleich zu gering emittierenden Staaten herausstellen. Zum Beispiel haben stark emittierende Staaten tendenziell weniger Verluste und Schäden sowie niedrigere Adaptationskosten aufgrund eines prozentuell niedrigeren Anteils von Sektoren an der Wohlstandssicherung, die von den Konsequenzen des Klimawandels besonders stark betroffen sind (z. B. Agrarwirtschaft). Zudem und angesichts der positiven Korrelation von (historischem) Emissions- und Wohlstandsniveau dürften Staaten mit weit überdurchschnittlichem Emissionsniveau es sich eher leisten können, Adaptationsmaßnahmen umzusetzen und haben entsprechend mehr, und im Sinne der Vermeidung von Substitutionskosten und

---

[11] Für Diskussion danke ich Keith Williges, Karl Steininger und Gottfried Kirchengast.

Verlusten auch bessere Optionen. Aufgrund solcher Faktoren dürften Länder mit weit überdurchschnittlich hohen Emissionsniveaus geringere kollektiven Kosten haben und deshalb ihre Bewohner*innen durchschnittlich geringere Reduktionskosten. Es scheint also wenigstens zweifelhaft, dass Menschen mit heute weit überdurchschnittlichem Emissionsniveau durchschnittlich höhere Kosten aufgrund der Transformation zu einem Netto-Null-Emissionsniveau haben werden.

Darüber hinaus könnte argumentiert werden, dass, selbst wenn spezielle und höhere Kosten für Bewohner*innen von Staaten mit weit überdurchschnittlichen Emissionsniveaus aufgrund der Frustration legitimer Status-quo-Erwartungen entstehen, diese sich nicht auf die Allokation des globalen Budgets an Emissionsrechten auswirken sollten. Dass sie sich auf die Allokation des globalen Budgets auswirken sollen, scheint abwegig. Denn für die Ausbildung der problematischen Status-quo-Erwartungen sind nicht alle Akteur*innen und auch nicht alle Staaten gleichermaßen verantwortlich. Die hoch industrialisierten Staaten haben eine konstitutive Rolle in der Formung dieser Erwartungen gespielt und tun dies weiterhin. Staaten haben einen maßgeblichen Einfluss darauf, welche Lebensweisen in einem gegebenen Land typisch sind. Da der Staat einige Lebensstile und langfristige Projekte (zu Lasten anderer) fördert, kann man sagen, dass er (a) in einem weitgefassten Sinne daran beteiligt ist, die Menge an Optionen festzulegen, aus denen seine Mitglieder (Menschen mit Lebensmittelpunkt im jeweiligen Staat) ihre Lebensstile und längerfristigen Projekte wählen können, und dass der Staat (b) seine Mitglieder darin bestärkt, die Erwartung auszubilden, dass sie auch weiterhin in der Verfolgung ihrer längerfristigen Projekte (inklusive des Ausmaßes an damit einhergehenden Emissionen) unterstützt werden.

Dazu kommt: Spätestens seit 1990 sind Staaten dafür verantwortlich, eine Strategie zur Transformation zu einer kohlenstoffarmen Gesellschaft zu verfolgen, mit der eine Änderung der Erwartungen der Mitglieder dieser Staaten in Bezug auf ein zulässiges Level an Emissionen einhergeht. Staaten verfügen über die Autorität und die Fähigkeit, eine solche Strategie zu verfolgen. Staaten unternehmen des Öfteren Schritte in die Richtung zu bestimmen, wie ihre Bewohner*innen ihre Emissionen reduzieren können, während sie weiterhin in der Lage bleiben, ihre Projekte zu verfolgen. Der Staat kann gewisse Handlungsweisen verbieten und Anreize für Verhaltensänderungen schaffen. Er kann die Kosten einer Emissionsverringerung bei andauernder Verfolgung der eigenen Projekte beeinflussen, entweder indem er die Kosten von weniger emissionsintensiven Mitteln z. B. der Energieproduktion oder Mobilität – die für die Verfolgung der meisten Projekte relevant sind – verändert oder indem er bestimmte Arten von Projekten wie zum Beispiel eine bestimmte Form des Ackerbaus subventioniert. Er kann in Infrastruktur investieren, die es erlaubt, dieselben Aktivitäten mit geringeren Emissionskosten zu verrichten, zum Beispiel indem er ein bequemes und effizientes öffentliches Verkehrswesen schafft. Zuletzt könnte der Staat auch eine Obergrenze an persönlichen Emissionen für private Aktivitäten festlegen und damit weiter Erwartungen seiner Mitglieder bezüglich Emissionen beeinflussen. Letzteres tut der Staat derzeit nicht. Dadurch vermittelt der Staat im Grunde, dass jedes Ausmaß an persönlichen Emissionen zulässig ist. Das wirkt sich auf die Projekte aus, die seine Mitglieder auswählen, sowie auf ihre Erwartungen über zukünftig zulässige Emissionen.

Drei Gründe sprechen also dafür, den Staaten mit weit überdurchschnittlichem Niveau an Emissionen die Kosten der Reduktion von Emissionen von einem besonders hohen auf Netto-Null-Niveau aufzuerlegen und, sofern diese Kosten höher sind als die entsprechenden Kosten von Staaten mit niedrigerem Ausgangsniveau, diese Kosten nicht von allen Staaten bzw. allen Menschen gleichermaßen mittragen zu lassen. Erstens sind die Staaten mit weit überdurchschnittlichem Niveau in starkem Maße für die Ausbildung dieses Niveaus historisch und kausal verantwortlich. Zweitens sind die Staaten selbst in der Lage, autoritative und effektive Maßnahmen zu setzen, die Emissionsniveaus so zu senken, dass die Reduktion mit der Fortführung der Lebensstile und der Projekte ihrer Bewohner*innen möglichst kompatibel ist. Drittens sind Staaten mit weit überdurchschnittlichem Emissionsniveau seit geraumer Zeit aus den genannten Gründen intergenerationeller und internationaler Gerechtigkeit verpflichtet, die Emissionsniveaus zu senken.

Zugleich ist es wahrscheinlich, dass für manche Menschen die Kosten der Reduktion auf ein deutlich niedrigeres Emissionsniveau besonders hoch sind – dies aus Gründen, welche die einzelne Person nicht zu verantworten hat, z. B., weil sie ein Projekt verfolgt, das mit sehr hohen Emissionen einhergeht oder für dessen Weiterverfolgung keine oder nur sehr teure weniger emissionsintensive Substitutionsmittel zur Verfügung stehen. Auch die Auswirkungen von staatlich gesetzten Maßnahmen zur Reduktion von Emissionsniveaus können sich sehr unterschiedlich auf die Möglichkeiten von Menschen auswirken, ihre Projekte weiterzuverfolgen. Das spricht dafür, dass erstens diese ungleichen Konsequenzen der Transformation berücksichtigt werden, indem Staaten bei der Wahl und Verfolgung ihrer Reduktionsstrategien besonders hohe Kosten für einzelne Menschen durch Frustration ihrer legitimen Status-quo-Erwartungen möglichst vermeiden und unterschiedliche Transformationskosten ihrer Bürger*innen nicht nur berücksichtigen, sondern auch ausgleichen. Zugleich spricht aber die besondere historische und kausale Verantwortung der Staaten mit weit überdurchschnittlichem Emissionsniveaus und ihre seit geraumer Zeit bestehende Pflicht, ihren intergenerationellen und internationalen Pflichten zur Emissionsreduktion zu genügen, dagegen, dass ihre vermeintlich besonders hohen Kosten der Emissionsreduktion allen auferlegt werden sollen, indem aufgrund dieser

Kosten diesen Staaten ein höherer Anteil der verbleibenden Emissionsrechte zuerkannt wird.

# 6 Schlussbemerkungen

Die Konsequenzen vergangener und historischer Emissionen generierender Aktivitäten können hohe normative Signifikanz aus Sicht distributiver Gerechtigkeit haben, sofern gezeigt werden kann, dass es distributiv relevant ungleich Betroffene gibt und die jeweils Betroffenen diese Ungleichheit nicht verdienen. Dann können diese Konsequenzen Grund für ausgleichende distributive Maßnahmen sein. Abhängig davon, welche ungleichen Konsequenzen dieser Art wir analysieren, unterscheiden sich aber ihre normativen Implikationen. Der Beitrag untersucht zwei Teilmengen dieser Konsequenzen, von denen Staatenvertreter*innen implizit oder explizit behaupten (siehe Abschnitt 1), sie seien für die Allokation der verbleibenden erlaubten globalen Emissionsrechte relevant. Für eine Teilmenge ist dies zutreffend, für die andere nicht.

Die ungleichen Begünstigungen aufgrund früherer eigener, aber nicht vorwerfbarer Emissionen generierender Handlungen und die ungleichen ererbten Begünstigungen heute und zukünftig Lebender aus Emissionen generierenden Aktivitäten früher Lebender sind für die faire Distribution der verbleibenden globalen Emissionsrechte relevant. Denn aus Sicht der distributiven Gerechtigkeit sollte (etwa gemäß dem Prinzip der Pro-Kopf-Gleichverteilung von Begünstigungen aus Emissionen generierenden Aktivitäten) ein Ausgleich der über die Gesamtlebenszeit von Menschen realisierten Begünstigungen aus Aktivitäten mit Emissionen als Nebenprodukt erreicht werden. Gegeben deutlich unterschiedlich vieler bereits realisierter Begünstigungen – durch eigene Emissionen generierende Aktivitäten und aufgrund entsprechender Aktivitäten früher Lebender – ist ein größerer Anteil des verbleibenden globalen Emissionsbudgets denen zuzuteilen, die weniger Begünstigungen realisiert haben oder realisieren werden. Dies ist eine Angelegenheit kosmopolitischer bzw. internationaler Gerechtigkeit.

Eine andere Teilmenge der Konsequenzen historischer Emissionen generierender Aktivitäten hat ebenfalls ungleiche Konsequenzen. Deren Berücksichtigung und Ausgleich ist aber Angelegenheit innerstaatlicher distributiver Gerechtigkeit. Ob hoch industrialisierte Staaten mit weit überdurchschnittlichen Emissionsniveaus besondere und besonders hohe Kosten bei der (aus Gründen intergenerationeller Gerechtigkeit geforderten) Transformation zu Netto-Null-Emissionen bis 2050 haben, ist eine empirische Frage und mindestens fragwürdig, wie in Abschnitt 5 erläutert. Für die Ausbildung der Status-quo-Erwartungen der Bewohner*innen der Staaten mit besonders hohen Emissionsniveaus sind jedenfalls die autoritativen Entscheidungen und Politiken dieser Staaten und über einen langen Zeitraum mitentscheidend. Bei hohem historischem und andauernd hohem Emissionsniveau haben hoch industrialisierte Staaten den institutionellen Rahmen für die in dem jeweiligen Gemeinwesen typischen Lebensweisen und Optionen geschaffen, deren Verfolgung mit Emissionen von durchschnittlich sehr hohem Niveau einhergehen. Die einzelnen Bürger*innen wählen aus einer Bandbreite von Lebensweisen und Optionen, zu deren Generierung sie selbst wenig beigetragen haben. Damit gehen Status-quo-Erwartungen einher und, wenn in bestimmter Weise qualifiziert, sind wenigstens einige dieser Erwartungen den Träger*innen individuell nicht vorwerfbar (Abschnitt 3). Menschen können auch aufgrund der Frustration ihrer legitimen Status-quo-Erwartungen hohe und unterschiedlich hohe Kosten (der Adaptation, Substitution und des Verlusts) bei der in kurzer Frist zu erzielenden Reduktion der von ihnen verursachten Emissionen auf netto Null haben. Wie diese Kosten unter den Bürger*innen verteilt sind, hängt nicht zuletzt von der Wahl der Strategie der Transformation und ihrer Implementierung ab (Abschnitt 5). Aus Sicht der distributiven Gerechtigkeit sollten Ungleichheiten dieser Kosten, wenn sie nicht vermeidbar sind, fair ausgeglichen werden. Dies ist eine Forderung innerstaatlicher Gerechtigkeit bei der Transition zu einer nahezu emissionsfreien Wirtschaft und Gesellschaft.

## Literatur

Baatz, Christian/Ott, Konrad (2017): „In Defense of Emissions Egalitarianism?". In: Meyer, Lukas H./Sanklecha, Pranay (Hg.): *Climate Justice and Historical Emissions*. Cambridge: Cambridge University Press, S. 165–197.
Baumert, Kevin/Herzog, Timothy/Pershing, Jonathan (2005): *Navigating the Numbers: Greenhouse Gas Data and International Climate Policy*. Washington, D.C.: World Resources Institute.
Butt, Daniel (2017): „Historical Emissions". In: Meyer, Lukas H./Sanklecha, Pranay (Hg.): *Climate Justice and Historical Emissions*. Cambridge: Cambridge University Press, S. 61–79.
Gosseries, Axel (2004): „Historical Emissions and Free Riding". In: *Ethical Perspectives* 11(1), S. 36–60.
Holtung, Nils/Lippert-Rasmussen, Kasper (2007): „An Introduction to Contemporary Egalitarianism". In: Holtung, Nils/Lippert-Rasmussen, Kasper (Hg.): *Egalitarianism: New Essays on the Nature and Vale of Equality*. Oxford: Oxford University Press, S. 1–37.
Houghton, J. T./Jenkins, G. J./Ephraums, J. J. (Hg.) (1990): *Climate Change: The IPCC Scientific Assessment*. Cambridge: Cambridge University Press.
Hurka, Thomas (1993): *Perfectionism*. Oxford: Oxford University Press.

Meyer, Lukas H. (2003): „Past and Future: The Case for a Threshold Conception of Harm". In: Meyer, Lukas H./Paulson, Stanley P./Pogge, Thomas W. (Hg.): *Rights, Culture, and the Law: Themes from the Legal and Political Philosophy of Joseph Raz*. Oxford: Oxford University Press, S. 143–159.

Meyer, Lukas H. (2009): „Intergenerationelle Suffizienzgerechtigkeit". In: Goldschmidt, Nils (Hg.): *Generationengerechtigkeit: Ordnungsökonomische Konzepte*. Tübingen: Mohr Siebeck, S. 281–322.

Meyer, Lukas H. (2013): „Why Historical Emissions Should Count". In: *Chicago Journal of International Law* 13(2), S. 597–613.

Meyer, Lukas H./Pölzler, Thomas (i. E.): „Basic Needs and Sufficiency: The Foundations of Intergenerational Justice". In: Gardiner, Stephen M. (Hg.): *Oxford Handbook of Intergenerational Ethics*. Oxford: Oxford University Press, im Erscheinen.

Meyer, Lukas H./Roser, Dominic (2010): „Climate Justice and Historical Emissions". In: *Critical Review of International Social and Political Philosophy* 13(1), S. 229–253.

Meyer, Lukas H./Sanklecha, Pranay (2011): „Individual Expectations and Climate Change". In: *Analyse & Kritik: Zeitschrift für Sozialtheorie* 33(2), S. 449–471.

Meyer, Lukas H./Sanklecha, Pranay (2014): „How Legitimate Expectations Matter in Climate Justice". In: *Politics, Philosophy & Economics* 13(4), S. 369–393.

Meyer, Lukas H./Sanklecha, Pranay (Hg.) (2017a): *Climate Justice and Historical Emissions*. Cambridge: Cambridge University Press.

Meyer, Lukas H./Sanklecha, Pranay (2017b): „Introduction: On the Significance of Historical Emissions for Climate Ethics". In: Meyer, Lukas H./Sanklecha, Pranay (Hg.): *Climate Justice and Historical Emissions*. Cambridge: Cambridge University Press, S. 1–21.

Ortner, Florian/Pölzler, Thomas/Meyer, Lukas H./Sass, Oliver (2017): „Natural Hazards and the Normative Significance of Expectations in Protecting Alpine Communities". In: European Geosciences Union (Hg.): *Geophysical Research Abstracts: Abstracts of the European Geosciences Union General Assembly 2017*. Wien/München: Copernicus, EGU2017–14139.

Parfit, Derek (1984): *Reasons and Persons*. Oxford: Clarendon Press.

Posner, Eric/Weisbach, David (2007): *Climate Change Justice*. Princeton, NJ: Princeton University Press.

Rawls, John (1999): *A Theory of Justice*. Revised Edition. Cambridge, MA: Belknap Press of Harvard University Press.

Thompson, Janna (2017): „Historical Responsibility and Climate Change". In: Meyer, Lukas H./Sanklecha, Pranay (Hg.): *Climate Justice and Historical Emissions*. Cambridge: Cambridge University Press, S. 46–60.

United Nations (2015): *Paris Agreement*. https://unfccc.int/files/essential_background/convention/application/pdf/english_paris_agreement.pdf, Zugriff 31. Juli 2020.

United Nations Population Fund (2014): *State of World Population 2014*. https://www.unfpa.org/sites/default/files/pub-pdf/EN-SWOP14-Report_FINAL-web.pdf, Zugriff 31. Juli 2020.

Wallimann-Helmer, Ivo/Meyer, Lukas H./Mintz-Woo, Kian/Schinko, Thomas/Serdeczny, Olivia (2019): „The Ethical Challenges in the Context of Climate Loss and Damage: Concepts, Methods and Policy Options". In: Mechler, Reinhard/Bouwer, Laurens M./Schinko, Thomas/Surminski, Swenja/Linnerooth-Bayer, JoAnne (Hg.): *Loss and Damage from Climate Change: Concepts, Methods and Policy Options*. Cham: Springer Open, S. 39–62.

Williams, Bernard (1973): „A Critique of Utilitarianism". In: Smart, J. J. C./Williams, Bernard (Hg.): *Utilitarianism: For and Against*. Cambridge: Cambridge University Press, S. 75–150.

Williges, Keith/Meyer, Lukas H./Steininger, Karl/Kirchengast, Gottfried (u. B.): „Fairness Critically Conditions the Carbon Budget Allocation Across Countries", unter Begutachtung.

Susana Monsó
# Is Predation Necessarily Amoral?

**Abstract:** The thesis that predation is necessarily amoral is widely regarded as an unquestionable assumption. In this paper, I begin by offering some empirical examples that suggest that predation could in some cases have a moral character. I then examine four different reasons that could be offered in support of the amorality of predation: (1) predators are not moral agents; (2) if predation were moral, it would imply an absurd duty to police nature; (3) predatory behaviour is not under the predator's control; (4) eating other animals is necessary for predators to survive. I argue that none of these reasons can successfully ground the necessary amorality of predation. While predation is likely amoral in most cases, it is not necessarily so.

**Keywords:** Animal ethics, amorality, predation, predator-prey problem

## 1 Introduction

Some animals prey on other animals, causing them unimaginable pain and suffering in the process. This simple fact of nature has given rise to the so-called 'predator-prey problem' in animal ethics. This problem arises because we have the intuition that we should not intervene to save prey animals from their predators, but this position is difficult to reconcile with a desire to protect animals from being harmed or having their lives cut short. Predation not only causes prey animals to die in horrific and painful ways, it also leads to a lifetime of stress and anxiety associated with the deaths of group members and the permanent threat of being eaten. If we care for these animals, it seems that we should do something about their suffering, but it is difficult to see how this can be made compatible with, on the one hand, caring for predatory species too and, on the other hand, respecting wild animals' wildness.

The traditional response to the predator-prey problem has its roots in Tom Regan's *The Case for Animal Rights*, where predation was postulated as amoral

---

**Note:** This research was funded by the Austrian Science Fund (FWF), under projects P 31466-G32 and M 2518-G32. The author would like to thank Kian Mintz-Woo for his comments on a previous draft of this paper, as well as the audience at the 42nd International Wittgenstein Symposium for their feedback. Additional thanks go to Antonio Osuna Mascaró, who provided empirical examples and helpful discussion.

https://doi.org/10.1515/9783110702255-025

(Regan 2004). Since predators are not moral agents, the argument goes, they have no duties, and so they cannot be said to violate the rights of prey when they hunt them down and eat them. Since there is no rights violation going on, it is not an unjust situation, and so there is no corresponding duty to intervene arising from it. Towards wild animals, all we have is a negative duty not to harm them, but we do not have any positive duty to aid them in those cases in which no rights violations are taking place. Therefore, we should adopt a laissez-faire position towards predation and steer clear of any interventions (Regan 2004: 285). Humans are "neither accountants nor managers of felicity in nature," and so "wildlife managers should be principally concerned with *letting animals be*" (Regan 2004: 357; emphasis in original).

Not everyone is satisfied with Regan's response. From a consequentialist perspective, it does not matter whether or not predators are moral agents but only the amount of suffering that they generate. Thus, some scholars who are strongly committed to reducing wild animal suffering defend that we should intervene to protect prey animals if we can do so without generating further bad consequences (e.g. Fink 2005; Horta 2015; Faria/Paez 2019). One can also find discomfort with Regan's response among animal rights theorists, who often consider that it is too simplistic and cannot be easily reconciled with positive duties that we owe to humans and other animals (e.g. Ebert/Machan 2012; Cochrane 2012; Milburn 2015; Kapembwa 2018). The details of the debate are unimportant for present purposes. What I want to point out is that neither side of the debate calls into question Regan's original assumption: that predation is necessarily amoral.

When discussing the claim that predation is amoral, I take the term 'amoral' to denote a lack of all moral character. To refer to the opposite of amoral, I will use the term 'moral,' understood in its descriptive, not normative sense. Something that is 'moral' in a descriptive sense simply has a moral character, but on its own the term does not specify whether there is rightness or wrongness involved. A behaviour that is 'moral' in a descriptive sense can therefore be either 'moral,' in its normative sense (i.e. roughly, conforming to moral standards) or 'immoral' (i.e. roughly, going against moral standards). Throughout this paper, I will always use the term 'moral' in its purely descriptive sense, in keeping with how it is usually used in the animal morality debate (Fitzpatrick 2017: 1154). Determining whether predation is amoral, therefore, amounts to establishing whether predation could ever be said to contain moral elements.

The structure of this paper is as follows. I begin by offering some examples from the empirical literature that suggest that, in some instances, predation could have moral aspects. I will then examine four reasons in support of the amorality of predation: (1) predators are not moral agents; (2) if predation were moral, it would imply an absurd duty to police nature; (3) predatory behaviour is not under the predator's control; (4) eating other animals is necessary for predators to survive. I will argue that none of them can successfully ground the necessary amorality of predation. Therefore, we should assume a more cautious stance. Predation, I will argue, is not necessarily amoral, but it may be contingently so, at least in most cases.

## 2 The possible morality of predation

My intention is to show that there is no necessary connection between predation and amorality. I do not intend to argue the direct opposite, namely, that predation is necessarily moral. This is clearly an absurd claim, most obviously because of the prevalence of predation in nature. A lion hunting and eating a gazelle is a paradigmatic case of predation, and the one we usually think of, but it is far from being the only one. In fact, predation extends far beyond the classical examples of lions, polar bears, and crocodiles, to cases like the bird who preys on a worm or the spider who preys on a fly. Even carnivorous plants could be regarded as predators. I will argue that the amorality of predation cannot be presupposed, by which I do not mean to imply that *all* forms of predation are moral. Rather, my claim is that we do not have enough grounds to claim that predation is *necessarily* amoral, or even that *all* forms of predation that we know of are *contingently* amoral.

To see this, let us begin by considering what it would take for predation to be necessarily amoral. This would mean that, of necessity, there are no moral elements involved in predation. I will consider some arguments in support of this conceptual claim in the following sections. But first, it will be useful to have a look at some empirical literature, to see whether we can find any support for the opposite idea: that there might be some moral elements in at least some forms of predation. Here is Biben (1979) describing the behaviour of a good candidate for moral predation, the common cat:

> [Predatory] behaviour patterns [...] show many properties commonly referred to as *playful*. [...] By play, I am referring to behaviour that is active, where the cat's attention is focused on the prey, or where the prey is touched, manipulated or approached, but not injured. These behaviour patterns can be considered *unnecessary for predation since the prey could easily be killed with minimal preliminaries* [...]. Instead, cats approached the prey, touched it, and picked it up in the mouth, but failed to bite. Such bouts of play were often repeated several times before the cat finally killed. However, *killing was only rarely an 'accident'* of vigorous play. In the great majority of cases, the killing bite was distinct from the preceding play activities. (Biben 1979: 86; emphasis added)

I have highlighted some of the elements that could provide this behaviour with a moral character. Predation is accompanied here by a number of playful interactions with the prey, which the author considers to be unnecessary for the end pursued and which undoubtedly prolong the prey's suffering. In addition, killing appears not to be an accident, but rather the result of a distinct killing bite, which suggests that the cat engages in this play behaviour as a separate activity, possibly one that she enjoys, and that she has some degree of control over when this activity begins and ends.

This sort of (apparent) intentional play with prey is also seen in wild predators. A notable example is provided by killer whales:

> Interviewees reported killer whales ramming narwhal to "break their ribs", and *killer whales will "play with" the narwhal, or pieces of them, and throw them around*. One interviewee provided a second-hand description of killer whales "playing soccer" with the narwhal, and another observed killer whales killing narwhal by slapping them with their tail. [...] One Pond Inlet interviewee described two killer whales biting a narwhal and pulling it apart, leaving the head and tail behind and taking the "meat in the middle". Two interviewees reported that killer whales will also drown narwhal. [...] Some participants noted that killer whales will sometimes *kill and eat only a little of their prey, leaving the rest*, and *sometimes even not eat anything at all*. [...] Eight interviewees noted that killer whales sometimes "*kill for fun*", kill without eating, or "play" with wildlife." (Ferguson/Higdon/Westdal 2012: 7, 11; emphasis added)

Here we not only see play behaviour involved in predation, but also that killing the narwhal is something that the orcas seem to enjoy and are willing to do for the sake of it, meaning that hunger is apparently not the sole motivation behind predation in this case. In addition, a variety of killing methods are used, which also suggests a degree of intentionality. Several of these methods are likely to be very painful and stressful for the prey. We see 'cruel' killing methods in other predatory species, like hyenas and lions, as the following quote shows:

> [H]yenas "kill the victim by eating it" (Kruuk 1972, p. 153), in that the animal may be *struggling and vocalising as feeding begins and may die up to a quarter hour later*. The belly and loins are torn open; the fetus is eaten if the prey is pregnant; the testicles or udder is eaten; the stomach is pulled out; and the stomach wall is eaten and the contents spilled on the ground (Kruuk 1972, p. 125). [...] *Lions kill by slow strangulation*, biting the throat of their prey: death is rapid for small prey but *may take an hour for an adult wildebeest* (Schaller 1973, p. 31) while it struggles to escape. (Nell 2006: 213; emphasis added)

Of course, none of this would be moral if it were purely mechanical. Compare: a fallen tree might cause a slow death to the unfortunate human it traps underneath it, but clearly the situation has no moral component to it. However, some predators are quite cognitively sophisticated, probably falling much closer to us on the spectrum of intentionality than to a fallen tree. In addition, and although there is too little work done on the proximate mechanisms of predation to generalise, it seems that high degrees of enjoyment can also be involved in this behaviour. For instance, here is a description of the reactions that predation typically invokes in chimpanzees:

> [T]he chimpanzees' visceral reaction to a hunt and kill is *intense excitement*. The forest comes alive with the barks and hoots and cries of the apes, and aroused newcomers race in from several directions. The monkey may be eaten alive, shrieking as it is torn apart. Dominant males try to seize the prey, leading to fights and charges and screams of rage. For one or two hours or more, the *thrilled* apes tear apart and devour the monkey. This is *blood lust in its rawest form*. (Wrangham/Peterson 1997: 216; emphasis added)

With these examples in mind, we can see that predation could contain the following, seemingly moral elements: (1) an intense emotional component of enjoyment or excitement apparently caused by, and possibly directed at, the hunt itself, (2) painful killing methods, often involving a (purposeful?) prolonging of the prey's suffering, (3) a variety of killing methods, which suggests a degree of control or intentionality over the behaviour, (4) playful interactions with prey and a surplus of killing, which suggests that hunger is not the sole motivation behind predation. Still, amongst philosophers, predation is for the most part assumed to be amoral. In the following sections, I examine the arguments that have been offered in support of this idea.

## 3 Objection: Predators are not moral agents

The claim that predators lack moral agency is the most commonly used to ground the amorality of predation, and this would probably be the most likely rebuttal against the examples I offered in the previous section. The behaviours described cannot be moral because only moral agents can engage in moral behaviour. The claim that predators are not moral agents can be traced back to Regan (2004: 151–156), who introduced the distinction between moral agents and moral patients into animal ethics. While (sentient) predators may be moral patients, and thus legitimate objects of moral consideration, they lack moral agency. This means that they cannot be said to have duties towards prey animals. So, they are not violating any duties when they hunt prey down and eat them, thus making predatory behaviour amoral.

In order to assess whether predators' purported lack of moral agency can truly ground the amorality of predation, we need to have a closer look at what Regan took moral agency to mean. He wrote:

> In contrast to moral agents, moral patients lack the prerequisites that would enable them to control their own behavior in ways that would make them *morally accountable* for what they do. A moral patient lacks the ability to formulate, let alone bring to bear, *moral principles* in deliberating about which one among the possible acts it would be right or proper to perform. Moral patients, in a word, *cannot do what is right, nor can they do what is wrong.* (Regan 2004: 152; emphasis added)

Regan is committing here what I termed the amalgamation fallacy (Monsó 2016). This consists of understanding moral agency as the amalgamation of three separate capacities: first, the capacity for moral responsibility (which allows moral agents to be "morally accountable"); second, the capacity for moral judgement (which allows them to understand and follow "moral principles"); third, the capacity for moral behaviour (which would allow them to "do what is right" or "what is wrong"). As I have argued elsewhere (Monsó 2016; 2017), these three capacities are distinct. However, Regan (as many other authors) amalgamates them and treats them as one. This has to do with the fact that the capacity he is interested in is the first one: moral responsibility. This is the relevant one for the case he is trying to make: the idea that we should not intervene in predator-prey relations. Moral responsibility is different from the other two capacities in that it does entail both moral judgement and moral behaviour, so focusing on moral responsibility can make it tempting to commit the amalgamation fallacy. However, while moral responsibility requires both moral judgement and moral behaviour, the opposite is not necessarily the case. Moral judgement and moral behaviour are both conceivable without the other two capacities.

It is probably true that predators lack the ability to entertain and act according to moral judgements, which means we cannot legitimately hold them morally accountable for their behaviour, but from this it does not follow that predation is amoral. This is because for predation to be moral all we need is moral behaviour, and moral behaviour can exist in the absence of both moral judgements and moral responsibility (Waller 1997; Rowlands 2012; Monsó 2017). Rowlands (2012) came up with a third moral category to express this idea: the notion of a moral subject. Moral subjects are beings whose behaviour can sometimes qualify as moral, even though they might not meet all the conditions to be held morally responsible. While all moral agents are moral subjects, not all moral subjects need be moral agents.

The category of a 'mere' moral subject allows us to make sense of the idea that children or people with certain mental illnesses or disabilities can sometimes behave in ways that we are inclined to describe in moral terms (they may be selfish, cruel, benevolent, generous, ...), but we might not want to praise or blame them for this behaviour because they do not meet various conditions for moral responsibility, like being able to fully comprehend and act in accordance with moral judgements. The notion of a moral subject could allow us to make sense of the moral character of their behaviour and, in turn, to make sense of the apparent morality of predation. A lack of moral judgement capacities may prevent predators from being regarded as full-blown moral agents, but they may still be moral subjects if their behaviour is at times moral. If this applies to their predatory behaviour, then we would have to conclude that predation could sometimes be moral.

What could make predatory behaviour moral? A sufficient (if not necessary) condition for moral behaviour to obtain is for it to have been triggered by a moral motivation (Rowlands 2012; Monsó 2017). Moral judgements are a type of moral motivation, but there are also other types, such as moral emotions. Rowlands (2012) defines moral emotions as intentional emotions that track moral propositions.[1] This means that they have to have intentional objects, rather than being mere affective states, and there must also be a truth-preserving relation between this intentional emotion and a moral proposition. With our current state of knowledge, we cannot confidently assert that moral emotions are at the basis of predatory behaviour, but we cannot exclude it a priori either. As we saw in the previous section, there are reasons to believe that intense emotions are present in some instances of predatory behaviour and that motivations other than hunger sometimes trigger the hunt and kill. It is in principle possible for some predatory behaviour to be caused by emotions akin to cruelty, schadenfreude, or blood lust – emotions that have as their intentional object the hunt or the prey's suffering and that track propositions like "This animal's suffering is good." On these grounds, it is implausible to exclude a priori the very possibility of moral predation.

## 4 Objection: An absurd duty to police nature?

If predation were moral, my opponent might argue, then this would imply that prey animals have their rights violated when they are hunted down and eaten by predators. This would have the implication that the state would be allowed, perhaps even required, to police nature in order to prevent this injustice from occurring. This implication is so absurd, the objection goes, that clearly predation cannot be moral. However, the first thing that should be said about this objection is that a duty to intervene in predator-prey relations is something that not

---

[1] For a careful explanation of what the notion of 'tracking' implies, see Rowlands (2012: chs. 2, 9) and Monsó (2017).

everyone would regard as an absurd conclusion. In fact, some ethicists who are very concerned about wild animal suffering might welcome it. So, this purported implication cannot be used as a *reductio ad absurdum*, and therefore it is not enough to conclude that predation cannot be moral. However, for those authors who, like myself, would rather adopt more of a hands-off stance towards predator-prey relations, it is important to point out that a duty to intervene would not automatically follow from the morality of predation.

The objection that the morality of predation implies a duty to police nature is very closely related to the claim examined in the previous section (that predation cannot be moral because predators are not moral agents), and rests upon the same conceptual confusion: an amalgamation of moral responsibility, moral judgement, and moral behaviour. If predators were moral subjects, rather than moral agents, this would mean that they have the capacity to behave on the basis of moral motivations, but lack the moral judgement abilities that would allow them to entertain duties, and to consequently be held morally responsible for their behaviour. If predators were moral subjects, instead of using the language of rights and duties, we would have to use the language of moral psychology to capture the moral quality of predation. We might say, for instance, that predatory behaviour is moral in those cases in which it is motivated by something akin to cruelty if the predator enjoys the prey's suffering and purposefully tries to prolong it as much as possible. This does not necessarily imply any duties of intervention. The description of predation as 'moral' says something about the psychology of the predator, but in and of itself it is not sufficient to ground a duty to intervene in predator-prey relations. Moral behaviour, as has been extensively argued by Rowlands (2011; 2012; 2017; see also Waller 2004; Monsó 2017), is conceptually independent from moral responsibility, so predation can be moral without it implying that predators ought to be blamed, punished, or even prevented from engaging in this behaviour.

# 5 Objection: Predation is not under the predator's control

Another way in which an opponent might defend the amorality of predation is by saying that this is a behaviour that is ultimately not under the control of the individual. The idea is that for a behaviour to count as moral, it must be 'chosen' by the actor. Since predation cannot be plausibly construed as 'chosen' by the predator but is rather a behaviour that she has no option but to engage in, it should be viewed as amoral. This objection can be tackled in different ways, depending on how we construct the link between control and morality and on what we mean when we say that the predator's behaviour is not under her control.

On the one hand, we might mean that behaviour can only be moral if one can be legitimately praised or blamed for it. And a certain behaviour will deserve praise or blame if and only if it is under the control of the individual. If one could not have done things differently, then obviously one does not deserve praise or blame, for there is no merit to the behaviour at all. This way of understanding the objection would, however, still fall prey to the amalgamation fallacy. Once we disentangle moral behaviour from moral responsibility, we can see how the absence of merit does not rule out the possibility of describing behaviour in moral terms. Getting rid of the amalgamation fallacy would not only enable us to make sense of the morality of the behaviour of children or people with certain mental illnesses or disabilities, it would also allow us to preserve morality if hard determinism turned out to be true. This was eloquently put by Rowlands:

> In determinism world – which may or may not be the actual world – hard determinism is true, and no one is, therefore, ever responsible for what they do. Would we really want to say that, in this world, there is no such thing as moral motivation? When Hitler (or the worldly equivalent thereof) starts a World War and attempts to exterminate various races, would we want to say that his motivations do not count as morally evil? We might, in such a world, justifiably rescind from evaluation of Hitler, the person: we might, that is, refuse to blame or hold him responsible for what he does. But refusing to classify his motivations as even falling into the category of the moral is highly counterintuitive. (Rowlands 2017: 471)

If predators indeed have no control whatsoever over their behaviour, they in themselves constitute a kind of determinism world. We might justifiably not want to blame them or hold them morally responsible, but if their behaviour fulfils a number of conditions, we might nevertheless want to classify it as moral, just as we would still consider Hitler's motivations as morally evil even if he had had no real choice.

There is another way of constructing the link between control and morality. When we say that predatory behaviour is not 'chosen' by the predator we might mean, following Korsgaard (2006), that predators lack normative self-government. While they might be able to choose how and when to engage in predatory behaviour, they cannot choose whether or not they want to be predators. They can, in other words, choose the means to their ends but not the ends in themselves. This, following Korsgaard, would mean that they do not have as high a level of intentionality as humans, the paradigmatic moral actors. We not only have motivations that can be classified as good or bad but can actually assess these motivations and decide whether or not to adopt them, whether or not they are in accordance with the sort of person we want to be. For Korsgaard, morality only emerges at this level.

However, normative self-government, thus understood, is quite intellectually demanding, to an extent that probably renders it implausible as a necessary condition for moral behaviour. It would mean a necessary exclusion from the realm of morality of anyone who lacks moral judgement capacities. But perhaps more importantly, as has been extensively argued by Rowlands (2011; 2012), higher-order reflection on our motivations cannot guarantee a deeper level of control over them than we have at the first-order level. There is nothing magical about higher-order cognition. Moving one level up simply changes the object of our reflections. Instead of asking ourselves, "Should I do it this way?" we ask, "Should I do it at all?" But whichever answer we give to the question, "Should I do it at all?" is one over which we might not have control either, so higher-order reflection gives nothing but the appearance of deeper control.

If we leave the requirement for normative self-government aside, one could still argue that predators cannot even control their behaviour at the first-order level, because predation obeys an uncontrollable drive. To this, one could counter-argue by pointing out that we have no qualms with describing as moral some human behaviour that obeys uncontrollable drives. The man who murders his wife in an irrepressible fit of rage, for instance, would not be regarded as having behaved 'amorally.' Still, one could object by saying that in this case we have an emotion with an intentional object that is motivating the behaviour, and to which we can attach a moral character. When saying that predation obeys an uncontrollable drive, what the defender of the amorality of predation might mean is that it is triggered by purely mechanical causes, with no cognitive or emotional mediation whatsoever. The lion slowly strangling the wildebeest would be analogous to the fallen tree slowly suffocating the person it fell upon or to a man who kills his wife entirely by accident. However, our current state of knowledge does not allow us to assert this. In fact, as we saw in section 2, the empirical literature offers some evidence in support of the opposite idea: that some predatory behaviour involves at least some degree of intentionality and that intense emotions may sometimes underlie the hunt and kill.

# 6 Objection: Predation is necessary for predators to survive

This final objection would consist in claiming that predation cannot be viewed as morally laden because it is necessary for the predators to survive. It is analogous to killing in self-defence, which is why it is more plausibly construed as amoral. Faced with this objection we would have to first of all point out that not all predation is necessary for survival. Chimpanzees in the wild, for example, mostly lead vegetarian lives but will occasionally prey on monkeys and insects. However, these non-plant foods make up a meagre 5% of their food intake (Stanford/Nkurunungi 2003). Domestic cats also often prey on mice and other small animals, even if they are supplied with all the food they need by their owners, so their predatory behaviour cannot be viewed as necessary for their survival, either. And we have already seen that other animals, like killer whales, will kill more than they actually eat.

However, even if all predation were necessary for survival, this would again not imply that predation is necessarily amoral. Imagine someone who, faced with a murderer, decides to kill him in self-defence, but purposely does it in the slowest way she can think of, enjoying the victim's suffering and trying to prolong it as much as possible. The killing might be justified, given the circumstances, but the way in which it is done can hardly be viewed as amoral in a descriptive sense. In fact, we might say that this is far from a virtuous form of killing in self-defence and that the killer has demonstrated somewhat of a sadistic character. It is as of yet unclear whether cruel, sadistic, or otherwise moral motivations ever underlie the behaviour of predators, but until this is determined we cannot confidently assert that all predation is amoral.

# 7 A final objection: Moral predation is unlikely

Assuming my opponent agrees with my arguments so far, two final arguments could be raised to defend the idea that moral predation is unlikely to happen very often in nature. The first one is that this sort of account of the morality of predation seems to require predators to be capable of attributing suffering to their prey. Therefore, it seems to require mindreading capacities. Given that there is still a significant amount of debate over whether chimpanzees, our closest relatives, possess mindreading capacities,[2] it is doubtful that these capacities are going to be very widely distributed in nature. The second objection is that it would not be fitness enhancing to expend more effort than necessary in killing prey, and so it is doubtful that predators are going to waste resources on prolonging their prey's suffering or engaging in other kinds of sadistic behaviours.[3]

---

[2] For an overview of the chimpanzee mindreading debate, see Andrews (2017).
[3] I owe these two objections to Kian Mintz-Woo.

The first thing that needs to be said with respect to these two objections is that they are not much of a problem for my argument. It is not my intention to show that *all* or even *some* predation is moral, but rather that we cannot exclude a priori the possibility of moral predation. So, considerations that make moral predation *unlikely* do not attack the core of my argument, since I am not committed to any claims regarding the actual distribution in nature of moral predation.

Still, there are reasons to think that these objections are not as strong as they might initially seem. On the one hand, the requirement that predators possess mindreading capacities in order for their behaviour to count as moral has some intuitive appeal, but it stems from the intuitive pull of the amalgamation fallacy. We are accustomed to thinking about moral behaviour as intertwined with moral judgement and moral responsibility, and the latter two probably do require mindreading capacities. But moral behaviour only requires a moral motivation, and as I have argued extensively elsewhere (Monsó 2015; 2016; 2017), some accounts of moral motivations do not demand mindreading capacities. Rowlands' (2012) account, for instance, requires a moral subject to have a reliable emotional sensitivity to good- or bad-making features of situations. While intentional directedness is opaque, emotional sensitivity is merely extensional or transparent, meaning that moral subjects only need to, for instance, reliably feel joyful in the presence of someone suffering, where this joy need only be directed at the superficial behavioural cues that accompany suffering. This is enough to speak of a reliable emotional sensitivity to suffering. In other words, mindreading is not necessary for minimal forms of morality; behaviour reading can suffice (Monsó 2015; 2016; 2017).

With respect to the objection that it would not be fitness enhancing for predators to waste resources by engaging in sadistic behaviours, this underestimates the importance that emotions can have in motivating and shaping behaviour. Due to the evolutionary arms race between predators and their prey, hunting prey down is a difficult and exhausting activity that results in very low success rates for predators. For instance, lions have about a 30% chance of catching a zebra or a gazelle, and it goes down to around 14% when it comes to antelopes (Schaller 1976: 389). In addition, prey animals have defence mechanisms that can sometimes make attacking them very dangerous. It is not uncommon, for instance, for lions to be crippled or even killed by their prey, who are often equipped with sharp horns or hooves (Schaller 1976: 189). It is therefore important for predators to be very motivated to hunt their prey, and while hunger surely plays an important role, finding high degrees of enjoyment in the hunt and kill might be a very effective motivator. Moreover, emotional contagion and other empathic mechanisms appear to be prevalent across mammalian species,[4] but it would be very problematic for a predator to feel sympathy towards her prey, so it would not be surprising for natural selection to have delivered mechanisms to counteract the possibility of an empathic reaction towards the prey's suffering. And finally, the time spent playing with dying or dead prey, rather than being a mere waste of resources, could be useful training for predators to perfect their hunting skills (Fox 1969; Špinka/Newberry/Bekoff 2001). Therefore, rather than being detrimental to a predator's fitness, having sadistic or cruel inclinations might actually be fitness enhancing.

# 8 Conclusion

Predation is generally presupposed to be amoral by philosophers discussing the predator-prey problem. In this short paper, I have examined four arguments that could be given in support of the necessary amorality of predation and found all of them lacking. While predation is likely amoral *in most cases*, it *could* be moral *in some cases*, if and when it was triggered by a moral motivation. The question of how widely distributed moral predation is in nature is an empirical issue on which I have not taken a stand. What I want to emphasise is that presupposing the amorality of predation without further qualification is unwarranted. Animal rights theorists need not worry about this conclusion, however, since predation can be moral without this necessarily implying any duty to intervene in predator-prey relations in the wild. In fact, as I have argued, making sense of the morality of predation requires disentangling moral behaviour from moral responsibility, and so it is likely that the case for the morality of predation will stand or fall with the case for moral behaviour without moral responsibility.

# References

Andrews, Kristin (2017): "Chimpanzee Mind Reading: Don't Stop Believing." In: *Philosophy Compass* 12(1), Article e12394.
Biben, Maxeen (1979): "Predation and Predatory Play Behaviour of Domestic Cats." In: *Animal Behaviour* 27(1), pp. 81–94.
Cochrane, Alasdair (2012): *Animal Rights without Liberation: Applied Ethics and Human Obligations*. New York, NY: Columbia University Press.
De Waal, Frans B. M./Preston, Stephanie D. (2017): "Mammalian Empathy: Behavioural Manifestations and Neural Basis." In: *Nature Reviews Neuroscience* 18(8), pp. 498–509.

---

[4] For a review, see De Waal/Preston (2017).

Ebert, Rainer/Machan, Tibor R. (2012): "Innocent Threats and the Moral Problem of Carnivorous Animals." In: *Journal of Applied Philosophy* 29(2), pp. 146–159.

Faria, Catia/Paez, Eze (2019): "It's Splitsville: Why Animal Ethics and Environmental Ethics Are Incompatible." In: *American Behavioral Scientist* 63(8), pp. 1047–1060.

Ferguson, Steven H./Higdon, Jeff W./Westdal, Kristin H. (2012): "Prey Items and Predation Behavior of Killer Whales (*Orcinus orca*) in Nunavut, Canada Based on Inuit Hunter Interviews." In: *Aquatic Biosystems* 8(3).

Fink, Charles K. (2005): "The Predation Argument." In: *Between the Species* 13(5), Article 3.

Fitzpatrick, Simon (2017): "Animal Morality: What Is the Debate About?" In: *Biology & Philosophy* 32(6), pp. 1151–1183.

Fox, M. W. (1969): "Ontogeny of Prey-Killing Behavior in Canidae." In: *Behaviour* 35(3–4), pp. 259–272.

Horta, Oscar (2015): "The Problem of Evil in Nature: Evolutionary Bases of the Prevalence of Disvalue." In: *Relations: Beyond Anthropocentrism* 3(1), pp. 17–32.

Kapembwa, Julius (2018): "Predation Catch-22: Disentangling the Rights of Prey, Predators, and Rescuers." In: *Journal of Agricultural and Environmental Ethics* 31(5), pp. 527–542.

Korsgaard, Christine M. (2006): "Morality and the Distinctiveness of Human Action." In: Macedo, Stephen/Ober, Josiah (Eds.): *Primates and Philosophers: How Morality Evolved*. Princeton, NJ: Princeton University Press, pp. 98–119.

Kruuk, Hans (1972): *The Spotted Hyena: A Study of Predation and Social Behavior*. Chicago: University of Chicago Press.

Milburn, Josh (2015): "Rabbits, Stoats and the Predator Problem: Why a Strong Animal Rights Position Need Not Call for Human Intervention to Protect Prey from Predators." In: *Res Publica* 21(3), pp. 273–289.

Monsó, Susana (2015): "Empathy and Morality in Behaviour Readers." In: *Biology & Philosophy* 30(5), pp. 671–690.

Monsó, Susana (2016): *Morality and Mindreading in Nonhuman Animals*. Doctoral dissertation. Madrid: Universidad Nacional de Educación a Distancia.

Monsó, Susana (2017): "Morality without Mindreading." In: *Mind & Language* 32(3), pp. 338–357.

Nell, Victor (2006): "Cruelty's Rewards: The Gratifications of Perpetrators and Spectators." In: *Behavioral and Brain Sciences* 29(3), pp. 211–224.

Regan, Tom (2004): *The Case for Animal Rights*. Updated with a new preface. Berkeley, CA: University of California Press.

Rowlands, Mark (2011): "Animals That Act for Moral Reasons." In: Beauchamp, Tom L./Frey, R. G. (Eds.): *The Oxford Handbook of Animal Ethics*. New York, NY: Oxford University Press, pp. 519–546.

Rowlands, Mark (2012): *Can Animals Be Moral?* New York, NY: Oxford University Press.

Rowlands, Mark (2017): "Moral Subjects." In: Andrews, Kristin/Beck, Jacob (Eds.): *The Routledge Handbook of Philosophy of Animal Minds*. Abingdon: Routledge, pp. 469–474.

Schaller, George B. (1976): *The Serengeti Lion: A Study of Predator-Prey Relations*. Chicago, IL: University of Chicago Press.

Špinka, Marek/Newberry, Ruth C./Bekoff, Marc (2001): "Mammalian Play: Training for the Unexpected." In: *The Quarterly Review of Biology* 76(2), pp. 141–168.

Stanford, Craig B./Nkurunungi, J. Bosco (2003): "Behavioral Ecology of Sympatric Chimpanzees and Gorillas in Bwindi Impenetrable National Park, Uganda: Diet." In: *International Journal of Primatology* 24(4), pp. 901–918.

Waller, Bruce N. (1997): "What Rationality Adds to Animal Morality." In: *Biology & Philosophy* 12(3), pp. 341–356.

Waller, Bruce N. (2004): "Virtue Unrewarded: Morality without Moral Responsibility." In: *Philosophia* 31(3–4), pp. 427–447.

Wrangham, Richard/Peterson, Dale (1997): *Demonic Males: Apes and the Origins of Human Violence*. Boston, MA: Mariner Books.

___
Part 7: **Wittgenstein**

Alice Crary
# Wittgenstein Does Critical Theory

**Abstract:** The aim of this article is to illuminate the distinctive challenges of liberating social criticism. The article's primary concern is an account of the nature of critical social thought that, while intuitively attractive, goes missing in many institutionally central philosophical conversations about such thought. This is because the account presupposes a heterodox conception of rationality that often is not even registered as a legitimate possibility, much less seriously discussed. Yet the relevant conception of rationality informs influential philosophical treatments of liberating social criticism, including, for instance, some notable contributions to Critical Theory. It is possible to mount a defense of this conception, thereby providing support for the appealing image of critique it brings within reach, by reconstructing – with some substantial criticisms and additions – an argument from mid twentieth-century Anglo-American philosophy of the social sciences, viz., the argument that forms the backbone of Peter Winch's *The Idea of a Social Science*. Winch draws his guiding insights from the later philosophy of Wittgenstein, and one payoff of reevaluating Winch's work against the backdrop of congenial work in Critical Theory is that this makes it possible not only to decisively contesting the deeply engrained idea that Wittgenstein's later thought has a politically conservative bent but, more positively, to demonstrate the great value of his thought for emancipatory criticism. The larger payoff of this ecumenical method is nothing more and nothing less than advancing the enterprise of critique.

**Keywords:** Ludwig Wittgenstein, Critical Theory, philosophy of language, analytic philosophy, critical social thought

## 1 The idea of widely rational critique

It is plausible but by no means uncontroversial to suggest that liberating social criticism needs to be conceived as capable of harnessing the cognitive power of critical gestures that shape our sense of what is important, inviting us to see social phenomena in new moral and political lights. Here we might think of the sorts of changes in our sense of significance that are sometimes affected by consciousness-raising social movements, counter publics, or political art. There is, admittedly, nothing contentious about the suggestion that activities, forms of social upheaval, images, utterances, or inscriptions that alter what strikes us as important – and that as a result change our conception of the social world – can affect our understanding of social situations in accidental or external ways. But suppose that what interests us is not merely a suggestion on these lines. Suppose that we are interested in the idea that the kinds of critical interventions that thus adjust our sense of significance can as such internally inform our understanding of decisive features of the social world. Then it will appear to us that, if we are to approach the task of criticism in a morally and politically responsible manner, we need critical methods and resources that take this possibility seriously.

Consider, as an initial example of the kind of critical exercise in question, the work of the legal scholar Kimberlé Crenshaw and, more specifically, portions of Crenshaw's work in which she undertakes to shed light on harms done to Black women in the United States who are victims of sexual violence. Crenshaw has written with great insight about, for instance, the case of Anita Hill, who in 1991 was subpoenaed to testify at the U.S. Senate hearings for Clarence Thomas' nomination to the Supreme Court because she told the FBI that, when she was working under Thomas at the Department of Education and the Equal Employment Opportunity Commission, he repeatedly subjected her to unwanted sexual attention (see Crenshaw 1992). Somewhat more recently, Crenshaw has discussed the case of Daniel Holtzclaw, a former Oklahoma City police officer, who while on the force systematically sought out women who were poor, Black, and had criminal records or legal troubles, sexually assaulting and raping them.[1]

One notable presupposition of Crenshaw's treatments of these and other cases is that – in order to appreciate the awfulness of unwelcome sexual behavior visited upon women – we need to have a vivid image of how, in our society, women experience disadvantages that are substantial, structural, and pervasive, and how women therefore have vulnerabilities that unwanted sexual activity both exploits and exacerbates. That is a theme from classic feminist accounts of rape and sexual harassment, and part of what is distinctive about Crenshaw's work is that, in addition to sounding this theme, she stresses that, if we are to do justice to harms done to Black women who are victims of sexual violence, we need to have a vivid sense of ways in which anti-Black racism in the United States affects Black women, interacting or – in Crenshaw's famous term of art – "intersecting" with sexism in a manner that effectively sexualizes it.[2] We

---

[1] See Amy Goodman's interview (2015) with Kimberlé Crenshaw and others. Thirteen women ultimately testified against Holtzclaw, and in 2015 he was convicted by an all-white jury of crimes (including four counts of first-degree rape) against eight of them.
[2] For Crenshaw's classic discussion of the importance of attention to "intersections" among forms of bias that affect women of color, see Crenshaw (1991).

need to be aware not only that rape and sexual assault have been conditions of Black women's work lives for centuries but also that today there are still institutional remnants of associated myths about Black women as "sexually voracious" and "sexually indiscriminate" (Crenshaw 1992: 411). For instance, we need to know that Black women's words are less likely to be taken as truth and, further, that even in situations in which a conviction is secured for a sex crime against a Black women the sentence is likely to be less severe than sentences imposed on men who commit the same crime against white women (see Crenshaw 1992: 412–413).

A guiding motif of Crenshaw's work in this area is that our sense of ways in which these aspects of U.S. history continue to shape social life need to inform our social vision if we are to be able to recognize and register the gravity of the harms done to Black women who are victims of sexual violence. Crenshaw accordingly proceeds as a critic by trying to get us to appreciate forms of social exposure produced by intertwined systems of racism and sexism. At the same time, she presents herself as, in this way, internally contributing to our ability to understand real aspects of social life (viz., specific injuries done to Black women). That is the sort of thing at stake in the claim that critical gestures that shape sense of salience or importance can as such directly inform genuine or objective understanding.

However unsurprising this claim may sound to feminists and critical race theorists (cf. Crary 2018c), there are philosophical circles in which it is taken to verge on heresy. At issue is a claim about how critical exercises that direct our attitudes may as such be rationally authoritative. To incorporate the claim, we have to challenge an entrenched philosophical understanding of rationality on which our ability to make the connections of a rational line of thought cannot essentially depend on our possession of any particular routes of feeling. We need to expand – or 'widen' – this familiar and, arguably, overly 'narrow' conception so that bits of discourse that encourage us to look at things from new cultural or evaluative perspectives may as such have rational power. We might speak here of a move away from a *narrower* and toward a *wider* conception of rationality.[3] Similarly, we might speak of a transition from *narrowly rational* to *widely rational* modes of critique.

A widely rational conception of critical social thought has a clear moral and political appeal. By its lights, social criticism is conceived so that critics cannot antecedently exclude the possibility of needing to explore and perhaps embrace

---

[3] For more detailed discussion of these competing conceptions of rationality, see Crary (2016: sec. 6.1).

cultural or ethical values, or historical perspectives, that shape the social settings they are investigating. It follows that efforts at social criticism need not be vulnerable to charges – of sorts sometimes leveled at Kantian-formalistic or consequentialist modes of social criticism – of an *elitist* or *ethnocentric* tendency to impose unacknowledged values cherished by other, possibly hegemonic societies while being insensitive to the local values at hand. (E. g., consider how Crenshaw and other antiracist feminists call on us to revise our understand what counts as grossly unjust and coercive treatment so that it includes some forms of sexual behavior that were not previously classified as such; it is essential to these theorists' procedures that they give us a feel for structurally produced social susceptibilities of women socially identified as nonwhite, specifically with a view opening our eyes to harms that are not otherwise visible.) Further, what is at issue is an understanding of social criticism as wholeheartedly rational. It follows that particular efforts at social criticism need not be vulnerable to charges – of sorts sometimes leveled at poststructuralist or other anti-universalistic modes of social criticism – of a *merely partisan* willingness to affirm whatever attitudes happen to be regarded as liberating at a given place and time. (E. g., there is no obstacle to taking Crenshaw and other feminist antiracists who talk about sexual violence against Black and other nonwhite women in a similar manner, i.e., in a manner that essentially presupposes the mobilization of specific evaluative attitudes, to be thereby speaking with rational authority.)

Despite its evident moral and political interest, a widely rational conception of social criticism often goes missing from discussions about what social criticism is like. It is not that theorists routinely consider and then reject as untenable widely rational accounts of social criticism. More commonly, the possibility of such accounts simply goes unregistered, and it is suggested that we are confronted with a choice between, on the one hand, conceptions of social criticism on which it is essentially in the business of exploring the perspective and values of specific social contexts – and on which it is in this strong sense 'context-bound' – and, on the other, conceptions on which it is rationally authoritative. For an illustration of this trend, consider the distinction that the Kantian moral and political philosopher Onora O'Neill draws between critique that is "weakly normative" and critique that is "strongly normative" (see O'Neill 2000; my translation). When O'Neill discusses weakly normative critique, she has in mind critique that as she sees it cannot help but represent "normative claims as [...] more limited and less deeply justified" because it is anchored in the "conceptions, obligations, and agreements of actual ethical codes as well as in the political institutions of a people" (O'Neill 2000: 719; my translation). When, in contrast, she talks about strongly normative critique, she has in mind critique that eschews the kind of context-groundedness characteristic of its weakly normative counterparts and can, in her view, thus lay claim to "norms that have cosmopolitan reach and that supply the ground of the action of all people" (O'Neill 2000: 720; my translation). The very terms in which O'Neill discusses these kinds of critique reveal that there is for her no prospect of social criticism that is both essentially grounded in particular values and rationally authoritative and that is thus capable of combining the respective virtues of social criticism in what she describes as its competing weakly and strongly normative instantiations. The very terms that she uses reveal, that is, that there is for her no prospect of widely rational social criticism. Nor is O'Neill alone in overlooking the possibility of such social criticism.[4] Among other things, the past several years have witnessed the emergence of a new set of debates about ideology and liberating critique within analytic philosophy that likewise mostly neglect the possibility of critique that uses widely rational resources.[5]

## 2 Widely rational critical theories

One place to look for calls for widely rational social criticism is the philosophical tradition, associated with the University of Frankfurt-based Institute for Social Research and placed under the heading of "Critical Theory," that aims to promote emancipatory politics by offering a special kind of theoretical image of society. It was in the late 1930s that affiliates of the Institute began to think that what united them was the pursuit of such an image or – as Max Horkheimer first put it – a *critical theory* of society (see Horkheimer 1972). Critical theories have generally been understood to possess the following elements. They are, to use a formulation by Raymond Geuss, essentially capable of serving as

---

4 Although it is possible to use the work of a Kantian, universalist critic like O'Neill to illustrate the tendency to overlook this possibility, it is equally possible to turn to an antiuniversalist to make the same point. For an antiuniversalist critic who believes we are obliged to choose between what O'Neill would call 'strongly normative' and 'weakly normative' critique, while differing from O'Neill in opting for the latter alternative, we could turn to the writings of Richard Rorty. See my discussion of relevant aspects of Rorty's work in Crary (2000). For further examples of both universalist and antiuniversalist varieties, see the text below.
5 Some of the most influential spokespeople for this emerging philosophical corpus are in effect 'universalist' theorists who do not represent critique as essentially context-sensitive, even if at some level they aim to do so. This includes Miranda Fricker (2007) – for relevant commentary on Fricker, see Crary (2018c) – and Jason Stanley (2015) – for relevant commentary on Stanley, see Crary (2017). Not that there are not analytically trained and engaged theorists, who are involved in new ideology debates, and who help themselves to widely rational resources. For one illuminating counterexample, see Mills (2017).

"guides to human action" in that they both reveal to the agents who hold them "what their true interests are" and emancipate agents by "free[ing them] from a kind of coercion which is at least partly self-imposed." Thus understood, critical theories are supposed to have a kind of "cognitive content" that is nonscientific (Geuss 1981: 1–2).[6] They are conceived in opposition to the 'positivist' idea that the kind of self-understanding that would free us from oppressive strictures is something we achieve by transcending all ethically loaded perspectives and adopting the standpoint of scientific experts.[7] This hostility to a scientific model is of a piece with a conception of critical theories as charged with exploring values embedded in particular social contexts and reflecting perspectives "immanent in human work" (Horkheimer 1972: 213). But a commitment to the exploration of immanent values is taken to be consistent with a theoretical vision possessed of context-transcendent rational authority. It is characteristic of critical theorists to summarize these desiderata by saying that they aim to do justice to the *dialectics of immanence and transcendence*. More succinctly, critical theorists sometimes say that they aspire to a satisfactory conception of *immanent critique*.

There is a striking measure of disagreement among critical theorists today about what a tenable account of what immanent critique is, or should be, would look like. A significant number accept the constraints of a philosophically orthodox, narrower conception of rationality. Indeed, it is possible to arrive at a reasonable classification of many of the accounts currently on offer by representing them as different strategies for achieving the core aims of immanent critique while respecting or at best modestly challenging these narrowly rational constraints. But it is not clear that early members of the Frankfurt School took themselves to be bound by similar restrictions, and any fair description of recent accounts of immanent critique should mention that there are critical theorists who, sometimes harking back to Critical Theory's origins, issue calls for widely rational modes of social criticism.[8]

---

6 For another helpful and congenial overview of the tradition of Critical Theory, see Honneth (2009: ch. 2).

7 Opposition to this positivist idea is a guiding theme of Max Horkheimer's classic "Traditional and Critical Theory" (1972: esp. 198–199, 232).

8 It would have been possible to frame this as a discussion about how to conceive the nature of *ideology critique*. The standard umbrella term for the theoretical images of society that critical theories aim to challenge is *ideology*, and, while in some conversational contexts "ideology" is used without any negative connotations, inside Critical Theory the term is typically employed pejoratively and in reference to ethically charged beliefs that are essentially woven into the fabric of, and inseparable from, social practices. For helpful remarks on how ideological beliefs are inextricably 'practice-soaked,' see, e.g., Geuss (1981: 5–7) and Jaeggi (2009: esp. 64). Any rea-

The contours of these widely rational projects emerge when they are considered against the backdrop of their more narrowly rational counterparts. The most high-profile forays into Critical Theory that operate with narrower assumptions about what rationality is like are projects that their cue from Kant's moral theory. The original model for these endeavors is Jürgen Habermas' approach to inheriting from Kant, an approach that has inspired a number of subsequent, in some respects quite different, Kantian accounts of immanent critique.

The roots of Habermas' Kantian strain lie in his inheritance, from members of the Frankfurt School's first generation, of the Marxian idea that a signature ill of modern capitalist societies is the takeover of political discourse by instrumental or "purposive-rational" reason. One of Habermas' signature ambitions, already very early in his career, is defending the authority of noninstrumental "communicative" or "interactive" forms of reason that are, he believes, capable of reviving the political sphere.[9] By the 1970s, Habermas is pursuing this goal by appealing to resources from John Searle's version of Austinian speech act theory and, more specifically, by appealing to the idea that individual utterances may have different illocutionary forces (see, e.g., Habermas 1979). Starting from this idea, Habermas goes on to insist that speech acts with different illocutionary forces raise validity claims that, although comparably authoritative, are established in different ways. While the validity claims of the sorts of theoretical or "cognitive" utterances that we rely on in the instrumental realm are established objectively, in terms of their adequacy to how things stand in the world, the validity claims of the sorts of "interactive" utterances that are decisive for the moral realm are established intersubjectively, in a manner aptly captured by Kant's conception of the categorical imperative in its universal law formulation. Habermas' Kantian thought is that the question of the truth of moral beliefs is one we settle by asking, not theoretical questions about whether the beliefs do descriptive justice to the world, but rather practical questions about whether the max-

---

sonable gloss on what is insidious about ideological beliefs would have to mention both an *epistemic* aspect having to do with ways in which ideological beliefs fail to truly capture the lives of the individuals caught up in the practices and institutions that they themselves support and stabilize and a *functional* aspect having to do with how these beliefs organize us "in relations of domination and subordination" (see Haslanger no date), thereby nevertheless assuming an aura of truth. Given that ideological beliefs have this sort of functional character, it seems clear that we need materially effective, nonneutral methods in order to combat them. Our answer to the question of whether these methods need to be regarded as in themselves nonrational – and hence as at best propaedeutic to ideology critique understood as a rationally respectable enterprise – or whether instead they may themselves qualify as rationally respectable ideology critique will reflect our views about the availability of a wider conception of rationality.
9 For a clear early statement of this view of Habermas, see Habermas (1987).

ims they encode are universalizable in the formal sense of being such that everyone could in principle consent to them (see Habermas 1999: esp. 64–65). Notice that, in thus borrowing from Kant's moral theory, Habermas is introducing a clear value-norm split. He is avoiding commitment to the idea of objective ethical values and construing norms as objective only in a formal or procedural sense.[10]

Consider now how Habermas uses these Kantian resources in arriving at a distinctive account of immanent critique. Habermas tends to distance himself from the monological aspect of Kant's categorical imperative procedure, representing normative rightness as achieved not by the in principle universalizability of practical maxims but by the concrete universalization of such maxims considered "from the perspective of real-life argumentation" (Habermas 1999: 65), when subject to idealizing conditions. The critical exercises Habermas describes – and that are pivotal for his mature "discourse ethics" – respect a demand for 'immanence' insofar as they in this way involve normative claims that arise from and are adjudicated within actual conversational contexts. But Habermas assumes that it would be right to worry that this institutionalization of Kant's transcendental moral project cannot by itself be relied upon to yield rationally authoritative conclusions, and so cannot be relied upon to qualify as critique in a full-blooded, context-transcendent sense. Because, as Hilary Putnam once put it, ethical values are for Habermas "as noncognitive as they are to positivists" (Putnam 2002: 112), it appears to Habermas that we need grounds for holding that it is possible to reason from our ethical starting points to rationally defensible conclusions. He addresses the putative problem by representing moves toward more reflective, posttraditional societies as moves toward progress. He embraces a philosophy of history on which, in his parlance, "there is progress in the de-centering of our perspectives when it comes to viewing the world as a whole" (Habermas 2013: 360). Habermas takes this philosophy of history to provide a teleological perspective from which 'we' reflective moderns can be confident that we are moving from our ethical starting points to authoritative conclusions. That is how he mobilizes narrowly rational, Kantian resources in trying to demonstrate his entitlement to represent the discourse-based critical maneuvers he champions not only as immanent but also as rationally authoritative and hence as cases of full-blooded critique.

Habermas' project has inspired other narrowly rational, Kantian accounts of immanent critique. This includes contributions to Critical Theory that proceed along more orthodox Kantian lines, such as, notably, the work of Rainer Forst.

---

[10] For a discussion of the centrality to Habermas' work of this sort of value-norm divide, see Putnam (2002).

Like Habermas and other Kantian moral philosophers, Forst steers clear of endorsing the idea of objective ethical values and adopts a strictly practical, formal approach to accounting for the universal authority of normative claims (see, e. g., Forst 2002: 156, 176, 180–181, 190; Forst 2014). But, unlike Habermas, Forst thinks it is possible to tell a tenable story about immanent critique in standard – transcendental – Kantian terms. He believes he can satisfy the demand for appropriate immanence by allowing for essential context-sensitivity in nonmoral spheres of thought and action and, additionally and more importantly, by underlining that even moral demands – that is, demands for universal justification – arise in concrete conversational contexts in which individuals make them.[11] The result is supposed to be a "contextualist universalism" that, in addition to having a claim to rational authority, has a good claim to immanence in virtue of its context-situatedness (see Forst 2002: 1, 60, 164, 172–173, 197–198; Forst 2014: 3, 9, 107). Forst thus endeavors to use familiar Kantian materials to accommodate the 'dialectics of immanence and transcendence.'

Suppose we speak generally of Kantian contributions to Critical Theory that aim to satisfy the conditions of a narrower conception of rationality. There is a notable political worry that arises in reference to these critical approaches. To say that the approaches are designed to satisfy narrowly rational constraints is to say that they take it for granted that we can make the connections internal to rational lines of thought apart from an even imaginative appreciation of any particular cultural or evaluative perspectives. This strategy is politically problematic insofar as it antecedently imposes substantial limits on the critical interest that exploration of such perspectives can have, excluding the possibility that we may need to enter into particular cultural perspectives in order to recognize the correctness of specific critical inferences. (E. g., it leaves no room for the possibility – insisted on by several generations of feminist theorists – that we need to look at society from a perspective informed by an appreciation of systematic and pervasive forms of sex-based discrimination in order to recognize that the concepts "objectification" and "harassment" apply to forms of some sexual behavior that have historically been regarded as at worst tasteless or annoying.[12]) So, despite the liberating aims of the thinkers who espouse them, narrowly rational critical approaches veer toward being dismissive of local values in a manner that pushes them irretrievably toward elitism or ethnocentrism.

---

[11] For Forst's own account of his inheritance from Habermas, see, e. g., Forst (2002: 192–197).
[12] For insightful discussion of the inability of Kantian approaches in ethics to do justice to feminist claims about *sexual objectification*, see Bauer (2015).

A prominent topic of conversation among critical theorists today is how best to combat such ethnocentrism.[13] A recognizable cohort of theorists contest what they see as the tradition's ethnocentric tendencies by taking their cue from strands of poststructuralist and postcolonialist thought.[14] It is possible to give a rough sketch of the stance that unites many of these theorists by referring to the basic theory of signs that at the heart of poststructuralist thought. At the core of the theory, which receives a classic treatment in Derrida's writings, is the idea that expressions acquire the status of signs as a result of being used in different contexts and that, when thus used, their meanings invariably suffer a displacement reflecting language-users' sense of the importance of similarities between previous contexts and the new context.[15] It is characteristic of the theorizing of self-avowed poststructuralists not merely to conclude from considerations along these lines that a value-neutral standpoint for thought about the world is forever beyond our grasp but also to take it for granted that neutrality is a necessary condition of true universality – and that the loss of a neutral standpoint is therefore tantamount to the loss of any claim to universal, rational authority. This skeptical conclusion depends for its apparent force on the coherence of the very – narrower – conception of rationality that poststructuralists typically represent as an unattainable ideal. It is only if we assume, in accordance with the conception, that rational moves of thought must be recognizable as such from a dispassionate standpoint that our invariable reliance on particular perspectives or attitudes seems to threaten the universal, rational authority of thought.

This inverted narrowly rational logic informs some of the signature political moves of poststructuralist theorists. A striking – and strikingly valuable – contribution of poststructuralist and postcolonialist thinkers has been to bring out how colonialist and racist violence often takes the form of the imposition of false universals, and it is certainly possible to accept this observation without being guided by any narrower assumptions about what rationality is like. But it is typical for poststructuralists to make a further pair of political-theoretical moves that are shaped by such assumptions. One of their characteristic gestures is insisting, in a manner that takes for granted that rationality is properly con-

---

[13] One notable recent collection that takes up this important question is Deutscher/Lafont (2017).
[14] Perhaps it merits mention that, although most self-identified poststructuralists accept versions of the type of skepticism about rationality sketched in this paragraph, it is in principle possible for poststructuralist theorists to reject such skepticism.
[15] See Derrida's discussion of what he calls "iterability" in "Signature Event Context" (Derrida 1988: 1–23).

strued in narrower terms, that our very willingness to represent our critical reflections as aspiring to universal or rational authority is inseparable from a slide into politically dangerous forms of ethnocentrism.[16] A second closely connected gesture is urging us to abandon our faith in narratives of "progress, right, sovereignty, free will, moral truth, [and] reason" (Brown 2001: 4) and to promote an emancipatory agenda without imagining that we can think and talk about the social world in a universally authoritative voice.

One ambitious recent attempt to use this basic strategy to inherit the mantle of Critical Theory is Amy Allen's *The End of Progress: Decolonizing the Normative Foundations of Critical Theory*. Allen's decolonizing efforts specifically target contributions to Critical Theory that she regards as Eurocentric and incapable of overcoming political sins of Europe's colonial past (see Allen 2016: 15). This is an undeniably important project. Allen should be credited with underlining how a number of prominent critical theorists' commitment to narrowly rational conceptions of the authority of their guiding normative ideals prevents them from recognizing forms of racism and ethnocentrism written into those ideals.[17] But Allen goes on from making this important point to making questionable theoretical moves that bear the imprint of an unacknowledged debt to a narrowly rational logic. She takes this logic for granted in calling on us to reject any sort of clearly universalist politics (see Allen 2016: 2). A central preoccupation of *The End of Progress* is developing this claim in connection with the notion of *progress*. While Allen is happy to avail herself of talk of progress insofar as it is forward-looking and used to underwrite efforts to identify and agitate for liberating forms of social life, she wants to distance herself from any suggestion that this stance commits her to allowing that particular social changes might rightly be established as progressive once and for all. This is because, however unwittingly, she tends to operate with the narrowly rational view that a given change could only be recognized as progressive as a matter of fact if, per impossibile, it was considered from an ideally dispassionate standpoint or "God's eye view" (Allen 2016: 19). Thus swayed by theory, Allen forfeits the very idea of progress (and its regressive opposite) as a fact. She tries to avoid the political dis-ease likely to be occasioned by this posture by denying that, in adopting her distinctive view of progress, she is committing herself to a "first-order moral relativism" that would disallow *talk* of truth or rationality (Allen 2016: 34, 65–66, 121, 212–215). Yet, insofar as she depicts moral and political assess-

---

[16] For an influential version of this view within poststructuralism, see Derrida (1976).
[17] For further helpful discussion of this basic point in reference to Axel Honneth's *Freedom's Right*, see McNay (2015) and Ng (2019).

ments as capable only of a type of 'truth' or 'rationality' that is a mere reflection of specific cultural values, it is fair to disregard the form of linguistic self-presentation she takes to be permissible and to insist that her preferred critical posture cannot avoid sliding into a politically and philosophically disempowering form of relativism. The resulting outlook is, in Allen's view, our best hope for achieving critical theorists' aspiration to liberating immanence and hence, as she sees it, the most satisfactory outcome of Critical Theory's pursuit of immanent critique (see Allen 2016: xi).

The political limitations of Allen's outlook are not trivial. Whereas Allen can consistently claim that it is open to us to employ nonrational methods to persuade people to adopt new perspectives, thereby bringing about liberating social changes, she is obliged to add that any such changes will fail to qualify as unequivocally progressive. She leaves herself vulnerable to the charge that she is advocating social remedies that, far from having an unambiguously emancipatory character, merely happen to seem emancipatory to particular groups of people at particular times. That is, she leaves herself open to the complaint that she is using theory to bully us into qualifying even our most careful critical conclusions.[18] (Suppose, e.g., that we affirm, as we should, Crenshaw's claim that Holtzclaw's selection of socially vulnerable victims made his actions especially pernicious. According to Allen's main line of reasoning, theoretical considerations oblige us to weaken our critical judgments by relativizing them, implicitly appending a disclaimer about how this is just how things appear in the cultural context in which we find ourselves.)[19] Reflection on the political pitfalls of an Allen-style approach to Critical Theory suggest the need to confront questions along the following lines. In trying to avoid the ethnocentric tendencies of accounts of immanent critique that strive satisfy constraints of a narrower concep-

---

**18** For an elegant treatment of this theme, see Lovibond (1989). See also my critique of Richard Rorty's view of political discourse – a view that in fundamental respects anticipates that of Allen and other poststructuralists – in Crary (2000).

**19** Poststructuralist theorists often present themselves as favoring *genealogical* methods (see, e.g., Allen 2016: ch. 5), so it is worth accenting that the attack on poststructuralism-leaning critical theories just sketched is *not* an attack on the interest of genealogy understood – as David Owen, e.g., understands it – as dedicated to freeing us from pictures of our lives that we experience as repressive; for Owen's view of genealogy, see esp. Owen (2002). It is possible to place value on genealogy, understood as a method of getting us to see that our current image of the world is not obligatory (say, by shifting our sense of what matters so that things look very different to us), without suggesting – as Allen effectively does – that it is incapable of contributing internally to a rationally authoritative, liberating theory of society. This article's concern with critical theories that have this poststructuralist bent is that their reliance on a narrower conception of rationality that seems to strip genealogy of this rational power.

tion of rationality, are we obliged to relinquish any claim to the rational authority of our conclusions? Are we obliged to maneuver, as cleverly as possible, within a narrowly rational conceptual space, endeavoring somehow to avoid both the Scylla of ethnocentrism and the Charybdis of skepticism about our critical conclusions' rational authority?

There is good reason to believe that this is not how members of the Frankfurt School's first generation conceived the project of giving a satisfactory account of immanent critique. It is possible to find suggestions of a quite different theoretical strategy in the work of leading figures in the early history of the Institute for Social Research. Already in the *Dialectic of Enlightenment*, Horkheimer and Adorno were taking their cue from the lesson of the method of Hegel's *Phenomenology of Spirit*, a book that tells the story of the education of consciousness in a manner that repudiates, with rigorous consistency, the idea of an external standpoint on the rapport between mind and world. Properly understood, this methodological precept has substantial implications for how we think about the nature of values, and of our mental contact with them. To get the basic idea, suppose that we understand social concepts as "thick" in the sense that an appreciation of particular cultural and evaluative perspectives is essential to the ability to authoritatively describe the patterns the concepts trace out. If we now reject in a thoroughly consistent manner the idea of a transcendent standpoint from which to determine that our modes of appreciation have an essential tendency to distort our view of the world, then we will not be in a position to insist that such thickness betokens a cognitive deficit. We will be in a position to allow that thick social concepts are real or metaphysically transparent concepts, and we will also be in a position to sanction, in reference to such concepts, an idea of objective values. That is, we will find ourselves wanting to sanction, in reference to social phenomena, an idea of objective values. This means that we will be in a position to allow – in a widely rational manner – that we may require specific sensitivities in order to recognize the correctness of intellectually respectable lines of thought about these values. Having arrived at this widely rational point, it will strike us as a relatively uncomplicated matter to produce an account of immanent critique. For now there is no tension between conceiving such critique as immanent, in the sense of being internally informed by specific cultural and historical perspectives, and conceiving it as possessing unqualified rational authority.

Today this sort of straightforward route to an account of immanent critique strikes many critical theorists as closed-off. In the decades after the Institute for Social Research's post-World War II return to Frankfurt, it became common for critical theorists to reject the idea of objective ethical values and the closely related idea of a conception of rationality wide enough to accommodate thought about a worldly landscape featuring such values.[20] It would not be unreasonable to trace the willingness of thinkers to make this two-fold gesture of rejection, at least in significant part, to Critical Theory's encounter with Anglophone philosophy in the 1960s. This includes, prominently, the so-called "positivism disputes" in which, for all their hostility to positivism, some representatives of Critical Theory took on board significant commitments of analytic meta-ethics.[21] Nevertheless, there are contributions to Critical Theory that clearly make use of widely rational resources.

This is true – to mention one significant recent example – of the image of immanent critique developed in Rahel Jaeggi's *Critique of Forms of Life*.[22] Jaeggi follows Horkheimer's and Adorno's leads in inheriting the method of the *Phenomenology of Spirit*, and, from the opening moments of her book, she makes it clear that she will contest narrowly rational strictures. She announces her interest in a construal of immanent critique on which its object is "forms of life," which for her is a label for those portions of our lives in which we develop and respond to ethical values. The guiding thesis of Jaeggi's book is that forms of life are constitutively ethical and such that there is no question of bringing them empirically into view while abstaining from ethical evaluation. Jaeggi sets out to show that the critique of forms of life is in this sense unavoidable. She is aware that many liberal political theorists take an openness to criticizing individuals' conceptions of the good to be inseparable from paternalism or even authoritarianism. In addition to attacking this posture as politically misconceived (see, e.g., Jaeggi 2018a: 9–15), she argues that it reflects a philosophical confusion about what our relation to forms of life is like.

Jaeggi's core account of forms of life starts with the claim that they are made up of social practices.[23] This matters, she maintains, because social practices are constituted by steps that are only authoritatively recognizable as such in terms of sensitivities that we come to possess in the process of learning to participate in the practices in question. So, learning a practice is inseparable from getting a feel for the practice's point, and – Jaeggi adds – this lesson bears not only on individual practices but on the constellations of practices that, for her, are con-

---

[20] The philosophical posture in question is sometimes dignified with the label "postmetaphysical." See, e.g., Habermas (1992).
[21] See esp. Habermas' contribution to Adorno et al. (1976).
[22] It is also true of the accounts of immanent critique presented in the work of a fair number of critical theorists, including some who take their cue from Horkheimer and Adorno.
[23] For Jaeggi's detailed account of forms of life and the conception of immanent critique they support, see Jaeggi (2018a: chs. 1–6). For a helpful, compressed account of forms of life, see Jaeggi (2018b).

stitutive of forms of life. It is possible to succinctly formulate these observations by saying that forms of life have ends. (To be sure, Jaeggi stresses that we are simply thrown into – without arriving at the point of thematizing – a fair number of our own practices and forms of life. Insofar as our explanations of our practices are thus not infrequently post hoc rationalizations, it follows that our forms of life may involve disorganized clusters of – acknowledged and unacknowledged – ends (see Jaeggi 2018b: 75).) When Jaeggi observes that forms of life have ends, she is noting that there is a sense in which, in reference to these ends, they can succeed or fail. That, very succinctly, is how she defends the view that, in our efforts to get forms of life in focus, we cannot help but concern ourselves with their normative happiness or unhappiness (see, e.g., Jaeggi 2018b: 78).

This view is pivotal for Jaeggi's preferred conception of immanent critique. To say that, in thinking and talking about forms of life as such, it is necessary to use irredeemably ethical categories, is to allow that it makes sense to describe forms of life as enterprises of dealing with "problems" and, more specifically, as enterprises of dealing with problems that – since, far from being brutely given, they are articulated in our practices – are appropriately described as "second order." To conceive forms of life as thus problem-involving is in turn to make room for conceiving the bundles of practices of which they are composed as susceptible to crises. For Jaeggi, criticizing forms of life is grappling with these sorts of internally arising crises, a task that, for her, we can only undertake by employing immanent, irreducibly ethical categories. When she characterizes the relevant categories as irreducibly ethical, she is, as noted above, suggesting that we can only authoritatively project them insofar as we enter into particular cultural perspectives. But she does not take it to follow that the concepts in question are therefore cognitively limited.

It is at this point in the presentation of her social theoretic vision that we see the significance of her reliance on the method of the *Phenomenology of Spirit* and, more specifically, of her reliance on its author's thoroughgoing attack on the idea of a God's eye view from which to antecedently determine that ethical perspectives as such veer toward hampering our ability to follow rational lines of thought (see, e.g., Jaeggi 2018a: 194). One of Jaeggi's typical ways of formulating her preferred conception of immanent critique is to say that such critique is not merely "internal" (i.e., in being somehow limited to determining the consistency of "practices and institutions with existing values and beliefs" (Jaeggi 2018b: 86; my translation)).[24] In presenting a notion of critique that counts as immanent

---

[24] Although Jaeggi insists on distinguishing her preferred critical methods from "internal"

without somehow needing to be disparaged as merely 'internal,' she is allowing that particular cultural and historical perspectives may directly contribute to our ability to make wholeheartedly rational inferences, a step she justifies by using the aforementioned gesture of Hegel to introduce a relevantly wide conception of rationality. A wider conception is thus pivotal for her effort to straightforwardly accommodate the 'dialectics of immanence and transcendence.'

Now we have before us an illustration of how, instead of working within a narrowly rational space to address apparently opposed worries about ethnocentrism and mere nonrational partisanship, one contemporary critical theorist orients herself in a widely rational space in which addressing both kinds of worries simultaneously is unproblematic. (Notice, to return to this article's guiding example, that the position thus equips us to accept on its own terms of the work of a social critic like Crenshaw – work that, taken at face value, seems to have rational power in virtue of provoking us to look at things from new, ethically laden, historical or cultural perspectives.) We have an illustration of one current contribution to Critical Theory that is dedicated to the sympathetic elaboration of widely rational modes of social criticism.

A Jaeggi-style account of immanent critique depends for its plausibility on a wider conception of rationality (i.e., a conception on which our sensitivities are internal to our rational abilities). Because this conception represents an affront to the current philosophical climate, we have good reason to suspect that, in the absence of a thoroughgoing defense, any theorist who helps herself to its resources will be perceived by many to be advocating critical exercises that fall short of rational authority. Despite the clear risk of misunderstanding along these lines, Jaeggi herself consistently, and quite deliberately, places greater emphasis on bringing out the political importance of her views than on mounting a defense of the philosophically unorthodox conception of rationality that animates them (see Jaeggi 2018a: 194).[25] Granted that she does not present a philosophical argument for this conception, we should expect that some readers of her work will complain that she is not entitled to depict immanent critique, as she understand it, as a rational enterprise. And this has in fact happened (see, e.g., Niederberger/Weihrauch 2015). If we are committed to following up on contributions to Critical Theory, like Jaeggi's, that make use of widely rational resources, we ought to be able to tell a story about why we are entitled to a wider conception of rationality. A reasonable place to turn is a core contribution to Anglo-Ameri-

---

modes of critique, she is too willing to sanction the coherence of the internal methods she rejects. See in this connection Crary (2019).

**25** For discussion of this feature of Jaeggi's work, see Crary (2019).

can analytic philosophy of the social sciences that takes as one of its organizing themes a question about whether it is possible to overcome antecedent obstacles that may seem to prevent us from conceiving rationality on wider lines.

## 3 A widely rational reading of Winch

Consider Peter Winch's landmark 1958 book *The Idea of a Social Science and Its Relation to Philosophy*.[26] Although one of Winch's goals in this work is to defend a nonrelativistic, widely rational account of social understanding, there has been a great deal of debate about whether he succeeds. Today it is not uncommon to find Winch represented as advocating a version of the very sort of culturally relativistic outlook he claimed to be avoiding.[27] To be sure, there is a small and – vocal set of readers who maintain that we should credit Winch with an antirelativistic outlook that is capable of accommodating rationally authoritative modes of social criticism.[28] This interpretative dispute, which has now run on for over half a century, is vexed and involved, and it makes sense to simply bypass it. Without getting distracted by exegetical questions about details of Winch's exposition, it is possible to isolate a pivotal strand of thought in *The Idea of a Social Science* – a strand of thought that develops themes from Wittgenstein's later philosophy and that is dedicated to motivating a view of the understanding of social phenomena on which such understanding is both objective and ineradicably ethical. Winch tends to formulate this view by saying that, as he conceives it, social understanding resists assimilation to the natural sciences. In connection with this reference to "the" natural sciences, some commentators have argued that Winch takes for granted a now discredited, positivistic claim about the unity of the sciences (see, e.g., Roth 2006). It is possible to sidestep this further exegetical dispute by observing that Winch's argument for his preferred view of social understanding can be run without any such unacceptable claim.[29] More important for the issues considered here, it is possible, by following up on his

---

**26** Issued with a new preface in 1990.
**27** This view was defended plausibly by some readers writing at roughly the same time as Winch (see, e.g., MacIntyre/Bell 1967), and it still receives thoughtful defenses in the work of a number of readers today (see, e.g., Diamond 2013; Diamond 2015; see also Risjord 2014: esp. 65–68).
**28** Lars Hertzberg defended this view as early as 1980 in Hertzberg (1980). For more recent efforts along the same lines, see Hutchinson/Read/Sharrock (2012) and Ahlskog/Lagerspetz (2015).
**29** For a defense of Winch against the charges Roth (2006) levels, see Cahill (2013).

argument for this view, to outline a defense of the sort of nonrelativistic and widely rational account of social criticism that is pivotal for politically liberating critical endeavors.

At the opening of *The Idea of a Social Science*, Winch announces that he is setting out not only to reject the (then venerable and today still widely held) view that to progress the social sciences must "emulate the natural sciences" (Winch 1990: 1)[30] but also to defend the different view that "any worthwhile study of society must be philosophical in character" (Winch 1990: 3). Although the latter view is questionable, it is worth considering what draws Winch to it. The view depends for its plausibility on the idea, which Winch seeks to defend in his book (and which is discussed below), that there is no such thing as a standpoint outside language from which to characterize the relationship between language and the world.[31] Suppose that, following Winch's lead, we abandon as incoherent the notion of a view on language "from sideways on."[32] Now it seems justified to represent the kinds of conceptual investigations undertaken in philosophy as capable of shedding light on what the world is like in a manner that is not merely a matter of limning the contingent structures of the disciplines within which the concepts in question are at home.[33] Taking his cue from an observation along these lines, Winch sets out to defend a view of the relationship between language and the world that would enable him to treat an investigation of the concept of *social phenomena* as genuinely illuminating. That is what he

---

**30** In his book, Winch critically examines the classic version of this view that is defended in the writings of John Stuart Mill (see Winch 1990: ch. 3). For a well-regarded, up to date defense of a view on these lines, see Rosenberg (2012). While the sort of natural-science oriented outlook that Rosenberg favors is today well received among analytic philosophers of the social sciences, it is much less well represented in European philosophy of social science.

**31** Winch offers his most quoted formulation of this view not in *The Idea of a Social Science* but a few years later in his influential article "Understanding a Primitive Society." In it he writes: "Reality is not what gives language sense. What is real and what is unreal shows itself *in* the sense that language has." (Winch 1964: 309)

**32** This is a well-known phrase from John McDowell.

**33** This is one side of the "pincer movement" that, at the outset of *The Idea of a Social Science*, Winch declares he is setting out to make. The accent here is on Winch's efforts to distance himself from classic "underlabourer" conceptions of philosophy on which it is a parasitic discipline that solves "problems thrown up in the course of non-philosophical investigations" (Winch 1990: 4). The other side of Winch's project is distancing himself from "master-scientist" conceptions on which philosophy "aims at [...] refuting scientific theories by purely *a priori* reasoning" (Winch 1990: 7). To appreciate this part of Winch's project, we need to see that, as Winch conceives them, conceptual investigations, while capable of giving us second-order awareness of knowledge of the world embodied in our concepts, do not result in the sort of new empirical information that would make them competitors of any of the natural sciences.

has in mind when he calls for a rapprochement of philosophy and the social sciences. His aspiration is to show that, as he puts it, "the central problem of sociology, that of giving an account of the nature of social phenomena in general, itself belongs to philosophy" (Winch 1990: 43). This is undoubtedly an important problem for sociology, though it is worth noting in passing that it is possible to grant its significance without holding, with Winch, that *any* worthwhile study of society must be philosophical in the sense of being addressed to it.

Winch starts his philosophical account of social phenomena from the uncontroversial idea that these phenomena are as such composed of actions or, as he puts it, of "meaningful behaviour" (Winch 1990: 45). He then claims that meaningful behavior is *"ipso facto* rule-governed" (Winch 1990: 52). This is a claim that, in the years after the publication of his book, he is eager to qualify. He revises it, he explains in 1990 in his Preface to the Second Edition of *The Idea of a Social Science*, both because he thinks it might wrongly seem to imply that all human activities are articulated in the same way and because he thinks it threatens to obscure the fact that "[d]ifferent aspects of social life [...] are frequently internally related in such a way that one cannot even be intelligibly conceived as existing in isolation from others" (Winch 1990: xv–xvi). Although Winch in these ways refines his position on the rule-governed character of meaningful behavior, he does not abandon the plausible thought that originally led him to bring up the topic of rule-following, namely, the thought that meaningful behavior is as such (at least unreflectively) articulated in terms of concepts or universal categories and that it accordingly admits questions about what counts as going on and doing the same.[34] Since there is good reason to think that we can defend this thought on independent grounds,[35] it seems reasonable to assume that Winch is right to introduce it. He introduces it because he wants to show that, however apparently uninteresting, the conceptually structured character of social activities is of philosophical moment. It is with an eye to showing this that Winch appeals to Wittgenstein's later philosophy and, more specifically, to Wittgenstein's later remarks on rule-following.

Operating with concepts or universal categories places us in the realm of rule-following, and a name is a universal category insofar as it can be applied in an indefinite number of circumstances. So, it should not surprise us that, when Winch first broaches the topic of rule-following he considers the practice

---

**34** Winch might plausibly be read as trying to find exceptions to this claim in his striking paper "The Universalizability of Moral Judgments" (1965). For reasons too involved to discuss here, this paper is problematic. Given that Winch does not mention relevant considerations in his 1990 remarks on *The Idea of a Social Science*, it seems reasonable simply to set it aside here.
**35** For a discussion of relevant topics, see Crary (2013).

of using a name, viz., the name "Mount Everest." Winch imagines a scenario in which someone who is giving him English-language instruction tries to teach him to use this name by gesturing at the mountain through the window of an airplane. There would, he claims, be nothing objectionable about saying that either this definition "lays down the meaning" or that "to use a word in its correct meaning is to use it in the same way as that laid down in the definition" (Winch 1990: 26). But, he adds, talk of using a term 'the same way' does not do much work by itself. In the scene of language-learning he is describing, it would be unclear whether his teacher was giving the name of the mountain or the word "mountain" and, by the same token, unclear what 'using the term the same way' amounts to.[36] What interests Winch here is not so much the possibility of misunderstanding but what this possibility reveals about what 'going on with a term in the same way' involves. What it reveals is that there is an element of context-sensitivity in the grasp of sameness that is internal to operating with a concept. Far from being the expression of a psychological mechanism that produces correct behavior in a manner independent of our sensitivities, such a grasp is inseparable from a sense of the importance of similarities uniting the context at hand with other contexts in which a concept is used.

Winch frequently speaks of "[t]he necessity for rules to have a social setting" (Winch 1990: 33), and when he does so he has in mind this basic view of conceptual understanding or rule-following (i.e., a construal of it as presupposing a feel for a given context). In developing this view, Winch is – as he himself stresses – inheriting from Wittgenstein's treatment of rule-following. Still borrowing from Wittgenstein, Winch goes on to suggest by means of a series of examples that the basic point he is making applies even to conceptual capacities – such as those we exercise in extending simple mathematical series – that may at first glance seem well suited to the context-independent model he rejects (see Winch 1990: 29–33).[37] Winch is preoccupied with these issues because they have a bearing on how we conceive social activities. Insofar as social activities as such involve conceptuality or rule-following, it is an implication of Winch's larger argument that a certain sensitivity to context or social setting is necessary for participating in any social activity.

This account of social activities, however apparently insignificant by itself, has significant consequences for how we construe the *understanding* of such ac-

---

[36] I.e., since using a name for a particular mountain consistently and using the general term "mountain" consistently are different things.

[37] Around the time of *The Idea of a Social Science*, Winch is independently concerned to stress that Wittgenstein's later remarks on rule-following represent a significant development in his philosophical outlook. See esp. Winch (1969).

tivities. To appreciate the kinds of consequences that interest Winch, it is helpful to accent an aspect of his argument that he himself does not underline. In defending his preferred account of social activities, he commits himself to a distinctive claim about understanding within the individual natural sciences.[38] When Winch is making a case for the account of social activities he favors, he claims that sensitivities contribute internally to all conceptual capacities. This means that, to the extent that modes of natural-scientific understanding involve conceptuality, sensitivities contribute internally to these modes of understanding.[39]

This view of understanding within the natural sciences forms the backdrop for the claims about social understanding that are the centerpiece of *The Idea of a Social Science*. Winch invites us to regard social understanding as resembling natural-scientific understanding in the following respect. Just as we require particular sensitivities to consistently apply the concepts internal to different forms of natural-scientific understanding, we require particular sensitivities to consistently apply the concepts internal to social understanding. At the same time, Winch brings out how social understanding is distinctive. He emphasizes that, in addition to resembling all other conceptual understanding in being rule-governed, social understanding takes rule-governed behavior as its object (see Winch 1990: 87–88). If we formulate Winch's claim that rule-governed behavior necessarily draws on particular sensitivities by saying that this behavior is as such structured by practical normativity, then we can bring into relief what is noteworthy about this view of social understanding by saying that, unlike concepts characteristic of the individual natural sciences, characteristically social concepts trace out patterns in a ground that is essentially structured by practical normativity or, in other words, in a ground that is essentially ethically nonneutral.[40] This means that we require sensitivities or modes of cultural appreciation

---

**38** Having already, at the opening of this section, flagged my awareness that the individual natural sciences involve different modes of understanding, it is worth stressing that the suggestion Winch is making here does not depend for its soundness on any failure to acknowledge differences among individual modes of natural-scientific understanding. All it depends on is the thought that all natural-scientific modes of understanding, however different in other respects, involve conceptuality.
**39** It seems reasonable to suppose that Winch selects his opening example of a rule-governed social activity with an eye to making just this point. That is, he chooses an activity – viz., use of the name "Mount Everest" – that involves concern with aspects of the physical world because he wants to impress on his readers that sensitivities are necessary prerequisites of the kind of consistent application of concepts that is internal even to various natural-scientific modes of understanding.
**40** It might seem reasonable to protest that Winch's line of reasoning here entitles him to represent social categories as irreducibly normative without representing the kind of normativity in

not merely to project these concepts consistently (something that is also true of mastery of concepts characteristic of individual natural sciences) but also to grasp their contents.[41] That is Winch's preferred conception of social understanding, and, as various commentators have noted, the passages in which he presents it are rightly taken to represent the climax of his early book (see, e. g., Hertzberg 1980: 168–169; Ahlskog/Lagerspetz 2015: 304–305).

One of the most arresting outcomes of the book's main argument is a conception of social understanding on which it is as such ethically charged. Granted that Winch as a rule represents social understanding, conceived in this manner, as genuine – not merely subjective – understanding, it follows that he is asking us to regard such understanding as both irreducibly ethical and objective. It follows, that is, that he is giving us an image of a region of objective reality as an intrinsically ethical realm and, by the same token, that he is placing himself in opposition to the sort of engrained conception of reality on which it is in itself bereft of ethical value. He is also thereby presenting a distinctive view of what the social is, a distinctive *social ontology*. It is an ontology on which objective features of the social world are irreducibly ethical and on which, in consequence, particular ethical attitudes may contribute internally to an objective understanding of these features. Here gestures that shape our attitudes may inform objective social understanding in a manner that is internal or direct (as opposed to merely external or accidental). This is what it comes to, to say that Winch's ontology of the social leaves room for the wider conception of rationality at issue in this article.

To say this is not to address the vexed exegetical question of whether Winch describes such a conception of rationality in a rigorously consistent manner, or whether instead he sometimes talks about his preferred conception of rationality in a qualified and relativizing style.[42] What matters here is that it is possible to

---

question as ethical. For considerations that effectively speak for regarding the relevant normativity as in fact ethical, see Crary (2016: ch. 2).

**41** A case could be made for thinking that the concepts characteristic of the part of biology, sometimes called natural history, that is concerned with the description and classification of organisms trace out patterns in a normatively structured ground. (For a defense of an account of natural history on these lines, see my commentary on Michael Thompson's work in Crary (2016: sec. 5.1.i).) But the kind of normativity in question is not practical or ethical and hence different from kind of normativity that forms the ground for projecting characteristically social concepts.

**42** There is good reason to hold with Cora Diamond – see, e. g., Diamond (2013) – that there are passages in Winch's early work, and perhaps above all in "Understanding a Primitive Society," in which he effectively slides into a relativistic posture. At the same time, it seems reasonable to think that Winch's core philosophical commitments early on speak for an attractive, contextualist and decidedly nonrelativistic account of social understanding.

find in *The Idea of a Social Science* an argument for this wider conception. Having now sketched the argument, we can explore the kind of philosophical opposition that it is likely to encounter, with an eye to building on Winch's efforts.

Consider what seems, in the eyes of many thinkers, to exclude the very idea of a wider conception of rationality. This idea is in tension with the entrenched view that objective reality is as such bereft of ethical value, and, by the same token, in tension with the kinds of philosophical reflections that are standardly taken to render this view obligatory. These reflections typically begin from some version of the following image of how the mind makes contact with the world. Here our subjective makeups have an essential tendency to block our view of things, and it is only to the extent that we abstract from elements of these makeups that we can bring reality into focus. The idea is that, in trying to distance ourselves from all contributions from subjectivity, we eliminate from our conception of the objective world every quality that is 'subjective' in the sense that it can only be brought into focus in reference to aspects of our subjective endowments. Starting from a suggestive picture of the relationship between mind and world, we wind up with a conception of reality that, insofar as it is intolerant of all subjective qualities, expels the ethically inflected qualities that Winch-style social understanding takes as its object.

*The Idea of a Social Science* is organized with an eye to resisting this basic line of thought.[43] The line of thought is driven by the idea of an obligation to abstract from all of our subjective endowments, and the book's argument is supposed to bring into question the very coherence of this idea by getting us to ask ourselves whether we have a clear notion of what satisfying such an obligation would be like. Recall Winch's reflections on Wittgenstein's view of rule-following. Winch credits Wittgenstein with showing that mastery of a concept necessarily presupposes a sense of the significance of similarities uniting its uses in different settings. As we saw, Winch brings out how this Wittgensteinian lesson

---

[43] Some interpreters who take *The Idea of a Social Science* to be propounding a relativist view arrive at this reading because they approach his work through the lens of this line of thought (see, e.g., Risjord 2014; Rosenberg 2012). Other who recognize that Winch is hostile to the line of thought nevertheless arrive at similar readings because they think he fails to fully distance himself from it (see, e.g., Diamond 2013; Diamond 2015). There are passages in Winch's writing that might plausibly be read as expressing sympathy for the kind of relativistic position that he officially disavows. For instance, in *The Idea of a Social Science* he tells us, "that criteria of logic [...] are only intelligible in the context of, ways of living or modes of social life" (Winch 1990: 100), and that, moreover, different ways of living each offer "a different account of the intelligibility of things" (Winch 1990: 103). Or, again, a few years later, in "Understanding a Primitive Society," he claims that different societies have different "standards of rationality" and that these standards "do not always coincide" (Winch 1964: 317).

applies even to those conceptual capacities – such as, say, simple mathematical ones – to which it may at first glance seem most foreign. In thus borrowing from Wittgenstein, Winch is inviting us to see that, even if we are inclined to believe otherwise, we have no clear notion of what it would be for a conceptual capacity to count as wholly abstract. Winch's thought seems to be that this conclusion counts not only against the idea of an obligation to abstract from all of our subjective endowments but also against the ethically neutral conception of reality that this idea is sometimes taken to underwrite.

This thought is bound to strike many philosophers as simply wrong. This is because today the idea of an obligation to abstract depends primarily for its philosophical influence on the assumption – not that one or another conceptual capacity meets the obligation but rather – that the obligation is satisfied by perceptual experience, where such experience is taken to be essentially a matter of the reception of content that is nonconceptual. Yet Winch does not criticize nonconceptualist views of perception. For this reason, both his attack on the idea of an obligation to abstract, and the case for a wider conception of rationality that he grounds in this attack, may seem unconvincing. The point is not that Winch is wrong to approach a defense of a wider conception of rationality by trying to dislodge the idea of obligatory abstraction. Nor is it that he is wrong to look for resources in Wittgenstein's later philosophy. Although Winch does not discuss these issues, Wittgenstein's writings do in fact contain resources for a direct assault on nonconceptualist views of perception. It follows that it is possible to employ Winch's strategy of inheriting from Wittgenstein to make a stronger case than Winch himself does against a call for abstraction, and to thereby also make a stronger case than Winch himself does for the sort of ethically-permissive conception of how things really are that is the ontological counterpart of a wider conception of rationality.

One place in Wittgenstein's writings to look for expressions of the antinonconceptualist – or 'conceptualist' – view that perception is conceptual all the way down is the discussion, in Part II, § xi of the *Philosophical Investigations*, of the phenomenon Wittgenstein calls *changes of aspect*. Wittgenstein's aim here is to illustrate how, far from being independent of what is seen, conceptuality directly informs our perception. He proceeds by presenting us with cases in which we see something new in an object (a new 'aspect') while recognizing that the object has not changed. (Thus, e.g., when gazing at a set of lines on a piece of paper, we may suddenly see a figure in it, although the drawing itself is unaltered.) This presentation of cases does not amount to an argument for a conceptualist view, but there are resources for an argument elsewhere in Wittgenstein's writings, for instance, in the passages in the *Philosophical Investigations* in which he is concerned with the privacy of experience. An important goal of some of these passages is – to simplify and condense quite a bit – to get us to see that nonconceptualists place inconsistent demands on what perceptual experience is like. With an eye to summarizing these considerations, we might start by noting that perceptual thought has a normative character that allows for questions about what justifies it. We might then add, plausibly but not uncontroversially, that, with regard to noninferential perceptual thought, we can appeal to experience to answer questions about what justifies perceptual beliefs, and that we thus ordinarily treat experience as having rational significance. Yet, if, following nonconceptualists, we represent perceptual experience as merely causal and essentially nonconceptual, we construe it as shorn of what by our own lights is its rational character. Now there can be no question of being in a position to depict experience as having what we ordinarily regard as its rational character. That is a sketch of a reconstructed Wittgensteinian case for thinking that nonconceptualism is internally inconsistent.

Debates about the prospects for a conceptualist account of perceptual experience are involved, and many philosophers maintain that there are insurmountable obstacles to a viable conceptualism. But the apparently most telling objections to conceptualism (viz., objections having to do with whether it can account for the perceptual capacities of babies and animals) can be answered.[44] Granted that this is so – and granted that nonconceptualist accounts of perception are the best case for making sense of the idea of an obligation to abstract – it follows that there is a good case for abandoning this idea as bankrupt.

This conclusion is of interest insofar as the idea of obligatory abstraction is what seems to force us to whittle away from our image of the world all qualities with a necessary reference to affect – and to, by this route, arrive at an image reality as in itself bereft of ethical values. Consistently forfeiting this idea is tantamount to conceding that we do not have a coherent enough account of what ideally abstract mental access to the world would be like to appeal to such access in antecedently impugning the cognitive credentials of nonabstract modes of thought. It is tantamount to conceding that we are not in a position to determine in advance that, any time we allow nonabstract or subjectively shaped considerations to inform our thought and speech, we thereby undermine our claim to do justice to how things really are. The result of our attempt to discredit the idea of ideal abstraction is thus that we are obliged to refashion our understanding of objective reality so that it no longer excludes everything subjective. It is a short step from here to accommodating within the objective realm the ethically

---

[44] For an argument to this effect, see Crary (2012). An expanded version of this materials is presented in Crary (2016: ch. 3).

nonneutral qualities that Winch urges us to see as objects of social understanding.⁴⁵

If we now allow that some objective qualities are as such ethically charged, we at the same time allow that modes of thought that shape our ethical sensibilities may as such directly contribute to our grasp of objective features of the world, thereby qualifying as rationally authoritative. By elaborating Winch's Wittgensteinian case for his suggestive and philosophically unorthodox social ontology, we accordingly equip ourselves to accommodate the wider conception of rationality that – as we have seen – we require in order to make sense of liberating social criticism, of the sort sought by contemporary critical theorists, that is rationally authoritative and capable of combatting forms of ethnocentrism. By the same token, we equip ourselves to account for the rational authority of critical gestures – such as those characteristic of Crenshaw and, indeed, many other radical social critics – that essentially involve bringing us to look at our lives from new evaluative perspectives.⁴⁶

## 4 Extending the argument

There is a respect in which the foregoing account of liberating social criticism needs to be supplemented. What drives the idea that we need widely rational modes of social criticism, both in the work of some contemporary critical theorists and in a Winchian strand of thought from analytic philosophy of the social sciences, is the conviction that social phenomena are irreducibly ethical and that they therefore reveal themselves to nonneutral modes of thought that only a wider conception equips us to recognize as rational. These are not, however, the only values that responsible social criticism needs to register. There are aspects both of human lives and of the lives of nonhuman animals, that despite not qualifying as social, likewise necessarily encode values. The Winchian argu-

---

**45** There is an extensive literature – one focused on a disanalogy between values and perceptual qualities – that is concerned with the thought that, even if we show that the objective realm includes qualities that count as subjective because they have essential reference to perceptual responses, there are special and additional a priori obstacles to representing the objective realm as including values or qualities that count as subjective because they have essential references to not to perceptual but to affective responses. The idea of such obstacles is, however, suspect. For discussion, see Crary (2007: ch. 1).
**46** The idea that critical gestures that mobilize evaluative perspectives can as such directly inform rational understanding is, according to the persuasive line of thought developed in Mills (1998), a common thread uniting Marxist, feminist, and Black epistemologies.

ment for the irreducibly ethical character of social phenomena starts from an understanding of social activities as modes of fully conceptual or rational expression, and it is possible to show that there are values necessarily encoded not only in all rational forms of animate life but also in all nonrational forms as well. Indeed, it is possible to show that the Winchian thesis about the irredeemably ethical character of rational human social life is a specific instance of a more general point about the irredeemably ethical character of animate life. We need to insist that social criticism be responsible to valuable aspects of nonrational animate life if we are to ensure that our practices and institutions are respectful both of the vulnerabilities of those human beings who (as a result of, say, congenital conditions, illness, or injury) are not fully rationally as well as of the vulnerabilities of nonrational animals. Although showing this is a task for another occasion, Wittgenstein is in fact a good guide to this expansion of the realm of values that are open for immanent critical exploration.[47] This marks another noteworthy point of contact with Critical Theory, above all, with prominent early members of the Frankfurt School, such as Adorno and Horkheimer, who held that doing justice to the worldly circumstances of animals as well as human beings called for affectively saturated "aesthetic reflection" (Horkheimer/Adorno 2002: 209). So, even bearing in mind the need to further develop this article's main line of argument in the manner just adumbrated, it is appropriate to see the larger conversation in question as combining themes from Wittgenstein and from Critical Theory.

## 5 Epilogue

If it is right to maintain, in accordance with sections 3 and 4 of this article, that Wittgenstein bequeaths to us a wider conception of rationality, then it is also fair to say that Wittgenstein gives us a straightforward method for incorporating what critical theorists call the logic of immanence and transcendence. Further, if with Habermas and his Frankfurt-based predecessors, we take as a key ill of late capitalism the overreach into the political sphere of instrumental reason, then we can add that the widely rational forms of reason Wittgenstein brings within reach are capable of countering this politically pernicious trend and reanimating the political domain. The relevant forms of reason are logically distinct

---

[47] For a detailed treatment of these themes, see Crary (2016: chs. 2–4). For further discussion of the case of cognitively disabled human beings, see Crary (2018a); for further discussion of the case of animals, see Crary (2018b).

from and, arguably, politically far more promising than the "communicative" forms proposed by Habermas himself.

The image of Wittgenstein that is operative here, an image of him as contributing decisively to an understanding of emancipatory criticism, is a far cry from the image many contemporary philosophers were brought up on. Since at least 1959, when Ernest Gellner published his polemical tract *Words and Things: An Examination of, and Attack on, Linguistic Philosophy*, the idea that Wittgenstein's later philosophy has an irredeemably conservative bent has enjoyed widespread acceptance. Despite the staying power of this idea, it seems clear that the push to depict Wittgenstein as a politically conservative thinker has been far stronger than any of the considerations offered in its favor (see Crary/De Lara 2019). There is good reason to rework our picture of Wittgenstein's philosophical and political legacy, bringing out how it is capable of directly informing our grasp of liberating social thought and how it provides support for the most promising accounts of such thought to emerge from Critical Theory. Or, as we might also put it, there is good reason to conclude that Wittgenstein can – help us to – do Critical Theory.[48]

# References

Adorno, Theodor W./Albert, Hans/Dahrendorf, Ralf/Habermas, Jürgen/Pilot, Harald/Popper, Karl R. (Eds.) (1976): *The Positivist Dispute in German Sociology*. Trans. by Glyn Adey and David Frisby. London: Heinemann.

Ahlskog, Jonas/Lagerspetz, Olli (2015): "Language-Games and Relativism: On Cora Diamond's Reading of Peter Winch." In: *Philosophical Investigations* 38(4), pp. 293–315.

Allen, Amy (2016): *The End of Progress: Decolonizing the Normative Foundations of Critical Theory*. New York, NY: Columbia University Press.

Bauer, Nancy (2015): *How to Do Things with Pornography*. Cambridge, MA: Harvard University Press.

---

[48] This chapter is a fundamental reworking of my article "Wittgenstein Goes to Frankfurt (and Finds Something Useful to Say)" (Crary 2018d), which appeared in the *Nordic Wittgenstein Review* in June 2018. That article's treatment of contemporary trends in Critical Theory came to me to seem unacceptably limited. After offering a set of lectures on these topics at Oxford in Hilary Term of 2019, I decided to revise the manuscript. I am grateful to the students and faculty members who attended the lectures for their provocative questions and helpful interventions. I subsequently presented versions of this material at the University of Essex as well as at the conference "Crisis and Critique: Philosophical Analysis and Current Events," in Kirchberg, and I am grateful for the productive feedback I received on those occasions. I owe special thanks to Sarah Bufkin, Patricia Cipollitti, Rebecca Duke, Matteo Falomi, Fabian Freyenhagen, Thomas Khurana, María Pía Lara, and Stella Villarmea. I am likewise thankful to Nathaniel Hupert and Hartmut von Sass for their generous and constructive comments during a final round of editing.

Brown, Wendy (2001): *Politics Out of History*. Princeton, NJ: Princeton University Press.
Cahill, Kevin M. (2013): "Naturalism and the Friends of Understanding." In: *Philosophy of the Social Sciences* 44(4), pp. 460–477.
Crary, Alice (2000): "Wittgenstein's Philosophy in Relation to Political Thought." In: Crary, Alice/Read, Rupert (Eds.): *The New Wittgenstein*. London: Routledge, pp. 118–145.
Crary, Alice (2007): *Beyond Moral Judgment*. Cambridge, MA: Harvard University Press.
Crary, Alice (2012): "Dogs and Concepts." In: *Philosophy* 87(2), pp. 215–237.
Crary, Alice (2013): "Freedom Is for the Dogs." In: Greif, Hajo/Weiss, Martin Gehrhard (Eds.): *Ethics, Society, Politics*. Berlin/Boston: De Gruyter, pp. 203–226.
Crary, Alice (2016): *Inside Ethics: On the Demands of Moral Thought*. Cambridge, MA: Harvard University Press.
Crary, Alice (2017): "Putnam and Propaganda." In: *The Graduate Faculty Philosophy Journal* 38(2), pp. 385–398.
Crary, Alice (2018a): "Cognitive Disability and Moral Status." In: Cureton, Adam/Wasserman, David (Eds.): *Oxford Handbook of Philosophy and Disability*. Oxford: Oxford University Press, pp. 451–467.
Crary, Alice (2018b): "Ethics." In: Gruen, Lori (Ed.): *Critical Terms in Animal Studies*. Chicago, IL: University of Chicago Press, pp. 154–169.
Crary, Alice (2018c): "The Methodological Is Political: What's the Matter with 'Analytic Feminism'?" In: *Radical Philosophy* 2(2), pp. 47–60.
Crary, Alice (2018d): "Wittgenstein Goes to Frankfurt (and Finds Something Useful to Say)." In: *Nordic Wittgenstein Review* 7(1), pp. 7–41.
Crary, Alice (2019): "Recovering the Core of Critique: Response to Jaeggi's 'Lebensformen als Problemlösungsinstanzen'." In: *Philosophisches Jahrbuch* 126(1), pp. 109–116.
Crary, Alice/De Lara, Joel (2019): "Who's Afraid of Ordinary Language Philosophy? A Plea for Reviving a Wrongly Revived Tradition." In: *The Graduate Faculty Philosophy Journal* 39(2), pp. 317–339.
Crenshaw, Kimberlé (1991): "Mapping the Margins: Intersectionality, Identity Politics and Violence Against Women of Color." In: *The Stanford Law Review* 43(6), pp. 1241–1299.
Crenshaw, Kimberlé (1992): "Whose Story Is It Anyway? Feminist and Anti-Racist Appropriations of Anita Hill." In: Morrison, Toni (Ed.): *Race-ing Justice, En-Gendering Power: Essays on Anita Hill, Clarence Thomas and the Construction of Social Reality*. New York, NY: Pantheon Books, pp. 402–440.
Derrida, Jacques (1976): *Of Grammatology*. Trans. by Gayatri Chakravorty Spivak. Baltimore, MD: The Johns Hopkins University Press.
Derrida, Jacques (1988): *Limited Inc.* Evanston, IL: Northwestern University Press.
Deutscher, Penelope/Lafont, Christina (2017): *Critical Theory in Critical Times: Transforming the Global Political and Economic Order*. New York, NY: Columbia University Press.
Diamond, Cora (2013): "Criticizing from 'Outside'." In: *Philosophical Investigations* 36(2), pp. 114–132.
Diamond, Cora (2015): "Putnam and Wittgensteinian Baby-Throwing: Variations on a Theme." In: Auxier, Randall E./Anderson, Douglas R./Hahn, Lewis Edwin (Eds.): *The Philosophy of Hilary Putnam*. Chicago, IL: Open Court, pp. 603–649.
Forst, Rainer (2002): *Contexts of Justice: Political Philosophy beyond Liberalism and Communitarianism*. Trans. by John M. M. Farrell. Berkeley, CA: University of California Press.

Forst, Rainer (2014): *Justification and Critique: Toward a Critical Theory of Politics.* Cambridge: Polity Press.

Fricker, Miranda (2007): *Epistemic Injustice: Power and the Ethics of Knowing.* Oxford: Oxford University Press.

Gellner, Ernest (2005): *Words and Things: An Examination of, and Attack on, Linguistic Philosophy.* London: Routledge.

Geuss, Raymond (1981): *The Idea of a Critical Theory: Habermas and the Frankfurt School.* Cambridge: Cambridge University Press.

Goodman, Amy (2015): "When Cops Rape: Daniel Holtzclaw & the Vulnerability of Black Women to Police Abuse." In: *Democracy Now!* 15 December 2015. https://www.democracynow.org/2015/12/15/daniel_holtzclaw_convicted_of_serial_rape, accessed 7 May 2018.

Habermas, Jürgen (1979): "What Is Universal Pragmatics?" In: *Communication and the Evolution of Society.* Trans. by Thomas McCarthy. Boston, MA: Beacon Press, pp. 1–68.

Habermas, Jürgen (1987): "Technology and Science as 'Ideology'." In: *Toward a Rational Society: Student Protest, Science, and Politics.* [1969]. Trans. by Jeremy J. Shapiro. Boston, MA: Beacon Press, pp. 81–122.

Habermas, Jürgen (1992): *Postmetaphysical Thinking: Philosophical Essays.* Trans. by William Mark Hohengarten. Cambridge, MA: MIT Press.

Habermas, Jürgen (1999): "Discourse Ethics: Notes on a Program of Philosophical Justification." In: *Moral Consciousness and Communicative Action.* Trans. by Christian Lenhardt and Shierry Weber Nicholsen. Cambridge, MA: MIT Press, pp. 43–115.

Habermas, Jürgen (2013): "Reply to My Critics." In: *Habermas and Religion.* Trans. by Ciaran Cronin. Edited by Craig Calhoun, Eduardo Mendieta, and Jonathan VanAntwerpen. Cambridge: Polity Press, pp. 347–390.

Haslanger, Sally (no date): "Critical Theory and Practice: Ideology and Morality." Unpublished manuscript.

Hertzberg, Lars (1980): "Winch on Social Interpretation." In: *Philosophy of the Social Sciences* 10(2), pp. 151–171.

Honneth, Axel (1995): *The Struggle for Recognition: The Moral Grammar of Social Recognition.* Trans. by Joel Anderson. Cambridge: Polity Press.

Honneth, Axel (2009): *Pathologies of Reason: On the Legacy of Critical Theory.* Trans. by John Ingram. New York, NY: Columbia University Press.

Honneth, Axel (2011): *Freedom's Right: The Social Foundations of Democratic Life.* New York, NY: Columbia University Press.

Honneth, Axel (2015): "Rejoinder." In: *Critical Horizons: A Journal of Philosophy and Social Theory* 16(2), pp. 204–226.

Horkheimer, Max (1972): "Traditional and Critical Theory." In: *Critical Theory: Collected Essays.* New York, NY: Continuum, pp. 190–243.

Horkheimer, Max/Adorno, Theodor W. (2002): *Dialectic of Enlightenment: Philosophical Fragments.* Edited by Gunzelin Schmid Noerr. Trans. by Edmund Jephcott. Stanford, CA: Stanford University Press.

Hutchinson, Phil/Read, Rupert/Sharrock, Wes (2012): *There Is No Such Thing as a Social Science: In Defence of Peter Winch.* Aldershot: Ashgate.

Jaeggi, Rahel (2009): "Rethinking Ideology." In: De Bruin, Boudewijn/Zurn, Christopher F. (Eds.): *New Waves in Political Philosophy.* Basingstoke: Palgrave Macmillan, pp. 63–86.

Jaeggi, Rahel (2018a): *Critique of Forms of Life*. Trans. by Ciaran Cronin. Cambridge, MA: Harvard University Press.

Jaeggi, Rahel (2018b): "Lebensformen als Problemlösungsinstanzen." In: *Philosophisches Jahrbuch* 125(1), pp. 64–89.

Lovibond, Sabina (1989): "Feminism and Postmodernism." In: *New Left Review* 178, pp. 5–28.

MacIntyre, Alasdair/Bell, D. R. (1967): "The Idea of a Social Science." In: *Proceedings of the Aristotelian Society* Supplementary Vol. 41, pp. 95–132.

McNay, Lois (2015): "Social Freedom and Progress in the Family: Reflections on Care, Gender and Inequality." In: *Critical Horizons* 16(2), pp. 170–186.

Mills, Charles W. (1998): "Alternative Epistemologies." In: *Blackness Visible: Essays on Philosophy and Race*. Ithaca, NY/London: Cornell University Press, pp. 21–39.

Mills, Charles W. (2017): "Ideology." In: Kidd, Ian James/Medina, José/Pohlhaus, Jr., Gail (Eds.): *The Routledge Handbook to Epistemic Injustice*. London/New York, NY: Routledge, pp. 100–111.

Ng, Karen (2019): "Social Freedom as Ideology." In: *Philosophy and Social Criticism* 45(7), pp. 795–818.

Niederberger, Andreas/Weihrauch, Tobias (2015): "Rahel Jaeggi: Kritik von Lebensformen." In: *Notre Dame Philosophical Reviews* 25 January 2015. https://ndpr.nd.edu/news/kritik-von-lebensformen/, accessed 20 August 2020.

O'Neill, Onora (2000): "Starke und schwache Gesellschaftskritik in einer Globalisierten Welt." In: *Deutsche Zeitschrift für Philosophie* 48(5), pp. 719–728.

Owen, David (2002): "Criticism and Captivity: On Genealogy and Critical Theory." In: *European Journal of Philosophy* 10(2), pp. 216–230.

Putnam, Hilary (2002): "Values and Norms." In: *The Collapse of the Fact/Value Distinction: And Other Essays*. Cambridge, MA: Harvard University Press, pp. 111–134.

Risjord, Mark (2014): *Philosophy of Social Science: A Contemporary Introduction*. New York, NY: Routledge.

Rosenberg, Arthur (2012): *Philosophy of Social Science*. Boulder, CO: Westview Press.

Roth, Paul A. (2006): "Naturalism without Fears." In: Turner, Stephen P./Risjord, Mark W. (Eds.): *Philosophy of Anthropology and Sociology*. Amsterdam: Elsevier, pp. 683–708.

Stanley, Jason (2015): *How Propaganda Works*. Princeton, NJ: Princeton University Press.

Winch, Peter (1964): "Understanding a Primitive Society." In: *American Philosophical Quarterly* 1(4), pp. 307–324.

Winch, Peter (1965): "The Universalizability of Moral Judgments." In: *The Monist* 49(2), pp. 196–214.

Winch, Peter (1969): "Introduction: The Unity of Wittgenstein's Philosophy." In: Winch, Peter (Ed.): *Studies in the Philosophy of Wittgenstein*. London: Routledge and Kegan Paul, pp. 1–19.

Winch, Peter (1990): *The Idea of a Social Science and Its Relation to Philosophy*. 2nd ed. London: Routledge.

Mélika Ouelbani
# Der Status der Mathematik in der Philosophie Wittgensteins

**Abstract:** [The Status of Mathematics in the Philosophy of Wittgenstein] In the *Tractatus*, mathematics plays a specific and important role. It epitomises a prototype of language although it may paradoxically seem not to convey any sense itself. After the *Tractatus*, mathematical language and calculation have clearly become for Wittgenstein the prototype for the functioning of our language. However, Wittgenstein is interested in mathematics per se; he asserts that he has taken it off its pedestal. Indeed, everything that he wrote on mathematics seeks to show that mathematical language is in no way different from other languages or superior to them. Thus, mathematics has served as a model for building the concept of language games and has itself become the language game that operates as the most common of them all.

**Keywords:** Ludwig Wittgenstein, *Tractatus logico-philosophicus*, mathematics, philosophy of mathematics, language, proposition

Die Philosophie Ludwig Wittgensteins steckt generell voller Paradoxien. Sie bestätigen die seiner Persönlichkeit innewohnende Dualität. Diese Dualität zu verstehen und aufzulösen, ist interessant. Dieser Charakterzug findet sich in der Rolle wieder, die er der Mathematik zuschrieb wie auch in seiner Philosophie der Mathematik und der Philosophie der Sprachspiele.

Ich möchte zunächst zeigen, dass die Mathematik im *Tractatus* zwar eine besondere, keineswegs jedoch eine privilegierte Rolle spielt. Die Mathematik hat eher den Status einer Anwendung in einem Projekt als den eines Modells, dem man als solches zu folgen hat.

Anschließend werde ich darlegen, dass dieses Modell in der Folge zu einer Art Prototyp der Sprache oder genauer ihrer Funktionsweise wird, um dann deutlich zu machen, dass Wittgenstein in seiner Post-*Tractatus*-Philosophie zwar bevorzugt die Analogie zum Kalkül und insbesondere zur Mathematik heranzieht, um die Funktionsweise unserer Sprache zu erklären, bei genauerer Betrachtung jedoch klar ersichtlich wird, dass es die Mathematik ist, die wie unsere Sprache funktioniert.

# 1 Die Mathematik im *Tractatus*

Wittgenstein wollte sich bekanntlich der Ingenieurslaufbahn widmen, fand jedoch über die Mechanik und ihre Gesetze Zugang zur Philosophie. Es war nämlich in erster Linie ihre Sprache, die sein Interesse weckte, insoweit als sie es ermöglicht, die Welt mit einer Einheitssprache zu beschreiben. Diese „bestimmt eine Form der Weltbeschreibung, indem sie sagt: Alle Sätze der Weltbeschreibung müssen aus einer Anzahl gegebener Sätze – den mechanischen Axiomen – auf eine gegebene Art und Weise erhalten werden." (TLP 6.341) Die Gesetze der Mechanik sind trotz ihres formalen, mathematischen Charakters in der Lage, die Phänomene zu erklären. Wittgenstein stellte sich somit die Frage, ob eine Einheitssprache die Möglichkeit bietet, die Welt, die Wirklichkeit auszudrücken, so wie es die Mechanik in der Physik machen kann. Diese Frage und dieses Interesse Wittgensteins lassen schon die Bedeutung erahnen, die er dem formalen Aspekt der Sprache in seinem Denken beimessen wird. Die Logik und die Mathematik – die ja eine logische Methode ist (TLP 6.2) – genießen in der Tat einen Sonderstatus und dies, obwohl sie aus Scheinsätzen bestehen. Diese a priori formale Einheitssprache, die, genauso wie die Mechanik, die Welt getreu abbilden könnte, muss zwangsläufig eine Gemeinsamkeit mit ihr aufweisen. Die Frage, wie sich Sprache und Wirklichkeit, wie wir sie erfahren, zueinander verhalten, war jedoch weder von Frege noch von Russell gestellt worden.

Diese Gemeinsamkeit wird gerade die Struktur sein: Die Tatsache und der Satz sind isomorph und die Logik stellt alle Möglichkeiten dessen dar, was geschehen kann. Man hat den Eindruck, alles beruhe auf der Form. Nach der wittgensteinschen Dreiteilung in sinnvolle, unsinnige und sinnlose Sätze sind jedoch nur die ersten echte Sätze.

Ein Satz ist sinnvoll, wenn er verifiziert werden kann, was bedeutet, dass es theoretisch möglich ist, ihn zu verifizieren. Anders ausgedrückt, damit eine Aussage ein Satz ist, reicht es aus, dass sie sich aus Namen zusammensetzt, die auf die Wirklichkeit verweisen, und dass sie syntaktisch korrekt gebildet ist. Die Aussage spricht eine Tatsache aus, die ihr entsprechen könnte.

Ein unsinniger Satz indessen enthält Wörter, die keine Bedeutung haben, wie dies im Allgemeinen bei spekulativen Aussagen der Fall ist. Diese Aussagen müssen folgerichtig absurd sein, insofern es unmöglich ist, sie zu verifizieren, da man nicht weiß, worauf sie sich beziehen.

So sind Tatsache und Sachverhalt eine Verbindung von Gegenständen. Sie bestehen somit aus denselben Gegenständen, die notwendigerweise zur Substanz gehören. Der einzige Unterschied zwischen beiden liegt in der Vorstellung, dass die Tatsache real ist, während der Sachverhalt lediglich möglich ist. Der Satz, der eine Tatsache ausdrückt, bringt eine reale Beziehung zwischen Gegenständen zum Ausdruck, wohingegen der Satz, der einen Sachverhalt ausdrückt, eine mögliche Verbindung von Gegenständen ausdrückt.

Ein Satz ist somit nicht notwendigerweise das Bild einer Tatsache, er kann auch einfach nur das Bild eines Sachverhaltes sein, was ausreicht, um ihm einen Sinn zu verleihen. Letztendlich ist es die Beziehung zwischen den Gegenständen, die realisiert oder nicht realisiert ist. Wenn die Sprache also die Wirklichkeit wie ein Spiegel reflektiert, wird es offensichtlich, dass der Begriff der Struktur oder der Form in der wittgensteinschen Auffassung sowohl der Sprache als auch der Welt grundlegend ist, zumindest zu Beginn seiner philosophischen Überlegungen. Diese Theorie des Bildes und des Sinns setzt nämlich voraus, dass:
- der Sinn sich über die Struktur oder die Form definiert,
- sich der Wahrheitswert ebenfalls über die Struktur definiert,
- die Sprache die Wirklichkeit nur abbilden kann, weil beide die gleiche Struktur haben. Folglich ist es die Logik, die die Verbindung zwischen Sprache und Wirklichkeit möglich macht.

Die entscheidende Rolle von Struktur und Form zur Erklärung der Verbindung zwischen Sprache und Wirklichkeit ergibt sich, wie zuvor erwähnt, aus dem Einfluss der hertzschen Mechanik. Es gibt letztlich keine Dualität zwischen Logik und Ontologie. In gewissem Sinne verschmelzen sie sogar miteinander, so dass man bei Wittgenstein von einer logischen Ontologie spricht. Hat nun die Sprache die gleiche Struktur wie das, was sie abbildet oder ausdrückt, dann sollten eigentlich die Sätze jeder beliebigen Sprache die gleiche Struktur haben wie das, was sie ausdrücken. Dies hat Wittgenstein vermutlich zu der folgenden Aussage veranlasst: „Die Übersetzung einer Sprache in eine andere geht nicht so vor sich, daß man jeden *Satz* der einen in einen *Satz* der anderen übersetzt, sondern nur die Satzbestandteile werden übersetzt." (TLP 4.025)

Der Atomist Wittgenstein stellte die Verbindung zwischen empirischer Wirklichkeit und Sprache zunächst über die Logik her. Diese Struktur, die Welt und Sprache gemein ist, dient demnach gleichsam als Behältnis/Form, das/die sowohl durch Worte und Sätze als auch durch Gegenstände und Tatsachen verkörpert werden kann. Der Logiker und Mathematiker Wittgenstein macht aus Welt und Sprache Modelle – im mathematischen Sinne des Begriffs – für dieselbe Struktur.

Der Status der Logik und der Mathematik, insoweit sie aus Scheinsätzen bestehen, ist folglich nicht abwertend, da die sogenannten Formalwissenschaften, wie gerade dargelegt, eine zentrale Rolle spielen. Das Paradox der Mathematik (und der Logik), die aufgrund ihres Formalismus Wegbereiter einer Sprache ist, die die Wirklichkeit getreu ausdrückt, und gleichzeitig absolut sinnlos ist, ist somit aufgelöst. Diese von Wittgenstein in den ersten Jahrzehnten des 20. Jahrhunderts angestrebte Stringenz und Perfektion hat sich jedoch als zu eingeschränkt erwiesen und als unfähig, die gesamte Realität auszudrücken; war es doch der Zweck des *Tractatus*, das Sagbare zu erfassen. Die Sprache, so wie wir sie verwenden, ist in Wirklichkeit viel undogmatischer, undurchdringlicher und vielschichtiger. Dennoch scheint es, dass Wittgenstein im Laufe der Entwicklung seiner Philosophie immer häufiger auf das Beispiel der Mathematik zurückgreift.

Da sich die referentielle, eher ideale Auffassung von Sprache als aporetisch erwiesen hatte, stellte Wittgenstein einige seiner eigenen Ideen in Frage. Er beschäftigte sich noch intensiver mit seinen Überlegungen zur Sprache und ihrer Funktionsweise und gelangte schließlich zu der Auffassung, dass die Sprache viel lebendiger, weniger starr und folglich viel komplexer ist. Sie kann sich mithin nicht mehr darauf beschränken, ein Spiegel zu sein, der eine eher begrenzte Wirklichkeit reflektiert. In diesem Fall ist es offensichtlich, dass sich der Satzbegriff deshalb wandeln musste. In der Tat befasst sich die erste nach dem *Tractatus* entwickelte revolutionäre und innovative Idee mit dem Satzbegriff als solchem.

## 2 Die neue Satzauffassung

Das Neuartige an dieser Idee ist die Möglichkeit, die Unvollständigkeit eines Satzes in Betracht zu ziehen. Ein Satz ist gemäß der Logik per Definition vollständig und im Gegensatz zu einer propositionalen Funktion frei von Widersprüchlichkeiten. Demnach ist „x ist Österreicher" eine Funktion, die eine Ergänzung erfordert wie etwa das Argument „Wittgenstein", um zu einem Satz zu werden (im vorliegenden Fall zu einem wahren Satz): „Wittgenstein ist Österreicher." Nur unter dieser Bedingung kann eine Aussage ein Satz sein und nach Wittgenstein somit das vollständige, perfekte Bild dessen, was er abbildet. Trotzdem kann eine Aussage durchaus Unbekannte enthalten und wahr oder falsch sein, wodurch sie automatisch und paradoxerweise zum Satz wird.

Ein unvollständiger Satz entspräche also einem notwendigerweise unvollständigen Bild. Er besteht darin, dass er Variablen enthält. Wittgenstein erklärte in einer Diskussion mit Moritz Schlick am 22. Dezember 1929, dass wenn man beispielsweise sagt: „Ich habe zwei Stoffe gesehen von der gleichen Farbe", das keineswegs heißt, „es waren beide grün oder beide blau oder …", sondern es meint: „wir haben einen Stoff gesehen von der Farbe x und einen anderen von der Farbe x." (siehe WWK 22.12.1929) Es wird folglich keinerlei Information über die Farbe des Stoffes gegeben und über die Farbe des Stoffes an sich wird nichts ausgesagt. Es handelt sich de facto um einen echten Satz, der eine Wirklichkeit abbildet, auch wenn diese nicht vollständig bestimmt ist. Er lässt bestimmte Informationen offen, d. h., er lässt „Möglichkeiten offen" (PB § 87). Das bedeutet, dass ein Satz eine Bedeutung haben, wahr oder falsch sein und dabei gleichzeitig allgemein sein kann und gewisse Punkte unbestimmt lassen kann. Somit hängt eine Antwort, die wir auf eine Frage geben können, zum Beispiel vom Äußerungskontext ab. Sie kann vollständig oder unvollständig sein, je nachdem, was wir von ihr erwarten. Ein wahrer oder falscher Satz kann Punkte offenlassen, die im Äußerungskontext belanglos sind. In dem genannten Beispiel kann es für uns irrelevant sein, die genaue Farbe des Stoffes zu kennen.

Dieser Gedanke ist im Entwicklungsprozess des wittgensteinschen Denkens und hinsichtlich des Status, den er der Mathematik beimisst, von grundlegender Bedeutung. Er bedeutet zunächst, dass mehrere Darstellungssysteme möglich sind. Demzufolge – und das ist von entscheidender Bedeutung – sind andere Systeme, andere logische Formen zur Darstellung der Wirklichkeit möglich. Es geht somit nicht mehr um eine alleinige Form der Darstellung, die zudem auch noch allen Sprachen gemein ist, wie dies noch im *Tractatus* der Fall war, weil die Beschaffenheit der Sätze dort nicht berücksichtigt wurde. Dieser Gedanke steht im Gegensatz zum logischen Atomismus, nach dem die atomaren Elementarsätze voneinander unabhängig sind. De facto steht jeder Satz in einer internen Beziehung zu den Sätzen des Systems, dem er angehört, wie das beispielsweise beim Farbsystem der Fall ist. Alles ist eine Frage der Kohärenz im Farbsystem (BÜF I § 22). Diese Kohärenz ergibt sich allerdings nicht zwangsläufig aus der Anwendung logischer Regeln.

Demzufolge sind diese also nicht immer bindend. So können etwa die logischen Konnektoren je nach Beschaffenheit des Satzes unterschiedlich verwendet werden, insofern als einen Satz gebrauchen bedeutet, eine Sprache zu gebrauchen, aus der man ihn nicht herauslösen kann. Sätze sind nicht isoliert und autonom.

Folglich wird kein System ausgeschlossen. Es wäre allerdings falsch, nunmehr weiterhin zu glauben, der *Tractatus* könne Sinn, Rede und Grammatik in ihrer Gesamtheit darstellen und erschöpfen. Wittgenstein bestätigt dies am 2. Januar 1930 in einem Gespräch mit Schlick, als er sagt: „Das was ich das erste Mal gar nicht beachtet hatte, war dies, dass die Syntax der logischen Konstanten nur einen Teil einer umfassenden Syntax bildet." (WWK 02.01.1930) Das Feld der Grammatik und des Sinns ist sehr viel weiter gefasst, als die Regeln der logischen Syntax es vorzugeben scheinen. Diese sind keinesfalls überholt oder wurden verworfen, sie sind jedoch in Bezug auf die Wirklichkeit ganz einfach unzureichend.

Diese Auffassung von Sprache und Sinn wirkt sich auf die Inferenzauffassung aus. Im logischen Kalkül vollzieht sich jede Inferenz abhängig von den Strukturmerkmalen der Sätze. Nach der neuen Satzauffassung lässt sich jedoch das

Nicht-Bestehen eines Satzes durchaus aus einem anderen schlussfolgern aufgrund der Tatsache, dass Sätze sich abhängig von den Systemen, denen sie angehören, ausschließen können (PB § 87).

In einer anderen Diskussion mit Waismann stellt Wittgenstein die Vorstellung, das Schlussfolgern entspräche einer rein wahrheitsfunktionalen Auffassung des Satzes, ganz klar in Frage: „Ich habe all das bei der Abfassung meiner Arbeit noch nicht gewusst und meinte damals, dass alles Schließen auf der Form der Tautologie beruhe. Ich hatte damals noch nicht gesehen, dass ein Schluss auch die Form haben kann: Ein Mensch ist 2 m groß, also ist er nicht 3 Meter groß. Das hängt damit zusammen, dass ich glaubte, die Elementarsätze müssten unabhängig sein; aus dem Bestehen eines Sachverhaltes könne man nicht auf das Nicht-Bestehen eines andern schließen. Wenn aber meine jetzige Auffassung mit dem Satzsystem richtig ist, ist es sogar die Regel, dass man aus dem Bestehen eines Sachverhaltes auf das Nicht-Bestehen aller übrigen schließen kann, die durch das Satzsystem beschrieben werden." (WWK 25.12.1929)

Somit gibt es zwei Arten von Inferenzen, die sich keineswegs ausschließen. Die eine beruht auf den logischen Konstanten, die andere auf den Regeln eines Sprachsystems, wie beispielsweise dem Farbsystem, anhand dessen man behaupten kann, dass A grün ist und somit weder blau noch rot usw. Entgegen der Behauptung des logischen Atomismus ist ein sogenannter einfacher Satz nicht unabhängig von den übrigen Sätzen, die zum gleichen System gehören. Nunmehr sind die Systeme und nicht mehr die Sätze unabhängig und autonom.

Diese Entwicklung im Denken Wittgensteins hat zur Folge, dass die Sprache wie unabhängige Systeme funktioniert – genauso wie die Mathematik oder der Kalkül. Diese Rolle der Logik und der Mathematik wird scheinbar geschmälert durch die Vorstellung einer nicht exklusiven, vermeintlich eher in der Grammatik enthaltenen logischen Syntax. In Wahrheit verstärkt sie jedoch den Einfluss des mathematischen Beispiels insofern, als die Sprache angesichts dieser Vielfalt und Pluralität nebeneinander existierender Systeme wie die Mathematik funktioniert.

## 3 Die Mathematik nach dem *Tractatus*

Dadurch, dass die Sprache nicht mehr von logischen, sondern von Gebrauchsregeln (philosophische Grammatik) geregelt wird, greift Wittgenstein zur Erklärung der Funktionsweise unserer Sprache auf die Analogie zum Kalkül und zur Mathematik zurück. Diese Analogie soll erklären, dass unsere Sprache als Ganzes funktioniert und ein untrennbares Ganzes bildet, das man als autonom bezeichnen kann. Somit kann man einen Satz nicht isoliert von der Sprache verstehen, der er angehört. „Einen Satz verstehen, heißt, eine Sprache verstehen. Ein

Satz ist ein Zeichen in einem System von Zeichen." (PG I § 84) Daher ist die Sprache wie die Mathematik ein System, genauer gesagt mehrere Systeme. So genügt es in der Mathematik beispielsweise „also nicht zu sagen ‚p ist beweisbar', sondern es muß heißen: beweisbar nach einem bestimmten System" (PG II § 25), d.h., p kann nicht in einem anderen System bewiesen werden. Das bedeutet gleichzeitig die Pluralität und Relativität der Wahrheiten und zwangsläufig des Sinns. So wie es mehrere mathematische Systeme gibt, gibt es somit mehrere Sprachen, die dank der Anwendung von Regeln funktionieren. Da das Hauptmerkmal des Kalküls jedoch darin besteht, dass es rein syntaktisch und formal ist, kann es möglicherweise zu Missverständnissen führen, da die Rolle unserer Sprache in der Vermittlung einer Intention besteht. Wittgenstein untermauert sie deshalb mit einer zweiten Analogie und zwar der Analogie zum Spiel, beispielsweise des Schachspiels oder des Ballspiels. Er möchte damit die Vorstellung von der zwangsläufigen Pluralität und Verschiedenartigkeit der Sprache unterstreichen und dass sie darin besteht, die Regeln eben dieser Systeme anzuwenden. Im Spiel wird sehr deutlich, dass die Regeln nicht ihre gesamten Anwendungen erschöpfen. Wenn wir Schach spielen, sind wir beispielsweise permanent dabei, neu zu erfinden. Dieses Merkmal der Regel und ihrer Anwendung im Spiel ist entscheidend und tritt dort sicher weitaus deutlicher zutage als im Kalkül. Die Analogie zum Kalkül verlangt folglich eine Ergänzung; sie bleibt jedoch dominierend und es hat den Anschein, dass Wittgenstein insbesondere dieser engen Beziehung zwischen Sprache und Kalkül hinsichtlich ihrer Funktionsweise eine ganz besondere Bedeutung beimaß. Zwischen 1929 und 1944 schrieb er viel über Mathematik und widmete ihr einen Großteil der Vorlesungen, die er in Cambridge vor einer ausgewählten Hörerschaft hielt, zu denen Alan Turing, Georg Henrik von Wright, Norman Malcolm, Rush Rhees, J. N. Findlay und weitere zählten. Die Manuskripte der *Bemerkungen über die Grundlagen der Mathematik* stammen aus den Jahren 1937 und 1938. Sie enthalten sehr aufschlussreiche Bemerkungen zu den Regeln und ihren Anwendungen, zum Kalkül, zur Inferenz, zum Spiel und zum Beweis sowie auch dazu, was ein Sprachspiel ist und wie es funktioniert.

Dieser doppelte Vergleich der Sprache mit dem Spiel und vor allem mit dem Kalkül ermöglicht Wittgenstein, den Schlüsselbegriff der Sprachspiele zu entwickeln. Was haben Sprachspiele mit Kalkül und Spiel gemeinsam? In welcher Beziehung stehen sie zueinander?

Diese Analogien müssen adäquat ausgewertet werden. Aus ihnen leitet sich die Vorstellung her, dass es die Regeln sind, die sowohl den Kalkül als auch das Spiel definieren und begründen. Kalkulieren wie auch Spielen besteht im Regelanwenden. Die Sprachspiele, die die Sprache begründen, definieren sich ebenfalls durch Regeln, deren Anwendung im Leben innerhalb dessen, was Wittgenstein *Lebensformen* nennt, geschieht. In Paragraph 7 der *Philosophischen*

*Untersuchungen* definiert er das Sprachspiel als „das Ganze: der Sprache und der Tätigkeiten, mit denen sie verwoben ist" (PU § 7). Verglichen mit der Idealsprache, mit der sich der *Tractatus* beschäftigt, wird dieses Interesse für unsere Sprache, so wie wir sie alltäglich gebrauchen, als Rückkehr auf den *rauen Boden* bezeichnet, d. h. eine Rückkehr zu Leben und Tätigkeit, mit denen die Sprache unausweichlich verflochten ist. Ein rauer Boden erschwert den Zugang und das in diesem Zusammenhang verwendete Adjektiv legt nahe, dass die Funktionsweise der Sprache nicht reibungslos und ohne Tücken ist. Wie wirkt sich das nun auf die Mathematik und ihren Status aus?

## 4 Die Schriften über Mathematik

Obwohl die Mathematik zu Hilfe genommen wurde, um die Funktionsweise der Sprache zu erklären, zeigen die Schriften über Mathematik paradoxerweise, dass die mathematische Sprache entgegen der gemeinhin verbreiteten Auffassung keineswegs frei von Unklarheiten ist und nicht weniger verschwommen ist als unsere Alltagssprache. Die mathematischen Unklarheiten betreffen sowohl Fachbegriffe als auch die „Wörter der gewöhnlichen Alltagssprache" (LFM I: 2) wie „Beweis", „Zahl", „Reihe" usw. Dabei sind letztere wesentlich hartnäckiger als erstere, derer man sich relativ leicht entledigen kann. Wie jede andere Sprache leidet folglich auch die Sprache der Mathematik darunter, dass man den gleichen Begriff für unterschiedliche Dinge verwenden kann, ohne zwischen den Verwendungen zu unterscheiden. „Wie primitive Menschen neigen wir dazu zu sagen, ‚obwohl all diese Dinge verschieden aussehen, sind sie in Wirklichkeit gleich' statt ‚obwohl all diese Dinge gleich aussehen, sind sie in Wirklichkeit verschieden.'" (LFM I: 3) Diese Bemerkung betrifft ungewöhnlicherweise die mathematische Sprache. Wenn die mathematischen Ausdrücke also eine „unendliche Anzahl von Verwendungen" haben, so kommt Wittgenstein nicht umhin, jegliche Möglichkeit, eine allgemeine Theorie des Beweises, der mathematischen Wahrheit, der Konsistenz vorzustellen, zu verwerfen und somit auch dem Logizismus, Formalismus und Intuitionismus abzuschwören.

Im *Tractatus* sind formale Aussagen – sowohl mathematische (Gleichungen) als auch logische (tautologische) – Scheinsätze, insofern als sie die Bedingung, aufgrund derer sie überhaupt Sätze sein können, nicht erfüllen, d. h. einen Sinn haben, der darin besteht, zumindest einen Sachverhalt auszudrücken. Wie verhält es sich nun mit den mathematischen Aussagen in den Schriften über Mathematik? Sind sie Sätze?

Es scheint, als habe Wittgenstein diese wichtige Frage nicht wirklich gestellt: Der mathematische Satz geht nämlich aus dem Kalkül hervor, er „ist *wesentlich* das letzte Glied einer Demonstration, die ihn als richtig oder unrichtig sichtbar macht", er „ist das letzte Glied einer Beweiskette" (PB § 162). In diesem Fall hat der mathematische Satz keinen Sinn, der seinem Wahrheitswert vorausgehen könnte. Im Gegenteil, es ist jener, welcher ihm einen Sinn gibt, denn er existiert erst, nachdem er bewiesen wurde. Ihn zu beweisen, bestimmt seinen Sinn.

Von nun an beugt sich die Mathematik der allgemeinen Auffassung von Sprache, die nach dem *Tractatus* eher pragmatisch ist, insofern als die mathematische Sprache durch Lernen und eine Art von Abrichtung erworben wird. „Die Mathematik [...] lehrt dich nicht einfach die Antwort auf eine Frage; sondern ein ganzes Sprachspiel, mit Fragen und Antworten." (BGM VII § 18) Eine mathematische Formel wird folglich gemeint, in der „Art und Weise, wie wir sie ständig gebrauchen, wie uns gelehrt wurde, sie zu gebrauchen" (PU § 190). Dies verleiht der Mathematik eine gewisse „Unerbittlichkeit", die in Wirklichkeit dem Gebrauch, den wir täglich von ihr machen, geschuldet ist. Die natürlichen Zahlenreihen und unsere Sprache sind folglich weder wahr noch falsch, sondern „brauchbar" und vor allem „verwendet". „[D]arum wird unerbittlich darauf gedrungen, daß wir Alle auf ‚eins' ‚zwei', auf ‚zwei' ‚drei' sagen, usf." (BGM I § 4)

Demnach verwendet man in der Mathematik und der Logik die Wörter „in der gleichen Weise, in der die anderen" sie in den gleichen Sprachspielen verwenden. Das wiederum bedeutet, dass richtig sprechen nichts bedeutet, da es die „unterschiedlichsten Weisen" gibt, Logik oder Mathematik zu betreiben. Diese unterliegen einer Übereinstimmung, „die darin besteht, das Gleiche zu tun, gleich zu reagieren". Im Gegensatz zur Funktionsweise der gewöhnlichen Sprache handelt es sich dabei nicht um eine Übereinstimmung der Meinungen (LFM XIX: 184– 187). Es ist eher eine Übereinstimmung im Handeln, eine Frage der Übung, denn „[z]um Rechnen gehört *wesentlich* dieser Consensus, das ist sicher. D.h.: zum Phänomen unseres Rechnens gehört dieser Consensus. In einer *Rechen*technik müssen Prophezeiungen möglich sein. Und das macht die Rechentechnik der Technik eines *Spieles*, wie des Schachs, ähnlich" (BGM III § 67). Die Sprache der Mathematik, der Kalkül könnten gar nicht anders funktionieren. Die Gesetze der Logik sind starr, vergleichbar etwa mit einem Rechtsgesetz, das ein Verbrechen streng bestraft. In der Anwendung können die Richter zwar mehr oder wenig nachsichtig sein, was uns jedoch nicht daran hindert zu sagen, dass das Gesetz unerbittlich ist. (LFM XX: 197) „Wir sagen nicht: ‚also *so* gehen wir!', sondern: ‚also *so* geht es!'" (BGM III § 69), eine Aussage, die Wittgenstein fast wortwörtlich geschrieben hat, um zu erklären, was ein Sprachspiel ist. „[...] *ein* Mensch könnte jedenfalls nicht nur *einmal* in seinem Leben rechnen." (BGM III § 67)

Da Wittgenstein keine Genealogie der Sprachen erstellt, ist jedwede Sprache einfach „ererbt". Wir finden sie vor und übernehmen sie, damit wir die Widersprüche, die uns in Schwierigkeiten bringen, „auf natürliche Weise" verwerfen

(LFM XXI: 206). Die Beherrschung der mathematischen Sprache ist eine Frage der Praxis und Übung, die dazu führt, dass ihr Gebrauch, wie der jeder anderen Sprache, gewöhnlich und „natürlich" wird.

Folglich ist auch in der Mathematik ein Satz das, was man daraus macht. Die Zeichen haben die Bedeutung, d. h. den Gebrauch (die Funktion), die man ihnen gibt. So ist ein Axiom ein Satz, dessen Gebrauch es ist, ein Axiom zu sein. Das wiederum bedeutet, dass ein Satz ein Axiom ist, wenn er als solches verwendet wird. Kein Satz existiert außerhalb seines Gebrauchs. Man kann sich also fragen, ob die Mathematik einen anderen Gebrauch als sich selbst hat oder ob sie lediglich eine Bequemlichkeit ist. (BGM IV § 52) Gewiss erwarten wir von ihr „gewisse Erfahrungen", die grundlegend sind, wie die Tatsache, dass die gleiche Multiplikation immer das gleiche Resultat ergibt. Es ist jedoch nicht die Mathematik, die diese Erwartungen zum Ausdruck bringt, auch wenn „[e]s [...] der Mathematik wesentlich [ist], daß ihre Zeichen auch im *Zivil* gebraucht werden". Dies ermöglicht den Zeichen, eine „mathematische Bedeutung" zu haben. Es ist der Gebrauch außerhalb der Mathematik, der das Zeichenspiel zur Mathematik macht (BGM V § 2). So erhält beispielsweise „300" eine Bedeutung durch den Kalkül, und in dem Satz „In diesem College befinden sich 300 Menschen" erhält 300 eine Bedeutung, so wie „Das ist ein Stuhl" „Stuhl" eine Bedeutung gibt. Gleichermaßen gilt, dass „Die Zahl dieser Dinge ist gleich der Zahl jener" ein Erfahrungssatz ist. Schaltet man dem gleichen Satz jedoch „per Definition" vor, wird er ein mathematischer Satz (LFM XXVI: 263). Es ist eine Frage des Kontextes und der Sprachspiele.

In Anbetracht der Tatsache, dass jede Sprache eine im Zusammenhang mit der ihr zugehörigen Lebensform autonom funktionierende Tätigkeit ist, stellt sich erneut die Frage nach der Nutzlosigkeit und sogar Unmöglichkeit der Grundlegung der Mathematik: Wozu braucht die Mathematik eine Grundlegung und nicht die Physik (BGM VII § 16)?

## 5 Zusammenfassung

Die Mathematik steht letztendlich nicht über den anderen Sprachtypen und genießt mitnichten den privilegierten Status, den man, gemessen an der Rolle, die sie in der Entwicklung der wittgensteinschen Sprachauffassung spielte, erwarten könnte. Wittgensteins Schriften über Mathematik zeigen somit, dass deren Sprache nicht perfekt ist und ihr Gebrauch irreführend und falsch sein kann. Im Übrigen kann die Widerspruchsfreiheit, die nur in der Praxis zum Ausdruck kommt, nicht das Kriterium ihrer Gültigkeit sein. Es ist die Grammatik des Gebrauchs, die die verschiedenen Verwendungen, die wir von ihr machen können, kontrolliert, und zwar genauso wie bei jeder anderen Sprache. Mit diesen Schlussfolgerungen verscherzte Wittgenstein sich übrigens die Gunst der Mathematiker seiner Zeit. Auf die Behauptung Hilberts „Aus dem Paradies, das Cantor uns geschaffen, soll uns niemand vertreiben können" erwiderte er, dass er nicht im Traum versuchen würde, jemanden daraus zu vertreiben, sondern vielmehr zeigen würde, dass es gar kein Paradies ist, indem er ihnen eine bestimmte Art der Forschung empfahl (LFM XI: 103), die ihrem Gebrauch der Sprache mehr Aufmerksamkeit beimisst.

Noch eine letzte Anmerkung: Die wittgensteinsche Philosophie der Mathematik veranschaulicht die Schwierigkeit, die behandelten Themen voneinander zu trennen, und stellt dadurch seine spiralförmig gewundene Betrachtungsweise dar, denn sie entfernt sich von ihrem Ausgangspunkt, um ununterbrochen mit neuen Klärungen dorthin zurückzukommen. Wittgenstein ging nämlich von dem Gedanken aus, die gewöhnliche Sprache sei keine Darstellung der Wirklichkeit, sondern funktioniere wie unterschiedliche, nur kohärente Kalküle, d. h. Kalküle, die die Regeln einhalten, wie das auch im Spiel der Fall ist. Diese beiden Analogien, von denen die zweite die erste noch verstärkt, ergeben den Begriff des Sprachspiels. Bei einer weiteren Vertiefung seiner Überlegungen erklärt Wittgenstein, dass es letztendlich die Mathematik ist, die wie unsere Sprache funktioniert, d. h. innerhalb von Sprachspielen. Dieses Hin und Her verdeutlicht die wittgensteinsche Philosophieauffassung als unablässige Suche nach einer Ordnung der Begriffe.

## Literatur

Wittgenstein, Ludwig (1989a) [WWK]: *Ludwig Wittgenstein und der Wiener Kreis*. Werkausgabe Band 3. Frankfurt a. M.: Suhrkamp.
Wittgenstein, Ludwig (1989b) [PU]: *Philosophische Untersuchungen*. Werkausgabe Band 1. Frankfurt a. M.: Suhrkamp.
Wittgenstein, Ludwig (1989c) [TLP]: *Tractatus logico-philosophicus*. Werkausgabe Band 1. Frankfurt a. M.: Suhrkamp.
Wittgenstein, Ludwig (1993a) [PB]: *Philosophische Bemerkungen*. Werkausgabe Band 2. Frankfurt a. M.: Suhrkamp.
Wittgenstein, Ludwig (1993b) [PG]: *Philosophische Grammatik*. Werkausgabe Band 4. Frankfurt a. M.: Suhrkamp.
Wittgenstein, Ludwig (1994) [BGM]: *Bemerkungen über die Grundlagen der Mathematik*. Werkausgabe Band 6. Frankfurt a. M.: Suhrkamp.
Wittgenstein, Ludwig (1995) [LFM]: *Cours sur les fondements des mathématiques: Cambridge, 1939*. Edition bilingue français-anglais. Paris: Trans-Europ-Repress.
Wittgenstein, Ludwig (1997) [BÜF]: *Bemerkungen über die Farben*. Werkausgabe Band 8. Frankfurt a. M.: Suhrkamp.

Georg Siller
# Hase oder Ente?
Wittgensteins Aspektwechsel und Identitätspolitik

**Abstract:** [Rabbit or Duck? Wittgenstein's Aspect Change and Identity Politics] Terms such as "identity" or "identity politics" are often accompanied by fierce controversy in public debates. Even independent of populist positioning, there is a clear uneasiness in the application of the concept of identity, as on the one hand the politically important, group-forming chances of identity concepts are welcomed, on the other hand their essentialist consequences are feared. The aim of this paper is to shed new light on such an identity dilemma by recourse to Wittgenstein's late philosophy. For this purpose, primarily his reflections on aspect-perception have been used. Analogous to his distinction between steady aspect-perceiving and noticing a change of aspect, a primary from a secondary use could be distinguished in the concept of identity.

**Keywords:** Identity, identity politics, Ludwig Wittgenstein, aspect change, secondary meaning

# 1 „Identität"

Wohl nur wenige Begriffe sind dermaßen vielfältig in ihren Bedeutungsnuancen und Anwendungsbereichen wie der Begriff der Identität. Seine Wurzeln liegen im lateinischen *identitas*, was eine Substantivierung von *idem* („dasselbe') darstellt. Der Begriff steht seit dem Mittelalter für die *Selbigkeit* von Dingen, er ist der Gegenbegriff zu *diversitas* („Verschiedenheit'). Was in diesem Sinne identisch ist, bildet eine Wesensgemeinschaft, wie etwa die drei Personen des christlichen Gottes. Später, in der Neuzeit, wird mit dem Begriff zunehmend auch die Selbigkeit *einer* Person bezeichnet, welche mit sich selbst in der Zeit übereinstimmt, also trotz aller Veränderungen noch dieselbe ist. Im 20. Jahrhundert kommt schließlich verstärkt der Begriff der *kollektiven Identität* auf, nach der es bestimmte Merkmale gibt, die bei den Mitgliedern einer Gruppe identisch sind – oder zumindest von den Gruppenmitgliedern als gemeinsame Merkmale aufgefasst werden. Bis heute wird Identität einerseits als wesenhafte Zugehörigkeit zu einer Gruppe verstanden, andererseits aber auch als etwas, was gerade die einzelne Person in ihrer Einzigartigkeit kennzeichnet, ihr authentisches Ich ausmacht.

In der soziologischen Unterscheidung von *sozialer* und *personaler* Identität[1] finden sich diese beiden Dimensionen wieder: Während die soziale Identität in den sozialen Rollen besteht, an welche ganz bestimmte gesellschaftliche Erwartungen geknüpft sind, steht die personale Identität für die persönliche Unverwechselbarkeit, also gerade für die Nicht-Entsprechung gegenüber solchen Rollenerwartungen. Aber auch eine in der Philosophie gebräuchliche Unterscheidung verweist auf den doppelten Charakter von Identität: Während man von *qualitativer* Identität dann spricht, wenn bestimmte Merkmale verschiedenen Individuen gemeinsam sind (Gleichheit), bedeutet *numerische* Identität, dass alle Merkmale gleich sind, dass also die beiden Individuen *als eines gezählt* werden können (Selbigkeit). Es handelt sich um ein und dasselbe Individuum.[2]

In den jüngeren Debatten rund um „Identitätspolitik" steht der Identitätsbegriff mit zusätzlichen Konzepten wie Selbstbestimmung und Würde in Verbindung. Trotzdem finden sich die zwei grundsätzlichen Formen von Identität wieder: die Übereinstimmung mit einem Kollektiv, aber auch die Übereinstimmung mit sich selbst im Sinne von Differenz und Einzigartigkeit. Einerseits wird bestimmten Formen von Identitätspolitik eine repressive Orientierung an einem *Kollektiv* vorgeworfen, andererseits wird der Kampfbegriff „Identitätspolitik" mit einem immer stärker auftretenden Partikularismus gleichgesetzt.

Für begriffliche Klärungen verschiedenster Art stellt Ludwig Wittgensteins Philosophie generell eine Fundgrube dar. Deshalb soll hier der Vorschlag für eine Unterscheidung gemacht werden, die sich an seine Überlegungen zum Aspekt-Wahrnehmen anlehnt. Unterschieden werden soll a) „Identität" als Zugehörigkeit zu einer Gruppe aufgrund übereinstimmender Merkmale und b) „Identität" als Wesen oder innerstes Zentrum einer Person, das zu missachten auch die Würde dieser Person verletzt. Die erste Form von Identität wird mehr oder weniger implizit gewusst und ist grundsätzlich nicht abhängig von einem auf sie gerichteten Bewusstseinszustand, die zweite existiert nur als Gegenstand eines *Erlebnisses* (entweder in der ersten oder dritten Person).

---

[1] Beispielsweise führte Erving Goffman diese Unterscheidung in detaillierter Form durch (vgl. Goffman 2018: 72–74).

[2] Eine solche numerische Identität meinte Wittgenstein, wenn er im *Tractatus* erklärt: „Von *zwei* Dingen zu sagen, sie seien identisch, ist ein Unsinn, und von *Einem* zu sagen, es sei identisch mit sich selbst, sagt gar nichts." (TLP 5.5303)

## 2 Aspekt-Wahrnehmen

Im sogenannten zweiten Teil der *Philosophischen Untersuchungen* gibt es einen Abschnitt, der an Umfang alle anderen Abschnitte überragt. Es handelt sich um das Kapitel XI, das in der Suhrkamp-Ausgabe immerhin eine Länge von 60 Seiten aufweist und das auch den berühmten Hasen-Enten-Kopf als Beispiel enthält. Zentrales Thema dieses Kapitels ist das Aspekt-Wahrnehmen – auch in Verbindung mit dem Erleben von Bedeutungen. Unabhängig davon, was Wittgenstein tatsächlich mit diesen Texten vorhatte und ob er die verschiedenen Kapitel auch wirklich selbst so anordnete, steht fest, dass Aspektwahrnehmungen in seinem Denken der späten 1940er Jahre einen zentralen Platz einnehmen.

Gleich auf den ersten Seiten des Kapitels unterscheidet Wittgenstein zwischen dem stetigen Aspekt-Wahrnehmen und dem Bemerken eines Aspektwechsels. Stetig ist eine Aspektwahrnehmung dann, wenn es keinerlei Kippen, keinen Wechsel gibt, wenn wir den Aspekt selbstverständlich und alternativlos wahrnehmen. Wir nehmen in diesem Fall genau genommen auch nicht den Aspekt als solchen wahr, sondern der Aspekt ist integriert in die bloße Wahrnehmung. Wenn wir z. B. vor uns eine Gabel liegen sehen, dann sehen wir nicht einerseits ein Ding und zusätzlich noch, dass es sich bei diesem Ding um eine Gabel handelt (PU: 521). Der Aspekt des Gabel-Seins ist nicht getrennt von der Wahrnehmung des Dings. Wir sehen einfach eine Gabel. Es wäre unsinnig, unter normalen Umständen davon zu sprechen, dass wir dieses Ding für eine Gabel halten. So wie es unsinnig wäre, davon zu sprechen, dass wir eine uns bekannte Person für einen Menschen halten und nicht für einen Roboter.

Das stetige Wahrnehmen von Aspekten ist nicht für sich ein Bewusstseinszustand. Wenn wir uns im eigenen Zimmer auskennen (BPP I § 295) oder wenn wir eine Landschaft als dreidimensional wahrnehmen (PU: 526, 547), dann geschieht die Wahrnehmung dieses Aspekts ganz nebenbei. Es würde unter gewöhnlichen Umständen sehr konstruiert wirken, die Wahrnehmung der Landschaft von der Wahrnehmung ihrer Dreidimensionalität zu unterscheiden. Dann müssten wir nach Wittgenstein auch das Grüne da draußen als „blatthaft" wahrnehmen, diese beiden Dinge da als „augenhaft" und jeweils von einem Bewusstseinszustand des „Blatthaft-Sehens" oder des „Augenhaft-Sehens" ausgehen (BPP I § 1006).

Analog verhält es sich beim Hasen-Enten-Kopf, den Wittgenstein vom US-amerikanischen Psychologen Joseph Jastrow übernommen hat, der aber schon 1892 in deutschen Satirezeitschriften auftauchte: Kennen wir nur die eine Sichtweise, nach der die Zeichnung z. B. einen Hasen darstellt, werden wir einfach einen Hasen wahrnehmen. Wir werden nicht sagen „Jetzt sehe ich es als einen Hasen!" Erst wenn uns auffällt, dass dieselbe Zeichnung sowohl eine Ente als auch einen Hasen darstellen könnte, wird das Sehen-als zum eigenen Bewusstseinszustand, wir sagen z. B. „Jetzt sehe ich es als einen Hasen!" oder auch „Jetzt ist es ein Hase!" Aber das heißt für Wittgenstein eben nicht, dass wir damit den einen Aspekt isoliert wahrnehmen. Das Erlebnis beim Bemerken des Aspektwechsels ist auf das Kippen verschiedener Aspekte gerichtet. Unser Satz ist nicht Bericht einer Aspektwahrnehmung, sondern Ausdruck des Staunens über die Möglichkeit des Aspektwechsels (PU: 528). Wir nehmen die Relation zwischen einem Aspekt und einem anderen – ebenfalls möglichen – Aspekt wahr. Im Aufleuchten des Aspekts staunen wir darüber, dass dasselbe Ding zwei verschiedene Dinge sein kann, zwei verschiedene Aspekte haben kann. Und auch darüber, dass diese zwei Aspekte nicht zufällig existieren, sondern in einer *internen Relation* stehen, also gewissermaßen zum Ding selbst gehören. Sie waren schon da, bevor wir sie bemerkten.

Das scheinbar Selbstverständliche, nämlich *einen* Aspekt als solchen zu erleben bzw. bewusst wahrzunehmen, wird damit nach Wittgenstein unmöglich. Denn wenn wir es mit nur einem Aspekt zu tun haben, wird er nicht eigens erlebt; und wenn wir überhaupt Aspekte erleben können, dann nicht diese selbst, sondern den Wechsel zwischen ihnen.

Entscheidend für Wittgenstein ist hier die Verwendung des Begriffs „sehen". Dieser Begriff wird unterschiedlich verwendet, je nachdem, ob wir einfach einen Hasen sehen oder ob wir etwas als einen Hasen sehen. Das „Sehen-als" erscheint uns „halb Seherlebnis, halb ein Denken" (PU: 525). Wir nehmen eine Deutung vor, wir können z. B. beim Hasen-Enten-Kopf unser Sehen aktiv steuern, wir können das Kippen bewusst herbeiführen – so etwas ist beim stetigen Aspekt-Wahrnehmen nicht vorgesehen. Deshalb ist die Verwendung von „sehen" beim Bemerken des Aspektwechsels nicht dieselbe wie beim stetigen Aspekt-Wahrnehmen.

## 3 Bedeutungserlebnisse

Ähnlich verhält es sich nach Wittgenstein bei den Sprachspielen rund um den Begriff „Bedeutung". Wir können Bedeutung zwar erleben, aber auch hier erleben wir nur den Wechsel von Bedeutungen, also wieder das Kippen. Das geschieht etwa, wenn wir ein bestimmtes Wort in zwei verschiedenen Kontexten ausprobieren, z. B. das Wort „weiche" einmal als Adjektiv bei „weiche Eier" und einmal als Imperativ bei „Weiche *nicht* vom Platz!" (PU: 555); oder wenn wir ein Wort aus dem Kontext eines Satzes herausholen und isoliert zehnmal wiederholen, sodass es zum bloßen Klang wird (vgl. PU: 553). Solche Bedeutungserlebnisse sind für Wittgenstein vergleichbar mit dem Bemerken des Aspektwechsels.

Wir haben bei Bedeutungserlebnissen den Eindruck, als könnten wir die Bedeutung direkt an den Wörtern wahrnehmen. Wenn wir z. B. – auch das ein Beispiel Wittgensteins – festlegen, dass das Wort „Turm" ab sofort „Bank" bedeute und wir sprechen nun den Satz aus: „Geh jetzt zum Turm!" (PU: 553), dann fühlt es sich so an, als würden wir die neue Bedeutung „Bank" am Wort „Turm" kleben sehen. Entsprechend würden wir auch Sätze sagen wollen wie „Jetzt meine ich mit ‚Turm' eine Bank", „Turm" bedeutet für mich jetzt „Bank".

## 4 Sekundäre Verwendung von Begriffen

Doch bei diesem „Meinen" oder „Bedeuten" ist es ähnlich wie beim „Sehen-als". Die Verwendung der Begriffe ist eine andere als die übliche. Im üblichen Sprachspiel haben nämlich „meinen" und „Bedeutung" nichts mit speziellen Erlebnissen zu tun, so wie das stetige Aspekt-Wahrnehmen in unseren Sprachspielen auch kein spezielles Aspekt-Wahrnehmen kennt (ich sehe eine Gabel, und nicht ein Ding, das zudem eine Gabel ist). Trotzdem haben wir nach Wittgenstein die Neigung, die entsprechenden Begriffe aus den anderen Sprachspielen zu übernehmen (PU: 556), also ihre Bedeutung zu verschieben. Wir haben die Neigung, Begriffe wie „meinen" oder „verstehen" oder „Bedeutung" für spezielle Erlebnisse zu verwenden.

Diese Neigung akzeptiert Wittgenstein, er möchte nicht von einer falschen Verwendung der Begriffe „meinen" oder „Bedeutung" sprechen. Nur muss klar sein, dass eine solche Verwendung der entsprechenden Begriffe eine sekundäre ist. Ein anderes Beispiel für sekundäre Bedeutungen/Verwendungen wäre bei Wittgenstein die Verwendung der Begriffe „fett" und „mager" für Mittwoch und Dienstag. Der Mittwoch ist nicht wirklich fett. Was wir über den Mittwoch sagen möchten, können wir trotzdem durch den Begriff „fett" zum Ausdruck bringen – so sind nun mal unsere Sprachspiele bzw. unsere Lebensform (vgl. PU: 556). Ähnlich ist der Ausdruck „gelb" für den Vokal „e" sekundär verwendet. Oder auch der Begriff „Kopfrechnen" für das schnelle Durchführen einer Addition im Kopf, denn die Tätigkeit des Rechnens ist hier eine andere als beim schriftlichen oder mündlichen Rechnen. Oder wir können sagen, der Name „Schubert" passt irgendwie zu seinen Werken: Hier ist das Wort „passen" sekundär verwendet, weil wir ja nicht sagen können, wie der Name zu den Werken passt. Es handelt sich also nicht um die übliche, primäre Bedeutung von „passen". So wie es nicht die primäre Bedeutung von „Bedeutung" ist, auf ein Erlebnis anzuspielen, in dem Bedeutung zur Atmosphäre eines Wortes wird.

In der Literatur über Wittgenstein ist eine Interpretation sehr verbreitet, nach der sich das Bedeutungserlebnis auf die sekundäre Bedeutung bezieht.³ Das hieße, dass wir die (üblichen) primären Bedeutungen ohne Erlebnis erfassen, die sekundären hingegen mit. Es wären also ganz besondere Bedeutungen, die im Bedeutungs-Erleben aufleuchten, so etwa eine besondere Bedeutung des Namens „Schubert", die ihn zu Schuberts Werken passen lässt. – Stimmiger erscheint mir jedoch jene Interpretation, nach der die Bedeutung der beteiligten Begriffe eine sekundäre ist, und zwar die Bedeutung der Begriffe „meinen", „sehen", und eben „Bedeutung". Schließlich lautet schon der Eröffnungssatz von Kapitel XI: „Zwei Verwendungen des Wortes ‚sehen'." (PU: 518) Außerdem lässt sich diese Interpretation gut mit anderen Abschnitten der *Philosophischen Untersuchungen* oder auch der *Bemerkungen über die Philosophie der Psychologie* in Verbindung bringen. Es ist gerade die sekundäre Verwendung von Begriffen wie „Bedeutung", die uns zu jenem „Bild" führt, nach dem wir den Aspekt oder die Bedeutung eines Dinges direkt am Ding wahrnehmen, wie eine „Atmosphäre" oder einen „Dunstkreis" (vgl. dazu Siller 2018: 152–153).

## 5 „Bedeutung" und „Identität"

Was spricht für die Anwendung sprachanalytischer Überlegungen aus Wittgensteins Spätphilosophie auf den Begriff der Identität? Er selbst hat die Verbindung nicht explizit hergestellt und es erscheint auf den ersten Blick fragwürdig, die Identität von Personen mit der Bedeutung von Wörtern oder dem Motiv von Strichzeichnungen gleichzusetzen. Doch Wittgensteins Beispiele in Kapitel XI handeln durchaus von einzelnen Menschen, genaugenommen von einzelnen Menschen als Objekten unseres Verstehens. Schon das erste Beispiel bezieht sich auf das Bemerken der Ähnlichkeit zweier Menschen. Wir betrachten ein Gesicht und plötzlich bemerken wir die Ähnlichkeit mit einem anderen Gesicht (vgl. PU: 518). Genau das ist für Wittgenstein das Aufleuchten eines Aspektes: Das Kippen besteht darin, dass das Gesicht sich nicht geändert hat und wir es doch anders sehen.

Zum Ende des Kapitels XI hin werden Wittgensteins Beispiele auch grundsätzlich psychologischer, die untersuchten Sprachspiele beziehen sich auf Absichten, Motive oder auch auf den Ausdruck menschlicher Gefühle. Das Ding, das Aspekte aufweist, kann sehr gut auch ein einzelner Mensch sein. So spricht Wittgenstein etwa davon, dass das Beurteilen der Echtheit eines Gefühlsaus-

---

3 Vgl. etwa Cavell (2006: 565), Schulte (1990: 107–108) sowie Mulhall (2001: 259).

drucks zu einem eigenen Sprachspiel gehört, in dem so etwas wie ein „Bild" vom verborgenen Inneren einer Person mitklingt. Solche Bilder sind für Wittgenstein Teil unserer Lebensform, sie dürfen nur nicht über ihr Sprachspiel hinausgetragen und für eine allgemeine „Metaphysik" verwendet werden. Wittgenstein verwendet dabei dasselbe Muster wie bei seiner Kritik an einer naiven Bedeutungstheorie: Auch dort ist es das ganz spezielle Bild von Bedeutung als „Atmosphäre" des Wortes, aus dem (ohne Rücksicht auf die Verschiedenheit der Sprachspiele) eine allgemeine Bedeutungstheorie gemacht wird. Wittgenstein bietet somit selbst eine strukturelle Weiterführung seiner Überlegungen an, bei der Menschen und nicht nur Wörter oder Zeichnungen *gedeutet* werden.

## 6 Primärer und sekundärer Identitätsbegriff

Es sind vor allem zwei Punkte, die mir an den Überlegungen Wittgensteins in diesem Zusammenhang zentral erscheinen: Erstens die Unterscheidung von primärer und sekundärer Verwendung von Begriffen wie „Bedeutung", zweitens die Feststellung, dass das Objekt des Bedeutungserlebnisses nicht eine einzelne Bedeutung ist, sondern die Relation zwischen zwei Bedeutungen. Diese beiden Punkte möchte ich nun auf den Begriff der Identität anwenden. Um den ersten geht es in diesem Abschnitt, der zweite wird in den zwei darauffolgenden Abschnitten behandelt.

Zum ersten Punkt: Der Vorschlag ist also, zwischen einem primären und einem sekundären Begriff von Identität zu unterscheiden. Ist von „Identität" im *primären* Sinn die Rede, versteht man darunter die jeweiligen Merkmale bestimmter Gruppen bzw. die Möglichkeit, einzelne Individuen aufgrund ihrer Merkmale bestimmten Gruppen zuzuordnen. Das können auch ganz unterschiedliche Gruppen bei einem einzigen Individuum sein. Ist jedoch von „Identität" in einer *sekundären* Verwendung die Rede, so handelt es sich um ein Identitäts-Erlebnis, das sich auf den authentischen Kern oder das Wesen einer Person bezieht, egal ob das Erlebnis eines der ersten oder dritten Person ist (ob ich also meine Identität erlebe oder die einer anderen Person). Dieses Erlebnis kann Elemente wie Stolz, Würde oder Anerkennung aufweisen, aber auch Irritation oder Distanzierung. Der primäre Identitätsbegriff entspricht dem stetigen Aspekt-Wahrnehmen bzw. dem „blinden" Regelfolgen, der sekundäre dem Bemerken des Aspekt-Wechsels bzw. dem Bedeutungserlebnis.

Die Unterscheidung von primärer und sekundärer Bedeutung versteht Wittgenstein so, dass die sekundäre von der primären abhängig ist, auf sie verweisen muss, sich aber auch nicht auf sie zurückziehen kann. Darin besteht die Gefahr einer Vermischung der beiden Bedeutungen, z. B. der beiden Bedeutungen von

„Bedeutung". Besteht eine solche Vermischungsgefahr auch beim Begriff der Identität? Gibt es Anzeichen dafür, dass eine technische Form von Identität verwechselt wird mit einer emotionalen Form, die das Wesen einer Person zum Ausdruck bringt? Die Anzeichen dafür gibt es, und sogar sehr deutlich. In ganz verschiedenen Kontexten wird die Zugehörigkeit zu einer sozialen Gruppe zum Wesen einer Person hochstilisiert und das in der ersten wie in der dritten Person. Gerade das ist es, was angesichts ganz verschiedener Varianten von Identitätspolitik Befremdung auslöst, was aber vor allem zum Merkmal eines sogenannten Rechtspopulismus wurde.[4]

Wenn die beiden Identitätsbegriffe häufig vermischt werden – was spricht dann eigentlich für ihre Trennung? Wittgenstein selbst versucht bei seiner Unterscheidung von primärem und sekundärem Begriff aufzuzeigen, dass die beiden Begriffsverwendungen unterschiedlichen Sprachspielen angehören, vor allem im Zusammenhang mit dem Aspekt-Wahrnehmen. Der Satz „Ich sehe das als einen Hasen" ergibt im Sprachspiel des stetigen Aspekt-Wahrnehmens keinen Sinn. Denn wenn wir bereits wissen, dass die Zeichnung einen Hasen darstellt, müsste ein solcher Satz sofort mit der Frage „Wie meinst du das?" beantwortet werden. Anders im Sprachspiel des Aspekt-Erlebens: Hier hat der Satz durchaus seinen Platz genauso wie der Satz „Jetzt ist es eine Ente!" oder „So gesehen ist es ein Hase!" Der Begriff „sehen als" wird anders verwendet als der Begriff „sehen", denn er setzt die Möglichkeit verschiedener Sichtweisen voraus.

Werden mit den beiden Identitätsbegriffen auf analoge Weise zwei verschiedene Sprachspiele unterschieden, so müssen auch diese sich in unterschiedlichen Regeln äußern. Genau das lässt sich aber feststellen und zwar anhand von Sätzen wie „Im Grunde ist sie immer noch Albanerin", „Dass er in einer Favela von Rio aufgewachsen ist, hat ihn wohl nachhaltig geprägt" oder auch „Ich fühle mich jetzt mehr denn je als EU-Bürger, meine Identität ist letztlich eine europäische": Rund um den (sekundären) Erlebnis-Identitätsbegriff haben diese Sätze einen Sinn. Im Sprachspiel des (primären) Identitätsbegriffes hingegen wären solche Formulierungen nicht anschlussfähig, weil dort die Zuordnung zu Gruppen ohne Erlebnis geschieht. Hier ist klar, dass jedes „Ding" aufgrund bestimmter Merkmale bestimmten Gruppen zugeordnet werden kann, und das ganz ohne Ausdrücke wie „Im Grunde [...]" oder „Ich fühle mich jetzt [...]". Es geht auch nicht um den authentischen Kern einer Person, sondern um Merkmale wie die Blutgruppe, die Anzahl der Onkel und Tanten, die Eigenschaft, die Zunge rollen zu können – oder auch in einem bestimmten Supermarkt regelmäßig einzukaufen, im Schlaf

---

[4] Gegen eine solche dem Populismus zugrundeliegende Verwechslung von kulturellen Merkmalen und personaler Identität spricht sich z. B. Ursula Renz aus (vgl. Renz 2019: 95–100).

meist auf dem Rücken zu liegen etc. Sätze wie „Für mich bist du letztlich eine Person, die im Schlaf auf dem Rücken liegt" oder „Ich fühle mich heute mehr denn je wie jemand mit der Schuhgröße 44" sind nicht leicht einzuordnen. Die Frage „Wie meinst du das?" wäre eine naheliegende Reaktion.

Obwohl Sprachspielgrenzen nicht immer exakt zu ziehen sind, handelt es sich doch um grundsätzlich zwei verschiedene Arten, rund um den Begriff der Identität zu „spielen". Im primären Gebrauch ist Identität entweder die (sehr lange Liste) aller Merkmale, die eine Gruppenzugehörigkeit ermöglichen, oder die Liste der Merkmale, die Kontinuität aufweisen, deren Veränderung also bei dieser Person nicht vorstellbar sind. Im zweiten Fall ist es allerdings gar nicht so einfach, Beispiele zu finden. Am ehesten eignen sich noch Ereignisse und Gegebenheiten der Vergangenheit wie z. B. das Geburtsdatum oder die Farbe der Geburtstagstorte zur Feier des vierten Geburtstages. Aber man sieht an diesen Beispielen schon, dass solche unveränderlichen Merkmale einer Person meist gar nicht mit ihrem „Wesen" oder „authentischen Kern" zu tun haben. Sie prägen die Person in den allermeisten Fällen gar nicht.

Mit grundlegenden Prägungen hat es jedoch der sekundäre Identitätsbegriff zu tun. Hier geht es um so etwas wie das wahre Selbst der Person. Das ist der Identitätsbegriff, wie ihn Erik Erikson in den 1950er Jahren bekannt machte[5] oder wie ihn vor kurzem Francis Fukuyama verwendet hat (2019). Fukuyama führt den Begriff der Identität nicht nur auf den Gegensatz von „Innen" und „Außen" zurück, sondern auch auf die Würde des Menschen und auf seinen Anspruch auf Anerkennung. Insofern spielen für ihn bei Fragen der Identität immer Gefühle wie Stolz, Zorn oder Scham eine Rolle (vgl. Fukuyama 2019: 159).

Die dem sekundären Identitätsbegriff entsprechende Lebensform ist historisch gesehen wohl jene der „Moderne" seit dem Beginn der Industriellen Revolution. Während noch in der Aufklärung des 18. Jahrhunderts Würde und Größe der Person in ihrem universal gefassten Menschsein gründete, begeisterte sich die Romantik für die Einmaligkeit und Einzigartigkeit des Individuums. Das kann als Abwehr gegenüber den Anforderungen einer immer stärker organisierten Gesellschaft gewertet werden. Auch in den soziologischen und psychologischen Identitäts-Konzepten des 20. Jahrhunderts schwang häufig die Sorge mit, das menschliche Individuum könne von den sich vervielfältigenden Rollenerwartungen erdrückt werden.[6] Zunehmende Vielfalt von Lebenswelten stellte aber noch in einem anderen Sinn eine Herausforderung für Identitätsgefühle dar: Die sogenannte Pluralisierung förderte zwar die Freiheit des eigenen Identitätsent-

---

5 Zur Bedeutung Eriksons für den modernen Identitätsbegriff vgl. Abels (2017: 219–220).
6 Vgl. dazu z. B. die Ausführungen zu Habermas in Abels (2017: 345–349).

wurfes, machte diesen aber auch beliebiger und damit fragwürdiger. Der Wunsch nach festem Boden bzw. so etwas wie Heimat wurde zur verbreiteten Reaktion auf postmoderne Unübersichtlichkeit, beruht aber möglicherweise genau auf jenem Missverständnis, es hätte einmal eine Zeit geben, in der man die eigene Identität auf eindeutige Weise – ohne jede Ambiguität – erlebte.

# 7 Ambiguität und Identitätserfahrung in der ersten Person

Es spricht jedoch einiges dafür, dass Identitätsgefühle notwendig mit Mehrdeutigkeiten und Widersprüchen konfrontiert sind (womit wir beim oben genannten zweiten Punkt angelangt sind). Bei ethnischen Identitätsgefühlen ist es z. B. durchaus so, dass ein Aufenthalt im Ausland das Bewusstsein für die eigene „Herkunft" intensivieren kann. Wir erleben uns zwar in einer Hinsicht *gleich* wie die uns im Ausland umgebenden Menschen (schließlich teilen wir ihren Lebensraum), in einer anderen Hinsicht aber deutlich *anders*. Dass wir anders sind, erleben wir somit nur zusammen mit dem Erlebnis einer Gleichheit. Ganz ähnlich ist es beim Nationalitätsgefühl in globalisierten Zeiten: Wir sind zwar alle TeilnehmerInnen am globalen Markt, doch genau dieses Erlebnis von Gleichheit oder Uniformität kann in uns den Blickwinkel verstärken, als BewohnerInnen einer bestimmten „Ecke" des Globus etwas Besonderes zu sein. Und es ist kein Zufall, dass in Mitteleuropa lokale Trachten genau dann definiert wurden, als durch Industrialisierung und Ausbau des Nationalstaates im frühen 19. Jahrhundert Regionalität nicht mehr selbstverständlich war. „*Gleich, aber anders*" wäre die entsprechende Ambiguitätsformel. Doch auch in der Umkehrung gibt es diese Formel, als „*anders, aber gleich*". Diese zweite Variante findet sich etwa bei der Entstehung des Nationalbewusstseins, welches sich im Kontrast zu all den regionalen Unterschieden bildet: Wir kommen zwar aus ganz unterschiedlichen Realitäten wie Catania, Rom oder Bassano del Grappa, aber gemeinsam bilden wir das italienische Volk.

Identitätserlebnisse sind nicht einfach das Erleben *einer* Identität. Ihr Objekt ist das Kippen zweier (oder mehrerer) verschiedener Beschreibungsmöglichkeiten für dieselbe Person. Dass keine wirklich eindeutig zutrifft, macht gerade die „Selbigkeit" der Person aus. Das gilt auch für Identitätserlebnisse in der ersten Person – und auch für die Erfahrung von Diskriminierung. Erlebt sich eine Person als diskriminiert aufgrund einer ganz speziellen Zuschreibung von Merkmalen, so erfährt sie ihr Anderssein nur vor dem Hintergrund eines Anspruchs auf ein Gleichsein. Sie erlebt sich nicht nur als anders (in ihren faktischen Möglichkeiten), sondern eben auch als gleich (in ihren rechtlichen Ansprüchen). Dass solche Erfahrungen einander brauchen, zeigen soziologische Beobachtungen wie z. B. bei Aladin El-Mafaalani, der von einem Paradox der Integration spricht: Diskriminierungsklagen werden genau dann akuter, wenn die Integration voranschreitet und die Gleichstellungserwartungen der integrierten Gruppen steigen (vgl. El-Mafaalani 2019: 42–44). Dieses Paradox funktioniert nach El-Mafaalani sogar in die andere Richtung: MigrantInnen werden mit zunehmender Integration als fremd empfunden wie etwa beim Kopftuchstreit, welcher sich nicht an verschleierten Putzfrauen entzündete, sondern an der kopftuchtragenden Deutschlehrerin Fereshta Ludin. Mit ihrem Fremdsein hat sie erst in dem Moment irritiert, als sie „gleicher" wurde. Generell gilt wohl: Je stärker das Gleichsein, desto stärker auch das Kontrasterlebnis. Die verschiedenen Stadt-Derbys im Sport können eine lange Geschichte davon erzählen.[7]

Das Kippen verschiedener Zuschreibungen zeigt sich auch am Konzept des *strategischen Essentialismus*, welchen innerhalb der postkolonialen Theorie Gayatri Chakravorty Spivak bekannt machte:[8] Eine diskriminierte Gruppe kann sich nur zur Wehr setzen, wenn sie die zugeschriebene kollektive Identität als solche erst einmal übernimmt. Die Adressierung durch die diskriminierende Mehrheitsgesellschaft muss aufgegriffen werden, um die in ihr liegende Benachteiligung zu bekämpfen, denn die betroffenen Menschen müssen als Kollektiv aktiv werden. Es gibt hier so etwas wie ein Dilemma einer antiessentialistischen Identitätspolitik: Sie distanziert sich zwar von der essentialistischen Vorstellung eines dominanten Wir (und der darin inbegriffenen eigenen Ausgrenzung), fällt aber gerade in ihrem Widerstand leicht in einen neuen Essentialismus zurück, da nun von einer Homogenität der eigenen, diskriminierten Gruppe ausgegangen wird. Die „wesenhaften" gemeinsamen Merkmale stehen dermaßen im Vordergrund, dass die eigene Heterogenität im politischen Kampf ausgeblendet zu werden droht. Ein historisches Beispiel dafür ist der Umstand, dass Sansculotten der Französischen Revolution oder auch Arbeiterbewegungen des 19. Jahrhunderts in ihrem Kampf um Anerkennung häufig ebenjene Anerkennung den Frauen in ihren eigenen Reihen verweigerten. Sie nahmen die eigene diskriminierte Gruppe homogen-essentialistisch als grundsätzlich männlich wahr und verstanden die Diskriminierung von Frauen als „Nebenwiderspruch", wel-

---

**7** Gegenüber vollkommen anderen Objekten empfinden wir kein Anderssein. Dass eine Person ein Anders- oder Gleichsein gegenüber einem Wurzelzeichen oder der Zahl 45 *erlebt*, lässt sich eigentlich gar nicht vorstellen.
**8** Einen solchen strategisch vertretenen Essentialismus erläuterte Gayatri Chakravorty Spivak das erste Mal 1984 in einem Interview mit Elizabeth Grosz, vgl. Spivak (1990: 11).

cher sich nach erfolgter Revolution von alleine lösen sollte (vgl. Susemichel/ Kastner 2018: 99).

Der Postkolonialist Stuart Hall sprach 1991 von einer Identitätspolitik ersten und zweiten Grades, wobei es ihm um die Gruppenbildung der Schwarzen in Großbritannien ging (vgl. Hall 2012: 78): Dass sich Einwanderer ganz unterschiedlicher Herkunft als „Schwarze" zu verstehen begannen, hat für ihn eine defensive kollektive Identität geschaffen und so eine Zurückweisung von Rassismus ermöglicht. Eine solche Identitätspolitik ersten Grades dürfe aber nicht versäumen, in einem zweiten Schritt die kollektive Identität „schwarz" als bloße Positionierung (und nicht als Essenz) zu verstehen, da Identitäten bei Hall im Sinne des Poststrukturalismus notwendig „dezentriert, zerstreut und fragmentiert" sind (Hall 2012: 180).[9]

Das Kippen von Gleich- und Anderssein ist ein zentrales Thema in den Diskussionen rund um Identitätspolitik. Gerade wenn eine „identitäre" Politik vermieden werden soll, wenn also ein stabiles, gemeinsames Wesen aller Gruppenmitglieder nicht vorausgesetzt werden soll, kann das nur gelingen, wenn die *interne Relation*, also die notwendige Zusammengehörigkeit der Blickwinkel von Gleich- und Anderssein immer neu erlebbar gemacht wird. Fehlt dem Erlebnis jegliche Ambiguität, handelt es sich – wenn man die hier vorgeschlagenen Identitätsbegriffe akzeptiert – nicht um ein echtes Identitätserlebnis, sondern um bloße Rhetorik. Und leere Identitäts-Inszenierungen sind nicht fähig, so etwas wie solidarische Gefühle zu entfalten, nicht einmal innerhalb der eigenen Gruppe, denn Solidarität ist letztlich nur möglich, wenn sie aus der doppelten Erfahrung von Gemeinsamkeit und Differenz heraus geschieht (vgl. Susemichel/Kastner 2018: 137–138).

## 8 Ambiguität in der dritten Person

Auch die Identität anderer Personen kann Gegenstand unseres Erlebens sein. Doch auch hier erleben wir genau genommen nicht eine bestimmte Identität, sondern das Kippen bzw. die Ambiguität verschiedener Deutungen, die auf die andere Person angewendet werden können. Der Soziologe Lothar Krappmann sieht Identität im Anschluss an Erving Goffman als einen Balance-Akt des Individuums zwischen divergierenden normativen Erwartungen, mit denen es in seiner Interaktion notwendig konfrontiert ist. Denn nicht nur das Erfüllen von

---

[9] Silke van Dyk spricht in diesem Zusammenhang von einer „Dialektik von Affirmation und Überwindung von Differenz" (vgl. Van Dyk 2019: 29).

Rollenerwartungen, sondern auch die Artikulation eigener Bedürfnisse und damit das Nicht-Erfüllen von Rollenerwartungen werden letztlich vom Individuum erwartet. Geht es ohne Vorbehalte in einer von außen herangetragenen Rolle auf, verliert es jede Attraktivität, es wird „unkenntlich" (Krappmann 2016: 57). Obwohl es einerseits als zuverlässig bzw. rollenkonform erscheinen muss, soll es zugleich sichtbar machen, „dass es auch anders handeln kann, anders schon gehandelt hat und anders auch wieder handeln wird" (Krappmann 2016: 57).

Was vom Individuum hiermit gesellschaftlich erwartet wird, ist also immer schon widersprüchlich. Die einzelne Person kann ihre Identität nur plausibel machen, wenn sie diesen Widersprüchen in irgendeiner Form begegnet und sie nicht ignoriert. Da Identität als Balancieren zwischen den unterschiedlichen Erwartungen verstanden wird, kann sie für Krappmann deshalb nicht bloße psychische Instanz sein. Sie ist bereits in der Interaktion angelegt – eine Ausnahme können hier nur extrem repressive gesellschaftliche Bedingungen bilden, in denen jeder Spielraum und damit jede Chance auf Identität fehlt.

Vom Individuum wird dabei vor allem „Ambiguitäts-Toleranz" erwartet, denn ein Individuum, „das Ich-Identität behaupten will, muss auch widersprüchliche Rollenbeteiligungen und einander widerstrebende Motivationsstrukturen interpretierend nebeneinander dulden" (Krappmann 2016: 155). Ambiguität muss aber bei Krappmann nicht nur bei sich selbst ertragen werden, sondern auch bei anderen. Nur wenn sich andere in ihrer Identität zeigen dürfen, kann daraus eine Interaktion entstehen, die auch die eigene Identität zum Ausdruck bringt. Es geht also nicht nur um die Perspektive der ersten Person, sondern auch um die der dritten Person – Ambiguität ist grundlegende Voraussetzung für das Wahrnehmen anderer Personen als mit sich identisch bzw. als Personen mit Würde.

Es ist erstaunlich, wie ähnlich eine solche Berücksichtigung von Ambiguität in einem ganz anderen Zusammenhang beschrieben wird, und zwar in Bertolt Brechts Überlegungen zum Theater. Bekanntlich ging es Brecht darum, in seinem „epischen Theater" die Identifikation des Publikums mit einzelnen Figuren des Stücks zu vermeiden. Seine wichtigste Methode: Auch die SchauspielerInnen sollten sich nicht mit der von ihnen gespielten Figur identifizieren, sie sollten nicht in ihr aufgehen. Es ist für sie wichtig, die Figur nicht vorschnell begreifen zu wollen, sondern ihr gegenüber in einer Haltung des Staunens und Widersprechens zu verbleiben. Also gerade nicht sofort zu fragen: „Wie wäre ich, wenn mir dies und das passierte?" (Brecht 1985: 157), sondern Beobachtungen anzustellen, die auch über die Figur hinausgehen, und aus der Distanz heraus die Figur aufzubauen: „Die Einheit der Figur wird nämlich durch die Art gebildet, in der sich ihre einzelnen Eigenschaften widersprechen" (Brecht 1985: 157). Um solche Widersprüche gezielt aufzufinden, sollen die SchauspielerInnen die Methode des „Nicht-Sondern" (Brecht 1985: 109, 159) anwenden, d.h., sie sollen sich den wichtigen Handlungen ihrer Figuren auf eine Weise annähern, dass immer auch die Möglichkeit einer Handlungsalternative berücksichtigt wird: Die Figuren handeln nicht anders, sondern so – sie könnten auch anders handeln, tun es aber nicht. Nur wenn sie in ihrer „Uneinigkeit mit sich selbst" (Brecht 1985: 152) erfahrbar gemacht werden, sind sie für Brecht lebendige Figuren und können dem Publikum „auffallen" (Brecht 1985: 159).

Das sind zwar nicht exakt dieselben Begrifflichkeiten wie bei Wittgenstein oder Krappmann, die Parallelen sind aber kaum zu leugnen. Brecht verwendet weder den Begriff „Aspekt" noch den der „Identität", doch unterstützt er die Sichtweise, das Erleben der Lebendigkeit einer Person mit Ambiguität in Verbindung zu bringen. Obwohl sein Verfremdungs-Effekt den Zweck der Historisierung verfolgt, er also letztlich die Veränderbarkeit der dargestellten gesellschaftlichen Umstände aufzeigen möchte, ist er weit davon entfernt, nur Typen von Menschen auf die Bühne zu bringen, die jeweils eine bestimmte Gruppe von Menschen vertreten. Er möchte den „unverwechselbaren Menschen" zeigen, denjenigen, der „mit seinesgleichen nicht ganz gleich ist" (Brecht 1985: 149). So muss für ihn gerade das historisierende Abbild „etwas von den Skizzen an sich haben, die um die herausgearbeitete Figur herum noch die Spuren anderer Bewegungen und Züge aufweisen" (Brecht 1985: 149). Es gibt nicht wenige Figuren in Brechts Stücken, die auf diese Weise auffallen, und das können durchaus auch Nebenfiguren sein – wie etwa die Seeräuber-Jenny in der Dreigroschenoper.

Wenn bei Brecht Personen nur dann als unverwechselbare erfahren werden, wenn sie mit sich selbst uneins sind, schaut das nach einem handfesten Paradox aus: Identität ist einerseits Selbigkeit im Sinne von Übereinstimmung mit sich selbst, andererseits aber auch Widersprüchlichkeit. Eine solche Widersprüchlichkeit muss allerdings als Sich-Widersetzen gegenüber Kategorisierungsversuchen verstanden werden. Und hier löst sich das Paradox, denn wer ganz individuell nur mit sich selbst übereinstimmt, kann mit allgemeinen Kategorien oder Begriffen nun einmal nicht erfasst werden, insofern ist eine glatte Beschreibung einer Person immer auch ein Angriff auf ihre Identität. Zu sagen, dass begriffliche Einordnung Identität erst herstellt, setzt einen anderen Identitätsbegriff voraus, wie ihn z. B. Theodor W. Adorno in seiner Philosophie des Nichtidentischen verwendete (vgl. Adorno 1975: 17).

## 9 Fazit: Konsequenzen für Identitätspolitik

Die Analogie zu Wittgensteins Aspektwechsel ergab für den Begriff „Identität" erstens die Unterscheidung eines primären von einem sekundären Identitätsbegriff, zweitens die Beschränkung des sekundären Identitätsbegriffs auf Momente, in denen Ambiguität im Erlebnis von Identität (in der ersten oder dritten Person) auch tatsächlich eine Rolle spielt. Für eine solche begriffliche Unterscheidung erwies sich nicht nur der Vergleich mit Wittgensteins verschiedenen Formen des Aspekt-Wahrnehmens als nützlich, sondern auch die Beobachtung, dass die verschiedenen Identitätsbegriffe unterschiedlichen Sprachspielen angehören. Darüber hinaus ließ sich der Zusammenhang von sekundärer Identität und Ambiguität weiter konkretisieren und zwar durch die Einbeziehung soziologischer Theorien (des symbolischen Interaktionismus und des Postkolonialismus) sowie des Theaterkonzeptes von Bertolt Brecht.

Was kann nun die Unterscheidung der beiden Identitätsbegriffe für die verschiedensten Formen von *Identitätspolitik* bedeuten? Auch der Begriff „Identitätspolitik" wird unterschiedlich verwendet, es lässt sich aber als Gemeinsamkeit herausfiltern, dass eine Gruppe von Menschen zum Thema gemacht wird, für die mehr Anerkennung und Berücksichtigung von Bedürfnissen eingefordert wird. Das kann eine marginalisierte Minderheit sein, aber auch jene Mehrheit, welche einer Elite gegenübersteht. Betrachtet man Identitätspolitik vor dem Hintergrund der oben getroffenen Unterscheidung eines primären und eines sekundären Identitätsbegriffes, ergeben sich folgende Überlegungen:

Wenn „Identität" in einer primären Verwendung die zahlreichen, aber eindeutigen Zugehörigkeiten zu einer Gruppe aufgrund übereinstimmender Merkmale bedeutet, in einer sekundären Verwendung jedoch mit dem Erlebnis eines authentischen Kerns von Personen verknüpft ist, so wird schnell klar, dass die verschiedenen Formen von Identitätspolitik den sekundären Begriff verwenden. Identität wird als erlebbar verstanden, unabhängig davon, ob das entsprechende Erlebnis nun Stolz, Kränkung, Volkszorn oder sonst etwas ist. Deshalb muss der Versuchung widerstanden werden, die Besonderheiten des sekundären Identitätsbegriffes zu vernachlässigen und so Sprachspielgrenzen zu missachten. Es darf bei identitätspolitischen Forderungen nach mehr Anerkennung nicht von einer *eindeutigen* Gruppenzugehörigkeit der betroffenen Menschen ausgegangen werden, wie sie beim primären Identitätsbegriff durchaus möglich ist. Werden die beiden Begriffe von Identität verwechselt, führt das geradewegs in einen Essentialismus, für den das Wesen einer Person in gleichbleibender Gruppenzugehörigkeit besteht.

Was auch immer als Identitätspolitik bezeichnet wird, muss nach den hier entwickelten begrifflichen Unterscheidungen eine grundsätzliche Bereitschaft zur Ambiguität bzw. zur Mehrdeutigkeit aufweisen. Eine Identitätspolitik, die z. B. ausschließlich das *Anderssein* einer bestimmten Gruppe erlebbar macht, ist nicht nur moralisch ein Problem, sondern sie steht in Widerspruch zum eigenen Identitätserlebnis. Neben dem Anderssein muss auch der dazugehörige Alternativ-Aspekt des *Gleichseins* ernst genommen werden. Eine solche Ambiguität kann entweder die Form „anders, aber auch gleich" oder die Form „gleich, aber auch anders" haben. Und es genügt dabei nicht, den Alternativ-Aspekt nur prinzipiell vorauszusetzen („Natürlich sind das auch Menschen wie wir, das habe ich ja nicht bestritten, aber …"), sondern dieser muss selbst auch *erlebbar* gemacht werden.

Ob Identitätspolitik also tatsächlich begrifflich kohärent betrieben werden kann, hängt davon ab, ob sie auch Bereitschaft zur Ambiguität ist. Wird der sekundäre Identitätsbegriff ernst genommen, hat Identitätspolitik durchaus das Potenzial zum Universalismus und muss nicht notwendig in einen Partikularismus führen – wie ihr häufig vorgeworfen wird.

Die Frage „Hase oder Ente?" kann angesichts des Hasen-Enten-Kopfes nicht eindeutig beantwortet werden. Nehmen wir die Hase-oder-Ente-Frage als Modell für die Frage nach der Identität einzelner Personen, so lässt sich sagen: Diese Frage *darf* keine abschließende Antwort finden, denn nur so wird Identität von Personen erlebbar, nur so werden diese in ihrer Würde anerkannt.

## Literatur

Abels, Heinz (2017): *Identität*. Wiesbaden: Springer VS.
Adorno, Theodor W. (1975): *Negative Dialektik*. Frankfurt a. M.: Suhrkamp.
Brecht, Bertolt (1985): *Schriften zum Theater*. Frankfurt a. M.: Suhrkamp.
Cavell, Stanley (2006): *Der Anspruch der Vernunft: Wittgenstein, Skeptizismus, Moral und Tragödie*. Übers. von Christiana Goldmann. Frankfurt a. M.: Suhrkamp.
El-Mafaalani, Aladin (2019): „Alle an einem Tisch: Zwischen Teilhabe und Diskriminierung". In: *Aus Politik und Zeitgeschichte* 69(9–11), S. 41–45.
Fukuyama, Francis (2019): *Identität: Wie der Verlust der Würde unsere Demokratie gefährdet*. Hamburg: Hoffmann und Campe.
Goffman, Erving (2018): *Stigma: Über Techniken der Bewältigung beschädigter Identität*. Frankfurt a. M.: Suhrkamp.
Hall, Stuart (2012): *Rassismus und kulturelle Identität: Ausgewählte Schriften*. Hamburg: Argument Verlag.
Krappmann, Lothar (2016): *Soziologische Dimensionen der Identität: Strukturelle Bedingungen für die Teilnahme an Interaktionsprozessen*. Stuttgart: Klett-Cotta.
Mulhall, Stephen (2001): „Seeing Aspects". In: Glock, Hans-Johann (Hg.): *Wittgenstein: A Critical Reader*. Malden, MA: Blackwell, S. 246–267.
Renz, Ursula (2019): *Was denn bitte ist kulturelle Identität? Eine Orientierung in Zeiten des Populismus*. Basel: Schwabe.
Schulte, Joachim (1990): *Chor und Gesetz: Wittgenstein im Kontext*. Frankfurt a. M.: Suhrkamp.
Siller, Georg (2018): *Unsicheres Mitleid: Eine Begriffssuche im Ausgang von Wittgenstein*. Bielefeld: Transcript.
Spivak, Gayatri Chakravorty (1990): *The Post-Colonial Critic: Interviews, Strategies, Dialogues*. Hg. von Sarah Harasym. New York, NY: Routledge.

Susemichel, Lea/Kastner, Jens (2018): *Identitätspolitiken: Konzepte & Kritiken in Geschichte & Gegenwart der Linken*. Münster: Unrast.

Van Dyk, Silke (2019): „Identitätspolitik gegen ihre Kritik gelesen: Für einen rebellischen Universalismus". In: *Aus Politik und Zeitgeschichte* 69(9–11), S. 25–32.

Wittgenstein, Ludwig (1984a) [BPP]: „Bemerkungen über die Philosophie der Psychologie". In: *Werkausgabe* Band 7. Frankfurt a. M.: Suhrkamp, S. 5–346.

Wittgenstein, Ludwig (1984b) [PU]: „Philosophische Untersuchungen". In: *Werkausgabe* Band 1. Frankfurt a. M.: Suhrkamp, S. 225–580.

Wittgenstein, Ludwig (1984c) [TLP]: „Tractatus logico-philosophicus". In: *Werkausgabe* Band 1. Frankfurt a. M.: Suhrkamp, S. 7–85.

Ilse Somavilla
# Der Verlust an Wahrhaftigkeit

Wittgensteins Kritik an Kultur und Wissenschaft der modernen Zivilisation

**Abstract:** [The Loss of Veracity: Wittgenstein's Critique of the Culture and Science of Modern Civilisation] That Ludwig Wittgenstein was critical of the "vast stream of European and American civilization" is well known from his preface to the *Philosophical Remarks* and from other published notes, especially from *Culture and Value*. This paper will examine how much more these remarks imply, especially regarding Wittgenstein's ambivalent attitude towards the sciences and culture of his time. He sensed the loss of veracity in the ever-growing progress of civilisation, whose spirit was *"fremd & unsympathisch"* ("alien & uncongenial") to him. Its goals were oriented towards individual purposes and success while, for Wittgenstein, the pursuit of clarity and truth as ends in themselves was the top priority. His 'movement of thought' was different from that of the 'typical Western scientist,' from whom he resolutely distanced himself. Additionally, he was critical of the lack of a cultural understanding of his time due to the progressive disintegration of a common spirit. This was connected to his concept of the artist – a concept whose prerequisites were authenticity and veracity, and which had to be viewed *sub specie aeternitatis*. In other words, the concept should be linked to an ethical way of life.

**Keywords:** Veracity, Ludwig Wittgenstein, *sub specie aeternitatis*, cultural decay, astonishment

Dass Ludwig Wittgenstein dem „Geist des großen Stromes der europäischen und amerikanischen Zivilisation" kritisch gegenüberstand, ist aus seinem Vorwort zu den *Philosophischen Bemerkungen* und weiteren Aufzeichnungen, vor allem in den *Vermischten Bemerkungen*, hinlänglich bekannt. Wie viel mehr diese Äußerungen implizieren, soll in diesem Beitrag erörtert werden.

Die kritische Haltung gegenüber den Wissenschaften kündigt sich bereits im *Tractatus* an. War dieses Werk zwar im Geiste einer wissenschaftlichen Abhandlung geschrieben, so weist Wittgenstein doch schon im Vorwort und auf den letzten Seiten auf die Grenzen des Sagbaren und damit wissenschaftlich Erklärbaren hin.[1] Und obwohl er einerseits die Metaphysik aus der Philosophie ausklammern wollte, die „richtige Methode der Philosophie" darin sah, „[n]ichts zu sagen, als was sich sagen läßt, also Sätze der Naturwissenschaft – also etwas, was mit Philosophie nichts zu tun hat" (TLP 6.53), so schrieb er andererseits, dass die Philosophie keine der Naturwissenschaften sei, sondern „über oder unter", nicht aber neben diesen stünde (vgl. TLP 4.111).

Als sich Wittgenstein um die Publikation der *Logisch-philosophischen Abhandlung* vermutlich Ende November 1919 unter anderem auch an Ludwig von Ficker wandte, beschrieb er sein Werk als „streng philosophisch und zugleich literarisch" und dessen Sinn als einen ethischen, in dem nicht „geschwefelt" werde. Weiter schrieb er, dass sein Werk aus zwei Teilen bestehe – dem, der geschrieben, und dem, der nicht geschrieben sei, wobei dieser zweite Teil der eigentlich wichtige sei (vgl. CLF: 32–35).

Trotzdem fokussierte sich die Rezeption jahrzehntelang auf den „geschriebenen" bzw. sprachanalytischen Teil, während dem sogenannten „ungeschriebenen" Teil nicht näher nachgegangen wurde. Dies hat sich mittlerweile, unter anderem durch das Auftauchen persönlicher Schriften und Briefe, geändert – Dokumente, aus denen der Mensch, aber auch der Philosoph Wittgenstein spricht und worin seine Haltung gegenüber dem wissenschaftlich Nichterklärbaren – dem Bereich außerhalb der Welt der Tatsachen und daher der sprachlich nicht fassbaren Fragen – zum Ausdruck kommt.

Paul Engelmann hat zwar schon 1948 auf die ethische Grundhaltung Wittgensteins im *Tractatus* hingewiesen, doch wurde diesem Aspekt in Wittgensteins Philosophie erst nach Jahren die gebührende Beachtung geschenkt. Dies ist umso erstaunlicher, da Wittgenstein bereits im Frühwerk deutlich machte, dass es ihm vor allem um Klarheit bzw. das Klarwerden von Sätzen ging, die nur dann zu erreichen sei, wenn man dem „Ausdruck der Gedanken" eine Grenze ziehe (vgl. TLP Vorwort), eine Grenze, die in der Sprache gezogen wird und welche die Philosophie, gerade im Hinblick auf den wissenschaftlichen Aspekt, einzuhalten habe. Und dieser Einhaltung der Grenze liegt eine ethische Komponente inne, die sich in Wittgensteins Schreiben von Anbeginn an bis zum Spätwerk beobachten lässt.

---

**1** Vgl. TLP 6.52: „Wir fühlen, daß, selbst wenn alle *möglichen* wissenschaftlichen Fragen beantwortet sind, unsere Lebensprobleme noch gar nicht berührt sind. Freilich bleibt dann eben keine Frage mehr; und eben dies ist die Antwort."

# 1 Wittgensteins ethischer Anspruch: Wahrhaftigkeit, Selbsterkenntnis und Streben nach Vervollkommnung

Der ethische Impuls von Wittgensteins Philosophieverständnis beschränkt sich jedoch nicht nur auf die Distanzierung von Aussagen über Ethisches und Religiöses, sondern impliziert darüber hinaus eine Haltung, die sich im Streben nach Wahrhaftigkeit und Vervollkommnung äußert – in unermüdlicher Arbeit an der eigenen Sicht- und Denkweise gegenüber philosophischen Problemen, dabei als Arbeit an sich selbst. „Wie kann ich Logiker sein, wenn ich noch nicht Mensch bin", so schrieb er bereits um Weihnachten 1913 an Bertrand Russell und erläuterte sein Bemühen nach Besserung im Sinne von William James, um mit sich selbst „in's Reine" zu kommen (vgl. CC: 65–66).

Dieses Bemühen erstreckte sich über Jahrzehnte seines Lebens und fand in fortlaufenden Überarbeitungen, Streichungen und Änderungen seiner Schriften seinen Niederschlag – begleitet von Selbstzweifeln und Leiden. Sich selbst zu hinterfragen bis zu schmerzhafter Einsicht seiner „dunklen Seiten", sah Wittgenstein als unabdingbare Voraussetzung für Demut und damit Wahrhaftigkeit. Dementsprechend übte er schonungslose Kritik an sich – wie auch an anderen kreativ Tätigen –, wenn er nur einen Anflug von Eitelkeit und damit das Gegenteil von Wahrhaftigkeit witterte.

Die Ehrlichkeit mit sich selbst erfordere Mut – ein wesentlicher Aspekt für Originalität und Voraussetzung für Genialität. Mut, sich mit philosophischen Problemen auf stets neue Weise auseinanderzusetzen, in die Tiefe zu gehen, anstatt an der Oberfläche zu verharren. „Go the bloody hard way", sagte er zu Rush Rhees (1969: 169; zit. nach Citron 2019: 1) und Norman Malcolm schrieb er am 16. November 1944: „But anyway, if we live to see each other again let's not shirk digging. You can't think decently if you don't want to hurt yourself. I know all about it because I am a shirker." (Malcolm 1984: 93–94) Ludwig Hänsel riet er, in allem, was dieser tue, sein Äußerstes zu geben und nie etwas zu lehren, worüber er sich selbst nicht im Klaren sei, sondern seine Zweifel als Zweifel vorzutragen. Nur durch „innere Wahrheit" könne man anderen zu größerer Wahrheit verhelfen (vgl. CLH: 143–144).[2] Am 19. Februar 1938 schrieb Wittgenstein in Code:

---

[2] Als lobendes Beispiel für intellektuelle Ehrlichkeit nannte Wittgenstein G. E. Moore: Dieser habe vor seinen Studenten an den Problemen „genagt", anstatt diese als etwas bereits „Verdautes" darzustellen (vgl. CLH: 143–144). Wittgenstein selbst bezichtigte sich damit, in seinen Vorlesungen öfters geschwindelt zu haben, indem er vortäuschte, sich über ein Problem im Klaren

> Sich über sich selbst belügen, sich über die eigene Unechtheit belügen, muß einen schlimmen Einfluß auf den Stil haben; denn die Folge wird sein, daß man in ihm nicht Echtes von Falschem unterscheiden kann. So mag die Unechtheit des Stils Mahlers zu erklären sein & in der gleichen Gefahr bin ich. Wenn man vor sich selbst schauspielert, so muß der Stil davon der Ausdruck sein. Er kann nicht der Eigene sein. Wer sich selbst nicht kennen will, der schreibt eine Art Betrug. Wer in sich selbst nicht hinuntersteigen will, weil es zu schmerzhaft ist, bleibt natürlich auch mit dem Schreiben an der Oberfläche. (BEE: MS 120: 72v)

Im Bemühen um kompromisslose Ehrlichkeit, deren Voraussetzung kritische Auseinandersetzung mit den eigenen Unzulänglichkeiten bis zur Sündhaftigkeit ist, begibt sich Wittgenstein in die Nähe des Wahnsinns. Dieser, so schreibt er, sei „der strengste Richter" darüber, ob sein „Leben recht oder unrecht" sei (vgl. DB: 185; 20.02.1937), weshalb er ihn nicht fliehen wolle. Beim Hinabsteigen in die eigenen Tiefen zeige sich, wie viel man wert sei, und dies zu erkennen, führe im Falle eines eitlen Menschen zum Wahnsinn, da er die Wahrheit nicht ertragen kann.[3] Diese zu akzeptieren, führe hingegen zur Überwindung persönlicher Eitelkeit, damit zu Bescheidenheit und zu geistiger Gesundheit.[4]

Wittgensteins Vorstellung von Geistigkeit und Mut zur Überschreitung von Grenzen kommt auch in einem von ihm vermutlich 1925 verfassten Brief-Fragment zum Ausdruck, in dem er das Dasein der Menschen innerhalb einer bestimmten Kultur mit dem Befinden in einer roten Glasglocke vergleicht – ein Gleichnis, das Parallelen zu Platons Höhlengleichnis wachruft. Die sich nur mit Wissenschaft und Kunst zufriedengebenden Menschen sieht Wittgenstein als in einem begrenzten Raum Lebende, in den anstatt des eigentlichen Lichts des Geistes nur gefärbte Lichter dringen, die aber für das Kulturideal gehalten werden, solange die Menschheit noch nicht an die Grenze dieser Kultur gekommen sei (vgl. LUS: 44–45).[5] Zum reinen weißen Licht zu gelangen, hieße mit dem Kopf die Glas-

---

zu sein, während er noch hoffte, darüber Klarheit zu erreichen (vgl. DB: 145). Und er beklagte einen Mangel an „Ernst & Wahrheitsliebe" in seiner Arbeit als auch das Fehlen von „Frömmigkeit & Ergebenheit" in seinem Schreiben (vgl. DB: 162).

3 Vgl. Wittgensteins Hinweis auf Lenaus Faust, der aus intellektuellem Stolz die Wahrheit seiner persönlichen Schwächen nicht ertragen kann und daher wahnsinnig wird.

4 Sich selbst zu kennen als Voraussetzung für Wahrhaftigkeit in kreativer Tätigkeit ist damit die Grundlage für eigentliche Geistigkeit – für Weisheit. Diese fehle Spinoza, da er sich selbst nicht erkannt habe – was Wittgenstein auch von sich selbst sagte (vgl. DB: 95). Das Wort „Weisheit" schien ihm in Zusammenhang mit einem Zitat von Spinoza nur als ein „hohles Ding", hinter dem sich der eigentliche Mensch, wie er wirklich sei, vor sich selbst verstecke (vgl. DB: 96–97).

5 In Wittgensteins Brief-Fragment sind Anklänge an Spenglers kulturkritische Sicht im *Untergang des Abendlandes* nicht zu übersehen, wenn auch mit mehreren Unterschieden. Darüber hinaus gibt es zahlreiche Bemerkungen Wittgensteins zu Spengler, die ähnliche Gedanken demonstrie-

scheibe zu durchbrechen, wozu nur wenige den Mut hätten. Die meisten Menschen resignieren und bleiben in ihrem von Wissenschaft und Kunst begrenzten Raum gefangen; manche wagen den Versuch, geben jedoch auf, sobald sie sich den Kopf am Glas anstoßen. Diejenigen aber, die alles riskieren, um durch Überschreitung der Grenze zum wahren Licht zu gelangen, sind für Wittgenstein jene, die sich mit eigentlicher Geistigkeit befassen, was die Auseinandersetzung mit letzten Fragen – mit Religiosität – impliziert. Nur diese Menschen seien fähig, geniale Werke zu schaffen im Gegensatz zu bloßen Talenten. Und diese Werke berühren, sind zeitlos: „Die Auseinandersetzung mit dem Geist, mit dem Licht, ergreift." (LUS: 45)

Die Parallele zu Wittgensteins persönlicher Auseinandersetzung mit Religion als ein „Ergriffensein" liegt nahe.[6] Ein „Ergriffensein", das zu einer Umkehr im Denken und Philosophieren führt, damit zur Bereitschaft für fortlaufende Veränderung auf dem Weg zur Vervollkommnung. Eine leidenschaftliche Auseinandersetzung mit kreativer Tätigkeit, ein Aufgehen im Augenblick – in der Gegenwart, nicht in der Zeit, worunter Wittgenstein das Merkmal des glücklichen Menschen verstand (vgl. TB: 8.7.16).

Der Mut, den er vom wahrhaft Schaffenden und Genialen fordert, ist analog dem Mut zur Änderung bis zur Selbstaufgabe, bis zum Tode. Furcht vor dem Tode hingegen sei „das beste Zeichen eines falschen, d.h. schlechten Lebens" (TB: 8.7.16), wie es bereits in den Tagebüchern des Ersten Weltkriegs heißt.

Wahrer Mut erfordert Authentizität im Sinne einer Existenz, die dem Tod ins Auge blickt (vgl. Heidegger; zit. nach Arnswald 2006: 134), sowie Religiosität im genuinen Sinn, das heißt fern von jeglicher Orientierung an dogmatischer Or-

---

ren: So vergleichen beide die Kulturentwicklung mit dem Leben eines Organismus und hegen eine dunkle Ahnung für Zukünftiges (vgl. Kienzler 2013: 317–336). Wittgenstein nannte Spengler auch als einen der Denker, die ihn beeinflusst hätten, übte aber Kritik an ihm: Es sei schade, dass Spengler nicht bei seinen guten Gedanken geblieben, sondern weiter gegangen sei, als er verantworten konnte. Offenbar fehlte ihm dazu eine „größere Reinlichkeit" (vgl. DB: 19). Dies zeigt sich besonders im Hinblick auf das hier erörterte Brief-Fragment, wo Wittgenstein von der Reinheit des geistigen Lichts spricht, dem nur der religiöse Mensch sich nähern könne und wozu Spengler offenbar nicht im Stande war.

**6** Vgl. VB: 106: „Das Christentum sagt unter anderm, glaube ich, daß alle guten Lehren nichts nützen. Man müsse das *Leben* ändern. (Oder die *Richtung* des Lebens.) Daß alle Weisheit kalt ist; & daß man mit ihr das Leben so wenig in Ordnung bringen kann, wie man Eisen *kalt* schmieden kann. Eine gute Lehre nämlich muß einen nicht *ergreifen*; man kann ihr folgen, wie einer Vorschrift des Arzts. – Aber hier muß man von etwas ergriffen & umgedreht werden. – (D.h., so verstehe ich's.) Ist man umgedreht, dann muß man umgedreht *bleiben*. Weisheit ist leidenschaftslos. Dagegen nennt Kierkegaard den Glauben eine *Leidenschaft*." (BEE: MS 132: 167–168; 11.10.1946) thodoxie, sondern eine Religiosität im Sinne von Geistigkeit, gepaart mit der Erfahrung von Leid, dem Bewusstsein und der Akzeptanz der Gegebenheiten. Dass das Schwere überwiegt, geht bereits aus Wittgensteins frühen Tagebüchern hervor, wo er die „Annehmlichkeiten der Welt" nur als „so viele Gnaden des Schicksals" betrachtet (TB: 13.8.16).[7]

Einer der wenigen, der Wittgensteins Anforderung genialen Schaffens entsprach, war Georg Trakl. Dessen Gedichte berührten ihn durch deren „Ton", den er als „Ton der wahrhaft genialen Menschen" empfand.[8]

## 2 Die Betrachtung *sub specie aeternitatis*

„Ton" im Sinne Wittgensteins entspricht dem Stil eines Schreibenden, der dessen Tiefe oder Oberflächlichkeit offenbare – dessen Moralität, um mit Karl Kraus zu sprechen. Ein als tief zu bezeichnender Stil bedeutet Wahrhaftigkeit des Verfassers und impliziert dessen Orientierung am Gesichtspunkt *sub specie aeternitatis*[9] – der nach Spinoza höchsten Stufe menschlicher Erkenntnis.

Wittgensteins Gleichnis von der roten Glasglocke evoziert nicht nur, wie erwähnt, auffallende Parallelen zu Platons Höhlengleichnis, sondern auch zu Spinozas Unterscheidung zwischen den drei Erkenntnisarten des Menschen: die des bloßen Vorstellens und Meinens (die Wittgensteins Beschreibung vom gleichgültigen, nicht weiter reflektierenden Menschen entspräche), der Erkenntnis der Vernunft (also der wissenschaftlichen Betrachtung) und schließlich der höchsten Erkenntnisweise – der Betrachtung *sub specie aeternitatis* als ethische und religiöse, doch nicht rationale, sondern intuitive Erkenntnis. Nur sie führe zur Erkenntnis des „reinen geistigen Lichts" (Wittgenstein) bzw. zur Erkenntnis Gottes (Spinoza), wobei dies die Akzeptanz alles Gegebenen in der Welt zur Folge hat – also der streng determinierten, von Gott als *natura naturans* geschaffenen Gesetze in der Natur – der *natura naturata* – bzw. der nach logischen Gesetzen bestehenden Weltordnung.

---

[7] Vgl. auch DB: 188, wo Wittgenstein schreibt, dass „dies Leben mit allerlei Lust & Schmerz" doch nichts sei, es müsse etwas viel Absoluteres sein. Und das einzig Absolute sei, „wie ein kämpfender, ein stürmender Soldat das Leben durchzufechten auf den Tod los". Alles andere sei „Zaudern, Feigheit, Bequemlichkeit also Erbärmlichkeit".
[8] Vgl. Wittgensteins Brief (Poststempel 28.11.14) an Ludwig von Ficker (CLF: 22).
[9] Der von Spinoza geprägte Ausdruck war einer der wenigen philosophischen Termini, den Wittgenstein laut Aussagen von Engelmann, gerne und häufig, auch in mündlichen Konversationen, verwendete (vgl. Somavilla/McGuinness 2006: 152).

Ohne diese ethisch-religiös bestimmte Erkenntnis bleibt nach Wittgenstein der in Kultur und Wissenschaft befangene Mensch gleich einer Fliege im Fliegenglas, die vergeblich gegen die Wände des Fliegenglases anstößt – ein Mensch, auf den eine in späteren Jahren von ihm erfolgte Bemerkung über den Solipsisten passt, der in der Fliegenglocke „flattert & flattert", sich an den Wänden stößt und weiter flattert. „Wie ist er zur Ruhe zu bringen?", fragt Wittgenstein am Ende dieser Bemerkung (BEE: MS 149: 34r–34v).

Im Hinblick auf Wittgensteins solipsistische Position der frühen Tagebücher und auf den damaligen Subjektbegriff führt das Bewusstsein der *Einzigkeit seines Lebens* jedoch zu Religion, Wissenschaft und Kunst (vgl. TB: 1.8.16).

Bereits in den *Tagebüchern 1914–1916* thematisiert er den Zusammenhang zwischen Ethik und Kunst unter dem Gesichtspunkt „sub specie aeternitatis" und nimmt diesen Gedanken in den *Tractatus* auf (TB: 7.10.16; TLP 6.45). Anfang der 1930er Jahre stellt er die Arbeit des Philosophen und die des Künstlers auf dieselbe Ebene, insofern als ihnen die Betrachtung der Welt „sub specie aeterni" gemeinsam sei.[10] Und im selben Jahr notiert er: „Stil ist der Ausdruck einer allgemein menschlichen Notwendigkeit. Das gilt vom Schreibstil wie vom Baustil (und jedem anderen). Stil ist die allgemeine Notwendigkeit sub specie eterni gesehen." (DB: 28) Wiederum also heißt es, sich in kreativer Tätigkeit des Ethischen mit Blick auf das Ewige bewusst zu werden. Bei Nicht-Erfüllung dieses ethischen Anspruchs wird der „Stil" bzw. „Ton" nicht glaubwürdig, nicht wahrhaft genial.

## 3 Sagen versus Zeigen und die Bedeutung des Schweigens

Die von Wittgenstein geforderte und in seinem Schreiben angestrebte Wahrhaftigkeit betrifft nicht nur den Stil bzw. die Form, sondern gleichermaßen den Inhalt: das heißt, das Einhalten der Grenze zwischen dem, was sich sagen lässt, und dem, was sich nur *zeigt*, bzw. die Distanzierung von Spekulationen – einem „Schwefeln" – über Bereiche, die sich wissenschaftlicher Erklärung entziehen; denn: „In der Philosophie liegt die Schwierigkeit darin, nicht mehr zu sagen, als was wir wissen." (BBB: 75) Daraus folgt der Verzicht auf die Erörterung ethischer

---

**10** Vgl. BEE: MS 109: 29–30; 22.08.1930, vgl. auch VB: 27: „Nun scheint mir aber, gibt es außer der Arbeit des Künstlers noch eine andere, die Welt sub specie äterni einzufangen. Es ist – glaube ich – der Weg des Gedankens der gleichsam über die Welt hinfliegt & sie so läßt wie sie ist, – sie von oben im Fluge betrachtend."

und religiöser Fragen in Philosophie und Wissenschaft, folglich die Ablehnung jedweder Theorien über Ethik.[11]

Für den Stil gilt eine ähnliche Zurückhaltung, das heißt Ökonomisierung von Sprache, Reduzierung auf das Wesentliche. Es kommt darauf an, die subtile Grenze zwischen Reden und Schweigen einzuhalten, um nicht in Geschwätz zu verfallen – eine Gefahr, die sich auf das Verhalten, die Handlung, auswirken kann. In einer kritischen Analyse der Gesellschaft seiner Zeit ging Kierkegaard bereits 1846 auf diese Problematik ein und brachte sie folgendermaßen zum Ausdruck:

> Was ist das, S c h w ä t z e n ? Es ist die Aufhebung der leidenschaftlichen Disjunktion zwischen Schweigen und Reden. Nur der, der wesentlich schweigen kann, kann wesentlich reden, nur der, der wesentlich schweigen kann, kann wesentlich handeln. Verschwiegenheit ist Innerlichkeit. (Kierkegaard 1914: 870)

An die 100 Jahre später sah Wittgenstein in ähnlicher Weise den Verlust an Innerlichkeit und Wahrhaftigkeit als Folge von Geschwätzigkeit bzw. der Unfähigkeit zum Schweigen. Sowohl in den Wissenschaften als auch im gesamten Kulturbereich der modernen Zivilisation konstatierte er die rücksichtslose Verfolgung egoistischer Ziele und Zwecke einer lärmenden Zeit. Anstatt nach ständig wachsendem technischem Fortschritt zu streben, ging es ihm um Zweckfreiheit, Klarheit und Durchsichtigkeit. Er hatte nicht die Absicht, ein Gebäude aufzubauen, sondern die „Grundlagen der möglichen Gebäude durchsichtig" vor sich zu haben (VB: 31). Sein Geist sei ein anderer als der des „typischen westlichen Wissenschaftlers", sein Ziel ein anderes als das der Wissenschaftler seiner Zeit und seine „Denkbewegung von der ihrigen verschieden" (VB: 31). Maurice O'Connor Drury gegenüber bemerke er: „Meine Denkweise ist in der heutigen Zeit nicht gefragt, ich muß zu sehr gegen den Strom schwimmen." (Drury 1992: 120 – 121)

## 4 Wittgensteins Kritik an Kunst und Philosophie seiner Zeit

Nicht nur an den Wissenschaften und Wissenschaftlern übte Wittgenstein Kritik, sondern ebenso an der Architektur, Kunst und Musik seiner Zeit, die er in einer Krise aufgrund des Verlusts an einem eigentlichen Kulturverständnis sah. Der Geist der großen europäischen und amerikanischen Zivilisation, dessen „Aus-

---

11 Vgl. Wittgensteins Gespräche mit dem Wiener Kreis über Ethik und Werte (WWK: 116–117).

druck die Industrie, Architektur, Musik der Faschismus & Socialismus der Jetztzeit ist", war ihm ein „fremder & unsympathischer Geist" (VB: 29). Er schreibe daher nur für Freunde, die in „Winkeln der Welt verstreut" seien (vgl. VB: 30).

Der Grund für eine Zeit ohne Kultur liege im fortschreitenden Zerfall eines gemeinsamen Geistes. Unter Kultur verstand Wittgenstein nämlich „eine große Organisation die jedem der zu ihr gehört seinen Platz anweis[e] an dem er im Geist des Ganzen arbeiten kann und seine Kraft [könne] mit gewissem Recht an seinem Erfolg im Sinne des Ganzen gemessen werden" (BEE: MS 109: 205; 06.–07.11.1930; zit. nach VB: 30).

Ebenso sei der Nimbus der Philosophie verloren gegangen; stattdessen ginge es nun um „*skill*", um „Können" von Talenten, denen der Charakter fehle, um tief und genial zu sein:

> The nimbus of philosophy has been lost. For we now have a method of doing philosophy, and can speak of *skilful* philosophers. Compare the difference between alchemy and chemistry; chemistry has a method and we can speak of skilful chemists. But once a method has been found the opportunities for the expression of personality are correspondingly restricted. The tendency of our age is to restrict such opportunities; this is characteristic of an age of declining culture or without culture. A great man need be no less great in such periods, but philosophy is now being reduced to a matter of skill and the philosopher's nimbus is disappearing. (LWL: 21)

Im Angriff auf „*skilful methods*" nimmt Wittgenstein im Grunde ein Thema auf, das bis in die Zeit der Aufklärung und des Rationalismus verfolgt werden kann, in der sich ein Wandel im Wahrnehmungs-Bewusstsein des Menschen bemerkbar machte. Mit Hilfe wachsender technischer Kenntnisse und Fähigkeiten, der selbst geschaffenen und produzierten Mittel, der Möglichkeit der Messbarkeit kam es zu einem Eingreifen des Menschen in das Weltgeschehen, zu dem Versuch, Lebensprozesse zu steuern und zu regulieren. Zu Beginn der Neuzeit veränderte sich die Hierarchie der menschlichen Aktivitäten noch einmal: Die Fähigkeit zur „theoretischen Schau", die den Menschen der Antike auszeichnete, wurde durch die Tendenz, sich Natur und Welt zu unterwerfen, sie durch das „herstellende *Machen*" (*poiesis*) zu bezwingen und (neu) zu gestalten, verdrängt (vgl. Brinek 1991: 150). Auch in der Philosophie wurde Denken als „Arbeit" betrachtet, um neue Erkenntnisse zu gewinnen, während die interesselose, staunende Haltung des Philosophen als ein Untätig-Sein negativ bewertet wurde, sein Philosophieren als spekulativ abgetan. Descartes war maßgebend verantwortlich für diese Wende in der Philosophie und den eigentlichen Beginn des Rationalismus. In seiner Abhandlung *Von der Methode des richtigen Vernunftgebrauchs und der wissenschaftlichen Forschung* ging es ihm darum, „zu Kenntnissen zu kommen, die von großem Nutzen für das Leben sind, und statt jener spekulativen Philosophie, die in den Schulen gelehrt wird, eine praktische zu finden [...] so daß wir sie auf eben dieselbe Weise (wie die verschiedenen Techniken unserer Handwerker) zu allen Zwecken, für die sie geeignet sind, verwenden und uns so zu Herren und Eigentümern der Natur machen können" (Descartes 1997: 169–170).

Wie Winfried Böhm in seinem Buch *Theorie und Praxis* darlegt, sind die neuzeitlichen Begriffe „Theorie" und „Praxis" damit weit vom ursprünglichen Verständnis derselben entfernt. Theorie ist nun nicht mehr die interesselose Schau der Wahrheit, die mit dem Staunen beginnt, sondern bezeichnet ein instrumentelles Wissen, ein „Know-how" (vgl. Böhm 1985; zit. nach Brinek 1991: 152). Wie sich bei Wittgenstein in späteren Jahren zeigt, würde das Tätig-Sein im ursprünglichen, positiven Sinn dem Staunen nicht entgegenstehen, sondern äußert sich als aktives, dynamisches Element staunender Betrachtung in der Entdeckung stets neuer, vorher noch nicht wahrgenommener Aspekte, die die theoretische, doch zweckfreie Betrachtung bereichern und auf ein wesentliches Anliegen seines Philosophieverständnisses hinweisen: nämlich durch Einsicht unterschiedlicher Aspekte sich von festgefahrenen Ansichten zu lösen. Die Bereitschaft, ein philosophisches Problem aus verschiedenen Perspektiven zu beleuchten, um dadurch eine neue, veränderte Sichtweise zu erreichen, anstatt starr an immer gleichbleibenden Positionen festzuhalten, liegt auf derselben Ebene wie sich Fehler einzugestehen – eine Haltung, die Mut und Demut erfordert.[12]

Wittgenstein selbst bekannte ja bereits im Vorwort zu den *Philosophischen Untersuchungen*, dass er im *Tractatus* schwere Irrtümer begangen habe, und es war charakteristisch für ihn, seine Sichtweise ständig zu erneuern und gerade Entworfenes wieder zu verwerfen.[13] Denn in seiner Arbeit wollte er „gehen", nicht bloß sitzen (vgl. DB: 207–208), wie er auch im Leben unaufhörlich nach Änderung im Sinne von moralischer Besserung strebte.

Und er, der sich selbst als „Terminus ad quem der großen abendländischen Philosophie – gleichsam wie der Name dessen, der die Alexandrinische Bibliothek verbrannt hat" (DB: 64) sah, stellt nun die Frage, was die Aufgabe der Philosophie sei. Die Welt zu beschreiben? Es sei die Aufgabe, unsere Begriffe zu säubern („*to tidy up our notions*"), um zu klären, was über die Welt gesagt werden kann (vgl. LWL: 21). Und wie bereits im *Tractatus* betont er, dass philosophische Tätigkeit Klärung sei: „*This activity of clearing up is philosophy.*" (LWL: 22) Klar-

---

12 Vgl. DB: 97: „Selbsterkenntnis & Demut ist Eins. (Das sind billige Bemerkungen.)"
13 Vgl. Friedrich Waismann (WWK: 26). Diese Eigenheit Wittgensteins führte jedoch zu Konflikten mit Wissenschaftlern, die eine systematische, zielorientierte Arbeitsweise vertraten, und war wohl der Grund für das Scheitern eines von Waismann mit Wittgenstein geplanten Projekts. Vgl. auch VB: 63–64: „Es ist für mich wichtig beim Philosophieren immer meine Lage zu verändern, nicht zu lange auf *einem* Bein zu stehen."

heit, Transparenz durch die Logik – gleich einem Kristall, wie er in den *Philosophischen Untersuchungen* präzisiert.[14]

Der Philosoph müsse diesem „Instinkt" zur Klärung folgen – ähnlich einem Kind, dessen „Warum" Erstaunen, Verwunderung ausdrücke, ohne eine präzise Antwort zu erwarten (vgl. LWL: 22).

Doch befänden sich die jungen Menschen heute in der Lage, „daß der normale, gute Verstand für die seltsamen Ansprüche des Lebens nicht mehr ausreich[e]. Es sei alles so verzwickt geworden, daß zu seiner Bewältigung ein ausnahmsweiser Verstand gehörte. Denn es genüg[e] nicht mehr, das Spiel gut spielen zu können, sondern die Frage [sei] immer wieder: was für ein Spiel ist jetzt überhaupt zu spielen?" (BEE: MS 118: 20v; 27.08.1937; zit. nach VB: 63)

Das Überhandnehmen von „*skill*" bzw. von bloßen Fertigkeiten wirkt sich nicht nur in der Philosophie, sondern ebenso in der Kunst aus, die gleichermaßen auf technische Perfektion statt Ausdruck des Künstlers abzielt – einem Ausdruck, dessen Voraussetzung Authentizität, gepaart mit Hingabe, sei. „Die Kunst ist ein Ausdruck. Das gute Kunstwerk ist der vollendete Ausdruck", notierte Wittgenstein bereits am 19. September 1916 (BEE: MS 103: 54r).

Unter „vollendeter Ausdruck" ist demnach keineswegs technische Perfektion zu verstehen, sondern das Erreichen eines Ideals im ethischen Sinne, dem Wahrhaftigkeit innewohnt. Das bedeutet die „völlige Angemessenheit des Ausdrucks an das Empfinden", wie es Engelmann mit Hinweis auf Ricarda Huchs Bemerkung über Gottfried Keller „[s]eine Wahrhaftigkeit, die den Ton nicht um eine Schwingung lauter werden läßt als sein Empfinden" hinsichtlich Wittgensteins Suche in der Kunst und in dessen Philosophieren sah (vgl. Somavilla/McGuinness 2006: 103).

Anstatt sich selbst zu inszenieren, plädiert Wittgenstein für ein selbstvergessenes, leidenschaftliches Aufgehen in kreativer Tätigkeit – sei es im Schreiben, Malen oder Musizieren – ohne Verfolgung eitler Zwecke oder Anpassung an gängige Moden, die im Grunde nichts anderes sei, als sich selbst und andere zu belügen.

Abweichend von Schopenhauers oder Nietzsches Verherrlichung des Genies, findet sich bei Wittgenstein eine Auffassung, die in erster Linie auf Wahrhaftigkeit

---

**14** Vgl. PU § 97: „Das Denken ist mit einem Nimbus umgeben. – Sein Wesen, die Logik, stellt eine Ordnung dar, und zwar die Ordnung a priori der Welt, d. i. die Ordnung der *Möglichkeiten*, die Welt und Denken gemeinsam sein muß. Diese Ordnung aber, scheint es, muß *höchst einfach* sein. Sie ist *vor* aller Erfahrung; muß sich durch die ganze Erfahrung hindurchziehen; ihr selbst darf keine erfahrungsmäßige Trübe oder Unsicherheit anhaften. – Sie muß vielmehr vom reinsten Kristall sein. Dieser Kristall aber erscheint nicht als eine Abstraktion; sondern als etwas Konkretes, ja als das Konkreteste, gleichsam *Härteste*. (*Log. Phil. Abh.* No. 5.5563.)"

des Charakters gerichtet ist, in zweiter Linie bzw. damit in Zusammenhang, auf Selbsterkenntnis, die zu Bescheidenheit, leidenschaftlicher Hingabe und persönlichem Ausdruck im Schaffen führt. „Genie ist das Talent, worin der Charakter sich ausspricht." (BEE: MS 136: 59a; 04.01.1948; zit. nach VB: 127)

Wahrhaftigkeit und Demut durch Mut zur Selbsterkenntnis, zur Änderung und Loslösung von eitlem Festhalten einmal gewonnener Erkenntnisse und Mut, der Realität ins Auge zu blicken – Aspekte, die Gabriel Citron als „*philosophical virtues*" bezeichnet (vgl. Citron 2019) – sind meines Erachtens in einer Betrachtung *sub specie aeternitatis* vereint, da all diese Tugenden zu eigentlicher Tugendhaftigkeit im Sinne einer heroischen Haltung gegenüber dem Leid der Welt führen – durch stillschweigende Annahme der von der *natura naturans* geschaffenen, nach logischen Gesetzen bestehenden Weltordnung. In dieser Erkenntnis und Bejahung unabwendbaren Leids durch innerliche Stärke liegt eigentliche Freiheit, die den Philosophen auszeichnet. Gerade darin sah Wittgenstein einen Mangel – durch die heutige Erziehung, die Leidensfähigkeit zu verringern, da es Leiden nicht geben solle (vgl. BEE: MS 137: 42a; 30.05.1948; zit. nach VB: 137).

Leidensunfähigkeit, Leidenschaftslosigkeit, Egoismus und Vereinzelung statt Mitgefühl (in der Durchbrechung des *principium individuationis*, wie es Schopenhauer in seiner Ethik im Anklang an die indische Philosophie der Upanishaden vorschwebte), kein persönlicher künstlerischer Ausdruck aufgrund fehlender Selbsterkenntnis (durch Hinabsteigen in die eigenen Tiefen) oder leidenschaftliches Aufgehen in der Sache durch Hingabe – dies waren weitere Charakteristika und Mängel der modernen Zivilisation, die Wittgenstein mit Argwohn konstatierte.

Mut in seinem Sinne bedeutet des weiteren Mut zum Überschreiten von Grenzen, das heißt Mut, das scheinbar Unerreichbare anzustreben, da in dem „Spannungsverhältnis des Möglichen mit dem Unmöglichen eine Erweiterung der eigenen Möglichkeiten" liege, auf die es im Leben ankomme.[15]

Die Auseinandersetzung mit den Grenzen des Möglichen schließt jedoch nicht aus, sich der eigenen Grenzen sowie der Grenzen von Sprache und Wissenschaft bewusst zu sein, und daher die Grenze zwischen *Sagen* und *Zeigen* einzuhalten – eine Grenze, die Wittgenstein bereits im Frühwerk wahrte, indem er das „Nicht Sagbare" im Schweigen festhielt, da er diesen Weg als unbedingt notwendig erachtete, um das Ethische „von Innen her" zu begrenzen (vgl. CLF: 35).

---

**15** Vgl. Ingeborg Bachmann, die in ihrer Rede „Die Wahrheit ist dem Menschen zumutbar" den Wunsch ausdrückt, die Grenzen zu überschreiten, das Unerreichbare, Vollkommene anzustreben – „sei es in der Liebe, der Freiheit oder jeder reinen Größe". Bachmann appelliert dafür, „daß wir uns orientieren an einem Ziel, das freilich, wenn wir uns nähern, sich noch einmal entfernt" (Bachmann 1978: 455).

## 5 Die Dimension des Staunens

Wittgensteins Erkenntnis der Grenzen der Sprache und die daraus resultierende Position des Schweigens kommt in seiner Auseinandersetzung mit philosophischen Fragen und Problemen insbesondere an jenen Stellen zum Ausdruck, wo er der Vielfalt der Welt in einer Haltung des Staunens begegnet – einer Haltung, die er in seiner Zeit verloren gegangen sah – nicht zuletzt durch die Erklärungen der Wissenschaften. Dies wird bereits im *Tractatus* deutlich, wo er die Problematik wissenschaftlicher Aussagen in einer Weise anspricht, der eine von Staunen getragene Haltung gegenüber dem über die Tatsachenwelt hinausgehenden Bereich innewohnt (vgl. TLP 6.432, 6.44, 6.45, 6.522, 6.54, 7).

Im Hinweis auf die eigentlichen Probleme des Lebens, die durch die Wissenschaften nicht gelöst werden können (vgl. TLP 6.52; zit. in Fußnote 1), scheint mit dem Wort „fühlen" die Bedeutung einer Dimension angesprochen, die sich vom Bereich des wissenschaftlich Sagbaren abhebt und eine mystische Erfassung des Ganzen nahelegt.[16] Wörter wie „fühlen", „meinen" und dergleichen sind als Ausdruck des Nicht-Rationalen und Intuitiven zu sehen und stehen für die Grenzziehung zwischen wissenschaftlich Sagbarem und Unsagbarem. Gleichzeitig weisen sie auf eine Richtungsänderung in Wittgensteins Denken hin, die sich auch in sprachlicher Hinsicht äußert, das heißt, sich vom Ton seiner bestimmten, Endgültigkeit beanspruchenden Behauptungen abhebt. In den späteren philosophischen Manuskripten lassen sich immer häufiger Ausdrücke der Unbestimmtheit und Unsicherheit beobachten. Indem ihm bei der Untersuchung sprachphilosophischer Probleme die Schwierigkeiten eindeutiger Festlegungen und Definitionen bewusst werden, da unsere Worte im Gebrauch verschwommen, vage und vielschichtig sind und auf unterschiedlichste Weise interpretiert werden können, geht er nicht mehr mit jener Bestimmtheit vor, in der er nach der Abfassung des *Tractatus* im Vorwort verkündet hatte, „die Probleme im Wesentlichen endgültig gelöst zu haben".

Das bestimmte, zielgerichtete und oftmals überhebliche Vorgehen mancher Wissenschaftler sowie die Anmaßung der Richtigkeit wissenschaftlicher Aussagen ist Wittgenstein suspekt – zum einen, da sie den Anspruch stellen, alles erklären zu können, zum anderen, da er durch rationale Erklärungen das Staunen des Menschen gefährdet sieht. Die Bemerkung „Zum Staunen muß der Mensch – und vielleicht Völker – aufwachen. Die Wissenschaft ist ein Mittel um ihn wieder einzuschläfern" trägt Wittgenstein am 5. November 1930 ein, also ca. ein Jahr nach dem *Vortrag über Ethik* und ca. zwei Monate nach neu aufgegriffenen Gedanken

---

16 Vgl. TLP 6.45: „Das Gefühl der Welt als begrenztes Ganzes ist das mystische."

zur Betrachtung *sub specie aeternitatis*. Zur selben Zeit äußert er auch sein Abseitsstehen vom „typischen westlichen Wissenschaftler", der den Geist, in dem er schreibe, nicht verstehe (vgl. VB: 30 – 31).

1931 notiert er: „Beiläufig gesprochen hat es in der alten Auffassung – etwa der, der (großen) westlichen Philosophien – zwei Arten von Problemen im wissenschaftlichen Sinne gegeben: wesentliche, große, universelle, & unwesentliche, quasi accidentelle Probleme. Und dagegen ist unsere Auffassung daß es kein *großes*, wesentliches Problem im Sinne der Wissenschaft gibt." (BEE: MS 110: 200; 22.06.1931; vgl. auch VB: 46)

Trotz seiner Vorbehalte gegen wissenschaftliche Erklärungen, gibt es auch Bemerkungen Wittgensteins, wo er die Erklärung von den Menschen einst rätselhaften Naturerscheinungen *nicht* als Hindernis für einen Verlust an Bewunderung sieht. Im Gegenteil, gerade der denkende, geistig und kulturell orientierte Mensch sollte sich der Bedeutung auch von wissenschaftlich erklärten Phänomenen bewusst sein und diesen in einer Haltung der Ehrfurcht begegnen, anstatt sie als etwas selbstverständlich Gewordenes nicht mehr zu beachten.

In seinen *Bemerkungen über Frazers Golden Bough* notiert er: „Denn keine Erscheinung ist an sich besonders geheimnisvoll, aber jede kann es uns werden, und das ist eben das Charakteristische am erwachenden Geist des Menschen, daß ihm eine Erscheinung bedeutend wird." (VE: 35)

Dieser Zugang setzt eine Wachheit voraus, die im Gegensatz zu der vorhin erwähnten, von den Wissenschaften verursachten „Einschläferung" steht, die mit Gleichgültigkeit und Stumpfheit gegenüber dem unmittelbar Gegebenen und nicht mehr Beachteten, da alltäglich Gesehenen und Erlebten, zusammenhängt.[17] In dieser Hinsicht ist auch die ethische Bedeutung des im *Vortrag über Ethik* beschriebenen „Staunens über die Existenz der Welt" zu sehen – als Appell zum „Wachsein" im Sinne intensiver Wahrnehmung und staunender Bewunderung. In diesem Vortrag trifft Wittgenstein eine klare Scheidung zwischen der wissenschaftlichen Betrachtung einer Tatsache und der Betrachtung einer Tatsache als Wunder, wobei er ein Beispiel davon gibt, wie wissenschaftliche Erklärung unser Staunen zerstören kann.

Die kritische Haltung gegenüber den Wissenschaften und einer analytischen Betrachtungsweise in der Philosophie findet sich noch in späten Jahren, als er am Beispiel der Betrachtung von Bäumen erörtert, wie durch einen rationalen Zugang unsere Bewunderung einen Riss bekäme, der erst zu heilen sei. Wittgenstein spricht dabei von einer „philosophischen Trübe", die das Staunenswerte ver-

---

17 Vgl. dazu auch PU § 129.

schleiere.[18] Im Gegensatz dazu geht es ihm um ein intuitives Verstehen, eine Haltung der Anschauung, die sich mit dem Gesamteindruck des Geschauten zufriedengibt, ohne rationale Erwägungen anzustellen. Denn im abstrakten und begrifflichen Denken wittert er die Gefahr, dass der Blick für das Wesentliche „getrübt", die Fähigkeit zum Staunen verloren gehe.

Diese, offenbar durch rational-wissenschaftliche Annäherung verursachte „Trübe", scheint zu seinen sprachanalytischen Untersuchungen in Widerspruch zu stehen – insbesondere im Hinblick auf den *Tractatus*, wo er gerade durch eine analytische Vorgangsweise Klarheit und Transparenz in philosophischen Sätzen anstrebt. Doch weist er bereits zu dieser Zeit, wie erwähnt, auf die Bedeutung einer staunenden Haltung im Sinne einer mystischen Annährung an das Unaussprechbare hin, die keiner Worte oder gar Erklärung bedarf. „Nicht *wie* die Welt ist, ist das Mystische, sondern *daß* sie ist", heißt es im *Tractatus* (TLP 6.44). Und im 1929 gehaltenen *Vortrag über Ethik* erklärt er das „Staunen über die Existenz der Welt" als sein erstes und wichtigstes Beispiel – als sein „Erlebnis par excellence" für sein Verständnis des Ethischen im absoluten Sinn.

Es ist die Ethik, die im Grunde im Zentrum seines Lebens und Philosophierens lag und sein Schreiben auf eine Art und Weise bestimmte, wie es sich bei oberflächlicher Betrachtung kaum erahnen ließe. Da es jedoch keine Sätze der Ethik gibt, jedweder Versuch der Verbalisierung in Unsinn münden würde, führt das ethisch begründete Staunen gleichermaßen zu einem ethisch begründeten Schweigen.

Den Verlust an Respekt und Ehrfurcht vor der Schöpfung sah Wittgenstein gerade in der modernen Zivilisation, gegen deren fortschrittsorientiertes und zweckbetontes Denken er sich entschieden aussprach – bewusst der zerstörerischen Folgen durch gewaltsame Ausbeutung der Natur. Wie auch Edith Stein feststellte, die durch das Überschreiten der Grenzen wissenschaftlicher Erkenntnis und durch die in der Folge willkürliche und gierige Bemächtigung der Güter der Erde bis zur Zerstörung die Klarheit des geistigen Blicks getrübt sah (vgl. Stein 1959: 30).

---

**18** Vgl. BEE: MS 134: 15r; 15.03.1947, zit. nach VB: 113: „Auch der Mathematiker kann natürlich die Wunder (das Krystall) der Natur anstaunen; aber kann er es, wenn es einmal problematisch geworden ist, <u>was</u> er sieht? Ist es wirklich möglich, solange eine philosophische Trübe das <u>ver-schleiert</u>, was das Staunenswerte oder Angestaunte ist?
  Ich könnte mir denken, daß Einer Bäume bewundert, & auch die Schatten, oder Spiegelungen von Bäumen, die er für Bäume hält. Sagt er sich aber einmal, daß dies doch keine Bäume sind & wird es für ihn problematisch, was sie sind, oder was ihre Beziehung zu Bäumen ist, dann hat die Bewunderung einen Riss, der erst zu heilen ist."

Um die Ehrfurcht vor der Schöpfung nicht zu verlieren, heißt es, die eigenen Grenzen einzusehen, die Wittgenstein mit dem bekannten Satz „*Die Grenzen meiner Sprache* bedeuten die Grenzen meiner Welt" (TLP 5.6; TB: 23.5.15) angesprochen hat.[19]

Da der Bereich jenseits des Sagbaren sich jedweder rationalen Erfassung entzieht, weist er auf andere Wege und Möglichkeiten hin, sich damit auseinanderzusetzen. Diese sah Wittgenstein in der Kunst. Doch gerade darin verspürte er einen Niedergang, verursacht durch das Fehlen eigentlicher Geistigkeit, die für ihn von Anfang an im Zentrum seiner Weltanschauung, seines Philosophierens lag und das Streben nach Wahrheit unter dem Gesichtspunkt des Ewigen voraussetzte. Es war das Festhalten an diesen Werten, dieser Form von Geistigkeit, die ihm half, in jeder Not des Lebens – wie der während des Ersten Weltkriegs – zu bestehen. Ein Leben im Geiste – in der Erkenntnis –, das sich auf seine philosophische Arbeit, auf das Streben nach moralischer Reinheit sowie auf ein Leben „[i]m guten & schönen" konzentrierte (vgl. BEE: MS 101: 35v; 7.10.14).

Die Verknüpfung von Ethik, Geistigkeit und künstlerischem Ausdruck vermisste Wittgenstein in seiner Zeit, was zu seiner persönlichen Desillusionierung über die Bedeutung von Kunst und Werten führte. 1949 notierte er:

> Mein eigenes Denken über Kunst & Werte ist weit desillusionierter, als es das der Menschen vor 100 Jahren sein *konnte*. Und doch heißt das nicht, daß es deswegen richtiger ist. Es heißt nur, daß im Vordergrund meines Geistes Untergänge sind, die nicht im *Vordergrund* jener waren. (BEE: MS 138: 4a; 18.01.1949; zit. nach VB: 151)

Angesichts des Zerfalls eines gemeinsamen Geistes und des damit zusammenhängenden kulturellen Niedergangs verlor er nicht ganz die Hoffnung auf den Geist des Vergangenen, den er über dem gegenwärtigen „Trümmerhaufen" – der „Asche" der Kultur – schweben sah (vgl. BEE: MS 107: 230; 11.01.1930).

In der großstädtischen Zivilisation sah er den Geist jedoch nur in einen Winkel gedrückt – „als (ewiger) Zeuge – – quasi als Rächer der Gottheit" (BEE: MS 183: 46; 08.10.1930; zit. nach DB: 46).

## Literatur

Arnswald, Ulrich (2006): „Zur Entwicklung eines Konzepts der Authentizität im Werke Wittgensteins". In: Lütterfelds, Wilhelm/Majetschak, Stefan/Raatzsch,

---

[19] Vgl. auch TLP 5.62: „Daß die Welt *meine* Welt ist, das zeigt sich darin, daß die Grenzen *der* Sprache (der Sprache, die allein ich verstehe) die Grenzen *meiner* Welt bedeuten."

Richard/Vossenkuhl, Wilhelm (Hg.): *Wittgenstein-Jahrbuch 2003/2006*. Frankfurt a. M.: Peter Lang, S. 133–156.

Bachmann, Ingeborg (1978): „Die Wahrheit ist dem Menschen zumutbar". In: *Gedichte und Erzählungen*. Ausgewählt von Helmut Koopmann. Stuttgart/München: Piper, S. 454–456.

Böhm, Winfried (1985): *Theorie und Praxis*. Würzburg: Königshausen & Neumann.

Brinek, Gertrude (1991): *Erziehung des Staunens: Zur pädagogischen Bedeutung eines emotiven Phänomens*. Wien: WUV Universitätsverlag.

Citron, Gabriel (2019): „Honesty, Humility, Courage, & Strength: Later Wittgenstein on the Difficulties of Philosophy and the Philosophical Virtues". In: *Philosophers' Imprint* 19(25), S. 1–24.

Descartes, René (1997): *Descartes: Philosophie jetzt!* Ausgewählt und vorgestellt von Stephan Meier-Oeser. Hg. von Peter Sloterdijk. München: Eugen Diederichs.

Drury, Maurice O'Connor (1992): „Bemerkungen zu einigen Gesprächen mit Wittgenstein". In: Rhees, Rush (Hg.): *Ludwig Wittgenstein: Porträts und Gespräche*. Frankfurt a. M.: Suhrkamp, S. 117–141.

Kienzler, Wolfgang (2013): „Wittgenstein und Spengler". In: Rothhaupt, Josef G. F./Vossenkuhl, Wilhelm (Hg.): *Kulturen und Werte: Wittgensteins Kringel-Buch als Initialtext*. Berlin: De Gruyter, S. 317–336.

Kierkegaard, Søren (1914): „Kritik der Gegenwart". Ins Deutsche übertragen und mit einem Nachwort von Theodor Haecker. In: *Der Brenner* 4(20), S. 869–908.

Malcolm, Norman (1984): *Ludwig Wittgenstein: A Memoir by Norman Malcolm with a Biographical Sketch by G. H. von Wright and with Wittgenstein's Letters to Malcolm*. Oxford: Oxford University Press.

Rhees, Rush (1969): *Without Answers*. London: Routledge & Kegan Paul.

Schopenhauer, Arthur (1977) [WWV]: *Die Welt als Wille und Vorstellung I und II*. Hg. von Angelika Hübscher. Zürich: Diogenes.

Somavilla, Ilse (2012): „Das philosophische Staunen bei den Griechen und bei Wittgenstein". In: Somavilla, Ilse/Thompson, James M. (Hg.): *Wittgenstein und die Antike/Wittgenstein and Ancient Thought*. Berlin: Parerga, S. 15–83.

Somavilla, Ilse (2016): „Wittgensteins kritische Betrachtung seiner Zeit". In: De Gennaro, Ivo et al. (Hg.): *Wirtliche Ökonomie: Philosophische und dichterische Quellen*. 2. Teilband. Nordhausen: Traugott Bautz, S. 343–365.

Somavilla, Ilse/McGuinness, Brian (Hg.) (2006): *Wittgenstein – Engelmann: Briefe, Begegnungen, Erinnerungen*. Innsbruck: Haymon.

Somavilla, Ilse/Unterkircher, Anton/Berger, Christian Paul (Hg.) (1994) [CLH]: *Ludwig Hänsel – Ludwig Wittgenstein: Eine Freundschaft: Briefe, Aufsätze, Kommentare*. Innsbruck: Haymon.

Stein, Edith (1959): *Die Frau: Ihre Aufgabe nach Natur und Gnade*. Freiburg: Herder.

Weininger, Otto (1918): *Über die letzten Dinge*. 4. Auflage. Wien/Leipzig: Wilhelm Braumüller.

Wittgenstein, Ludwig (1969) [CLF]: *Briefe an Ludwig von Ficker*. Hg. von Georg Henrik von Wright unter Mitarbeit von Walter Methlagl. Salzburg: Otto Müller.

Wittgenstein, Ludwig (1980) [LWL]: *Wittgenstein's Lectures: Cambridge, 1930–1932*. From the Notes of John King and Desmond Lee. Hg. von Desmond Lee. Oxford: Basil Blackwell.

Wittgenstein, Ludwig (1989a) [WWK]: *Ludwig Wittgenstein und der Wiener Kreis*. Werkausgabe Band 3. Frankfurt a. M.: Suhrkamp.

Wittgenstein, Ludwig (1989b) [VE]: *Vortrag über Ethik und andere kleine Schriften*. Hg. von Joachim Schulte. Frankfurt a. M.: Suhrkamp.
Wittgenstein, Ludwig (1990a) [PU]: *Philosophische Untersuchungen*. Werkausgabe Band 1. Frankfurt a. M.: Suhrkamp.
Wittgenstein, Ludwig (1990b) [TB]: *Tagebücher 1914–1916*. Werkausgabe Band 1. Frankfurt a. M.: Suhrkamp.
Wittgenstein, Ludwig (1990c) [TLP]: *Tractatus logico-philosophicus*. Werkausgabe Band 1. Frankfurt a. M.: Suhrkamp.
Wittgenstein, Ludwig (1991) [BBB]: *Das Blaue Buch*. Werkausgabe Band 5. Frankfurt a. M.: Suhrkamp.
Wittgenstein, Ludwig (1994) [VB]: *Vermischte Bemerkungen*. Eine Auswahl aus dem Nachlaß. Hg. von Georg Henrik von Wright unter Mitarbeit von Heikki Nyman. Neubearbeitung des Textes durch Alois Pichler. Frankfurt a. M.: Suhrkamp.
Wittgenstein, Ludwig (1995) [CC]: *Cambridge Letters: Correspondence with Russell, Keynes, Moore, Ramsey and Sraffa*. Hg. von Brian McGuinness und Georg Henrik von Wright. Oxford. Blackwell.
Wittgenstein, Ludwig (1997) [DB]: *Denkbewegungen: Tagebücher 1930–1932, 1936–1937*. Hg. von Ilse Somavilla. Innsbruck: Haymon [Seitenzahl = Manuskriptseite, nicht Buchseite].
Wittgenstein, Ludwig (2000) [BEE]: *Wittgenstein's Nachlass: The Bergen Electronic Edition*. Bergen/Oxford: Oxford University Press.
Wittgenstein, Ludwig (2004) [LUS]: *Licht und Schatten: Ein nächtliches (Traum-)Erlebnis und ein Brief-Fragment*. Hg. von Ilse Somavilla. Innsbruck: Haymon.

# Index of Names

Abels, Heinz 437
Adams, John 53
Adichie, Chimamanda Ngochi 236
Adler, Jonathan 254f., 258
Adloff, Frank 177, 179f.
Adorno, Theodor W. 28, 35f., 291, 397f., 411, 442
Aeschbach, Sébastien 167
Agamben, Giorgio 106, 266
Ahlskog, Jonas 401, 406
Alexander, Jeffrey C. 180
Allabadi, Fadwa 183
Allen, Amy 395f.
Allen, Danielle 153
Alloa, Emmanuel 259
Althusser, Louis 20
Andersen, Niels Åkerstrøm 4
Anderson, Chris 129
Anderson, Elizabeth 142, 144, 152
Anderson, Malcolm 105
Andrews, Kristin 377
Annas, Julia 340
Anscombe, G. E. M. 258f.
Apel, Karl-Otto 47, 292, 298
Appiah, Kwame Anthony 221, 225–228
Arendt, Hannah 18, 36, 50, 53f., 56f., 222
Aristotle 13, 258, 331f., 334f., 339, 341
Arnswald, Ulrich 451
Arrhenius, Svante 348
Assange, Julian 185
Assmann, Aleida 266f.
Atkinson, Colin 133
Augustine 257, 318
Aumann, Robert J. 270
Austin, J. L. 55, 391

Baatz, Christian 351
Bachmann, Ingeborg 458
Bacon, Francis 299, 305
Badiou, Alain 25f.
Baeza, Laura 75
Bajohr, Hannes 80, 82, 84, 87f., 90, 92
Balkin, Jack M. 148, 151

Banerjee, Abhijit 144
Barnosky, Anthony D. 306
Basu, Rima 211–213, 216f., 219
Bauer, Nancy 393
Bauman, Zygmunt 106
Baumert, Kevin 346
Bayes, Thomas 270
Bekoff, Marc 379
Bell, D. R. 401
Bellah, Robert N. 56
Ben Ali, Zine el-Abidine 63f., 70
Benhabib, Seyla 89
Benjamin, Walter 25–27, 35
Bennett, Christopher 161
Berkowitz, Dan 184
Berlin, Isaiah 272
Bernays, Edward 233, 240–244
Betzler, Monika 190, 197
Biben, Maxeen 369
Bielefeldt, Heiner 112
Binmore, Ken 270
Birnbacher, Dieter 325
Bishop, Claire 26
Bizas, Konstantinos 7f.
Blum, Lawrence 206
Bobbio, Norberto 107
Böckenförde, Ernst-Wolfgang 104, 106
Boddington, Paula 124
Böhm, Winfried 456
Boland, Richard 126
Bolsonaro, Jair 309
Boltanski, Luc 31–35
Bourdieu, Pierre 32
Bourguiba, Habib 64, 71
Brashear, Jeffrey 124
Brecht, Bertolt 441–443
Breyer, Stephen 44
Brinek, Gertrude 455f.
Brodnig, Ingird 194
Brown, Wendy 55f., 395
Brundtland, Gro Harlem 289, 300–302
Bruner, Jerome 135
Burke, Edmund 16

Bush, George H. W. 301
Butt, Daniel 356
Butterwegge, Christoph 109 f.

Cáceres, Berta 310
Caesar, Gaius Julius 258
Cahill, Kevin M. 401
Cameron, David 29
Campagna, Norbert 83
Carroll, Sean 133
Castells, Manuel 183
Cavell, Stanley 434
Celikates, Robin 19, 143
Chambers, Simone 178, 183
Chennoufi, Ridha 75
Cherry, Myisha 164, 169
Christensen, David 271–274
Citron, Gabriel 449, 458
Coady, C. A. J. 252, 258 f.
Cochrane, Alasdair 368
Collopy, Fred 126
Comte, Auguste 325
Condorcet (Nicolas de Caritat) 279
Conway, Erik M. 274
Cook, John 275 f.
Cooke, Maeve 10, 12, 19 f.
Cottle, Simon 183
Crapanzano, Vincent 52
Crary, Alice 152, 387, 389, 396, 400, 403, 406, 409–412
Crenshaw, Kimberlé 386–388, 396, 400, 410
Crippa, Monica 302
Cummings, Elijah 42

Dallal, Jenine Abboushi 183
Daniels, Norman 281
Dardot, Pierre 27 f.
Darwall, Stephen 168, 267
Darwin, Charles 282
Dashkova, Yekaterina Romanovna 15
Däubler, Theodor 91
De Angelis, Massimo 28
De Boer, Karin 21
De Lara, Joel 412
De Sousa Santos, Boaventura 287
De Waal, Frans B. M. 379

Deleuze, Gilles 246, 307
Deng, Xiaoping 289
Derrida, Jacques 54 f., 57 f., 62–64, 69, 106, 128, 289, 292, 298, 394 f.
Descartes, René 257, 260, 294, 455 f.
Deutscher, Penelope 394
DeWitt, Bryce S. 133
Di Paola, Marcello 104
Diamond, Cora 401, 406 f.
Diderot, Denis 15 f.
Dockx, Nico 27
Domingos, Pedro 124, 130
Dostoyevsky, Fyodor 299
Drexhage, John 301
Driver, Julia 191
Drury, Maurice O'Connor 454
Duflo, Esther 144
Dummett, Michael 206
Dussel, Enrique 287
Dworkin, Ronald 149

Ebert, Rainer 368
Ehrenfeld, David 322, 327
Eko, Lyombe 184
El-Mafaalani, Aladin 439
El-Nawawy, Mohammed 183
Elitok, Seçil Paçacı 303
Ellis, Erle 331
Emerson, Ralph Waldo 82
Engelmann, Paul 448, 452, 457
Engels, Friedrich 20
Erb, Volker 111
Erdoğan, Recep Tayyip 61
Erhardt, Andreas 324
Erikson, Erik 437
Escobar, Arturo 287, 306
Essebsi, Béji Caïd 62, 69, 77
Ester, Peter 183
Etzioni, Amitai 178
Euchner, Walter 107
Everett, Hugh 133

Fabian, Jordan 206
Faria, Catia 368
Fassin, Didier 19, 22
Faulkner, Paul 254
Ferguson, Adam 246

Ferguson, Steven H. 370
Feuerbach, Ludwig 19
Fichte, Johann Gottlieb 18
Ficker, Ludwig von 448, 452
Findlay, J. N. 423
Fink, Charles K. 368
Finlayson, James Gordon 18
Fitzpatrick, Simon 368
Fleiner, Rebekka 94
Flores, Fernando 117, 126 f.
Forrester, Katrina 82
Forst, Rainer 392 f.
Foucault, Michel 21 f., 31 f., 34, 71, 74, 76 f., 223, 233, 244–246, 292
Fox, M. W. 379
Frank, Ulrich 121, 123, 132 f.
Frankena, William K. 323
Frankfurt, Harry 199
Fraser, Nancy 36, 289
Frazer, James George 238, 460
Frege, Gottlob 280, 292 f., 418
Freud, Sigmund 21, 240–242
Fricker, Miranda 389
Friedman, Marilyn 192
Frings, Manfred S. 168
Frye, Marilyn 205, 207, 220
Fukuyama, Francis 437
Fullinwider, Robert K. 191

Gabriel, Oscar W. 178
Gadamer, Hans-Georg 20
Galen 14
Galilei, Galileo 280
Gamwell, Franklin 42, 45–48, 51 f., 55
Gandhi, Mohandas Karamchand 287, 299
Gandhi, Rahul 303
Garcia, J. L. A. 206
Gardiner, Stephen M. 332
Gaus, Gerald 214
Geertz, Clifford 230
Gelfert, Axel 255
Gellner, Ernest 412
Gerry, Elbridge 43
Geuss, Raymond 389 f.
Giddens, Anthony 104 f.
Gielen, Pascal 27
Gießen, Bernhard 267

Gilbert, Jeremy 29–31
Ginsburg, Ruth Bader 44
Giotto di Bondone 86
Gkliati, Mariana 303
Glasgow, Joshua 206
Goffman, Erving 430, 440
Gogou, Kondylia 303
Goodman, Amy 386
Gosseries, Axel 348
Gramsci, Antonio 31, 34 f.
Grimes, Marcia 176
Grimm, Dieter 106, 108
Grosz, Elizabeth 439
Guattari, Félix 307
Gumbrecht, Hans Ulrich 287

Habermas, Jürgen 9–12, 16, 20, 47, 107, 118, 244, 246, 287, 289 f., 292, 302, 306, 308 f., 391–393, 398, 411 f., 437
Hájek, Alan 277
Hall, Stuart 67, 243, 440
Hallich, Oliver 191
Hamilton, Clive 332
Hampshire, Stuart 147
Hänsel, Ludwig 449
Haraway, Donna 31, 34
Hardt, Michael 27, 30, 246
Harney, Stefano 26
Harsanyi, John 270
Harvey, David 27
Haslanger, Sally 140, 206, 209, 391
Hegel, Georg Wilhelm Friedrich 4, 8, 11, 18–20, 225, 238, 287, 291 f., 397, 400
Heidegger, Martin 291, 299, 451
Held, David 289
Hempel, Carl G. 129
Herbert, Ulrich 180
Hertz, Heinrich 419
Hertzberg, Lars 401, 406
Herzog, Timothy 346
Hess, Andreas 82
Hibou, Béatrice 61
Higdon, Jeff W. 370
Hilbert, David 427
Hill, Anita 386
Hippocrates 14
Hirsch, Alfred 89

Hirschman, Albert O.   179
Hitler, Adolf   93, 375
Hobbes, Thomas   11, 29, 41, 44, 83, 87f., 93, 105
Hochschild, Arlie Russell   165, 170f.
Höller, Christian   34
Holmes, Stephen   94
Holtung, Nils   348
Holtzclaw, Daniel   386, 396
Holzleithner, Elisabeth   94
Homer   7
Honig, Bonnie   56
Honneth, Axel   292, 390, 395
hooks, bell   233, 235–238, 246
Horkheimer, Max   291, 389f., 397f., 411
Horta, Oscar   368
Huch, Ricarda   457
Hughes, Mike   273
Hume, David   18, 225
Hurka, Thomas   348
Hutchinson, Phil   401

Ibn Khaldūn, 'Abd ar-Rahmān   63, 65, 71f.
Inglehart, Ronald   326
Inhofe, James M.   274
Irwin, T. H.   334

Jacobi, Friedrich Heinrich   18
Jaeggi, Rahel   390, 398–400
Jakobs, Günther   111
James, William   449
Jameson, Fredric   26
Jamieson, Dale   104, 273
Jastrow, Joseph   431
Jefferson, Thomas   49, 54, 56
Jenkins, Willis   331
Jonas, Hans   325

Kagan, Elena   44
Kahn, Paul W.   52
Kant, Immanuel   8–10, 18f., 25f., 36, 80, 83, 88, 93, 108, 176, 214, 225, 238, 287, 291f., 307, 309, 388f., 391–393
Kapembwa, Julius   368
Kaplan, Mark   274f., 277f.
Käßmann, Margot   194f.
Kastner, Jens   440

Keane, Michael   183
Kekes, John   86
Keller, Gottfried   457
Keller, Simon   217
Kersting, Wolfgang   110
Keynes, John Maynard   110
Khamis, Sahar   183
Khashoggi, Jamal   303
Kienzler, Wolfgang   451
Kierkegaard, Søren   451, 454
King, Anna   183
Kiwan, Dina   176
Klvaňa, Tomáš P.   183
Kocka, Jürgen   180
Kopstein, Jeffrey   178, 183
Korsgaard, Christine M.   375f.
Koselleck, Reinhart   3–18, 21f., 287
Kossow, Niklas   176
Kothari, Rajni   287
Krappmann, Lothar   440–442
Kraus, Karl   34, 452
Kraybill, Donald   184
Kretschmann, Winfried   189
Krieger, Martin H.   323
Kripke, Saul   258f.
Kruuk, Hans   370
Kühne, Thomas   133
Kukutschka, Roberto Martínez Barranco   176
Kusch, Martin   258
Kvaløy, Sigmund   300f.
Kymlicka, Will   149

Lacan, Jacques   292, 298
Laclau, Ernesto   20, 30, 234
Lafont, Christina   394
Lagerspetz, Olli   401, 406
Lanier, Jaron   135
Latour, Bruno   20, 25f.
Laval, Christian   27f.
Le Bon, Gustave   29, 233, 238–242
Leibniz, Gottfried Wilhelm   18, 318, 320, 322
Lenau, Nikolaus   450
Lenin (Vladimir Ilyich Ulyanov)   66
Leopold, Aldo   321
Lessig, Lawrence   27

Levey, Geoffrey Brahm 184
Levi, Isaac 272, 274
Levitsky, Steven 96
Lewandowsky, Stephan 275f., 279–281
Lewis, C. I. 278, 323
Lewis, David 136
Liebsch, Burkhard 90
Lindzen, Richard S. 274
Lippert-Rasmussen, Kasper 348
Lippmann, Walter 240–242
Lloyd, Elizabeth 275f.
Locke, John 83, 93, 105, 107f., 214, 225
Lohmann, Georg 308
Lonzi, Carla 238
Lovejoy, Arthur O. 320
Lovibond, Sabina 396
Ludin, Fereshta 439
Lugones, María 222
Luhmann, Niklas 308
Luther, Martin 53

Machan, Tibor R. 368
Machiavelli, Niccolò 86
MacIntyre, Alasdair 401
MacLachlan, Alice 163f., 166, 169
MacLeod, Alan 175
Madison, James 44
Maier, Eva Maria 109, 111
Malcolm, Norman 423, 449
Malthus, Thomas Robert 299
Marcuse, Herbert 244
Margalit, Avishai 256, 261, 266f.
Marggraf, Rainer 322
Marglin, Stephen A. 308
Marx, Karl 17, 19–21, 30, 34, 36, 308, 310, 391, 410
Marx, Reinhard 112
Maus, Ingeborg 108
Mayr, Erasmus 191
Mbembe, Achille 221–225, 228, 230
McCarthy, Thomas 308
McClintock, Barbara 274
McDowell, John 402
McKittrick, Katherine 55
McLuhan, Marshall 244
McMyler, Benjamin 267
McNay, Lois 395

Meadows, Donella H. 300
Mehring, Reinhard 88
Meier, Heinrich 92
Meister, Robert 85, 94
Merkel, Angela 198, 302f.
Merkel, Wolfgang 103, 108
Meyer, Kirsten 322
Meyer, Lukas H. 343–347, 352–357
Mieth, Corinna 191f.
Mignolo, Walter D. 228f.
Mikkola, Mari 141
Milburn, Josh 368
Mill, John Stuart 214f., 272, 325, 402
Mills, Charles W. 389, 410
Modi, Narendra 303, 309
Modood, Tariq 184
Monckton, Christopher 274
Monsó, Susana 372–374, 378
Montaigne, Michel de 85, 87
Montesquieu (Charles-Louis de Secondat) 83, 87
Moore, G. E. 449
Moran, Richard 255, 259f., 265
Moten, Fred 26
Mouffe, Chantal 30, 84
Muhammad 184
Mulhall, Stephen 178, 434
Müller, Heiner 279
Müller, Jan-Werner 92
Murphy, Deborah 301
Murphy, Kevin P. 123, 131
Murphy, Liam 140
Mussolini, Benito 178

Næss, Arne 295
Nancy, Jean-Luc 28, 35
Nandy, Ashis 287
Nederveen Pieterse, Jan 228f.
Negri, Antonio 27, 30, 246
Nell, Victor 370
Nero Claudius Caesar Augustus Germanicus 16
Neuhäuser, Christian 191
Newberry, Ruth C. 379
Newton, Isaac 280
Ng, Karen 395
Nichtweiß, Barbara 92

Niederberger, Andreas 400
Nietzsche, Friedrich 22, 158, 166, 168, 291, 307, 458
Nkurunungi, John Bosco 377
Nordmann, Alfred 238
Nozick, Robert 178

Obama, Barack 170, 302
Offe, Claus 102
Olesen, Thomas 184
Olsen, Niklas 4
Olsson, Erik J. 276, 278 f.
O'Neill, Onora 388 f.
Orbán, Viktor 21, 80, 95
Oreskes, Naomi 274
Ortega y Gasset, José 29, 235, 240
Ortner, Florian 355
Ostrom, Elinor 27
Ott, Konrad 351
Owen, David 22, 396

Paez, Eze 368
Paine, Thomas 16
Parfit, Derek 347
Pasanen, Jarna 288
Pascal, Blaise 53
Patomäki, Heikki 289
Pauen, Michael 196
Peirce, Charles Sanders 272
Pentland, Alex 128 f.
Pershing, Jonathan 346
Peterson, Dale 371
Pimlott, Douglas H. 324
Plato 295, 325, 332, 450, 452
Plessner, Helmuth 91
Pogge, Thomas W. 226
Pölzler, Thomas 357
Pommerehne, Werner W. 326
Posner, Eric 346 f.
Powers, Shawn 184
Pratap, Vijay 309
Precht, Richard David 124
Preston, Stephanie D. 379
Putnam, Hilary 392
Putnam, Robert 178

Rabotnikof, Nora 11

Ramsey, Frank P. 277
Rawls, John 139, 145 f., 178, 214, 272, 290, 292, 307, 309, 355
Raz, Joseph 215
Read, Rupert 307, 401
Regan, Tom 367 f., 371 f.
Reichold, Anne 160
Renz, Ursula 436
Rescher, Nicholas 129, 318, 322, 327
Rhees, Rush 423, 449
Richter, Melvin 9, 13
Richter, Michaela W. 9, 13
Ricœur, Paul 19, 21, 65, 67, 70 f., 74 f.
Riedel, Manfred 105
Risjord, Mark 401, 407
Roberts, John 43 f.
Robespierre, Maximilien 53
Robin, Corey 79
Rölli, Marc 239
Rolston III, Holmes 325
Roosevelt, Franklin D. 87
Rorty, Richard 90, 128, 132, 292, 298, 389, 396
Rosenberg, Arthur 402, 407
Rosenthal, Jacob 191 f.
Roser, Dominic 343 f.
Roth, Paul A. 401
Rousseau, Jean-Jacques 8, 15 f., 44, 53, 287, 299, 307
Rowlands, Mark 372–376, 378
Rucho, Robert A. 43
Russell, Bertrand 292 f., 418, 449
Rüstow, Alexander 245

Saage, Richard 107
Sadinmaa, Antti 289
Salvini, Matteo 21, 303
Sanford, John F. A. 49, 51
Sanklecha, Pranay 343 f., 353–356
Santana, Arthur D. 195
Scanlon, T. M. 139, 145 f.
Scarry, Elaine 88
Schaal, Gary S. 94
Schaller, George B. 370, 378
Scheler, Max 158, 166 f., 171, 325
Scheppele, Kim Lane 80
Schiller, Friedrich 17

Schinkel, Willem 26
Schlick, Moritz 420f.
Schmidt, Sybille 266
Schmitt, Carl 11f., 79f., 83–85, 87–94
Schön, Donald A. 134
Schopenhauer, Arthur 458
Schroeder, Mark 212f.
Schulte, Joachim 434
Schulz, Daniel 106
Schumpeter, Joseph A. 102f., 107, 307
Scott, Dred 41, 49–51, 54
Searle, John 391
Sen, Amartya 307
Sextus Empiricus 294f., 297
Shacklady, John 124
Sharrock, Wes 401
Shelby, Tommie 141–144, 206
Shklar, Judith N. 79–90, 92–94, 96
Sieyès, Emmanuel Joseph 53
Siller, Georg 434
Sinclair, Andrew 124
Singer, Peter 227
Sloterdijk, Peter 26
Smith, Adam 164
Smith, Angela 161f.
Socrates 291, 294–297, 306, 310, 332f.
Solnit, Rebecca 140, 154
Sombart, Werner 244
Sonderegger, Ruth 21
Soon, Willie W.-H. 274
Sotomayor, Sonia 44
Spengler, Oswald 299, 450f.
Špinka, Marek 379
Spinoza, Baruch de 30, 105, 246, 450, 452
Spivak, Gayatri Chakravorty 222, 439
Srnicek, Nick 29
Stahl, Titus 143
Stanford, Craig B. 377
Stanley, Jason 389
Stavrides, Stavros 27
Stedman Jones, Gareth 17
Stein, Edith 461f.
Steinvorth, Ulrich 318
Stemploska, Zofia 145
Stockdale, Katie 163
Strawson, P. F. 158–161, 212
Streb, Sabine 322

Stullerova, Kamila 93
Suler, John 197
Susemichel, Lea 440
Sussman, David 88
Svampa, Lucila 9
Swift, Adam 141, 178
Szigetvári, Viktor 95

Tai, John W. 183
Taney, Roger B. 50
Tarde, Gabriel 240, 242
Taylor, Charles 287
Taylor, Craig 191
Taylor, Paul C. 143
Taylor, Paul W. 321
Theunissen, Michael 306
Thévenot, Laurent 32
Thiel, Thorsten 194, 197
Thomas Aquinas 318
Thomas, Clarence 386
Thompson, Allen 331f.
Thompson, Janna 356
Thompson, Michael 406
Thucydides 13
Tocqueville, Alexis de 102, 112
Toivakainen, Niklas 299, 304
Tolstoy, Leo 299
Tordai, Csaba 95
Tosi, Justin 192, 199
Trakl, Georg 452
Trump, Donald 14, 16, 21, 42f., 57, 80f., 96, 166, 206, 302f., 309
Truth, Sojourner 235
Tugendhat, Ernst 306
Turing, Alan 423

Ulvila, Marko 288
Unrau, Christine 90
Urban, Hans-Jürgen 109

Van Dyk, Silke 440
Van Laak, Dirk 84
Van Reekum, Rogier 26
Van Reybrouck, David 135
Vető, Balázs 95
Vinken, Henk 183

Virno, Paolo 30 f.
Vlastos, Gregory 296

Wägele, Johann-Wolfgang 321
Waismann, Friedrich 422, 456
Wallace, Kathleen A. 194
Waller, Bruce N. 372, 374
Wallgren, Thomas 289, 292, 296, 304
Wallimann-Helmer, Ivo 346
Walzer, Michael 22
Ward, James D. 302
Warmke, Brandon 192, 199
Wartofsky, Marx W. 133
Weber, Max 310
Weber-Guskar, Eva 189, 200
Weihrauch, Tobias 400
Weisbach, David 346 f.
Welch, John R. 276
Welzer, Harald 196
Wenar, Leif 214
Wendt, Fabian 198
Westdal, Kristin H. 370
Whannel, Paddy 243
Wichert, Andreas 130
Widdicombe, Lizzie 117
Wiedmann, Thomas O. 302

Williams, Alex 29
Williams, Bernard 355
Williams, Rhys H. 176
Williges, Keith 344, 352, 360
Winch, Peter 44 f., 385, 401–408, 410 f.
Wingert, Lutz 266
Winograd, Terry 117, 126 f.
Wittgenstein, Ludwig 4, 6, 22, 128, 238, 258 f., 285 f., 291–298, 385, 401, 403 f., 407–412, 417–427, 429–436, 442 f., 447–462
Wolff, Christian 18
Wolff, Jonathan 147, 149 f.
Wood, Denis 133
Wrangham, Richard 371
Wright, Erik Olin 140, 152
Wright, Georg Henrik von 293, 299, 423
Wulff, Christian 194 f.
Wynter, Sylvia 55

Young, Iris 147, 151
Young, Peyton 279

Zakaria, Fareed 81
Ziblatt, Daniel 96
Žižek, Slavoj 292

# List of Contributors

**Richard Amesbury**
Arizona State University, USA

**Dieter Birnbacher**
University of Düsseldorf, Germany

**Christine Bratu**
University of Göttingen, Germany

**Ridha Chennoufi**
University of Tunis, Tunisia

**Alice Crary**
The New School for Social Research, NY, USA

**Eva-Maria Engelen**
University of Konstanz, Germany

**Ulrich Frank**
University of Duisburg-Essen, Germany

**Marie-Luisa Frick**
University of Innsbruck, Austria

**Stephen M. Gardiner**
University of Washington, USA

**Anke Graness**
University of Hildesheim, Germany

**Sally Haslanger**
Massachusetts Institute of Technology, USA

**Elisabeth Holzleithner**
University of Vienna, Austria

**María Pía Lara**
National Autonomous University of Mexico

**Thijs Lijster**
University of Groningen, The Netherlands

**Eva Maria Maier**
University of Vienna, Austria

**Ulrich Metschl**
University of Innsbruck, Austria

**Lukas H. Meyer**
University of Graz, Austria

**Susana Monsó**
University of Veterinary Medicine Vienna, Austria

**Andreas Oberprantacher**
University of Innsbruck, Austria

**Mélika Ouelbani**
Faculty of Humanities at Tunis, Tunisia

**Anne Reichold**
University of Flensburg, Germany

**Marc Rölli**
Academy of Fine Arts Leipzig, Germany

**Anne Siegetsleitner**
University of Innsbruck, Austria

**Georg Siller**
Meran, Italy

**Ilse Somavilla**
University of Innsbruck, Austria

**Thomas Wallgren**
University of Helsinki, Finland

**Karsten Weber**
OTH Regensburg, Germany

**Eva Weber-Guskar**
University of Bochum, Germany